THE COMPLETE SLOW COOKER

THE COMPLETE
SLOW COOKER

From Appetizers to Desserts—400 Must-Have
Recipes That Cook While You Play (or Work)

THE EDITORS AT
AMERICA'S TEST KITCHEN

Library of Congress Cataloging-in-Publication Data
Names: America's Test Kitchen (Firm)
Title: The complete slow cooker : from appetizers to desserts-
    400 must-have recipes that cook while you play (or work) /
    the editors at America's Test Kitchen.
Description: Boston, MA : America Test Kitchen, [2017] | Includes
    bibliographical references and index.
Identifiers: LCCN 2017020591 | ISBN 9781940352787 (alk. paper)
Subjects: LCSH: Electric cooking, Slow. | LCGFT: Cookbooks.
Classification: LCC TX827 .C653 2017 | DDC 641.5/884--dc23
LC record available at https://lccn.loc.gov/2017020591

AMERICA'S TEST KITCHEN
21 Drydock Avenue, Suite 210E, Boston, MA 02210

Printed in Canada
10 9 8 7 6 5 4 3 2 1

Distributed by Penguin Random House Publisher Services
Tel: 800–733–3000

CHIEF CREATIVE OFFICER: Jack Bishop
EDITORIAL DIRECTOR, BOOKS: Elizabeth Carduff
EXECUTIVE EDITOR: Julia Collin Davison
EXECUTIVE FOOD EDITOR: Dan Zuccarello
SENIOR MANAGING EDITOR: Debra Hudak
SENIOR EDITOR: Sara Mayer
ASSOCIATE EDITORS: Leah Colins and Lawman Johnson
TEST COOKS: Joseph Gitter and Katherine Perry
EDITORIAL ASSISTANT: Alyssa Langer
DESIGN DIRECTOR, BOOKS: Carole Goodman
PRODUCTION DESIGNER: Reinaldo Cruz
GRAPHIC DESIGNER: Katie Barranger
PHOTOGRAPHY DIRECTOR: Julie Bozzo Cote
SENIOR STAFF PHOTOGRAPHER: Daniel J. van Ackere
STAFF PHOTOGRAPHERS: Steve Klise and Kevin White
PHOTOGRAPHY PRODUCER: Mary Ball
ADDITIONAL PHOTOGRAPHY: Keller + Keller and Carl Tremblay
FOOD STYLING: Catrine Kelty, Kendra McKnight, Marie Piraino,
    Elle Simone Scott, and Sally Staub
PHOTOSHOOT KITCHEN TEAM:
    MANAGER: Timothy McQuinn
    SENIOR EDITOR: Chris O'Connor
    TEST COOK: Daniel Cellucci
    ASSISTANT TEST COOKS: Mady Nichas and Jessica Rudolph
ILLUSTRATION: Jay Layman
PRODUCTION DIRECTOR: Guy Rochford
SENIOR PRODUCTION MANAGER: Jessica Lindheimer Quirk
PRODUCTION MANAGER: Christine Walsh
IMAGING MANAGER: Lauren Robbins
PRODUCTION AND IMAGING SPECIALISTS: Heather Dube, Dennis Noble,
    and Jessica Voas
COPY EDITOR: Jeff Schier
PROOFREADER: Pat Jalbert-Levine
INDEXER: Elizabeth Parson

CONTENTS

Welcome to America's Test Kitchen

This book has been tested, written, and edited by the folks at America's Test Kitchen. Located in Boston's Seaport District in the historic Innovation and Design Building, it features 15,000 square feet of kitchen space including multiple photography and video studios. It is the home of *Cook's Illustrated* magazine and *Cook's Country* magazine and is the workday destination for more than 60 test cooks, editors, and cookware specialists. Our mission is to test recipes over and over again until we understand how and why they work and until we arrive at the "best" version.

We start the process of testing a recipe with a complete lack of preconceptions, which means that we accept no claim, no technique, and no recipe at face value. We simply assemble as many variations as possible, test a half-dozen of the most promising, and taste the results blind. We then construct our own recipe and continue to test it, varying ingredients, techniques, and cooking times until we reach a consensus. As we like to say in the test kitchen, "We make the mistakes so you don't have to." The result, we hope, is the best version of a particular recipe, but we realize that only you can be the final judge of our success (or failure). We use the same rigorous approach when we test equipment and taste ingredients.

All of this would not be possible without a belief that good cooking, much like good music, is based on a foundation of objective technique. Some people like spicy foods and others don't, but there is a right way to sauté, there is a best way to cook a pot roast, and there are measurable scientific principles involved in producing perfectly beaten, stable egg whites. Our ultimate goal is to investigate the fundamental principles of cooking to give you the techniques, tools, and ingredients you need to become a better cook. It is as simple as that.

To see what goes on behind the scenes at America's Test Kitchen, check out our social media channels for kitchen snapshots, exclusive content, video tips, and much more. You can watch us work (in our actual test kitchen) by tuning in to *America's Test Kitchen* or *Cook's Country from America's Test Kitchen* on public television or on our websites. Listen to test kitchen experts on public radio (SplendidTable.org) to hear insights that illuminate the truth about real home cooking. Want to hone your cooking skills or finally learn how to bake—with an America's Test Kitchen test cook? Enroll in one of our online cooking classes. However you choose to visit us, we welcome you into our kitchen, where you can stand by our side as we test our way to the best recipes in America.

facebook.com/AmericasTestKitchen
twitter.com/TestKitchen
youtube.com/AmericasTestKitchen
instagram.com/TestKitchen
pinterest.com/TestKitchen
google.com/+AmericasTestKitchen

AmericasTestKitchen.com
CooksIllustrated.com
CooksCountry.com
OnlineCookingSchool.com

SLOW COOKER 101

INTRODUCTION

ALTHOUGH SLOW COOKERS HAVE ALWAYS BEEN POPULAR, in the past few years they have become wildly so. Many chefs and fine food magazines are now embracing them as well—and they're not just making pot roast, either. Suddenly everyone seems to have discovered that the slow cooker is a ticket to an exotic chicken tagine, Asian-braised short ribs, killer homemade chicken stock, and even desserts—the sorts of exciting and classic dishes America's Test Kitchen has been making in the slow cooker for the past 10 years. Now, three best-selling books and 600 recipes later, we've pulled our collective knowledge into this comprehensive cookbook, and in the process have refined our techniques and developed even more innovative recipes.

For this new collection, we listened to what our fans have said about our recipes and used their feedback to shape the mix: Readers wanted more recipes that can cook all day (at least 8 hours) and more easy-prep recipes (no more than 15 minutes' prep time and no stovetop work), and healthier recipes, too. (Icons highlight each of these types of recipes in the book, and nutritional information for the lighter recipes is at the back of the book.) Perhaps most important, we developed nearly 100 new and exciting recipes. And since it is handy to have lots of variations on slow-cooker basics, we devised a feature called "Make It 5 Ways": These recipe spreads present a bulletproof technique and master recipe for a dish plus four ways to vary it so dinner is never boring. Among these recipes you'll find whole "roasted" chicken (the slow cooker renders the meat ultratender, while spice rub options keep flavors interesting), beef stews, meatloaves, big batch marinara sauces, lentil salads, and poached salmon.

In the pages that follow, we highlight what the test kitchen has learned, share our secrets for slow-cooker success, and give you our one-of-a-kind guide to how a great slow cooker is made, along with our tested recommendations for the best slow cooker your money can buy.

Despite all the testing we have done to make our recipes foolproof, using a slow cooker isn't an exact science; the heating power varies tremendously among brands of slow cookers. Consequently, there are a few basics you need to know as you are making the recipes in this book.

USE THE TIME RANGES

You will find both 1- and 2-hour cooking ranges for the recipes in this book. The 2-hour ranges are largely for soups and stews and pasta sauces—recipes where bringing a lot of liquid up to temperature can take some time, especially in a smaller slow cooker. So for these recipes, such as Hearty Beef Stew (page 64) or Classic Marinara Sauce (page 256), where a smaller slow cooker (like 4 quarts) is an option, you'll find a longer cooking range to accommodate this. Note also that all the more delicate and exacting recipes using fish and leaner cuts of meat have the shorter time range (and shorter cooking times); we found this narrower range to be more reliable. We recommend that the first time you make one of these recipes you check for doneness at the lower end of the range.

KNOW YOUR SLOW COOKER

While all ovens set to 350 degrees will perform the same (assuming all the ovens are properly calibrated), temperatures vary widely among slow cookers. We tested more than a dozen models and prepared every recipe in this book in two different models. It's hard to make blanket statements that apply to all slow cookers; some models run hot and fast, while others heat more slowly and gently. In our testing, we have found that some slow cookers run hot or cool on just one of the settings (either low or high). This is where the cook's experience comes into play. If you have been using a slow cooker for some time, ask yourself if dishes are generally finished cooking at the beginning or at the end of the times provided in the recipes. The answer should tell you whether you have a "fast" slow cooker or a "slow" model. If you are just getting started with your slow cooker, check all recipes at the lower end of the time range, but allow some extra time to cook food longer if necessary. NOTE: To reiterate, all of our recipes were developed using traditional slow cookers. Be aware that there are appliances on the market, such as a multicooker, that have a slow-cooker setting or function but perform very differently and may not produce the same results.

MATCH RECIPES TO SLOW-COOKER SIZES

Slow cookers come in a variety of sizes, from the ridiculously small (1 quart) to the very big (7 quarts or more). In general, we like 6-quart models. That said, we tested our recipes in slow cookers of different sizes. Each recipe in this book includes the size range that will work for that particular recipe, though the majority of the recipes work with 4- to 7-quart slow cookers. Note that some

Test Cook Joe Gitter carefully lowers a 6-inch cake pan containing a Key lime pie into a slow-cooker insert.

recipes must be made in a large slow cooker (at least 5 quarts) or you run the risk of overfilling the insert. The shape of the slow cooker also matters for some of our recipes: Oval slow cookers are needed to accommodate some roasts, casseroles, braised vegetable dishes, and rice and grains. Some foods just won't fit in a round slow cooker, and some are more successful due to the greater surface area in the oval type. For example, in the case of rice and grains, an oval slow cooker allows for more even cooking because the rice or grain is spread out more. If you don't know the size of your slow cooker, check the underside of the insert (where the size is usually stamped), or simply measure how much water it takes to fill the insert to just above the lip.

KEEP FOOD SAFE

Using a slow cooker is a safe way to cook food, but there are a few things to keep in mind to ensure it is a safe process. First, make sure your slow cooker and your utensils have been properly cleaned. Do not let your meat or fish sit out on the counter for any length of time before adding to the slow cooker. And never put frozen food into your slow cooker, as this greatly increases the risk that your food will not reach a safe bacteria-killing temperature. You should also follow our guidelines in recipes where we specify the doneness temperature of meat, fish, or poultry.

A slow cooker promises to be a little fantasy grandmother who sits in the kitchen all day cooking for you, but use the wrong cooker and that dream could fizzle. A cooker might run hotter than expected, drying out the food or turning it mushy, or slower than you want, so dinner isn't ready when you are. Then there can be issues with hot spots, which make food cook unevenly. And what if operating your machine is so confusing that you have to pore over the manual each time you use it?

To find the ideal machine that would deliver a properly cooked meal and be absolutely simple and intuitive to use, we went shopping. Previous experience taught us that glass lids were a must, as they allow you to see progress without losing heat. So were oval-shaped crocks, as these can accommodate large roasts and offer more versatility than round crocks. We also wanted a generous 6- to 7-quart capacity. With these criteria in mind, we rounded up eight models priced from $39.99 to $148.71.

Slow cookers rely on covered moist-heat cooking, so of course we wanted to evaluate how well each model performed the classic task of turning a tough cut of meat tender. But since people these days use their slow cookers for much more than just braises and stews, we'd throw a few other recipe challenges at them, too. We chose recipes that presented a range of cooking times and that offered both low and high temperature settings. (Most recipes give you the option to cook for a shorter span on high or about twice as long on low. Generally the choice is about convenience, though delicate foods often require the low setting.)

SET AND FORGET?

We started by asking testers to evaluate how easy the slow cookers were to fill, set, turn off, and empty. Only the least-expensive model in our lineup had a manual control (a simple dial, with no timer or automatic switch-off). We much preferred digital programmable cookers, which automatically switch to "warm" when the cooking time is up.

But setting the programmable cookers wasn't always easy. We wanted intuitive controls, but several models had so many buttons and confusing layouts that our testers couldn't tell if they'd set them correctly. Then there was the "smart" slow cooker that ran via a phone app—it left most testers frustrated. Yet another cooker's controls let you set only even-numbered cooking times (2, 4, 6, 8, or 10 hours) and indicated cooking progress with a cryptic series of lights. But one model in particular was a pleasure to use: Its controls were unambiguous, each button clicked satisfyingly and lit up when pressed, and within a few seconds the clock began counting down so you knew that it was running.

Handling the slow cookers presented new challenges. The handles on some became red-hot during cooking or were set too close to the hot rim of the housing. While we liked that the three products in our lineup with metal inserts were featherlight and we didn't have to worry about cracking them, two of them became too hot

With the help of a mechanical engineer from MIT, Lisa McManus evaluated the inner workings of each slow cooker.

to touch. Surprisingly, the heaviest crock in the lineup, a ceramic model, was also the easiest to use. It had protruding handles that were easy to grip and stayed cool. We found that this cooker was the only model that held close to the advertised capacity of 6 to 7 quarts and was also the only one with clear minimum and maximum fill lines.

COOKIN' GOOD

It was time to start cooking. First up: braising chuck roast into pot roast. Two models produced mixed results, slightly overcooking some pieces and leaving others a bit underdone and chewy. A third model never rendered the meat fully fork-tender, even after extended cooking.

Next we made delicate boneless, skinless chicken breasts. Our recipe calls for laying four breasts in a row across the bottom of the crock. In three models (two of which were guilty of unevenly cooking the chuck roast), the breasts at either end cooked too fast. They climbed as high as 185 degrees, becoming dry and rubbery, before the pair in the center reached the target doneness temperature of 160 degrees. While cooking speed varied, all models fell within the range indicated in our recipe.

Next up: turkey breast. In previous testings, we found that some slow cookers had a hot spot along the back wall of the cooker, which risked overcooking larger cuts that pressed up against it.

This time around we were pleased to find that this hot spot wasn't an issue, although one cooker that unevenly cooked chicken breasts overcooked the turkey where it touched the narrow ends of the crock. Again, cooking times varied, but all models finished within our time range of 5 to 6 hours on low.

Aside from the unevenly cooked chicken and turkey, all of the food was passable. But our front-runner produced evenly cooked food every time.

UNDER THE HOOD

Why did some cookers run fast and others slow? Why did some cook food evenly and others not? To find out, we dismantled a duplicate set of cookers with the help of Gregory Thiel, a postdoctoral associate in mechanical engineering at the Massachusetts Institute of Technology. Here's what we found: Most of our models were "traditional" slow cookers, meaning that food goes into a ceramic stoneware crock that absorbs and transmits heat slowly. These models have heating element strips made of nickel and chrome wire that wrap around a fiberglass strip that belts the crock. When the cooker is on, this wire heats up to a greater or lesser degree depending on the wattage and the setting. This construction tends to create hot spots near the element—particularly at the curved ends of the cookers, where the element surrounds the food more closely.

But two models with this belt-style construction actually did manage to cook food evenly, even at the ends. Opening up their housing revealed thick, heat-resistant padding and foil heat shields packed inside (the other models were empty except for the heating element). The insulation shields the pot from contact with the heating elements, preventing hot spots, and also explains why these two models—one of them our front-runner, from KitchenAid— tended to run a bit slower.

Two other models were designed very differently, with lightweight, nonstick-coated aluminum pots that sit directly on a hot plate made of stove-style electric coils embedded inside cast aluminum that also heat more or less powerfully depending on the setting. This design encourages even cooking from end to end, though the thin metal pots of these slow cookers (by Cuisinart and Ninja) cooked hotter and faster than ceramic-crock models.

The remaining cooker was a hybrid style made by Crock-Pot, with a metal crock and a traditional belt-style heater. Like the other two models with metal pots, it cooked a little fast.

The KitchenAid model that we liked so much has a useful feature: a sensor that automatically monitors and adjusts the cooking temperature so that it levels off and stays below boiling (ideally, food should stay at a simmer), helping further guard against overcooking food. Without such a sensor, the temperature of the crock pot's contents will just keep climbing to a boiling point, whether set to low or high, simply because the heat is on (when set to low, the crock just takes longer to get there).

This was made clear in our final test: We tracked the temperature as each model heated 4 quarts of water over a period of 6 hours on high and then 12 hours on low.

A CLEAR WINNER

The **KitchenAid 6-Quart Slow Cooker with Solid Glass Lid** ($99.99), our former winner, handled every recipe with perfect results, albeit a bit slowly. Its thick stoneware crock, insulated housing, built-in thermal sensor, and crystal-clear controls are well thought-out—at a moderate price. The **Cuisinart 6-Quart 3-in-1 Cook Central** ($148.71) is also a solid choice. It offers the advantages of an unbreakable metal crock with stay-cool plastic handles, as well as a brown-and-sear function that lets you skip using a skillet before slow-cooking in recipes that call for it.

Winning Inner Workings

Our top-rated slow cooker from **KitchenAid** doesn't boast much power—just 350 watts— but its smart design ensures even, steady heat that maintains a simmer and delivers perfectly cooked food every time.

1. CERAMIC STONEWARE CROCK Holds lots of heat; heats up slowly and transmits heat slowly for gentle, steady cooking; maintains stable temperature more easily than metal crocks.

2. HEATING ELEMENT Nichrome wire on fiberglass strip wraps around crock like a belt. Strip is located around lower third of crock, enclosed in metal casing.

3. TWO LAYERS OF INSULATION Buffer crock as element warms, preventing hot spots near element, and helping conserve and employ heat efficiently.

4. TEMPERATURE SENSOR Monitors cooking temperature and adjusts automatically to stay below boiling.

LARGE SLOW COOKERS

We tested eight 6- to 7-quart slow cookers, preparing a variety of recipes using both low and high temperature settings and varied cooking times. We used temperature probes to map heating patterns, and a panel of testers evaluated the cookers for ease of use and cleaning. We also dismantled a set of the cookers to understand the placement and type of heating elements they contained. The slow cookers were all purchased online and appear in order of preference.

HIGHLY RECOMMENDED

	CRITERIA		TESTERS' COMMENTS

KITCHENAID 6-Quart Slow Cooker with Solid Glass Lid
MODEL: KSC6223SS
PRICE: $99.99
CROCK MATERIAL: Ceramic stoneware
FEATURES: 24-hour cooking time display; warm, low, medium, high settings; keeps warm for 4 hours after cooking

COOKING ★★★
EASE OF USE ★★★
CLEANUP ★★★

Our former champion won again for its well-designed, straightforward control panel that made it simple to set and monitor progress at a glance. The roomy crock cooked gently and evenly and never boiled, so food emerged tender and juicy. Its broad, protruding handles with grippy textured undersides stayed cool. Thick insulation kept heat directed toward the crock, and a built-in internal temperature sensor kept the temperature below boiling.

CUISINART 6-Quart 3-in-1 Cook Central
MODEL: MSC-600
PRICE: $148.71
CROCK MATERIAL: Aluminum with nonstick coating
FEATURES: Low, high, simmer, and warm settings; brown/sauté and steam functions; metal rack for steaming; keeps warm for 24 hours after cooking

COOKING ★★★
EASE OF USE ★★½
CLEANUP ★★★

We loved the lightweight crock and stay-cool plastic handles. The crock is set directly over a built-in hot plate, so it ran a little hot and fast. That said, it cooked evenly, in part due to a built-in temperature control. Its brown/sauté function saves using a skillet, though it took longer and food steamed a little due to the crock's high sides. A great choice if you hate to lift heavy crocks or worry about breakage.

RECOMMENDED

	CRITERIA		TESTERS' COMMENTS

NINJA 3-in-1 Cooking System
MODEL: MC750
PRICE: $99.99
CROCK MATERIAL: Aluminum with nonstick coating
FEATURES: Brown/sauté function; low, high, buffet (warm) settings; keeps warm for 12 hours after cooking

COOKING ★★★
EASE OF USE ★★
CLEANUP ★★★

This model has a thin rectangular metal pot and cooked fast but evenly. It has both a built-in hot plate and a belt-like heating element for different cooking functions. It is easy to set, though its controls are a little complicated. Its slick metal handles got very hot, and while its brown/sauté function works, it was noticeably slower at browning food, probably due to its lower wattage.

RECOMMENDED WITH RESERVATIONS

	CRITERIA		TESTERS' COMMENTS

CROCK-POT 6-Quart Slow Cooker with Stovetop-Safe Cooking Pot
MODEL: SCCPVI600-S
PRICE: $56.80
CROCK MATERIAL: Cast aluminum with ceramic nonstick coating (PTFE- and PFOA-free)
FEATURES: Warm, low, high settings; 20-hour countdown timer

COOKING ★★★
EASE OF USE ★★
CLEANUP ★★

The metal crock got very hot, so it ran slightly fast, though it cooked evenly. The crock can be used on the stovetop for browning and searing before placing it into the cooker to slow-cook. A few design issues: Its metal handles became quite hot, the slick ceramic coating still felt greasy after repeated hand washing, and the thin lip of the crock meant its lid sometimes slipped into the pot when jostled. Some testers found the controls confusing.

NOT RECOMMENDED

These slow cookers did not make the cut: **HAMILTON BEACH Stay or Go 6-Quart Programmable Slow Cooker; CROCK-POT Smart Wifi-Enabled WeMo 6-Quart Slow Cooker; GOURMIA SlowSmart Express 7 Qt Digital Programmable Slow Cooker;** and the **BLACK + DECKER 7-Quart Slow Cooker—Teal.**

SMALL SLOW COOKERS

Although we recommend buying a 5½- to 6-quart slow cooker because it is the most versatile, we recognize that for smaller households, or for those where space is tight, a 4-quart slow cooker might be more appropriate. That said, the actual footprint of 4-quart slow cookers is not that much smaller than the larger ones. To assess this smaller version, we bought eight 4-quart models priced from about $20 to $130. Half featured digital programmable timers; the rest had manual controls that can't be programmed. We much preferred cookers with digital programmable controls that automatically switched over to "warm."

In the end, we can recommend two small slow cookers. The **Cuisinart 4-Quart Cook Central 3-in-1 Multicooker** ($129.95) was simple to set, and its digital timer meant that we could just walk away. It cooked food well if a little more slowly than other models. If your kitchen is cramped, be aware that it is nearly as big as a full-size slow cooker. Our Best Buy is the **Hamilton Beach Stay or Go 4-Quart Slow Cooker** ($26.99). With manual controls and no timer, it was far less convenient, but it performed perfectly.

Mini Slow Cookers

You're probably wondering, "Do I really need a baby slow cooker?" We were skeptical, too, but they can do everything from keep dips warm at parties to slow-cook scaled-down meals for two from start to finish, not to mention that they easily stow away in small kitchens, tiny dorm rooms, or campers. They're also inexpensive. To find the best one, we gathered four models priced from $13.79 to $24.02—all with 1½-quart capacities—and used them to make slow-cooker recipes for cheese fondue and chicken soup, as well as keep hot spinach and artichoke dip and queso fundido warm (tracking the temperature of each for 3 hours).

All of the mini slow cookers we tested handled the fondue, soup, and spinach dip well, but two—those without "warm" settings—had problems with the more finicky queso dip, which can separate if it gets too hot. Our favorite, the **Elite Cuisine 1.5 Quart Mini Slow Cooker** ($24.02), aced every test.

RECOMMENDED		CRITERIA		TESTERS' COMMENTS
CUISINART 4-Quart Cook Central 3-in-1 Multicooker MODEL: MSC-400 PRICE: $129.95 CONTROLS: Digital programmable		COOKING DESIGN	★ ★ ★ ★ ★ ★	This new "multicooker"—a slow cooker that can also brown, sauté, and steam—produced perfect chicken, steaks, and ribs. Its programmable timer can be set to cook for up to 24 hours, then it automatically switches to "keep warm." We liked its lightweight, easy-clean, sturdy metal insert with extra-large handles and its oval shape, clear lid, and intuitive controls. The browning function is a nice plus for searing food or reducing sauces.
HAMILTON BEACH Stay or Go 4-Quart Slow Cooker `BEST BUY` MODEL: 33246T PRICE: $26.99 CONTROLS: Manual		COOKING DESIGN	★ ★ ★ ★ ★	This cooker performed well, producing perfect ribs, steak, and chicken. A gasket and clips on the lid let you take your cooker to a potluck without risking spills. It's comparatively low-tech: The "off," "low," "high," and "warm" settings are on a manual dial—which is its drawback. You can't set it to turn off or to switch to "keep warm" on its own.

RECOMMENDED WITH RESERVATIONS		CRITERIA		TESTERS' COMMENTS
WEST BEND 4-Quart Oval Crockery Cooker MODEL: 84384 PRICE: $29.99 CONTROLS: Manual		COOKING DESIGN	★ ★ ★ ½	This model produced tender chicken and steak (although the sauce scorched slightly). But ribs developed a leathery crust wherever they touched the hot bottom of the insert.

THE TEST KITCHEN'S TOP SECRETS TO SLOW-COOKER SUCCESS

After years of developing slow-cooker recipes we've learned that a simple "dump-and-go" approach often leads to second-rate recipes. Here are some tricks and techniques that are key to turning out great-tasting food from your slow cooker.

1 GET OUT A SKILLET (SOMETIMES)

We understand that you're using a slow cooker because life is busy and you don't have lots of time to spare. It can seem like a pain in the neck to pull out your skillet first, but we think it is often-times the best route to building flavor. (We never put raw aromatics or spices directly into the slow cooker.) For some recipes, spending just 5 or 10 minutes sautéing aromatics or browning meat makes all the difference between a meal that is expedient and one that is great. Browning creates a flavorful fond in the bottom of the pan that provides the basis for a rich sauce such as for Osso Buco (page 125). Browning a whole roast, like the eye-round roast in our Roast Beef with Hearty Mushroom Gravy (page 160), or a halved roast, as in Cider-Braised Pork Roast (page 166), adds both extra flavor and attractive color.

2 PRESS THE MICROWAVE INTO SERVICE

The fastest appliance in your kitchen is your ally when it comes to using your slow cooker. When the microwave will suffice, we turn to it instead of the stove-top. We use the microwave to quickly and easily soften aromatics, bloom spices, parcook vegetables, and more in many recipes. Tossed with a little oil, aromatics and spices meld and allow a head start on flavor building once they are added to the slow cooker, as in Chicken Tikka Masala (page 91). When you need to add hot broth or coconut milk to a dish at the end of cooking, the microwave is the easy answer. Same with delicate vegetables, like the snow peas in Thai Green Curry with Shrimp and Sweet Potatoes (page 193), that are added to the slow cooker right before serving—a quick spin in the microwave and you can stir them right in.

3 BULK UP ON SPICES, AROMATICS, AND OTHER FLAVORINGS

The flavors in a slow-cooker dish can become muted over the long cooking time. So we up the amounts of aromatics and spices in our slow cooker recipes beyond what is normally used. To increase the flavor of the spices, we bloom them in either a skillet or the microwave. For most stews, chilis, pasta sauces, and many braises, flavor building starts with sau-téing the aromatics or browning meat, resulting in a flavorful fond that can be deglazed with wine or broth for deep, rich flavor. We often season roasts with robust spice rubs.

Aiming to cut down on stovetop work, in many cases we call upon glutamate-rich ingredients like tomato paste, porcini mushrooms, and soy sauce, which can mimic the deep flavor that comes from browning and traditional sauce making. And many slow-cooker dishes need a flavor boost before serving, so we turn to herbs, citrus juice, vinegar, or other flavorful ingredients like brown sugar or coconut milk.

4 THINK DIFFERENTLY ABOUT THICKENERS

Since there is no opportunity for stews and chilis to reduce and thicken naturally in the moist environment of the slow cooker, thickeners are often necessary. Sometimes we use a classic fat-and-flour-based roux, but whenever possible we try to use ingredients already in the dish to help thicken it. For instance, we have found success processing portions of canned beans and frozen corn before building the stew base, as we do in our Pork and White Bean Stew with Kale (page 67), or finishing a dish by mashing some of the cooked beans and vegetables, such as in Black Bean Chili (page 84). If all else fails, we typically reach for instant tapioca, which we have found over the years to be a great no-fuss thickener that can be stirred in at the start. A few tablespoons of tapioca added to the slow cooker with the lamb in Lamb Vindaloo (page 151) ensure that the sauce is thick and clingy.

5 PAY ATTENTION TO TEMPERATURE WHEN COOKING LEAN PROTEINS

After you've been using your slow cooker for a while, you become attuned to whether it runs fast or slow and whether your recipes will be done toward the beginning or the end of the time ranges. This will help inform timing when you're making more temperature-sensitive foods like leaner roasts (pork loin, pork tenderloin, whole chicken, eye-round roast) and fish. While well-marbled roasts like a chuck-eye roast can cook all day without fear of overcooking, these more delicate foods, or a beef roast you want to serve medium-rare, need more precise timing. To make sure these roasts remain moist, we cook them on low and use 1-hour time ranges. Start monitoring their temperature at the lower end of the time range and take them out of the slow cooker as soon as they reach the desired temperature. After you've made these recipes once, you'll know how long to cook them in the future.

6 JUMP-START THE COOKING OF RICE AND PASTA

Both pasta and rice are tricky to cook perfectly in a slow cooker. And there is nothing worse than crunchy rice or mushy pasta. A technique we use with both of them to combat uneven cooking is to begin with hot or boiling water or broth to jump-start the cooking. When we used room-temperature water, we found them to be unevenly cooked—mushy at the bottom and dried out at the top. By the time the water or broth heated up enough to cook the rice or pasta, the bottom of the dish had overcooked and the top portion had dried out.

We also use a few other techniques for each of them in concert with the hot water trick—for information on toasting pasta see page 208, and on using a parchment shield when making rice casseroles or sides see page 177.

7 TOAST THE PASTA

After much testing, we found that recipes that included pasta could be very difficult to cook perfectly in the slow cooker, which is why you will find only a handful of them in this collection. What we did learn was that when making slow-cooker casseroles with pasta, how you handle the pasta makes a huge difference in the success of the dish. For Grown-Up Macaroni and Cheese with Comté and Porcini (page 208), raw or partially cooked pasta does not work, but toasting it with a little extra-virgin olive oil in the microwave does. This technique prevents the pasta from becoming bloated. We found that microwaving the pasta at 50 percent power, and stirring it occasionally, gently toasts the pasta (note that only a portion will look toasted and blistered). For more information on toasting pasta, see page 208.

8 BUILD SUPPORT WITH ALUMINUM FOIL

Since most slow cookers have a hotter side (typically the back side, opposite the side with the controls), some dense foods like casseroles can burn. To solve this problem we line the slow cooker insert with an aluminum foil collar (see page 208). For dishes that we want to lift out of the insert intact, like meatloaf, lasagna, and monkey bread, a simple foil sling (see page 180) makes this a snap. Foil packets come in handy, too: when cooking a stew loaded with vegetables, placing the vegetables in this packet keeps them fresh and prevents them from overcooking.

Other times, particularly with our slow-cooker desserts, we found a foil rack to be useful (see page 333). This ring elevates cakes above the bottom of the pan, where we add a water bath to create more even heat in the slow cooker. As a result, no part of the pan is getting direct heat, and the slow cooker functions more like an oven in this situation. We do this with our Carrot Cake (page 336), Flourless Chocolate Cake (page 337), and cheesecakes (pages 338–339).

9 RESIST LIFTING THE LID TO STIR (MOST OF THE TIME)

It's hard to resist lifting the lid early to check on how your pot roast or casserole is coming along. Don't do it! The slow cooker builds up heat over time and maintains a relatively low even temperature; lifting the lid releases steam and ruins the slow cooker's effectiveness. Doing so will throw off the timing we've carefully tested for these recipes.

That said, there are some recipes that are temperature-driven, and timing (and doneness) is tricky, as with poached fish or pork tenderloin, and some custardy desserts like cheesecake; for these recipes we recommend that you do lift the lid and check the temperature partway through the cooking time to avoid the risk of overcooking. After you've had experience with these recipes, you will know how to anticipate the timing for perfect results.

Note that there are a handful of recipes like granola, party mix, and spiced nuts where lifting the lid and stirring are essential, but these are the exception.

10 ADD VEGETABLES AT THE RIGHT TIME

Vegetables are tricky to get right in the slow cooker, so we focused a lot of attention on making sure our vegetables were perfectly cooked.

For sturdy vegetables like potatoes and carrots, to ensure they cook through perfectly it is sometimes necessary to give them a head start on the stovetop or in the microwave before adding them to, for instance, Homey Chicken Stew (page 68); in this case the chicken needs far less time than the potato chunks and sliced carrots to be perfectly cooked. In other cases, as with Braised Steaks with Horseradish Smashed Potatoes (page 121), we can add raw small whole potatoes to the slow cooker along with the meat for perfect results. Delicate vegetables like frozen peas, baby spinach, and chopped tomatoes turn mushy and lackluster when added at the beginning of cooking, so stir them in at the end. Fresh stir-ins like sliced red bell pepper or zucchini can take just 20 minutes or less to soften.

11 MAKE THE MOST OF THE BRAISING LIQUID

The juice left behind after braising a roast is like liquid gold, but how you handle it to turn it into a rich sauce can be tricky in the slow cooker. Often all it needs is a quick skim to remove the excess fat from the surface, and some salt and pepper for seasoning, as we do with pot roast. For our Cider-Braised Pork Roast (page 166) the resulting sauce (flavored with apple butter, cider, and vinegar) is so delicious that all we need to do is skim off the fat and serve it with the meat. Other times, as with Turkey Breast with Gravy (page 159), we reduce the remaining sauce to intensify the flavor; we also sometimes put braising liquid in the blender for an unctuous sauce. Before serving we frequently stir in some acidic citrus juice or vinegar, or some chopped fresh herbs, to brighten and balance the flavors, such as in our Cuban Pork Roast with Mojo Sauce (page 167).

12 FINISH UNDER THE BROILER (SOMETIMES)

Since the slow cooker is a moist cooking vehicle, you will never get a nice char or crisp skin when using it. So a technique we picked up to get a nice crisp texture is to cook a dish all the way through and then finish it under the broiler. (We also like to use a glaze before and after broiling to build layers of flavor and to help ensure a crisp crust.) We use this technique with our meatloaves (pages 204–206) to get the signature caramelized crust. We also pass ribs (pages 142–143) and chicken wings (pages 32–33) under the broiler to give them that "grilled" char and crisp skin often associated with these dishes.

You'll find more than 60 soups, stews, and chilis in this book since they are perennial favorites for slow cooking and many of them can cook all day long. Here is what we learned to deliver perfect results.

BROTH IS ESSENTIAL

Broth is a key ingredient in soups and stews, adding flavor as well as keeping things moist. We start many of our soups and stews with broth instead of water to give them a back-bone of flavor. Broth from scratch is easy to make in the slow cooker (pages 40–41) and always tastes the best. While nothing compares with the flavor of homemade, sometimes even in the test kitchen we reach for convenient store-bought broth. We have tasted commercial chicken, beef, and vegetarian broths and can recommend these brands: **Swanson Chicken Stock**, **Better Than Bouillon Roasted Beef Base**, and **Orrington Farms Vegan Chicken Flavored Broth Base & Seasoning.**

When we need bold, briny flavor for a seafood dish such as Manhattan Clam Chowder (page 54), we reach for bottled clam juice, which is made by briefly steaming fresh clams in salted water and filtering the resulting broth before bottling. Our winner is **Bar Harbor Clam Juice.**

Bottled clam juice, along with the juice from canned clams, adds briny seafood flavor to our Manhattan clam chowder.

BROWN ONLY HALF THE MEAT

We found that we could streamline the process for many of our stews, chilis, and braises, such as Beef Burgundy (page 66), by browning only half of the meat to get rich flavor from the fond. The other half of the meat can then be added to the slow cooker raw.

ADD A PANADE TO GROUND MEAT

Lean ground meat can easily over-cook in the slow cooker and turn dry and gritty. After much trial and error during our chili making and beyond, we found that mixing the ground meat with a panade, a mixture of bread and milk or broth, produced the best results. For instance, a panade ensures that the ground turkey in our Turkey Chili (page 79) stays moist, and the ground beef in Shepherd's Pie (page 201) stays tender, after hours in the slow cooker.

HANDLE VEGETABLES WITH CARE

We worked hard to pack our stews with interesting combinations of vegetables, so naturally we also focused a lot of attention on ensuring they were perfectly cooked. For stews that have a short stay in the slow cooker, sturdier vegetables like potatoes and carrots, depending on how large they are cut, just do not cook through properly. Instead we parcook them before adding them to the slow cooker. For an all-day stew like Farro and Butternut Squash Stew (page 75), we cook the squash in a foil packet on top of the stew so that it stays flavorful and colorful.

USE YOUR NOODLES

Try as we might, we found we could not cook egg noodles in soup in the slow cooker; the heat of the slow cooker just isn't hot enough to cook them properly. So we cook our egg noodles on the stovetop and stir them into the soup at the end of cooking. We did, however, happily discover that finicky rice noodles work perfectly in the slow cooker. The noodles cook gently and don't break apart or turn mushy, making them the perfect addition to Vietnamese Beef and Noodle Soup (page 44), as well as Pork Pad Thai (page 145).

FINISH WITH FRESH FLAVOR

Because many dishes need a flavor boost before serving, we often finish our stews (and other dishes) with fresh herbs, citrus juice, vinegar, or other flavorful ingredients, like brown sugar or coconut milk.

In a slow cooker it can be really tricky to ensure moist, flavorful poultry. Here are the keys to achieving great results every time.

SHORTER COOKING TIME IS KEY

We found that the only way to cook chicken (and turkey) in a slow cooker is on the low setting and for a relatively short amount of time. We recommend that until you have experience cooking poultry in your slow cooker, start checking the temperature of chicken breasts (boneless and bone-in), whole chicken, and turkey breasts at the low end of the temperature range to ward off dry, overcooked poultry. Chicken thighs are more forgiving, making them especially well suited to the slow cooker because their dark meat becomes meltingly tender during the long cooking time; for this reason we cook them longer than bone-in or boneless breasts, and we don't check their temperature. Longer cooking times are also needed in soups or casseroles where the meat is insulated by other ingredients.

This one-pot chicken dinner features tender chicken finished with a basil vinaigrette and couscous, tomatoes, and fennel.

PROPER COOKING TIMES FOR POULTRY

Type of Poultry	Cooking Time*
Boneless, Skinless Chicken Breasts	1 to 2 hours on low
Bone-in Split Chicken Breasts	2 to 3 hours on low
Chicken Thighs	4 to 5 hours on low
Whole Chicken	4 to 5 hours on low
Turkey Breast	5 to 6 hours on low

*Note that cooking times vary in our Dinner for Two chapter

REMOVE THE SKIN

When left on the chicken, the skin becomes flabby and rubbery in the slow cooker, and the corresponding sauce superfatty—an unappealing result. We address this problem in two ways: We either remove the skin before cooking, or keep it on long enough to hold in flavor during cooking and then remove it afterward. Removing the skin before cooking usually left us with a plain, bland-tasting piece of meat, so we often drizzle our chicken with bright vinaigrettes or herbs to infuse flavor, such as in our Curried Chicken Thighs with Acorn Squash (page 110). Chicken skin is typically slippery, so a paper towel provides extra grip to help remove it. Because the skin is more difficult to remove from whole chickens, we wait until they are fully cooked and carved before removing the skin.

ADD A RUB UNDER AND OVER

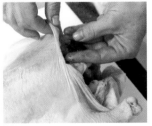

Distributing a flavorful rub both over and under the skin of the chicken ensures the best flavor. We do this with our Five Ways with Chicken in a Pot (page 156) and Herbed Chicken with Warm Spring Vegetable Salad (page 154). For a whole chicken, loosen the skin over the thighs and breast and rub half of the spice mixture under the skin, directly on the meat. Rub the remaining mixture on the skin of the entire chicken. Once the chicken is cooked and fully infused with the rub's flavor, you can easily remove the skin, or not— cook's choice.

POSITION A WHOLE CHICKEN CAREFULLY

Our testers discovered that when a whole chicken is placed breast side down, a moister bird results because the juices from the dark meat render down into the breast, keeping it from becoming over-cooked as the dark meat reaches the proper temperature.

SHAPE ALSO MATTERS

Buying the right pork loin roast makes all the difference. Look for a roast that is wide and short, and steer clear of those that are long and narrow. Narrow pork loins don't fit as easily into the slow cooker and are prone to overcooking because they cook through more quickly.

SPLIT ONE ROAST INTO TWO

A great method for ensuring even cooking is to break a large roast into two smaller roasts, as we do in Classic Pot Roast with Carrots and Potatoes (page 163); they cook for a shorter amount of time so as to cook to perfection.

SECURE POT ROASTS AND PORK LOINS WITH TWINE

Our favorite cuts for pot roast are beef chuck-eye roast and pork butt roast (also called Boston butt), because they are well marbled and become very tender over the long braising time. In our experience, these roasts often come unevenly cut or oddly shaped, so to ensure that they cook evenly, we tie them once or twice around the center with kitchen twine to produce a more uniformly shaped roast that will cook through evenly.

Brisket can cook all day in a slow cooker, and here it is given an overnight spice rub and cooked with lots of sliced onion.

The slow cooker is a great vehicle for cooking roasts, especially for the busy cook who doesn't have time to spend monitoring the oven. But you can't just set it and forget it in the slow cooker either; you have to make sure you've properly prepped and positioned your roasts to ensure ideal results. Here are a few important tips to guarantee your roasts are foolproof every time.

PICK THE RIGHT ROAST

The easiest roasts to cook in a slow cooker are the tougher, fattier roasts, like beef chuck-eye roast, beef brisket, and pork butt, because low-and-slow cooking turns the meat meltingly tender. That said, with a few tricks we found success with leaner roasts, too.

BROWNING ADDS COLOR AND FLAVOR

For some of our roasts, we chose to brown them in a skillet first. This step is often overlooked in slow-cooker recipes because of the added work and extra dishes, but we felt it provides a welcome depth of flavor not only to our finished roast but to the final sauce or gravy made with the braising liquid. For more information about using a skillet to brown a roast, see page 8.

POSITION CORRECTLY

In our testing we learned that getting juicy roasts has a lot to do with how we position them in the slow cooker. Nestling two pork tenderloins side by side, alternating the narrow and thicker ends, helps to insulate the lean meat and prevent it from overcooking. Positioning larger roasts, like brisket and pork loins, fat and/or skin side up allows more fat to render and baste the meat as it cooks.

MAXIMIZE FLAVOR WITH RUBS AND AROMATICS

No one wants to serve up a pale, bland-looking pork loin, pork tenderloin, or beef roast. The moist environment and extended cooking times of the slow cooker are notorious for producing dull, washed-out flavors. To prevent our roasts from turning out bland, we season them liberally with spice rubs, like in our Braised Brisket and Onions (page 161), and flavor-packed sauces. We also create concentrated bases for braising with plenty of aromatics and spices. As the roasts cook, they are infused with the bold flavor of the braising liquid, like with our Southwestern Pork Roast (page 169).

LET IT REST

After almost any piece of meat finishes cooking, it is crucial to allow it to rest. During this time the proteins relax and reabsorb any accumulated meat juices and redistribute them throughout the meat, resulting in juicier and more tender cuts and less pooled drippings. For lean cuts of meat that are prone to drying out and turning tough, this resting time is especially important for ensuring that they stay moist and tender. We often call for tenting meat with aluminum foil to keep it warm while it rests. Unless a recipe calls for something more specific, we found that tenting a roast works best when one sheet of foil is loosely placed on top of the meat in an upside-down V. Do not crimp the edges as this can trap steam and sog out a crust.

PROPER COOKING TIMES FOR ROASTS

Type of Roast	Cooking Time on Low	Cooking Time on High
Top Sirloin Beef Roast	1 to 2 hours	—
Boneless Beef Chuck-Eye Roast	9 to 10 hours	6 to 7 hours
Beef Brisket	9 to 10 hours	6 to 7 hours
Pork Tenderloin	1 to 2 hours	—
Boneless Pork Loin	2 to 3 hours	—
Boneless Pork Butt Roast	9 to 10 hours	6 to 7 hours
Ham	5 to 6 hours	—

MAKE IT A MEAL

What's even better than making a no-fuss roast in the slow cooker? Having a side dish to serve along with it. To get a complete meal all in one pot, we sometimes add beans, rice, and vegetables including potatoes, carrots, onions, or sweet potatoes to the slow cooker along with our roasts. Then, while our roasts rest, we quickly mash the sweet potatoes or toss the potatoes in dressing for easy salads. In other cases, we add fresh vegetables or grains to the slow cooker as the roast rests and up the heat to high to cook them through in a flash, such as for our Spiced Pork Tenderloin with Raisin-Almond Couscous (page 138).

Adding small potatoes and carrot pieces to the slow cooker alongside savory pot roast makes a hearty one-pot meal.

Overcooked fish and rubbery shrimp are all too common, but the combination of the slow cooker's low temperature and mild heat is terrific for producing moist fish fillets and tender shrimp and scallops. Here are a few key points to keep in mind to successfully cook seafood in the slow cooker.

KEEP A RULER HANDY

Ensuring moist fish in the slow cooker starts at the fish counter, where we choose 1- to 1½-inch-thick fillets and steaks, which can cook for a longer period of time without drying out. It is also important to choose fillets or steaks that are similar in size and thickness so that each piece will cook at the same rate.

TEMP YOUR FISH

To further guarantee that the fish is properly cooked, we use the low setting and short time ranges to reduce the opportunity for overcooking. Start monitoring the fish's temperature at the low end of the range until you have experience cooking it in your slow cooker.

This cod peperonata features a bold base of bell peppers, tomatoes, paprika, and wine, into which we nestle the fish.

STIR IN SHRIMP AND SCALLOPS AT THE END

Yes, you can cook shrimp and scallops in a slow cooker, but the key is to add them toward the end of the cooking time and let the moist heat of the slow cooker gently cook them through. For instance, we learned it takes just 30 to 40 minutes to cook shrimp in a slow cooker, so for a seafood stew or soup we let the base of broth, vegetables, and aromatics simmer for several hours to soften the vegetables and meld flavors before we add the shrimp. The same principle holds true for scallops, such as our Scallops with Creamy Braised Leeks (page 188), where we use the majority of the slow-cooker time to braise the leeks in wine and cream, then add the scallops for the last 30 to 40 minutes.

USE A SLING WHEN POACHING

To make it easy to remove delicate fish from the slow cooker after poaching, we often use a foil sling. To form a sling, fold a sheet of aluminum foil into a 12 by 9-inch rectangle and press it widthwise into the slow cooker. Use the ends of the sling as handles to lift the fish out of the slow cooker fully intact.

SHALLOW POACH

Poaching is an easy method for cooking fish, but it typically requires prepping a slew of ingredients for the poaching broth, only to dump it out at the end of cooking. Plus, much of the fish's flavor leaches out into the liquid. Fortunately, in the slow cooker these problems can be easily solved using a shallow poaching technique: We simply rest the fish on top of a few citrus slices and herb stems to keep it elevated for even cooking, and we use just enough liquid to gently steam, not simmer, the fish. During our testing we also learned that adding wine to the poaching liquid helps to achieve perfectly cooked fish quickly at a lower temperature. This is because wine lowers water's boiling point and produces more vapor to cook the fillets. This steamy environment gave us perfectly poached fish every time.

DON'T COOK CLAMS OR MUSSELS

After much testing with clams and mussels, we learned that by the time they become hot enough for the shells to open up (and sometimes they don't open), their tender meat is tough and inedible. In short, the slow cooker doesn't get hot enough fast enough to safely cook clams or mussels.

With exacting cooking times and in most cases precise amounts of liquid required, rice, grain, and bean dishes can be tricky to cook perfectly in your slow cooker. Here is what we learned.

USE AN OVAL SLOW COOKER

We found that an oval slow cooker is the perfect vessel in which to cook perfect rice, lentils, wheat berries, and more. The oval shape provides more surface area over which to spread the rice and grains to allow for more even cooking.

TRAP STEAM WITH PARCHMENT

In addition to the right ratio of rice to water, the key to perfectly cooked rice is a parchment shield (see page 177). Crimping a piece of parchment over the top of the rice creates a vacuum that prevents the grains on top from drying out as the water is absorbed. In addition, condensation builds up on the parchment shield and drips back down onto the rice, creating a superbly even, moist environment. This works beautifully for sides like Wild Rice Pilaf with Cranberries and Pecans (page 279) and more elaborate dishes with lots of rice like Mushroom Biryani (page 246) and Paella (page 199).

ADD BOILING WATER

We learned that long-grain white rice, basmati rice, and brown rice all need a head start with boiling water in the slow cooker. We found that cooking them on high is best, as is using a layer of parchment over the rice to protect the grains on top from drying out as the liquid is absorbed.

A WORD ABOUT INSTANT RICE

In some recipes where rice plays a supporting role, as in Lemony Chicken and Rice with Spinach and Feta (page 110), we found that traditional rice takes too long to cook. Raw rice doesn't cook through evenly and is blown out and mushy by the time the chicken or beans are done. Instant white rice, also known as minute rice, stirred in toward the end of cooking, holds its shape and absorbs the rich flavors of the cooking liquid and other ingredients.

Topping basmati rice with a layer of mushrooms and then a sheet of parchment paper ensures it cooks evenly.

NO SOAKING NEEDED

When starting with dried beans, we add them right to the slow cooker, no advance soaking or simmering needed. The beans require no prep other than being picked over and rinsed. Dried beans are well suited to low-and-slow cooking, and the gentle simmering heat of the slow cooker helps the beans to cook through evenly.

COOK BEANS ON HIGH

The gentle, steady heat of the slow cooker produces perfectly tender beans and chickpeas after 8 or 9 hours of cooking them on the high setting. But we weren't able to get the same result from cooking on low; even after 16 hours of cooking, we still had crunchy beans. So we cook our Baked Beans (pages 288–289) and other bean recipes exclusively on high.

CHAPTER 1

EASY APPETIZERS

■ EASY PREP ■ VEGETARIAN ■ LIGHT ■ COOK ALL DAY
Photo: Garlicky Shrimp

Easy Spiced Nuts

SERVES 10 TO 14 **EASY PREP** **VEG** **LIGHT**
COOKING TIME 2 TO 3 HOURS ON HIGH
SLOW COOKER SIZE 4 TO 7 QUARTS

WHY THIS RECIPE WORKS Crunchy and addictive, spiced nuts make a great hors d'oeuvre or snack. And while most recipes call for toasting the nuts in the oven, we wanted to see if we could use a slow cooker instead and avoid the pitfall of burning them. We decided to go with a simple spice combination of cinnamon, ginger, and coriander, using just enough to complement the flavor of the nuts without overpowering them. The addition of just ¼ cup sugar provided some background sweetness, which played well against the warm spices. To make sure the spices adhered to the nuts, we also needed a liquid component. Some spiced nut recipes call for using butter or syrup, but these liquids don't necessarily do a good job of coating everything; we found that an egg white mixed with a little water and salt worked best. To avoid unappealing clumps of egg white on the roasted nuts, we drained them thoroughly before adding the spices. You can use any combination of nuts here; just be sure to have 3 cups in total. You will need an oval slow cooker for this recipe. This recipe can be doubled; you will need to cool the nut mixture on two rimmed baking sheets.

- 1 large egg white
- 1 tablespoon water
- 1 teaspoon salt
- 3 cups (15 ounces) whole unblanched almonds, cashews, pecans, and/or walnuts
- ¼ cup sugar
- 2 teaspoons ground cinnamon
- 1 teaspoon ground ginger
- 1 teaspoon ground coriander

1. Lightly coat slow cooker with vegetable oil spray. Whisk egg white, water, and salt together in large bowl. Add almonds and toss to coat; drain thoroughly in fine-mesh strainer.

2. Combine sugar, cinnamon, ginger, and coriander in second large bowl. Add almonds and toss to coat. Transfer almond mixture to prepared slow cooker, cover, and cook, stirring every 30 minutes, until almonds are toasted and fragrant, 2 to 3 hours on high.

3. Transfer almond mixture to rimmed baking sheet and spread into even layer. Let cool to room temperature, about 20 minutes. Serve. (Almonds can be stored at room temperature for up to 1 week.)

NOTES FROM THE TEST KITCHEN

All About Nuts

With their meaty texture, great flavor, and abundant healthy fats and protein, nuts are an essential ingredient in many recipes. Here's what you need to know.

STORING NUTS All nuts are high in oil and will become rancid rather quickly. In the test kitchen, we store all nuts in the freezer in freezer-safe zipper-lock bags. Frozen nuts will keep for months, and there's no need to defrost before toasting or chopping.

TOASTING NUTS Toasting nuts brings out their flavors and gives them a satisfying crunchy texture. To toast a small amount (under 1 cup), put the nuts (or seeds) in a dry small skillet over medium heat. Shake the skillet occasionally to prevent scorching and toast until they are lightly browned and fragrant, 3 to 8 minutes. Watch them closely since they can go from golden to burnt very quickly. To toast more than 1 cup of nuts, spread the nuts in a single layer on a rimmed baking sheet and toast in a 350-degree oven. To promote even toasting, shake the baking sheet every few minutes, and toast until the nuts are lightly browned and fragrant, 5 to 10 minutes.

SKINNING NUTS The skins from some nuts, such as walnuts and hazelnuts, can impart a bitter flavor and an undesirable texture in some dishes. To remove the skins, simply rub the hot toasted nuts inside a clean dish towel.

ALMOND PRIMER Most nuts can be found either raw, toasted, or roasted, but almonds are sold in a dizzying array of varieties: raw, roasted, blanched, slivered, sliced, and smoked. So which almonds do we prefer? When it comes to decorating cookies, we like the clean presentation of whole skinless blanched almonds. For other baked goods, leafy salads, and simple side dishes, we find that thinly sliced raw almonds (with or without their skins) deliver a nice, light flavor and texture. In stir-fries and pilafs, we love the substantial crunch of thick-cut slivered almonds. Roasted almonds are best for eating out of hand. As for smoked almonds, we find their bold flavor and crunch are best in snacks like spiced nuts or party mixes. Like all nuts, almonds are highly perishable (the oils in the nuts go rancid quickly) and are best stored in the freezer to prevent spoilage.

Stirring the party mix a couple of times while in the slow cooker is the key to an appealingly crisp mix.

Party Mix

SERVES 10 TO 12   `EASY PREP`
COOKING TIME 3 TO 4 HOURS ON HIGH
SLOW COOKER SIZE 4 TO 7 QUARTS

WHY THIS RECIPE WORKS Crunchy, salty, and borderline addictive, homemade party snack mix is guaranteed to disappear quickly at any gathering. But after making a back-of-the-box party mix recipe, we felt there was room for improvement. We decided to sidestep the conventional oven method in favor of using the slow cooker to create a perfectly toasted party mix every time. We started with the classic combination of Corn, Rice, and Wheat Chex cereals, to which we added pita chips, minipretzels, and dry-roasted peanuts. Tasters preferred the nutty sweetness of melted butter to margarine or olive oil, each of which left a greasy finish. Since Worcestershire sauce was integral to getting that trademark party mix flavor, we decided to add a generous amount to ensure its flavor didn't become muted in the slow cooker. We also doubled the usual amount of garlic powder and added a little cayenne pepper for subtle heat. To help release excess moisture and ensure our mix wouldn't get soggy, we removed the lid every hour to stir, which also redistributed the mix so it wouldn't burn. To finish, we spread the mix out on a rimmed baked sheet to dry and crisp. You can use any combination of cereal here; just be sure to have 9 cups of cereal in total. You will need an oval slow cooker for this recipe.

9 cups (10 ounces) Corn, Rice, and/or Wheat Chex cereal
2 ounces pita chips, broken into 1-inch pieces (1 cup)
1 cup (1½ ounces) minipretzels
1 cup (5 ounces) dry-roasted peanuts
8 tablespoons unsalted butter, melted
¼ cup Worcestershire sauce
1½ teaspoons garlic powder
¼ teaspoon cayenne pepper

1. Combine cereal, pita chips, minipretzels, and peanuts in slow cooker. Whisk melted butter, Worcestershire, garlic powder, and cayenne together in bowl. Drizzle butter mixture over cereal mixture and gently toss until evenly coated. Cover and cook, stirring every hour, until cereal mixture is toasted and fragrant, 3 to 4 hours on high.

2. Transfer cereal mixture to rimmed baking sheet and spread into even layer. Let cool to room temperature, about 20 minutes. Serve. (Party mix can be stored at room temperature for up to 1 week.)

Warm Marinated Artichoke Hearts

SERVES 8 TO 10   `EASY PREP`   `VEG`
COOKING TIME 1 TO 2 HOURS ON LOW
SLOW COOKER SIZE 4 TO 7 QUARTS

WHY THIS RECIPE WORKS Marinated artichoke hearts are a classic antipasto, but when flavored with little more than oil and garlic they can be boring and one-dimensional. We wanted to revive this dish by using the gentle heat of the slow cooker to infuse the artichokes with deep, complex flavor. Fresh artichokes are not always readily available and can be a hassle to prepare for cooking, so we started with jarred artichoke hearts. Available year-round, they come fully prepped right out of the jar; we simply needed to halve and rinse them, then pat them dry before tossing them in the slow cooker. To flavor the basic marinade, we added some bright lemon zest and juice, red pepper flakes, and a few sprigs of fresh thyme along with the requisite olive oil and garlic. Briny kalamata olives and rich, tangy feta cheese fit in nicely with the Mediterranean theme; we simply stirred the cheese in at the end of cooking to ensure that the cubes wouldn't lose their shape. While we prefer the flavor and texture of jarred whole baby artichokes, you can substitute 18 ounces frozen artichoke hearts, thawed and patted dry, for the jarred. Serve with crusty bread for dipping in the infused oil.

3 cups jarred whole baby artichokes packed in water, halved, rinsed, and patted dry
1 cup extra-virgin olive oil
½ cup pitted kalamata olives, halved
3 garlic cloves, peeled and smashed
2 sprigs fresh thyme
¾ teaspoon grated lemon zest plus 2 tablespoons juice
Salt and pepper
¼ teaspoon red pepper flakes
4 ounces feta cheese, cut into ½-inch cubes (1 cup)

1. Combine artichokes, oil, olives, garlic, thyme sprigs, lemon zest and juice, 1 teaspoon salt, and pepper flakes in slow cooker. Cover and cook until heated through and flavors meld, 1 to 2 hours on low.

2. Discard thyme sprigs. Gently stir in feta and let sit until heated through, about 5 minutes. Season with salt and pepper to taste. Serve warm or at room temperature. (Marinated artichokes can be held on warm or low setting for up to 2 hours.)

NOTES FROM THE TEST KITCHEN

The Best Supermarket Extra-Virgin Olive Oil

Extra-virgin oils range wildly in price, color, and quality, so it's hard to know which to buy. While many things can affect the quality and flavor of olive oil, the type of olive, the time of harvest (earlier means greener, more bitter, and pungent; later, more mild and buttery), and the processing are the most important factors. The best-quality olive oil comes from olives pressed as quickly as possible without heat (which coaxes more oil from the olives at the expense of flavor). Our favorite supermarket extra-virgin olive oil, **California Olive Ranch Everyday Extra Virgin Olive Oil** ($9.99 for 500 ml), is a standout for its "fruity," "fragrant" flavor. In fact, its flavor rivaled that of our favorite high-end extra-virgin oil.

Warm Marinated Mushrooms

SERVES 8 TO 10 EASY PREP VEG
COOKING TIME 1 TO 2 HOURS ON LOW
SLOW COOKER SIZE 4 TO 7 QUARTS

WHY THIS RECIPE WORKS A classic Italian antipasto, marinated mushrooms are rich with earthy flavor. The right combination of bright acidity, heady herbs, and a fine extra-virgin olive oil should pack each bite with a punch. To create the most flavorful mushrooms possible, we started by microwaving them, which released their moisture and avoided a diluted marinade. Then we simply combined the mushrooms and the marinade ingredients in the slow cooker; after just 2 hours they were tender but not mushy and had absorbed the warm, herb-infused oil. For a finishing touch, we built up the flavor even more by adding Dijon mustard, sherry vinegar, and fresh tarragon to turn that nice herb oil into a great warm vinaigrette. Tasters couldn't get enough of the mushrooms as a result of this flavor boost. Look for small mushrooms, about 1¼ inches in diameter, for this recipe. If your mushrooms are larger, halve or quarter them before cooking. Serve with crusty bread for dipping in the infused oil.

2 pounds small cremini or white mushrooms, trimmed
½ cup extra-virgin olive oil
4 garlic cloves, minced
3 sprigs fresh thyme
Salt and pepper
2 tablespoons minced fresh tarragon
1 tablespoon Dijon mustard
1 tablespoon sherry vinegar

1. Toss mushrooms with 2 tablespoons oil in bowl and microwave, stirring occasionally, until mushrooms release their liquid and shrink in size, about 10 minutes; drain thoroughly.

2. Combine mushrooms, garlic, thyme sprigs, ¾ teaspoon salt, ¼ teaspoon pepper, and remaining 6 tablespoons oil in slow cooker. Cover and cook until mushrooms are tender and flavors meld, 1 to 2 hours on low.

3. Discard thyme sprigs. Stir in tarragon, mustard, and vinegar and season with salt and pepper to taste. Serve warm or at room temperature. (Marinated mushrooms can be held on warm or low setting for up to 2 hours.)

Convenient jarred artichokes and frozen spinach are quickly transformed into this flavorful, fresh-tasting dip.

Spinach and Artichoke Dip

SERVES 6 TO 8   `EASY PREP`   `VEG`
COOKING TIME 1 TO 2 HOURS ON LOW
SLOW COOKER SIZE 1½ TO 7 QUARTS

WHY THIS RECIPE WORKS Spinach and artichoke dip is a bona fide crowd-pleaser, but it often ends up watery, bland, and left behind on the buffet table. We wanted a reliable dip that was rich, creamy, and packed with flavorful chunks of artichokes and earthy spinach. We discarded versions with flour-thickened cream mixtures in favor of an easy-prep combination of softened cream cheese and mayonnaise that gave our dip both the creaminess we were after and a subtle tanginess that tasters enjoyed. Jarred artichoke hearts and frozen spinach were easier options than their fresh counterparts; we just made sure to rid them of excess moisture. With a sprinkle of fresh chives, our dip was ready for the party. While we prefer the flavor and texture of jarred whole baby artichokes, you can substitute 18 ounces frozen artichoke hearts, thawed and patted dry, for the jarred. Serve with crusty bread, crackers, and/or Crostini.

6 ounces cream cheese, softened
½ cup mayonnaise
2 tablespoons water
1 tablespoon lemon juice
3 garlic cloves, minced
¼ teaspoon salt
¼ teaspoon pepper
3 cups jarred whole baby artichokes packed in water, rinsed, patted dry, and chopped
10 ounces frozen spinach, thawed and squeezed dry
2 tablespoons minced fresh chives

1. Whisk cream cheese, mayonnaise, water, lemon juice, garlic, salt, and pepper in large bowl until well combined. Gently fold in artichokes and spinach.

2A. FOR 1½- TO 5-QUART SLOW COOKER Transfer mixture to slow cooker, cover, and cook until heated through, 1 to 2 hours on low.

2B. FOR 5½- TO 7-QUART SLOW COOKER Transfer mixture to 1½-quart soufflé dish. Set dish in slow cooker and pour water into slow cooker until it reaches about one-third up sides of dish (about 2 cups water). Cover and cook until heated through, 1 to 2 hours on low. Remove dish from slow cooker, if desired.

3. Gently stir dip to recombine. Sprinkle with chives and serve. (Dip can be held on warm or low setting for up to 2 hours.)

SIMPLE ACCOMPANIMENTS

CROSTINI
MAKES 25 TO 30 TOASTS
Crostini taste best straight from the oven.

1 large (12- to 15-inch) baguette, cut into ½-inch-thick slices on bias
1 garlic clove, peeled and sliced in half
2 tablespoons extra-virgin olive oil
Salt and pepper

Adjust oven rack to middle position and heat oven to 400 degrees. Arrange bread in single layer on baking sheet. Bake bread until dry and crisp, about 10 minutes, flipping slices over halfway through baking. Rub garlic clove over 1 side of each piece of toasted bread, then brush with oil. Season with salt and pepper to taste and serve.

You can serve this warm crab dip right from a small slow cooker, or put it in a soufflé dish if using a large one.

Creamy Crab Dip

SERVES 6 TO 8   **EASY PREP**
COOKING TIME 1 TO 2 HOURS ON LOW
SLOW COOKER SIZE 1½ TO 7 QUARTS

WHY THIS RECIPE WORKS For an elegant crab dip that tasted first and foremost of crab, we included a full pound of crabmeat and limited the amount of filler. Patting the crabmeat dry was key to ensuring that the dip was creamy but not watery, and adding some traditional Old Bay seasoning balanced the sweet richness of the crabmeat. We tried adding raw onions to the slow cooker, but they never turned tender, so we softened them in the microwave with butter first to give them a head start. We liked a combination of cream cheese and mayonnaise for the mild tanginess and rich texture it lent to our dip. Finishing with a sprinkle

of chives instead of the traditional cheese layer gave our creamy dip a lighter, fresher flavor. Do not substitute imitation crabmeat here. Serve with crusty bread, crackers, and/or Crostini (page 23).

    1 small onion, chopped fine
    2 tablespoons unsalted butter
    2 teaspoons Old Bay seasoning
    8 ounces cream cheese, softened
    ¼ cup mayonnaise
    ¼ teaspoon pepper
    1 pound lump crabmeat, picked over for shells
       and pressed dry between paper towels
    2 tablespoons minced fresh chives

1. Microwave onion, butter, and Old Bay in large bowl, stirring occasionally, until onion is softened, about 5 minutes. Whisk in cream cheese, mayonnaise, and pepper until well combined. Gently fold in crabmeat.

2A. FOR 1½- TO 5-QUART SLOW COOKER Transfer mixture to slow cooker, cover, and cook until heated through, 1 to 2 hours on low.

2B. FOR 5½- TO 7-QUART SLOW COOKER Transfer mixture to 1½-quart soufflé dish. Set dish in slow cooker and pour water into slow cooker until it reaches about one-third up sides of dish (about 2 cups water). Cover and cook until heated through, 1 to 2 hours on low. Remove dish from slow cooker, if desired.

3. Gently stir dip to recombine. Sprinkle with chives and serve. (Dip can be held on warm or low setting for up to 2 hours.)

NOTES FROM THE TEST KITCHEN

Buying Crabmeat

Check the fish counter for containers of fresh or pasteurized crabmeat. These do cost more than the small cans you'll find near the tuna, but they're well worth the additional cost. Depending upon the season, pasteurized crabmeat can cost significantly less than fresh, and it has a long shelf life. You should always use fresh crabmeat for crab cakes, where the texture and flavor of the crab take center stage, but pasteurized crabmeat is fine for dips and casseroles. Jumbo lump is the highest-quality crabmeat (and the most expensive, too) and, as the name suggests, consists of large lumps of meat.

It's worth using your best extra-virgin olive oil for this simple white bean dip.

Rosemary and Garlic White Bean Dip

SERVES 6 TO 8   **EASY PREP**   **VEG**   LIGHT
COOKING TIME 1 TO 2 HOURS ON LOW
SLOW COOKER SIZE 1½ TO 7 QUARTS

WHY THIS RECIPE WORKS For a simple white bean dip to really stand out, it needs to have both a little texture and a lot of flavor. To transform humble legumes into a rich, warm dip worthy of a dinner party, we started with delicately flavored cannellini beans. We processed most of the beans into a smooth puree along with a good dose of extra-virgin olive oil, but we reserved a third of the beans to pulse in at the end for an appealing chunky texture. For bold, aromatic flavor, we stirred in a little garlic, rosemary, lemon zest, and lemon juice. Serve with crusty bread, crackers, and/or Crostini (page 23).

3 (15-ounce) cans cannellini beans, rinsed
¼ cup extra-virgin olive oil, plus extra for serving
1 garlic clove, minced
1 teaspoon minced fresh rosemary
¼ teaspoon grated lemon zest plus 1 tablespoon juice
¼ teaspoon salt

1. Process two-thirds of beans, oil, garlic, rosemary, lemon zest and juice, and salt in food processor until smooth, about 10 seconds, scraping down sides of bowl as needed. Add remaining beans and pulse until just incorporated (mixture will be chunky), about 2 pulses.

2A. FOR 1½- TO 5-QUART SLOW COOKER Transfer mixture to slow cooker, cover, and cook until heated through, 1 to 2 hours on low.

2B. FOR 5½- TO 7-QUART SLOW COOKER Transfer mixture to 1½-quart soufflé dish. Set dish in slow cooker and pour water into slow cooker until it reaches about one-third up sides of dish (about 2 cups water). Cover and cook until heated through, 1 to 2 hours on low. Remove dish from slow cooker, if desired.

3. Gently stir dip to recombine and adjust consistency with hot water as needed. Drizzle dip with extra oil and serve. (Dip can be held on warm or low setting for up to 2 hours.)

NOTES FROM THE TEST KITCHEN

Canned Cannellini Beans

We go through a lot of cannellini beans here in the test kitchen. Their creamy texture and mildly nutty flavor round out soups, casseroles, pasta dishes, and salads alike, and they can also be used to make appealing dips. Our readers love them, too. Seventy-one percent say that they regularly buy canned cannellini beans. We've always appreciated the convenience of canned beans for use in quick recipes and their ability to be pureed into perfectly creamy spreads.

Modern canning practices, which vary from brand to brand, generally call for cleaning, sorting, and blanching the beans before sealing them in their cans with water and, often, salt, which flavors the beans and tenderizes the skins. All but one of the products we tasted add calcium chloride, which maintains firmness and prevents splitting, and calcium disodium EDTA, a preservative that binds iron in the water and prevents white beans from turning brown. Sampling the beans plain, in dip, and in soup. we found that seasoning ended up playing the biggest role in our results: Our winning can, made by **Goya**, was the saltiest in the bunch, while our last-place contender was a no-salt-added organic product.

Refried Bean Dip

SERVES 6 TO 8 `EASY PREP` `VEG`
COOKING TIME 1 TO 2 HOURS ON LOW
SLOW COOKER SIZE 1½ TO 7 QUARTS

WHY THIS RECIPE WORKS Refried bean dip is a staple at any game-day gathering, but it's often lacking in the flavor department. We ditched the dull-tasting canned refried beans. Instead, we started with canned pinto beans, processed most of them until smooth, then pulsed in some more whole beans to give the dip a chunky texture. Next, we packed in bold flavor with chili powder, garlic, and cumin, as well as a can of spicy Ro-tel Diced Tomatoes & Green Chilies. Finishing it with Monterey Jack cheese and bright cilantro balanced the hearty beans and flavorful spices. Serve with tortilla chips and/or Easy Homemade Pita Chips.

3 (15-ounce) cans pinto beans, rinsed
½ cup chicken or vegetable broth
2 teaspoons chili powder
1 garlic clove, minced
1 teaspoon salt
½ teaspoon ground cumin
1 (10-ounce) can Ro-tel Diced Tomatoes & Green Chilies, drained
2 ounces Monterey Jack cheese, shredded (½ cup)
2 tablespoons minced fresh cilantro

1. Process two-thirds of beans, broth, chili powder, garlic, salt, and cumin in food processor until smooth, about 10 seconds, scraping down sides of bowl as needed. Add tomatoes and remaining beans and pulse until incorporated (mixture will be chunky), about 2 pulses.

2A. FOR 1½- TO 5-QUART SLOW COOKER Transfer mixture to slow cooker, cover, and cook until heated through, 1 to 2 hours on low. Gently stir dip to recombine. Sprinkle with Monterey Jack, cover, and cook on low until cheese is melted, about 5 minutes.

2B. FOR 5½- TO 7-QUART SLOW COOKER Transfer mixture to 1½-quart soufflé dish. Set dish in slow cooker and pour water into slow cooker until it reaches about one-third up sides of dish (about 2 cups water). Cover and cook until heated through, 1 to 2 hours on low. Gently stir dip to recombine, then sprinkle with Monterey Jack. Cover and cook on low until cheese is melted, about 5 minutes. Remove dish from slow cooker, if desired.

3. Sprinkle dip with cilantro and serve. (Dip can be held on warm or low setting for up to 2 hours.)

SIMPLE ACCOMPANIMENTS

EASY HOMEMADE PITA CHIPS

MAKES 48 CHIPS
An oil mister works best here, but you can also use olive oil spray. These chips work well with any type of dip.

4 (8-inch) white or whole-wheat pita breads
  Olive oil spray
1 teaspoon salt

1. Adjust oven racks to upper-middle and lower-middle positions and heat oven to 350 degrees. Using kitchen shears, cut around perimeter of each pita bread to yield 2 thin rounds. Stack pita rounds and, using a chef's knife, cut into 6 wedges each. Spread pita wedges, smooth side down, over 2 rimmed baking sheets. Spray top of each chip with oil, then sprinkle with salt.

2. Bake chips until beginning to crisp and brown lightly, 8 to 10 minutes. Flip chips over so smooth side is facing up and continue to bake until chips are fully toasted, 8 to 10 minutes longer. Remove baking sheets from oven and let cool before serving. (Chips can be stored at room temperature for up to 3 days.)

Beef and Black Bean Taco Dip

SERVES 6 TO 8 `EASY PREP`
COOKING TIME 1 TO 2 HOURS ON LOW
SLOW COOKER SIZE 3 TO 7 QUARTS

WHY THIS RECIPE WORKS We set out to develop a hearty, meaty taco dip worthy of eating while watching the big game. We wanted our dip to include plenty of flavorful ground beef, but when we simply stirred raw ground beef into the slow cooker, the dip was a watery, greasy mess. So we partially cooked the ground beef in the microwave to remove moisture and render excess fat. A packet of taco seasoning and a little garlic made quick work of seasoning the beef and helped shorten our ingredient list. To bulk up the meat, we added lots of hearty black beans. Mashing half of the beans and stirring in some shredded Monterey Jack cheese helped to bind everything together. To finish, we topped the dip with more gooey Monterey Jack and a sprinkling of scallions. Serve with tortilla chips and/or Easy Homemade Pita Chips.

This taco dip easily delivers great Tex-Mex flavor thanks to store-bought taco seasoning and Ro-tel canned tomatoes.

1 pound 85 percent lean ground beef
1 (1-ounce) packet taco seasoning
2 garlic cloves, minced
2 (15-ounce) cans black beans, rinsed
2 (10-ounce) cans Ro-tel Diced Tomatoes & Green Chilies, drained with ¼ cup juice reserved
8 ounces Monterey Jack cheese, shredded (2 cups)
2 scallions, sliced thin

1. Microwave ground beef, taco seasoning, and garlic in bowl, stirring occasionally, until beef is no longer pink, about 5 minutes. Break up any large pieces of beef with spoon, then drain off excess fat.

2. Using potato masher, mash half of beans with reserved tomato juice in large bowl until mostly smooth. Stir in beef mixture, tomatoes, 1½ cups Monterey Jack, and remaining beans until well combined.

3A. FOR 3- TO 5-QUART SLOW COOKER Transfer mixture to slow cooker, cover, and cook until heated through, 1 to 2 hours on low. Gently stir dip to recombine, then sprinkle with remaining ½ cup Monterey Jack. Cover and cook on low until cheese is melted, about 5 minutes.

3B. FOR 5½- TO 7-QUART SLOW COOKER Transfer mixture to 1½-quart soufflé dish. Set dish in slow cooker and pour water into slow cooker until it reaches about one-third up sides of dish (about 2 cups water). Cover and cook until heated through, 1 to 2 hours on low. Gently stir dip to recombine, then sprinkle with remaining ½ cup Monterey Jack. Cover and cook on low until cheese is melted, about 5 minutes. Remove dish from slow cooker, if desired.

4. Sprinkle dip with scallions and serve. (Dip can be held on warm or low setting for up to 2 hours.)

Pepperoni Pizza Dip

SERVES 6 TO 8 `EASY PREP`
COOKING TIME 1 TO 2 HOURS ON LOW
SLOW COOKER SIZE 3 TO 7 QUARTS

WHY THIS RECIPE WORKS Too often pizza dips try to incorporate the flavors of pizza but end up as dense, greasy cheese bombs. We wanted a pizza-inspired dip that we could actually dip into—without losing half our chip along the way. To start, we combined rich, meltable cream cheese and flavorful pizza sauce for a creamy, tangy base. Then we gradually added mozzarella until we found the perfect balance between a creamy dip and stringy, chewy pizza cheese. Next we added our favorite pizza toppings—spicy pepperoni and earthy mushrooms. To remove the mushrooms' excess moisture and the pepperoni's grease, we briefly microwaved them before stirring them into the slow cooker. Though we liked the idea of further imitating pizza by sprinkling an extra layer of cheese over the top, in practice the extra cheese made our dip over-the-top greasy. Instead we reserved a quarter of the mushrooms and pepperoni for the top and garnished it with a little fresh basil. Serve with tortilla chips and/or Easy Homemade Pita Chips (page 26).

1 pound white mushrooms, trimmed and sliced thin
4 ounces thinly sliced pepperoni, quartered
1 pound cream cheese, softened
1 cup canned pizza sauce
8 ounces mozzarella cheese, shredded (2 cups)
2 tablespoons chopped fresh basil

1. Line large plate with double layer of coffee filters. Spread mushrooms and pepperoni in even layer over filters and microwave until mushrooms have released their liquid and fat begins to render from pepperoni, about 3 minutes. Set aside one-quarter of mushroom-pepperoni mixture for topping.

2. Whisk cream cheese and pizza sauce in large bowl until well combined. Fold in remaining mushroom-pepperoni mixture and mozzarella.

3A. FOR 3- TO 5-QUART SLOW COOKER Transfer mixture to slow cooker and top with reserved mushroom-pepperoni mixture. Cover and cook until heated through, 1 to 2 hours on low.

3B. FOR 5½- TO 7-QUART SLOW COOKER Transfer mixture to 1½-quart soufflé dish and top with reserved mushroom-pepperoni mixture. Set dish in slow cooker and pour water into slow cooker until it reaches about one-third up sides of dish (about 2 cups water). Cover and cook until heated through, 1 to 2 hours on low. Remove dish from slow cooker, if desired.

4. Gently stir dip to recombine. Sprinkle dip with basil and serve. (Dip can be held on warm or low setting for up to 2 hours.)

NOTES FROM THE TEST KITCHEN

Pepperoni

Pepperoni dates back to ancient Rome, where it was a convenient food for soldiers on the march. It reached America with the Italian immigrants who arrived around 1900. Pepperoni started being used as a pizza topping in New York City, and its production underwent a total transformation from artisanal to commercial. Today pepperoni is the most-ordered pizza topping in the United States. Pepperoni is made from cured and fermented pork along with just a little beef, and it is seasoned with black pepper, sugar, anise, cayenne, paprika (the source of its orange color), and lots of salt. It should have spice, heat, and chew, and the flavors shouldn't get lost once baked. Our favorite supermarket brand is **Margherita Italian Style Pepperoni.**

Cream cheese and a little cornstarch stabilize our flavorful slow-cooker fondue.

Beer and Cheddar Fondue

SERVES 8 TO 10   EASY PREP   VEG
COOKING TIME 1 TO 2 HOURS ON LOW
SLOW COOKER SIZE 1½ TO 7 QUARTS

WHY THIS RECIPE WORKS Fondue can be tricky because it tends to be fussy; to prevent the cheese from separating, it needs to be melted slowly and gently. Once melted, it must be kept at just the right temperature and frequently stirred to keep the fondue from breaking. We wanted to take advantage of the gentle, steady heat of the slow cooker to make a beer and cheddar fondue that would stay creamy for hours unattended. Sharp cheddar had great flavor, but its texture was consistently grainy when melted. We switched to mild cheddar and added highly meltable American cheese to make it even creamier, but our fondue still turned grainy as it sat. To further stabilize it, we added a mixture of cornstarch and cream cheese. Now we had a fondue that stayed creamy without constant stirring. To bring out the flavor of the cheddar, we added some garlic and dry mustard. Finally, for the characteristic malty flavor, we added some mild lager—tasters preferred its milder, less bitter flavor over other styles of beer. This fondue tasted best when made with block cheese that we shredded ourselves; you can find block American cheese at the deli counter. Preshredded cheese will work, but the fondue will be much thicker. For dipping we like to use bread, apple slices, steamed broccoli and cauliflower florets, and cured meats. Be sure to have long skewers on hand for easy dipping.

 1 cup mild lager, such as Budweiser
 4 ounces cream cheese
 1 tablespoon cornstarch
 1 garlic clove, minced
 1 teaspoon dry mustard
 ¼ teaspoon pepper
 8 ounces mild cheddar cheese, shredded (2 cups)
 8 ounces American cheese, shredded (2 cups)

1. Microwave beer, cream cheese, cornstarch, garlic, mustard, and pepper in large bowl, whisking occasionally, until smooth and thickened, about 5 minutes. Stir in cheddar and American cheeses until combined.

2A. FOR 1½- TO 5-QUART SLOW COOKER Transfer mixture to slow cooker, cover, and cook until cheese is melted, 1 to 2 hours on low.

2B. FOR 5½- TO 7-QUART SLOW COOKER Transfer mixture to 1½-quart soufflé dish. Set dish in slow cooker and pour water into slow cooker until it reaches about one-third up sides of dish (about 2 cups water). Cover and cook until cheese is melted, 1 to 2 hours on low. Remove dish from slow cooker, if desired.

3. Whisk fondue until smooth. Serve. (Fondue can be held on warm or low setting for up to 2 hours. Adjust consistency with hot water as needed, adding 2 tablespoons at a time.)

NOTES FROM THE TEST KITCHEN

The Color of Cheddar

If you live in the Midwest, your cheddar is probably orange. If you live in the Northeast, your cheddar is definitely white. Our test cooks have strong opinions about which color cheese tastes better (lining up with where they grew up). To settle the matter, we blindfolded 10 cooks and editors and had them taste two national brands of sharp white and orange (sometimes labeled yellow) cheddar, plain and in macaroni and cheese. Only one taster was able to distinguish flavor differences between the two colors of cheddar (and was that just blind luck?). Orange cheddars are colored with ground annatto seeds. These seeds, called *achiote* in Latin cooking, are used to color butter and margarine, too. Don't let regionalism color your perception: Color has no flavor.

A combination of shredded American cheese and Monterey Jack gives this queso dip its melty texture and big flavor.

Chile con Queso

SERVES 8 TO 10   EASY PREP   VEG
COOKING TIME 1 TO 2 HOURS ON LOW
SLOW COOKER SIZE 1½ TO 7 QUARTS

WHY THIS RECIPE WORKS Chile con queso has fallen on hard times; often it's just Ro-tel Diced Tomatoes & Green Chilies mixed with Velveeta, microwaved, and stirred. We wanted to keep the simplicity but ditch the plastic flavor and waxy texture. We started with a base of chicken broth, cream cheese, and cornstarch to help stabilize the cheese and prevent it from breaking. For the cheeses, we chose Monterey Jack for its great flavor and American cheese for its superior meltability. We kept the classic Ro-tel tomatoes but bumped up their flavor even more with garlic and canned chipotle chile. This dip tasted best when made with block cheese that we shredded ourselves; you can find block American cheese at the deli counter. Preshredded cheese will work, but the dip will be much thicker. If you prefer a mild chili con queso, omit the chipotle. Serve with tortilla chips and/or Easy Homemade Pita Chips (page 26).

1 cup chicken or vegetable broth

4 ounces cream cheese

1 tablespoon cornstarch

1 tablespoon minced canned chipotle chile in adobo sauce

1 garlic clove, minced

¼ teaspoon pepper

8 ounces Monterey Jack cheese, shredded (2 cups)

4 ounces American cheese, shredded (1 cup)

1 (10-ounce) can Ro-tel Diced Tomatoes & Green Chilies, drained

1. Microwave broth, cream cheese, cornstarch, chipotle, garlic, and pepper in large bowl, whisking occasionally, until smooth and thickened, about 5 minutes. Stir in Monterey Jack and American cheeses until well combined.

2A. FOR 1½- TO 5-QUART SLOW COOKER Transfer mixture to slow cooker, cover, and cook until cheese is melted, 1 to 2 hours on low.

2B. FOR 5½- TO 7-QUART SLOW COOKER Transfer mixture to 1½-quart soufflé dish. Set dish in slow cooker and pour water into slow cooker until it reaches about one-third up sides of dish (about 2 cups water). Cover and cook until cheese is melted, 1 to 2 hours on low. Remove dish from slow cooker, if desired.

3. Whisk dip until smooth, then stir in tomatoes. Serve. (Dip can be held on warm or low setting for up to 2 hours. Adjust consistency with hot water as needed, adding 2 tablespoons at a time.)

NOTES FROM THE TEST KITCHEN

Using a Soufflé Dish in the Slow Cooker

While a large slow cooker is great for cooking up big batches of soups, stews, and braises for a crowd, the large amount of space is problematic for smaller dishes like dips, which end up spreading out too thin and burning or cooking unevenly. To solve this problem, we assemble the recipe in a 1½-quart soufflé dish, then place the dish in the slow cooker. To encourage even heat transfer, we pour about 2 cups of water into the slow cooker to make a simple water bath. Once the dip is cooked, the soufflé dish can be removed from the slow cooker for serving.

Supermarket Brie is completely transformed into an elegant starter when figs, herbs, walnuts, and honey are added.

Baked Brie with Figs, Walnuts, and Herbs

SERVES 8 TO 10 **EASY PREP** **VEG**

COOKING TIME ABOUT 1 HOUR ON LOW

SLOW COOKER SIZE 3½ TO 7 QUARTS

WHY THIS RECIPE WORKS Baked Brie is a party favorite, but all too often it winds up a congealed mess as it cools instead of the warm, dippable concoction that everyone finds so irresistible. Enter the slow cooker, where making it is supereasy plus you can serve it right out of the slow cooker or out of a warm soufflé dish—ensuring that it will stay appealing longer. For an elegant take on the classic, we decided to pair the Brie with earthy dried figs and toasted chopped walnuts. For sweet and creamy flavor in every bite, we first trimmed off the rind (which doesn't melt that well) and cut the cheese into cubes. Slicing the figs in half allowed for better distribution of fruit without the pieces getting lost in the cheese. The addition of thyme provided a little earthiness that complemented both the cheese and the fruit. The result? Our fig-herb mixture was evenly distributed throughout the dish, not just spooned on top. A drizzle of honey and some minced chives before serving reinforced the sweet-savory flavor profile, while toasted walnuts added a subtle smoky crunch. Be sure to use a firm, fairly unripe Brie for this recipe. Serve with crusty bread, crackers, and/or Crostini (page 23).

1½ pounds firm Brie cheese, rind removed, cut into 1-inch pieces
1 cup dried figs, stemmed and halved
1 teaspoon minced fresh thyme
¼ teaspoon pepper
2 tablespoons honey
¼ cup walnuts, toasted and chopped
1 tablespoon minced fresh chives

1A. FOR 3½- TO 5-QUART SLOW COOKER Lightly coat slow cooker with vegetable oil spray. Combine Brie, figs, thyme, and pepper in prepared slow cooker. Cover and cook until Brie is heated through and begins to soften around edges, about 1 hour on low.

1B. FOR 5½- TO 7-QUART SLOW COOKER Lightly coat 1½-quart soufflé dish with vegetable oil spray. Combine Brie, figs, thyme, and pepper in prepared dish. Set dish in slow cooker and pour water into slow cooker until it reaches about one-third up sides of dish (about 2 cups water). Cover and cook until Brie is heated through and begins to soften around edges, about 1 hour on low. Remove dish from slow cooker, if desired.

2. Drizzle Brie with honey and sprinkle with walnuts and chives. Serve. (Brie can be held on warm or low setting for up to 2 hours.)

CUTTING RIND OFF BRIE

1. Using serrated knife, carefully slice top and bottom rind off wheel of Brie.

2. Trim rind from sides.

Barbecued Kielbasa Bites

SERVES 8 TO 10   `EASY PREP`
COOKING TIME 1 TO 2 HOURS ON LOW
SLOW COOKER SIZE 4 TO 7 QUARTS

WHY THIS RECIPE WORKS Cocktail franks are a classic kid-friendly party favorite. For an adult take on this hors d'oeuvre, we decided to go with kielbasa. And this appealing appetizer was made even easier by using the slow cooker, where the kielbasa could gently simmer hands-free in a flavorful sauce without worry of scorching. Since the sauce was to be the star here, we skipped the bottled variety in favor of creating a simple homemade sauce. Starting with tangy ketchup, we added some molasses for its rich sweetness and Dijon mustard and cider vinegar for a dose of acidity. A combination of chili powder and cayenne added complex but not overwhelming heat.

1 cup ketchup
½ cup molasses
3 tablespoons cider vinegar
3 tablespoons Dijon mustard
1 tablespoon packed brown sugar
2 teaspoons chili powder
⅛ teaspoon cayenne pepper
3 pounds kielbasa sausage, sliced on bias ½ inch thick

Combine ketchup, molasses, vinegar, mustard, sugar, chili powder, and cayenne in slow cooker. Stir in kielbasa, cover, and cook until heated through and flavors meld, 1 to 2 hours on low. Serve. (Kielbasa can be held on warm or low setting for up to 2 hours. Adjust sauce consistency with hot water as needed, adding 2 tablespoons at a time.)

NOTES FROM THE TEST KITCHEN

Kielbasa

Kielbasa, or Polish sausage, is a smoked pork sausage that sometimes has beef added and is usually sold precooked.  We tasted five national supermarket brands, and we highly recommend **Wellshire Farms Smoked Polska Kielbasa**. It is naturally smoked and had a meaty, complex flavor and a hearty texture compared to the springy, hot dog–like textures of the others.

MAKE IT 5 WAYS CHICKEN WINGS

Buffalo Chicken Wings

SERVES 4 TO 6   **EASY PREP**
COOKING TIME 4 TO 5 HOURS ON LOW
SLOW COOKER SIZE 4 TO 7 QUARTS

Great wings should have juicy, tender meat and a crisp coating. You might not consider making them in your slow cooker, especially when trying to achieve both is challenging to do simultaneously. The gentle heat of the slow cooker is great for achieving meltingly tender wings, but terrible at producing a good crisp coating. However, great wings are possible in the slow cooker with a little re-imagination. To add serious flavor, we first tossed the wings with a hefty blend of spices and aromatics. We then cooked the wings on low for 4 to 5 hours, which ensured they remained moist and became perfectly tender. For a crisp exterior, a few minutes under the broiler was all it took. We found that basting the wings with sauce while they broiled kept the skin from fully crisping. Instead, we broiled the wings sans sauce and gently tossed them with it after broiling. These recipes can easily be doubled in a 7-quart slow cooker; you will need to broil the wings in two batches.

1 BUFFALO CHICKEN WINGS

4 pounds chicken wings, cut at joints and trimmed, wingtips discarded
1 tablespoon paprika
1 teaspoon cayenne pepper
1 teaspoon salt
½ teaspoon pepper
½ cup Frank's RedHot Original Cayenne Pepper Sauce
6 tablespoons unsalted butter, melted
2 tablespoons molasses

1. Lightly coat slow cooker with vegetable oil spray. Toss chicken with paprika, cayenne, salt, and pepper in slow cooker. Cover and cook until chicken is tender, 4 to 5 hours on low.

2. Adjust oven rack 6 inches from broiler element; heat broiler. Set wire rack in aluminum foil–lined rimmed baking sheet; coat with vegetable oil spray. Transfer chicken to prepared rack. Broil chicken until lightly charred and crisp, 15 to 20 minutes, flipping chicken halfway through broiling.

3. Whisk hot sauce, melted butter, and molasses in large bowl until combined. Gently toss chicken with sauce to coat. Serve.

2 KOREAN CHICKEN WINGS

Gochujang, a Korean chile-soybean paste, can be found in Asian markets and in some supermarkets. If you can't find gochujang, substitute an equal amount of Sriracha sauce and add only 2 tablespoons of water to the sauce.

4 pounds chicken wings, cut at joints and trimmed, wingtips discarded
2 tablespoons grated fresh ginger
3 garlic cloves, minced
1 teaspoon pepper
½ teaspoon salt
¼ cup sugar
¼ cup gochujang
¼ cup water
2 tablespoons soy sauce
1 tablespoon sesame oil

1. Lightly coat slow cooker with vegetable oil spray. Toss chicken with 5 teaspoons ginger, two-thirds of garlic, pepper, and salt in slow cooker. Cover and cook until chicken is tender, 4 to 5 hours on low.

2. Adjust oven rack 6 inches from broiler element; heat broiler. Set wire rack in aluminum foil–lined rimmed baking sheet; coat with vegetable oil spray. Transfer chicken to prepared rack. Broil chicken until lightly charred and crisp, 15 to 20 minutes, flipping chicken halfway through broiling.

3. Whisk sugar, gochujang, water, soy sauce, sesame oil, remaining 1 teaspoon ginger, and remaining garlic in large bowl until sugar is dissolved. Gently toss chicken with sauce to coat. Serve.

3 SMOKY BARBECUE CHICKEN WINGS

4 pounds chicken wings,
  cut at joints and trimmed,
  wingtips discarded
1 tablespoon paprika
1 tablespoon chili powder
1 teaspoon salt
½ teaspoon pepper
¼ teaspoon cayenne pepper
½ cup ketchup
6 tablespoons molasses
2 tablespoons Dijon mustard
1 tablespoon cider vinegar
1 tablespoon packed brown sugar
½ teaspoon liquid smoke

1. Lightly coat slow cooker with vegetable oil spray. Toss chicken with paprika, chili powder, salt, pepper, and cayenne in slow cooker. Cover and cook until chicken is tender, 4 to 5 hours on low.

2. Adjust oven rack 6 inches from broiler element; heat broiler. Set wire rack in aluminum foil–lined rimmed baking sheet; coat with vegetable oil spray. Transfer chicken to prepared rack. Broil chicken until lightly charred and crisp, 15 to 20 minutes, flipping chicken halfway through broiling.

3. Whisk ketchup, molasses, mustard, vinegar, sugar, and liquid smoke in large bowl until sugar is dissolved. Gently toss chicken with sauce to coat. Serve.

4 MANGO-CURRY CHICKEN WINGS

4 pounds chicken wings,
  cut at joints and trimmed,
  wingtips discarded
1 tablespoon paprika
1 tablespoon curry powder
2 teaspoons ground cumin
1 teaspoon salt
½ teaspoon pepper
¾ cup mango chutney
1 shallot, minced
3 tablespoons water
1 tablespoon minced fresh cilantro
1 teaspoon grated lime zest

1. Lightly coat slow cooker with vegetable oil spray. Toss chicken with paprika, curry powder, cumin, salt, and pepper in slow cooker. Cover and cook until chicken is tender, 4 to 5 hours on low.

2. Adjust oven rack 6 inches from broiler element; heat broiler. Set wire rack in aluminum foil–lined rimmed baking sheet; coat with vegetable oil spray. Transfer chicken to prepared rack. Broil chicken until lightly charred and crisp, 15 to 20 minutes, flipping chicken halfway through broiling.

3. Whisk chutney, shallot, water, cilantro, and lime zest together in bowl. Gently toss chicken with sauce to coat. Serve.

5 HONEY-MUSTARD CHICKEN WINGS

4 pounds chicken wings,
  cut at joints and trimmed,
  wingtips discarded
1 tablespoon onion powder
1 teaspoon salt
½ teaspoon pepper
½ teaspoon cayenne pepper
⅓ cup spicy brown mustard
¼ cup honey

1. Lightly coat slow cooker with vegetable oil spray. Toss chicken with onion powder, salt, pepper, and cayenne in slow cooker. Cover and cook until chicken is tender, 4 to 5 hours on low.

2. Adjust oven rack 6 inches from broiler element; heat broiler. Set wire rack in aluminum foil–lined rimmed baking sheet; coat with vegetable oil spray. Transfer chicken to prepared rack. Broil chicken until lightly charred and crisp, 15 to 20 minutes, flipping chicken halfway through broiling.

3. Whisk mustard and honey together in large bowl. Gently toss chicken with sauce to coat. Serve.

CUTTING UP CHICKEN WINGS

1. Using kitchen shears or sharp chef's knife, cut through joint between drumette and wingette.
2. Cut off and discard wingtip.

Garlicky Shrimp

SERVES 8 TO 10 **EASY PREP**

COOKING TIME ABOUT 1 HOUR ON HIGH

SLOW COOKER SIZE 4 TO 7 QUARTS

WHY THIS RECIPE WORKS Delicate, fast-cooking shrimp and the slow cooker may seem like an impossible pairing, but the slow, gentle heat of the slow cooker is actually terrific for producing tender shrimp without the fear of overcooking. With that in mind, we set out to create a classic garlic shrimp recipe that would infuse the shrimp with plenty of rich, garlicky flavor. We started by cooking sliced garlic and spices in oil for 30 minutes to soften the raw flavor of the garlic and allow the spices' flavors to bloom. Once the oil was sufficiently flavored, we stirred in the shrimp. A mere 20-minute poach in the garlicky oil was enough to cook and season the shrimp. Serve with crusty bread for dipping in the infused oil.

- ¾ cup extra-virgin olive oil
- 6 garlic cloves, sliced thin
- 1 teaspoon smoked paprika
- 1 teaspoon salt
- ¼ teaspoon pepper
- ¼ teaspoon red pepper flakes
- 2 pounds large shrimp (26 to 30 per pound), peeled and deveined
- 1 tablespoon minced fresh parsley

Combine oil, garlic, paprika, salt, pepper, and pepper flakes in slow cooker. Cover and cook until flavors meld, about 30 minutes on high. Stir in shrimp, cover, and cook on high until opaque throughout, about 20 minutes, stirring halfway through cooking. Transfer shrimp and oil mixture to serving dish. Sprinkle with parsley and serve.

PEELING AND DEVEINING SHRIMP

1. Break shell under swimming legs, which will come off as shell is removed. Leave tail intact if desired, or tug tail to remove.

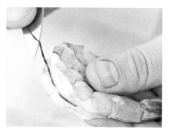

2. Use paring knife to make shallow cut along back of shrimp to expose vein. Use tip of knife to lift out vein. Discard vein by wiping blade against paper towel.

Shrimp Basics

BUYING SHRIMP Virtually all of the shrimp sold in supermarkets today have been previously frozen, either in large blocks of ice or by a method called "individually quick-frozen," or IQF for short. Supermarkets simply defrost the shrimp before displaying them on ice at the fish counter. We highly recommend purchasing bags of still-frozen shrimp and defrosting them as needed at home, since there is no telling how long "fresh" shrimp may have been kept on ice at the market. IQF shrimp have a better flavor and texture than shrimp frozen in blocks, and they are convenient because it's easy to defrost just the amount you need. Shrimp are sold both with and without their shells, but we find shell-on shrimp to be firmer and sweeter. Also, shrimp should be the only ingredient listed on the bag; some packagers add preservatives, but we find treated shrimp to have an unpleasant, rubbery texture.

SORTING OUT SHRIMP SIZES Shrimp are sold both by size (small, medium, etc.) and by the number needed to make 1 pound, usually given in a range. Choosing shrimp by the numerical rating is more accurate, because the size labels vary from store to store. Here's how the two sizing systems generally compare:

Small	51 to 60 per pound
Medium	41 to 50 per pound
Medium-Large	31 to 40 per pound
Large	26 to 30 per pound
Extra-Large	21 to 25 per pound
Jumbo	16 to 20 per pound

DEFROSTING SHRIMP You can thaw frozen shrimp overnight in the refrigerator in a covered bowl. For a quicker thaw, place them in a colander under cold running water; they will be ready in a few minutes. Thoroughly dry the shrimp before cooking.

Swedish Meatballs

SERVES 10 TO 12
COOKING TIME 4 TO 5 HOURS ON LOW
SLOW COOKER SIZE 4 TO 7 QUARTS

WHY THIS RECIPE WORKS Swedish meatballs have long been standard cocktail party fare, but rolling and browning dozens of little meatballs and then building a sauce leave little time to get everything (including the host) ready before company arrives. Enter our recipe for Swedish Meatballs—prepared in the slow cooker. To keep our recipe's sauce from becoming greasy, we put our meatballs in the oven for 15 minutes, allowing much of their fat to render and collect on the bottom of the pan. Cooking our meatballs in the oven also allowed us to brown them before adding them to the slow cooker. For a quick sauce, we started with a base of flour-and-butter roux and beef broth, which cooked down to the perfect consistency to coat the meatballs. A couple tablespoons of soy sauce gave our sauce a rich, meaty backbone without overpowering the other ingredients. Lingonberry preserves are a traditional accompaniment for Swedish meatballs. If you can't find lingonberry preserves, cranberry preserves can be used.

We bake these party-worthy meatballs briefly before adding them to the slow cooker to remove excess fat.

6	tablespoons unsalted butter
2	onions, chopped fine
4	slices caraway-rye bread, crusts removed, torn into 1-inch pieces
3½	cups beef broth
1	cup sour cream
2	large egg yolks
½	teaspoon ground allspice
¼	teaspoon ground nutmeg
	Salt and pepper
1	pound 90 percent lean ground beef
1	pound ground pork
½	cup all-purpose flour
2	tablespoons soy sauce
2	teaspoons minced fresh dill, plus extra for serving

1. Adjust oven rack to middle position and heat oven to 475 degrees. Set wire rack in aluminum foil–lined rimmed baking sheet and coat with vegetable oil spray. Melt 1 tablespoon butter in 12-inch skillet over medium heat. Add onions and cook until softened, about 8 minutes; transfer to large bowl. Add bread, ¼ cup broth, ¼ cup sour cream, egg yolks, allspice, nutmeg, ½ teaspoon salt, and ¼ teaspoon pepper and mash with fork until smooth. Add ground beef and ground pork and knead with hands until well combined.

2. Pinch off and roll meat mixture into tablespoon-size meatballs (about 60 meatballs) and arrange on prepared rack. Bake until lightly browned, about 15 minutes. Transfer meatballs to slow cooker.

3. Melt remaining 5 tablespoons butter in now-empty skillet over medium heat. Add flour and cook, whisking often, until beginning to brown, about 3 minutes. Slowly whisk in remaining 3¼ cups broth, smoothing out any lumps, and bring to simmer; transfer to slow cooker. Cover and cook until meatballs are tender and sauce is slightly thickened, 4 to 5 hours on low.

4. Using large spoon, skim excess fat from surface of sauce. Whisk ½ cup sauce, soy sauce, dill, and remaining ¾ cup sour cream together in bowl (to temper), then gently stir mixture back into slow cooker. Season with salt and pepper to taste. Sprinkle with extra dill and serve. (Meatballs can be held on warm or low setting for up to 2 hours. Adjust sauce consistency with hot water as needed, adding 2 tablespoons at a time.)

Homemade pesto adds rich flavor to these turkey meatballs.

Turkey-Pesto Cocktail Meatballs

SERVES 12 TO 14   LIGHT
COOKING TIME 4 TO 5 HOURS ON LOW
SLOW COOKER SIZE 4 TO 7 QUARTS

WHY THIS RECIPE WORKS Slow-cooker cocktail meatballs are a great way to feed a crowd—a big batch can gently simmer away before guests arrive, then be served warm right out of the slow cooker. We wanted a classic Italian-inspired turkey meatball and marinara dish that would be easy to prepare and would deliver on flavor, with a tangy tomato sauce and tender meatballs. Fresh pesto gave our meatballs bright flavor, while Parmesan both added complexity and reinforced the Italian flavors. The addition of panko bread crumbs and egg yolks acted as a binder and kept the meatballs moist and tender. Before adding the meatballs to the slow cooker we baked them to get rid of excess fat and to firm them up just enough so they wouldn't fall apart in the slow cooker's moist environment. A little reserved pesto added just before serving kept this dish fresh and bright. Be sure to use ground turkey, not ground turkey breast (also labeled 99 percent fat-free), in this recipe.

    4 cups fresh basil leaves, lightly bruised
    4 garlic cloves, minced
    ⅓ cup extra-virgin olive oil
    2 ounces Parmesan cheese, grated (1 cup)
 1⅓ cups panko bread crumbs
    2 large egg yolks
       Salt and pepper
    2 pounds ground turkey
    1 (28-ounce) can crushed tomatoes

1. Adjust oven rack to middle position and heat oven to 475 degrees. Set wire rack in aluminum foil–lined rimmed baking sheet and coat with vegetable oil spray. Process basil and garlic in food processor until finely ground, about 30 seconds, scraping down sides of bowl as needed. With processor running, slowly add oil and process until smooth, about 30 seconds. Measure out and reserve 2 tablespoons pesto for serving. Transfer remaining pesto to large bowl.

2. Stir Parmesan, panko, egg yolks, ½ teaspoon salt, and ¼ teaspoon pepper into remaining pesto. Add ground turkey and knead with hands until well combined. Pinch off and roll turkey mixture into tablespoon-size meatballs (about 60 meatballs) and arrange on prepared rack. Bake until no longer pink, about 10 minutes. Transfer meatballs to slow cooker.

3. Gently stir tomatoes and ½ teaspoon salt into slow cooker, cover, and cook until meatballs are tender, 4 to 5 hours on low.

4. Using large spoon, skim excess fat from surface of sauce. Stir reserved pesto into meatballs and season with salt and pepper to taste. Serve. (Meatballs can be held on warm or low setting for up to 2 hours. Adjust sauce consistency with hot water as needed, adding 2 tablespoons at a time.)

BRUISING BASIL

To release the full range of flavor from basil, place the leaves in a zipper-lock bag and gently pound with a meat pounder or the end of a rolling pin until the leaves are darkened in color.

Studded with potatoes and red bell pepper, this classic tortilla turns out perfectly in the slow cooker.

Spanish Tortilla

SERVES 8 `VEG`

COOKING TIME 3 TO 4 HOURS ON LOW
SLOW COOKER SIZE 4 TO 7 QUARTS

WHY THIS RECIPE WORKS Served with a garlicky aïoli, Spanish tortilla makes a great tapas dish. Worried that the simplest version of a tortilla would be bland after emerging from a slow cooker, we chose to add red bell pepper and peas to the mix, along with a hefty dose of minced garlic and fresh oregano. To ensure that the potatoes were perfectly cooked, we sliced them thin and then microwaved them before adding them to the slow cooker. Placing an aluminum foil collar and a foil liner (see page 208) in the slow cooker before assembling the tortilla prevented overbrowning and made the tortilla easy to remove and serve. You will need an oval slow cooker for this recipe. Serve with Garlic Aïoli.

  2 pounds russet potatoes, peeled, quartered lengthwise, and sliced ⅛ inch thick
  2 onions, chopped fine
  1 red bell pepper, stemmed, seeded, and cut into ½-inch pieces
 ¼ cup extra-virgin olive oil
  6 garlic cloves, minced
  1 tablespoon minced fresh oregano or 1 teaspoon dried
 ¼ teaspoon red pepper flakes
  1 cup frozen peas
 12 large eggs
  1 teaspoon salt
 ½ teaspoon pepper

1. Line slow cooker with aluminum foil collar, then line with foil liner and lightly coat with vegetable oil spray. Microwave potatoes, onions, bell pepper, oil, garlic, oregano, and pepper flakes in large covered bowl, stirring occasionally, until potatoes are nearly tender, about 9 minutes. Stir in peas, then transfer potato mixture to prepared slow cooker.

2. Whisk eggs, salt, and pepper together in bowl, then pour mixture evenly over potato mixture. Gently press potato mixture into egg mixture. Cover and cook until center of tortilla is just set, 3 to 4 hours on low.

3. Turn slow cooker off and let tortilla rest, covered, until fully set, about 20 minutes. Using foil liner, transfer tortilla to serving platter and serve.

SIMPLE ACCOMPANIMENTS

GARLIC AÏOLI

MAKES 1¼ CUPS

Using a combination of vegetable oil and extra-virgin olive oil is crucial to the flavor of the aïoli.

  2 large egg yolks
  2 teaspoons Dijon mustard
  2 teaspoons lemon juice
  1 garlic clove, minced
 ¾ cup vegetable oil
  1 tablespoon water
 ½ teaspoon salt
 ¼ teaspoon pepper
 ¼ cup extra-virgin olive oil

Process egg yolks, mustard, lemon juice, and garlic in food processor until combined, about 10 seconds. With processor running, slowly drizzle in vegetable oil, about 1 minute. Transfer mixture to medium bowl and whisk in water, salt, and pepper. Whisking constantly, slowly drizzle in olive oil. (Aïoli can be refrigerated for up to 4 days.)

BOTTOMLESS BOWLS

■ EASY PREP ■ VEGETARIAN ■ LIGHT ■ COOK ALL DAY
Photo: Farro and Butternut Squash Stew

One of the best (and simplest) ways to stock your freezer with chicken broth is to make it in the slow cooker.

All-Purpose Chicken Broth

MAKES 3 QUARTS **ALL DAY**
COOKING TIME 6 TO 8 HOURS ON LOW OR 4 TO 6 HOURS ON HIGH
SLOW COOKER SIZE 4 TO 7 QUARTS

WHY THIS RECIPE WORKS Chicken broth is one of the most versatile and often-used ingredients in any kitchen. But while making a successful broth on the stovetop can be a tedious task, an equally tasty slow-cooker version is a breeze. Searching for a broth with unadulterated chicken flavor, we tested many combinations of chicken parts, finding a whole cut-up chicken too fussy, and chicken backs, legs, and necks too liver-y. Chicken wings were the surprise winner—the resulting broth was remarkably clear and refined, and the long simmering time eked out every last bit of flavor from the chicken bones. Roasting the chicken wings was an easy way to incorporate dark color and pleasantly deep caramelized flavor. Additionally, we found that an onion, a little garlic, and some salt were all we needed to complement, and not distract from, the chicken.

3 pounds chicken wings
1 onion, chopped
3 quarts water
3 garlic cloves, peeled and smashed
½ teaspoon salt

1. Adjust oven rack to lower-middle position and heat oven to 450 degrees. Line rimmed baking sheet with aluminum foil and lightly spray with vegetable oil spray. Distribute chicken and onion evenly on prepared sheet and roast until golden, about 40 minutes; transfer to slow cooker.

2. Stir water, garlic, and salt into slow cooker, cover, and cook until broth is deeply flavored and rich, 6 to 8 hours on low or 4 to 6 hours on high.

3. Strain broth through fine-mesh strainer into large container, pressing on solids to extract as much liquid as possible. Using large spoon, skim fat from surface of broth. (Broth can be refrigerated for up to 4 days or frozen for up to 2 months.)

All-Purpose Beef Broth

MAKES 3 QUARTS
COOKING TIME 4 TO 6 HOURS ON LOW
SLOW COOKER SIZE 4 TO 7 QUARTS

WHY THIS RECIPE WORKS Rich, deep beef broth is a must-have in any cook's kitchen, and with the help of the slow cooker it can be whipped up with ease. Hoping to avoid the work involved in cutting up beef chuck or in dealing with beef bones, we turned to ground beef for a quicker beef broth—its increased surface area enables more beef flavor to be absorbed by the liquid. For additional meaty undertones, we included a full pound of white mushrooms, which we sautéed with onions and tomato paste before browning the beef, and we also added some soy sauce to the slow cooker (both tomato paste and soy sauce add depth of flavor without calling attention to themselves). To round out our broth, we added red wine for color and acidity, and an onion, carrot, and celery rib for sweetness.

1 tablespoon vegetable oil
1 pound white mushrooms, trimmed and halved
1 onion, chopped
3 tablespoons tomato paste
1½ pounds 85 percent lean ground beef
¾ cup dry red wine
3 quarts water
1 carrot, peeled and chopped
1 celery rib, chopped
2 tablespoons soy sauce
3 bay leaves

1. Heat oil in 12-inch skillet over medium heat until shimmering. Add mushrooms, onion, and tomato paste, cover, and cook until mushrooms are softened, 5 to 10 minutes. Uncover and continue to cook until mushrooms are dry and browned, 5 to 10 minutes.

2. Stir in ground beef and cook, breaking up any large pieces with wooden spoon, until no longer pink, about 5 minutes. Stir in wine, scraping up any browned bits, and cook until nearly evaporated, 5 to 7 minutes; transfer to slow cooker.

3. Stir water, carrot, celery, soy sauce, and bay leaves into slow cooker. Cover and cook until broth is deeply flavored and rich, 4 to 6 hours on low.

4. Strain broth through fine-mesh strainer into large container, pressing on solids to extract as much liquid as possible. Using large spoon, skim fat from surface of broth. (Broth can be refrigerated for up to 4 days or frozen for up to 2 months.)

NOTES FROM THE TEST KITCHEN

Storing and Freezing Broth

Broth can be refrigerated in an airtight container for up to four days or frozen for up to two months. When freezing broth, we like to portion it into either a nonstick muffin tin or freezer-safe zipper-lock bags. To release frozen broth from a muffin tin, simply twist the tin as you would an ice-cube tray; once frozen, the blocks of broth can be stored more efficiently in a zipper-lock bag. If portioning the broth directly into zipper-lock bags, use a 4-cup liquid measure (or a large yogurt container) to support the bag and hold it open while filling it; the bags of broth can be laid flat in the freezer to save space.

All-Purpose Vegetable Broth

MAKES 3 QUARTS **VEG** **ALL DAY**
COOKING TIME 9 TO 11 HOURS ON LOW OR 6 TO 8 HOURS ON HIGH
SLOW COOKER SIZE 4 TO 7 QUARTS

WHY THIS RECIPE WORKS Vegetable broth is essential to full-flavored vegetarian cooking, enhancing meat-free dishes with clean vegetal flavor. It needs gentle cooking, and the slow cooker is the perfect medium in which to bring out the subtlety of many types of vegetables. First, we found that a base of onions, scallions, carrots, and celery along with a generous dose of garlic provided a strong background to the broth that was neither too vegetal nor too sweet. The addition of half a head of cauliflower, cut into florets and added with the water, gave our broth pleasant earthiness and nuttiness. Finally, a single tomato added acidic balance, and thyme sprigs, bay leaves, and peppercorns rounded out the flavors. Although we wanted to be able to dump all the vegetables into the cooker raw, we found that we needed the additional flavor developed from browning the aromatics. We chose a longer cooking time than we used for our meat-based broths so that the flavor of all the different vegetables could shine through. To avoid a cloudy broth, do not press on the solids when straining.

1 tablespoon vegetable oil
3 onions, chopped
4 scallions, chopped
2 carrots, peeled and chopped
2 celery ribs, chopped
15 garlic cloves, peeled and smashed
3 quarts water
½ head cauliflower (1 pound), cored and cut into 1-inch florets
1 tomato, cored and chopped
8 sprigs fresh thyme
1 teaspoon black peppercorns
½ teaspoon salt
3 bay leaves

1. Heat oil in 12-inch skillet over medium heat until shimmering. Add onions, scallions, carrots, celery, and garlic and cook until vegetables are softened and lightly browned, 8 to 10 minutes. Stir in 1 cup water, scraping up any browned bits; transfer to slow cooker.

2. Stir remaining 11 cups water, cauliflower, tomato, thyme sprigs, peppercorns, salt, and bay leaves into slow cooker. Cover and cook until broth is deeply flavored and rich, 9 to 11 hours on low or 6 to 8 hours on high.

3. Strain broth through fine-mesh strainer into large container, without pressing on solids. (Broth can be refrigerated for up to 4 days or frozen for up to 2 months.)

REMOVING FAT FROM BROTH

Let the broth settle, then use a large, flat spoon to skim the fat off the surface. Be sure to hold the spoon parallel to the surface of the soup; you want to collect as little broth as possible.

Blade steaks become meltingly tender in the slow cooker and can be easily shredded at the end of the cooking time.

Beef and Barley Soup

SERVES 6 TO 8   **ALL DAY**

COOKING TIME 9 TO 10 HOURS ON LOW OR 6 TO 7 HOURS ON HIGH

SLOW COOKER SIZE 5 TO 7 QUARTS

WHY THIS RECIPE WORKS To build a flavorful base for this simple but comforting soup in a slow cooker, we needed to get out our skillet to sauté a hefty amount of onions with tomato paste and thyme and then deglaze the pan with wine, scraping up the flavorful browned bits left behind. This simple step made a world of difference in the soup's flavor and allowed us to skip the tedious process of browning the meat. To simplify things further we used trimmed beef blade steak, which we shredded after it had become meltingly tender in the slow cooker—no need to cut the meat into pieces to start. The addition of soy sauce to the broth base added a surprising amount of flavor. Since pearl barley can absorb two to three times its volume in cooking liquid, we needed to be judicious in the quantity we added to the soup. A modest ¼ cup was all that

was needed to lend a pleasing velvety texture without overfilling the slow cooker with swollen grains. Do not substitute hulled, hull-less, quick-cooking, or presteamed barley (read the ingredient list on the package to determine this) in this recipe. You can substitute an equal amount of beef flat-iron steaks, if desired.

  2 tablespoons vegetable oil
  2 onions, chopped fine
  ¼ cup tomato paste
  1 tablespoon minced fresh thyme or 1 teaspoon dried
  ½ cup dry red wine
  1 (28-ounce) can diced tomatoes
  4 cups beef broth
  2 carrots, peeled and chopped
  ⅓ cup soy sauce
  ¼ cup pearl barley, rinsed
  2 bay leaves
  2 pounds beef blade steaks, ¾ to 1 inch thick, trimmed
    Salt and pepper
  2 tablespoons minced fresh parsley

1. Heat oil in 12-inch skillet over medium heat until shimmering. Add onions and cook until softened and lightly browned, 8 to 10 minutes. Stir in tomato paste and thyme and cook until fragrant, about 30 seconds. Stir in wine, scraping up any browned bits; transfer to slow cooker.

2. Stir tomatoes and their juice, broth, carrots, soy sauce, barley, and bay leaves into slow cooker. Season steaks with salt and pepper and nestle into slow cooker. Cover and cook until steaks are tender, 9 to 10 hours on low or 6 to 7 hours on high.

3. Discard bay leaves. Transfer steaks to cutting board, let cool slightly, then shred into bite-size pieces using 2 forks; discard fat and gristle. Stir beef into soup and let sit until heated through, about 5 minutes. Stir in parsley and season with salt and pepper to taste. Serve.

TRIMMING BLADE STEAKS

To trim blade steaks, halve each steak lengthwise, leaving the gristle on one half. Then simply cut the gristle away.

Old-fashioned oxtail soup is tailor-made for the slow cooker, and here we load it up with carrots and parsnips.

Hearty Beef Oxtail Soup

SERVES 6 TO 8　EASY PREP　ALL DAY

COOKING TIME 9 TO 10 HOURS ON LOW OR 6 TO 7 HOURS ON HIGH

SLOW COOKER SIZE 5 TO 7 QUARTS

WHY THIS RECIPE WORKS Oxtail soup rarely shows up on the dinner table these days. While it offers deep flavor, rich body, and fall-apart-tender meat (thanks to a significant amount of gelatin), it requires hours of gentle simmering to extract the flavor of the marrow inside the bones and to break down the collagen. We wanted to put the slow cooker to work and bring oxtail soup back to the menu. All the oxtails needed was some salt and pepper and plenty of hands-off time in the slow cooker to become meltingly tender. To complement the rich meat, we chose hearty, earthy carrots and parsnips for our vegetables. To round out the soup, we added store-bought beef broth and a combination of onions, tomato paste, and thyme. A sprinkle of fresh parsley before serving added an herbal flavor. Oxtails can often be found in the freezer section of the grocery store; if using frozen oxtails, be sure to thaw them completely before using.

2 onions, chopped fine
¼ cup tomato paste
2 tablespoons vegetable oil
1 tablespoon minced fresh thyme or
　1 teaspoon dried
8 cups beef broth
3 carrots, peeled and sliced ½ inch thick
3 parsnips, peeled and sliced ½ inch thick
2 bay leaves
3 pounds oxtails, trimmed
　Salt and pepper
2 tablespoons minced fresh parsley

1. Microwave onions, tomato paste, oil, and thyme in bowl, stirring occasionally, until onions are softened, about 5 minutes; transfer to slow cooker. Stir in broth, carrots, parsnips, and bay leaves. Season oxtails with salt and pepper and nestle into slow cooker. Cover and cook until oxtails are tender, 9 to 10 hours on low or 6 to 7 hours on high.

2. Transfer oxtails to cutting board, let cool slightly, then shred into bite-size pieces using 2 forks; discard fat and bones. Discard bay leaves. Using large spoon, skim fat from surface of soup.

3. Stir beef into soup and let sit until heated through, about 5 minutes. Stir in parsley and season with salt and pepper to taste. Serve.

NOTES FROM THE TEST KITCHEN

Buying Oxtails

Depending on which part of the tail they come from, oxtail pieces can vary in diameter from ¾ inch to 4 inches. (Thicker pieces are cut close to the body; thinner pieces come from the end of the tail.) Try to buy oxtail packages with pieces approximately 2 inches thick and between 2 and 4 inches in diameter; they will yield more meat for the soup. Thicker pieces also lend more flavor to the broth. It's fine to use a few small pieces; just don't rely on them exclusively.

Beefy blade steaks can cook all day in the slow cooker, making them the perfect choice for this aromatic soup.

Vietnamese Beef and Noodle Soup

SERVES 6 TO 8 | EASY PREP | ALL DAY |

COOKING TIME 9 TO 10 HOURS ON LOW OR 6 TO 7 HOURS ON HIGH

SLOW COOKER SIZE 5 TO 7 QUARTS

WHY THIS RECIPE WORKS With its richly perfumed broth and mix of raw/cooked and hot/cold ingredients, this Southeast Asian soup (called *pho*) seemed like a long shot for the slow cooker. But it turned out to be one of our easiest soups. Fish sauce and soy sauce punched up store-bought broth, which we further enhanced with bruised lemon grass, star anise, and cloves. And blade steak was a great and easy choice for this soup since it is so full of rich beefy flavor. Surprisingly, finicky rice noodles worked perfectly in the slow cooker; since the liquid didn't come to a full boil, the noodles cooked gently and did not break apart or turn mushy. Finishing with the requisite garnishes created a perfectly balanced soup. You can substitute an equal amount of beef flat-iron steaks, if desired.

2 onions, chopped fine
6 garlic cloves, minced
2 tablespoons vegetable oil
8 cups beef broth
2 cups water
¼ cup fish sauce, plus extra for serving
2 tablespoons soy sauce
1 lemon grass stalk, trimmed to bottom 6 inches and bruised with back of knife
4 star anise pods
4 whole cloves
2 pounds beef blade steaks, ¾ to 1 inch thick, trimmed
Salt and pepper
8 ounces (¼-inch-wide) rice noodles
⅓ cup chopped fresh cilantro
2 scallions, sliced thin
Bean sprouts
Sprigs fresh Thai or Italian basil
Lime wedges
Hoisin sauce
Sriracha sauce

1. Microwave onions, garlic, and oil in bowl, stirring occasionally, until onions are softened, about 5 minutes; transfer to slow cooker. Stir in broth, water, fish sauce, soy sauce, lemon grass, star anise, and cloves. Season steaks with salt and pepper and nestle into slow cooker. Cover and cook until steaks are tender, 9 to 10 hours on low or 6 to 7 hours on high.

2. Transfer steaks to cutting board, let cool slightly, then shred into bite-size pieces using 2 forks; discard fat and gristle. Discard lemon grass, star anise, and cloves.

3. Stir noodles into soup, cover, and cook on high until tender, 10 to 20 minutes. Stir in beef and let sit until heated through, about 5 minutes. Stir in cilantro and scallions. Serve, passing bean sprouts, basil sprigs, lime wedges, hoisin, Sriracha, and extra fish sauce separately.

Japanese Pork and Ramen Soup

SERVES 6 TO 8 | EASY PREP |

COOKING TIME 6 TO 7 HOURS ON LOW OR 4 TO 5 HOURS ON HIGH

SLOW COOKER SIZE 5 TO 7 QUARTS

WHY THIS RECIPE WORKS A great ramen soup requires a great broth, and to accomplish this in a slow cooker we enhanced store-bought chicken broth with onions, garlic, and ginger at the beginning of cooking, then stirred in white miso (fermented soybean paste), soy sauce, mirin (Japanese rice wine), and sesame oil at the end. The combination of boneless country-style pork ribs, which are easy to shred after cooking, and hearty shiitakes imparted an intense, meaty flavor to the finished soup. Fresh spinach, stirred in toward the end, added an earthy flavor, and supermarket ramen noodles cooked perfectly in the same amount of time as the spinach. The spinach may seem like a lot at first, but it wilts down substantially. Look for country-style pork ribs with lots of fat and dark meat, and stay away from ribs that look overly lean with pale meat, as they will taste very dry after the extended cooking time.

2 onions, chopped fine
6 garlic cloves, minced
2 tablespoons grated fresh ginger
2 tablespoons vegetable oil
8 cups chicken broth
12 ounces shiitake mushrooms, stemmed and sliced thin
1½ pounds boneless country-style pork ribs, trimmed
   Salt and pepper
2 (3-ounce) packages ramen noodles, broken into
   1-inch pieces, seasoning packets discarded
6 ounces (6 cups) baby spinach
2 tablespoons white miso
1 tablespoon soy sauce, plus extra for seasoning
1 tablespoon mirin
1 teaspoon toasted sesame oil
2 scallions, sliced thin
1 tablespoon sesame seeds, toasted

1. Microwave onions, garlic, ginger, and vegetable oil in bowl, stirring occasionally, until onions are softened, about 5 minutes; transfer to slow cooker. Stir in broth and mushrooms. Season ribs with salt and pepper and nestle into slow cooker. Cover and cook until ribs are tender, 6 to 7 hours on low or 4 to 5 hours on high.

2. Transfer ribs to cutting board, let cool slightly, then shred into bite-size pieces using 2 forks; discard fat.

3. Stir noodles and then spinach, 1 handful at a time, into soup, cover, and cook on high until noodles are tender, about 8 minutes. Whisk miso, soy sauce, mirin, and sesame oil together in bowl until miso is fully dissolved. Stir miso mixture and pork into soup and let sit until heated through, about 5 minutes. Stir in scallions and season with extra soy sauce to taste. Serve, sprinkling individual portions with sesame seeds.

Italian Meatball and Escarole Soup

SERVES 6 LIGHT

COOKING TIME 4 TO 6 HOURS ON LOW OR 3 TO 5 HOURS ON HIGH
SLOW COOKER SIZE 4 TO 7 QUARTS

WHY THIS RECIPE WORKS Hearty beans, delicate meatballs, and wilted greens make for a classic Italian soup, but timing this dish in a slow cooker took extra care. While most bean-based soups start with cooking dried beans for hours before adding the meatballs, this just would not work in the slow cooker. Rather than settle for tough meatballs or undercooked beans, we reached for canned beans and broth to which we added onion, garlic, and red pepper flakes. For the meatballs we used ground turkey, which was lean but still full of flavor. To protect the lean meat from drying out, we mixed it with a panade (a combination of bread and milk) as well as some Parmesan and an egg yolk for flavor and richness. Searing the meatballs in a skillet before adding them to the slow cooker allowed them to keep their shape and added meaty flavor to the broth. Since we had the skillet out, we used it to sauté our aromatics to further enhance their flavor. Escarole, stirred in toward the end, rounded out our soup perfectly, adding freshness and color. The escarole may seem like a lot at first, but it all wilts down. Be sure to use ground turkey, not ground turkey breast (also labeled 99 percent fat-free), in this recipe.

2 slices hearty white sandwich bread,
   torn into 1-inch pieces
¼ cup whole milk
1 ounce Parmesan cheese, grated (½ cup)
3 tablespoons minced fresh parsley
1 large egg yolk
1½ teaspoons minced fresh oregano or ½ teaspoon dried
4 garlic cloves, minced
   Salt and pepper
1 pound ground turkey
2 teaspoons vegetable oil
1 onion, chopped fine
¼ teaspoon red pepper flakes
6 cups chicken broth
1 (15-ounce) can cannellini beans, rinsed
1 head escarole (1 pound), trimmed and sliced 1 inch thick

1. Mash bread, milk, Parmesan, parsley, egg yolk, oregano, half of garlic, and ½ teaspoon pepper into paste in large bowl using fork. Add ground turkey and hand-knead until well combined. Pinch off and roll turkey mixture into tablespoon-size meatballs (about 24 meatballs).

2. Heat 1 teaspoon oil in 12-inch nonstick skillet over medium heat until shimmering. Brown half of meatballs on all sides, about 5 minutes; transfer to slow cooker. Repeat with remaining 1 teaspoon oil and remaining meatballs; transfer to slow cooker.

3. Add onion and ¼ teaspoon salt to fat left in skillet and cook over medium heat until onion is softened, about 5 minutes. Stir in pepper flakes and remaining garlic and cook until fragrant, about 30 seconds; transfer to slow cooker. Gently stir in broth and beans, cover, and cook until meatballs are tender, 4 to 6 hours on low or 3 to 5 hours on high.

4. Stir escarole into soup, 1 handful at a time, cover, and cook on high until tender, 15 to 20 minutes. Season with salt and pepper to taste. Serve.

Old-Fashioned Chicken Noodle Soup

SERVES 6 TO 8   LIGHT
COOKING TIME 3 TO 4 HOURS ON LOW
SLOW COOKER SIZE 5 TO 7 QUARTS

Making a deeply flavored chicken noodle soup in the slow cooker is surprisingly easy, but it requires getting out a skillet to start things off right. We found that searing skin-on chicken breasts and using the flavorful fat to sweat our vegetables and aromatics gave us unbelievable depth of flavor. We then removed the skin from the chicken to prevent too much fat from getting into our soup. Using chicken broth instead of water also gave us a backbone of flavor. We tried many iterations of cooking our noodles in the soup but found that the heat of the slow cooker was not sufficient to cook the noodles (or pasta or couscous, depending on the recipe) properly, so we cooked them on the side and added them at the end; ramen noodles, however, which we used in our Chinese take on chicken soup, can be added right to the slow cooker at the end. You can substitute bone-in chicken thighs for the bone-in breasts, if desired; increase the cooking time to 4 to 5 hours.

1 OLD-FASHIONED CHICKEN NOODLE SOUP

1½ pounds bone-in split chicken breasts, trimmed
   Salt and pepper
4 teaspoons vegetable oil
3 carrots, peeled and cut into ½-inch pieces
2 celery ribs, cut into ½-inch pieces
1 onion, chopped fine
1 teaspoon tomato paste
1 teaspoon minced fresh thyme
10 cups chicken broth
2 ounces wide egg noodles
½ cup frozen peas
2 tablespoons minced fresh parsley

1. Pat chicken dry with paper towels; season with salt and pepper. Heat 1 tablespoon oil in 12-inch skillet over medium-high heat until just smoking. Brown chicken, 3 to 4 minutes per side; transfer to plate and discard skin.

2. Add carrots, celery, onion, and ¾ teaspoon salt to fat left in skillet; cook over medium heat until softened, about 8 minutes. Stir in tomato paste and thyme; cook until fragrant, about 30 seconds. Stir in 1 cup broth, scraping up any browned bits; transfer to slow cooker.

3. Stir in remaining 9 cups broth. Nestle chicken into slow cooker, cover, and cook until chicken is tender, 3 to 4 hours on low.

4. Bring 2 quarts water to boil in large saucepan. Add noodles and 1½ teaspoons salt; cook until al dente. Drain noodles, rinse with cold water, then toss with remaining 1 teaspoon oil.

5. Transfer chicken to cutting board, let cool slightly, then shred into bite-size pieces; discard bones. Stir noodles, chicken, and peas into soup; let sit for 5 minutes. Stir in parsley; season with salt and pepper to taste. Serve.

2 SPRING VEGETABLE CHICKEN SOUP

1½ pounds bone-in split chicken breasts, trimmed
   Salt and pepper
4 teaspoons vegetable oil
1 onion, chopped fine
1 teaspoon tomato paste
1 teaspoon minced fresh thyme
10 cups chicken broth
2 ounces medium shells
2 cups frozen lima beans, thawed
1 zucchini, quartered lengthwise and sliced ¼ inch thick
½ cup grated Parmesan cheese
2 tablespoons minced fresh basil

1. Pat chicken dry with paper towels; season with salt and pepper. Heat 1 tablespoon oil in 12-inch skillet over medium-high heat until just smoking. Brown chicken, 3 to 4 minutes per side; transfer to plate and discard skin.

2. Add onion and ¾ teaspoon salt to fat left in skillet; cook over medium heat until softened, about 5 minutes. Stir in tomato paste and thyme; cook until fragrant, about 30 seconds. Stir in 1 cup broth, scraping up any browned bits; transfer to slow cooker.

3. Stir in remaining 9 cups broth. Nestle chicken into slow cooker, cover, and cook until chicken is tender, 3 to 4 hours on low.

4. Bring 2 quarts water to boil in large saucepan. Add pasta and 1½ teaspoons salt; cook until al dente. Drain pasta, rinse with cold water, then toss with remaining 1 teaspoon oil.

5. Transfer chicken to cutting board, let cool slightly, then shred into bite-size pieces; discard bones. Stir lima beans and zucchini into soup, cover, and cook on high until tender, about 30 minutes. Stir in noodles and chicken; let sit for 5 minutes. Stir in Parmesan and basil; season with salt and pepper to taste. Serve.

3 SPICY CHIPOTLE CHICKEN NOODLE SOUP

1½ pounds bone-in split chicken
  breasts, trimmed
  Salt and pepper
4 teaspoons vegetable oil
4 teaspoons minced canned
  chipotle chile in adobo sauce
3 garlic cloves, minced
1 tablespoon tomato paste
1 teaspoon minced fresh oregano
1 teaspoon ground cumin
10 cups chicken broth
1 (28-ounce) can diced
  tomatoes, drained
2 ounces wide egg noodles
2 cups frozen corn, thawed
2 tablespoons minced fresh cilantro

1. Pat chicken dry with paper towels;
season with salt and pepper. Heat
1 tablespoon oil in 12-inch skillet over
medium-high heat until just smoking.
Brown chicken, 3 to 4 minutes per side;
transfer to plate and discard skin.

2. Add chipotle, garlic, tomato paste,
oregano, cumin, and ¾ teaspoon salt
to fat left in skillet; cook until fragrant,
about 30 seconds. Stir in 1 cup broth,
scraping up any browned bits; transfer
to slow cooker.

3. Stir in remaining 9 cups broth and
tomatoes. Nestle chicken into slow
cooker, cover, and cook until chicken is
tender, 3 to 4 hours on low.

4. Bring 2 quarts water to boil in
large saucepan. Add noodles and
1½ teaspoons salt; cook until al dente.
Drain noodles, rinse with cold water,
then toss with remaining 1 teaspoon oil.

5. Transfer chicken to cutting board,
let cool slightly, then shred into bite-
size pieces; discard bones. Stir noodles,
chicken, and corn into soup; let sit for
5 minutes. Stir in cilantro; season with
salt and pepper to taste. Serve.

4 CURRIED CHICKEN AND COUSCOUS SOUP

1½ pounds bone-in split chicken
  breasts, trimmed
  Salt and pepper
4 teaspoons vegetable oil
12 ounces Swiss chard, stems and
  leaves separated and chopped
3 carrots, peeled and cut into
  ½-inch pieces
2 tablespoons grated fresh ginger
2 teaspoons curry powder
1 teaspoon tomato paste
10 cups chicken broth
⅓ cup Israeli couscous
2 tablespoons minced fresh mint

1. Pat chicken dry with paper towels;
season with salt and pepper. Heat
1 tablespoon oil in 12-inch skillet over
medium-high heat until just smoking.
Brown chicken, 3 to 4 minutes per side;
transfer to plate and discard skin.

2. Add chard stems, carrots, and
¾ teaspoon salt to fat left in skillet;
cook over medium heat until softened,
about 8 minutes. Stir in ginger, curry
powder, and tomato paste and cook
until fragrant, about 30 seconds. Stir in
1 cup broth, scraping up any browned
bits; transfer to slow cooker.

3. Stir in remaining 9 cups broth.
Nestle chicken into slow cooker, cover,
and cook until chicken is tender, 3 to
4 hours on low.

4. Bring 2 quarts water to boil in
large saucepan. Add couscous and
1½ teaspoons salt; cook until al dente.
Drain couscous, rinse with cold water,
then toss with remaining 1 teaspoon oil.

5. Transfer chicken to cutting board,
let cool slightly, then shred into bite-
size pieces; discard bones. Stir chard
leaves into soup, cover, and cook on
high until tender, about 30 minutes. Stir
in couscous and chicken; let sit for
5 minutes. Stir in mint and season with
salt and pepper to taste. Serve.

5 CHINESE CHICKEN AND RAMEN SOUP

1½ pounds bone-in split chicken
  breasts, trimmed
  Salt and pepper
1 tablespoon vegetable oil
2 carrots, peeled and sliced
  ¼ inch thick
2 tablespoons grated fresh ginger
3 garlic cloves, minced
10 cups chicken broth
3 tablespoons soy sauce
2 star anise pods
1 (3-ounce) package ramen noodles,
  broken into 1-inch pieces,
  seasoning packet discarded
½ small head napa cabbage,
  cored and shredded (4 cups)
3 scallions, sliced thin
1 teaspoon toasted sesame oil

1. Pat chicken dry with paper towels;
season with salt and pepper. Heat
1 tablespoon vegetable oil in 12-inch
skillet over medium-high heat until
just smoking. Brown chicken, 3 to
4 minutes per side; transfer to plate and
discard skin.

2. Add carrots to fat left in skillet;
cook over medium heat until softened,
about 8 minutes. Stir in ginger and
garlic and cook until fragrant, about
30 seconds. Stir in 1 cup broth,
scraping up any browned bits; transfer
to slow cooker.

3. Stir in remaining 9 cups broth, soy
sauce, and star anise. Nestle chicken
into slow cooker, cover, and cook until
chicken is tender, 3 to 4 hours on low.

4. Transfer chicken to cutting board,
let cool slightly, then shred into bite-
size pieces; discard bones. Discard star
anise. Stir noodles and cabbage into
soup, cover, and cook on high until
noodles are tender, about 8 minutes.
Stir in chicken; let sit for 5 minutes. Stir
in scallions and sesame oil; season with
salt and pepper to taste. Serve.

We add pieces of corn tortilla to the slow cooker for flavor and thickening, and then crisp up strips for the topping.

Tortilla Soup

SERVES 6 TO 8
COOKING TIME 4 TO 5 HOURS ON LOW
SLOW COOKER SIZE 5 TO 7 QUARTS

WHY THIS RECIPE WORKS This turbocharged take on chicken soup features a spicy, tomatoey broth overflowing with garnishes and tender shredded chicken. To replicate the traditionally deep, smoky, roasted flavor of the broth in a slow cooker, typically achieved by charring the vegetables, we browned some of the vegetables in a skillet before adding them to the slow cooker. Using chipotle chiles in adobo sauce (which are dried, smoked jalapeños in a spicy chile sauce) also added some smokiness along with a spicy kick. For even more heat, include the jalapeño seeds. Don't omit the garnishes; the flavor of the soup depends heavily on them.

    1 cup plus 1 tablespoon vegetable oil
    2 tomatoes, cored and chopped
    1 onion, chopped fine
    2 jalapeño chiles, stemmed, seeded, and minced
    6 garlic cloves, minced
    1 tablespoon minced canned chipotle chile in adobo sauce

    1 tablespoon tomato paste
    6 cups chicken broth
   10 (6-inch) corn tortillas (4 torn into ½-inch pieces,
      6 halved and cut crosswise into ½-inch strips)
  1½ pounds boneless, skinless chicken thighs, trimmed
      Salt and pepper
    8 ounces Cotija cheese, crumbled (2 cups)
    1 avocado, halved, pitted, and cut into ½-inch pieces
   ½ cup sour cream
   ½ cup minced fresh cilantro
      Lime wedges

1. Heat 1 tablespoon oil in 12-inch nonstick skillet over medium-high heat until shimmering. Add tomatoes, onion, half of jalapeños, garlic, 2 teaspoons chipotle, and tomato paste and cook until onion is softened and beginning to brown, 8 to 10 minutes. Stir in 1 cup broth, scraping up any browned bits; transfer to slow cooker.

2. Stir remaining 5 cups broth and tortilla pieces into slow cooker. Season chicken with salt and pepper and nestle into slow cooker. Cover and cook until chicken is tender, 4 to 5 hours on low.

3. Meanwhile, wipe skillet clean with paper towels. Heat remaining 1 cup oil in skillet over medium-high heat until shimmering. Add tortilla strips and cook, stirring occasionally, until golden brown, 4 to 6 minutes. Using slotted spoon, transfer tortilla strips to paper towel–lined plate; discard remaining oil. Season tortilla strips with salt to taste and let cool slightly to crisp.

4. Transfer chicken to cutting board, let cool slightly, then shred into bite-size pieces using 2 forks. Whisk soup vigorously for 30 seconds to break down tortilla pieces. Stir in chicken, remaining jalapeños, and remaining 1 teaspoon chipotle and let sit until heated through, about 5 minutes. Season with salt and pepper to taste. Serve, passing tortilla strips, Cotija, avocado, sour cream, cilantro, and lime wedges separately.

NOTES FROM THE TEST KITCHEN

Chipotle Chiles in Adobo

Canned chipotle chiles are jalapeños that have been ripened until red, then smoked and dried. They are sold either as is, ground to a powder, or packed in a tomato-based sauce (which we prefer). These chiles will keep for two weeks in the refrigerator, or they can be frozen for up to two months. To freeze, puree the chiles and quick-freeze teaspoonfuls on a plastic wrap–covered plate. Once the chiles are hard, transfer them to a zipper-lock freezer bag.

Thai Chicken and Coconut Soup

SERVES 6 TO 8   `EASY PREP`

COOKING TIME 4 TO 5 HOURS ON LOW

SLOW COOKER SIZE 5 TO 7 QUARTS

WHY THIS RECIPE WORKS Thai-style chicken soup (aka *tom kha gai*) is famous for its exotic balance of sweet, spicy, and sour flavors. Though recipes for this soup usually call for foreign ingredients like galangal, kaffir lime leaves, and bird's-eye chiles, we swapped them out for supermarket staples like ginger, limes, and Thai red curry paste. Adding some of the coconut milk to the soup just before serving (warmed, so it doesn't cool off the soup) helped deepen the sweet coconut flavor.

2 onions, chopped fine

6 garlic cloves, minced

2 tablespoons grated fresh ginger

2 tablespoons vegetable oil

4 cups chicken broth

2 (13.5-ounce) cans coconut milk

2 lemon grass stalks, trimmed to bottom 6 inches and bruised with back of knife

2 carrots, peeled and sliced ¼ inch thick

3 tablespoons fish sauce, plus extra for seasoning

10 sprigs fresh cilantro, plus leaves for serving

1½ pounds boneless, skinless chicken thighs, trimmed
   Salt and pepper

8 ounces white mushrooms, trimmed and sliced thin

3 tablespoons lime juice, plus lime wedges for serving

1 tablespoon sugar

2 teaspoons Thai red curry paste

2 scallions, sliced thin

1. Microwave onions, garlic, ginger, and oil in bowl, stirring occasionally, until onions are softened, about 5 minutes; transfer to slow cooker. Stir in broth, 1 can coconut milk, lemon grass, carrots, 1 tablespoon fish sauce, and cilantro sprigs. Season chicken with salt and pepper and nestle into slow cooker. Cover and cook until chicken is tender, 4 to 5 hours on low.

2. Transfer chicken to cutting board, let cool slightly, then shred into bite-size pieces using 2 forks. Discard lemon grass and cilantro sprigs.

3. Stir mushrooms into soup, cover, and cook on high until tender, 10 to 15 minutes. Meanwhile, microwave remaining 1 can coconut milk, remaining 2 tablespoons fish sauce, lime juice, sugar, and curry paste in bowl, whisking occasionally, until hot, about 3 minutes. Stir hot coconut milk mixture and chicken into soup and let sit until heated through, about 5 minutes. Season with extra fish sauce to taste. Serve, passing cilantro leaves, lime wedges, and scallions separately.

Buying Broth

Even though homemade broths taste better (pages 40–41), the reality is that the majority of home cooks rely on supermarket broth for most recipes. When selecting store-bought broth, it's important to choose wisely since what you use can have a big impact on your final dish. We prefer chicken broth to beef broth and vegetable broth for its stronger, cleaner flavor, though all have their place in our recipes.

CHICKEN BROTH We like chicken broths with short ingredient lists that include a relatively high percentage of meat-based protein and flavor-boosting vegetables like carrots, celery, and onions. We also like a lower sodium content—less than 700 milligrams per serving. Our favorite brand is **Swanson Chicken Stock**.

VEGETABLE BROTH We've found that the top brands of vegetable broth have a hefty amount of salt and enough vegetable content to be listed on the ingredient list. Because store-bought vegetable broths tend to be sweet, we often mix vegetable broth with chicken broth for the best flavor. Our favorite brand is **Orrington Farms Vegan Chicken Flavored Broth Base & Seasoning**.

BEEF BROTH We've found the best beef broths have concentrated beef stock and flavor-enhancing ingredients such as tomato paste and yeast extract near the top of their ingredient lists. Our favorite brand is **Better Than Bouillon Roasted Beef Base**.

CLAM JUICE Bottled clam juice conveniently brings a bright and mineral-y flavor to seafood dishes. Our favorite, **Bar Harbor Clam Juice**, comes from the shores of clam country in Maine.

SHREDDING MEAT

To shred chicken, beef, or pork into bite-size pieces or large chunks, hold a fork in each hand, with the tines facing down. Insert the tines into the cooked meat and gently pull the forks away from each other, breaking the meat apart and into the desired pieces.

Turkey thighs get star billing in this hearty soup, which also includes brown rice that is added after the turkey is tender.

Turkey and Rice Soup

SERVES 6 TO 8 **EASY PREP** **LIGHT**
COOKING TIME 6 TO 7 HOURS ON LOW
SLOW COOKER SIZE 5 TO 7 QUARTS

WHY THIS RECIPE WORKS Turkey soup is a dish perfectly suited for a slow cooker. The hearty flavor of turkey translates easily into a full-flavored soup without requiring any tricks, and turkey thighs (which we prefer for soup) seem to have been designed for the slow cooker's low and steady cooking environment. Turkey thighs, which are made up entirely of dark meat, are quite big and thick, which means they are nearly impossible to overcook, and they have lots of flavor to spare. (As a bonus, they're cheap, too!) Be sure to use instant rice (sometimes labeled minute rice); traditional rice takes much longer to cook and won't work here. You can substitute an equal amount of bone-in chicken thighs for the turkey, if desired; reduce the cooking time to 4 to 5 hours.

2 onions, chopped fine
4 garlic cloves, minced
1 tablespoon vegetable oil
1 tablespoon tomato paste
2 teaspoons minced fresh thyme or ½ teaspoon dried
  Salt and pepper
8 cups chicken broth
3 carrots, peeled and sliced ¼ inch thick
2 celery ribs, sliced ¼ inch thick
2 bay leaves
2 pounds bone-in turkey thighs, skin removed, trimmed
2 cups instant brown rice
2 tablespoons minced fresh parsley

1. Microwave onions, garlic, oil, tomato paste, thyme, and ¾ teaspoon salt in bowl, stirring occasionally, until onions are softened, about 5 minutes; transfer to slow cooker. Stir in broth, carrots, celery, and bay leaves. Season turkey with salt and pepper and nestle into slow cooker. Cover and cook until turkey is tender, 6 to 7 hours on low.

2. Transfer turkey to cutting board, let cool slightly, then shred into bite-size pieces using 2 forks; discard bones. Discard bay leaves.

3. Stir rice into soup, cover, and cook on high until tender, 30 to 40 minutes. Stir in turkey and let sit until heated through, about 5 minutes. Stir in parsley and season with salt and pepper to taste. Serve.

Hearty Turkey and Vegetable Soup

SERVES 6 TO 8 **EASY PREP** **LIGHT**
COOKING TIME 6 TO 7 HOURS ON LOW
SLOW COOKER SIZE 5 TO 7 QUARTS

WHY THIS RECIPE WORKS In this recipe, turkey delivers a full-flavored soup without requiring a lot of extra steps. To complement the meaty turkey thighs, we microwaved leeks and colorful chard stems to bring out their sweetness, which added valuable depth to the broth. Chopped chard leaves were added during the last 20 minutes of cooking for an earthy, colorful contrast. Orzo was the perfect addition to this soup, adding substance. You can substitute an equal amount of bone-in chicken thighs for the turkey, if desired; reduce the cooking time to 4 to 5 hours.

1½ pounds leeks, white and light green parts only, halved lengthwise, sliced ¼ inch thick, and washed thoroughly
8 ounces Swiss chard, stems chopped, leaves cut into 1-inch pieces
1 tablespoon plus 1 teaspoon vegetable oil
1 teaspoon tomato paste
1 teaspoon minced fresh thyme or ¼ teaspoon dried
  Salt and pepper

8   cups chicken broth
2   carrots, peeled and cut into ½-inch pieces
2   bay leaves
2   pounds bone-in turkey thighs, trimmed
¼   cup orzo

1. Microwave leeks, chard stems, 1 tablespoon oil, tomato paste, thyme, and ¾ teaspoon salt in bowl, stirring occasionally, until vegetables are softened, about 5 minutes; transfer to slow cooker. Stir in broth, carrots, and bay leaves. Season turkey with salt and pepper and nestle into slow cooker. Cover and cook until turkey is tender, 6 to 7 hours on low.

2. Meanwhile, bring 2 quarts water to boil in large saucepan. Add orzo and 1½ teaspoons salt and cook, stirring often, until al dente. Drain orzo, rinse with cold water, then toss with remaining 1 teaspoon oil in bowl; set aside.

3. Transfer turkey to cutting board, let cool slightly, then shred into bite-size pieces using 2 forks; discard bones. Discard bay leaves.

4. Stir chard leaves into soup, cover, and cook on high until tender, 20 to 30 minutes. Stir in orzo and turkey and let sit until heated through, about 5 minutes. Season with salt and pepper to taste. Serve.

PREPARING HEARTY GREENS

1. Cut away leafy portion from either side of stalk or stem using chef's knife.

2. Stack several leaves and either slice leaves crosswise or cut into pieces as directed in recipe. Wash and dry cut leaves using salad spinner.

3. If using Swiss chard stems in recipe, cut into pieces as directed after separating from leafy portion. (Discard collard and kale stems.)

After making an ultra-flavorful broth in the slow cooker, we add the cod and squid and cook them for just 20 minutes.

Spanish Seafood Soup

SERVES 6   LIGHT   ALL DAY
COOKING TIME 6 TO 8 HOURS ON LOW OR 4 TO 6 HOURS ON HIGH
SLOW COOKER SIZE 4 TO 7 QUARTS

WHY THIS RECIPE WORKS Just about every country with a coastline has a seafood soup specialty, and this one takes its inspiration from Spain's classic version known as *zarzuela*. Chock full of fish, this tomato-based soup is seasoned with saffron and paprika and finished with a picada, a flavorful mixture of bread crumbs, finely chopped almonds, and olive oil. We began with a sofrito of onion, bell pepper, and garlic, to which we added tomato paste and a large amount of paprika, plus saffron, red pepper flakes, and bay leaves to create a rich foundation for our broth. A bottle of clam juice added the requisite briny seafood flavor, and a little wine added depth. And since the base of our soup was so rich and fragrant, we found that we could simply add water to achieve the right consistency. Adding the seafood at the end ensured that it was cooked perfectly. Finished with the picada and a drizzle of olive oil, this seafood soup tasted rich and hearty. Halibut and haddock are good substitutes for the cod. If desired, you can omit the squid in this recipe and increase the amount of cod to 1½ pounds. Serve with crusty bread or Garlic Toasts (page 58) to dip into the broth.

1 onion, chopped fine
1 red bell pepper, stemmed, seeded, and chopped fine
6 garlic cloves, minced
2 tablespoons extra-virgin olive oil, plus extra for serving
2 tablespoons tomato paste
1 tablespoon paprika
Salt and pepper
¼ teaspoon saffron threads, crumbled
⅛ teaspoon red pepper flakes
1 (28-ounce) can diced tomatoes
2 cups water
1 (8-ounce) bottle clam juice
¼ cup dry white wine
2 bay leaves
1 pound skinless cod fillets, 1 to 1½ inches thick, cut into 1-inch pieces
8 ounces small squid bodies, sliced crosswise into ½-inch-thick rings
½ cup panko bread crumbs
2 tablespoons slivered almonds, chopped fine
2 tablespoons minced fresh parsley

1. Microwave onion, bell pepper, garlic, 1 tablespoon oil, tomato paste, paprika, ½ teaspoon salt, saffron, and pepper flakes in bowl, stirring occasionally, until vegetables are softened, about 5 minutes; transfer to slow cooker. Stir in tomatoes and their juice, water, clam juice, wine, and bay leaves. Cover and cook until flavors meld, 6 to 8 hours on low or 4 to 6 hours on high.

2. Season cod and squid with salt and pepper and stir into soup. Cover and cook on high until cod flakes apart when gently prodded with paring knife, 20 to 30 minutes.

3. Meanwhile, heat remaining 1 tablespoon oil in 12-inch skillet over medium heat until shimmering. Add panko and almonds and cook, stirring often, until golden brown, 5 to 7 minutes. Transfer panko mixture to bowl and season with salt and pepper to taste; set aside until ready to serve.

4. Discard bay leaves. Gently stir parsley into soup and season with salt and pepper to taste. Serve, topping individual portions with panko mixture and drizzling with extra oil.

Lemon grass, ginger, and fish sauce are the keys to this sweet and spicy Thai soup.

Spicy Thai Shrimp Soup

SERVES 6 **EASY PREP** **LIGHT**
COOKING TIME 6 TO 8 HOURS ON LOW OR 4 TO 6 HOURS ON HIGH
SLOW COOKER SIZE 4 TO 7 QUARTS

WHY THIS RECIPE WORKS Inspired by the popular *tom yum* soup from Thailand, a sweet and spicy soup packed with herbs and spices, we set out to create a version in our slow cooker that was both light and complexly flavored, balancing hot, salty, sweet, and sour elements. Microwaving our aromatics with sesame oil allowed the ingredients to meld and the scallions to release their flavor once added to the soup. A small amount of chili-garlic sauce provided heat, and the saltiness came via fish sauce. Lemon grass was an essential ingredient in this soup, lending a subtle, fragrant lemon essence without harsh citrus notes. This dish traditionally includes shrimp, and to ensure that the shrimp didn't overcook, we added them at the end and let them cook through on high for 15 minutes. The sweet and fresh flavors of a papaya salad seasoned with Thai basil and sesame oil made a zesty and bright topping. The final result: an easy, aromatic, and tasty Thai-style soup.

4 scallions, white parts minced, green parts
   cut into 1-inch pieces
3 garlic cloves, minced
2 teaspoons toasted sesame oil
7 cups chicken broth
2 lemon grass stalks, trimmed to bottom 6 inches
   and bruised with back of knife
1 (2-inch) piece ginger, peeled and sliced
   into ½-inch-thick rounds
1 tablespoon fish sauce, plus extra for seasoning
2 teaspoons Asian chili-garlic sauce
1½ teaspoons sugar
1½ pounds medium-large shrimp (31 to 40 per pound),
   peeled, deveined, and tails removed
8 ounces white mushrooms, trimmed and sliced thin
1 green papaya, peeled, seeded, and shredded
⅓ cup chopped fresh Thai or Italian basil
1 teaspoon lime juice
8 ounces cherry tomatoes, quartered
   Salt and pepper

1. Microwave scallion whites, garlic, and 1 teaspoon oil in bowl, stirring occasionally, until fragrant, about 1 minute; transfer to slow cooker. Stir in broth, lemon grass, ginger, fish sauce, chili-garlic sauce, and sugar. Cover and cook until flavors meld, 6 to 8 hours on low or 4 to 6 hours on high.

2. Discard lemon grass and ginger. Stir shrimp and mushrooms into soup, cover, and cook on high until shrimp are opaque throughout, 15 to 20 minutes.

3. Combine papaya, basil, lime juice, and remaining 1 teaspoon oil in bowl. Stir tomatoes and scallion greens into soup. Season with salt, pepper, and extra fish sauce to taste. Serve, topping individual portions with papaya mixture.

BRUISING LEMON GRASS

Trim and discard all but bottom 6 inches of stalk. Peel off discolored outer layer, then lightly smash stalk with back of chef's knife.

Cajun Shrimp and Corn Chowder

SERVES 6 TO 8   **EASY PREP**

COOKING TIME 5 TO 7 HOURS ON LOW OR 3 TO 5 HOURS ON HIGH

SLOW COOKER SIZE 4 TO 7 QUARTS

WHY THIS RECIPE WORKS Achieving fresh corn flavor in a chowder can be a challenge, but we were determined to develop a foolproof recipe for corn chowder in a slow cooker. We started with frozen corn, which was convenient and available any time of year. We found that the trick to getting fresh corn flavor from frozen corn was to puree a portion of the corn in a blender before adding it to the soup. Not only did this amplify the corn's flavor, but the starch released by the pureed corn helped to thicken the chowder. We added the remaining corn at the end of cooking for color and a satisfying crunch. To give our chowder a Cajun feel, we added shrimp, andouille sausage, bell pepper, and Cajun seasoning. Stirring the shrimp in toward the end of cooking allowed us to monitor them closely and ensure they did not overcook.

6 cups frozen corn, thawed
3 cups chicken broth
8 ounces andouille sausage, cut into ¼-inch pieces
2 garlic cloves, minced
1½ teaspoons Cajun seasoning
12 ounces red potatoes, unpeeled, cut into ½-inch pieces
1 pound medium-large shrimp (31 to 40 per pound),
   peeled, deveined, and tails removed
1 red bell pepper, stemmed, seeded, and chopped fine
½ cup heavy cream
   Salt and pepper

1. Process 4 cups corn and 2 cups broth in blender until smooth, about 1 minute, scraping down sides of blender jar as needed; transfer to slow cooker.

2. Microwave andouille, garlic, and Cajun seasoning in bowl, stirring occasionally, until fragrant, about 2 minutes; transfer to slow cooker. Stir in potatoes and remaining 1 cup broth, cover, and cook until flavors meld and potatoes are tender, 5 to 7 hours on low or 3 to 5 hours on high.

3. Stir remaining 2 cups corn, shrimp, and bell pepper into soup. Cover and cook on high until shrimp are opaque throughout, 15 to 20 minutes. Stir in cream and let sit until heated through, about 5 minutes. Season with salt and pepper to taste. Serve.

For meaty depth of flavor, we simply add uncooked slices of bacon to the chowder as it simmers in the slow cooker.

Manhattan Clam Chowder

SERVES 6 LIGHT ALL DAY

COOKING TIME 8 TO 10 HOURS ON LOW OR 5 TO 7 HOURS ON HIGH

SLOW COOKER SIZE 4 TO 7 QUARTS

WHY THIS RECIPE WORKS Manhattan clam chowder has a delicate harmony of briny seafood, acidic notes, and creamy potatoes, all in a rich, tomatoey broth. Getting the proper balance of tomato to clam took some ingenuity. After pureeing a large can of whole tomatoes to set up our base, we used a bottle of clam juice along with the juice from canned clams to give us the seafood flavor we were looking for. Because the acidity of the tomatoes slowed the breakdown of starches in the potatoes, we had to give the potato pieces enough time to cook all the way through. For a meaty flavor we did something unortho-dox: We added uncooked slices of bacon directly to the slow cooker and removed them before serving. This gave the soup a savory depth without the presence of bits of bacon and avoided an overt pork taste. To finish, we added a little sherry for sweetness and parsley for brightness.

1 (28-ounce) can whole peeled tomatoes
1 onion, chopped fine
2 tablespoons tomato paste
4 garlic cloves, minced
1½ teaspoons minced fresh oregano or ½ teaspoon dried
1 tablespoon vegetable oil
1½ pounds Yukon Gold potatoes, peeled and cut into ½-inch pieces
4 (6.5-ounce) cans chopped clams, drained, juice reserved
1 (8-ounce) bottle clam juice
2 slices bacon
2 bay leaves
2 tablespoons minced fresh parsley
1 tablespoon dry sherry
Salt and pepper

1. Process tomatoes and their juice in food processor until smooth, about 30 seconds; transfer to slow cooker.

2. Microwave onion, tomato paste, garlic, oregano, and oil in bowl, stirring occasionally, until onion is softened, about 5 minutes; transfer to slow cooker. Stir in potatoes, reserved clam juice, bottled clam juice, bacon, and bay leaves. Cover and cook until potatoes are tender, 8 to 10 hours on low or 5 to 7 hours on high.

3. Discard bacon and bay leaves. Stir clams into chowder and let sit until heated through, about 5 minutes. Stir in parsley and sherry and season with salt and pepper to taste. Serve.

French Onion Soup

SERVES 6 TO 8 ALL DAY

COOKING TIME 10 TO 12 HOURS ON HIGH

SLOW COOKER SIZE 5 TO 7 QUARTS

WHY THIS RECIPE WORKS This soup is so rich and flavorful and so packed with darkly caramelized onions that no one would ever imagine it was made in a slow cooker. The secret? For the roasted beefy flavor that usually comes only with homemade beef broth, we microwaved beef bones before tucking them into the slow cooker around the onions. As for the onions, we had to be inventive given the moist heat of the slow cooker; through trial and error, we found that a mix of apple butter and soy sauce gave the onions a silken texture and deep color that made them taste like they had spent hours browning on the stovetop. Beef bones can often be found in the freezer section of the grocery store; if using frozen beef bones, be sure to thaw them completely before using.

3. Discard beef bones. Bring broth to boil in saucepan, then stir into slow cooker. Season with salt and pepper to taste.

4. Just before serving, position oven rack 6 inches from broiler element and heat broiler. Lay baguette slices on rimmed baking sheet and broil until crisp and golden, about 2 minutes per side. Sprinkle Gruyère over 1 side of croutons and continue to broil until melted and bubbly, 3 to 5 minutes. Ladle soup into individual serving bowls and top with cheese croutons. Serve.

All About Onions

Many supermarkets stock a half-dozen types of onions. Here are the onions that you will find in most markets.

YELLOW ONIONS These strong-flavored onions maintain their potency when cooked, making them our first choice for cooking.

WHITE ONIONS These pungent onions are similar to yellow onions but lack some of their complexity.

RED ONIONS These crisp onions have a sweet, peppery flavor when raw and are often used in salads.

SWEET ONIONS Vidalia, Maui, and Walla Walla are three common sweet varieties. Their texture can become stringy when cooked, so they are best used raw.

PEARL ONIONS These crunchy small onions are generally used in soups, stews, and side dishes. Peeling them is a chore, so we recommend buying frozen pearl onions that are already peeled.

SHALLOTS Shallots have a complex, subtly sweet flavor. When cooked, they become very soft and almost melt away, making them the perfect choice for sauces.

SCALLIONS Scallions have an earthy flavor and a delicate crunch and are best in dishes that involve little cooking.

BUYING AND STORING ONIONS Choose rock-hard onions with dry, papery skins. Avoid onions with green sprouts. Store at room temperature, away from light. Store scallions in the refrigerator, covered loosely with a plastic bag.

Apple butter and soy sauce mimic the sweet caramelized flavor that is the hallmark of French onion soup.

2	pounds beef bones
6	onions, halved and sliced ¼ inch thick
4	tablespoons unsalted butter, melted
1	tablespoon packed brown sugar
	Salt and pepper
1	teaspoon minced fresh thyme or ¼ teaspoon dried
5	tablespoons all-purpose flour
¾	cup apple butter
¾	cup dry sherry
¼	cup soy sauce
4	cups beef broth
1	(24-inch) loaf French baguette, sliced ½ inch thick
10	ounces Gruyère cheese, shredded (2½ cups)

1. Line large plate with double layer of coffee filters. Working in batches, arrange beef bones on prepared plate and microwave until well browned, 8 to 10 minutes.

2. Toss onions with melted butter, sugar, 1 teaspoon salt, 1 teaspoon pepper, and thyme in slow cooker. Whisk flour, apple butter, sherry, and soy sauce in bowl until smooth, then stir into slow cooker. Nestle bones into slow cooker, cover, and cook until onions are softened and deep golden brown, 10 to 12 hours on high.

A little cream and dry sherry take the flavor and texture of this tomato soup up a notch at the end of the slow cooking.

Creamy Tomato Soup

SERVES 6 TO 8 **EASY PREP** **VEG**
COOKING TIME 4 TO 6 HOURS ON LOW OR 3 TO 5 HOURS ON HIGH
SLOW COOKER SIZE 4 TO 7 QUARTS

WHY THIS RECIPE WORKS Making a deeply flavored tomato soup is hard enough on the stovetop, but getting the consistency right in a slow cooker seemed daunting at best. First, there was the issue of the tomatoes (fresh or canned?), and second, the matter of technique (how to add flavor and texture to the soup). Since perfectly ripe tomatoes are available just a few weeks a year, we turned to our trusty standby, canned diced tomatoes, which are reliable and prep-free. As for technique, we started by building an aromatic base by microwaving onion and other aromatic ingredients. To add richness, we incorporated heavy cream and dry sherry after the soup was pureed. Serve with Classic Croutons.

1 onion, chopped fine
2 tablespoons unsalted butter
2 tablespoons all-purpose flour
1 tablespoon packed brown sugar
1 tablespoon tomato paste
    Salt and pepper
    Pinch cayenne pepper
3 (14.5-ounce) cans diced tomatoes
3 cups chicken or vegetable broth,
    plus extra as needed
2 bay leaves
½ cup heavy cream
2 teaspoons dry sherry

1. Microwave onion, butter, flour, sugar, tomato paste, ½ teaspoon salt, and cayenne in bowl, stirring occasionally, until onion is softened, about 5 minutes; transfer to slow cooker. Stir in tomatoes and their juice, broth, and bay leaves. Cover and cook until flavors meld, 4 to 6 hours on low or 3 to 5 hours on high.

2. Discard bay leaves. Working in batches, process soup in blender until smooth, 1 to 2 minutes. Return soup to slow cooker and stir in cream and sherry. Adjust consistency with extra hot broth as needed. Season with salt and pepper to taste. Serve.

SIMPLE ACCOMPANIMENTS

CLASSIC CROUTONS

MAKES 3 CUPS

Either fresh or stale bread can be used in this recipe, although stale bread is easier to cut and crisps more quickly in the oven.

6 slices hearty white sandwich bread, crusts removed, cut into ½-inch cubes (3 cups)
3 tablespoons unsalted butter, melted, or extra-virgin olive oil
    Salt and pepper

Adjust oven rack to middle position and heat oven to 350 degrees. Toss bread with melted butter, season with salt and pepper, and spread onto rimmed baking sheet. Bake until golden brown and crisp, 20 to 25 minutes, stirring halfway through baking. Let cool and serve. (Croutons can be stored at room temperature for up to 3 days.)

VARIATION

GARLIC CROUTONS
Whisk 1 minced garlic clove into melted butter before tossing with bread.

Pureeing Soup

Here's what you need to know for the best results. And because pureeing hot soup can be dangerous, follow our safety tips.

BLENDER IS BEST The blade on the blender does the best job with soups because it pulls ingredients down from the top of the container. No stray bits go untouched by the blade. And as long as plenty of headroom is left at the top of the blender, there is no leakage.

IMMERSION BLENDER LEAVES BITS BEHIND The immersion blender is appealing given that it travels to the pot, but we found that it can leave unblended bits of food behind.

PROCESS WITH CAUTION The food processor does a decent job of pureeing, but small bits of vegetables can get trapped under the blade. More troubling is the fact that a food processor tends to leak hot liquid.

WAIT BEFORE BLENDING, AND BLEND IN BATCHES
When blending hot soup, wait 5 minutes for moderate cooling, and fill the blender only two-thirds full; otherwise, the soup can explode out the top. In addition, hold the lid securely with a folded dish towel to keep it in place and to protect your hand from hot steam. And pulse several times before blending continuously.

Garden Minestrone

SERVES 6 TO 8   `EASY PREP`   `VEG`   `LIGHT`   `ALL DAY`
COOKING TIME 8 TO 10 HOURS ON HIGH
SLOW COOKER SIZE 4 TO 7 QUARTS

WHY THIS RECIPE WORKS Creating anything garden-fresh in a slow cooker is a tall order, but we were willing to try to beat the odds and develop a recipe for a bright, lively tasting minestrone that married a flavorful tomato broth with fresh vegetables, beans, and pasta. The base of our soup would be our broth, and after microwaving the aromatics we added broth and canned tomato sauce along with carrots and dried beans—both of which could sustain a long stay in a slow cooker. Sliced zucchini and chopped chard were simply added during the last 20 minutes of cooking, and the precooked pasta was stirred in at the end. Serve with crusty bread or Garlic Toasts (page 58) to dip into the broth.

You can add dried beans right to the slow cooker—no soaking required when making this fresh and easy minestrone.

1 onion, chopped fine
4 garlic cloves, minced
1 tablespoon plus 1 teaspoon extra-virgin olive oil, plus extra for serving
1½ teaspoons minced fresh oregano or ½ teaspoon dried
⅛ teaspoon red pepper flakes
8 cups chicken or vegetable broth
1 (15-ounce) can tomato sauce
1 cup dried great Northern or cannellini beans, picked over and rinsed
2 carrots, peeled and cut into ½-inch pieces
½ cup small pasta, such as ditalini, tubettini, or elbow macaroni
Salt and pepper
1 zucchini, quartered lengthwise and sliced ¼ inch thick
8 ounces Swiss chard, stemmed and sliced ½ inch thick
½ cup chopped fresh basil
Grated Parmesan cheese

1. Microwave onion, garlic, 1 tablespoon oil, oregano, and pepper flakes in bowl, stirring occasionally, until onion is softened, about 5 minutes; transfer to slow cooker. Stir in broth, tomato sauce, beans, and carrots. Cover and cook until beans are tender, 8 to 10 hours on high.

2. Meanwhile, bring 2 quarts water to boil in large saucepan. Add pasta and 1½ teaspoons salt and cook, stirring often, until al dente. Drain pasta, rinse with cold water, then toss with remaining 1 teaspoon oil in bowl; set aside.

3. Stir zucchini and chard into soup, cover, and cook on high until tender, 20 to 30 minutes. Stir in pasta and let sit until heated through, about 5 minutes. Stir in basil and season with salt and pepper to taste. Serve, passing Parmesan and extra oil separately.

SIMPLE ACCOMPANIMENTS

GARLIC TOASTS

MAKES 8 SLICES

Be sure to use a high-quality crusty bread, such as a baguette; do not use sliced sandwich bread.

- 8 (1-inch-thick) slices rustic bread
- 1 large garlic clove, peeled
- 3 tablespoons extra-virgin olive oil
  Salt and pepper

Adjust oven rack 6 inches from broiler element and heat broiler. Spread bread evenly in rimmed baking sheet and broil, flipping as needed, until well toasted on both sides, about 4 minutes. Briefly rub 1 side of each toast with garlic, drizzle with oil, and season with salt and pepper to taste. Serve.

Miso Soup with Shiitakes and Sweet Potatoes

SERVES 6 EASY PREP VEG LIGHT

COOKING TIME 4 TO 6 HOURS ON LOW OR 3 TO 5 HOURS ON HIGH

SLOW COOKER SIZE 4 TO 7 QUARTS

WHY THIS RECIPE WORKS A great miso soup is all about the rich, flavorful broth. We started with water for the liquid base and infused it with a hearty amount of shiitake mushrooms, scallions, ginger, garlic, sesame oil, and red pepper flakes. We tried different types of miso, but tasters preferred the traditional white variety for its mild and slightly sweet flavor. Before adding the miso to the slow cooker, we found it best to thin the thick paste with a small

amount of water to ensure that it would be fully incorporated into the soup. For extra protein we bumped up the amount of tofu, which is traditional in miso soup, and selected the extra-firm variety, as it held its shape best during cooking. For an interesting twist we added sweet potatoes for a little sweetness, and stirred in watercress for a fresh, peppery finish. You can substitute firm tofu here if desired; avoid silken, soft, or medium-firm tofu, as these varieties will break down while cooking.

- 12 ounces shiitake mushrooms, stemmed and sliced thin
- 2 scallions, sliced thin
- 1 (2-inch) piece ginger, peeled and sliced into ¼-inch-thick rounds
- 4 garlic cloves, minced
- 2 teaspoons toasted sesame oil
  Salt and pepper
- ⅛ teaspoon red pepper flakes
- 6 cups water
- ½ cup white miso
- 14 ounces extra-firm tofu, cut into ½-inch cubes
- 12 ounces sweet potatoes, peeled and cut into ½-inch pieces
- 1 tablespoon soy sauce, plus extra for seasoning
- 3 ounces (3 cups) watercress, cut into 2-inch pieces

1. Microwave mushrooms, scallions, ginger, garlic, oil, ¼ teaspoon salt, and pepper flakes in bowl, stirring occasionally, until mushrooms are softened, about 5 minutes; transfer to slow cooker.

2. Whisk 1 cup water and miso in now-empty bowl until miso is fully dissolved. Stir miso mixture, tofu, potatoes, soy sauce, and remaining 5 cups water into slow cooker. Cover and cook until potatoes are tender, 4 to 6 hours on low or 3 to 5 hours on high.

3. Discard ginger. Stir in watercress and let sit until slightly wilted, about 3 minutes. Season with salt, pepper, and extra soy sauce to taste. Serve.

NOTES FROM THE TEST KITCHEN

Miso

Made from a fermented mixture of soybeans and rice, barley, or rye, miso is incredibly versatile, as it is suitable for use in soups, braises, dressings, and sauces. This salty, deep-flavored paste ranges in strength and color from mild pale yellow (referred to as white) to stronger-flavored red or brownish black, depending on the fermentation method and ingredients.

This rustic soup is supereasy to make, and a hefty dose of kale, added at the end, adds bright flavor.

Portuguese Potato and Kale Soup

SERVES 6 TO 8   **EASY PREP**

COOKING TIME 4 TO 6 HOURS ON LOW OR 3 TO 5 HOURS ON HIGH

SLOW COOKER SIZE 4 TO 7 QUARTS

WHY THIS RECIPE WORKS Most recipes for this classic Portuguese soup use spicy chorizo sausage. While this sausage imparted smoky, meaty flavor, its flavors became dull while in the slow cooker. Looking for ways to compensate for the loss of flavor, we added chili powder, oregano, and minced chipotle chile. And microwaving them with the aromatics bloomed their flavors further. Stirring in kale toward the end prevented the hearty greens from tasting washed out but ensured they would be perfectly tender. Serve with crusty bread or Garlic Toasts (page 58) to dip into the broth.

  1 onion, chopped fine
  4 garlic cloves, minced
  1 tablespoon extra-virgin olive oil, plus extra for serving
  1 tablespoon chili powder
1½ teaspoons minced fresh oregano or ½ teaspoon dried
  ½ teaspoon minced canned chipotle chile in adobo sauce
  6 cups chicken broth
  1 pound red potatoes, unpeeled, cut into ½-inch pieces
  8 ounces chorizo sausage, halved lengthwise
    and sliced ½ inch thick
  8 ounces kale, stemmed and sliced ¼ inch thick
    Salt and pepper

1. Microwave onion, garlic, oil, chili powder, oregano, and chipotle in bowl, stirring occasionally, until onion is softened, about 5 minutes; transfer to slow cooker. Stir in broth, potatoes, and chorizo, cover, and cook until potatoes are tender, 4 to 6 hours on low or 3 to 5 hours on high.

2. Stir kale into soup, cover, and cook on high until tender, 20 to 30 minutes. Season with salt and pepper to taste. Serve, passing extra oil separately.

Split Pea Soup

SERVES 6 TO 8   **EASY PREP**   **ALL DAY**

COOKING TIME 8 TO 10 HOURS ON LOW OR 5 TO 7 HOURS ON HIGH

SLOW COOKER SIZE 4 TO 7 QUARTS

WHY THIS RECIPE WORKS To give our split pea soup a rich, smoky flavor, we used a 1-pound ham steak in addition to a smoked ham hock. After the soup was done, we removed the ham steak and ham hock. We then shredded the ham steak (and discarded the ham hock) and returned the meat to the soup. Merely whisking the soup right before serving ensured that all the peas had broken down and that the soup was smooth. Ham hocks often can be found near the ham and bacon in the supermarket.

  2 onions, chopped fine
  1 celery rib, chopped fine
  2 tablespoons unsalted butter
  3 garlic cloves, minced
  1 tablespoon minced fresh thyme or ¾ teaspoon dried
    Salt and pepper
  ¼ teaspoon red pepper flakes
  7 cups water
  1 pound (2 cups) split peas, picked over and rinsed
  1 pound ham steak, rind removed, quartered
  1 (12-ounce) smoked ham hock, rinsed
  2 bay leaves

1. Microwave onions, celery, butter, garlic, thyme, ¾ teaspoon salt, and pepper flakes in bowl, stirring occasionally, until onions are softened, about 5 minutes; transfer to slow cooker. Stir in water, peas, ham steak, ham hock, and bay leaves. Cover and cook until peas are tender, 8 to 10 hours on low or 5 to 7 hours on high.

2. Transfer ham steak to cutting board, let cool slightly, then shred into bite-size pieces using 2 forks. Discard ham hock and bay leaves.

3. Whisk soup vigorously until peas are broken down and soup thickens, about 30 seconds. Stir in ham and let sit until heated through, about 5 minutes. Season with salt and pepper to taste. Serve.

Tuscan White Bean Soup

SERVES 6 TO 8   `EASY PREP`   `LIGHT`   `ALL DAY`
COOKING TIME 8 TO 10 HOURS ON HIGH
SLOW COOKER SIZE 4 TO 7 QUARTS

WHY THIS RECIPE WORKS With few ingredients to distract from flaws like mushy beans or a thin broth, Tuscan White Bean Soup is rarely well prepared in a slow cooker. To create a richly perfumed base for our soup, we microwaved a hefty amount of flavorful pancetta along with a lot of onion and garlic. We added dried beans straight to the slow cooker, where the gentle simmering heat helped them cook through evenly. Rosemary is traditional in this soup, but after several hours it gave the broth a bitter, medicinal taste. Placing a sprig of rosemary in the soup to steep for a few minutes at the end of cooking allowed us to achieve just the right amount of fresh rosemary flavor. Serve with crusty bread or Garlic Toasts (page 58) to dip into the broth.

2 onions, chopped fine
6 ounces pancetta, chopped fine
8 garlic cloves, minced
1 tablespoon extra-virgin olive oil,
  plus extra for serving
¼ teaspoon red pepper flakes
4 cups chicken broth
4 cups water
1 pound (2½ cups) dried great Northern or
  cannellini beans, picked over and rinsed
1 Parmesan cheese rind (optional),
  plus grated Parmesan for serving
2 bay leaves
1 sprig fresh rosemary
  Salt and pepper

1. Microwave onions, pancetta, garlic, oil, and pepper flakes in bowl, stirring occasionally, until onions are softened, about 5 minutes; transfer to slow cooker. Stir in broth, water, beans, Parmesan rind (if using), and bay leaves. Cover and cook until beans are tender, 8 to 10 hours on high.

2. Nestle rosemary sprig into soup, cover, and cook on high until rosemary is fragrant, about 15 minutes.

3. Discard rosemary sprig, bay leaves, and Parmesan rind, if using. Season with salt and pepper to taste. Serve, passing grated Parmesan and extra oil separately.

PICKING OVER AND RINSING DRIED BEANS

Before cooking dried beans, you should pick them over for any small stones or debris and then rinse them. The easiest way to check for small stones is to spread the beans out over a large plate or rimmed baking sheet.

U.S. Senate Navy Bean Soup

SERVES 6 TO 8   `EASY PREP`   `ALL DAY`
COOKING TIME 8 TO 10 HOURS ON HIGH
SLOW COOKER SIZE 4 TO 7 QUARTS

WHY THIS RECIPE WORKS This simple ham and bean soup is a long-standing tradition on the U.S. Senate lunch menu, but it doesn't always live up to its reputation. Often the beans are tough or overcooked, the ham flavor is weak, and the broth is thin. We wondered if we could add more heft to this humble soup. To give the soup more robust ham flavor, we found that a combination of ham hock and ham steak was ideal for both a nice smoky flavor and lots of meaty bites of ham. To keep the soup's saltiness under control, we rinsed the ham hock before cooking and replaced the chicken broth with water. We added dried navy beans straight to the slow cooker, where the gentle simmering heat helped them cook through evenly. By the time the ham hock was tender, the beans were perfectly cooked. Carrots made our soup even heartier, and onions and garlic deepened its flavor. A splash of red wine vinegar added just before serving helped to balance the rich, meaty soup with a little acidity. Ham hocks often can be found near the ham and bacon in the supermarket.

2 onions, chopped fine
2 garlic cloves, minced
2 tablespoons vegetable oil

A ham steak and ham hock combo guarantees that this navy bean soup has deep, meaty, smoky flavor.

2 teaspoons minced fresh thyme or ½ teaspoon dried
7 cups water
1 pound (2½ cups) dried navy beans, picked over and rinsed
1 (12-ounce) smoked ham hock, rinsed
8 ounces ham steak, rind removed, quartered
3 carrots, peeled and sliced ½ inch thick
2 bay leaves
1 teaspoon red wine vinegar, plus extra for seasoning
  Salt and pepper

1. Microwave onions, garlic, oil, and thyme in bowl, stirring occasionally, until onions are softened, about 5 minutes; transfer to slow cooker. Stir in water, beans, ham hock, ham steak, carrots, and bay leaves. Cover and cook until beans are tender, 8 to 10 hours on high.

2. Transfer ham hock and ham steak to cutting board, let cool slightly, then shred into bite-size pieces using 2 forks; discard fat, skin, and bones. Discard bay leaves.

3. Stir ham into soup and let sit until heated through, about 5 minutes. Stir in vinegar and season with salt, pepper, and extra vinegar to taste. Serve.

Black Bean Soup

SERVES 6 TO 8   EASY PREP   LIGHT   ALL DAY
COOKING TIME 8 TO 10 HOURS ON HIGH
SLOW COOKER SIZE 4 TO 7 QUARTS

WHY THIS RECIPE WORKS To create an easy black bean soup that was robust even after hours in the slow cooker, we added chili powder to our microwaved aromatics, tossed in a smoked ham hock (which we later shredded), and included chopped celery and carrot. We added dried black beans straight to the slow cooker where the gentle simmering heat would help them cook through evenly. As for texture, we tried thickeners such as flour, but they only muted the overall flavor of the soup. Mashing some of the cooked beans and stirring them back into the finished soup worked best, providing excellent body and intensifying flavors as well. To add a touch of brightness, we stirred in minced fresh cilantro. Serve this soup with minced red onion, sour cream, and hot sauce.

2 onions, chopped fine
6 garlic cloves, minced
2 tablespoons vegetable oil
2 tablespoons chili powder
3 cups chicken broth
3 cups water
1 pound (2½ cups) dried black beans, picked over and rinsed
1 (12-ounce) smoked ham hock, rinsed
3 celery ribs, cut into ½-inch pieces
2 carrots, peeled and cut into ½-inch pieces
2 bay leaves
2 tablespoons minced fresh cilantro
  Salt and pepper

1. Microwave onions, garlic, oil, and chili powder in bowl, stirring occasionally, until onions are softened, about 5 minutes; transfer to slow cooker. Stir in broth, water, beans, ham hock, celery, carrots, and bay leaves. Cover and cook until beans are tender, 8 to 10 hours on high.

2. Transfer ham hock to cutting board, let cool slightly, then shred into bite-size pieces using 2 forks; discard fat, skin, and bones. Discard bay leaves.

3. Mash portion of beans with potato masher until soup is thickened to desired consistency. Stir in ham and let sit until heated through, about 5 minutes. Stir in cilantro and season with salt and pepper to taste. Serve.

Storing and Reheating Soups, Stews, and Chilis

As tempting as it might seem, do not transfer hot foods straight to the refrigerator. This can increase the fridge's internal temperature to unsafe levels, which is dangerous for all the other food stored there. Letting the pot cool on the countertop for an hour helps its temperature drop to about 75 degrees, at which point you can transfer it safely to the fridge.

To reheat soups, stews, and chilis, we prefer to simmer them gently on the stovetop in a heavy-bottomed pot, but a spin in the microwave works, too. Just be sure to cover the dish to prevent a mess. And note that while most soups, stews, and chilis freeze just fine, those that contain dairy or pasta do not—the dairy curdles as it freezes, and the pasta turns bloated and mushy. Instead, make and freeze the dish without including the dairy or pasta. After thawing the soup, stew, or chili, and heating it through, stir in the uncooked pasta and simmer until just tender, or stir in the dairy and continue to heat gently until hot (do not boil).

Convenient 15-bean soup mix and already cooked chicken sausage yield a soup with surprising heartiness and flavor.

15-Bean Soup with Sausage and Spinach

SERVES 6 **EASY PREP** **LIGHT** **ALL DAY**

COOKING TIME 8 TO 10 HOURS ON HIGH
SLOW COOKER SIZE 4 TO 7 QUARTS

WHY THIS RECIPE WORKS With 15-bean soup mix as our inspiration, we set out to make an easy bean soup with meaty undertones, a bright flavor, and an appealingly chunky texture. Our first step was to ditch the flavoring packets that come with these soup mixes because their dried seasonings and bits of vegetables offered up zero flavor but a lot of sodium. Instead, a combination of onion, garlic, thyme, and red pepper flakes provided a nice balance of oniony aromatics and herbs, and fresh white mushrooms (for mild mushroom flavor) rounded out the flavor of this simple soup. For heartiness we added precooked chicken sausage, which held up during the long cooking time and kept this soup on the lighter side. We stirred in spinach at the end of cooking and allowed it to wilt slightly, adding a fresh, bright element to the soup.

- 8 ounces cooked hot or sweet Italian chicken sausage, sliced ½ inch thick
- 1 onion, chopped fine
- 6 garlic cloves, minced

- 1 tablespoon minced fresh thyme or
  ¾ teaspoon dried
- ¼ teaspoon red pepper flakes
  Salt and pepper
- 6 cups chicken broth
- 2 cups water
- 8 ounces (1¼ cups) 15-bean soup mix, seasoning packet discarded, beans picked over and rinsed
- 8 ounces white mushrooms, trimmed and quartered
- 2 bay leaves
- 4 ounces (4 cups) baby spinach

1. Microwave sausage, onion, garlic, thyme, pepper flakes, and ¼ teaspoon salt in bowl, stirring occasionally, until onion is softened, about 5 minutes; transfer to slow cooker. Stir in broth, water, beans, mushrooms, and bay leaves. Cover and cook until beans are tender, 8 to 10 hours on high.

2. Discard bay leaves. Stir in spinach, 1 handful at a time, and let sit until wilted, about 5 minutes. Season with salt and pepper to taste. Serve.

Moroccan Lentil Soup with Mustard Greens

SERVES 6   **EASY PREP**   **VEG**   **LIGHT**   **ALL DAY**

COOKING TIME 7 TO 9 HOURS ON LOW OR 4 TO 6 HOURS ON HIGH

SLOW COOKER SIZE 4 TO 7 QUARTS

WHY THIS RECIPE WORKS To create a cohesive lentil soup in the slow cooker, we started by microwaving aromatics with Moroccan spices—coriander, garam masala, and cayenne—for a deep, round flavor. For our base we used vegetable broth for its light and slightly sweet flavor. As for the type of lentils, we found that French green lentils did the best job of retaining their texture, shape, and flavor through the long simmer. To finish, we wanted a new and interesting flavor. Dates are a common Moroccan ingredient, and we found that they imparted a nutty, sweet flavor to the broth. Also added at the end, mustard greens offered the perfect balance to the warm spices in this dish, adding a subtle peppery bitterness. To add a little acidity and tang we topped the soup with a mixture of Greek yogurt, parsley, and lemon juice for a perfect balance. We prefer French green lentils, or *lentilles du Puy*, for this recipe, but it will work with any type of lentil except red or yellow. If you can't find mustard greens, you can substitute kale.

1 onion, chopped fine
1 tablespoon vegetable oil
2 garlic cloves, minced
1 teaspoon garam masala
¾ teaspoon ground coriander
  Salt and pepper
⅛ teaspoon cayenne pepper
8 cups vegetable or chicken broth
1 cup French green lentils, picked over and rinsed
12 ounces mustard greens, stemmed and sliced ½ inch thick
4 ounces pitted dates, chopped (¾ cup)
½ cup plain Greek yogurt
¼ cup chopped fresh parsley
1 tablespoon lemon juice

1. Microwave onion, oil, garlic, garam masala, coriander, ¼ teaspoon salt, and cayenne in bowl, stirring occasionally, until onion is softened, about 5 minutes; transfer to slow cooker. Stir in broth and lentils, cover, and cook until lentils are tender, 7 to 9 hours on low or 4 to 6 hours on high.

2. Stir mustard greens and dates into soup, cover, and cook on high until greens are tender, 20 to 30 minutes. Season with salt and pepper to taste.

3. Combine yogurt, parsley, lemon juice, and ⅛ teaspoon pepper in bowl. Season with salt and pepper to taste. Serve, topping individual portions with yogurt mixture.

Getting to Know Lentils

Lentils come in dozens of sizes and colors, and the variations in flavor and color are considerable. We evaluated the most commonly available types of lentils in terms of taste, texture, and appearance. Here's what we found.

BROWN AND GREEN LENTILS These larger lentils are what you'll find in every supermarket. They are a uniform drab brown or green. They have a mild yet light and earthy flavor and a creamy texture. They hold their shape well when cooked and have tender insides. These are all-purpose lentils, great in soups and salads or tossed with olive oil and herbs.

LENTILLES DU PUY These French lentils are smaller than the common brown and green varieties. They are a dark olive-green, almost black. We love them for their rich, earthy, complex flavor and firm yet tender texture. They keep their shape and look beautiful on the plate when cooked, so they're perfect for salads and dishes where the lentils take center stage.

RED AND YELLOW LENTILS These small, split orange-red or golden-yellow lentils completely disintegrate when cooked. If you are looking for a lentil that will quickly break down into a thick puree, this is the one to use.

BLACK LENTILS Like lentilles du Puy, black lentils are slightly smaller than the standard brown and green lentils. They have a deep black hue similar to the color of caviar. In fact, some markets refer to them as beluga lentils. They have a robust, earthy flavor and hold their shape well when cooked, but their skins can make dishes dark and muddy.

WHITE LENTILS White lentils are simply skinned and split black lentils. They have a unique flavor similar to that of mung beans. Like red and yellow lentils, they disintegrate as they cook, and they boast a particularly viscous, starchy texture that makes for a great soup.

MAKE IT 5 WAYS BEEF STEW

Hearty Beef Stew

SERVES 6 TO 8 **ALL DAY**
COOKING TIME 9 TO 10 HOURS ON LOW
OR 6 TO 7 HOURS ON HIGH
SLOW COOKER SIZE 5 TO 7 QUARTS

Achieving big, bold flavor in beef stew usually requires browning the meat, a tedious task that is done in stages and takes time. We wanted to streamline the process while still getting the beefy flavor. To this end, we found that browning only half of the beef still gave us the same flavor without the extra work. We then bolstered the base of the stews with hearty tomato paste, garlic, and onions to achieve maximum impact, deglazing our pan to preserve our precious flavors. We chose to thicken most of the stews with flour, blooming it in the fat of the meat and creating a simple roux. The Catalan Beef Stew also benefited from the addition of chopped nuts and parsley, which acted as both thickener and flavor enhancer. Switching out our vegetables and aromatics in each stew gave us a wide variety of hearty stews from which to choose for a satisfying slow-cooked dinner.

1 HEARTY BEEF STEW

4 pounds boneless beef chuck-eye roast, pulled apart at seams, trimmed, and cut into 1½-inch pieces
  Salt and pepper
2 tablespoons vegetable oil
2 onions, chopped fine
⅓ cup all-purpose flour
¼ cup tomato paste
1 teaspoon minced fresh thyme
2 cups beef broth
½ cup dry red wine
1½ pounds red potatoes, unpeeled, cut into 1-inch pieces
1 pound carrots, peeled, halved lengthwise, and sliced 1 inch thick
2 bay leaves
2 cups frozen peas, thawed
2 tablespoons minced fresh parsley

1. Pat beef dry with paper towels and season with salt and pepper. Heat oil in 12-inch skillet over medium-high heat until just smoking. Brown half of beef on all sides, about 8 minutes; transfer to slow cooker with remaining uncooked beef.

2. Add onions to fat left in skillet and cook over medium heat until softened and lightly browned, about 10 minutes. Stir in flour, tomato paste, and thyme and cook until fragrant, about 1 minute. Slowly whisk in broth and wine, scraping up any browned bits and smoothing out any lumps; transfer to slow cooker.

3. Stir potatoes, carrots, and bay leaves into slow cooker. Cover and cook until beef is tender, 9 to 10 hours on low or 6 to 7 hours on high.

4. Discard bay leaves. Stir in peas and let sit until heated through, about 5 minutes. Stir in parsley and season with salt and pepper to taste. Serve.

2 PROVENÇAL BEEF STEW

4 pounds boneless beef chuck-eye roast, pulled apart at seams, trimmed, and cut into 1½-inch pieces
  Salt and pepper
2 tablespoons vegetable oil
2 onions, chopped fine
⅓ cup all-purpose flour
¼ cup tomato paste
¼ ounce dried porcini mushrooms, rinsed and minced
3 garlic cloves, minced
2 teaspoons minced fresh rosemary
1 anchovy fillet, minced
2 cups beef broth
½ cup dry red wine
1½ pounds carrots, peeled, halved lengthwise, and sliced 1 inch thick
1 (14.5-ounce) can diced tomatoes, drained
2 (2-inch) strips orange zest
½ cup pitted kalamata olives, chopped

1. Pat beef dry with paper towels and season with salt and pepper. Heat oil in 12-inch skillet over medium-high heat until just smoking. Brown half of beef on all sides, about 8 minutes; transfer to slow cooker with remaining uncooked beef.

2. Add onions to fat left in skillet and cook over medium heat until softened and lightly browned, about 10 minutes. Stir in flour, tomato paste, mushrooms, garlic, rosemary, and anchovy and cook until fragrant, about 1 minute. Slowly whisk in broth and wine, scraping up any browned bits and smoothing out any lumps; transfer to slow cooker.

3. Stir carrots, tomatoes, and orange zest into slow cooker. Cover and cook until beef is tender, 9 to 10 hours on low or 6 to 7 hours on high. Stir in olives and season with salt and pepper to taste. Serve.

3 CATALAN BEEF STEW

4 pounds boneless beef chuck-eye roast, pulled apart at seams, trimmed, and cut into 1½-inch pieces
Salt and pepper
2 tablespoons vegetable oil
1 pound cremini mushrooms, trimmed and quartered
2 onions, chopped fine
⅓ cup all-purpose flour
¼ cup tomato paste
3 garlic cloves, minced
1 teaspoon smoked paprika
¾ teaspoon ground cinnamon
2 cups beef broth
½ cup dry white wine
2 (14.5-ounce) cans diced tomatoes, drained
¼ cup slivered almonds, toasted and chopped fine
2 tablespoons minced fresh parsley
1 tablespoon sherry vinegar

1. Pat beef dry with paper towels and season with salt and pepper. Heat oil in 12-inch skillet over medium-high heat until just smoking. Brown half of beef on all sides, about 8 minutes; transfer to slow cooker with remaining uncooked beef.

2. Add mushrooms and onions to fat left in skillet and cook over medium heat until softened and lightly browned, about 10 minutes. Stir in flour, tomato paste, garlic, paprika, and cinnamon and cook until fragrant, about 1 minute. Slowly whisk in broth and wine, scraping up any browned bits and smoothing out any lumps; transfer to slow cooker.

3. Stir tomatoes into slow cooker, cover, and cook until beef is tender, 9 to 10 hours on low or 6 to 7 hours on high. Stir in almonds, parsley, and vinegar, and season with salt and pepper to taste. Serve.

4 MOROCCAN-SPICED BEEF STEW

4 pounds boneless beef chuck-eye roast, pulled apart at seams, trimmed, and cut into 1½-inch pieces
Salt and pepper
2 tablespoons vegetable oil
2 onions, chopped fine
⅓ cup all-purpose flour
¼ cup tomato paste
3 garlic cloves, minced
1 teaspoon paprika
1 teaspoon garam masala
Pinch cayenne pepper
3 cups beef broth
½ cup dry white wine
2 (15-ounce) cans chickpeas, rinsed
2 carrots, peeled, halved lengthwise, and sliced 1 inch thick
1 cup dried figs, stemmed and cut into ½-inch pieces
2 bay leaves

1. Pat beef dry with paper towels and season with salt and pepper. Heat oil in 12-inch skillet over medium-high heat until just smoking. Brown half of beef on all sides, about 8 minutes; transfer to slow cooker with remaining uncooked beef.

2. Add onions to fat left in skillet and cook over medium heat until softened and lightly browned, about 10 minutes. Stir in flour, tomato paste, garlic, paprika, garam masala, and cayenne and cook until fragrant, about 1 minute. Slowly whisk in broth and wine, scraping up any browned bits and smoothing out any lumps; transfer to slow cooker.

3. Stir chickpeas, carrots, figs, and bay leaves into slow cooker. Cover and cook until beef is tender, 9 to 10 hours on low or 6 to 7 hours on high. Discard bay leaves. Season with salt and pepper to taste. Serve.

5 SPICY KOREAN BEEF STEW

4 pounds boneless beef chuck-eye roast, pulled apart at seams, trimmed, and cut into 1½-inch pieces
Salt and pepper
2 tablespoons vegetable oil
2 onions, chopped fine
⅓ cup all-purpose flour
2 tablespoons grated fresh ginger
3 garlic cloves, minced
2 cups beef broth
½ cup mirin
3 cups cabbage kimchi, drained and chopped
2 tablespoons sugar
1 tablespoon soy sauce, plus extra for seasoning
1 tablespoon toasted sesame oil
1 ounce (1 cup) bean sprouts
4 scallions, sliced thin

1. Pat beef dry with paper towels and season with salt and pepper. Heat vegetable oil in 12-inch skillet over medium-high heat until just smoking. Brown half of beef on all sides, about 8 minutes; transfer to slow cooker with remaining uncooked beef.

2. Add onions to fat left in skillet and cook over medium heat until softened and lightly browned, about 10 minutes. Stir in flour, ginger, and garlic and cook until fragrant, about 1 minute. Slowly whisk in broth and mirin, scraping up any browned bits and smoothing out any lumps; transfer to slow cooker.

3. Stir 2 cups kimchi into slow cooker, cover, and cook until beef is tender, 9 to 10 hours on low or 6 to 7 hours on high.

4. Stir sugar, soy sauce, sesame oil, and remaining 1 cup kimchi into stew and let sit for 5 minutes. Season with extra soy sauce to taste. Serve, topping individual portions with bean sprouts and scallions.

Beef Burgundy

SERVES 8 **ALL DAY**

COOKING TIME 9 TO 10 HOURS ON LOW OR 6 TO 7 HOURS ON HIGH

SLOW COOKER SIZE 5 TO 7 QUARTS

WHY THIS RECIPE WORKS To ensure a rich-tasting, company-worthy beef burgundy, we decided it was worth a little extra prep time. So to start, we browned half the meat in a skillet (the other half can be added raw to the slow cooker). Then we boosted the base of the stew by sautéing bacon with a hefty amount of garlic and thyme and adding tomato paste for sweetness and soy sauce for extra meatiness. To keep the flavor of the wine in balance, we added half of it at the outset and then reduced the remaining half to mellow its sharpness before adding it to the stew at the end. Frozen pearl onions made things easy; we simply cooked them through and browned them in a skillet before adding them and browned mushrooms to the finished stew. Use a good-quality medium-bodied wine, such as a Côtes du Rhône or Pinot Noir, for this stew.

5 pounds boneless beef chuck-eye roast,
   pulled apart at seams, trimmed, and cut
   into 1½-inch pieces
   Salt and pepper
2 tablespoons vegetable oil
4 slices bacon, chopped fine
2 onions, chopped fine
1 carrot, peeled and chopped fine
⅓ cup all-purpose flour
¼ cup tomato paste
6 garlic cloves, minced
1 tablespoon minced fresh thyme or
   ¾ teaspoon dried
2½ cups dry red wine
1½ cups beef broth, plus extra as needed
⅓ cup soy sauce
2 bay leaves
2 cups frozen pearl onions
3 tablespoons unsalted butter
2 teaspoons sugar
1 pound cremini mushrooms, trimmed and
   halved if small or quartered if large
2 tablespoons minced fresh parsley

1. Pat beef dry with paper towels and season with salt and pepper. Heat oil in 12-inch skillet over medium-high heat until just smoking. Brown half of beef on all sides, about 8 minutes; transfer to slow cooker along with remaining uncooked beef.

2. Add bacon to fat left in skillet and cook over medium heat until crisp, 5 to 7 minutes. Stir in onions and carrot and cook until softened and lightly browned, 8 to 10 minutes. Stir in flour, tomato paste, garlic, and thyme and cook until fragrant, about 1 minute. Slowly whisk in 1¼ cups wine, scraping up any browned bits and smoothing out any lumps; transfer to slow cooker.

3. Stir broth, soy sauce, and bay leaves into slow cooker, cover, and cook until beef is tender, 9 to 10 hours on low or 6 to 7 hours on high.

4. About 30 minutes before serving, bring pearl onions, ½ cup water, butter, and sugar to simmer in 12-inch skillet over medium heat. Cover and cook until onions are fully thawed and tender, 5 to 8 minutes. Uncover and continue to cook until all liquid evaporates, about 4 minutes. Stir in mushrooms and cook until vegetables are browned and glazed, 8 to 12 minutes. Discard bay leaves and stir onion-mushroom mixture into stew.

5. Bring remaining 1¼ cups wine to simmer in now-empty skillet and cook until reduced by half, 6 to 8 minutes; stir into stew. Adjust consistency with extra hot broth as needed. Stir in parsley and season with salt and pepper to taste. Serve.

CUTTING STEW MEAT

1. Pull apart roast at its major seams (delineated by lines of fat and silverskin). Use knife as necessary.

2. With knife, trim off excess fat and silverskin.

3. Cut meat into pieces as directed in recipe.

A hefty dose of whole-grain mustard added before serving brings zesty flavor to this rustic pork and bean stew.

Pork and White Bean Stew with Kale

SERVES 6   EASY PREP   ALL DAY

COOKING TIME 6 TO 8 HOURS ON LOW OR 4 TO 6 HOURS ON HIGH

SLOW COOKER SIZE 4 TO 7 QUARTS

WHY THIS RECIPE WORKS For a real stick-to-your-ribs meal, we used a classic white bean stew as a starting point and incorporated meaty pork and earthy kale. Boneless country-style pork ribs required minimal prep work, and thanks to plenty of intramuscular fat they were moist and fall-apart tender after several hours in the slow cooker. Dried beans were still undercooked by the time the pork was done, but canned white beans cooked through perfectly in the same amount of time and required little preparation. To give the stew body, we pureed a portion of the beans with broth before adding them to the slow cooker. To boost the fresh flavor of the stew and complement the rich pork and beans, we added 2 tablespoons of whole-grain mustard after the kale had cooked through. Cutting the kale into 1-inch pieces allowed the hearty green to become tender in just 20 minutes of cooking time. Look for country-style pork ribs

with lots of fat and dark meat, and stay away from ribs that look overly lean with pale meat, as they will taste very dry after the extended cooking time.

   3 (15-ounce) cans cannellini beans, rinsed
   4 cups chicken broth, plus extra as needed
   2 onions, chopped fine
   2 tablespoons extra-virgin olive oil, plus extra for serving
   4 garlic cloves, minced
   1 tablespoon minced fresh thyme or ¾ teaspoon dried
     Salt and pepper
1½ pounds boneless country-style pork ribs, trimmed and cut into 1½-inch pieces
   8 ounces kale, stemmed and cut into 1-inch pieces
   2 tablespoons whole-grain mustard

1. Process one-third of beans and 1 cup broth in blender until smooth, about 30 seconds; transfer to slow cooker.

2. Microwave onions, oil, garlic, thyme, and ¼ teaspoon salt in bowl, stirring occasionally, until onions are softened, about 5 minutes; transfer to slow cooker. Stir in remaining beans and remaining 3 cups broth. Season pork with salt and pepper and stir into slow cooker. Cover and cook until pork is tender, 6 to 8 hours on low or 4 to 6 hours on high.

3. Stir in kale, cover, and cook on high until tender, 20 to 30 minutes. Adjust consistency with extra hot broth as needed. Stir in mustard and season with salt and pepper to taste. Serve, drizzling individual portions with extra oil.

Brazilian Black Bean and Pork Stew

SERVES 6 TO 8   ALL DAY

COOKING TIME 8 TO 9 HOURS ON HIGH

SLOW COOKER SIZE 5 TO 7 QUARTS

WHY THIS RECIPE WORKS Inspired by the meaty Brazilian stew known as *feijoada*, this slow-cooker recipe is packed with creamy black beans and tender, juicy chunks of pork and has an intense, smoky flavor. To start, we relied on sautéing bacon with onions, garlic, tomato paste, and a trio of spices—chili powder, cumin, and coriander—to build a strong foundation. Since the black beans didn't require soaking, we simply added them to the slow cooker next, along with the pork and broth, and allowed everything to cook until tender. The addition of a little kielbasa sausage to the mix was untraditional but added even more smoky, meaty flavor. Serving this stew with the traditional salsa-like Brazilian hot sauce added the perfect tangy background for the rich flavors of the dish. Pork butt roast is often labeled Boston butt in the supermarket.

STEW

- 6 slices bacon, chopped fine
- 2 onions, chopped fine
- ¼ cup tomato paste
- 6 garlic cloves, minced
- 2 tablespoons chili powder
- 2 teaspoons ground cumin
- 1 teaspoon ground coriander
- 1 cup water
- 4 cups chicken broth, plus extra as needed
- 1 pound (2½ cups) dried black beans, picked over and rinsed
- 1 pound kielbasa sausage, halved lengthwise and sliced ½ inch thick
- 2 bay leaves
- 1 (3-pound) boneless pork butt roast, pulled apart at seams, trimmed, and cut into 1½-inch pieces
  Salt and pepper

HOT SAUCE

- 2 tomatoes, cored and chopped
- 1 onion, chopped fine
- 1 green bell pepper, stemmed, seeded, and chopped fine
- ⅓ cup white wine vinegar
- 1 jalapeño chile, stemmed, seeded, and minced
- 3 tablespoons extra-virgin olive oil
- 1 tablespoon minced fresh cilantro
- ½ teaspoon salt

1. FOR THE STEW Cook bacon in 12-inch skillet over medium heat until crisp, 5 to 7 minutes. Stir in onions and cook until softened and lightly browned, 8 to 10 minutes. Stir in tomato paste, garlic, chili powder, cumin, and coriander and cook until fragrant, about 1 minute. Stir in water, scraping up any browned bits; transfer to slow cooker.

2. Stir broth, beans, kielbasa, and bay leaves into slow cooker. Season pork with salt and pepper and stir into slow cooker. Cover and cook until pork is tender, 8 to 9 hours on high.

3. FOR THE HOT SAUCE Combine all ingredients in bowl and let sit at room temperature until flavors meld, about 30 minutes. (Hot sauce can be refrigerated for up to 2 days.)

4. Discard bay leaves. Adjust consistency with extra hot broth as needed. Season with salt and pepper to taste. Serve with hot sauce.

Browning boneless, skinless chicken thighs imparts extra flavor to this classic and rich chicken stew.

Homey Chicken Stew

SERVES 6 TO 8
COOKING TIME 4 TO 5 HOURS ON LOW
SLOW COOKER SIZE 5 TO 7 QUARTS

WHY THIS RECIPE WORKS To make a chicken stew in which the simple, pure flavor of a rich broth married with tender chicken and vegetables would shine through, we had to start by browning boneless, skinless thighs, which both gave them extra flavor and rendered some of their fat and juice (which later made their way into the slow cooker). We also sautéed aromatics with a little tomato paste, which added richness without a noticeable tomatoey presence. In early tests we discovered that our chunky potatoes as well as the sliced carrots were just not tender by the time the chicken had finished cooking. So we gave them a head start by briefly simmering them in the skillet with the aromatics, which ensured that we could have tender vegetables in our finished stew.

- 3 pounds boneless, skinless chicken thighs, trimmed
  Salt and pepper
- 3 tablespoons vegetable oil

2 onions, chopped fine

⅓ cup all-purpose flour

6 garlic cloves, minced

1 tablespoon tomato paste

2 teaspoons minced fresh thyme or ½ teaspoon dried

4 cups chicken broth, plus extra as needed

½ cup dry white wine

12 ounces red potatoes, unpeeled, cut into ½-inch pieces

4 carrots, peeled and sliced ¼ inch thick

2 bay leaves

1 cup frozen peas

2 tablespoons minced fresh parsley

1. Pat chicken dry with paper towels and season with salt and pepper. Heat 1 tablespoon oil in 12-inch skillet over medium-high heat until just smoking. Brown half of chicken, about 4 minutes per side; transfer to slow cooker. Repeat with 1 tablespoon oil and remaining chicken; transfer to slow cooker.

2. Heat remaining 1 tablespoon oil in now-empty skillet over medium heat until shimmering. Add onions and cook until softened and lightly browned, 8 to 10 minutes. Stir in flour, garlic, tomato paste, and thyme and cook until fragrant, about 1 minute. Slowly whisk in 2 cups broth and wine, scraping up any browned bits and smoothing out any lumps. Stir in potatoes and carrots and bring to simmer. Cover, reduce heat to medium-low, and simmer until vegetables just begin to soften, about 10 minutes; transfer to slow cooker.

3. Stir remaining 2 cups broth and bay leaves into slow cooker, cover, and cook until chicken is tender, 4 to 5 hours on low.

4. Transfer chicken to cutting board, let cool slightly, then pull apart into large chunks using 2 forks. Discard bay leaves.

5. Stir chicken and peas into stew and let sit until heated through, about 5 minutes. Adjust consistency with extra hot broth as needed. Stir in parsley and season with salt and pepper to taste. Serve.

Chicken Stew with Sausage and White Beans

SERVES 6 TO 8

COOKING TIME 4 TO 5 HOURS ON LOW

SLOW COOKER SIZE 5 TO 7 QUARTS

WHY THIS RECIPE WORKS This hearty stew takes its inspiration from classic Tuscan white bean stew, only here we combined meaty chicken thighs with sausage. We found it was worth getting out the skillet to brown the chicken and sausage and sauté the aromatics and fennel, as this step added a richer, deeper flavor. The sliced fennel, thyme, and red pepper flakes complemented the flavors of the Italian sausage. The spinach may seem like a lot at first, but

For welcome fresh flavor we add 6 ounces of baby spinach to this stew and let it wilt down before serving.

it wilts down substantially. A sprinkling of grated Parmesan cheese enhances the other flavors in the stew. Serve with crusty bread or Garlic Toasts (page 58).

2 pounds boneless, skinless chicken thighs, trimmed
 Salt and pepper

3 tablespoons vegetable oil

1 pound hot or sweet Italian sausage, casings removed

2 onions, chopped fine

1 fennel bulb, stalks discarded, bulb halved, cored, and sliced thin

⅓ cup all-purpose flour

6 garlic cloves, minced

1 tablespoon tomato paste

2 teaspoons minced fresh thyme or ½ teaspoon dried

⅛ teaspoon red pepper flakes

4 cups chicken broth, plus extra as needed

½ cup dry white wine

2 (15-ounce) cans cannellini beans, rinsed

2 bay leaves

6 ounces (6 cups) baby spinach
 Grated Parmesan cheese

1. Pat chicken dry with paper towels and season with salt and pepper. Heat 1 tablespoon oil in 12-inch skillet over medium-high heat until just smoking. Brown half of chicken, about 4 minutes per side; transfer to slow cooker. Repeat with 1 tablespoon oil and remaining chicken; transfer to slow cooker.

2. Heat remaining 1 tablespoon oil in now-empty skillet over medium-high heat until just smoking. Add sausage and cook, breaking up meat into rough 1-inch pieces with wooden spoon, until browned, about 5 minutes. Using slotted spoon, transfer sausage to slow cooker.

3. Pour off all but 1 tablespoon fat from skillet, add onions and fennel, and cook over medium heat until softened and lightly browned, 8 to 10 minutes. Stir in flour, garlic, tomato paste, thyme, and pepper flakes and cook until fragrant, about 1 minute. Slowly whisk in 1 cup broth and wine, scraping up any browned bits and smoothing out any lumps; transfer to slow cooker.

4. Stir remaining 3 cups broth, beans, and bay leaves into slow cooker, cover, and cook until chicken is tender, 4 to 5 hours on low.

5. Transfer chicken to cutting board, let cool slightly, then pull apart into large chunks using 2 forks. Discard bay leaves.

6. Stir chicken into stew, then stir in spinach, 1 handful at a time, and let sit until wilted, about 5 minutes. Adjust consistency with extra hot broth as needed. Season with salt and pepper to taste. Serve with Parmesan.

Chicken Bouillabaisse

SERVES 6 TO 8
COOKING TIME 4 TO 5 HOURS ON LOW
SLOW COOKER SIZE 5 TO 7 QUARTS

WHY THIS RECIPE WORKS Swapping in readily available chicken thighs for the numerous and expensive varieties of fish in traditional bouillabaisse made this update of the classic Provençal recipe an equally delicious but far more practical dish, especially for the slow cooker. It is still a stunningly flavorful dish rich with garlic, fennel, orange, and saffron, not to mention the classic rouille, which you can make on the side. The ingredients that give bouillabaisse its robust traditional flavor could withstand hours in the slow cooker, making for an intensely flavorful broth at the end of cooking. But to ensure the deepest flavor in this stew, we had to get our skillet and brown the chicken in batches, sauté the aromatics, and make a simple roux. Every ingredient counts here—from the traditional saffron, white wine, and cayenne to the orange zest and fresh tarragon. A small amount of licorice-flavored liqueur (we prefer pastis) intensified the traditional anise backbone of this stew, while canned tomatoes lent welcome acidity and brightness.

Served with a rouille and garlic toasts, our slow-cooker chicken bouillabaisse will be the star of any dinner party.

STEW

- 3 pounds boneless, skinless chicken thighs, trimmed
  Salt and pepper
- 3 tablespoons extra-virgin olive oil
- 1 leek, white and light green parts only, halved lengthwise, sliced thin, and washed thoroughly
- 1 small fennel bulb, stalks discarded, bulb halved, cored, and sliced thin
- ¼ cup all-purpose flour
- 4 garlic cloves, minced
- 1 tablespoon tomato paste
- ¼ teaspoon saffron threads, crumbled
- ⅛ teaspoon cayenne pepper
- 4 cups chicken broth, plus extra as needed
- ½ cup dry white wine
- ¼ cup pastis or Pernod
- 12 ounces Yukon Gold potatoes, peeled and cut into ½-inch pieces
- 1 (14.5-ounce) can diced tomatoes, drained
- 1 (3-inch) strip orange zest
- 1 tablespoon minced fresh tarragon or parsley

 2 tablespoons water

 ⅛ teaspoon saffron threads, crumbled

 1 slice hearty white sandwich bread,
 crusts removed, torn into 1-inch pieces

 2 teaspoons lemon juice

 1 large egg yolk

 1 teaspoon Dijon mustard

 1 small garlic clove, minced
 Pinch cayenne pepper

 ½ cup extra-virgin olive oil
 Salt and pepper

 1 recipe Garlic Toasts (page 58)

1. FOR THE STEW Pat chicken dry with paper towels and season with salt and pepper. Heat 1 tablespoon oil in 12-inch skillet over medium-high heat until just smoking. Brown half of chicken, about 4 minutes per side; transfer to slow cooker. Repeat with 1 tablespoon oil and remaining chicken; transfer to slow cooker.

2. Heat remaining 1 tablespoon oil in now-empty skillet over medium heat until shimmering. Add leek and fennel and cook until softened and lightly browned, 8 to 10 minutes. Stir in flour, garlic, tomato paste, saffron, and cayenne and cook until fragrant, about 1 minute. Slowly whisk in 2 cups broth, wine, and pastis, scraping up any browned bits and smoothing out any lumps. Stir in potatoes and bring to simmer. Cover, reduce heat to medium-low, and simmer until potatoes are softened, about 15 minutes; transfer to slow cooker.

3. Stir remaining 2 cups broth, tomatoes, and orange zest into slow cooker, cover, and cook until chicken is tender, 4 to 5 hours on low.

4. FOR THE ROUILLE Microwave water and saffron in medium bowl until steaming, about 10 seconds; let steep for 5 minutes. Stir in bread and lemon juice and let sit until bread is softened and beginning to break down, about 5 minutes. Mash bread with fork until smooth paste forms. Whisk in egg yolk, mustard, garlic, and cayenne. Whisking constantly, slowly drizzle in oil until mixture resembles smooth mayonnaise. Season with salt and pepper to taste. (Rouille can be refrigerated for up to 2 days.)

5. Transfer chicken to cutting board, let cool slightly, then pull apart into large chunks using 2 forks. Discard orange zest.

6. Stir in chicken and let sit until heated through, about 5 minutes. Adjust consistency with extra hot broth as needed. Stir in tarragon and season with salt and pepper to taste. Serve with rouille and Garlic Toasts.

Fisherman's Stew

SERVES 6 TO 8   **EASY PREP**   **LIGHT**
COOKING TIME 5 TO 7 HOURS ON LOW OR 3 TO 5 HOURS ON HIGH
SLOW COOKER SIZE 4 TO 7 QUARTS

WHY THIS RECIPE WORKS To make a slow-cooker fish stew with tender and moist cod and shrimp, a full-flavored broth, spicy chorizo, and hearty potatoes, the key was to allow the stew to simmer and build flavor, then add the fish and shrimp at the end and poach them gently just until they were done. For the broth, we started with white wine, clam juice, and diced tomatoes. We simmered onion, garlic, chorizo, and chunks of red potatoes in the broth until the potatoes were tender and the broth was richly flavored. Then we added the seafood and gently cooked it in the flavorful broth for 30 minutes. All the stew needed was a sprinkle of fresh parsley to finish. Halibut and haddock are good substitutes for the cod. For a richer fish stew, serve with Garlic Aïoli (page 37).

 1 onion, chopped

 8 ounces chorizo sausage, cut into ¼-inch pieces

 4 garlic cloves, minced

 1 pound red potatoes, unpeeled, cut into ½-inch pieces

 2 (8-ounce) bottles clam juice

 1 (14.5-ounce) can diced tomatoes, drained

 ¼ cup dry white wine

 1½ pounds skinless cod fillets, 1 to 1½ inches thick,
 cut into 2- to 3-inch pieces

 8 ounces large shrimp (26 to 30 per pound),
 peeled, deveined, and tails removed
 Salt and pepper

 2 tablespoons minced fresh parsley

1. Microwave onion, chorizo, and garlic in bowl, stirring occasionally, until onion is softened, about 5 minutes; transfer to slow cooker. Stir in potatoes, clam juice, tomatoes, and wine. Cover and cook until flavors meld and potatoes are tender, 5 to 7 hours on low or 3 to 5 hours on high.

2. Season cod and shrimp with salt and pepper and stir into stew. Cover and cook on high until shrimp are opaque throughout and cod flakes apart when gently prodded with paring knife, about 30 minutes. Gently stir in parsley and season with salt and pepper to taste. Serve.

This humble fish stew delivers more satisfying flavor than its simple ingredient list would lead you to believe.

Sicilian Fish Stew

SERVES 6 TO 8 **EASY PREP** **LIGHT**

COOKING TIME 4 TO 6 HOURS ON LOW OR 3 TO 5 HOURS ON HIGH

SLOW COOKER SIZE 4 TO 7 QUARTS

WHY THIS RECIPE WORKS In Sicily, fish is combined with tomatoes and local ingredients to create a simple stew that relies on the intermingling of salty, sweet, and sour flavors. For our slow cooker riff on this stew we created a balanced tomatoey broth base from a basic trio of ingredients: onions, celery, and garlic, which we bloomed in the microwave along with tomato paste and thyme. Some clam juice gave us the brininess of the sea, and a little white wine gave us much needed acidity. Golden raisins and capers imparted nice punches of sweet and salty flavor. This stew is typically made with firm white-fleshed fillets, such as snapper. However, tasters felt that the snapper's mild flavor was lost amid the bold flavors of the stew and preferred the stronger flavor and meaty texture of swordfish. Cooking the swordfish for only the last half-hour ensured tender, flaky fish that remained moist. And since many fish stews feature a nutty herb topping for a hit of texture and flavor, we decided to include that. We went with a slight twist on gremolata,

a classic Italian herb condiment, swapping in mint and orange for the usual lemon and parsley to give us nuanced freshness. Halibut is a good substitute for the swordfish. Serve with crusty bread or Garlic Toasts (page 58) to dip into the broth.

 2 onions, chopped fine
 1 celery rib, chopped fine
 2 tablespoons extra-virgin olive oil
 2 tablespoons tomato paste
 4 garlic cloves, minced
 1 teaspoon minced fresh thyme or ¼ teaspoon dried
    Salt and pepper
    Pinch red pepper flakes
 2 (8-ounce) bottles clam juice
 1 (14.5-ounce) can diced tomatoes, drained
 ¼ cup dry white wine
 ¼ cup golden raisins
 2 tablespoons capers, rinsed
 1½ pounds skinless swordfish steaks, 1 to 1½ inches thick,
    cut into 1-inch pieces
 ¼ cup pine nuts, toasted and chopped
 ¼ cup minced fresh mint
 1 teaspoon grated orange zest

1. Microwave onions, celery, oil, tomato paste, three-quarters of garlic, thyme, ½ teaspoon salt, ¼ teaspoon pepper, and pepper flakes in bowl, stirring occasionally, until vegetables are softened, about 5 minutes; transfer to slow cooker. Stir in clam juice, tomatoes, wine, raisins, and capers, cover, and cook until flavors meld, 4 to 6 hours on low or 3 to 5 hours on high.

2. Season swordfish with salt and pepper and stir into stew. Cover and cook on high until swordfish flakes apart when gently prodded with paring knife, about 30 minutes.

3. Combine pine nuts, mint, orange zest, and remaining garlic in bowl. Season stew with salt and pepper to taste. Serve, topping individual portions with pine nut mixture.

CUTTING UP SWORDFISH FOR STEW

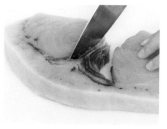

1. Using sharp knife, trim skin and dark lines from flesh.

2. Cut trimmed flesh into 1-inch pieces.

Browning the eggplant before adding it to the slow cooker ensures it holds its shape and does not turn soggy.

Italian Vegetable Stew

SERVES 6   **VEG**   **ALL DAY**

COOKING TIME 8 TO 9 HOURS ON LOW OR 5 TO 6 HOURS ON HIGH

SLOW COOKER SIZE 5 TO 7 QUARTS

WHY THIS RECIPE WORKS Creating any vegetable stew in the slow cooker so that the vegetables remain bright and flavorful requires just a few tricks. For this Italian-inspired stew we found that we needed to brown the eggplant first to keep it from becoming soggy and wan-tasting in the final stew. And since we had our skillet out already, we added more oil to it and browned the chopped tomatoes, along with a little tomato paste and the aromatics and oregano, which gave them a deeper flavor. The potatoes cooked perfectly in this stew, but we needed to add the zucchini at the end to ensure that it remained green and crisp-tender.

¼ cup extra-virgin olive oil, plus extra for serving
1 pound eggplant, cut into 1-inch pieces
1 (28-ounce) can whole peeled tomatoes, drained with juice reserved, chopped
1 onion, chopped fine
1 red bell pepper, stemmed, seeded, and cut into 1-inch pieces
4 garlic cloves, minced
1 tablespoon tomato paste
1 tablespoon minced fresh oregano or ¾ teaspoon dried
3 cups chicken or vegetable broth, plus extra as needed
1 pound Yukon Gold potatoes, peeled and cut into ½-inch pieces
2 zucchini, quartered lengthwise and sliced 1 inch thick
2 tablespoons chopped fresh basil
Salt and pepper
Grated Parmesan cheese

1. Heat 2 tablespoons oil in 12-inch skillet over medium-high heat until shimmering. Brown eggplant lightly on all sides, 5 to 7 minutes; transfer to slow cooker.

2. Heat remaining 2 tablespoons oil in now-empty skillet over medium-high heat until shimmering. Add tomatoes, onion, and bell pepper and cook until dry and beginning to brown, 8 to 10 minutes. Stir in garlic, tomato paste, and oregano and cook until fragrant, about 30 seconds. Stir in 1 cup broth, scraping up any browned bits; transfer to slow cooker.

3. Stir remaining 2 cups broth, reserved tomato juice, and potatoes into slow cooker, cover, and cook until vegetables are tender, 8 to 9 hours on low or 5 to 6 hours on high.

4. Stir zucchini into stew, cover, and cook on high until tender, 20 to 30 minutes. Adjust consistency with extra hot broth as needed. Stir in basil and season with salt and pepper to taste. Serve, drizzling individual portions with extra oil and passing Parmesan separately.

CUTTING UP EGGPLANT

1. To cut eggplant into tidy pieces, first cut eggplant crosswise into 1-inch-thick rounds.

2. Then cut each round into pieces as directed in recipe.

Colorful and fresh-tasting, our quinoa stew benefits from a variety of toppings like avocado and queso fresco.

Quinoa and Vegetable Stew

SERVES 6 EASY PREP VEG LIGHT

COOKING TIME 5 TO 7 HOURS ON LOW OR 3 TO 5 HOURS ON HIGH

SLOW COOKER SIZE 4 TO 7 QUARTS

WHY THIS RECIPE WORKS In countries along the Andean high-lands, such as Peru, quinoa plays a starring role in many dishes, including a hearty stew that also features potatoes and corn. We set about making our own version of this stew using the slow cooker, where the flavors could meld over time for a richer-tasting dish. Red potatoes were a given, and microwaving them with onion and garlic provided a flavorful base for our stew. Diced tomatoes offered brightness and acidity. Along with the corn—we opted for the frozen variety for convenience and consistent flavor year-round—we included peas for more color and sweetness. To keep our quinoa from overcooking, we stirred it in near the end of the cooking time. For thickening, we simply mashed a portion of the cooked potatoes and tomatoes and stirred them back in when we added the quinoa. Be sure to rinse the quinoa in a fine-mesh strainer before using; rinsing removes the quinoa's bitter protective coating (called saponins).

1 onion, chopped
3 garlic cloves, minced
1 tablespoon vegetable oil
1 tablespoon chili powder
  Salt and pepper
6 cups vegetable or chicken broth, plus extra as needed
1 pound red potatoes, unpeeled, cut into ½-inch pieces
1 (14.5-ounce) can diced tomatoes, drained
1 cup prewashed white quinoa, rinsed
1 cup frozen peas, thawed
1 cup frozen corn, thawed
2 tablespoons minced fresh cilantro
8 ounces queso fresco cheese, crumbled (2 cups)
1 avocado, halved, pitted, and cut into ½-inch pieces
  Lime wedges

1. Microwave onion, garlic, oil, chili powder, and ½ teaspoon salt in bowl, stirring occasionally, until onion is softened, about 5 minutes; transfer to slow cooker. Stir in broth, potatoes, and tomatoes, cover, and cook until flavors meld and potatoes are tender, 5 to 7 hours on low or 3 to 5 hours on high.

2. Transfer 2 cups potato-tomato mixture to bowl and mash with potato masher until mostly smooth. Stir quinoa and mashed potato-tomato mixture into stew, cover, and cook on high until quinoa is tender, 20 to 30 minutes.

3. Stir in peas and corn and let sit until heated through, about 5 minutes. Adjust consistency with extra hot broth as needed. Stir in cilantro and season with salt and pepper to taste. Serve, passing queso fresco, avocado, and lime wedges separately.

NOTES FROM THE TEST KITCHEN

All About Quinoa

Quinoa originated in the Andes Mountains of South America, and while it is generally treated as a grain, it is actually the seed of the goosefoot plant. Sometimes referred to as a "super grain," quinoa is high in protein, and its protein is complete, which means it possesses all of the amino acids in the balanced amounts that our bodies require.

Beyond its nutritional prowess, we love quinoa for its addictive crunchy texture, nutty taste, and ease of preparation. It's important to rinse your quinoa in order to remove the bitter-tasting compounds called saponins on the surface of the seed. We tested prewashed and unwashed brands and found that both benefit from rinsing at home.

You can use white and red quinoa interchangeably in most recipes; however, white quinoa is best for dishes like stews because it is starchier and will hold together better.

French Lentil Stew

SERVES 6 `LIGHT` `ALL DAY`

COOKING TIME 7 TO 9 HOURS ON LOW OR 4 TO 6 HOURS ON HIGH

SLOW COOKER SIZE 4 TO 7 QUARTS

WHY THIS RECIPE WORKS For a warming lentil stew with a deep flavor profile and hearty texture, we turned to French green lentils. Also known as *lentilles du Puy*, these legumes retain some of their texture during cooking without getting too soft, and since they are high in fiber they make for a healthy and filling stew. Caramelizing the onions required getting out a skillet, but our patience was rewarded with a richly flavored foundation. For a truly satisfying stew, we added brown rice to the mix, which added depth of flavor and broke down slightly as it cooked, helping to thicken the stew. Searching for a hearty green to offer a colorful contrast to the dark lentils, we settled on shredded Brussels sprouts, which we added at the end of the cooking time. A little sherry vinegar stirred in just before serving helped to brighten the stew. We prefer French green lentils for this recipe, but it will work with any type of lentil except red or yellow. Short-grain brown rice can be substituted for the long-grain rice, if desired.

   2 slices bacon, chopped fine
   3 onions, chopped fine
   ½ teaspoon brown sugar
     Salt and pepper
   3 garlic cloves, minced
   1 tablespoon minced fresh thyme or
     ¾ teaspoon dried
   1 tablespoon mustard seeds
   1½ teaspoons ground coriander
     Pinch cayenne pepper
   8 cups chicken broth, plus extra as needed
   4 carrots, peeled, halved lengthwise, and
     sliced ½ inch thick
   1 cup French green lentils, picked over and rinsed
   ½ cup long-grain brown rice
   8 ounces Brussels sprouts, trimmed, halved, and
     sliced thin
   2 tablespoons sherry vinegar

1. Cook bacon in 12-inch skillet over medium heat until crisp, 5 to 7 minutes. Add onions, sugar, and ½ teaspoon salt, cover, and cook until onions are softened, about 5 minutes. Uncover, reduce heat to medium-low, and continue to cook, stirring often, until onions are caramelized, about 20 minutes. Stir in garlic, thyme, mustard seeds, coriander, and cayenne and cook until fragrant, about 30 seconds. Stir in 1 cup broth, scraping up any browned bits; transfer to slow cooker.

2. Stir remaining 7 cups broth, carrots, lentils, and rice into slow cooker. Cover and cook until lentils are tender, 7 to 9 hours on low or 4 to 6 hours on high.

3. Stir Brussels sprouts into stew and let sit until softened, about 5 minutes. Adjust consistency with extra hot broth as needed. Stir in vinegar and season with salt and pepper to taste. Serve.

SLICING BRUSSELS SPROUTS

1. Trim stem end of each sprout and then cut each sprout in half through cut end.

2. With flat surface on cutting board, thinly slice each half.

Farro and Butternut Squash Stew

SERVES 6 `VEG` `LIGHT` `ALL DAY`

COOKING TIME 10 TO 12 HOURS ON LOW OR 7 TO 9 HOURS ON HIGH

SLOW COOKER SIZE 4 TO 7 QUARTS

WHY THIS RECIPE WORKS Perfect for a cold winter's night, this farro stew is substantial and flavorful. We began with sweet, nutty farro and added mushrooms for meaty depth and butternut squash for substance. To start, we microwaved the mushrooms and aromatics with just a tablespoon of oil until the mushrooms softened, released some of their moisture, and were flavored by the aromatics. Vegetable broth worked well for the cooking liquid and provided a subtly sweet backbone. To give it a boost, we stirred in some white wine, which contributed complexity and brightness to our hearty stew. We cooked the squash in a foil packet on top of the stew to make sure it would retain its sweet flavor and bright color. Fresh, peppery arugula provided color and freshness. We prefer the flavor and texture of whole farro; pearled farro can be used, but the texture may be softer. Do not use quick-cooking or presteamed farro (the ingredient list on the package will specify the type) in this recipe. The arugula may seem like a lot at first, but it wilts down substantially.

1½ pounds cremini mushrooms, trimmed
and quartered
1 onion, chopped fine
2 tablespoons tomato paste
3 garlic cloves, minced
1 tablespoon extra-virgin olive oil,
plus extra for serving
Salt and pepper
6 cups chicken or vegetable broth,
plus extra as needed
1 cup whole farro
¼ cup dry white wine
2 bay leaves
1½ pounds butternut squash, peeled, seeded,
and cut into ½-inch pieces (4 cups)
5 ounces (5 cups) baby arugula
Grated Parmesan cheese

1. Microwave mushrooms, onion, tomato paste, garlic, oil, and
½ teaspoon salt in bowl, stirring occasionally, until vegetables are
softened, 8 to 10 minutes; transfer to slow cooker.

2. Stir broth, farro, wine, and bay leaves into slow cooker. Season
squash with salt and pepper, wrap in aluminum foil packet, and
place on top of stew. Cover and cook until farro is tender, 10 to
12 hours on low or 7 to 9 hours on high.

3. Carefully open foil packet and stir squash, along with any
accumulated juices, into stew. Discard bay leaves. Stir in arugula,
1 handful at a time, and let sit until wilted, about 5 minutes. Adjust
consistency with extra hot broth as needed. Season with salt and
pepper to taste. Serve, passing Parmesan and extra oil separately.

MAKING A FOIL PACKET

1. Place vegetables on 1 side of
large sheet of aluminum foil.
Fold foil over vegetables and
crimp 3 open edges to seal.

2. Place packet on top of
ingredients in slow cooker,
pressing it gently to fit.

The combination of hearty wheat berries and two kinds of
mushrooms makes for a filling vegetarian stew.

Wheat Berry and Wild Mushroom Stew

SERVES 6 `EASY PREP` `VEG` `LIGHT` `ALL DAY`
COOKING TIME 8 TO 9 HOURS ON LOW OR 5 TO 6 HOURS
ON HIGH
SLOW COOKER SIZE 4 TO 7 QUARTS

WHY THIS RECIPE WORKS For this hearty vegetarian stew, we
started with sweet, nutty wheat berries and added mushrooms for
earthy, meaty depth. The wheat berries were hearty enough to withstand the long cooking time of the slow cooker and still maintain
their chewy texture. Including two types of mushrooms—sliced
cremini and dried porcini—ensured that our stew had tender bites
of mushroom and intense, earthy flavor. To reinforce the woodsy
notes of the mushrooms, we included dried thyme. To give the stew
a boost, we stirred in some Madeira, adding an extra splash of the
fortified wine at the end of cooking for brightness. Baby spinach
provided color and freshness. Finally, for a hint of richness, we
stirred in a couple of pats of butter. If using quick-cooking or
presteamed wheat berries (the ingredient list on the package specifies the type), you will need to decrease the cooking time in step 1.

The wheat berries will retain a chewy texture once fully cooked. You can substitute dry sherry for the Madeira if desired. The spinach may seem like a lot at first, but it wilts down substantially.

2 pounds cremini mushrooms, trimmed and sliced thin
½ ounce dried porcini mushrooms, rinsed and minced
3 garlic cloves, minced
3 tablespoons extra-virgin olive oil, plus extra for drizzling
2 teaspoons minced fresh thyme or ½ teaspoon dried
  Salt and pepper
6 cups chicken or vegetable broth, plus extra broth as needed
1½ cups wheat berries
½ cup dry Madeira
6 ounces (6 cups) baby spinach
  Grated Parmesan cheese

1. Microwave cremini mushrooms, porcini mushrooms, garlic, 1 tablespoon oil, thyme, and ½ teaspoon salt in bowl, stirring occasionally, until mushrooms are softened, about 5 minutes; transfer to slow cooker. Stir in broth, wheat berries, and 6 tablespoons Madeira. Cover and cook until wheat berries are tender, 8 to 9 hours on low or 5 to 6 hours on high.

2. Stir in spinach, 1 handful at a time, and let sit until wilted, about 5 minutes. Adjust consistency with extra hot broth as needed. Stir in remaining 2 tablespoons oil and remaining 2 tablespoons Madeira and season with salt and pepper to taste. Serve, drizzling individual portions with extra oil and sprinkling with Parmesan.

Red Beans and Rice Stew

SERVES 6   EASY PREP   ALL DAY
COOKING TIME 8 TO 10 HOURS ON HIGH
SLOW COOKER SIZE 4 TO 7 QUARTS

WHY THIS RECIPE WORKS When we think of New Orleans we long for a bowl of smoky, spicy red beans and rice, perhaps the region's most notable specialty. When done right, this dish elevates ordinary ingredients—onions, celery, green bell peppers, kidney beans, and rice—to extraordinary heights. With its tender rice, creamy beans, and robustly flavored slow-simmered sauce, this dish is well suited to the slow cooker. We found the classic Cajun trinity of onions, celery, and green peppers a must, and stirring in the peppers (along with the rice) for the last 15 minutes of cooking preserved their texture and color. In addition to paprika and cayenne, spicy andouille sausage provided just the intensity we were seeking, though a milder andouille or kielbasa can be substituted. A splash of red wine vinegar and a sprinkling of

This New Orleans favorite can withstand a day in the slow cooker and still deliver creamy beans and perfect rice.

scallions before serving provide welcome brightness and are a must. Be sure to use instant rice (sometimes labeled minute rice); traditional rice takes much longer to cook and won't work here.

2 onions, chopped fine
1 celery rib, chopped fine
6 garlic cloves, minced
2 tablespoons vegetable oil
2 teaspoons minced fresh thyme or ½ teaspoon dried
2 teaspoons paprika
¼ teaspoon cayenne pepper
4 cups chicken broth, plus extra as needed
4 cups water
1 pound (2½ cups) dried red kidney beans, picked over and rinsed
1 pound spicy andouille sausage, sliced ½ inch thick
2 bay leaves
2 green bell peppers, stemmed, seeded, and chopped
½ cup instant white rice
3 scallions, sliced thin
  Salt and pepper
  Red wine vinegar

1. Microwave onions, celery, garlic, oil, thyme, paprika, and cayenne in bowl, stirring occasionally, until vegetables are softened, about 5 minutes; transfer to slow cooker. Stir in broth, water, beans, sausage, and bay leaves. Cover and cook until beans are tender, 8 to 10 hours on high.

2. Discard bay leaves. Stir bell peppers and rice into stew, cover, and cook on high until tender, 15 to 20 minutes. Adjust consistency with extra hot broth as needed. Sir in scallions and season with salt, pepper, and vinegar to taste. Serve.

White Chicken Chili

SERVES 6 TO 8
COOKING TIME 4 TO 5 HOURS ON LOW
SLOW COOKER SIZE 5 TO 7 QUARTS

WHY THIS RECIPE WORKS White chicken chili is a fresher, lighter cousin of the thick red chili most Americans know and love. Its appeal is not surprising. First, it is a healthier alternative, and second, because there are no tomatoes to mask the other flavors, the chiles, herbs, and spices take center stage. Unlike red chili, which uses any combo of dried chiles, chili powders, and cayenne pepper, white chicken chili gets its backbone from fresh green chiles, which contribute vibrant flavor and spiciness. To achieve a great white chicken chili in the slow cooker, we needed to build flavor every step of the way. We started by browning boneless chicken thighs to ensure our chili had big chicken flavor. Sautéing the aromatics—including four jalapeño chiles—and spices together in the skillet also added a richer, deeper flavor, plus deglazing the pan ensured all the rich browned bits we developed ended up in the slow cooker. For convenience, instead of multiple types of chiles, we relied on jalapeño chiles only. Serve with your favorite chili garnishes.

3 cups chicken broth, plus extra as needed
1 (15-ounce) can white or yellow hominy, rinsed
3 pounds boneless, skinless chicken thighs, trimmed
  Salt and pepper
3 tablespoons vegetable oil
2 onions, chopped fine
4 jalapeño chiles, stemmed, seeded, and minced
6 garlic cloves, minced
4 teaspoons ground cumin
2 teaspoons ground coriander
3 (15-ounce) cans cannellini beans, rinsed
¼ cup minced fresh cilantro
2 tablespoons minced jarred jalapeños
2 avocados, halved, pitted, and cut into ½-inch pieces

Pureeing a can of hominy with broth gives this white chicken chili just the right appealing texture and base of corn flavor.

1. Process 2 cups broth and hominy in blender until smooth, about 1 minute; transfer to slow cooker.

2. Pat chicken dry with paper towels and season with salt and pepper. Heat 1 tablespoon oil in 12-inch skillet over medium-high heat until just smoking. Brown half of chicken, about 4 minutes per side; transfer to slow cooker. Repeat with 1 tablespoon oil and remaining chicken; transfer to slow cooker.

3. Heat remaining 1 tablespoon oil in now-empty skillet over medium heat until shimmering. Add onions and cook until softened and lightly browned, 8 to 10 minutes. Stir in fresh jalapeños, garlic, cumin, and coriander and cook until fragrant, about 30 seconds. Stir in remaining 1 cup broth, scraping up any browned bits; transfer to slow cooker.

4. Stir beans into slow cooker, cover, and cook until chicken is tender, 4 to 5 hours on low.

5. Transfer chicken to cutting board, let cool slightly, then pull apart into large chunks using 2 forks. Stir chicken into chili and let sit until heated through, about 5 minutes. Adjust consistency with extra hot broth as needed. Stir in cilantro and jarred jalapeños and season with salt and pepper to taste. Serve with avocados.

Turkey Chili

SERVES 8 TO 10

COOKING TIME 4 TO 5 HOURS ON LOW

SLOW COOKER SIZE 5 TO 7 QUARTS

WHY THIS RECIPE WORKS Turkey chili is a great alternative to classic beef chili, providing a leaner but no less flavorful meal for the dinner table. To help protect our ground turkey from drying out, we enlisted the help of a panade—a paste of bread and milk—to provide added moisture. We also found the addition of broth and a little soy sauce helped reinforce the meatiness of the leaner meat. Be sure to use ground turkey, not ground turkey breast (also labeled 99 percent fat-free), in this recipe. Serve with your favorite chili garnishes.

2	slices hearty white sandwich bread, torn into 1-inch pieces
¼	cup soy sauce
2	pounds ground turkey
3	tablespoons vegetable oil
3	onions, chopped fine
1	red bell pepper, stemmed, seeded, and chopped
¼	cup chili powder
¼	cup tomato paste
6	garlic cloves, minced
1	tablespoon ground cumin
¾	teaspoon dried oregano
1¼	cups chicken broth, plus extra as needed
2	(15-ounce) cans kidney beans, rinsed
1	(28-ounce) can diced tomatoes, drained
1	(15-ounce) can tomato sauce
1	tablespoon packed brown sugar
2	teaspoons minced canned chipotle chile in adobo sauce
	Salt and pepper

1. Mash bread and soy sauce into paste in large bowl using fork. Add ground turkey and knead with hands until well combined.

2. Heat oil in 12-inch skillet over medium heat until shimmering. Add onions and bell pepper and cook until softened and lightly browned, 8 to 10 minutes. Stir in chili powder, tomato paste, garlic, cumin, and oregano and cook until fragrant, about 1 minute.

3. Add half of turkey mixture and cook, breaking up turkey with wooden spoon, until no longer pink, about 5 minutes. Repeat with remaining turkey mixture. Stir in broth, scraping up any browned bits; transfer to slow cooker.

4. Stir beans, tomatoes, tomato sauce, sugar, and chipotle into slow cooker. Cover and cook until turkey is tender, 4 to 5 hours on low. Break up any remaining large pieces of turkey with spoon. Adjust consistency with extra hot broth as needed. Season with salt and pepper to taste. Serve.

A hefty amount of chili powder, canned chipotles, and some soy sauce add big flavor to our ground beef chili.

Classic Beef Chili

SERVES 8 TO 10

COOKING TIME 6 TO 7 HOURS ON LOW OR 4 TO 5 HOURS ON HIGH

SLOW COOKER SIZE 5 TO 7 QUARTS

WHY THIS RECIPE WORKS Gently simmered ground beef chili is certainly well suited for the slow cooker, but achieving the characteristic rich flavors and tender meat can be a challenge. To develop the all-American chili we were looking for, we started with the base, choosing a combination of diced and pureed tomatoes to create the proper consistency. Next, we incorporated a generous combination of chili powder, cumin, oregano, and red pepper flakes, bumping up the flavors even further with smoky chipotles. Browning the beef to develop flavor is standard in most traditional chilis, but this produced overcooked, gritty meat in the slow cooker. To fix this, we found mixing the raw beef with a panade—a mixture of bread and milk often used in meatballs—before browning it worked wonders. We also stirred in a little soy sauce to help boost the meaty flavor—maybe a tad unconventional for chili, but it worked. Serve with your favorite chili garnishes.

2 slices hearty white sandwich bread, torn into 1-inch pieces
¼ cup whole milk
 Salt and pepper
2 pounds 85 percent lean ground beef
3 tablespoons vegetable oil
3 onions, chopped fine
¼ cup chili powder
¼ cup tomato paste
6 garlic cloves, minced
1 tablespoon ground cumin
¾ teaspoon dried oregano
½ teaspoon red pepper flakes
1 (28-ounce) can tomato puree
1 (28-ounce) can diced tomatoes
2 (15-ounce) cans red kidney beans, rinsed
3 tablespoons soy sauce
1 tablespoon packed brown sugar
2 teaspoons minced canned chipotle chile in adobo sauce

1. Mash bread, milk, ½ teaspoon salt, and ½ teaspoon pepper into paste in large bowl using fork. Add ground beef and knead with hands until well combined.

2. Heat oil in 12-inch skillet over medium heat until shimmering. Add onions and cook until softened and lightly browned, 8 to 10 minutes. Stir in chili powder, tomato paste, garlic, cumin, oregano, and pepper flakes and cook until fragrant, about 1 minute.

3. Add half of beef mixture and cook, breaking up beef with wooden spoon, until no longer pink, about 5 minutes. Repeat with remaining beef mixture. Stir in 1 cup tomato puree, scraping up any browned bits; transfer to slow cooker.

4. Stir remaining tomato puree, diced tomatoes and their juice, beans, soy sauce, sugar, and chipotle into slow cooker. Cover and cook until beef is tender, 6 to 7 hours on low or 4 to 5 hours on high.

5. Using large spoon, skim fat from surface of chili. Break up any remaining large pieces of beef with spoon. Adjust consistency with hot water as needed. Season with salt and pepper to taste. Serve.

MAKING A PANADE

Using fork, mash bread and milk (or other liquid) into paste.

Texas Chili

SERVES 8 TO 10   **ALL DAY**

COOKING TIME 9 TO 10 HOURS ON LOW OR 6 TO 7 HOURS ON HIGH

SLOW COOKER SIZE 5 TO 7 QUARTS

WHY THIS RECIPE WORKS Texans are famous for their style of chili featuring big chunks of beef slowly simmered in a chile-infused sauce. For our slow-cooker version we chose generous chunks of beef chuck-eye roast, which remained moist while still turning impressively tender. We found that we needed to brown only half of the beef to give us the deep, rich beefy flavor from the fond, saving us a little prep time. To achieve the characteristic rich and smooth sauce, we used pureed diced tomatoes and seasoned them with a hefty amount of onions, garlic, and jalapeños mixed with an equally generous amount of spices. Canned chipotle chile added even more flavor complexity. To thicken our chili, we hydrated some corn tortillas, which we then pureed with our tomatoes, giving us a nice richness and an added depth of flavor. While beans are traditionally served alongside this chili, we liked the creaminess that they provided when cooked with the meat, so we included them in the mix. Serve with your favorite chili garnishes.

5 (6-inch) corn tortillas, torn into 2-inch pieces
1½ cups chicken broth, plus extra as needed
1 (14.5-ounce) can diced tomatoes
2 tablespoons minced canned chipotle chile in adobo sauce
2 teaspoons packed dark brown sugar
4 pounds boneless beef chuck-eye roast, pulled apart at seams, trimmed, and cut into 1½-inch pieces Salt and pepper
2 tablespoons vegetable oil
2 onions, chopped
2 jalapeño chiles, stemmed, seeded, and minced
3 tablespoons chili powder
4 garlic cloves, minced
1 tablespoon ground cumin
½ teaspoon dried oregano
2 (15-ounce) cans red kidney beans, rinsed

1. Microwave tortillas and ½ cup broth in bowl, stirring occasionally, until tortillas are fully hydrated, about 3 minutes. Process tortilla mixture, tomatoes and their juice, chipotle, and sugar in food processor until smooth, about 1 minute, scraping down sides of bowl as needed; transfer to slow cooker.

2. Pat beef dry with paper towels and season with salt and pepper. Heat oil in 12-inch skillet over medium-high heat until just smoking. Brown half of beef on all sides, about 8 minutes; transfer to slow cooker with remaining uncooked beef.

3. Add onions and ¼ teaspoon salt to fat left in skillet and cook over medium heat until onions are softened and lightly browned, 8 to 10 minutes. Stir in jalapeños, chili powder, garlic, cumin, and oregano and cook until fragrant, about 1 minute. Slowly whisk in remaining 1 cup broth, scraping up any browned bits; transfer to slow cooker.

4. Stir beans into slow cooker, cover, and cook until beef is tender, 9 to 10 hours on low or 6 to 7 hours on high. Adjust consistency with extra hot broth as needed. Season with salt and pepper to taste. Serve.

A little brewed coffee is traditional in this pork chili and kicks up the bittersweet nuances perfectly.

New Mexican Red Pork Chili

SERVES 8 **EASY PREP** **ALL DAY**
COOKING TIME 9 TO 10 HOURS ON LOW OR 6 TO 7 HOURS ON HIGH
SLOW COOKER SIZE 5 TO 7 QUARTS

WHY THIS RECIPE WORKS Inspired by the traditional New Mexican stew carne adovada, this chili features meltingly tender chunks of pork in an intense, richly flavored red chile sauce. For this long-simmered chili, we found that the considerable marbling of fat in pork butt produced supremely tender chunks of meat that didn't dry out. As for the sauce, chili powder, oregano, and chipotle chiles provided a solid baseline of warmth and depth, while fresh coffee brought a balance of robust, bittersweet flavors. And, since the flavor of dried chiles is sometimes described as raisiny, we went to the source, adding raisins before serving to achieve the desired fruity nuance. Stirring in fresh cilantro, lime zest, and lime juice at the end helped to brighten this earthy dish. Pork butt roast is often labeled Boston butt in the supermarket. Serve with your favorite chili garnishes.

2 onions, chopped fine

¼ cup chili powder

6 garlic cloves, minced

2 tablespoons vegetable oil

2 tablespoons tomato paste

¾ teaspoon dried oregano

2 cups chicken broth, plus extra as needed

½ cup brewed coffee

¼ cup instant tapioca

1 tablespoon minced canned chipotle chile in adobo sauce

1 tablespoon packed brown sugar, plus extra for seasoning

2 bay leaves

1 (4-pound) boneless pork butt roast, pulled apart at seams, trimmed, and cut into 1½-inch pieces
Salt and pepper

½ cup raisins

¼ cup minced fresh cilantro

1 teaspoon grated lime zest plus 1 tablespoon juice, plus extra juice for seasoning

1. Microwave onions, chili powder, garlic, oil, tomato paste, and oregano in bowl, stirring occasionally, until onions are softened, about 5 minutes; transfer to slow cooker.

2. Stir in broth, coffee, tapioca, chipotle, sugar, and bay leaves. Season pork with salt and pepper and stir into slow cooker. Cover and cook until pork is tender, 9 to 10 hours on low or 6 to 7 hours on high.

3. Discard bay leaves. Stir raisins into chili and let sit until heated through, about 5 minutes. Stir in cilantro and lime zest and juice. Adjust consistency with extra hot broth as needed. Season with salt, pepper, extra sugar, and extra lime juice to taste. Serve.

Broiling the tomatillos and onion adds a lot of smoky flavor to this classic Mexican-style green chili.

Tomatillo Chili with Pork and Hominy

SERVES 8 TO 10 `ALL DAY`

COOKING TIME 9 TO 10 HOURS ON LOW OR 6 TO 7 HOURS ON HIGH

SLOW COOKER SIZE 5 TO 7 QUARTS

WHY THIS RECIPE WORKS In this classic green chili, chunks of pork slowly simmer in a bright sauce made from chiles and tomatillos. The key to achieving the bold flavors of this chili in a slow cooker was broiling the tomatillos along with the other aromatics and spices. Once charred, the vegetables and spices took on a rustic, smoky flavor, and we pureed them to create a flavorful base. Hominy also contributed to the heartiness of the dish and helped thicken the sauce. If you can't find fresh tomatillos, you can substitute three 11-ounce cans of tomatillos, drained, rinsed, and patted dry; broil as directed in step 1. Pork butt roast is often labeled Boston butt in the supermarket. Serve with your favorite chili garnishes.

1½ pounds tomatillos, husks and stems removed, rinsed well, dried, and halved

1 onion, cut into 1-inch pieces

3 tablespoons vegetable oil

4 garlic cloves, minced
¾ teaspoon dried oregano
1 teaspoon ground cumin
  Pinch ground cloves
  Pinch ground cinnamon
2 (15-ounce) cans white or yellow hominy, rinsed
2½ cups chicken broth, plus extra as needed
3 poblano chiles, stemmed, seeded, and chopped fine
3 tablespoons instant tapioca
2 teaspoons sugar
2 bay leaves
1 (4-pound) boneless pork butt roast, pulled apart
  at seams, trimmed, and cut into 1½-inch pieces
  Salt and pepper
¼ cup minced fresh cilantro

1. Position oven rack 6 inches from broiler element and heat broiler. Toss tomatillos and onion with oil, garlic, oregano, cumin, cloves, and cinnamon, then spread onto aluminum foil–lined rimmed baking sheet. Broil vegetables until blackened and beginning to soften, 5 to 10 minutes, rotating sheet halfway through broiling; let cool slightly.

2. Pulse vegetables, along with any accumulated juices, in food processor until almost smooth, about 10 pulses, scraping down sides of bowl as needed; transfer to slow cooker.

3. Stir hominy, broth, poblanos, tapioca, sugar, and bay leaves into slow cooker. Season pork with salt and pepper and stir into slow cooker. Cover and cook until pork is tender, 9 to 10 hours on low or 6 to 7 hours on high.

4. Discard bay leaves. Adjust consistency with extra hot broth as needed. Stir in cilantro and season with salt and pepper to taste. Serve.

HUSKING AND RINSING TOMATILLOS

1. Pull papery husks and stems off of tomatillos; discard.

2. Rinse tomatillos in colander to rid them of sticky residue from husks. Dry tomatillos thoroughly.

Hearty Vegetarian Chili

SERVES 6 TO 8 `EASY PREP` `VEG` `LIGHT` `ALL DAY`
COOKING TIME 8 TO 10 HOURS ON HIGH
SLOW COOKER SIZE 4 TO 7 QUARTS

WHY THIS RECIPE WORKS Vegetarian chilis often rely on a mix of beans and vegetables for heartiness, but neither one really adds meaty depth. We wanted a hearty chili that was as rich, savory, and deeply satisfying as any meat chili out there. We started with dried navy beans, which turned tender and creamy with the long simmer. To up the heartiness of our dish, we tried adding a variety of ingredients, but only bulgur provided the textural dimension our chili had been missing. After a quick rinse and a few minutes in the microwave, it needed just 5 to 10 minutes in the slow cooker to fully soften and absorb the rich flavors. Finally, we ramped up the intensity and depth of our chili with soy sauce, dried shiitakes, and tomato paste. When shopping, don't confuse bulgur with cracked wheat, which has a much longer cooking time and will not work in this recipe. Serve with your favorite chili garnishes.

2 onions, chopped fine
3 tablespoons chili powder
¼ cup tomato paste
2 tablespoons vegetable oil
4 teaspoons dried oregano
1 tablespoon ground cumin
  Salt and pepper
1 pound (2½ cups) dried navy beans, picked
  over and rinsed
3 tablespoons soy sauce
½ ounce dried shiitake mushrooms, rinsed
  and minced
⅔ cup medium-grind bulgur, rinsed

1. Microwave onions, chili powder, tomato paste, oil, oregano, cumin, and 1 teaspoon salt in bowl, stirring occasionally, until onions are softened, about 5 minutes; transfer to slow cooker. Stir in beans, 9 cups water, soy sauce, and mushrooms. Cover and cook until beans are tender, 8 to 10 hours on high.

2. Microwave bulgur, 2 cups water, and ¼ teaspoon salt in covered bowl until bulgur is softened, about 5 minutes; drain bulgur and stir into chili. Cover and cook on high until bulgur is tender, 5 to 10 minutes. Adjust consistency with extra hot water as needed. Season with salt and pepper to taste. Serve.

This rich, hearty bean chili is so satisfying and flavorful, no one will miss the meat.

Black Bean Chili

SERVES 6 TO 8 **VEG** **LIGHT** **ALL DAY**
COOKING TIME 8 TO 10 HOURS ON HIGH
SLOW COOKER SIZE 4 TO 7 QUARTS

WHY THIS RECIPE WORKS Vegetarian versions of black bean chili can be tricky since there are no ham products, like meaty, smoky ham hocks, to build flavor over the long cooking time. To achieve the full flavors we expected from black bean chili, we started by browning a generous amount of aromatics and spices. This additional step was promising, but the chili still seemed pretty lean. Though a bit odd for a chili, a surprise ingredient, mustard seeds, added an appealing pungency and the level of complexity we were looking for. To bulk up the chili, we added bell peppers, white mushrooms, and canned tomatoes. We added the tomatoes at the end because otherwise their acidity prevented the beans from cooking through fully. Minced cilantro and a spritz of fresh lime provide welcome brightness and are a must. Serve with your favorite chili garnishes.

2 tablespoons vegetable oil
2 onions, chopped fine
2 red bell peppers, stemmed, seeded, and chopped fine
2 jalapeño chiles, stemmed, seeded, and minced
9 garlic cloves, minced
3 tablespoons chili powder
4 teaspoons mustard seeds
1 tablespoon minced canned chipotle chile in adobo sauce
1 tablespoon ground cumin
1 tablespoon dried oregano
2½ cups vegetable or chicken broth, plus extra as needed
2½ cups water
1 pound (2½ cups) dried black beans, picked over and rinsed
10 ounces white mushrooms, trimmed and halved if small or quartered if large
2 bay leaves
1 (28-ounce) can whole peeled tomatoes, drained and cut into ½-inch pieces
2 tablespoons minced fresh cilantro
   Salt and pepper
   Lime wedges

1. Heat oil in 12-inch skillet over medium heat until shimmering. Add onions and bell peppers and cook until vegetables are softened and lightly browned, 8 to 10 minutes. Stir in jalapeños, garlic, chili powder, mustard seeds, chipotle, cumin, and oregano and cook until fragrant, about 1 minute. Stir in 1 cup broth, scraping up any browned bits; transfer to slow cooker.

2. Stir remaining 1½ cups broth, water, beans, mushrooms, and bay leaves into slow cooker. Cover and cook until beans are tender, 8 to 10 hours on high.

3. Discard bay leaves. Transfer 1 cup cooked beans to bowl and mash with potato masher until mostly smooth. Stir mashed beans and tomatoes into chili and let sit until heated through, about 5 minutes. Adjust consistency with extra hot broth as needed. Stir in cilantro and season with salt and pepper to taste. Serve with lime wedges.

SEEDING JALAPEÑOS

Most of a chile pepper's heat is in the ribs and seeds. To remove both easily, cut the pepper in half lengthwise, then use a melon baller to scoop along the inside of each half. (The sharp edge of the melon baller can also be used to cut off the stem.)

Cuban White Bean and Plantain Chili

SERVES 6 **VEG** **LIGHT** **ALL DAY**

COOKING TIME 8 TO 10 HOURS ON HIGH

SLOW COOKER SIZE 4 TO 7 QUARTS

WHY THIS RECIPE WORKS This satisfying vegetarian chili brings the flavors of Cuba home to your slow cooker. To replicate the intricate spice profiles of Latin cuisine, we used a combination of citrusy coriander, earthy cumin, warm oregano, and a fresh jalapeño for complexity. Added to the chili, plantains became tender during the cooking process, and when we mashed a portion with some of the beans, they became a natural thickener. Seasoning with cider vinegar at the end of cooking brought fresh acidity to the finished chili. We prefer the softer texture and added sweetness of ripe plantains in this dish. Green plantains can be substituted; however, they will have a much firmer texture and a starchier flavor.

- 2 onions, chopped fine
- 6 garlic cloves, minced
- 1 jalapeño chile, stemmed, seeded, and minced
- 2 tablespoons vegetable oil
- 1½ tablespoons ground cumin
- 1 tablespoon ground coriander
- 1 teaspoon dried oregano
  Salt and pepper
- 6 cups vegetable or chicken broth, plus extra as needed
- 3 cups water
- 1¾ pounds ripe plantains, peeled, quartered lengthwise, and sliced 1 inch thick
- 1 pound (2½ cups) dried small white beans, picked over and rinsed
- 2 bay leaves
- 1½ cups frozen corn, thawed
- ¼ cup minced fresh cilantro
- 1 tablespoon cider vinegar, plus extra for seasoning

1. Microwave onions, garlic, jalapeño, oil, cumin, coriander, oregano, and ½ teaspoon salt in bowl, stirring occasionally, until onions are softened, about 5 minutes; transfer to slow cooker. Stir in broth, water, plantains, beans, and bay leaves. Cover and cook until beans are tender, 8 to 10 hours on high.

2. Discard bay leaves. Transfer 1 cup cooked beans and plantains to bowl and mash with potato masher until mostly smooth. Stir mashed bean mixture and corn into chili and let sit until heated through, about 5 minutes. Adjust consistency with extra hot broth as needed. Stir in cilantro and vinegar, and season with salt, pepper, and extra vinegar to taste. Serve.

All About Fresh Chile Peppers

Chiles get their heat from a group of chemical compounds called capsaicinoids, the best known being capsaicin. If you like a lot of heat, you can use the entire chile when cooking. If you prefer a milder dish, remove the ribs and seeds. Here are the chiles we reach for most in the test kitchen.

JALAPEÑO Perhaps the best-known chile, jalapeños are moderately hot and have a bright, grassy flavor similar to a green bell pepper. They can be dark green or scarlet red.

POBLANO These chiles are very dark green in color. When ripe, they turn a reddish-brown. They have a fruity, subtly spicy flavor. Thanks to their large size, they are also ideal for stuffing. Poblanos can be found in Latin markets and many supermarkets.

ANAHEIM With their acidic, lemony flavor, mild spiciness, and crisp texture, these popular chiles can be eaten raw, roasted, or fried; they are also frequently stuffed or used in salsa. Anaheim chiles are medium green in color and have a long, tapered shape.

SERRANO Similar in appearance to jalapeños but with a slightly thinner shape and brazen heat, these chiles have a fresh, clean, fruity flavor. They are good both raw in salsa and cooked in chilis and curries.

HABANERO These small, lantern-shaped chiles pack intense heat. They have a floral, fruity flavor that makes them a great addition to marinades, salsas, and cooked dishes. They range from light green to orange or red in color.

THAI These tiny multicolored chiles look ornamental, but they mean business. They have a flavor similar to that of black peppercorns and a bold, lingering heat. They are best when used sparingly in cooked dishes.

CHICKEN EVERY WAY

For more chicken and turkey recipes, see pages 154–159 in A Roast in Every Pot chapter

■ EASY PREP   ■ LIGHT   ■ COOK ALL DAY
Photo: Sweet and Tangy Pulled Chicken

Cranberry-Orange Chicken

SERVES 4 EASY PREP LIGHT

COOKING TIME 1 TO 2 HOURS ON LOW

SLOW COOKER SIZE 4 TO 7 QUARTS

WHY THIS RECIPE WORKS Boneless, skinless chicken breasts can be easily overcooked but not in the slow cooker, where gentle heat ensures moist, tender results. To make simple chicken breasts more interesting, we decided to use canned whole-berry cranberry sauce, which we livened up with orange juice and zest and fresh thyme. As the chicken cooked in this mixture, it took on the sweet flavors of the sauce base. We added red wine vinegar to cut the sweetness, and a tablespoon of soy sauce for depth of flavor. When the chicken was perfectly cooked, we simmered the vibrant sauce briefly to thicken it. Toasted almonds added an appealing crunchy finish to the sauced chicken. You will need an oval slow cooker for this recipe. Check the chicken's temperature after 1 hour of cooking and continue to monitor until it registers 160 degrees.

    1 (14-ounce) can whole-berry cranberry sauce
    1 tablespoon soy sauce
    2 teaspoons red wine vinegar
    1 teaspoon minced fresh thyme or ¼ teaspoon dried
    ½ teaspoon grated orange zest plus ¼ cup juice
       Pinch cayenne pepper
    4 (6- to 8-ounce) boneless, skinless chicken
       breasts, trimmed
       Salt and pepper
    ⅓ cup sliced almonds, toasted

1. Combine cranberry sauce, soy sauce, vinegar, thyme, orange zest and juice, and cayenne in slow cooker. Season chicken with salt and pepper and arrange in even layer in slow cooker. Cover and cook until chicken registers 160 degrees, 1 to 2 hours on low.

2. Transfer chicken to serving dish and tent loosely with aluminum foil. Transfer cooking liquid to medium saucepan, bring to simmer over medium heat, and cook until sauce is slightly thickened, about 5 minutes. Season with salt and pepper to taste. Spoon sauce over chicken and sprinkle with almonds. Serve.

POUNDING CHICKEN BREASTS

To create chicken breasts of even thickness, simply pound the thicker ends of the breasts until they are all of uniform thickness. Though some breasts will still be larger in size, at least they will cook at the same rate.

Putting the ham and cheese on the outside makes this classic French chicken dish a snap to prepare.

Unstuffed Chicken Cordon Bleu

SERVES 4 EASY PREP

COOKING TIME 1 TO 2 HOURS ON LOW

SLOW COOKER SIZE 4 TO 7 QUARTS

WHY THIS RECIPE WORKS Traditional recipes for chicken cordon bleu require carefully stuffing bone-in breasts, but we wanted an easier approach. To streamline the method and adapt it to the slow cooker, we wrapped boneless chicken breasts in thin slices of deli ham, nestled them in the slow cooker, then topped them with Swiss cheese for a no-fuss approach that kept prep work to a minimum. Poaching the breasts in a flavorful mixture of broth, mustard, and aromatics seasoned the chicken and allowed it to cook more gently. Once the chicken was cooked through, we whisked some cream into the cooking liquid to make an easy mustard cream sauce. Our slow-cooker version had all the classic flavors of chicken cordon bleu—

the only thing we lost was the fussy technique. You will need an oval slow cooker for this recipe. Check the chicken's temperature after 1 hour of cooking and continue to monitor until it registers 160 degrees.

½ cup chicken broth
2 tablespoons Dijon mustard
1 tablespoon instant tapioca
1 teaspoon minced garlic
1 teaspoon minced fresh thyme or ¼ teaspoon dried
  Salt and pepper
4 (6- to 8-ounce) boneless, skinless chicken
  breasts, trimmed
8 thin slices deli ham (8 ounces)
4 thin slices deli Swiss cheese (4 ounces)
¼ cup heavy cream

1. Combine broth, mustard, tapioca, garlic, thyme, and ½ teaspoon pepper in slow cooker. Season chicken with salt and pepper. Working with 1 breast at a time, shingle 2 slices of ham on counter, overlapping edges slightly, and lay chicken in center of slices. Fold ham around chicken and arrange in even layer in slow cooker. Cover and cook until chicken registers 160 degrees, 1 to 2 hours on low.

2. Top each breast with 1 slice Swiss cheese. Cover and cook on high until cheese is melted, about 5 minutes.

3. Transfer chicken to serving dish. Whisk cream into cooking liquid until smooth, about 1 minute. Season with salt and pepper to taste. Spoon sauce over chicken and serve.

MAKING CHICKEN CORDON BLEU

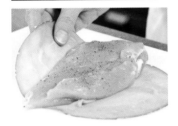 

1. Shingle 2 slices of ham on counter, overlapping edges slightly; lay chicken breast in center of slices.

2. Fold ham ends neatly over chicken breast and press on overlapping ends to adhere.

Quick, cheesy homemade bread crumbs add a crunchy finishing touch on our chicken Parm.

Chicken Parmesan

SERVES 6
COOKING TIME 3 TO 4 HOURS ON LOW
SLOW COOKER SIZE 4 TO 7 QUARTS

WHY THIS RECIPE WORKS Traditional chicken Parmesan, with its crispy fried-crumb coating and blanket of melted cheese, was not well suited to the slow cooker, we soon discovered, but we were determined to make a version that was. We started with boneless, skinless chicken breasts, and to account for the moisture they gave off in the cooker, we made a superconcentrated tomato sauce. Once the chicken was cooked, we found that a reverse method was best for the coating: First, we sprinkled basil and mozzarella and Parmesan cheeses over the breasts in the cooker. Once the cheeses melted, we added a flavorful topping of pretoasted panko, along with more Parmesan, basil, and oregano. You will need an oval slow cooker for this recipe. Check the chicken's temperature after 3 hours of cooking and continue to monitor until it registers 160 degrees.

2 tablespoons extra-virgin olive oil
1 onion, chopped fine
  Salt and pepper
1 (6-ounce) can tomato paste
4 garlic cloves, minced
1 tablespoon minced fresh oregano or 1 teaspoon dried
⅛ teaspoon red pepper flakes
1 (28-ounce) can diced tomatoes, drained
1 tablespoon cornstarch
1 tablespoon water
6 (6- to 8-ounce) boneless, skinless chicken
  breasts, trimmed
6 ounces mozzarella cheese, shredded (1½ cups)
¼ cup grated Parmesan cheese
3 tablespoons shredded fresh basil
⅓ cup panko bread crumbs
1 tablespoon minced fresh parsley

1. Heat 1 tablespoon oil in 12-inch nonstick skillet over medium heat until shimmering. Add onion, ¼ teaspoon salt, and ¼ teaspoon pepper and cook until onion is softened and lightly browned, 5 to 7 minutes. Stir in tomato paste, garlic, 1½ teaspoons oregano, and pepper flakes and cook until tomato paste is rust-colored, about 4 minutes; transfer to slow cooker.

2. Stir tomatoes into slow cooker. Dissolve cornstarch in water in bowl and stir into tomato mixture. Season chicken with salt and pepper and shingle in even layer in slow cooker. Cover and cook until chicken registers 160 degrees, 3 to 4 hours on low.

3. Combine mozzarella and 2 tablespoons Parmesan in bowl. Sprinkle chicken with 2 tablespoons basil, followed by mozzarella mixture. Cover and cook on high until cheese is melted, about 5 minutes.

4. Meanwhile, toss panko with remaining 1 tablespoon oil in shallow dish. Microwave crumbs, stirring often, until deep golden brown, 2 to 4 minutes. Let cool slightly, then combine with parsley, remaining 2 tablespoons Parmesan, remaining 1 tablespoon basil, remaining 1½ teaspoons oregano, ⅛ teaspoon salt, and ⅛ teaspoon pepper. Serve, sprinkling individual portions of chicken and sauce with bread-crumb mixture.

SHREDDING BASIL

To shred basil or other leafy herbs, simply stack several leaves on top of one another, roll them up, and slice. For basil, we find rolling leaves from tip to tail minimizes bruising and browning.

Fresh Versus Supermarket Mozzarella

Mozzarella is the leading cheese in the United States in per-capita consumption, with most supermarkets stocking two main varieties: fresh (usually packed in brine) and supermarket, or low-moisture (available either as a block or preshredded).

WHAT'S THE DIFFERENCE? Both varieties are made by stretching and pulling the curds by hand or machine, which aligns the proteins into long chains and gives the cheese its trademark elasticity. However, the final products differ considerably when it comes to water weight. According to federal standards, fresh mozzarella must have a moisture content between 52 percent and 60 percent by weight, making it highly perishable. Drier, firmer low-moisture mozzarella hovers between 45 percent and 52 percent and can last in the fridge for weeks.

WHEN TO USE FRESH We prefer the sweet richness and tender bite of the fresh stuff for snacking, sandwiches, and Caprese salad but tend not to use it in cooked applications, since heat can destroy its delicate flavor and texture.

WHEN TO USE SUPERMARKET For most baked dishes we turn to the low-moisture kind. Its mellow flavor blends seamlessly with bolder ingredients and melts nicely in everything from lasagna to pizza. We prefer supermarket mozzarella that, when baked, is creamy and clean-tasting and has a bit of soft (not rubbery) chew, plenty of gooey stretch, and flavorful browning.

HOW TO STORE MOZZARELLA As it sits, mozzarella releases moisture. If this moisture evaporates too quickly, the cheese dries out. But if the moisture stays on the cheese's surface, it encourages mold. To find the best storage method, we wrapped mozzarella in various materials, refrigerated the samples for six weeks, and monitored them for mold and dryness. Those wrapped in plastic wrap or zipper-lock bags were the first to show mold. Those in waxed or parchment paper alone lost too much moisture and dried out. The best method: First wrap the cheese in waxed or parchment paper, then loosely wrap in aluminum foil. The paper wicks moisture away, while the foil cover traps enough water to keep the cheese from drying out. Fresh mozzarella does not store well and is best eaten within a day or two.

Savory tomato paste and garam masala punch up the sauce for this Indian chicken, and yogurt makes it smooth and rich.

Chicken Tikka Masala

SERVES 4 **EASY PREP**

COOKING TIME 2 HOURS ON LOW
SLOW COOKER SIZE 4 TO 7 QUARTS

WHY THIS RECIPE WORKS We wanted to create a flavorful take on chicken tikka masala that had tender, moist pieces of chicken napped in a robustly spiced creamy tomato sauce. While traditionally this dish calls for marinating the chicken overnight to infuse flavor and cooking the sauce separately, we turned to our slow cooker for an easy hands-off version that would infuse big flavor into the chicken while cooking the entire dish to perfection. For a tikka masala recipe with assertive flavor, we needed the perfect sauce. Fresh tomatoes and canned sauce both released too much liquid during cooking, which created a thin sauce made worse by the juices released by the chicken. Switching to drained canned diced tomatoes along with flavor-packed tomato paste proved to be the answer; and when we added the perfect mix of aromatics plus garam masala, our sauce had the bold, zesty tomato flavor that is the hallmark of this dish. To finish the dish, we tempered in yogurt after cooking to ensure a velvety rich sauce. For a spicier dish, do not remove the ribs and seeds from the chile.

1 onion, chopped fine
3 tablespoons vegetable oil
1 serrano chile, stemmed, seeded, and minced
2 tablespoons tomato paste
4 teaspoons garam masala
3 garlic cloves, minced
1 tablespoon grated fresh ginger
2 teaspoons sugar
  Salt and pepper
1 (14.5-ounce) can diced tomatoes, drained
2 pounds boneless, skinless chicken breasts, trimmed and cut into 1½-inch pieces
¾ cup plain whole-milk yogurt
¼ cup minced fresh cilantro

1. Microwave onion, oil, serrano, tomato paste, garam masala, garlic, ginger, sugar, and ½ teaspoon salt in bowl, stirring occasionally, until onion is softened, about 5 minutes; transfer to slow cooker. Stir in tomatoes. Season chicken with salt and pepper and stir into slow cooker. Cover and cook until chicken is tender, 2 to 3 hours on low.

2. Whisk ½ cup sauce and yogurt together in bowl (to temper), then stir mixture back into slow cooker and let sit until heated through, about 5 minutes. Stir in cilantro and season with salt and pepper to taste. Serve.

NOTES FROM THE TEST KITCHEN

Shopping for Garam Masala

Garam masala is a northern Indian combination of up to 12 dry-roasted, ground spices and is used in a wide range of dishes. The most common ingredients include black peppercorns, cinnamon, cloves, cardamom, coriander, cumin, dried chiles, fennel, mace, nutmeg, and bay leaves. Ginger and caraway seeds also make frequent appearances. While we've found that commercial mixtures tend to be less aromatic and more muted than batches we toast and grind fresh ourselves, grinding whole spices to concoct this blend is time-consuming and expensive. In search of a good-tasting, commercially available garam masala, we tested a handful of top products. The tasters' favorite was **McCormick Gourmet Collection Garam Masala**, chosen for its ability to both blend into dishes and round out their acidic and sweet notes. It also won praise for adding a mellow, well-balanced aroma to most dishes.

Chicken with "Roasted" Garlic Sauce

SERVES 4   LIGHT

COOKING TIME 2 TO 3 HOURS ON LOW
SLOW COOKER SIZE 4 TO 7 QUARTS

WHY THIS RECIPE WORKS It's often the simplest meals that are the hardest to re-create in the slow cooker; tender, perfectly cooked bone-in chicken with a garlicky gravy is no exception. For a richly flavored and satisfying gravy, we turned to 15 whole cloves of garlic plus a shallot to lend a roasted flavor and body to our sauce. To end up with aromatics soft enough to puree into a smooth gravy, we found it necessary to jump-start their cooking by sautéing them on the stovetop until lightly browned. Giving the shallots and garlic time to brown also added to the subtle roasted taste and deepened their overall flavor, which became sweeter and mellower after hours in the slow cooker. With the aromatics already in the skillet, adding a small amount of flour was a quick and easy way to thicken the sauce, and deglazing with wine and broth ensured that the flavorful browned bits in the bottom of the pan ended up in the slow cooker. The addition of soy sauce helped to round out the overall flavor of the sauce. Rosemary and chives enlivened the gravy with fresh flavors. You will need an oval slow cooker for this recipe. Check the chicken's temperature after 2 hours of cooking and continue to monitor until it registers 160 degrees.

- 4 (12-ounce) bone-in split chicken breasts, trimmed
  Salt and pepper
- 1 tablespoon vegetable oil
- 15 garlic cloves, peeled
- 1 shallot, peeled and quartered
- 3 tablespoons all-purpose flour
- ½ teaspoon minced fresh rosemary or ⅛ teaspoon dried
- ⅔ cup dry white wine
- ½ cup chicken broth
- 1 tablespoon soy sauce
- 1 tablespoon minced fresh chives

1. Pat chicken dry with paper towels and season with salt and pepper. Heat oil in 12-inch skillet over medium-high heat until just smoking. Brown chicken, 3 to 4 minutes per side; transfer to plate and discard skin.

2. Add garlic and shallot to fat left in skillet and cook over medium-low heat until lightly browned and fragrant, 8 to 10 minutes. Stir in flour and rosemary and cook for 1 minute. Slowly whisk in wine, broth, and soy sauce, scraping up any browned bits and smoothing out any lumps; transfer to slow cooker.

3. Arrange chicken, skinned side up, in even layer in slow cooker, adding any accumulated juices. Cover and cook until chicken registers 160 degrees, 2 to 3 hours on low.

4. Transfer chicken to serving dish. Process cooking liquid in blender until smooth, about 30 seconds. Stir in chives and season with salt and pepper to taste. Serve chicken with sauce.

NOTES FROM THE TEST KITCHEN

All About Garlic

Here's everything you need to know about buying, storing, and cooking with garlic.

BUYING GARLIC Pick heads without spots, mold, or sprouting. Squeeze them to make sure they are not rubbery or missing cloves. The garlic shouldn't have much of a scent. Of the various garlic varieties, your best bet is soft-neck garlic, since it stores well and is heat-tolerant. This variety features a circle of large cloves surrounding a small cluster at the center. Hard-neck garlic has a stiff center staff surrounded by large, uniform cloves and boasts a more intense flavor. But since it's easily damaged and doesn't store as well as soft-neck garlic, wait to buy it at the farmers' market.

STORING GARLIC Whole heads of garlic should last at least a few weeks if stored in a cool, dark place with plenty of air circulation to prevent spoiling and sprouting.

PREPARING GARLIC Keep in mind that garlic's pungency emerges only after its cell walls are ruptured, triggering the creation of a compound called allicin. The more a clove is broken down, the more allicin that is produced. Thus you can control the amount of bite garlic contributes to a recipe by how fine or coarse you cut it. It's also best not to cut garlic in advance; the longer cut garlic sits, the harsher its flavor.

COOKING GARLIC Garlic's flavor is sharpest when raw. Once it is heated above 150 degrees, its enzymes are destroyed and no new flavor is produced. This is why roasted garlic, which is cooked slowly and takes longer to reach 150 degrees, has a mellow, slightly sweet flavor. Garlic browned at very high temperatures (300 to 350 degrees) results in a more bitter flavor. To avoid the creation of bitter compounds, wait to add garlic to the pan until other ingredients have softened. And don't cook garlic over high heat for much longer than 30 seconds.

An easy-to-make cream sauce takes this slow-cooker chicken from everyday to special in a flash.

Chicken with Mushrooms and Tarragon Cream Sauce

SERVES 4
COOKING TIME 2 TO 3 HOURS ON LOW
SLOW COOKER SIZE 4 TO 7 QUARTS

WHY THIS RECIPE WORKS To get the richest and deepest chicken flavor for this creamy, company-worthy braised chicken, we opted to get out a skillet and brown bone-in chicken breasts. Since we had our skillet out, we also browned the mushrooms and aromatics and deglazed the pan with white wine, seriously elevating the overall flavor. We further boosted the flavor with an unusual ingredient, soy sauce, which brought an extra level of meatiness without taking over. We added cream at the end of the cooking time, along with a hefty dose of fresh tarragon for bright flavor. You will need an oval slow cooker for this recipe. Check the chicken's temperature after 2 hours of cooking and continue to monitor until it registers 160 degrees.

4 (12-ounce) bone-in split chicken breasts, trimmed
  Salt and pepper
2 tablespoons vegetable oil
1¼ pounds cremini mushrooms, trimmed and halved if small or quartered if large
2 onions, chopped fine
¼ cup all-purpose flour
4 garlic cloves, minced
2 teaspoons minced fresh thyme or ½ teaspoon dried
¾ cup dry white wine
2 tablespoons soy sauce
2 bay leaves
¼ cup heavy cream
2 tablespoons minced fresh tarragon

1. Pat chicken dry with paper towels and season with salt and pepper. Heat 1 tablespoon oil in 12-inch skillet over medium-high heat until just smoking. Brown chicken, 3 to 4 minutes per side; transfer to plate and discard skin.

2. Heat remaining 1 tablespoon oil in now-empty skillet over medium heat until shimmering. Add mushrooms, onions, and ¼ teaspoon salt, cover, and cook until vegetables are softened and mushrooms have released their liquid, about 5 minutes. Uncover and continue to cook until vegetables are dry and lightly browned, 5 to 7 minutes. Stir in flour, garlic, and thyme and cook until fragrant, about 1 minute. Slowly stir in wine, scraping up any browned bits and smoothing out any lumps; transfer to slow cooker.

3. Stir soy sauce and bay leaves into slow cooker. Arrange chicken, skinned side up, in even layer in slow cooker, adding any accumulated juices. Cover and cook until chicken registers 160 degrees, 2 to 3 hours on low.

4. Transfer chicken to serving dish. Discard bay leaves. Stir cream and tarragon into cooking liquid. Adjust consistency with hot water as needed. Season with salt and pepper to taste. Spoon vegetables and sauce over chicken and serve.

TRIMMING SPLIT CHICKEN BREASTS

Using kitchen shears, trim off rib section from each breast, following vertical line of fat from tapered end of breast up to socket where wing was attached.

Browning the chicken and building the foundation of the sauce in a skillet first ensures a boldly flavored sauce.

Lemony Chicken with Artichokes and Capers

SERVES 4
COOKING TIME 2 TO 3 HOURS ON LOW
SLOW COOKER SIZE 4 TO 7 QUARTS

WHY THIS RECIPE WORKS For an easy braise with bright citrus flavor, we used the slow cooker to gently simmer chicken and artichokes with strips of lemon zest. As the chicken cooked, the lemon zest infused the meat and the sauce with bright flavor. Bone-in chicken breasts stayed moist and juicy even after hours of simmering. Some onion and garlic gave the dish additional depth and savory flavor. For the sauce, we loved the combination of bold, briny capers with the bright lemon and hearty artichokes. A squeeze of fresh lemon juice added at the end reinforced the citrus flavor, and a little heavy cream thickened and enriched the sauce. While we prefer the flavor and texture of jarred whole baby artichokes, you can substitute 18 ounces frozen artichoke hearts, thawed and patted dry, for the jarred. You will need an oval slow cooker for this recipe. Check the chicken's temperature after 2 hours of cooking and continue to monitor until it registers 160 degrees.

4 (12-ounce) bone-in split chicken breasts, trimmed
  Salt and pepper
1 tablespoon extra-virgin olive oil
1 onion, chopped fine
2 tablespoons all-purpose flour
2 garlic cloves, minced
1 teaspoon minced fresh thyme or ¼ teaspoon dried
½ cup chicken broth
3 cups jarred whole baby artichokes packed in water, halved, rinsed, and patted dry
1 (2-inch) strip lemon zest plus 2 tablespoons juice
½ cup heavy cream
2 tablespoons capers, rinsed
2 tablespoons minced fresh parsley

1. Pat chicken dry with paper towels and season with salt and pepper. Heat oil in 12-inch skillet over medium-high heat until just smoking. Brown chicken, 3 to 4 minutes per side; transfer to plate and discard skin.

2. Add onion, ½ teaspoon salt, and ½ teaspoon pepper to fat left in skillet and cook over medium heat until onion is softened and lightly browned, 5 to 7 minutes. Stir in flour, garlic, and thyme and cook until fragrant, about 1 minute. Slowly whisk in broth, scraping up any browned bits and smoothing out any lumps; transfer to slow cooker.

3. Stir artichokes and lemon zest into slow cooker. Arrange chicken, skinned side up, in even layer in slow cooker, adding any accumulated juices. Cover and cook until chicken registers 160 degrees, 2 to 3 hours on low.

4. Transfer chicken to serving dish and tent loosely with aluminum foil. Discard lemon zest. Stir cream, capers, parsley, and lemon juice into cooking liquid and let sit until heated through, about 5 minutes. Season with salt and pepper to taste. Spoon sauce over chicken and serve.

NOTES FROM THE TEST KITCHEN

Buying Processed Artichokes

Because fresh artichokes are limited by seasonality, we often turn to prepared artichokes. When buying them, avoid premarinated versions; we prefer to control the seasonings ourselves. We also don't recommend canned hearts, which tend to taste waterlogged and have tough leaves. We think that smaller whole jarred artichoke hearts, labeled "baby" or "cocktail," are best. Our favorite brand is Pastene Baby Artichokes, which have a sweet, earthy flavor.

Latin Chicken with Tomatoes and Olives

SERVES 4 `EASY PREP` `LIGHT`
COOKING TIME 2 TO 3 HOURS ON LOW
SLOW COOKER SIZE 4 TO 7 QUARTS

WHY THIS RECIPE WORKS This classic Latin-style chicken features tender chicken braised in a chunky tomato sauce; gently simmering the chicken in the sauce helps it to remain moist while enriching the flavors of both. Most slow-cooker recipes result in a dull, waterlogged tomato sauce, so we looked to give our dish a richer texture with a bright and assertive tomato flavor. Our testing revealed that canned diced tomatoes with their juice had the fresh tomato taste we wanted but created too much liquid during cooking. Compounded with the juices from the chicken, they created a thin, dull sauce. Draining the diced tomatoes, plus adding tomato paste and a small amount of tapioca, created the thickened sauce we were after. Finishing the sauce with green olives gave our dish a briny contrast, and a sprinkling of fresh cilantro and lime juice tied it all together. You will need an oval slow cooker for this recipe. Check the chicken's temperature after 2 hours of cooking and continue to monitor until it registers 160 degrees.

- 1 onion, halved and sliced thin
- 4 garlic cloves, sliced thin
- 1 tablespoon vegetable oil
- 1 tablespoon tomato paste
- 2 teaspoons minced fresh oregano or ½ teaspoon dried
- ¼ teaspoon ground cumin
- 1 (14.5-ounce) can diced tomatoes, drained
- 1 teaspoon instant tapioca
- 4 (12-ounce) bone-in split chicken breasts, skin removed, trimmed
  Salt and pepper
- ⅓ cup pitted large brine-cured green olives, chopped coarse
- 2 tablespoons minced fresh cilantro
- 1 tablespoon lime juice

1. Microwave onion, garlic, oil, tomato paste, oregano, and cumin in bowl, stirring occasionally, until onion is softened, about 5 minutes; transfer to slow cooker. Stir in tomatoes and tapioca. Season chicken with salt and pepper and arrange, skinned side up, in even layer in slow cooker. Cover and cook until chicken registers 160 degrees, 2 to 3 hours on low.

2. Transfer chicken to serving dish. Stir olives, cilantro, and lime juice into sauce and season with salt and pepper to taste. Spoon sauce over chicken and serve.

All About Olives

BRINE-CURED VERSUS SALT-CURED Jarred olives come in three basic types at the supermarket: brine-cured green, brine-cured black, and salt-cured black (often labeled "oil-cured"). Brine-cured olives are soaked in a salt solution for periods of up to a year to remove bitterness and develop flavor. Salt-cured olives are packed in salt until nearly all their liquid has been extracted, then covered in oil to be replumped. Both processes traditionally take weeks or even months. Generally we find that brine-cured black and green olives can be used interchangeably in any recipe based on personal preference. Among our test cooks, only a few olive aficionados favored the concentrated, bitter taste of salt-cured olives—we don't recommend cooking with them unless a recipe specifically calls for them. And as for canned olives? We avoid them entirely, finding them almost tasteless, and with a firm yet oddly slippery texture.

GREEN OLIVES Often labeled "Spanish" olives, green olives are picked before they fully ripen, and their mild flavor adds a bright, acidic dimension to food. Manzanillas, produced in Spain and California, are the pimento-stuffed olives best known for garnishing martinis. Add these olives at the end of cooking to avoid bitterness.

BLACK OLIVES Picked when mature, black olives lend a more robust, fruity taste. The most common types are kalamata olives, which have an earthy flavor and creamy flesh, and niçoise olives, which boast an assertive, somewhat bitter flavor. We prefer the fresher kalamatas from the refrigerator section of the supermarket; the jarred shelf-stable ones are bland and mushy in comparison. If you can't find kalamatas in the refrigerator section of your market, look for them at the salad bar.

PITTED VERSUS UNPITTED Pitted olives are certainly convenient, but they lack the complex, fruity flavors of unpitted olives and often have a mushier texture. After being brined for up to a year, the pitted olives are returned to the brine for packing, which can penetrate the inside of the olive and turn it mushy and pasty, as well as increase the absorption of salt. That saltier taste can mask subtler flavors. If you have the time, we recommend that you buy unpitted olives and pit them yourself.

Thai Chicken with Asparagus and Mushrooms

SERVES 4 `EASY PREP`

COOKING TIME 2 TO 3 HOURS ON LOW
SLOW COOKER SIZE 4 TO 7 QUARTS

WHY THIS RECIPE WORKS Thai dishes are known for their complex, long-simmered flavor. A few shortcut ingredients and the slow cooker were all we needed to create a boldly flavored, but easy-to-prepare, Thai chicken dinner. Thai red curry paste was an easy swap for an overwhelming list of traditional seasonings. We enriched it with coconut milk to deepen the flavor of our sauce. Stirring in a portion of the coconut milk just before serving helped to deepen the coconut flavor, which otherwise can taste washed out after several hours in the slow cooker. A little instant tapioca helped to thicken the sauce to a curry-like consistency that went perfectly with rice. Bone-in chicken breasts stayed moist and tender as the sauce simmered and the rich flavors melded. We liked light, fresh asparagus and delicate shiitakes in this dish, but they turned to mush in the slow cooker. Luckily, just 5 minutes in the microwave was enough to turn them tender, then we added them to the dish at the end. We finished the sauce with lime juice, fish sauce, and fresh cilantro to brighten its rich flavors. You will need an oval slow cooker for this recipe. Check the chicken's temperature after 2 hours of cooking and continue to monitor until it registers 160 degrees.

- 1 cup canned coconut milk
- 2 tablespoons Thai red curry paste
- 1 tablespoon instant tapioca
  Salt and pepper
- 4 (12-ounce) bone-in split chicken breasts, skin removed, trimmed
- 1 pound asparagus, trimmed and cut into 1-inch lengths
- 1 pound shiitake mushrooms, stemmed and sliced ½ inch thick
- 1 tablespoon vegetable oil
- 2 tablespoons lime juice, plus extra for seasoning
- 1 tablespoon fish sauce, plus extra for seasoning
- ¼ cup minced fresh cilantro

1. Whisk ½ cup coconut milk, curry paste, tapioca, ½ teaspoon salt, and ½ teaspoon pepper together in slow cooker. Season chicken with salt and pepper and arrange, skinned side up, in even layer in slow cooker. Cover and cook until chicken registers 160 degrees, 2 to 3 hours on low.

2. Microwave asparagus, mushrooms, and oil in bowl, stirring occasionally, until vegetables are tender, about 5 minutes.

3. Transfer chicken to serving dish and tent loosely with aluminum foil. Stir vegetables, remaining ½ cup coconut milk, lime juice, and fish sauce into cooking liquid and let sit until heated through, about 5 minutes. Stir in cilantro and season with extra lime juice and fish sauce to taste. Spoon sauce over chicken and serve.

TRIMMING ASPARAGUS

1. Remove 1 spear of asparagus from bunch and bend it at thicker end until it snaps.

2. With broken asparagus spear as guide, trim tough ends from remaining asparagus bunch using chef's knife.

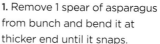

NOTES FROM THE TEST KITCHEN

Curry Paste

Curry pastes, which can be either green or red, are a key ingredient for adding deep, well-rounded flavor to Thai curries. They are made from a mix of lemon grass, kaffir lime leaves, shrimp paste, ginger, garlic, chiles (fresh green Thai chiles for green curry paste, and dried red Thai chiles for red curry paste), and other spices. So it's not surprising that making curry paste at home can be quite a chore. We have found that the store-bought variety does a fine job and saves significant time in terms of both shopping and prep. It is usually sold in small jars next to other Thai ingredients at the supermarket. Be aware that these pastes can vary in spiciness depending on the brand, so use more or less as desired.

Chicken with Fennel and Tomato Couscous

SERVES 4   `EASY PREP`

COOKING TIME 2 TO 3 HOURS ON LOW
SLOW COOKER SIZE 4 TO 7 QUARTS

WHY THIS RECIPE WORKS For a simple braised chicken dinner with fresh Italian flavors, we combined bone-in chicken breasts with fennel and bright cherry tomatoes. Store-bought chicken broth flavored with garlic, salt, and pepper made a simple cooking liquid that seasoned the chicken as it simmered and helped it to cook gently and evenly. Once the chicken was cooked, we used the flavorful cooking liquid, enriched with the chicken's juices, to cook couscous for a quick and easy side dish. A quick basil vinaigrette brought freshness and acidity when drizzled over both the chicken and the couscous. Be sure to use regular (or fine-grain) couscous; large-grain couscous, often labeled "Israeli-style," takes much longer to cook and won't work in this recipe. You will need an oval slow cooker for this recipe. Check the chicken's temperature after 2 hours of cooking and continue to monitor until it registers 160 degrees.

- 1 fennel bulb, stalks discarded, bulb halved, cored, and sliced thin
- 5 tablespoons extra-virgin olive oil
- 3 garlic cloves, minced
  Salt and pepper
- ½ cup chicken broth
- 4 (12-ounce) bone-in split chicken breasts, skin removed, trimmed
- 8 ounces cherry tomatoes, halved
- 1 cup couscous
- ¼ cup chopped fresh basil
- 2 tablespoon white wine vinegar
- 2 teaspoons honey
- ½ teaspoon Dijon mustard

For a one-dish meal, we cook couscous in the flavorful cooking liquid once the chicken is done.

1. Microwave fennel, 1 tablespoon oil, two-thirds of garlic, ½ teaspoon salt, and ½ teaspoon pepper in bowl, stirring occasionally, until fennel is tender, about 5 minutes; transfer to slow cooker. Stir in broth. Season chicken with salt and pepper and arrange, skinned side up, in even layer in slow cooker. Sprinkle tomatoes over chicken, cover, and cook until chicken registers 160 degrees, 2 to 3 hours on low.

PREPARING FENNEL

1. Cut off tops and feathery fronds.

2. Trim thin slice from base and remove any tough or blemished outer layers.

3. Cut bulb in half through base. Use small sharp knife to remove pyramid-shaped core.

4. Slice fennel halves as directed in recipe.

2. Transfer chicken to serving dish and tent loosely with aluminum foil. Strain cooking liquid into fat separator, reserving vegetables. Return vegetables and 1 cup defatted liquid to now-empty slow cooker; discard remaining liquid. Stir in couscous, cover, and cook on high until tender, about 15 minutes.

3. Whisk remaining ¼ cup oil, remaining garlic, basil, vinegar, honey, and mustard together in bowl. Season with salt and pepper to taste. Add 3 tablespoons dressing to cooked couscous and fluff with fork to combine. Drizzle chicken with remaining dressing and serve with couscous.

Spiced Chicken with Carrot Couscous

SERVES 4   **EASY PREP**

COOKING TIME 2 TO 3 HOURS ON LOW

SLOW COOKER SIZE 4 TO 7 QUARTS

WHY THIS RECIPE WORKS Looking for an alternative to the classic pairing of chicken and rice, we turned to the flavors and ingredients of Morocco for inspiration. We made a Moroccan spice rub by blooming garlic, garam masala, and turmeric with a small amount of olive oil in the microwave. To complete our meal with an easy but flavorful side, we stirred couscous, shredded carrots, and some of our spiced cooking liquid into the slow cooker while the chicken rested. After just 15 minutes, the couscous had cooked through and was ready to be served. A quick vinaigrette brought freshness and acidity when drizzled over both the chicken and the couscous. Be sure to use regular (or fine-grain) couscous; large-grain couscous, often labeled "Israeli-style," takes much longer to cook and won't work in this recipe. You will need an oval slow cooker for this recipe. Check the chicken's temperature after 2 hours of cooking and continue to monitor until it registers 160 degrees.

- 1 cup chicken broth
- 3 tablespoons extra-virgin olive oil
- 3 garlic cloves, minced
- 1 teaspoon garam masala
   Salt and pepper
- ¼ teaspoon ground turmeric
- 4 (12-ounce) bone-in split chicken breasts, skin removed, trimmed
- 1 cup couscous
- 2 carrots, peeled and shredded
- ½ cup orange juice
- 3 tablespoons minced fresh cilantro
- 1 tablespoon sherry vinegar
- 2 tablespoons sliced almonds, toasted

1. Add broth to slow cooker. Microwave 1 tablespoon oil, garlic, garam masala, ½ teaspoon salt, ¼ teaspoon pepper, and turmeric in bowl until fragrant, about 30 seconds; let cool slightly. Rub chicken with spice mixture, then arrange, skinned side up, in even layer in slow cooker. Cover and cook until chicken registers 160 degrees, 2 to 3 hours on low.

2. Transfer chicken to serving dish and tent loosely with aluminum foil. Transfer cooking liquid to fat separator. Return 1 cup defatted liquid to now-empty slow cooker; discard remaining liquid. Stir in couscous and carrots, cover, and cook on high until couscous is tender, about 15 minutes.

3. Whisk orange juice, cilantro, vinegar, and remaining 2 tablespoons oil together in bowl. Season with salt and pepper to taste. Add almonds and 3 tablespoons dressing to cooked couscous and fluff with fork to combine. Drizzle chicken with remaining dressing and serve with couscous.

NOTES FROM THE TEST KITCHEN

Getting to Know Couscous

Couscous is a starch made from durum semolina, the high-protein wheat flour that is also used to make Italian pasta. However, while pasta is made with ground durum semolina that is mixed with water to form a dough, traditional Moroccan couscous is made by rubbing crushed durum semolina and water between the hands to form small granules. The couscous is then dried and, traditionally, cooked over a simmering stew in a steamer called a couscoussier. About the size of bread crumbs, the couscous found in most supermarkets is a precooked version that needs only a few minutes of steeping in hot liquid in order to be fully cooked. Pearl couscous, also known as Israeli couscous, is larger than traditional couscous (about the size of a caper) and, like Italian pasta, is made from durum semolina flour. However, it is toasted, rather than dried, which gives it its unique, nutty flavor.

Couscous   Pearl Couscous

Fresh oregano and lemon zest give both the chicken and the hearty bulgur bold flavor.

Greek Chicken with Warm Tabbouleh

SERVES 4 **EASY PREP**
COOKING TIME 2 TO 3 HOURS ON LOW
SLOW COOKER SIZE 4 TO 7 QUARTS

WHY THIS RECIPE WORKS Most grains need to cook for much longer than chicken to become tender enough to eat, making it a challenge to adapt this dish to a slow cooker. Looking for bright and fresh flavors to pair with our Greek-inspired chicken, we turned to the classic tabbouleh salad. Fortunately, our testing revealed that medium-grind bulgur is one of the few hearty grains that can cook through in the slow cooker without breaking down and becoming gummy. Rubbing the chicken with an aromatic mixture of garlic, oregano, and lemon zest seasoned not only the chicken but also the bulgur as it cooked. We drained the bulgur at the end of cooking to remove excess liquid and seasoned it with olive oil, lemon juice, parsley, and tomatoes to turn the hearty grain into a vibrant salad. When shopping, don't confuse bulgur with cracked wheat, which has a much longer cooking time and will not work in this recipe. You will need an oval slow cooker for this recipe. Check the chicken's temperature after 2 hours of cooking and continue to monitor until it registers 160 degrees.

1 cup medium-grind bulgur, rinsed
1 cup chicken broth
  Salt and pepper
3 tablespoons extra-virgin olive oil
4 teaspoons minced fresh oregano
1¼ teaspoons grated lemon zest plus
  3 tablespoons juice
1 garlic clove, minced
4 (12-ounce) bone-in split chicken breasts, skin removed, trimmed
½ cup plain Greek yogurt
½ cup minced fresh parsley
3 tablespoons water
8 ounces cherry tomatoes, quartered

1. Lightly coat slow cooker with vegetable oil spray. Combine bulgur, broth, and ¼ teaspoon salt in slow cooker. Microwave 1 tablespoon oil, 1 tablespoon oregano, 1 teaspoon lemon zest, garlic, ½ teaspoon salt, and ¼ teaspoon pepper in bowl until fragrant, about 30 seconds; let cool slightly. Rub chicken with oregano mixture, then arrange, skinned side up, in even layer in prepared slow cooker. Cover and cook until chicken registers 160 degrees, 2 to 3 hours on low.

2. Whisk yogurt, 1 tablespoon parsley, water, remaining 1 teaspoon oregano, remaining ¼ teaspoon lemon zest, and ⅛ teaspoon salt together in bowl. Season with salt and pepper to taste.

3. Transfer chicken to serving dish, brushing any bulgur that sticks to breasts back into slow cooker. Drain bulgur mixture, if necessary, and return to now-empty slow cooker. Add tomatoes, lemon juice, remaining 7 tablespoons parsley, and remaining 2 tablespoons oil and fluff with fork to combine. Season with salt and pepper to taste. Serve chicken with tabbouleh and yogurt sauce.

NOTES FROM THE TEST KITCHEN

Curly Versus Flat-Leaf Parsley

We find flat-leaf parsley to have a sweet, bright flavor that's much nicer than the bitter, grassy tones of curly-leaf. It's also much more fragrant than its curly cousin.

Curly-Leaf Parsley   Flat-Leaf Parsley

MAKE IT 5 WAYS CHICKEN AND POTATOES

Mediterranean Chicken and Potatoes

SERVES 4
COOKING TIME 2 TO 3 HOURS ON LOW
SLOW COOKER SIZE 4 TO 7 QUARTS

These five recipes feature chicken and potatoes and a variety of spices, aromatics, and vegetables, giving you lots of choices for interesting dinners. We started each recipe by using the microwave to bloom an aromatic oil mixture, then letting it cool slightly before rubbing it directly onto bone-in chicken breasts (skin removed) for a big flavor boost. Microwaving the potatoes before placing them in the bottom of the slow cooker ensured that our vegetables would be fully tender when the chicken finished cooking. Once our chicken and potatoes were perfectly cooked, we whisked together a quick pantry-friendly dressing to accompany the finished dish, along with fresh garnishes to make for a simple and satisfying slow-cooker meal with a vibrant appeal. You will need an oval slow cooker for these recipes. Check the chicken's temperature after 2 hours of cooking and continue to monitor until it registers 160 degrees.

1 LEMON-ROSEMARY CHICKEN AND POTATOES

- 6 tablespoons extra-virgin olive oil
- 4 garlic cloves, minced
- 1 teaspoon minced fresh rosemary
- ¼ teaspoon red pepper flakes
  Salt and pepper
- 1½ pounds red potatoes, unpeeled, cut into 1-inch pieces
- 4 (12-ounce) bone-in split chicken breasts, skin removed, trimmed
- 1 tablespoon water
- 2 teaspoons whole-grain mustard
- 1 teaspoon grated lemon zest plus 2 tablespoons juice
- 1 cup frozen peas, thawed

1. Microwave 2 tablespoons oil, garlic, rosemary, pepper flakes, ½ teaspoon salt, and ½ teaspoon pepper in bowl until fragrant, about 30 seconds; let cool slightly.

2. Toss potatoes with 1 tablespoon oil, ½ teaspoon salt, and ¼ teaspoon pepper in large bowl. Cover potatoes and microwave, stirring occasionally, until softened, 8 to 10 minutes; transfer to slow cooker. Rub chicken with oil mixture; arrange skinned side up in even layer in slow cooker. Cover and cook until chicken registers 160 degrees, 2 to 3 hours on low.

3. Whisk remaining 3 tablespoons oil, water, mustard, lemon zest and juice, and ⅛ teaspoon salt in separate bowl until combined. Season with salt and pepper to taste. Transfer chicken to serving dish; tent loosely with aluminum foil. Stir peas into slow cooker; let sit until heated through, about 5 minutes. Using slotted spoon, transfer vegetables to dish with chicken; drizzle with half of dressing. Serve, passing remaining dressing separately.

2 MEDITERRANEAN CHICKEN AND POTATOES

- ¼ cup extra-virgin olive oil
- 4 garlic cloves, minced
- 2 teaspoons minced fresh thyme or ¾ teaspoon dried
- 2 oranges, plus 2 teaspoons grated orange zest
  Salt and pepper
- 1 pound red potatoes, unpeeled, cut into 1-inch pieces
- 1 small fennel bulb, stalks discarded, bulb halved, cored, and sliced thin
- 4 (12-ounce) bone-in split chicken breasts, skin removed, trimmed
- ¼ cup pitted kalamata olives, chopped
- 2 tablespoons minced fresh parsley
- 1 tablespoon red wine vinegar

1. Microwave 2 tablespoons oil, garlic, thyme, orange zest, ½ teaspoon salt, and ½ teaspoon pepper in bowl until fragrant, about 30 seconds; let cool slightly.

2. Toss potatoes and fennel with 1 tablespoon oil, ½ teaspoon salt, and ¼ teaspoon pepper in large bowl. Cover vegetables and microwave, stirring occasionally, until softened, 8 to 10 minutes; transfer to slow cooker. Rub chicken with oil mixture; arrange skinned side up in even layer in slow cooker. Cover and cook until chicken registers 160 degrees, 2 to 3 hours on low.

3. Cut away peel and pith from oranges. Quarter oranges, then slice crosswise into ½-inch-thick pieces. Combine oranges, olives, parsley, vinegar, and remaining 1 tablespoon oil in bowl. Season with salt and pepper to taste. Transfer chicken to serving dish. Using slotted spoon, transfer vegetables to dish with chicken. Serve with orange relish.

3 FRENCH CHICKEN AND WARM POTATO SALAD

6 tablespoons extra-virgin olive oil
1 shallot, minced
2 teaspoons minced fresh thyme or ¾ teaspoon dried
  Salt and pepper
1½ pounds Yukon Gold potatoes, unpeeled, cut into 1-inch pieces
4 (12-ounce) bone-in split chicken breasts, skin removed, trimmed
3 tablespoons water
2 tablespoons Dijon mustard
2 tablespoons minced fresh chives
1 tablespoon lemon juice
1 teaspoon sugar
5 radishes, trimmed and sliced thin

1. Microwave 2 tablespoons oil, shallot, thyme, ½ teaspoon salt, and ½ teaspoon pepper in bowl until fragrant, about 30 seconds; let cool slightly.

2. Toss potatoes with 1 tablespoon oil, ½ teaspoon salt, and ¼ teaspoon pepper in separate bowl. Cover potatoes and microwave, stirring occasionally, until softened, 8 to 10 minutes; transfer to slow cooker. Rub chicken with oil mixture; arrange skinned side up in even layer in slow cooker. Cover and cook until chicken registers 160 degrees, 2 to 3 hours on low.

3. Whisk remaining 3 tablespoons oil, water, mustard, chives, lemon juice, sugar, and ⅛ teaspoon salt in large bowl until combined. Set aside ¼ cup dressing for serving. Transfer chicken to serving dish. Using slotted spoon, transfer potatoes to bowl with remaining dressing. Add radishes; gently toss to combine. Season with salt and pepper to taste. Serve chicken with salad and reserved dressing.

4 SESAME-GINGER CHICKEN AND SWEET POTATOES

3 tablespoons vegetable oil
4 teaspoons grated fresh ginger
3 garlic cloves, minced
  Salt and pepper
1½ pounds sweet potatoes, peeled, cut into 1-inch pieces
1 red bell pepper, stemmed, seeded, and cut into ¼-inch-wide strips
4 (12-ounce) bone-in split chicken breasts, skin removed, trimmed
2 tablespoons toasted sesame oil
1 tablespoon water
1 tablespoon rice vinegar
1 teaspoon honey
1 teaspoon Asian chili-garlic sauce
2 teaspoons sesame seeds, toasted
2 scallions, sliced thin on bias

1. Microwave 2 tablespoons vegetable oil, 1 tablespoon ginger, garlic, ½ teaspoon salt, and ½ teaspoon pepper in bowl until fragrant, about 30 seconds; let cool slightly.

2. Toss potatoes with remaining 1 tablespoon vegetable oil, ½ teaspoon salt, and ¼ teaspoon pepper in large bowl. Cover potatoes and microwave, stirring occasionally, until almost tender, 8 to 10 minutes; transfer to slow cooker with bell pepper. Rub chicken with oil mixture; arrange skinned side up in even layer in slow cooker. Cover and cook until chicken registers 160 degrees, 2 to 3 hours on low.

3. Whisk sesame oil, water, vinegar, honey, chili-garlic sauce, and remaining 1 teaspoon ginger in bowl until combined. Season with salt and pepper to taste. Transfer chicken to serving dish. Using slotted spoon, transfer vegetables to dish with chicken; drizzle with half of dressing. Sprinkle with sesame seeds and scallions. Serve, passing remaining dressing separately.

5 SPICY PERUVIAN CHICKEN AND SWEET POTATOES

3 tablespoons extra-virgin olive oil
1 habanero chile, stemmed, seeded, and minced
5 garlic cloves, minced
2½ teaspoons grated lime zest plus 1 tablespoon juice
1¼ teaspoons paprika
1 teaspoon ground cumin
1 teaspoon dried oregano
  Salt and pepper
1½ pounds sweet potatoes, peeled, cut into 1-inch pieces
4 (12-ounce) bone-in split chicken breasts, skin removed, trimmed
½ cup mayonnaise
1 teaspoon sugar
2 tablespoons minced fresh mint
2 tablespoons roasted pepitas

1. Microwave 2 tablespoons oil, habanero, garlic, 2 teaspoons lime zest, 1 teaspoon paprika, cumin, oregano, ½ teaspoon salt, and ½ teaspoon pepper in bowl until fragrant, about 30 seconds; let cool slightly.

2. Toss potatoes with remaining 1 tablespoon oil, ½ teaspoon salt, and ¼ teaspoon pepper in bowl. Cover potatoes and microwave, stirring occasionally, until almost tender, 8 to 10 minutes; transfer to slow cooker. Rub chicken with oil mixture; arrange skinned side up in even layer in slow cooker. Cover and cook until chicken registers 160 degrees, 2 to 3 hours on low.

3. Whisk mayonnaise, sugar, lime juice, remaining ½ teaspoon lime zest, and remaining ¼ teaspoon paprika in bowl until combined. Season with salt and pepper to taste. Transfer chicken to serving dish. Using slotted spoon, transfer potatoes to dish with chicken. Sprinkle with mint and pepitas. Serve with sauce.

Chicken Provençal

SERVES 4 **EASY PREP** LIGHT

COOKING TIME 4 TO 5 HOURS ON LOW

SLOW COOKER SIZE 4 TO 7 QUARTS

WHY THIS RECIPE WORKS Chicken Provençal represents the best of French peasant cooking—chicken on the bone is slowly simmered with tomatoes, garlic, herbs, and olives—and translating it to a quick and easy slow-cooker dish was a snap. We preferred bone-in chicken thighs to breasts because their richness holds up to the strong garlicky tomato flavor of this classic dish. Once again, strong, bold flavors allowed us to eliminate any browning, simplifying the process. The long-stewed flavor is accented at the end with an addition of olives, parsley, and a dose of good-quality extra-virgin olive oil.

1 onion, chopped fine
12 garlic cloves, minced
1 tablespoon extra-virgin olive oil,
   plus extra for serving
2 tablespoons tomato paste
2 teaspoons minced fresh oregano or
   ½ teaspoon dried
1 (28-ounce) can crushed tomatoes
½ cup dry white wine
2 bay leaves
8 (5- to 7-ounce) bone-in chicken thighs,
   skin removed, trimmed
   Salt and pepper
½ cup pitted niçoise olives, chopped coarse
¼ cup minced fresh parsley
   Lemon wedges

1. Microwave onion, garlic, oil, tomato paste, and oregano in bowl, stirring occasionally, until onion is softened, about 5 minutes; transfer to slow cooker. Stir in tomatoes, wine, and bay leaves. Season chicken with salt and pepper and nestle into slow cooker. Cover and cook until chicken is tender, 4 to 5 hours on low.

2. Transfer chicken to serving dish. Discard bay leaves. Stir in olives and parsley and season with salt and pepper to taste. Spoon 1 cup sauce over chicken. Serve, drizzling individual portions with extra oil and passing lemon wedges and remaining sauce separately.

Buying Chicken

Here's what you need to know when buying chicken.

DECIPHERING LABELS A lot of labeling doesn't (necessarily) mean much. Companies can exploit loopholes to qualify for "Natural/All-Natural," "Hormone-Free," and "Vegetarian Diet/Fed" labeling. "USDA Organic," however, isn't all hype: The chickens must eat all organic feed without animal byproducts, be raised without antibiotics, and have access to the outdoors.

PAY ATTENTION TO PROCESSING Our research showed that processing is the major player in chicken's texture and flavor. We found that brands labeled "water-chilled" (soaked in a water bath in which it absorbs up to 14 percent of its weight in water, which you pay for since chicken is sold by the pound) or "enhanced" (injected with broth and flavoring) are unnaturally spongy and are best avoided. Labeling laws say water gain must be shown on the product label, so these should be easily identifiable. When buying whole chickens or chicken parts, look for those that are labeled "air-chilled." Without the excess water weight, these brands are less spongy in texture (but still plenty juicy) and have more chicken flavor.

BONELESS, SKINLESS BREASTS AND CUTLETS Try to pick a package with breasts of similar size, and pound them to an even thickness so they will cook at the same rate. You can buy cutlets ready to go at the grocery store, but we don't recommend it. These cutlets are usually ragged and of various sizes; it's better to cut your own cutlets from breasts.

BONE-IN PARTS You can buy a whole chicken or chicken parts at the supermarket, but sometimes it's hard to tell by looking at the package if it's been properly butchered. If you have a few extra minutes, consider buying a whole chicken and butchering it yourself.

WHOLE CHICKENS Whole chickens come in various sizes. Broilers and fryers are younger chickens that weigh 2½ to 4½ pounds. A roaster (or "oven-stuffer roaster") is an older chicken and usually clocks in between 5 and 7 pounds. Stewing chickens, which are older laying hens, are best used for stews since the meat is tougher and stringier. A 3½- to 4-pound bird will feed four people.

Chicken Adobo

SERVES 4   `EASY PREP`   `LIGHT`

COOKING TIME   4 TO 5 HOURS ON LOW
SLOW COOKER SIZE   4 TO 7 QUARTS

WHY THIS RECIPE WORKS Chicken adobo is a popular Filipino dish made by slowly simmering chicken in a mixture of vinegar, soy sauce, garlic, bay leaves, and black pepper. The beauty of this dish is that it features a short ingredient list and requires very little prep work, while still delivering tender, moist chicken and a boldly flavored sauce. In traditional recipes the chicken is marinated, then the marinade is reduced to create a thick sauce. Since we would be cooking the chicken thighs for a full 4 hours, we skipped the marinade and simply cooked the chicken directly in the sauce. So that we wouldn't have to reduce the sauce over the stove, we scaled it down and added a little tapioca to thicken it as it cooked. Some creamy coconut milk helped to balance the tart and salty flavors of the sauce. Stirring in a portion of the coconut milk just before serving helped to deepen the coconut flavor, which can taste dull after several hours in the slow cooker.

½ cup canned coconut milk
3 tablespoons cider vinegar
2 tablespoons soy sauce
2 garlic cloves, minced
2 tablespoons instant tapioca
2 bay leaves
   Salt and pepper
8 (5- to 7-ounce) bone-in chicken thighs,
   skin removed, trimmed
2 scallions, sliced thin

1. Whisk ¼ cup coconut milk, 2 tablespoons vinegar, soy sauce, garlic, tapioca, bay leaves, and 1 teaspoon pepper together in slow cooker. Season chicken with salt and pepper and nestle into slow cooker. Cover and cook until chicken is tender, 4 to 5 hours on low.

2. Transfer chicken to serving dish. Discard bay leaves. Whisk remaining ¼ cup coconut milk and remaining 1 tablespoon vinegar into cooking liquid until smooth. Season with salt and pepper to taste. Spoon 1 cup sauce over chicken and sprinkle with scallions. Serve, passing remaining sauce separately.

We made a simple mole sauce using pantry staples for this easy Mexican chicken.

Chicken Mole

SERVES 4   `EASY PREP`   `LIGHT`

COOKING TIME   4 TO 5 HOURS ON LOW
SLOW COOKER SIZE   4 TO 7 QUARTS

WHY THIS RECIPE WORKS A great mole (a rich Mexican chile sauce) requires hours of slow cooking to develop the deep, complex flavors for which it is so well known, making it a perfect match for the slow cooker. For our mole, we chose meaty bone-in chicken thighs, which paired well with the spicy sauce. We cooked the chicken directly in the mole so it would absorb that smoky-sweet flavor, and after 4 hours in the slow cooker it was fall-off-the-bone tender. Traditionally mole boasts an extensive list of ingredients, but we streamlined the recipe by relying on pantry staples, including chili powder, cocoa powder, and peanut butter, for complex flavor without the work. Canned diced tomatoes added acidity, and raisins gave us just the right sweetness; finishing with cilantro brightened things up.

1 (14.5-ounce) can diced tomatoes,
    drained with ½ cup juice reserved
⅓ cup raisins
2 tablespoons unsweetened cocoa powder
2 tablespoons peanut butter
1 tablespoon chili powder
4 garlic cloves, minced
    Salt and pepper
8 (5- to 7-ounce) bone-in chicken thighs,
    skin removed, trimmed
¼ cup minced fresh cilantro

1. Combine tomatoes and reserved juice, raisins, cocoa, peanut butter, chili powder, garlic, ½ teaspoon salt, and ½ teaspoon pepper in slow cooker. Season chicken with salt and pepper and nestle into slow cooker. Cover and cook until chicken is tender, 4 to 5 hours on low.

2. Transfer chicken to serving dish. Process cooking liquid in blender until smooth, about 30 seconds. Season with salt and pepper to taste. Pour 1 cup sauce over chicken and sprinkle with cilantro. Serve, passing remaining sauce separately.

REMOVING CHICKEN SKIN

Chicken skin is often slippery, making it a challenge to remove by hand, even when the chicken has been browned. To simplify the task, use a paper towel to provide extra grip while pulling.

Chinese Barbecued Chicken Thighs

SERVES 4   `EASY PREP`

COOKING TIME 4 TO 5 HOURS ON LOW
SLOW COOKER SIZE 4 TO 7 QUARTS

WHY THIS RECIPE WORKS Chinese barbecued chicken is not something most people would associate with a slow cooker, but this dish comes surprisingly close to the labor-intensive classic. The process for making it in a slow cooker is quite simple: First, we made a quick sauce layered with Asian flavors including five-spice powder, hoisin, honey, soy sauce, sesame oil, and ginger. Cooking the chicken in the slow cooker with half of the sauce helped to tenderize the meat and infused it with the sauce's flavors. And since this classic's hallmark lies in its deeply caramelized exterior, we moved our chicken from the slow cooker to the broiler. We brushed

These Chinese barbecued chicken thighs get their deep caramelization from the broiler after they are cooked.

the meat with the remaining sauce and gave it a few minutes under a hot broiler to caramelize. In the end we were left with beautiful mahogany barbecued chicken.

2 tablespoons hoisin sauce
2 tablespoons ketchup
2 tablespoons honey
1 tablespoon soy sauce
1 tablespoon dry sherry
1½ teaspoons toasted sesame oil
1½ teaspoons grated fresh ginger
1 garlic clove, minced
½ teaspoon five-spice powder
8 (5- to 7-ounce) bone-in chicken thighs, trimmed

1. Lightly coat slow cooker with vegetable oil spray. Combine hoisin, ketchup, honey, soy sauce, sherry, oil, ginger, garlic, and five-spice powder in bowl. Place chicken in prepared slow cooker and pour half of hoisin mixture over top. Turn chicken to coat evenly. Cover and cook until chicken is tender, 4 to 5 hours on low.

2. Adjust oven rack 6 inches from broiler element and heat broiler. Set wire rack in aluminum foil–lined rimmed baking sheet and coat with vegetable oil spray. Transfer chicken to prepared rack; discard cooking liquid. Broil chicken until browned, about 10 minutes, flipping chicken halfway through broiling.

3. Brush chicken with half of sauce and continue to broil until lightly charred, about 5 minutes, flipping and brushing chicken with remaining sauce halfway through broiling. Serve.

Barbecued Chicken Drumsticks

SERVES 4 TO 6 **EASY PREP**
COOKING TIME 4 TO 5 HOURS ON LOW
SLOW COOKER SIZE 4 TO 7 QUARTS

WHY THIS RECIPE WORKS Although our slow-cooker barbecued drumsticks required some time under the broiler at the end to caramelize their skin until glossy brown, they were otherwise prep-free—it took only a few minutes to measure out the spices and sauce and get them under way.

4 pounds chicken drumsticks, trimmed
1 tablespoon paprika
1 tablespoon chili powder
  Salt and pepper
¼ teaspoon cayenne pepper
½ cup ketchup
6 tablespoons molasses
2 tablespoons Dijon mustard
1 tablespoon cider vinegar
1 tablespoon packed brown sugar
½ teaspoon liquid smoke

1. Lightly coat slow cooker with vegetable oil spray. Toss chicken with paprika, chili powder, 1 teaspoon salt, ½ teaspoon pepper, and cayenne in prepared slow cooker. Cover and cook until chicken is tender, 4 to 5 hours on low.

2. Adjust oven rack 6 inches from broiler element and heat broiler. Set wire rack in aluminum foil–lined rimmed baking sheet and coat with vegetable oil spray. Transfer chicken to prepared rack. Broil chicken until lightly charred, about 10 minutes, flipping chicken halfway through broiling.

3. Whisk ketchup, molasses, mustard, vinegar, sugar, and liquid smoke in bowl until sugar is dissolved. Brush chicken with one-third of sauce and continue to broil until lightly charred, about 5 minutes, flipping and brushing chicken with more sauce halfway through broiling. Brush chicken with remaining sauce. Serve.

Fig preserves, balsamic vinegar, and orange zest elevate ordinary drumsticks to new heights.

Fig-Balsamic Glazed Chicken Drumsticks

SERVES 4 TO 6 **EASY PREP**
COOKING TIME 4 TO 5 HOURS ON LOW
SLOW COOKER SIZE 4 TO 7 QUARTS

WHY THIS RECIPE WORKS Following our success with slow-cooker chicken wings (page 32), we wanted to use our easy method to make tender slow-cooked drumsticks with a delicious sticky-sweet glaze. The method translated perfectly to the drumsticks; we simply seasoned them with salt, pepper, and a little aromatic rosemary and cooked them until tender. Then we set them on a wire rack and broiled them until the skin was crisp and browned, glazing them partway through. For the glaze, we decided on the classic Italian combination of figs and balsamic vinegar. To keep our glaze as simple as possible, we relied on fig preserves, which had great flavor and an ideal thick consistency. We simply added some balsamic vinegar and orange zest to round out the flavor. These drumsticks cook up charred and sticky after a short time under the broiler.

4 pounds chicken drumsticks, trimmed
2 tablespoons minced fresh rosemary or
  2 teaspoons dried, crumbled
  Salt and pepper
¾ cup fig preserves
3 tablespoons balsamic vinegar
1½ teaspoons grated orange zest

1. Lightly coat slow cooker with vegetable oil spray. Toss chicken with rosemary, 1 teaspoon salt, and ½ teaspoon pepper in prepared slow cooker. Cover and cook until chicken is tender, 4 to 5 hours on low.

2. Adjust oven rack 6 inches from broiler element and heat broiler. Set wire rack in aluminum foil–lined rimmed baking sheet and coat with vegetable oil spray. Transfer chicken to prepared rack. Broil chicken until lightly charred, about 10 minutes, flipping chicken halfway through broiling.

3. Whisk preserves, vinegar, orange zest, 1 teaspoon pepper, and ½ teaspoon salt together in bowl. Brush chicken with one-third of sauce and continue to broil until lightly charred, about 5 minutes, flipping and brushing chicken with more sauce halfway through broiling. Brush chicken with remaining sauce. Serve.

Jerk Chicken

SERVES 4 TO 6 `EASY PREP`
COOKING TIME 4 TO 5 HOURS ON LOW
SLOW COOKER SIZE 4 TO 7 QUARTS

WHY THIS RECIPE WORKS We wanted to use a slow cooker to create an authentic-tasting jerk chicken recipe—with fiery chiles, warm spices, and fragrant herbs—that tasted just as good as its more commonly grilled counterpart. First, we used a food processor to make a smooth paste of the traditional mix of aromatics—scallions, garlic, habanero chiles (also called Scotch bonnets), and ginger—along with sticky molasses, dried thyme, allspice, salt, and oil to bind everything together. We coated the chicken with some of this paste before cooking and saved the rest for basting later on. Following a slow braise in the slow cooker, after which the chicken was tender but still intact, we finished it under the broiler, basting it with more of the paste until it was lightly charred and crisp. If you can't find habanero chiles, substitute 2 to 4 jalapeño chiles. For even more heat, include the chile seeds.

8 scallions, chopped
¼ cup vegetable oil
2 habanero chiles, stemmed and seeded
1 (1-inch) piece ginger, peeled and sliced into
  ¼-inch-thick rounds

Our charred jerk chicken was so appealing that tasters questioned whether we had a grill hidden somewhere.

2 tablespoons molasses
3 garlic cloves, peeled
1 tablespoon dried thyme
2 teaspoons ground allspice
1 teaspoon salt
4 pounds bone-in chicken pieces (thighs
  and/or drumsticks), trimmed
  Lime wedges

1. Process scallions, oil, habaneros, ginger, molasses, garlic, thyme, allspice, and salt in food processor until smooth, about 30 seconds.

2. Lightly coat slow cooker with vegetable oil spray. Transfer ½ cup mixture to prepared slow cooker; reserve remaining mixture separately. Add chicken to slow cooker and turn to coat evenly with scallion mixture. Cover and cook until chicken is tender, 4 to 5 hours on low.

3. Adjust oven rack 6 inches from broiler element and heat broiler. Set wire rack in aluminum foil–lined rimmed baking sheet and coat with vegetable oil spray. Transfer chicken to prepared rack; discard cooking liquid. Broil chicken until browned, about 10 minutes, flipping chicken halfway through broiling.

4. Brush chicken with half of reserved scallion mixture and continue to broil until lightly charred, about 5 minutes, flipping and brushing chicken with remaining scallion mixture halfway through broiling. Serve with lime wedges.

PREPARING CHILES SAFELY

Wear gloves when working with very hot peppers like habaneros to avoid direct contact with oils that supply heat. Wash your hands, knife, and cutting board well after prepping chiles.

Huli Huli Chicken

SERVES 4
COOKING TIME 4 TO 5 HOURS ON LOW
SLOW COOKER SIZE 4 TO 7 QUARTS

WHY THIS RECIPE WORKS We wanted to create a slow-cooker version of this Hawaiian chicken, with its tropical flavor and mahogany coating. The chicken's deep color gets a little help from a salty-sweet sauce (called *huli huli*), which contains brown sugar, ketchup, and soy sauce. Slow-cooker chicken emerges rather pale at the end of the cooking time, so we knew we'd have to finish the chicken under the broiler to get the level of caramelization we were seeking. Precooking the sauce on the stovetop was ideal, as it thickened the mixture and concentrated its flavor. To balance the intensity of the soy sauce, we added pineapple juice and lime juice, which provided sweetness and acidity, while fresh garlic and ginger rounded things out. We added half of our sauce to the slow cooker to infuse flavor into the chicken as it braised. Basting the chicken with the remaining sauce while finishing it under the broiler enabled us to achieve a traditional-looking mahogany lacquer.

⅔ cup pineapple juice
½ cup packed brown sugar
½ cup ketchup
¼ cup lime juice (2 limes)
¼ cup soy sauce
6 garlic cloves, minced
2 tablespoons grated fresh ginger
4 (10-ounce) chicken leg quarters, trimmed
   Salt and pepper

Precooking the sweet-salty huli huli sauce is the key to keeping it from becoming too diluted in the slow cooker.

1. Bring pineapple juice, sugar, ketchup, lime juice, soy sauce, garlic, and ginger to simmer in medium saucepan over medium heat and cook until thickened and measures 1 cup, 15 to 20 minutes.

2. Lightly coat slow cooker with vegetable oil spray. Transfer ½ cup sauce to prepared slow cooker; reserve remaining sauce separately. Season chicken with salt and pepper, add to slow cooker, and turn to coat evenly with sauce. Cover and cook until chicken is tender, 4 to 5 hours on low.

3. Adjust oven rack 6 inches from broiler element and heat broiler. Set wire rack in aluminum foil–lined rimmed baking sheet and coat with vegetable oil spray. Transfer chicken to prepared rack; discard cooking liquid. Broil chicken until browned, about 10 minutes, flipping chicken halfway through broiling.

4. Brush chicken with ¼ cup reserved sauce and continue to broil until chicken is lightly charred, about 5 minutes, flipping and brushing chicken with remaining ¼ cup sauce halfway through broiling. Serve.

Chicken Cacciatore

SERVES 4 `LIGHT`

COOKING TIME 4 TO 5 HOURS ON LOW
SLOW COOKER SIZE 4 TO 7 QUARTS

WHY THIS RECIPE WORKS A combination of sliced cremini mushrooms and diced tomatoes made a great start to a rustic Cacciatore sauce for bone-in chicken thighs, but it still needed some work. We wanted a sauce that would cling to the chicken and lightly coat a bed of noodles or rice. Instead, by the end of cooking, the mushrooms, tomatoes, and chicken had released so much liquid that the sauce was thin, watery, and dull. To cut back on moisture, first we switched from diced tomatoes to crushed, which still gave us great simmered tomato flavor but added a lot less moisture. Then, we briefly sautéed the mushrooms along with the aromatics to release their moisture. A dose of fresh parsley added at the end contributed a bright note and rounded out the hearty flavors of this rustic meal.

1 tablespoon extra-virgin olive oil
1 pound cremini mushrooms, trimmed and quartered
1 onion, chopped fine
  Salt and pepper
¼ cup tomato paste
¼ ounce dried porcini mushrooms, rinsed and minced
4 garlic cloves, minced
2 teaspoons dried oregano
½ teaspoon red pepper flakes
½ cup dry red wine
1 (28-ounce) can crushed tomatoes
8 (5- to 7-ounce) bone-in chicken thighs, skin removed, trimmed
2 tablespoons minced fresh parsley
1 tablespoon red wine vinegar

1. Heat oil in 12-inch skillet over medium heat until shimmering. Add cremini mushrooms, onion, and ¼ teaspoon salt, cover, and cook until vegetables are softened and mushrooms have released their liquid, about 5 minutes. Uncover and continue to cook until vegetables are dry and lightly browned, 5 to 7 minutes. Stir in tomato paste, porcini mushrooms, garlic, oregano, and pepper flakes and cook until fragrant, about 30 seconds. Stir in wine, scraping up any browned bits; transfer to slow cooker.

2. Stir tomatoes into slow cooker. Season chicken with salt and pepper and nestle into slow cooker. Cover and cook until chicken is tender, 4 to 5 hours on low.

3. Transfer chicken to serving dish. Stir parsley and vinegar into sauce and season with salt and pepper to taste. Spoon 1 cup sauce over chicken. Serve, passing remaining sauce separately.

SIMPLE SIDES

CREAMY PARMESAN POLENTA

SERVES 4 TO 6

Coarse-ground degerminated cornmeal such as yellow grits (with uniform grains the size of couscous) works best in this recipe. Avoid instant or quick-cooking products, as well as whole-grain, stone-ground, and regular cornmeal. Do not omit the baking soda—it reduces the cooking time and makes for a creamier polenta. This recipe can easily be doubled in a Dutch oven.

7½ cups water
  Salt and pepper
  Pinch baking soda
1½ cups coarse-ground cornmeal
2 ounces Parmesan cheese, grated (1 cup)
2 tablespoons extra-virgin olive oil

1. Bring water to boil in large saucepan over medium-high heat. Stir in 1½ teaspoons salt and baking soda. Slowly pour cornmeal into water in steady stream while stirring back and forth with wooden spoon or rubber spatula. Bring mixture to boil, stirring constantly, about 1 minute. Reduce heat to lowest setting and cover.

2. After 5 minutes, whisk polenta to smooth out any lumps that may have formed, about 15 seconds. (Make sure to scrape down sides and along bottom of saucepan.) Cover and continue to cook, without stirring, until polenta grains are tender but slightly al dente, about 25 minutes longer. (Polenta should be loose and barely hold its shape; it will continue to thicken as it cools.)

3. Off heat, stir in Parmesan and oil, and season with pepper to taste. Cover and let sit for 5 minutes. Serve.

Kimchi-Braised Chicken Thighs

SERVES 4 `EASY PREP` `LIGHT`

COOKING TIME 4 TO 5 HOURS ON LOW
SLOW COOKER SIZE 4 TO 7 QUARTS

WHY THIS RECIPE WORKS This Korean-inspired dish came together quickly and highlighted the spicy flavor of kimchi (a fermented Korean condiment made from cabbage). The strong flavor of kimchi matched well with chicken thighs, which are fattier and meatier than breasts. We reinforced the Asian flavors by making a broth boosted by scallions, garlic, soy sauce, sugar, sesame oil, and fresh ginger. To get the most flavor from the kimchi and prevent it from tasting washed out, we added it toward the end of cooking.

1 cup chicken broth

4 scallions, white and green parts separated
and sliced thin

6 garlic cloves, minced

2 tablespoons instant tapioca

1 tablespoon soy sauce

1 tablespoon sugar

1 tablespoon toasted sesame oil

1 teaspoon grated fresh ginger

8 (5- to 7-ounce) bone-in chicken thighs,
skin removed, trimmed
Pepper

2 cups cabbage kimchi, drained and chopped coarse

1. Combine broth, scallion whites, garlic, tapioca, soy sauce, sugar, oil, and ginger in slow cooker. Season chicken with pepper and nestle into slow cooker. Cover and cook until chicken is tender, 4 to 5 hours on low.

2. Stir in kimchi, cover, and cook on high until tender, 20 to 30 minutes. Transfer chicken and kimchi to serving dish. Spoon 1 cup sauce over chicken and sprinkle with scallion greens. Serve, passing remaining sauce separately.

Chicken Thighs with Swiss Chard and Mustard

SERVES 4 EASY PREP LIGHT

COOKING TIME 4 TO 5 HOURS ON LOW

SLOW COOKER SIZE 5 TO 7 QUARTS

WHY THIS RECIPE WORKS Tender chicken, spicy mustard, and earthy Swiss chard are a great combination for a warming winter supper. Quick-cooking Swiss chard may not seem like a good match for the slow cooker, but we found that we could add it for just the last 30 minutes of cooking and get it perfectly crisp-tender without dirtying an extra pot. To complement the slightly bitter chard, we wanted a rich, mustardy sauce. We found that a combination of dry and whole-grain mustard was the key to getting the right amount of mustard flavor. Dry mustard added to the slow cooker at the beginning of cooking infused the chicken with a subtle flavor, and finishing the sauce with bold whole-grain mustard punched up its acidity. Onion, garlic, and some thyme rounded out the dish's flavors.

1 onion, chopped fine

4 garlic cloves, minced

1 tablespoon vegetable oil

1 teaspoon dry mustard

We use both dry mustard and whole-grain mustard in this dish to create the best flavor.

2 teaspoons minced fresh thyme or
½ teaspoon dried

8 (5- to 7-ounce) bone-in chicken thighs,
skin removed, trimmed
Salt and pepper

2 pounds Swiss chard, stemmed and cut
into 1-inch pieces

2 tablespoons whole-grain mustard

1. Microwave onion, garlic, oil, dry mustard, and thyme in bowl, stirring occasionally, until onion is softened, about 5 minutes; transfer to slow cooker. Season chicken with salt and pepper and nestle into slow cooker. Cover and cook until chicken is tender, 4 to 5 hours on low.

2. Transfer chicken to plate. Stir chard, 1 handful at a time, into slow cooker. Arrange chicken evenly on top of chard, adding any accumulated juices. Cover and cook on high until chard is wilted, 20 to 30 minutes.

3. Transfer chicken to serving dish. Stir whole-grain mustard into Swiss chard and season with salt and pepper to taste. Serve.

Arranging the squash along the bottom of the slow cooker ensures that the large wedges are perfectly cooked.

Curried Chicken Thighs with Acorn Squash

SERVES 4 `EASY PREP` `LIGHT`
COOKING TIME 4 TO 5 HOURS ON LOW
SLOW COOKER SIZE 5 TO 7 QUARTS

WHY THIS RECIPE WORKS Meaty chicken thighs are a perfect match for the slow cooker, as they become meltingly tender in its moist heat environment. Here we opted to pair them with wedges of acorn squash, which are hearty enough to withstand a few hours in the slow cooker and still hold their shape. To give this dish a distinct flavor profile we rubbed the chicken with curry powder that we had bloomed in the microwave with a little bit of oil. To finish, we microwaved a mixture of honey and cayenne, to which we added lime juice, then drizzled the mixture over the chicken and squash. This simple step tied together the flavors of this easy one-dish meal. You will need an oval slow cooker for this recipe.

2 small acorn squashes (1 pound each),
   quartered pole to pole and seeded
1 tablespoon vegetable oil
2 teaspoons curry powder

½ teaspoon salt
¼ teaspoon pepper
8 (5- to 7-ounce) bone-in chicken thighs,
   skin removed, trimmed
3 tablespoons honey
⅛ teaspoon cayenne pepper
1 tablespoon lime juice
¼ cup fresh cilantro leaves

1. Shingle squash wedges, cut side down, into slow cooker, then add ½ cup water. Microwave oil, curry powder, salt, and pepper in bowl until fragrant, about 30 seconds; let cool slightly. Rub chicken with curry mixture and arrange in single layer on top of squash. Cover and cook until chicken is tender, 4 to 5 hours on low.

2. Transfer chicken and squash to serving dish; discard cooking liquid. Microwave honey and cayenne in bowl until heated through, about 30 seconds. Stir in lime juice. Drizzle chicken and squash with honey mixture and sprinkle with cilantro. Serve.

PREPARING ACORN SQUASH

1. Set squash on damp dish towel to hold in place. Position chef's knife on top of squash and strike with mallet to drive it into squash. Continue to hit knife with mallet until it cuts completely through squash.

2. After scooping out seeds with spoon, place squash halves cut side down on cutting board and cut in half, pole to pole, using mallet if necessary.

Lemony Chicken and Rice with Spinach and Feta

SERVES 4 `EASY PREP`
COOKING TIME 4 TO 5 HOURS ON LOW
SLOW COOKER SIZE 4 TO 7 QUARTS

WHY THIS RECIPE WORKS For a chicken and rice dinner that was big on flavor but light on prep, we looked to the Mediterranean for inspiration. We included feta for its briny tang, lemon for its brightness, and baby spinach for freshness and color. To start, we microwaved simple aromatics to bloom and develop their flavor

1. Microwave onion, oil, garlic, oregano, and ½ teaspoon salt in bowl, stirring occasionally, until onion is softened, about 5 minutes; transfer to slow cooker. Stir in broth. Season chicken with salt and pepper and nestle into slow cooker. Cover and cook until chicken is tender, 4 to 5 hours on low.

2. Transfer chicken to plate. Stir rice into slow cooker. Arrange chicken on top of rice, adding any accumulated juices. Cover and cook on high until rice is tender, 20 to 30 minutes.

3. Transfer chicken to serving dish and tent loosely with aluminum foil. Gently stir spinach into slow cooker, 1 handful at a time, and let sit until wilted, about 5 minutes. Stir in lemon zest and juice, and season with salt and pepper to taste. Transfer rice to dish with chicken and sprinkle with feta and parsley. Serve.

NOTES FROM THE TEST KITCHEN

Instant Rice

While we aren't very impressed with how instant rice tastes on its own, it is the perfect choice for slow-cooker rice-based dishes. By comparison, raw long-grain white rice cooked very unevenly, while precooked homemade rice and packaged fully cooked rice retained their distinct texture and didn't bind well. Not only did instant rice cook very evenly, but its slightly starchy texture helped to thicken soups and stews and to bind casseroles together.

Chicken Thighs with Black-Eyed Pea Ragout

SERVES 4 LIGHT
COOKING TIME 4 TO 5 HOURS ON LOW
SLOW COOKER SIZE 5 TO 7 QUARTS

WHY THIS RECIPE WORKS Juicy chicken, tender black-eyed peas, and earthy kale are a great combination for a healthy and comforting supper. Sturdy kale is a perfect match for the slow cooker; after a quick spin in the microwave (along with onion, garlic, and oil) it could be added to the slow cooker to fully soften and cook through. To complement the bitter kale we wanted rich, slightly spicy black-eyed peas. We found that a combination of dry mustard and hot sauce was the key to getting the right balance between heat and spice. Dry mustard added to the slow cooker at the beginning of cooking infused the chicken with a subtle flavor, and finishing the peas with hot sauce punched up the heat and acidity of the dish. Pureeing a portion of the peas also helped to thicken the juices released from the chicken during cooking.

We dress up quiet chicken and rice with bright Mediterranean flavors.

before adding them to the slow cooker. We then added meaty bone-in chicken thighs for their deep flavor and cooked them on low to tender perfection. Once the chicken was cooked, we removed the thighs and stirred in instant rice, then nestled the chicken on top and continued to cook just until the rice was cooked through. Be sure to use instant rice (sometimes labeled minute rice); traditional rice takes much longer to cook and won't work here.

- 1 onion, chopped fine
- 2 tablespoons extra-virgin olive oil
- 3 garlic cloves, minced
- 2 teaspoons minced fresh oregano or ½ teaspoon dried
  Salt and pepper
- ½ cup chicken broth
- 8 (5- to 7-ounce) bone-in chicken thighs, skin removed, trimmed
- 1½ cups instant white rice
- 4 ounces (4 cups) baby spinach
- 1 teaspoon grated lemon zest plus 2 tablespoons juice
- 2 ounces feta cheese, crumbled (½ cup)
- 2 tablespoons minced fresh parsley

- 1 pound kale, stemmed and chopped coarse
- 1 onion, chopped fine
- 4 garlic cloves, minced
- 1 tablespoon vegetable oil
- 1 teaspoon dry mustard
- 2 teaspoons minced fresh thyme or ½ teaspoon dried
- ½ cup chicken broth
- 2 (15-ounce) cans black-eyed peas, rinsed
- 8 (5- to 7-ounce) bone-in chicken thighs, skin removed, trimmed
    Salt and pepper
- 2 teaspoons hot sauce

1. Microwave kale, onion, garlic, oil, mustard, and thyme in covered bowl, stirring occasionally, until vegetables are softened, 5 to 7 minutes; transfer to slow cooker.

2. Process broth and one-third of peas in food processor until smooth, about 30 seconds; transfer to slow cooker. Stir in remaining peas. Season chicken with salt and pepper and nestle into slow cooker. Cover and cook until chicken is tender, 4 to 5 hours on low.

3. Transfer chicken to serving dish. Stir hot sauce into ragout and season with salt and pepper to taste. Serve chicken with ragout.

Coq au Vin

SERVES 4

COOKING TIME 4 TO 5 HOURS ON LOW

SLOW COOKER SIZE 5 TO 7 QUARTS

WHY THIS RECIPE WORKS Julia Child put this dish (with all of the components cooked separately) on the American food map in the early 1960s. For an easier version made in the slow cooker, we first browned flavorful chicken thighs in a skillet and then transferred them to the slow cooker. Next, we crisped bacon in the skillet and set it aside so that it would still be crispy when we added it back at the end of cooking. Though we discarded most of the fat from the chicken and bacon to control greasiness, we used a bit of it to help build a quick sauce, sautéing mushrooms in 4 tablespoons of the combined fat before adding tomato paste, garlic, and flour to the skillet. Just 1¾ cups of dry red wine was all we needed to finish our sauce, along with thyme to add some depth. After a few hours on low, our slow-cooker Coq au Vin was ready to finish with minced fresh parsley and pieces of crispy bacon.

- 8 (5- to 7-ounce) bone-in chicken thighs, trimmed
    Salt and pepper
- 1 tablespoon vegetable oil

To develop intense flavor, we sauté mushrooms in bacon fat to start our quick sauce.

- 1 cup frozen pearl onions
- 4 slices thick-cut bacon, cut into 1-inch pieces
- 10 ounces cremini mushrooms, trimmed and quartered
- ¼ cup all-purpose flour
- 1 tablespoon tomato paste
- 2 garlic cloves, minced
- 2 teaspoons minced fresh thyme or ½ teaspoon dried
- 1¾ cups dry red wine
- 2 tablespoons minced fresh parsley

1. Pat chicken dry with paper towels and season with salt and pepper. Heat oil in 12-inch skillet over medium-high heat until just smoking. Cook half of chicken, skin side down, until well browned, 7 to 10 minutes. Transfer chicken, skin side up, to slow cooker; repeat with remaining chicken. Add onions to slow cooker.

2. Reserve chicken fat left in skillet. Add bacon to now-empty skillet and cook over medium heat until crisp, 5 to 7 minutes. Using slotted spoon, transfer bacon to paper towel–lined bowl; set aside until ready to serve.

3. Pour off all but ¼ cup fat left in skillet. If necessary, add reserved chicken fat to equal ¼ cup. Add mushrooms and cook until softened and well browned, 5 to 7 minutes. Stir in flour, tomato paste, garlic, and thyme and cook until fragrant, about 1 minute. Slowly whisk in wine, scraping up any browned bits and smoothing out any lumps. Bring to simmer and cook until thickened and spatula leaves trail in sauce, about 2 minutes; transfer to slow cooker. Cover and cook until chicken is tender, 4 to 5 hours on low.

4. Transfer chicken to serving dish. Using large spoon, skim excess fat from surface of sauce. Season with salt and pepper to taste. Spoon 1 cup sauce over chicken and sprinkle with reserved bacon and parsley. Serve, passing remaining sauce separately.

NOTES FROM THE TEST KITCHEN

Buying Bacon

Good bacon is meaty, smoky, salty, and sweet; it has what industry experts call "balanced bacon flavor." To find the best, we tasted six thick strips (based partly on actual thickness rather than labels, since some fatter slices weren't identified as such) and four traditional slices from nationally available supermarket brands (choosing both styles from the same brand when possible). We highly recommend two thick-cut bacons, **Farmland Thick Sliced Bacon** and **Plumrose Premium Thick Sliced Bacon**, and one traditional bacon, **Oscar Mayer Naturally Hardwood Smoked Bacon**. The thick-cut Farmland strip was the meatiest strip we tried, with its saltiness nicely offset by its sweetness. The Plumrose bacon was "pleasantly smoky and substantially meaty." Tasters described the traditional slice of Oscar Mayer bacon as having "a nice ratio of fat to lean meat," and being "perfect in terms of crispness."

Southern Smothered Chicken

SERVES 4

COOKING TIME 4 TO 5 HOURS ON LOW

SLOW COOKER SIZE 4 TO 7 QUARTS

WHY THIS RECIPE WORKS The traditional Southern style of "smothered" chicken involves cooking the chicken low-and-slow in a rich gravy. Too often, though, versions of smothered chicken taste like whatever else is in the dish, rather than the chicken itself. But smothered chicken is designed to coax out as much flavor as possible from the chicken, and the slow cooker is the perfect tool for the job. To start, we tossed chicken thighs in flour and browned them in batches to render some fat and build a base of flavor. Once the chicken was browned, we moved it to the slow cooker and used some of the residual fat to sauté the aromatic ingredients for the sauce. A simple mix of onion, celery, garlic, and sage gave a clean, savory base that enhanced the rich chicken flavor. Achieving the right consistency for the sauce took some tinkering. In the end, we found that just 1 cup of chicken broth with 2 tablespoons of flour made for a velvety rich sauce, and was plenty to smother the chicken for serving. Once the sauce was added to the slow cooker, we cooked everything until the chicken was tender and our sauce was deeply flavorful. This simple braise may not be flashy, but its robust chicken flavor, brought to life in the slow cooker, is deeply satisfying.

8 (5- to 7-ounce) bone-in chicken thighs, trimmed
   Salt and pepper
½ cup plus 2 tablespoons all-purpose flour
¼ cup vegetable oil
2 onions, chopped fine
2 celery ribs, chopped fine
3 garlic cloves, minced
1 tablespoon minced fresh sage or 1 teaspoon dried
1 cup chicken broth
1 tablespoon cider vinegar
1 tablespoon minced fresh parsley

1. Pat chicken dry with paper towels and season with salt and pepper. Spread ½ cup flour in shallow dish. Working with 1 piece at a time, dredge chicken in flour, shaking off excess, and transfer to plate.

2. Heat oil in 12-inch skillet over medium-high heat until just smoking. Cook half of chicken until deep golden brown, 4 to 6 minutes per side. Transfer chicken, skin side up, to slow cooker; repeat with remaining chicken, adjusting heat as needed if flour begins to burn.

3. Pour off all but 2 tablespoons fat from skillet. Add onions, celery, 1 teaspoon salt, and ½ teaspoon pepper and cook over medium heat until vegetables are softened, about 8 minutes. Stir in garlic, sage, and remaining 2 tablespoons flour and cook until fragrant, about 1 minute. Slowly whisk in broth, scraping up any browned bits and smoothing any lumps; transfer to slow cooker. Cover and cook until chicken is tender, 4 to 5 hours on low.

4. Transfer chicken to serving dish. Using large spoon, skim excess fat from surface of sauce. Stir in vinegar and parsley, and season with salt and pepper to taste. Spoon 1 cup sauce over chicken. Serve, passing remaining sauce separately.

The homemade barbecue sauce for our pulled chicken starts in the microwave.

Sweet and Tangy Pulled Chicken

SERVES 4 `EASY PREP` `LIGHT`
COOKING TIME 2 TO 3 HOURS ON LOW
SLOW COOKER SIZE 4 TO 7 QUARTS

WHY THIS RECIPE WORKS A simple spice mixture and a quick homemade barbecue sauce made it easy to turn slow-cooked bone-in chicken into tangy, silky, shredded chicken—perfect for piling onto buns for an easy dinner. Quickly microwaving the aromatics together with the chili powder, paprika, and cayenne softened the onions and infused them with layers of barbecue flavor while at the same time blooming the spices. We found that simply seasoning the chicken with salt and pepper before nestling the breasts into our quick sauce mixture of ketchup, molasses, and the aromatics was enough to infuse the chicken with the rich essence of the sauce. Stirring in vinegar at the beginning of cooking made the sauce too thin and dulled its acidity, but adding 2 tablespoons of vinegar at the end of cooking, along with a small amount of mustard, ensured that the sauce was the perfect consistency and retained its bright flavors.

Check the chicken's temperature after 2 hours of cooking and continue to monitor until it registers 160 degrees. Serve with pickle chips and Sweet and Tangy Coleslaw (page 148).

- 1 onion, chopped fine
- ¼ cup tomato paste
- 1 tablespoon chili powder
- 1 tablespoon vegetable oil
- 1 teaspoon paprika
  Salt and pepper
- ⅛ teaspoon cayenne pepper
- ¼ cup ketchup
- 2 tablespoons molasses
- 2 (12-ounce) bone-in split chicken breasts, skin removed, trimmed
- 2 tablespoons cider vinegar
- 2 teaspoons Dijon mustard
- 4 hamburger buns

1. Lightly coat slow cooker with vegetable oil spray. Microwave onion, tomato paste, chili powder, oil, paprika, ½ teaspoon salt, ¼ teaspoon pepper, and cayenne in bowl, stirring occasionally, until onion is softened, about 5 minutes; transfer to prepared slow cooker. Stir in ketchup and molasses. Add chicken to slow cooker and coat evenly with sauce mixture. Cover and cook until chicken registers 160 degrees, 2 to 3 hours on low.

2. Transfer chicken to cutting board, let cool slightly, then shred into bite-size pieces using 2 forks; discard bones. Stir vinegar and mustard into sauce. Adjust consistency with hot water as needed. Stir in chicken and season with salt and pepper to taste. Serve on hamburger buns.

Tomatillo Chicken Soft Tacos

SERVES 4 TO 6 `EASY PREP` `LIGHT`
COOKING TIME 4 TO 5 HOURS ON LOW
SLOW COOKER SIZE 4 TO 7 QUARTS

WHY THIS RECIPE WORKS To make great chicken soft tacos, we needed a tender, flavorful chicken filling. Cooking chicken in tomatillo salsa flavored the chicken in a big way without the involved prep of using fresh tomatillos. Fresh poblano chile peppers lent a little heat to the sauce and created a more complex flavor profile than salsa alone. We found that boneless chicken thighs worked best here; after 4 to 5 hours in the slow cooker they were meltingly tender and could be shredded easily. Finishing with a little lime juice and cilantro added fresh flavor. Jarred tomatillo salsa is also called *salsa verde*. We don't discard any of the cooking liquid so as

We create a flavorful cooking liquid for boneless, skinless chicken thighs using store-bought salsa verde.

to help season the chicken and keep the filling moist; a slotted spoon works best for serving the filling. Serve with lime wedges, diced avocado, queso fresco, and/or sour cream.

1 cup jarred tomatillo salsa
2 poblano chiles, stemmed, seeded, and chopped
  Salt and pepper
1 teaspoon minced fresh oregano or ¼ teaspoon dried
3 pounds boneless, skinless chicken thighs, trimmed
¼ cup minced fresh cilantro
2 tablespoons lime juice
12–18 (6-inch) flour tortillas, warmed

1. Combine salsa, poblanos, ¼ teaspoon salt, ¼ teaspoon pepper, and oregano in slow cooker. Season chicken with salt and pepper and nestle into slow cooker. Cover and cook until chicken is tender, 4 to 5 hours on low.

2. Using tongs, break chicken into bite-size pieces. Stir in cilantro and lime juice, and season with salt and pepper to taste. Serve with warmed tortillas.

Warming Tortillas

ON THE STOVETOP When warming tortillas on the stovetop, work with one tortilla at a time. For a gas stove, place the tortilla over a medium flame until slightly charred, about 30 seconds per side. For an electric stove, toast the tortilla in a skillet over medium-high heat until it is softened and speckled with brown spots, 20 to 30 seconds per side. Transfer the toasted tortillas to a plate and cover with a dish towel to keep them warm.

IN THE OVEN Wrap up to six tortillas in aluminum foil and place them in a 350-degree oven for about 5 minutes. To warm more than six tortillas, divide them into multiple foil packets. To keep the tortillas warm, simply leave them wrapped in foil until ready to use.

Chicken Curry

SERVES 6 TO 8
COOKING TIME 4 TO 5 HOURS ON LOW
SLOW COOKER SIZE 4 TO 7 QUARTS

WHY THIS RECIPE WORKS Curries are especially well suited to the slow cooker. When the ingredients have the opportunity to cook for hours, the flavors meld and the result is a deeply flavorful and complex dish. To pack the most flavor into our curry, we focused on the essentials: curry powder, garlic, ginger, chiles, and garam masala, and bloomed them in oil in the microwave before adding them to the slow cooker. Creamy, slightly nutty chickpeas and hearty cauliflower worked well with the flavors of the curry and accented the mild flavor of the chicken. With the steady heat of the slow cooker, the vegetables and chicken cooked to tender perfection in the same rate of time without the worry of overcooking. For additional thickening power, we added instant tapioca to the slow cooker along with the chicken broth. Yogurt tempered into the stew after cooking helped balance its heat and added velvety richness.

2 onions, chopped fine
1 jalapeño chile, stemmed, seeded, and minced
3 tablespoons vegetable oil
6 garlic cloves, minced
2 tablespoons grated fresh ginger
2 tablespoons curry powder
1 tablespoon tomato paste
1 teaspoon garam masala

We found that instant tapioca is an easy way to thicken the sauce in this chicken curry.

    Salt and pepper
 1 (15-ounce) can chickpeas, rinsed
 ½ head cauliflower (1 pound), cored and
    cut into 1-inch florets
 1 (14.5-ounce) can diced tomatoes, drained
 ½ cup chicken broth
 1 tablespoon instant tapioca
 2 pounds boneless, skinless chicken thighs, trimmed
 1 cup plain whole-milk yogurt
 1 cup frozen peas, thawed
 ¼ cup minced fresh cilantro
    Lime wedges

1. Microwave onions, jalapeño, oil, garlic, ginger, curry powder, tomato paste, garam masala, and 1 teaspoon salt in bowl, stirring occasionally, until vegetables are softened, about 5 minutes; transfer to slow cooker. Stir in chickpeas, cauliflower, tomatoes, broth, and tapioca. Season chicken with salt and pepper and nestle into slow cooker. Cover and cook until chicken is tender, 4 to 5 hours on low.

2. Transfer chicken to cutting board, let cool slightly, then shred into bite-size pieces using 2 forks.

3. Whisk ½ cup cooking liquid and yogurt together in bowl (to temper), then stir mixture back into slow cooker. Stir in chicken and peas and let sit until heated through, about 5 minutes. Stir in cilantro and season with salt and pepper to taste. Serve with lime wedges.

CUTTING CAULIFLOWER INTO FLORETS

1. Pull off any leaves, then cut out core of cauliflower using paring knife.

2. Separate florets from inner stem using tip of paring knife.

3. Cut larger florets into smaller pieces by slicing through stem.

Braised Chicken Sausages with White Bean Ragout
SERVES 4   **EASY PREP**
COOKING TIME 3 TO 4 HOURS ON LOW
SLOW COOKER SIZE 4 TO 7 QUARTS

WHY THIS RECIPE WORKS For this hearty winter braise, a simple combination of sausage, beans, and rosemary is transformed into a rich, warming bean ragout by the gentle simmer of the slow cooker. For the main components of the dish, we chose delicately flavored cannellini beans and Italian chicken sausage, which was full of spices like fennel and caraway that would flavor the dish. We combined broth, wine, minced garlic, and rosemary for a flavorful cooking liquid that would season the beans as they cooked. Cherry tomatoes

Flavorful Italian chicken sausages are the centerpiece of this rustic one-dish meal.

added a pop of bright color and fresh flavor. Once the sausage was cooked and the beans were tender, we mashed a portion of the beans and tomatoes together to help thicken the ragout. Stirring in some baby spinach right before serving brightened up this comforting dish. Italian turkey sausage can be substituted for the chicken sausage.

  2 (15-ounce) cans cannellini beans, rinsed
  ¼ cup chicken broth
  ¼ cup dry white wine
  2 garlic cloves, minced
  1 sprig fresh rosemary
     Salt and pepper
1½ pounds hot or sweet Italian chicken sausage
  8 ounces cherry tomatoes
  4 ounces (4 cups) baby spinach
  2 tablespoons extra-virgin olive oil

1. Combine beans, broth, wine, garlic, rosemary sprig, ½ teaspoon salt, and ½ teaspoon pepper in slow cooker. Nestle sausage into slow cooker and top with tomatoes. Cover and cook until sausage is tender, 3 to 4 hours on low.

2. Transfer sausage to serving dish and tent loosely with aluminum foil. Discard rosemary sprig. Transfer 1 cup bean-tomato mixture to bowl and mash with potato masher until mostly smooth.

3. Stir spinach, 1 handful at a time, and mashed bean mixture into slow cooker and let sit until spinach is wilted, about 5 minutes. Stir in oil and season with salt and pepper to taste. Serve sausages with ragout.

Italian Braised Turkey Sausages

SERVES 4 `LIGHT`
COOKING TIME 3 TO 4 HOURS ON LOW
SLOW COOKER SIZE 5 TO 7 QUARTS

WHY THIS RECIPE WORKS For this hearty dinner, a combination of sausage, peppers, onions, and potatoes is transformed into a satisfying meal by the gentle and moist heat of the slow cooker. For the main components, we chose creamy red potatoes, bell peppers, onions, and Italian turkey sausage, which is packed with spices like fennel and caraway that would flavor the dish. We microwaved tomato paste, garlic, oregano, and red pepper flakes with the vegetables, both to give the potatoes, peppers, and onions a head start and to infuse them with layers of flavor. Some fresh basil stirred in right before serving brightened up this dish. Italian chicken sausage can be substituted for the turkey sausage.

 12 ounces red potatoes, unpeeled, quartered and
     sliced ¼ inch thick
  3 red or green bell peppers, stemmed, seeded,
     and cut into ¼-inch-wide strips
  1 onion, halved and sliced ½ inch thick
  ¼ cup tomato paste
  2 tablespoons water
  3 garlic cloves, minced
  2 teaspoons minced fresh oregano or ½ teaspoon dried
  ¼ teaspoon red pepper flakes
  ¼ cup chicken broth
1½ pounds hot or sweet Italian turkey sausage
  2 tablespoons chopped fresh basil
     Salt and pepper

1. Microwave potatoes, bell peppers, onion, tomato paste, water, garlic, oregano, and pepper flakes in covered bowl, stirring occasionally, until vegetables are almost tender, about 15 minutes; transfer to slow cooker. Stir in broth. Nestle sausage into slow cooker, cover, and cook until sausage and vegetables are tender, 3 to 4 hours on low.

2. Transfer sausage to serving dish. Stir basil into vegetable mixture and season with salt and pepper to taste. Spoon vegetable mixture over sausage. Serve.

STEAKS, CHOPS, RIBS, AND MORE

■ EASY PREP   ■ LIGHT   ■ COOK ALL DAY
Photo: Classic Barbecued Spareribs

A little heavy cream, stirred into the sauce left behind in the slow cooker, enriches these beefy blade steaks.

Braised Steaks with Mushrooms and Onions

SERVES 4 `ALL DAY`

COOKING TIME 8 TO 9 HOURS ON LOW OR 5 TO 6 HOURS ON HIGH

SLOW COOKER SIZE 4 TO 7 QUARTS

WHY THIS RECIPE WORKS This dish promises meltingly tender blade steaks smothered in a sauce of sweet onions and earthy mushrooms, a combination that works perfectly in the slow cooker. To get the deep, robust flavor we were after, we browned the onions (to bring out their natural sweetness) and the mushrooms (to deepen their inherent earthiness), and added flour as a thickener and a splash of sherry to deglaze the pan and complement the flavors of the onions and mushrooms. After hours in the slow cooker the steaks melded with the onions and mushrooms, turning fork-tender and rich-tasting. To finish the dish, we added a bit of cream to round out the flavors, and some parsley for freshness. You can substitute an equal amount of beef flat-iron steaks, if desired.

1 tablespoon vegetable oil
1 pound white mushrooms, trimmed and sliced ¼ inch thick
1 onion, halved and sliced thin
  Salt and pepper
¼ cup all-purpose flour
1 tablespoon minced fresh thyme or 1 teaspoon dried
1½ teaspoons paprika
¾ cup chicken broth
¼ cup dry sherry
4 (6- to 8-ounce) beef blade steaks, ¾ to 1 inch thick, trimmed
¼ cup heavy cream
2 tablespoons minced fresh parsley

1. Heat oil in 12-inch skillet over medium heat until shimmering. Add mushrooms, onion, and ¼ teaspoon salt, cover, and cook until vegetables are softened and mushrooms have released their liquid, about 5 minutes. Uncover and continue to cook until vegetables are dry and lightly browned, 5 to 7 minutes. Stir in flour, thyme, and paprika and cook until fragrant, about 1 minute. Slowly stir in broth and sherry, scraping up any browned bits and smoothing out any lumps; transfer to slow cooker.

2. Season steaks with salt and pepper and nestle into slow cooker. Cover and cook until beef is tender and fork slips easily in and out of meat, 8 to 9 hours on low or 5 to 6 hours on high.

3. Transfer steaks to serving dish. Using large spoon, skim fat from surface of sauce. Stir in cream and parsley and season with salt and pepper to taste. Spoon 1 cup sauce over steaks and serve, passing remaining sauce separately.

Provençal Braised Steaks

SERVES 4 `EASY PREP` `ALL DAY`

COOKING TIME 8 TO 9 HOURS ON LOW OR 5 TO 6 HOURS ON HIGH

SLOW COOKER SIZE 4 TO 7 QUARTS

WHY THIS RECIPE WORKS We wanted to complement rich, tender braised steaks with a bright, aromatic tomato sauce. Blade steaks, a reasonably priced cut that turns meltingly tender when slow-cooked, had lots of meaty flavor. For a flavor-packed base for our sauce, we microwaved onions, tomato paste, garlic, anchovy, and red pepper flakes to bring out their flavors. We added this potent mixture to the slow cooker with the steaks; as the steaks cooked, their juices melded with the aromatics to create a deeply flavorful sauce. Once the meat was tender, we simply stirred in briny olives and capers and plenty of fresh parsley for a bright sauce that perfectly balanced the rich steak. You can substitute an equal amount of beef flat-iron steaks, if desired.

2 onions, chopped
6 garlic cloves, minced
2 tablespoons tomato paste
1 tablespoon extra-virgin olive oil
1 anchovy fillet, rinsed and minced
⅛ teaspoon red pepper flakes
4 (6- to 8-ounce) beef blade steaks,
   ¾ to 1 inch thick, trimmed
   Salt and pepper
½ cup pitted kalamata olives, halved
¼ cup minced fresh parsley
2 tablespoons capers, rinsed

1. Microwave onions, garlic, tomato paste, oil, anchovy, and pepper flakes in bowl, stirring occasionally, until onions are softened, about 5 minutes; transfer to slow cooker. Season steaks with salt and pepper and nestle into slow cooker. Cover and cook until beef is tender and fork slips easily in and out of meat, 8 to 9 hours on low or 5 to 6 hours on high.

2. Transfer steaks to serving dish. Using large spoon, skim fat from surface of sauce. Stir in olives, parsley, and capers, and season with salt and pepper to taste. Spoon sauce over steaks and serve.

Braised Steaks with Horseradish Smashed Potatoes

SERVES 4   **EASY PREP**   **ALL DAY**
COOKING TIME 8 TO 9 HOURS ON LOW OR 5 TO 6 HOURS ON HIGH
SLOW COOKER SIZE 5 TO 7 QUARTS

WHY THIS RECIPE WORKS Steak and smashed potatoes are a classic pairing that we wanted to bring to the slow cooker. We knew our biggest challenge would be getting the steak and potatoes to cook through in the same amount of time. The key to success turned out to be pairing the right-size potatoes to the cooking time of the steaks and arranging the potatoes above the steaks in order for them to cook through more gently. Once they were fully cooked, we smashed the potatoes with milk, cream cheese, butter, fresh chives, and spicy horseradish. We braised blade steaks in a mix of onions, garlic, and tomato paste until they were nearly fall-apart tender. To make the sauce, we simply defatted the braising liquid and then served it with the rich steak and creamy, tangy potatoes. Look for small red potatoes measuring 1 to 2 inches in diameter; if your potatoes are larger, cut them into 1-inch pieces to ensure that they cook through properly. Buy refrigerated prepared horseradish, not the shelf-stable kind, which contains preservatives and additives. You can substitute an equal amount of beef flat-iron steaks, if desired.

2 onions, chopped fine
6 garlic cloves, minced
2 tablespoons tomato paste
1 tablespoon vegetable oil
4 (6- to 8-ounce) beef blade steaks,
   ¾ to 1 inch thick, trimmed
   Salt and pepper
1½ pounds small red potatoes, unpeeled
¾ cup milk, warmed, plus extra as needed
2 ounces cream cheese, softened
3 tablespoons unsalted butter, melted
3 tablespoons prepared horseradish, drained
2 tablespoons minced fresh chives

1. Microwave onions, garlic, tomato paste, and oil in bowl, stirring occasionally, until onions are softened, about 5 minutes; transfer to slow cooker.

2. Season steaks with salt and pepper and nestle into slow cooker. Arrange potatoes on top of steaks. Cover and cook until beef and potatoes are tender and fork slips easily in and out of meat, 8 to 9 hours on low or 5 to 6 hours on high.

3. Using slotted spoon, transfer potatoes to large bowl. Transfer steaks to serving dish, tent loosely with aluminum foil, and let rest while finishing potatoes and jus.

4. Break potatoes into large chunks with back of large spoon. Fold in warm milk, cream cheese, melted butter, horseradish, and chives until incorporated and only small chunks of potato remain. Adjust potatoes' consistency with extra warm milk as needed. Using large spoon, skim fat from surface of jus. Season potatoes and jus with salt and pepper to taste. Spoon jus over steaks and serve with potatoes.

NOTES FROM THE TEST KITCHEN

Buying Blade Steaks

One of our favorite cuts for the slow cooker, this surprisingly tender steak is a small cut from the cow's shoulder, or chuck, where most other cuts are quite tough. Blade steaks are inexpensive because they have a line of gristle that runs down the middle, but when slow-cooked these steaks turn fall-apart tender and the gristle is easily removed, yielding a richly flavored, beefy steak.

Storing Meat Safely

Throwing away meat because it went bad before you had a chance to cook it is frustrating, particularly when you've spent a lot of money on a nice steak or cut of lamb. Proper storage is the best way to prolong its shelf life and prevent waste.

REFRIGERATING MEAT Raw meat should be refrigerated well wrapped and never on shelves that are above other food. Check regularly to ensure your refrigerator's temperature is between 35 and 40 degrees. Most raw and cooked meat will keep for two to three days in the refrigerator. Raw ground meat and raw poultry will keep for two days, while smoked ham and bacon will keep for up to two weeks.

FREEZING MEAT In general, meat tastes best when it hasn't been frozen. If you're going to freeze meat, wrap it well in plastic wrap and then place the meat in a zipper-lock bag and squeeze out excess air. Label the bag and use the meat within a few months.

THAWING MEAT All meat can be thawed safely on a plate or rimmed baking sheet in the refrigerator (and this is the only safe method for large cuts like whole chickens). Never thaw meat on the counter, where bacteria will rapidly multiply. According to the U.S. Department of Agriculture, frozen food that is properly thawed is safe to refreeze. However, a second freeze-thaw cycle aggravates moisture loss, reducing the quality of the meat, so we don't recommend it.

QUICK THAW FOR SMALL CUTS Flat cuts like chicken breasts, pork chops, and steaks will thaw more quickly when left on a metal surface rather than on a wood or a plastic one, because metal can transfer ambient heat much more quickly. To thaw frozen wrapped steaks, chops, or ground meat (flattened to 1 inch thick before freezing), place in a skillet (heavy steel and cast-iron skillets work best) in a single layer. Flip the meat every half-hour until it's thawed. Small cuts can also be sealed in zipper-lock bags and submerged in hot (140-degree) water—this method will safely thaw chicken breasts, steaks, and chops in under 15 minutes.

We "roast" the bones in the microwave, which removes unwanted fat and deepens the flavor of this classic braise.

Red Wine–Braised Short Ribs

SERVES 4   `ALL DAY`

COOKING TIME 8 TO 9 HOURS ON LOW OR 5 TO 6 HOURS ON HIGH

SLOW COOKER SIZE 5 TO 7 QUARTS

WHY THIS RECIPE WORKS Short ribs are all about the meat and the sauce, so to get a deeply flavored sauce, we first focused on the bones, which we knew were one key to flavor. Not wanting to roast the bones in the oven, we turned to the microwave, which helped in two ways: It rendered out unwanted fat (and short ribs are notoriously greasy), and it gave the bones a roasted flavor, which, in turn, deepened the sauce during the long cooking time. One taste of these long-cooked ribs with their dark, glossy sauce and you'll be glad you put your microwave and skillet to work first. Look for short ribs that are well marbled with at least 1 inch of meat above the bone.

- 5 pounds bone-in English-style short ribs, trimmed, meat and bones separated
- 1 tablespoon vegetable oil
- 2 onions, chopped

1 carrot, peeled and chopped
1 celery rib, chopped
3 tablespoons all-purpose flour
2 tablespoons tomato paste
1 tablespoon minced fresh thyme or
  1 teaspoon dried
2 cups dry red wine
2 tablespoons balsamic vinegar
2 cups chicken broth
2 bay leaves
  Salt and pepper
2 tablespoons minced fresh parsley

1. Line large plate with double layer of coffee filters. Working in batches, arrange beef bones on prepared plate and microwave until well browned, 8 to 10 minutes; transfer to slow cooker.

2. Heat oil in 12-inch skillet over medium heat until shimmering. Add onions, carrot, and celery and cook until softened and lightly browned, 8 to 10 minutes. Stir in flour, tomato paste, and thyme and cook until fragrant, about 1 minute. Slowly stir in wine and vinegar, scraping up any browned bits and smoothing out any lumps. Bring to simmer and cook until sauce is thickened, about 5 minutes; transfer to slow cooker.

3. Stir broth and bay leaves into slow cooker. Season short ribs with salt and pepper and nestle into slow cooker. Cover and cook until beef is tender and fork slips easily in and out of meat, 8 to 9 hours on low or 5 to 6 hours on high.

4. Transfer short ribs to serving dish, tent loosely with aluminum foil, and let rest while finishing sauce. Strain cooking liquid into fat separator and let sit for 5 minutes; discard bones and solids. Combine defatted sauce and parsley in bowl and season with salt and pepper to taste. Spoon 1 cup sauce over short ribs and serve, passing remaining sauce separately.

PREPARING SHORT RIBS

1. To remove meat from bones, insert sharp knife between rib and meat, staying as close to bone as possible, and cut meat off bone.

2. Using knife, trim away large piece of fat on top, and any fat on bottom of each rib.

A microwaved base of aromatics, including 10 garlic cloves, creates a hearty tomato sauce for braised short ribs.

Rustic Italian Braised Beef Short Ribs

SERVES 4 **EASY PREP** **ALL DAY**

COOKING TIME 8 TO 9 HOURS ON LOW OR 5 TO 6 HOURS ON HIGH

SLOW COOKER SIZE 5 TO 7 QUARTS

WHY THIS RECIPE WORKS For braised beef short ribs with an Italian spin, we made a flavorful braise with classic Italian ingredients. Starting with the aromatics, we softened onions and bloomed tomato paste, garlic, oil, oregano, and red pepper flakes in the microwave. We added this flavor-packed mixture to the slow cooker with a can of whole peeled tomatoes. As the short ribs simmered, the tomatoes softened and melded with the aromatic ingredients and meaty short ribs to create a hearty tomato sauce reminiscent of a traditional Sunday gravy. Once the short ribs were meltingly tender, we defatted the sauce, then stirred it back into the tomatoes, breaking the tomatoes into large chunks. A generous sprinkling of fresh basil finished the dish on a bright note. Look for boneless short ribs that are well marbled and measure about 2 inches wide and 1 inch thick.

2 onions, chopped
10 garlic cloves, sliced thin
3 tablespoons tomato paste
1 tablespoon extra-virgin olive oil
1 tablespoon minced fresh oregano or 1 teaspoon dried
½ teaspoon red pepper flakes
1 (28-ounce) can whole peeled tomatoes, drained
2½ pounds boneless English-style short ribs, trimmed
   Salt and pepper
¼ cup chopped fresh basil

1. Microwave onions, garlic, tomato paste, oil, oregano, and pepper flakes in bowl, stirring occasionally, until onions are softened, about 5 minutes; transfer to slow cooker. Stir in tomatoes. Season short ribs with salt and pepper and nestle into slow cooker. Cover and cook until beef is tender and fork slips easily in and out of meat, 8 to 9 hours on low or 5 to 6 hours on high.

2. Transfer short ribs to serving dish, tent loosely with aluminum foil, and let rest while finishing sauce. Strain sauce into fat separator, reserving tomatoes, and let sit for 5 minutes. Add reserved tomatoes to large bowl and break into large chunks with back of large spoon. Add defatted sauce and season with salt and pepper to taste. Spoon sauce over short ribs and sprinkle with basil. Serve.

NOTES FROM THE TEST KITCHEN

Buying Beef Short Ribs

Short ribs are just what their name says they are: short ribs cut from any location along the length of a cow's rib section. Short ribs can be butchered in a variety of ways. In most supermarkets, you'll find English-style short ribs (top). This widely available choice  contains a single bone, 4 to 5 inches long, with a thick piece of meat below it. In some supermarkets you can also buy boneless short ribs (bottom); when doing so, look for meat that's uniform in shape and at least 4 inches long and 1 inch thick. It is best to avoid tapered pieces of meat, which will cook up unevenly.

Browning the oxtails before adding them to the slow cooker gives this humble dish richness through and through.

Braised Oxtails with White Beans and Tomatoes

SERVES 6 TO 8   **ALL DAY**

COOKING TIME 9 TO 10 HOURS ON LOW OR 6 TO 7 HOURS ON HIGH

SLOW COOKER SIZE 5 TO 7 QUARTS

WHY THIS RECIPE WORKS Succulent, beefy oxtails play the starring role in this simple Mediterranean-inspired braised dish featuring creamy white beans and an aromatic sauce. To ensure this dish had rich, meaty flavor, we began by browning the oxtails in a skillet before sautéing the aromatics. For aroma we added a simple yet flavorful combination of eastern Mediterranean ingredients to give the braising liquid its character: sweet diced tomatoes, warm and earthy paprika and red pepper flakes, and pungent oregano. We then deglazed the skillet with broth to ensure a flavorful liquid for braising—the key to this humble peasant dish that is surprisingly rich and satisfying. After braising, we were careful to remove the fat from the cooking liquid using a fat separator. To finish our hearty dish, we stirred in a splash of sherry vinegar and some more fresh oregano. Try to buy oxtails that are approximately 2 inches thick and 2 to 4 inches in diameter. Oxtails can often be found in the freezer section of the grocery store; if using frozen oxtails, be sure to thaw them completely before using.

4 pounds oxtails, trimmed
  Salt and pepper
2 tablespoons extra-virgin olive oil
1 onion, chopped fine
1 carrot, peeled and chopped fine
6 garlic cloves, minced
2 tablespoons tomato paste
1 tablespoon minced fresh oregano
1 teaspoon paprika
½ teaspoon red pepper flakes
2 cups chicken broth
2 (15-ounce) cans diced tomatoes, drained
1 (15-ounce) can navy beans, rinsed
1 tablespoon sherry vinegar

1. Pat oxtails dry with paper towels and season with salt and pepper. Heat oil in 12-inch skillet over medium-high heat until just smoking. Brown half of oxtails on all sides, 8 to 10 minutes; transfer to plate. Repeat with remaining oxtails; transfer to plate.

2. Add onion, carrot, and 1 teaspoon salt to fat left in skillet and cook over medium heat until vegetables are softened, about 5 minutes. Stir in garlic, tomato paste, 1 teaspoon oregano, paprika, and pepper flakes and cook until fragrant, about 30 seconds. Stir in broth, scraping up any browned bits; transfer to slow cooker.

3. Stir tomatoes and beans into slow cooker. Nestle oxtails into slow cooker, adding any accumulated juices. Cover and cook until oxtails are tender and fork slips easily in and out of meat, 9 to 10 hours on low or 6 to 7 hours on high.

4. Transfer oxtails to serving dish, tent loosely with aluminum foil, and let rest while finishing sauce. Strain cooking liquid into fat separator, reserving solids, and let sit for 5 minutes. Transfer reserved solids and defatted liquid to serving bowl. Stir in vinegar and remaining 2 teaspoons oregano, and season with salt and pepper to taste. Spoon 1 cup sauce over oxtails and serve, passing remaining sauce separately.

For osso buco with a lush consistency, we process the marrow from the veal shanks with the braising liquid.

Osso Buco

SERVES 6
COOKING TIME 5 TO 6 HOURS ON LOW OR 3 TO 4 HOURS ON HIGH
SLOW COOKER SIZE 5 TO 7 QUARTS

WHY THIS RECIPE WORKS There are some recipes that you could argue are even better when made in a slow cooker, and *ossobuco*, the famous Italian classic, is such a dish. This venerable Old World braise extracts incredible flavor from a handful of simple ingredients: veal shanks (which we brown), aromatics (onions, carrots, and celery, all sautéed), and liquids (usually a blend of wine, stock, and tomatoes). Here in the test kitchen we certainly have tackled the traditional version, but now it was time to put the slow cooker to the test and see if we could turn out a version that rivaled it. To provide a savory backbone for the veal shanks we started with the stock. Veal stock is traditional, but few cooks have access to it. We found that chicken broth, along with garlic, onions, carrots, and celery, made a sturdy yet subtle flavor base for our braising liquid. A combination of tomato paste and fresh tomatoes worked perfectly to create plenty of deep tomato flavor. To serve six people, we called for good-size shanks and tied them around the equator to keep the meat attached to the bone. While many recipes suggest flouring the veal before browning it, we got better results by searing the meat seasoned only with salt and pepper. Browning the shanks in two batches prevented overcrowding, while deglazing the pan with wine after softening the aromatics enriched the sauce. At the end of cooking, we processed the marrow from the supertender veal shanks with the braising liquid to give it a lush, thick consistency. Gremolata—a classic component of osso buco comprising a mixture of minced garlic, parsley, and lemon zest—is sometimes used just as a garnish, but often some of it is stirred into the sauce as well. We stirred a quarter of the gremolata right into the braise, and used the remaining to garnish each serving for a final hit of fresh flavor. You will need an oval slow cooker for this recipe.

6 (14- to 16-ounce) veal shanks, 1½ inches thick, trimmed and tied around equator
   Salt and pepper
6 tablespoons extra-virgin olive oil
2 onions, chopped
2 carrots, peeled and sliced ¼ inch thick
2 celery ribs, cut into ½-inch pieces
3 tablespoons tomato paste
¼ ounce dried porcini mushrooms, rinsed and minced
¼ teaspoon red pepper flakes
12 garlic cloves, minced
½ cup dry white wine
1½ cups chicken broth
2 tomatoes, cored and chopped
2 bay leaves
1 sprig fresh thyme
½ cup minced fresh parsley
1 tablespoon grated lemon zest

1. Pat shanks dry with paper towels and season with salt and pepper. Heat 2 tablespoons oil in 12-inch skillet over medium-high heat until just smoking. Brown half of shanks on all sides, 8 to 10 minutes; transfer to large plate. Repeat with 2 tablespoons oil and remaining shanks; transfer to plate.

2. Add remaining 2 tablespoons oil, onions, carrots, celery, and 1 teaspoon salt to fat left in skillet and cook until vegetables are softened, 8 to 10 minutes. Stir in tomato paste, mushrooms, pepper flakes, and half of garlic and cook until fragrant, about 1 minute. Stir in wine, scraping up any browned bits; transfer to slow cooker.

3. Stir broth, tomatoes, bay leaves, and thyme sprig into slow cooker. Nestle shanks into slow cooker, adding any accumulated juices. Cover and cook until shanks are tender and fork slips easily in and out of meat, 5 to 6 hours on low or 3 to 4 hours on high.

4. Transfer shanks to serving dish and discard twine. Extract marrow from bones using end of small spoon and reserve. Tent shanks loosely with aluminum foil and let rest while finishing sauce.

5. Combine parsley, lemon zest, and remaining garlic in bowl. Discard bay leaves and thyme sprig. Process reserved marrow and 1½ cups cooking liquid in blender until smooth, about 30 seconds. Stir marrow mixture and one-quarter of parsley mixture into remaining cooking liquid and season with salt and pepper to taste. Place shanks in individual serving bowls, ladle sauce over top, and sprinkle with remaining parsley mixture. Serve.

TYING VEAL SHANKS

Tie piece of twine around thickest portion of each shank to keep meat attached to bone while cooking.

Hungarian Goulash

SERVES 6 TO 8   ALL DAY

COOKING TIME 8 TO 9 HOURS ON LOW OR 5 TO 6 HOURS ON HIGH

SLOW COOKER SIZE 5 TO 7 QUARTS

WHY THIS RECIPE WORKS Because the sauce for this recipe is so packed with flavor, we found that we could skip the standard step of browning the meat and instead brown only the hefty amount of onions and carrots. Adding ⅓ cup of sweet paprika, blended with jarred roasted red peppers, tomato paste, and vinegar, ensured a deep, rich sauce. To thicken the sauce to the proper noodle-coating consistency, we added 3 tablespoons of flour and a judicious amount of water (just 5 tablespoons) to compensate for the moisture that the meat would release as it cooked. To add richness and tang, we stirred in ½ cup of sour cream after the goulash finished cooking and the meat was incredibly tender. Since paprika is vital to this recipe, it is best to use a fresh container. Do not substitute hot or smoked Spanish paprika for the sweet paprika. Serve over egg noodles.

1½ cups jarred roasted red peppers, rinsed
⅓ cup paprika
2 tablespoons tomato paste
1 tablespoon distilled white vinegar
2 tablespoons vegetable oil

A paste made with roasted red peppers and paprika plus 4 pounds of onions gives this goulash bold flavor.

4 pounds onions, chopped
4 carrots, peeled and cut into 1-inch pieces
Salt and pepper
3 tablespoons all-purpose flour
1 bay leaf
5 tablespoons water
4 pounds boneless beef chuck-eye roast, pulled apart at seams, trimmed, and cut into 1½-inch pieces
½ cup sour cream
2 tablespoons minced fresh parsley

1. Process red peppers, paprika, tomato paste, and vinegar in food processor until smooth, about 2 minutes, scraping down sides of bowl as needed.

2. Heat oil in Dutch oven over medium heat until shimmering. Add onions, carrots, and 1 teaspoon salt, cover, and cook, stirring occasionally, until vegetables are softened, 8 to 10 minutes. Stir in flour, bay leaf, and red pepper mixture and cook, uncovered, until mixture begins to brown and stick to bottom of pot, about 2 minutes. Stir in water, scraping up any browned bits; transfer to slow cooker.

3. Season beef with salt and pepper and stir into slow cooker. Cover and cook until beef is tender, 8 to 9 hours on low or 5 to 6 hours on high.

4. Discard bay leaf. Using large spoon, skim fat from surface of sauce. Whisk ½ cup sauce and sour cream together in bowl (to temper), then stir mixture back into slow cooker. Season with salt and pepper to taste. Serve, sprinkling individual portions with parsley.

Buying Sweet and Smoked Paprika

"Paprika" is a generic term for a spice made from ground dried red peppers. Whether paprika is labeled sweet or smoked is determined by the variety (or varieties) of pepper used and how the peppers are cultivated and processed.

SWEET PAPRIKA (sometimes called Hungarian paprika or simply paprika) is the most common. Typically made from a combination of mild red peppers, sweet paprika is prized more for its deep scarlet hue than for its very subtle flavor. Our favorite sweet paprika is **The Spice House Hungarian Sweet Paprika**, which we found outshone the competition. This brand is available only through mail-order, but we think the complexity of its "earthy," "fruity" flavors and its "toasty" aroma make this slight inconvenience well worthwhile.

SMOKED PAPRIKA which is traditionally called for in many Spanish recipes, is produced by drying peppers (either sweet or hot) over smoldering oak embers. Since smoked paprika has a deep, musky flavor all its own, we do not recommend using it for all paprika applications; it is best used to season hearty meats or to add a smoky aroma to boldly flavored dishes. Our favorite smoked paprika is **Simply Organic Smoked Paprika**. Compared with other brands, this made-in-Spain smoked paprika was more redolent with richer, "deeper" smoky flavor. With "the perfect balance of paprika and smokiness," it was "bright and warm" and "sweet and rounded," with smoke that "lingered" "without being overpowering."

Two types of mushrooms, fresh and dried, make them a key player in this beefy stroganoff.

Beef Stroganoff

SERVES 6 TO 8   `ALL DAY`

COOKING TIME 8 TO 9 HOURS ON LOW OR 5 TO 6 HOURS ON HIGH

SLOW COOKER SIZE 5 TO 7 QUARTS

WHY THIS RECIPE WORKS To make sure our slow-cooker version of beef stroganoff delivered tender beef in a meaty mushroom sauce, we started by getting out our skillet and browning the mushrooms to concentrate their flavor, augmenting them with dried porcini mushrooms for an even deeper mushroom flavor that wouldn't be muted by hours in the slow cooker. Then, since we had our skillet out to brown the white mushrooms, we sautéed the aromatics and created a flour-thickened base for the stew to produce the proper consistency. With such a flavorful base, we didn't need to brown the meat but could add it directly to the slow cooker—a real timesaver. Serve over egg noodles.

  2 tablespoons vegetable oil
1½ pounds white mushrooms, trimmed and
      halved if small or quartered if large
  3 onions, chopped fine
    Salt and pepper
  ⅓ cup all-purpose flour
  ¼ cup tomato paste
  6 garlic cloves, minced
  ½ ounce dried porcini mushrooms, rinsed and minced
  1 tablespoon minced fresh thyme or 1 teaspoon dried
  ½ cup dry white wine
1½ cups chicken broth
  ⅓ cup soy sauce
  2 bay leaves
  4 pounds boneless beef chuck-eye roast, pulled apart
      at seams, trimmed, and cut into 1½-inch pieces
  ⅓ cup sour cream
  2 teaspoons Dijon mustard
  2 tablespoons minced fresh dill

1. Heat oil in 12-inch skillet over medium heat until shimmering. Add white mushrooms, onions, and ¼ teaspoon salt, cover, and cook until vegetables are softened and mushrooms have released their liquid, about 5 minutes. Uncover and continue to cook until vegetables are dry and lightly browned, 5 to 7 minutes. Stir in flour, tomato paste, garlic, porcini mushrooms, and thyme and cook until fragrant, about 1 minute. Slowly stir in wine and ½ cup broth, scraping up any browned bits and smoothing out any lumps; transfer to slow cooker.

2. Stir remaining 1 cup broth, soy sauce, and bay leaves into slow cooker. Season beef with salt and pepper and stir into slow cooker. Cover and cook until beef is tender, 8 to 9 hours on low or 5 to 6 hours on high.

3. Discard bay leaves. Using large spoon, skim fat from surface of sauce. Whisk ½ cup sauce, sour cream, mustard, and dill together in bowl (to temper), then stir mixture back into slow cooker. Season with salt and pepper to taste. Serve.

Sloppy Joes

SERVES 6

COOKING TIME 3 TO 4 HOURS ON LOW OR 2 TO 3 HOURS ON HIGH

SLOW COOKER SIZE 4 TO 7 QUARTS

WHY THIS RECIPE WORKS Since the texture of the meat is important when it comes to Sloppy Joes, we found it necessary to get out our skillet and brown the beef before adding it to the slow cooker; this simple step ensured small but consistent pieces of tender ground beef. We used a combination of ketchup and canned tomato sauce to give our sandwiches the right combination of gentle sweetness and strong tomato flavor; a bit of brown sugar, chili powder, and hot sauce kept the sauce balanced. We limited the amount of ketchup

This family-friendly Sloppy Joe filling tastes world's better than those made with a store-bought seasoning packet.

and tomato sauce to only 2 cups, enough so that the meat was moist and saucy but was still able to fit on a bun. Another bonus: This recipe doubles easily if you're planning on feeding a crowd.

- 2 slices hearty white sandwich bread, torn into 1-inch pieces
- ¼ cup whole milk
  Salt and pepper
- 2 pounds 85 percent lean ground beef
- 2 tablespoons vegetable oil
- 2 onions, chopped fine
- 4 garlic cloves, minced
- 1 teaspoon chili powder
- 1 (15-ounce) can tomato sauce
- 1 cup ketchup
- 2 teaspoons packed brown sugar
- ½ teaspoon hot sauce
- 8 hamburger buns

1. Mash bread, milk, ½ teaspoon salt, and ½ teaspoon pepper into paste in large bowl using fork. Add ground beef and knead with hands until well combined.

2. Heat oil in 12-inch skillet over medium heat until shimmering. Add onions and cook until softened and lightly browned, 8 to 10 minutes. Stir in garlic and chili powder and cook until fragrant, about 30 seconds.

3. Add half of beef mixture and cook, breaking up beef with wooden spoon, until no longer pink, about 5 minutes. Add remaining ground beef and continue to cook until no longer pink, about 5 minutes. Stir in tomato sauce, scraping up any browned bits; transfer to slow cooker.

4. Stir ketchup, sugar, and hot sauce into slow cooker. Cover and cook until beef is tender, 3 to 4 hours on low or 2 to 3 hours on high.

5. Using large spoon, skim fat from surface of sauce. Break up any remaining large pieces of beef with spoon. Adjust consistency with hot water as needed. Season with salt and pepper to taste. Spoon mixture onto buns and serve.

Ground Beef Tacos

SERVES 4 TO 6
COOKING TIME 3 TO 4 HOURS ON LOW OR 2 TO 3 HOURS ON HIGH
SLOW COOKER SIZE 4 TO 7 QUARTS

WHY THIS RECIPE WORKS When it comes to tacos, it's all about the filling. We started by getting out our skillet and sautéing the aromatics and beef before adding them to the slow cooker; this step ensured maximum flavor and small but consistent pieces of tender ground beef. We found tomato sauce was a great base for our taco filling, and intensified the flavor with chili powder, cumin, coriander, and oregano as well as a splash of cider vinegar and touch of brown sugar. The meat, however, was a bit dry, so we added a panade (a paste of milk and bread) to the raw meat before cooking to keep it moist. Serve with your favorite taco toppings.

-    1 slice hearty white sandwich bread, torn into 1-inch pieces
-    3 tablespoons whole milk
     Salt and pepper
- 1½ pounds 85 percent lean ground beef
-    2 tablespoons vegetable oil
-    1 onion, chopped fine
-    3 tablespoons chili powder
-    4 garlic cloves, minced
-    2 teaspoons minced fresh oregano or ½ teaspoon dried
-    1 teaspoon ground cumin
-    1 teaspoon ground coriander
-    1 (8-ounce) can tomato sauce
-    1 teaspoon cider vinegar
-    1 teaspoon packed brown sugar
- 8-12 taco shells, warmed

1. Mash bread, milk, ¼ teaspoon salt, and ⅛ teaspoon pepper into paste in large bowl using fork. Add ground beef and knead with hands until well combined.

2. Heat oil in 12-inch skillet over medium heat until shimmering. Add onion and cook until softened and lightly browned, 5 to 7 minutes. Stir in chili powder, garlic, oregano, cumin, and coriander and cook until fragrant, about 1 minute.

3. Add half of beef mixture and cook, breaking up beef with wooden spoon, until no longer pink, about 5 minutes. Add remaining ground beef and continue to cook until no longer pink, about 5 minutes. Stir in tomato sauce, vinegar, and sugar, scraping up any browned bits; transfer to slow cooker. Cover and cook until beef is tender, 3 to 4 hours on low or 2 to 3 hours on high.

4. Using large spoon, skim fat from surface of sauce. Break up any remaining large pieces of beef with spoon. Adjust consistency with hot water as needed. Season with salt and pepper to taste. Serve with taco shells.

Shredded Beef Tacos with Cabbage-Carrot Slaw

SERVES 4 TO 6   EASY PREP   ALL DAY

COOKING TIME 7 TO 8 HOURS ON LOW OR 4 TO 5 HOURS ON HIGH

SLOW COOKER SIZE 4 TO 7 QUARTS

WHY THIS RECIPE WORKS This easy-to-prepare slow-cooker beef filling makes a great weeknight meal. We turned to chuck roast, with its big beefy flavor, as the basis for the filling because it becomes meltingly tender and shreddable in the slow cooker—plus it's inexpensive and easy to find. Cutting the roast into 1½-inch pieces helped it cook faster and, as a result, become even more tender than when left whole. To make our red sauce we built a flavorful mixture of dried ancho chiles, chipotle chiles, tomato paste, and a hint of cinnamon. The different types of chiles created layers of heat without turning the sauce overly spicy. We bloomed the aromatics, including the dried chiles, with oil in the microwave to bring out their full flavor and added them to the slow cooker with a little honey to balance the heat, and water to distribute the spices evenly. Once the beef was pull-apart tender, we simply pureed the braising liquid into a rich, smooth sauce and tossed it with the shredded beef. To complement the warm spices of the beef, we topped our tacos with a cool and tangy cabbage slaw, which we kept simple with just a splash of lime juice.

½ onion, chopped fine
1 ounce (2 to 3) dried ancho chiles, stemmed, seeded, and torn into 1-inch pieces (½ cup)
3 garlic cloves, minced
1 tablespoon tomato paste

Dried ancho chiles and chipotle chile give these easy-to-make shredded beef tacos their flavor punch.

1 tablespoon vegetable oil
1 teaspoon minced canned chipotle chile in adobo sauce
½ teaspoon ground cinnamon
¾ cup water
1 tablespoon honey
2 pounds boneless beef chuck-eye roast, pulled apart at seams, trimmed, and cut into 1½-inch pieces
Salt and pepper
½ head napa cabbage, cored and sliced thin (6 cups)
1 carrot, peeled and shredded
1 jalapeño chile, stemmed, seeded, and sliced thin
¼ cup lime juice (2 limes), plus lime wedges for serving
¼ cup chopped fresh cilantro
12–18 (6-inch) corn tortillas, warmed
Crumbled queso fresco

1. Microwave onion, anchos, garlic, tomato paste, oil, chipotle, and cinnamon in bowl, stirring occasionally, until onion is softened, about 5 minutes; transfer to slow cooker. Stir in water and honey. Season beef with salt and pepper and stir into slow cooker. Cover and cook until beef is tender, 7 to 8 hours on low or 4 to 5 hours on high.

2. Combine cabbage, carrot, jalapeño, lime juice, cilantro, and ½ teaspoon salt in large bowl. Cover and refrigerate until ready to serve.

3. Using slotted spoon, transfer beef to another large bowl. Using potato masher, smash beef until coarsely shredded; cover to keep warm.

4. Process cooking liquid in blender until smooth, about 1 minute. Adjust sauce consistency with extra hot water as needed. Season with salt and pepper to taste. Toss beef with 1 cup sauce. Toss slaw to recombine. Serve beef with tortillas, slaw, and queso fresco, passing lime wedges and remaining sauce separately.

NOTES FROM THE TEST KITCHEN

Corn Tortillas

While we love homemade corn tortillas, we usually rely on the convenience of store-bought. Good corn tortillas should be soft and pliable, with a fresh, light corn flavor. We compared tortillas in two blind taste tests, first assessing them warmed in an oven and served plain, and then pitting the top four products against one another in enchiladas. Tasters faulted many of the tortillas for being either too sweet or bland. Our winner had a hint of sweetness from its light, fresh corn flavor but no added sugar. It also had the most sodium by far, but no one found them too salty. Actually, they were quite flavorful, which makes sense because salt is a flavor booster. Texture is where supermarket corn tortillas can really go wrong; they're often crumbly and dry, and they break as you try to bend them around a filling. Our winner maintained pliability by adding wheat gluten, which binds with water to make the dough more cohesive and elastic, which in turn creates a softer, stronger tortilla. This also means that unlike most corn tortillas, our winner is not gluten-free. The bottom line: Low sugar and high salt make the best combination for great flavor. If you're not worried about gluten, a corn tortilla with added protein from wheat, like our winner, **Maria and Ricardo's Handmade Style Soft Corn Tortillas**, is the strongest and most supple option. For those who need gluten-free tortillas, our second-place finisher, Mission White Corn Tortillas, Restaurant Style, while lacking our winner's firm structure, is still a good option.

The filling for these lettuce wraps is addictively delicious and is supereasy to make using boneless short ribs.

Korean Lettuce Wraps

SERVES 4 TO 6   **EASY PREP**   **ALL DAY**

COOKING TIME 8 TO 9 HOURS ON LOW OR 5 TO 6 HOURS ON HIGH

SLOW COOKER SIZE 4 TO 7 QUARTS

WHY THIS RECIPE WORKS Tender short ribs covered in a sweet/spicy glaze are classic Korean BBQ fare, but when they're made in a slow cooker, that bold flavor tends to become watered-down. For a signature Korean glaze, we created a base of fruity hoisin sauce, *gochujang* (a Korean chile-soybean paste), minced ginger, garlic, and a little toasted sesame oil. Instead of adding extra liquid (broth or water) to our base as we do for most braises, we allowed the meat's natural juices to meld with the glaze base to build a flavor-rich sauce. A tablespoon of instant tapioca helped to ensure the glaze was properly thickened. The addition of rice vinegar and more hoisin after cooking brightened the flavor of the dish, while scallions provided welcome notes of freshness. We prefer to eat these tender short rib pieces wrapped in a lettuce leaf and eaten like a taco, but they are equally delicious served over rice. Gochujang can be found in Asian markets and in some supermarkets. If you can't find gochujang, substitute an equal amount of Sriracha sauce.

½ cup plus 1 tablespoon hoisin sauce
2 tablespoons gochujang
4 teaspoons grated fresh ginger
4 garlic cloves, minced
1 tablespoon instant tapioca
3 pounds boneless English-style short ribs, trimmed
Salt and pepper
1 tablespoon rice vinegar
2 teaspoons toasted sesame oil
2 scallions, sliced thin
2 heads Bibb lettuce (8 ounces each), leaves separated

1. Combine ½ cup hoisin, gochujang, ginger, garlic, and tapioca in slow cooker. Season short ribs with pepper and nestle into slow cooker. Cover and cook until beef is tender and fork slips easily in and out of meat, 8 to 9 hours on low or 5 to 6 hours on high.

2. Transfer short ribs to cutting board, let cool slightly, then pull apart into large chunks using 2 forks; tent with aluminum foil to keep warm.

3. Transfer cooking liquid to fat separator and let sit for 5 minutes. Whisk defatted liquid, vinegar, oil, and remaining 1 tablespoon hoisin together in large bowl. Add beef and scallions and toss to combine. Season with salt and pepper to taste. Serve beef with lettuce leaves.

Shredded Barbecued Beef

SERVES 8 TO 10   **ALL DAY**

COOKING TIME 9 TO 10 HOURS ON LOW OR 6 TO 7 HOURS ON HIGH

SLOW COOKER SIZE 5 TO 7 QUARTS

WHY THIS RECIPE WORKS Piled high on soft buns, saucy barbecued shredded beef is a real crowd-pleaser. We chose a boneless chuck-eye roast for the beef since we knew it would become tender and shreddable after hours in a slow cooker. For a richly flavored sauce, we got out our skillet, first browning bacon for smoky flavor, and then sautéing onions and spices in the rendered bacon fat. We then added ketchup, mustard, and brown sugar plus a somewhat unusual ingredient—coffee—which, when reduced down along with all the other sauce ingredients, lent just the complexity we were seeking.

4 slices bacon, chopped
2 onions, chopped fine
2 tablespoons chili powder
1 tablespoon paprika
1½ cups brewed coffee
1½ cups ketchup
¼ cup packed dark brown sugar

2 tablespoons brown mustard
1 (4- to 5-pound) boneless beef chuck-eye roast, trimmed and quartered
Salt and pepper
1 tablespoon hot sauce
1 tablespoon cider vinegar
1 teaspoon liquid smoke

1. Cook bacon in 12-inch skillet over medium heat until crisp, 5 to 7 minutes. Stir in onions and cook until softened and lightly browned, 8 to 10 minutes. Stir in chili powder and paprika and cook until fragrant, about 30 seconds. Stir in coffee, ketchup, sugar, and 1 tablespoon mustard. Bring to simmer and cook until ketchup mixture is thickened and measures 4 cups, about 10 minutes. Transfer 2 cups of ketchup mixture to slow cooker; reserve remaining mixture separately.

2. Season beef with salt and pepper and nestle into slow cooker. Cover and cook until beef is tender and fork slips easily in and out of meat, 9 to 10 hours on low or 6 to 7 hours on high.

3. Transfer beef to cutting board, let cool slightly, then shred into bite-size pieces using 2 forks; discard fat. Transfer beef to large bowl and cover to keep warm.

4. Strain cooking liquid into fat separator and let sit for 5 minutes; discard solids. Bring defatted liquid to simmer in saucepan over medium heat and cook until thickened and measures 1 cup, 20 to 30 minutes. Whisk in reserved ketchup mixture, hot sauce, vinegar, remaining 1 tablespoon mustard, and liquid smoke. Season with salt and pepper to taste. Toss beef with 1½ cups sauce and serve, passing remaining sauce separately.

NOTES FROM THE TEST KITCHEN

Liquid Smoke

We were among the many people who assume that there must be some kind of synthetic chemical chicanery going on in the making of "liquid smoke" flavoring. But that's not the case. Liquid smoke is made by channeling smoke from smoldering wood chips through a condenser, which quickly cools the vapors, causing them to liquefy (just like the drops that form when you breathe on a piece of cold glass). The water-soluble flavor compounds in the smoke are trapped within this liquid, while the nonsoluble carcinogenic tars and resins are removed by a series of filters, resulting in a clean, smoke-flavored liquid. Our top-rated brand, **Wright's Liquid Smoke**, contains nothing but smoke and water.

The vibrant pairing of sweet red bell peppers and onions plus cumin and oregano are the base of this Cuban favorite.

Ropa Vieja

SERVES 4 TO 6
COOKING TIME 6 TO 7 HOURS ON LOW OR 4 TO 5 HOURS ON HIGH
SLOW COOKER SIZE 4 TO 7 QUARTS

WHY THIS RECIPE WORKS *Ropa vieja*, Cuba's national dish and a favorite in Cuban neighborhoods throughout the United States, is elemental and beautifully simple—a beefy braise of flank steak in a sauce that balances tomato and white wine with sweet peppers, onions, and garlic. Cumin and oregano add warmth, while briny olives and bright vinegar cut the richness of the meat and make the flavors pop. Versions we tried in the slow cooker identified two problems: meat that was too difficult to shred, and a final stew that was too soupy. Choosing the cut of beef was easy: Flank steak, the traditional choice, won out with tasters over chuck ("greasy" and hard to shred), skirt ("mushy" after long cooking), and brisket (a "little fibrous" and not always easy to find). Flank, with its lean, large muscle fibers all running in one direction, not only was the easiest cut to shred, but also stood up best to long, slow cooking without turning greasy. Serve with Basmati Rice Pilaf (page 134).

3 tablespoons vegetable oil
2 onions, halved and sliced thin
2 red bell peppers, stemmed, seeded, and cut into ½-inch-wide strips
¼ cup tomato paste
4 garlic cloves, minced
2 teaspoons ground cumin
1½ teaspoons dried oregano
Salt and pepper
½ cup dry white wine
2 tablespoons soy sauce
2 bay leaves
1 (2-pound) flank steak, trimmed and cut crosswise against grain into 4 equal pieces
¾ cup pitted large brine-cured green olives, sliced
1 tablespoon distilled white vinegar

1. Heat oil in 12-inch skillet over medium-high heat until shimmering. Add onions and peppers, cover, and cook, stirring occasionally, until softened and spotty brown, 8 to 10 minutes.

2. Push vegetables to sides of skillet. Add tomato paste, garlic, cumin, oregano, and ½ teaspoon salt to center of skillet and cook, uncovered, until fragrant, about 1 minute. Stir tomato paste mixture into vegetables. Stir in wine and cook until nearly evaporated, about 2 minutes; transfer to slow cooker.

3. Stir soy sauce and bay leaves into slow cooker. Season steak with salt and pepper and nestle into slow cooker. Cover and cook until beef is tender and fork slips easily in and out of meat, 6 to 7 hours on low or 4 to 5 hours on high.

4. Transfer steak to cutting board, let cool slightly, then shred into bite-size pieces using 2 forks. Discard bay leaves. Stir beef and olives into slow cooker and let sit until heated through, about 5 minutes. Stir in vinegar and season with salt and pepper to taste. Serve.

CUTTING BELL PEPPERS

1. Slice off top and bottom, remove core, then slice down through side of pepper.

2. Lay pepper flat on cutting board, cut away any remaining ribs, then cut pepper into pieces as directed in recipe.

Beef and Broccoli Stir-Fry

SERVES 4 TO 6   `EASY PREP`   `ALL DAY`

COOKING TIME 7 TO 8 HOURS ON LOW OR 4 TO 5 HOURS ON HIGH

SLOW COOKER SIZE 4 TO 7 QUARTS

WHY THIS RECIPE WORKS Normally, stir-fry includes splattering hot oil and hectic, last-minute ingredient additions that require lots of advance work. We found a way to simulate a stir-fry in the slow cooker for an easy, light, and mess-free dinner without piles of prep bowls and greasy pans. We chose boneless chuck-eye roast because it contains a fair amount of connective tissue that breaks down and makes the meat meltingly tender after hours in the slow cooker (and since chuck roasts have chunks of visible fat, it's easy to remove the excess when cutting up the roast for braising). A combination of chicken broth and soy sauce created the body of our "stir-fry" sauce, and instant tapioca gave it the perfect clingy consistency. Sesame oil and dry mustard added richness and depth, and we studded the sauce with ginger and red pepper flakes for two different dimensions of heat. A little extra sesame oil and soy sauce stirred in at the end reinforced the meaty, savory flavors of the sauce. At the same time, we stirred in a splash of acidic orange juice to brighten the dish and add a hint of balancing sweetness. To keep the broccoli bright and fresh, we waited until the end of cooking and briefly steamed it in the microwave before combining it with the tender chunks of beef.

- 3 scallions, white parts minced, green parts sliced thin on bias
- 2 tablespoons grated fresh ginger
- 4 garlic cloves, minced
- 2 teaspoons toasted sesame oil
- ¼ teaspoon red pepper flakes
- ¼ teaspoon dry mustard
- 2 pounds boneless beef chuck-eye roast, pulled apart at seams, trimmed, and cut into 1½-inch pieces
- ½ cup chicken broth
- 2 tablespoons soy sauce, plus extra for seasoning
- 2 tablespoons packed brown sugar
- 1½ tablespoons instant tapioca
- 1½ pounds broccoli florets, cut into 1-inch pieces
- ¼ cup orange juice

1. Microwave scallion whites, ginger, garlic, 1 teaspoon oil, pepper flakes, and mustard in bowl, stirring occasionally, until fragrant, about 1 minute; transfer to slow cooker. Stir in beef, broth, 1 tablespoon soy sauce, sugar, and tapioca. Cover and cook until beef is tender, 7 to 8 hours on low or 4 to 5 hours on high.

2. Microwave broccoli and ¼ cup water in covered bowl, stirring occasionally, until tender, about 6 minutes. Drain broccoli, then stir into slow cooker along with orange juice, remaining 1 teaspoon oil, and remaining 1 tablespoon soy sauce. Let sit until heated through, about 5 minutes. Season with extra soy sauce to taste. Sprinkle with scallion greens and serve.

SIMPLE SIDES

BASMATI RICE PILAF

SERVES 4 TO 6

Long-grain white, jasmine, or Texmati rice can be substituted for the basmati. You will need a large saucepan with a tight-fitting lid for this recipe. A nonstick saucepan will help prevent the rice from sticking. This recipe can be easily doubled; increase the amount of water to only 3¾ cups.

- 1 tablespoon extra-virgin olive oil
- 1 small onion, chopped fine
  Salt and pepper
- 1½ cups basmati rice, rinsed
- 2¼ cups water

1. Heat oil in large saucepan over medium heat until shimmering. Add onion and ¼ teaspoon salt and cook until onion is softened, about 5 minutes. Add rice and cook, stirring often, until grain edges begin to turn translucent, about 3 minutes.

2. Stir in water and bring to simmer. Reduce heat to low, cover, and continue to simmer until rice is tender and all water is absorbed, 16 to 18 minutes.

3. Remove saucepan from heat and lay clean folded dish towel underneath lid. Let sit for 10 minutes. Fluff rice with fork, season with salt and pepper to taste, and serve.

NOTES FROM THE TEST KITCHEN

Broccoli Florets

Broccoli florets add a nice crunch and bright green color to many dishes. Most supermarkets sell broccoli florets already trimmed and ready to go, which helps cut back on prep time and waste. But note that if the florets you've purchased are large or unevenly cut, you may need to trim them further before cooking.

Stuffed peppers are easier to make in the slow cooker and require no preblanching of the peppers.

Tex-Mex Stuffed Bell Peppers

SERVES 4

COOKING TIME 4 TO 5 HOURS ON LOW OR 3 TO 4 HOURS ON HIGH

SLOW COOKER SIZE 5 TO 7 QUARTS

WHY THIS RECIPE WORKS Creating an easy stuffed pepper recipe in the slow cooker required some tinkering since, in our experience, even good traditional versions can be problematic—bland fillings and tough or mushy peppers are the norm. We didn't want to spend time at the stove sautéing the beef, nor did we want to parcook the peppers; luckily, we found the long cooking time guaranteed that beef added raw would emerge fully cooked, and the bell peppers would soften perfectly in the moist environment (as long as a little water was added at the outset). Getting perfectly cooked rice was more of a challenge. After trying many varieties of rice, both cooked and raw, we discovered that instant rice, a parcooked product, was the best option and turned out perfectly tender by the time the peppers were finished cooking. As for flavoring, we wanted to up the ante by pairing the classic beef, rice, and cheese trio with strong Tex-Mex spices. We added a healthy dose of Monterey Jack cheese to help hold the filling together,

frozen corn, and chili powder and chipotles for heat. A sprinkling of cilantro at the end added brightness. Try to choose peppers with flat bottoms so that they stay upright in the slow cooker. Be sure to use instant rice (sometimes labeled minute rice); traditional rice takes much longer to cook and won't work here. You will need an oval slow cooker for this recipe.

    4   red, yellow, or orange bell peppers (8 ounces each)
    1   onion, chopped fine
    6   garlic cloves, minced
    2   tablespoons chili powder
    1   tablespoon vegetable oil
    1   slice hearty white sandwich bread, torn into
        1-inch pieces
    ¼   cup whole milk
        Salt and pepper
    5   ounces Monterey Jack cheese, shredded (1¼ cups)
    1   cup frozen corn
    ¾   cup instant white rice
    2   teaspoons minced canned chipotle chile in adobo sauce
    12 ounces 85 percent lean ground beef
    2   tablespoons minced fresh cilantro

1. Trim ½ inch off top of each pepper, then remove core and seeds. Finely chop pepper tops, discarding stems. Microwave chopped pepper tops, onion, garlic, chili powder, and oil in bowl, stirring occasionally, until onion is softened, about 5 minutes.

2. Mash bread, milk, 1½ teaspoons salt, and ½ teaspoon pepper into paste in large bowl using fork. Stir in pepper mixture, 1 cup Monterey Jack, corn, rice, and chipotle. Add ground beef and knead with hands until well combined. Divide filling evenly among bell peppers, mounding slightly.

3. Pour ⅓ cup water into slow cooker. Place stuffed peppers upright in slow cooker and sprinkle with remaining ¼ cup Monterey Jack. Cover and cook until peppers are tender, 4 to 5 hours on low or 3 to 4 hours on high.

4. Using tongs and slotted spoon, transfer peppers to serving dish; discard cooking liquid. Sprinkle with cilantro. Serve.

MAKING STUFFED PEPPERS

Arrange stuffed peppers in slow cooker, leaning them against one another and sides of slow-cooker insert, so that they remain upright during cooking.

Italian Stuffed Bell Peppers

SERVES 4

COOKING TIME 4 TO 5 HOURS ON LOW OR 3 TO 4 HOURS ON HIGH

SLOW COOKER SIZE 5 TO 7 QUARTS

WHY THIS RECIPE WORKS Stuffed with Italian sausage and two kinds of cheese, these slow-cooker stuffed peppers are anything but boring. Keeping with our Italian theme and following the technique we established for making stuffed peppers in the slow cooker, we added tomato paste to the microwaved aromatics, as well as chopped zucchini to the filling, and a topping of Parmesan and chopped fresh basil. Try to choose peppers with flat bottoms so that they stay upright in the slow cooker. Be sure to use instant rice (sometimes labeled minute rice); traditional rice takes much longer to cook and won't work here. You will need an oval slow cooker for this recipe.

- 4 red, yellow, or orange bell peppers (8 ounces each)
- 1 small zucchini, cut into ¼-inch pieces
- 1 onion, chopped fine
- 6 garlic cloves, minced
- 1 tablespoon extra-virgin olive oil
- 1 tablespoon tomato paste
- ¼ teaspoon red pepper flakes
- 1 slice hearty white sandwich bread, torn into 1-inch pieces
- ¼ cup whole milk
  Salt and pepper
- 3 ounces Monterey Jack cheese, shredded (¾ cup)
- ¾ cup instant white rice
- ¼ cup grated Parmesan cheese, plus extra for serving
- 12 ounces hot or sweet Italian sausage, casings removed
- 2 tablespoons chopped fresh basil

1. Trim ½ inch off top of each pepper, then remove core and seeds. Finely chop pepper tops, discarding stems. Microwave chopped pepper tops, zucchini, onion, garlic, oil, tomato paste, and pepper flakes in bowl, stirring occasionally, until vegetables are softened, about 5 minutes.

2. Mash bread, milk, 1 teaspoon salt, and ½ teaspoon pepper into paste in large bowl using fork. Stir in pepper mixture, Monterey Jack, rice, and Parmesan. Add sausage and knead with hands until well combined. Divide filling evenly among bell peppers, mounding slightly.

3. Pour ⅓ cup water into slow cooker. Place stuffed peppers upright in slow cooker. Cover and cook until peppers are tender, 4 to 5 hours on low or 3 to 4 hours on high.

4. Using tongs and slotted spoon, transfer peppers to serving dish; discard cooking liquid. Sprinkle with basil and extra Parmesan. Serve.

A mixture of spicy chorizo and ground beef plus a binder of instant white rice deliver tender and flavorful meatballs.

Mexican Meatballs with Chorizo and Rice

SERVES 4 TO 6

COOKING TIME 4 TO 5 HOURS ON LOW

SLOW COOKER SIZE 4 TO 7 QUARTS

WHY THIS RECIPE WORKS *Albondigas en chipotle* is a classic Mexican dish that features a smoky, spicy, chipotle chile–infused tomato sauce and tender meatballs. Usually the meatballs also contain rice as the binder, so the trick here was to figure out how to make ultraflavorful meatballs whereby the rice became super-tender and melded into the meat, and the meatballs themselves were also tender and perfectly cooked. First, we focused on the flavor and texture of our meatballs, which we wanted to have the kick and flavor of traditional albondigas. Instead of relying on a laundry list of spices, we turned to a commonly used Mexican ingredient with plenty of its own seasoning: Mexican chorizo. By substituting chorizo for a portion of the ground beef, we were able to quickly elevate our meatballs with spicy, rich flavor. We mixed milk and bread into a paste to form a panade. This was essential to ensure moisture and lightness in our meatballs. After trying many varieties of rice, both cooked and raw, we discovered that instant rice was the best option and turned out perfectly tender by the time the meatballs were finished cooking. To develop a rich sauce, we used a combination of tomato paste and canned diced tomatoes, which welcomed the deep, smoky flavors of the chipotle chile. The addition of red wine vinegar and brown sugar helped to balance the sauce with tart and sweet notes. Canned chipotle chile in adobo sauce was easy to use and provided additional heat, smokiness, and a bit of acidity. We braised the meatballs in the sauce for several hours, which not only tenderized the meatballs further but also infused the sauce with great flavor. Be sure to use instant rice (sometimes labeled minute rice); traditional rice takes much longer to cook and won't work here.

2 slices hearty white sandwich bread,
   torn into 1-inch pieces
½ cup whole milk
   Salt and pepper
12 ounces Mexican-style chorizo sausage,
   casings removed
12 ounces 85 percent lean ground beef
½ cup instant white rice
2 tablespoons extra-virgin olive oil
1 onion, chopped fine
3 tablespoons tomato paste
3 garlic cloves, minced
1 tablespoon minced fresh oregano or
   1 teaspoon dried
1 tablespoon minced canned chipotle
   chile in adobo sauce
¼ teaspoon ground cumin
1 cup chicken broth
1 (14.5-ounce) can diced tomatoes
2 tablespoons red wine vinegar
1 tablespoon packed brown sugar
1 bay leaf
2 tablespoons chopped fresh cilantro

1. Mash bread, milk, 1 teaspoon pepper, and ½ teaspoon salt into paste in large bowl using fork. Add chorizo, ground beef, and rice and knead with hands until well combined. Pinch off and roll mixture into 2-inch meatballs (about 16 meatballs).

2. Heat oil in 12-inch nonstick skillet over medium-high heat until just smoking. Brown meatballs on all sides, about 5 minutes; transfer to slow cooker.

3. Add onion to fat left in skillet and cook over medium heat until softened, about 5 minutes. Stir in tomato paste, garlic, oregano, chipotle, and cumin and cook until fragrant, about 30 seconds. Stir in broth, tomatoes, vinegar, sugar, and bay leaf, scraping up any browned bits; transfer to slow cooker. Cover and cook until meatballs are tender, 4 to 5 hours on low.

4. Discard bay leaf. Using large spoon, skim fat from surface of sauce. Stir in cilantro and season with salt and pepper to taste. Serve.

The key to cooking lean pork tenderloins in the slow cooker is the way we position them side by side.

Teriyaki Pork Tenderloin

SERVES 4   `EASY PREP`   `LIGHT`

COOKING TIME 1 TO 2 HOURS ON LOW
SLOW COOKER SIZE 4 TO 7 QUARTS

WHY THIS RECIPE WORKS Cooking a lean roast like pork tenderloin in a slow cooker is tricky because it can quickly turn overcooked and dry. We discovered that nestling two tenderloins side by side, alternating the narrow and thicker ends, helped to insulate the meat and prevented it from overcooking. Once we had the method in hand, we developed the flavor, coating the pork with a teriyaki glaze made with equal parts sugar and soy sauce and seasoned with fresh ginger, garlic, and mirin. To ensure a properly clingy glaze, we simply thickened the sauce with some cornstarch before applying it to the pork, and then we ran the tenderloins under the broiler before serving. To prevent the pork from overcooking under the broiler, we removed it from the slow cooker just shy of 145 degrees. You will need an oval slow cooker for this recipe. Because they are cooked gently and not browned, the tenderloins will be rosy throughout. Check the tenderloins' temperature after 1 hour of cooking and continue to monitor until they register 145 degrees.

⅓ cup soy sauce
⅓ cup sugar
2 tablespoons mirin
½ teaspoon grated fresh ginger
1 garlic clove, minced
2 (12- to 16-ounce) pork tenderloins, trimmed
1½ teaspoons cornstarch
1 tablespoon water
2 scallions, sliced thin
1 teaspoon sesame seeds, toasted

1. Combine soy sauce, sugar, mirin, ginger, and garlic in slow cooker. Nestle tenderloins into slow cooker, side by side, alternating thicker end to thinner end. Cover and cook until pork registers 145 degrees, 1 to 2 hours on low.

2. Adjust oven rack 6 inches from broiler element and heat broiler. Transfer tenderloins to aluminum foil–lined rimmed baking sheet. Transfer cooking liquid to small saucepan and bring to simmer over medium heat. Whisk cornstarch and water together in bowl, then whisk into cooking liquid and simmer until thickened, 3 to 5 minutes.

3. Liberally brush tenderloins with glaze and broil until spotty brown on top, about 5 minutes. Transfer tenderloins to carving board, tent loosely with foil, and let rest for 5 minutes. Slice tenderloins ¼ inch thick, then transfer to serving dish. Drizzle with remaining glaze and sprinkle with scallions and sesame seeds. Serve.

NOTES FROM THE TEST KITCHEN

Natural Versus Enhanced Pork

Because modern pork is so lean and therefore somewhat bland and prone to dryness if overcooked, many producers now inject their fresh pork products with a sodium solution. So-called enhanced pork is now the only option at many supermarkets, especially when buying lean cuts like the tenderloin. (You can determine the difference by reading the label; if the pork has been enhanced it will have an ingredient list.) Enhanced pork is injected with a solution of water, salt, sodium phosphates, sodium lactate, potassium lactate, sodium diacetate, and varying flavor agents, generally adding 7 to 15 percent extra weight. While enhanced pork does cook up juicier (it has been pumped full of water!), we find the texture almost spongy, and the flavor is often unpleasantly salty. We prefer the genuine pork flavor of natural pork and rely on brining to keep it juicy. Also, enhanced pork loses six times the moisture that natural pork loses when frozen and thawed—yet another reason to avoid enhanced pork.

Spiced Pork Tenderloin with Raisin-Almond Couscous

SERVES 4 `EASY PREP`
COOKING TIME 1 TO 2 HOURS ON LOW
SLOW COOKER SIZE 4 TO 7 QUARTS

WHY THIS RECIPE WORKS We wanted to make succulent pork tenderloin with warm spices and an easy side dish—all in the slow cooker. First, we seasoned the pork with fragrant spice. Instead of a laundry list of spices, we used garam masala (an Indian spice blend) for complex flavor. Once the pork was cooked, we repurposed the potent cooking liquid to make couscous. We simply stirred the couscous into the slow cooker along with some raisins, and 15 minutes later we had a richly flavored couscous salad, which we finished with some sliced almonds. An easy fresh parsley vinaigrette rounded out the flavors of the spiced pork and couscous. Be sure to use regular (or fine-grain) couscous; large-grain couscous, often labeled "Israeli-style," takes much longer to cook and won't work in this recipe. You will need an oval slow cooker for this recipe. Because they are cooked gently and not browned, the tenderloins will be rosy throughout. Check the tenderloins' temperature after 1 hour of cooking and continue to monitor until they register 145 degrees.

1 cup chicken broth
4 garlic cloves, minced
2 (12- to 16-ounce) pork tenderloins, trimmed
2 teaspoons garam masala
  Salt and pepper
1 cup couscous
½ cup raisins
¼ cup sliced almonds, toasted
½ cup extra-virgin olive oil
½ cup minced fresh parsley
2 tablespoons red wine vinegar

1. Combine broth and half of garlic in slow cooker. Sprinkle tenderloins with garam masala and season with salt and pepper. Nestle tenderloins into slow cooker, side by side, alternating thicker end to thinner end. Cover and cook until pork registers 145 degrees, 1 to 2 hours on low.

2. Transfer tenderloins to carving board, tent loosely with aluminum foil, and let rest while finishing couscous. Measure out and reserve 1 cup cooking liquid; discard remaining liquid. Combine reserved liquid, couscous, and raisins in now-empty slow cooker. Cover and cook on high until couscous is tender, about 15 minutes. Fluff couscous with fork, then stir in almonds.

3. Whisk oil, parsley, vinegar, and remaining garlic together in bowl, and season with salt and pepper to taste. Slice tenderloins ¼ inch thick and serve with couscous and vinaigrette.

Herbed Pork Tenderloin with Ratatouille

SERVES 4   `LIGHT`

COOKING TIME 1 TO 2 HOURS ON LOW

SLOW COOKER SIZE 5 TO 7 QUARTS

WHY THIS RECIPE WORKS For this simple braised pork tenderloin, we turned to Provence for inspiration, pairing this lean cut with a robust ratatouille. Traditionally, ratatouille is a labor of love, with many recipes demanding that each vegetable be cooked separately for the perfect texture. We found that the slow cooker eliminated much of this fussy preparation with just a little up-front prep. Broiling the eggplant, zucchini, and aromatics together before adding them to the slow cooker ensured browned and flavorful vegetables with no excess water. The flavor of fresh tomatoes was far too muted after slow cooking, so we opted for a can of crushed tomatoes, which added the perfect combination of tomato pieces and flavorful sauce needed to braise our tenderloins. We stirred in a tablespoon of olive oil, along with peppery fresh basil, to brighten and enrich the finished dish. You will need an oval slow cooker for this recipe. Because they are cooked gently and not browned, the tenderloins will be rosy throughout. Check the tenderloins' temperature after 1 hour of cooking and continue to monitor until they register 145 degrees.

1 pound eggplant, cut into ½-inch pieces

1 pound zucchini, cut into ½-inch pieces

1 onion, chopped

2 tablespoons extra-virgin olive oil

3 garlic cloves, minced

1 tablespoon tomato paste

1 teaspoon minced fresh thyme or ¼ teaspoon dried
   Salt and pepper

1 (28-ounce) can crushed tomatoes

2 (12- to 16-ounce) pork tenderloins, trimmed

¼ cup chopped fresh basil

1. Adjust oven rack 6 inches from broiler element and heat broiler. Toss eggplant, zucchini, and onion with 1 tablespoon oil, garlic, tomato paste, thyme, ¼ teaspoon salt, and ¼ teaspoon pepper in bowl. Spread vegetable mixture evenly over aluminum foil–lined rimmed baking sheet and broil until softened and spotty brown, 8 to 10 minutes; transfer to slow cooker.

2. Stir tomatoes into slow cooker. Season tenderloins with salt and pepper and nestle into slow cooker, side by side, alternating thicker end to thinner end. Cover and cook until pork registers 145 degrees, 1 to 2 hours on low.

3. Transfer tenderloins to carving board, tent loosely with foil, and let rest for 5 minutes. Stir basil and remaining 1 tablespoon oil into ratatouille and season with salt and pepper to taste. Slice tenderloins ¼ inch thick and serve with ratatouille.

These pork chops have a lush, bacon-infused sauce that rivals any made on the stovetop.

Smothered Pork Chops with Onions and Bacon

SERVES 4   `ALL DAY`

COOKING TIME 7 TO 8 HOURS ON LOW OR 4 TO 5 HOURS ON HIGH

SLOW COOKER SIZE 5 TO 7 QUARTS

WHY THIS RECIPE WORKS This Southern staple promises fork-tender chops covered in a rich, oniony gravy. For our slow-cooker take on smothered chops, bone-in blade-cut chops were the perfect choice because they contain a good amount of fat and connective tissue that help them stay tender and juicy during hours of braising. We started by rendering chopped bacon, which helped create a savory foundation for our sauce. We then sautéed onions, garlic, and some thyme in the fat before adding a little flour and some chicken broth, which gave us the makings for a full-bodied gravy. To further boost the gravy's flavor, we added some soy sauce (for an extra bit of meatiness) and just a little brown sugar. We livened up the finished gravy with a splash of cider vinegar and a tablespoon of minced parsley. You will need an oval slow cooker for this recipe.

4 slices bacon, chopped

3 onions, halved and sliced ½ inch thick

⅓ cup all-purpose flour

3 garlic cloves, minced

1 tablespoon minced fresh thyme or 1 teaspoon dried

1 cup chicken broth

2 tablespoons soy sauce

4 teaspoons packed brown sugar

2 bay leaves

4 (8- to 10-ounce) bone-in blade-cut pork chops, ¾ inch thick, trimmed

Salt and pepper

1 tablespoon cider vinegar

1 tablespoon minced fresh parsley

1. Cook bacon in 12-inch skillet over medium heat until crisp, 5 to 7 minutes. Add onions and cook until softened and lightly browned, about 10 minutes. Stir in flour, garlic, and thyme and cook until fragrant, about 1 minute. Slowly stir in broth, scraping up any browned bits and smoothing out any lumps; transfer to slow cooker.

2. Stir soy sauce, sugar, and bay leaves into slow cooker. Cut 2 slits about 2 inches apart through fat on edges of each pork chop. Season chops with salt and pepper and nestle into slow cooker. Cover and cook until pork is tender and fork slips easily in and out of meat, 7 to 8 hours on low or 4 to 5 hours on high.

3. Transfer chops to serving dish, tent loosely with aluminum foil, and let rest for 5 minutes. Discard bay leaves. Using large spoon, skim fat from surface of sauce. Stir in vinegar and parsley and season with salt and pepper to taste. Spoon 1 cup sauce over chops and serve, passing remaining sauce separately.

NOTES FROM THE TEST KITCHEN

Buying Blade-Cut Pork Chops

Pork chops come from the loin of the pig and can be cut into blade chops, rib chops, center-cut chops, and sirloin chops. Cut from the shoulder end of the loin, blade chops are the toughest cut—but they are also the fattiest, juiciest, and most flavorful. We put the slow cooker to work to cook these chops gently until they are tender. Look for bone-in chops with plenty of dark meat and good marbling.

Braised Pork Chops with Dried Fruit Compote

SERVES 4 `EASY PREP` `ALL DAY`

COOKING TIME 7 TO 8 HOURS ON LOW OR 4 TO 5 HOURS ON HIGH

SLOW COOKER SIZE 5 TO 7 QUARTS

WHY THIS RECIPE WORKS Pork and fruit are a natural combination, but fresh fruit in a slow cooker is a dicey proposition unless you are using it just for flavor. So since we wanted the fruit to play a starring role alongside the pork, we turned to dried fruit, along with applesauce, to make a simple fruit compote for our slow-cooker pork chops. Balanced with shallots, brown sugar, and vinegar, plus a cinnamon stick, this lively compote was packed with flavor. This recipe was a snap to make—the only prep work was cutting the apricots and mincing the shallots. You will need an oval slow cooker for this recipe.

1 cup applesauce

1 cup dried apricots, quartered

½ cup dried cherries

2 shallots, minced

2 tablespoons packed brown sugar

1 tablespoon cider vinegar, plus extra for seasoning

2 bay leaves

1 cinnamon stick

4 (8- to 10-ounce) bone-in blade-cut pork chops, ¾ inch thick, trimmed

Salt and pepper

2 tablespoons minced fresh parsley

1. Combine applesauce, apricots, cherries, shallots, sugar, vinegar, bay leaves, and cinnamon stick in slow cooker. Cut 2 slits about 2 inches apart through fat on edges of each pork chop. Season chops with salt and pepper and nestle into slow cooker. Cover and cook until pork is tender and fork slips easily in and out of meat, 7 to 8 hours on low or 4 to 5 hours on high.

2. Transfer chops to serving dish, tent loosely with aluminum foil, and let rest for 5 minutes. Discard bay leaves and cinnamon stick. Using large spoon, skim fat from surface of sauce. Stir in parsley and season with salt, pepper, and extra vinegar to taste. Spoon 1 cup sauce over chops and serve, passing remaining sauce separately.

Molasses, ketchup, and liquid smoke infuse meaty blade steaks and pinto beans with deep smoky flavor.

Braised Pork Chops with Campfire Beans

SERVES 4 **EASY PREP** **ALL DAY**

COOKING TIME 7 TO 8 HOURS ON LOW OR 4 TO 5 HOURS ON HIGH

SLOW COOKER SIZE 5 TO 7 QUARTS

WHY THIS RECIPE WORKS Beans are a classic accompaniment to pork dishes, and we wanted to complement our meaty pork chops with a side of hearty barbecued beans. To create a deeply flavored sauce, we used a small amount of ketchup and molasses for the necessary sweetness and viscosity, then amped up the flavor with onion, chili powder, and liquid smoke. Canned pinto beans turned creamy and tender in the slow cooker as they absorbed the smoky flavor of the sauce and helped to braise the chops. We chose blade-cut pork chops, which contain a good amount of fat and connective

tissue that help them stay tender and juicy during hours of braising. To really wake up the flavor of the beans before serving, we stirred in cider vinegar and Dijon mustard for a hit of piquant freshness. You will need an oval slow cooker for this recipe.

    1 onion, chopped fine
    2 garlic cloves, minced
    1 teaspoon chili powder
    1 tablespoon vegetable oil
    2 (15-ounce) cans pinto or navy beans, rinsed
    ¼ cup ketchup
    1 tablespoon molasses
    ½ teaspoon liquid smoke
    4 (8- to 10-ounce) bone-in blade-cut pork
      chops, ¾ inch thick, trimmed
      Salt and pepper
    1 tablespoon cider vinegar
    1 tablespoon Dijon mustard
    2 scallions, sliced thin

1. Microwave onion, garlic, chili powder, and oil in bowl, stirring occasionally, until onion is softened, about 5 minutes; transfer to slow cooker. Stir in beans, ketchup, molasses, and liquid smoke.

2. Cut 2 slits about 2 inches apart through fat on edges of each pork chop. Season chops with salt and pepper and nestle into slow cooker. Cover and cook until pork is tender, 7 to 8 hours on low or 4 to 5 hours on high.

3. Transfer chops to serving dish, tent loosely with aluminum foil, and let rest for 5 minutes. Using large spoon, skim fat from surface of sauce. Transfer 1 cup beans to bowl and mash with potato masher until mostly smooth. Stir mashed beans, vinegar, mustard, and scallions into remaining beans, and season with salt and pepper to taste. Serve chops with beans.

PREVENTING CURLED PORK CHOPS

Pork chops—especially thin-cut chops—have a tendency to buckle and curl as they cook. To prevent this, cut two small slits, about 2 inches apart, into the fat and connective tissue on the edges of each chop.

MAKE IT 5 WAYS BARBECUED SPARERIBS

Classic Barbecued Spareribs

SERVES 4 TO 6 `EASY PREP` `ALL DAY`
COOKING TIME 7 TO 8 HOURS ON LOW OR 4 TO 5 HOURS ON HIGH
SLOW COOKER SIZE 5 TO 7 QUARTS

For fall-off-the-bone-tender barbecued pork spareribs with grilled flavor, we started by covering the ribs with a dry spice rub for deep flavor. To fit two racks of spareribs into the slow cooker, we cut them in half and stood the racks upright around the slow cooker's perimeter, overlapping them slightly. We found that leaving the membrane coating the underside of the ribs attached helped hold the racks together as they cooked Once the ribs were fully tender, we transferred them to a wire rack set in a baking sheet, brushed them with a simple pantry barbecue sauce, and broiled them to develop a lightly charred exterior. Avoid buying ribs labeled "spareribs"; their large size and irregular shape make them unwieldy in a slow cooker. St. Louis–style spareribs are smaller and more uniform in size. You can substitute an equal amount of baby back ribs; reduce the cooking time to 4 to 5 hours on low or 3 to 4 hours on high. You will need an oval slow cooker for these recipes.

1 CLASSIC BARBECUED SPARERIBS

- 3 tablespoons paprika
- 2 tablespoons packed brown sugar
- 2 teaspoons onion powder
- 2 teaspoons garlic powder
- ¼ teaspoon cayenne pepper
  Salt and pepper
- 2 (2½- to 3-pound) racks St. Louis–style spareribs, trimmed, halved
- ½ cup ketchup
- 6 tablespoons molasses
- 2 tablespoons Dijon mustard
- 1 tablespoon cider vinegar
- ½ teaspoon liquid smoke

1. Combine paprika, sugar, onion powder, garlic powder, cayenne, 2 teaspoons salt, and 1 tablespoon pepper in bowl. Pat ribs dry with paper towels; rub with spice mixture.

2. Arrange ribs upright in slow cooker, with thick ends pointing down and meaty sides against wall (ribs will overlap). Cover and cook until ribs are just tender, 7 to 8 hours on low or 4 to 5 hours on high.

3. Adjust oven rack 4 inches from broiler element and heat broiler. Set wire rack in aluminum foil–lined rimmed baking sheet; coat with vegetable oil spray. Transfer ribs meaty side up to prepared rack; let sit until surface is dry, about 10 minutes.

4. Whisk ketchup, molasses, mustard, vinegar, and liquid smoke together in bowl. Brush ribs with half of sauce; broil until sauce is bubbling and beginning to char, about 5 minutes. Brush ribs with remaining sauce, tent loosely with foil, and let rest for 10 minutes. Cut ribs in between bones to separate. Serve.

2 SWEET AND SOUR BARBECUED SPARERIBS

- 2 tablespoons grated fresh ginger
- 6 garlic cloves, minced
- 1 tablespoon ground allspice
  Salt and pepper
- 2 (2½- to 3-pound) racks St. Louis–style spareribs, trimmed, halved
- ½ cup pineapple preserves
- ¼ cup ketchup
- ¼ cup packed dark brown sugar
- 1 tablespoon distilled white vinegar
- 1 tablespoon soy sauce
- ¼ teaspoon red pepper flakes

1. Combine 1 tablespoon ginger, two-thirds of garlic, allspice, 2 teaspoons salt, and ½ teaspoon pepper in bowl. Pat ribs dry with paper towels; rub with spice mixture.

2. Arrange ribs upright in slow cooker, with thick ends pointing down and meaty sides against wall (ribs will overlap). Cover and cook until ribs are just tender, 7 to 8 hours on low or 4 to 5 hours on high.

3. Adjust oven rack 4 inches from broiler element and heat broiler. Set wire rack in aluminum foil–lined rimmed baking sheet; coat with vegetable oil spray. Transfer ribs meaty side up to prepared rack; let sit until surface is dry, about 10 minutes.

4. Whisk pineapple preserves, ketchup, sugar, vinegar, soy sauce, pepper flakes, remaining 1 tablespoon ginger, and remaining garlic together in bowl until sugar is dissolved. Brush ribs with half of sauce; broil until sauce is bubbling and beginning to char, about 5 minutes. Brush ribs with remaining sauce, tent loosely with foil, and let rest for 10 minutes. Cut ribs in between bones to separate. Serve.

3 SPICY MUSTARD BARBECUED SPARERIBS

5 tablespoons packed brown sugar
1 tablespoon onion powder
1 tablespoon garlic powder
2 teaspoons ground cumin
½ teaspoon cayenne pepper
  Salt and pepper
2 (2½- to 3-pound) racks St. Louis–style spareribs, trimmed, halved
1 cup yellow mustard
¼ cup cider vinegar
1 teaspoon hot sauce
1 teaspoon Worcestershire sauce

1. Combine 2 tablespoons sugar, onion powder, garlic powder, cumin, cayenne, ½ teaspoon salt, and ½ teaspoon pepper in bowl. Pat ribs dry with paper towels; rub with spice mixture.

2. Arrange ribs upright in slow cooker, with thick ends pointing down and meaty sides against wall (ribs will overlap). Cover and cook until ribs are just tender, 7 to 8 hours on low or 4 to 5 hours on high.

3. Adjust oven rack 4 inches from broiler element and heat broiler. Set wire rack in aluminum foil–lined rimmed baking sheet; coat with vegetable oil spray. Transfer ribs meaty side up to prepared rack; let sit until surface is dry, about 10 minutes.

4. Whisk mustard, vinegar, hot sauce, Worcestershire, ½ teaspoon pepper, and remaining 3 tablespoons sugar together in bowl until sugar is dissolved. Brush ribs with half of sauce; broil until sauce is bubbling and beginning to char, about 5 minutes. Brush ribs with remaining sauce, tent loosely with foil, and let rest for 10 minutes. Cut ribs in between bones to separate. Serve.

4 CHINESE BARBECUED SPARERIBS

1 tablespoon five-spice powder
  Salt and pepper
2 (2½- to 3-pound) racks St. Louis–style spareribs, trimmed, halved
⅓ cup hoisin sauce
⅓ cup honey
¼ cup sugar
¼ cup soy sauce
¼ cup ketchup
2 tablespoons dry sherry
1 tablespoon toasted sesame oil
1 tablespoon grated fresh ginger
2 garlic cloves, minced

1. Combine five-spice powder, 1½ teaspoons salt, and 1 teaspoon pepper in bowl. Pat ribs dry with paper towels; rub with spice mixture.

2. Arrange ribs upright in slow cooker, with thick ends pointing down and meaty sides against wall (ribs will overlap). Cover and cook until ribs are just tender, 7 to 8 hours on low or 4 to 5 hours on high.

3. Adjust oven rack 4 inches from broiler element and heat broiler. Set wire rack in aluminum foil–lined rimmed baking sheet; coat with vegetable oil spray. Transfer ribs meaty side up to prepared rack; let sit until surface is dry, about 10 minutes.

4. Whisk hoisin, honey, sugar, soy sauce, ketchup, sherry, oil, ginger, and garlic together in bowl until sugar is dissolved. Brush ribs with half of sauce; broil until sauce is bubbling and beginning to char, about 5 minutes. Brush ribs with remaining sauce, tent loosely with foil, and let rest for 10 minutes. Cut ribs in between bones to separate. Serve.

5 FIESTA BARBECUED SPARERIBS

¼ cup packed brown sugar
3 tablespoons chili powder
2 teaspoons ground cumin
2 teaspoons ground coriander
1 teaspoon garlic powder
  Salt and pepper
2 (2½- to 3-pound) racks St. Louis–style spareribs, trimmed, halved
1 cup chili sauce
¼ cup finely chopped jarred jalapeños
¼ cup chopped fresh cilantro
1 teaspoon grated lime zest plus 1 tablespoon juice

1. Combine 2 tablespoons sugar, chili powder, cumin, coriander, garlic powder, and 2 teaspoons salt in bowl. Pat ribs dry with paper towels; rub with spice mixture.

2. Arrange ribs upright in slow cooker, with thick ends pointing down and meaty sides against wall (ribs will overlap). Cover and cook until ribs are just tender, 7 to 8 hours on low or 4 to 5 hours on high.

3. Adjust oven rack 4 inches from broiler element and heat broiler. Set wire rack in aluminum foil–lined rimmed baking sheet; coat with vegetable oil spray. Transfer ribs meaty side up to prepared rack; let sit until surface is dry, about 10 minutes.

4. Whisk chili sauce, jalapeños, cilantro, lime zest and juice, ½ teaspoon salt, ¼ teaspoon pepper, and remaining 2 tablespoons sugar together in bowl until sugar is dissolved. Brush ribs with half of sauce; broil until sauce is bubbling and beginning to char, about 5 minutes. Brush ribs with remaining sauce, tent loosely with foil, and let rest for 10 minutes. Cut ribs in between bones to separate. Serve.

For the crispy edges that are the hallmark of this Chinese favorite, we broil the meat with extra sauce after cooking it.

Chinese Barbecued Pork

SERVES 6 TO 8 **EASY PREP**

COOKING TIME 5 TO 6 HOURS ON LOW OR 3 TO 4 HOURS ON HIGH

SLOW COOKER SIZE 5 TO 7 QUARTS

WHY THIS RECIPE WORKS For a slow-cooker version of the Chinatown favorite *char siu*, we started with a boneless pork butt cut into 1-inch-thick steaks. After seasoning the meat with five-spice powder, we "braised" it to tenderness. A coating of quick, no-cook sauce and a few minutes under the broiler rendered this pork glazed, crispy, deeply browned, and intensely delicious. Pork butt roast is often labeled Boston butt in the supermarket.

1½ teaspoons five-spice powder
1½ teaspoons salt
¾ teaspoon pepper
1 (4-pound) boneless pork butt roast, trimmed and sliced crosswise into 1-inch-thick steaks
⅓ cup hoisin sauce
⅓ cup honey
¼ cup sugar
¼ cup soy sauce
¼ cup ketchup
2 tablespoons dry sherry
1 tablespoon toasted sesame oil
1 tablespoon grated fresh ginger
2 garlic cloves, minced

1. Combine ¾ teaspoon five-spice powder, salt, and pepper in bowl. Rub pork with spice mixture and arrange in even layer in slow cooker. Cover and cook until pork is just tender, 5 to 6 hours on low or 3 to 4 hours on high.

2. Adjust oven rack 4 inches from broiler element and heat broiler. Set wire rack in aluminum foil–lined rimmed baking sheet and coat with vegetable oil spray. Whisk hoisin, honey, sugar, soy sauce, ketchup, sherry, oil, ginger, garlic, and remaining ¾ teaspoon five-spice powder together in bowl.

3. Transfer pork to prepared rack; discard cooking liquid. Brush pork with one-third of sauce and broil until lightly caramelized, about 10 to 15 minutes, flipping and brushing pork with more sauce halfway through broiling. Brush pork with remaining sauce and broil until deep mahogany and crispy around edges, about 3 minutes. Transfer pork to cutting board and let rest for 10 minutes. Slice pork crosswise into thin strips and serve.

PREPARING FRESH GINGER

1. To quickly peel knob of ginger, hold it firmly against cutting board and use edge of teaspoon to scrape away thin, brown skin.

2. To grate ginger, peel just small section of large piece of ginger, then grate peeled portion using rasp-style grater, using unpeeled ginger as handle to keep your fingers safely away from grater.

3. For smashed coins of ginger, slice peeled knob of ginger crosswise into coins, then use corner of heavy pan (or mallet) to gently smash ginger and release its flavor.

Pad thai is surprisingly easy to make in a slow cooker, with the noodles added at the end to soak up the sauce.

Pork Pad Thai

SERVES 4 TO 6 EASY PREP

COOKING TIME 6 TO 7 HOURS ON LOW OR 4 TO 5 HOURS ON HIGH

SLOW COOKER SIZE 4 TO 7 QUARTS

WHY THIS RECIPE WORKS Great pad thai should feature clean, fresh, not-too-sweet flavors, perfectly cooked noodles, and plenty of tender protein—not exactly a dish you would expect to come completely out of the slow cooker. But this recipe achieves just that. For our slow-cooker version, we began by considering the appropriate protein to include. Most recipes include shrimp and egg, but we decided to sidestep tradition in favor of boneless country-style pork ribs, which could take full advantage of the slow-cook time and yield tender, flavorful meat. Braising the pork in a combination of chicken broth, fish sauce, sugar, and tamarind juice created a distinct pad thai flavor profile. Blooming the aromatics (scallion whites, garlic, and a chile) in toasted sesame oil before adding them to the slow cooker elevated the flavors even further. Perfectly cooked noodles were next, and we found the simplest solution was

best. After removing the pork from the slow cooker, we placed the noodles in the remaining braising liquid and let them rehydrate for 20 minutes. To complete the dish, we returned the pork, now shredded into 1-inch pieces, to the slow cooker along with bean sprouts, scallion greens, cilantro, and peanuts for added freshness and crunch. Tamarind juice concentrate can be found at Asian markets as well as in the international food aisle of many supermarkets. Look for tamarind juice concentrate manufactured in Thailand, which is thinner and tastes brighter than the paste concentrate produced in other countries. If you can't find it, substitute 1½ tablespoons lime juice and 1½ tablespoons water, and omit the lime wedges. Look for country-style pork ribs with lots of fat and dark meat, and stay away from ribs that look overly lean with pale meat, as they will taste very dry after the extended cooking time.

- 3 tablespoons toasted sesame oil
- 4 scallions, white parts minced, green parts cut into 1-inch pieces
- 4 garlic cloves, minced
- 1 serrano chile, stemmed and sliced into thin rings
- 1¾ cups chicken broth
- ¼ cup sugar
- 3 tablespoons tamarind juice concentrate
- 3 tablespoons fish sauce
- 1½ pounds boneless country-style pork ribs, trimmed
  Salt and pepper
- 8 ounces (¼-inch-wide) rice noodles
- 4 ounces (2 cups) bean sprouts
- 2 tablespoons rice vinegar
- ¼ cup fresh cilantro leaves
- ¼ cup dry-roasted peanuts, chopped coarse
  Lime wedges

1. Microwave oil, scallion whites, garlic, and serrano in bowl, stirring occasionally, until fragrant, about 1 minute; transfer to slow cooker. Stir in broth, sugar, tamarind juice, and 2 tablespoons fish sauce.

2. Season pork with salt and pepper and nestle into slow cooker. Cover and cook until pork is tender and fork slips easily in and out of meat, 6 to 7 hours on low or 4 to 5 hours on high.

3. Transfer pork to cutting board, let cool slightly, then pull apart into large chunks using 2 forks. Nestle noodles into cooking liquid left in slow cooker, cover, and cook on high until tender, 20 to 30 minutes.

4. Add pork to noodles and gently toss to combine. Let sit until heated through, about 5 minutes. Add bean sprouts, scallion greens, vinegar, and remaining 1 tablespoon fish sauce and toss to combine. Sprinkle with cilantro and peanuts. Serve with lime wedges.

Carne Adovada

SERVES 6 TO 8 ALL DAY

COOKING TIME 8 TO 9 HOURS ON LOW OR 5 TO 6 HOURS ON HIGH

SLOW COOKER SIZE 4 TO 7 QUARTS

WHY THIS RECIPE WORKS For this recipe, we wanted to develop complexity without having to spend time browning meat and aromatics and grinding a heap of hard-to-find dried New Mexican chiles. In the end, we ditched stovetop browning in favor of seasoning the pork with soy sauce. (The sauce was so flavorful that we didn't miss the 20 to 30 minutes we would have spent browning the meat.) We softened the onion and bloomed the spices in the microwave, avoiding any stovetop prep altogether. We replicated the taste of dried chiles by using a combination of raisins, brewed coffee, and smoky chipotle chiles in adobo sauce. And finally, we pureed the sauce in a blender with just enough liquid and thickener to form a sauce that would coat the meat like a blanket. Pork butt roast is often labeled Boston butt in the supermarket. Serve with Basmati Rice Pilaf (page 134) and/or warm corn tortillas.

  2 onions, chopped
  ½ cup chili powder
  6 garlic cloves, minced
  3 tablespoons vegetable oil
  1 tablespoon minced canned chipotle chile in adobo sauce
  2 teaspoons dried oregano
    Salt and pepper
  ¾ cup chicken broth
  ½ cup brewed coffee
  ⅓ cup all-purpose flour
  ¼ cup raisins
  3 tablespoons soy sauce
  4 pounds boneless pork butt roast, pulled apart at seams, trimmed, and cut into 1½-inch pieces
  ¼ cup minced fresh cilantro
  1 teaspoon grated lime zest plus 1 tablespoon juice

1. Microwave onions, chili powder, garlic, oil, chipotle, oregano, and 1 teaspoon salt in bowl, stirring occasionally, until onions are softened, about 5 minutes. Transfer onion mixture to blender and process with broth, coffee, flour, raisins, and soy sauce until smooth, about 1 minute, scraping down sides of blender jar as needed; transfer to slow cooker.

2. Season pork with salt and pepper and stir into slow cooker. Cover and cook until pork is tender, 8 to 9 hours on low or 5 to 6 hours on high.

3. Using large spoon, skim fat from surface of sauce. Stir in cilantro and lime zest and juice. Season with salt and pepper to taste. Serve.

During the long cooking time, the pork becomes infused with bright citrus flavor and earthy spice notes.

Pork Carnitas

SERVES 6 TO 8 EASY PREP ALL DAY

COOKING TIME 8 TO 9 HOURS ON LOW OR 5 TO 6 HOURS ON HIGH

SLOW COOKER SIZE 4 TO 7 QUARTS

WHY THIS RECIPE WORKS To achieve a slow-cooker version of this Mexican pulled pork dish, we had to make some adjustments to compensate for the moist environment of the slow cooker. We cut pork shoulder into chunks and combined the meat with onion, orange zest and juice, lime zest and juice, garlic, ground cumin, oregano, and hefty amounts of salt and pepper. As the meat cooked, it released just the right amount of liquid to help it braise and become pull-apart tender. To get the characteristic crispiness of the dish, we turned to the stovetop and a nonstick skillet. We mashed the pork pieces, added them to the hot skillet along with some of the intensely flavorful juices, and cooked the mixture until the pork began to fry and turn crispy. Pork butt roast is often labeled Boston butt in the supermarket. Do not overtrim the pork; this extra fat is essential for keeping the pork moist and helping it brown when sautéed in step 3. Serve with sour cream, chopped onion, chopped cilantro, thinly sliced radishes, and/or lime wedges.

4 pounds boneless pork butt roast, pulled apart
  at seams, trimmed, and cut into 1½-inch pieces
1 small onion, peeled and halved
3 (2-inch) strips orange zest plus ½ cup juice
3 (2-inch) strips lime zest plus 2 tablespoons juice
5 garlic cloves, minced
1 tablespoon ground cumin
1 tablespoon dried oregano
  Salt and pepper
2 bay leaves
2 tablespoons vegetable oil
18–24 (6-inch) corn tortillas, warmed

1. Combine pork, onion, orange zest and juice, lime zest and juice, garlic, cumin, oregano, 2½ teaspoons salt, 1½ teaspoons pepper, and bay leaves in slow cooker. Cover and cook until pork is tender, 8 to 9 hours on low or 5 to 6 hours on high.

2. Using slotted spoon, transfer pork to large bowl. Using potato masher, smash pork until coarsely shredded. Strain cooking liquid into separate bowl; discard solids.

3. Heat oil in 12-inch nonstick skillet over medium-high heat until shimmering. Add pork to skillet. Whisk cooking liquid to recombine, then add 1 cup to skillet with pork. Cook, stirring occasionally, until liquid has evaporated and pork is evenly browned and crisp in spots, 10 to 15 minutes. Season with salt and pepper to taste. Transfer pork to serving dish and moisten with remaining cooking liquid as needed. Serve with tortillas.

NOTES FROM THE TEST KITCHEN

Juicing Lemons and Limes

We've tried countless methods and gizmos for juicing lemons and limes and have dismissed most of them. However, we do endorse rolling lemons vigorously on a hard surface before slicing them open to be juiced. Why? Rolling a lemon on a hard surface bruises, breaks up, and softens the rind's tissues as it also tears the membranes of the juice vesicles (the tear-shaped juice sacs), filling the inside of the lemon with juice before it is cut and squeezed. Once the lemon is rolled, we recommend either a wooden reamer or a juicer, which we have found to be especially easy and fast, and equally effective. However you squeeze lemon or lime juice, we strongly recommend that you do so at the last minute; our testing has proven that the flavor mellows quickly and the juice will taste bland in a short time.

Shredded Pork Mole Tacos

SERVES 4 `EASY PREP` `ALL DAY`
COOKING TIME 7 TO 8 HOURS ON LOW OR 4 TO 5 HOURS ON HIGH
SLOW COOKER SIZE 4 TO 7 QUARTS

WHY THIS RECIPE WORKS Weeknight tacos are usually limited to quick-cooking fillings like ground beef, but the slow cooker makes it easy to use cuts like pork butt that take several hours to turn tender. We wanted to make easy pulled pork tacos and pair them with a rich mole sauce. Traditionally mole requires an extensive list of ingredients to develop its complex flavor, but we simplified our version by relying on pantry staples like chili powder, cumin, and chipotle chiles. Canned tomato sauce added acidity, and raisins gave us just the right sweetness. Once the pork was cooked through, we quickly blended the sauce to give it the perfect consistency. A little lime juice and cilantro at the end balanced the flavors and completed the dish. Pork butt roast is often labeled Boston butt in the supermarket. Serve with sour cream, chopped onion, chopped cilantro, thinly sliced radishes, and/or lime wedges.

1 (15-ounce) can tomato sauce
1 cup raisins
2 tablespoons chili powder
2 tablespoons ground cumin
1 tablespoon minced canned chipotle chile
  in adobo sauce
3 garlic cloves, peeled
2 pounds boneless pork butt roast, pulled apart
  at seams, trimmed, and cut into 1½-inch pieces
  Salt and pepper
½ cup minced fresh cilantro
3 tablespoons lime juice (2 limes)
12 (6-inch) corn tortillas, warmed

1. Combine tomato sauce, raisins, chili powder, cumin, chipotle, and garlic in slow cooker. Season pork with salt and pepper and stir into slow cooker. Cover and cook until pork is tender, 7 to 8 hours on low or 4 to 5 hours on high.

2. Using slotted spoon, transfer pork to large bowl. Using potato masher, smash pork until coarsely shredded; cover to keep warm.

3. Process cooking liquid in blender until smooth, about 1 minute. Adjust sauce consistency with hot water as needed. Stir in cilantro and lime juice, and season with salt and pepper to taste. Toss pork with 1 cup sauce. Serve pork with tortillas, passing remaining sauce separately.

North Carolina Pulled Pork

SERVES 8 TO 10 `EASY PREP` `ALL DAY`

COOKING TIME 9 TO 10 HOURS ON LOW OR 6 TO 7 HOURS
ON HIGH

SLOW COOKER SIZE 5 TO 7 QUARTS

WHY THIS RECIPE WORKS To make authentic North Carolina pulled pork, with its succulent, smoky meat and tangy vinegar-based sauce, we began by smothering a pork butt roast with a sweet and spicy dry rub of brown sugar, paprika, chili powder, cumin, salt, and pepper. For smokiness we cooked the pork with smoked ham hocks, which we then shredded along with the roast. Reducing the defatted cooking liquid to a concentrated 1 cup on the stovetop, then stirring in cider vinegar, ketchup, more sugar, and liquid smoke, led to the perfect balance of tangy, sweet, and smoky flavors in the finished barbecue sauce. Note that this sauce is fairly thin compared to gooey molasses-based sauces. Don't shred the meat too fine in step 2; it will break up more as the meat is combined with the sauce. Pork butt roast is often labeled Boston butt in the supermarket. Serve on soft buns with pickle chips.

- 6 tablespoons packed dark brown sugar
- ¼ cup paprika
- 2 tablespoons chili powder
- 1 tablespoon ground cumin
   Salt and pepper
- 1 (4- to 5-pound) boneless pork butt roast, trimmed and quartered
- 3 (12-ounce) smoked ham hocks, rinsed
- 2 cups chicken broth
- 1 cup cider vinegar
- ¾ cup ketchup
- 1½ teaspoons liquid smoke

1. Combine 3 tablespoons sugar, paprika, chili powder, cumin, 2 teaspoons salt, and 1 tablespoon pepper in bowl. Rub pork with spice mixture and arrange in even layer in slow cooker along with ham hocks. Pour broth over pork. Cover and cook until pork is tender and fork slips easily in and out of meat, 9 to 10 hours on low or 6 to 7 hours on high.

2. Transfer pork and ham hocks to cutting board, let cool slightly, then shred into bite-size pieces; discard fat, skin, and bones. Transfer pork to large bowl and cover to keep warm.

3. Strain cooking liquid into fat separator and let sit for 5 minutes; discard solids. Bring defatted liquid to simmer in saucepan over medium heat and cook until thickened and measures 1 cup, 20 to 30 minutes. Whisk in vinegar, ketchup, liquid smoke, and remaining 3 tablespoons sugar. Season with salt and pepper to taste. Toss pork with 1½ cups sauce and serve, passing remaining sauce separately.

SIMPLE SIDES

SWEET AND TANGY COLESLAW

SERVES 4

If you don't have a salad spinner, use a colander to drain the cabbage, pressing out the excess moisture with a rubber spatula. This recipe can be easily doubled.

- ¼ cup cider vinegar, plus extra for seasoning
- 2 tablespoons vegetable oil
- ¼ teaspoon celery seeds
   Salt and pepper
- ½ head green or red cabbage, cored and shredded (6 cups)
- ¼ cup sugar, plus extra for seasoning
- 1 large carrot, peeled and shredded
- 2 tablespoons chopped fresh parsley

1. Whisk vinegar, oil, celery seeds, and ¼ teaspoon pepper together in medium bowl. Place bowl in freezer and chill until dressing is cold, at least 15 minutes or up to 30 minutes.

2. Meanwhile, in large bowl, toss cabbage with sugar and 1 teaspoon salt. Cover and microwave until cabbage is just beginning to wilt, about 1 minute. Stir briefly, cover, and continue to microwave until cabbage is partially wilted and has reduced in volume by one-third, 30 to 60 seconds.

3. Transfer cabbage mixture to salad spinner and spin until excess water is removed, 10 to 20 seconds. Remove bowl from freezer, add cabbage mixture, carrot, and parsley to cold dressing, and toss to coat. Season with salt, pepper, vinegar, and sugar to taste. Refrigerate until chilled, about 15 minutes. Toss coleslaw again before serving.

Game Day Brats and Beer

SERVES 4 `EASY PREP`

COOKING TIME 2 TO 3 HOURS ON LOW

SLOW COOKER SIZE 4 TO 7 QUARTS

WHY THIS RECIPE WORKS Nobody likes to be stuck in the kitchen on game day, so we wanted to develop a recipe for brats and beer that would simmer in the slow cooker while we enjoyed the party. To make sure the bratwurst had plenty of flavor, we stirred a mixture of savory soy sauce, punchy Dijon mustard, caraway seeds, and a little balancing brown sugar into the slow cooker. Onions were also a must; we microwaved them briefly to ensure that they were fully tender by the time the brats were cooked through.

As the bratwurst cooked, the flavors in the pot melded, giving us rich, juicy sausage and flavorful onions. For the finishing touch, we stirred some tangy sauerkraut into the onion mixture to round out the dish. Light-bodied American lagers, such as Budweiser, work best for this recipe. We prefer pouched sauerkraut, sold near the pickles in most supermarkets, to jarred or canned varieties. You will need an oval slow cooker for this recipe.

    1 pound onions, sliced into ½-inch-thick rounds
    1 tablespoon vegetable oil
 1½ pounds bratwurst
    1 cup mild lager, such as Budweiser
   ¼ cup Dijon mustard, plus extra for serving
   ¼ cup soy sauce
    2 tablespoons packed brown sugar
   ½ teaspoon caraway seeds
    1 cup sauerkraut, rinsed
    4 (6-inch) Italian sub rolls, split lengthwise

1. Microwave onions and oil in bowl, stirring occasionally, until onions are softened, about 5 minutes; transfer to slow cooker. Nestle sausage into slow cooker. Whisk beer, mustard, soy sauce, sugar, and caraway together in bowl, then pour over sausage and onions. Cover and cook until sausage is tender, 2 to 3 hours on low.

2. Transfer sausage to cutting board, tent loosely with aluminum foil, and let rest while finishing onion mixture. Stir sauerkraut into slow cooker and let sit until heated through, about 5 minutes. Strain onion-sauerkraut mixture, discarding cooking liquid, and transfer to bowl. Cut bratwurst into 2-inch pieces. Serve bratwurst on rolls with onion-sauerkraut mixture and extra mustard.

Street Fair Sausages with Peppers and Onions

SERVES 4 EASY PREP
COOKING TIME 2 TO 3 HOURS ON LOW
SLOW COOKER SIZE 4 TO 7 QUARTS

WHY THIS RECIPE WORKS For a fun and easy meal, we used the slow cooker to make superflavorful peppers and onions together with perfectly cooked Italian sausage. First, we jump-started the vegetables in the microwave to ensure that they'd cook through, then we added them to the slow cooker and nestled in raw Italian sausages. To season the vegetables as they cooked, we used a potent mixture of chicken broth, tomato paste, and garlic. As they simmered, the peppers and onions absorbed the flavors of the sausage and braising liquid. Once the sausages were cooked through, all we needed to do was strain the peppers and onions and pile them high on sub rolls with the tender, juicy sausages. You will need an oval slow cooker for this recipe.

No need to stand at the grill when you can make these tender sausages, peppers, and onions in your slow cooker.

    2 red or green bell peppers, stemmed, seeded,
      and cut into ¾-inch-wide strips
    2 onions, sliced into ½-inch-thick rounds
    2 tablespoons tomato paste
    1 tablespoon vegetable oil
    1 garlic clove, minced
   ½ cup chicken broth
 1½ pounds hot or sweet Italian sausage
      Salt and pepper
    4 (6-inch) Italian sub rolls, split lengthwise

1. Microwave peppers, onions, tomato paste, oil, and garlic in bowl, stirring occasionally, until vegetables are softened, about 8 minutes; transfer to slow cooker. Stir in broth. Nestle sausage into slow cooker, cover, and cook until sausage is tender, 2 to 3 hours on low.

2. Transfer sausage to cutting board. Strain pepper-onion mixture, discarding cooking liquid, and transfer to bowl. Season with salt and pepper to taste. Cut sausage into 2-inch pieces. Serve sausage on rolls with pepper-onion mixture.

Once the lamb shanks are meltingly tender, we strain the sauce and process it in a blender with harissa and vinegar.

Braised Lamb Shanks with Bell Peppers and Harissa

SERVES 6 ALL DAY

COOKING TIME 7 TO 8 HOURS ON LOW OR 4 TO 5 HOURS ON HIGH

SLOW COOKER SIZE 5 TO 7 QUARTS

WHY THIS RECIPE WORKS Lamb shanks are made for braising in a slow cooker. We found that browning the shanks before braising added complex, roasted flavors. What gives this dish its unique character is the combination of slow-cooked bell peppers, which we gave a head start on the stovetop along with some aromatics and the Tunisian condiment harissa—a potent blend of ground chiles, garlic, and spices. Chicken broth served as a perfect mild medium in which to meld the rich flavors of the lamb, the sweetness of the peppers, and the aromas of the harissa. To keep our sauce clean and light, we made sure to trim our shanks of all visible fat before cooking, and we defatted the cooking liquid after braising. To add richness and more flavor to the sauce, we ran the braised vegetables through the blender with the cooking liquid, and finished with mint for freshness. You will need an oval slow cooker for this recipe.

6 (10- to 12-ounce) lamb shanks, trimmed
    Salt and pepper
1 tablespoon extra-virgin olive oil
4 red bell peppers, stemmed, seeded, and cut
    into 1-inch pieces
1 onion, chopped fine
5 tablespoons harissa
2 tablespoons tomato paste
4 garlic cloves, minced
2 cups chicken broth
2 bay leaves
2 tablespoons red wine vinegar
2 tablespoons minced fresh mint

1. Pat lamb shanks dry with paper towels and season with salt and pepper. Heat oil in 12-inch skillet over medium-high heat until just smoking. Brown half of shanks on all sides, 8 to 10 minutes; transfer to large plate. Repeat with remaining shanks; transfer to plate.

2. Add bell peppers, onion, and 1 teaspoon salt to fat left in skillet and cook over medium heat until vegetables are softened, about 8 minutes. Stir in 3 tablespoons harissa, tomato paste, and garlic and cook until fragrant, about 30 seconds. Stir in broth and bay leaves, scraping up any browned bits; transfer to slow cooker.

3. Nestle lamb shanks into slow cooker, adding any accumulated juices. Cover and cook until lamb is tender and fork slips easily in and out of meat, 7 to 8 hours on low or 4 to 5 hours on high.

4. Transfer shanks to serving dish, tent loosely with aluminum foil, and let rest while finishing sauce. Discard bay leaves. Strain cooking liquid into fat separator, reserving solids, and let sit for 5 minutes. Process defatted liquid, reserved solids, vinegar, and remaining 2 tablespoons harissa in blender until smooth, about 1 minute. Season with salt and pepper to taste. Spoon 1 cup sauce over shanks and sprinkle with mint. Serve, passing remaining sauce separately.

NOTES FROM THE TEST KITCHEN

Buying Harissa

Harissa is a North African chili paste that's used as a condiment and as an ingredient. It's potent, so just a dollop adds a jolt of bright, spicy flavor to everything from soups and stews to sautéed vegetables and fried eggs. Harissa is always made with some combination of hot and/or mild chiles, garlic, and oil and often includes aromatic spices like cumin, coriander, and caraway. We recommend two products. Our top scorer, **Mina Harissa, Spicy,** packs a fiery, garlicky punch that is perfect for heat-seekers. Those who shy away from heat will enjoy our runner-up, the sweeter, milder **Les Moulins Mahjoub Traditional Harissa Spread.**

For a vindaloo sauce with just the right luxurious body, we found that adding a little instant tapioca was key.

Lamb Vindaloo

SERVES 6 TO 8 **ALL DAY**

COOKING TIME 9 TO 10 HOURS ON LOW OR 6 TO 7 HOURS ON HIGH

SLOW COOKER SIZE 5 TO 7 QUARTS

WHY THIS RECIPE WORKS With roots in India, this classic dish is a natural for the slow cooker, combining slowly simmered lamb with a rich tomato-based sauce perfumed with paprika, cumin, cardamom, and cayenne. We chose a hearty boneless lamb shoulder roast for this recipe, and it remained tender and juicy during the extended cooking time. A hefty amount of spices is key in this dish, but too much produced a chalky texture. Instead, we bloomed the spices with the aromatics so we could use a more moderate amount. Some sugar and red wine vinegar also enhanced the flavors of the dish.

3 onions, chopped fine
3 tablespoons vegetable oil
3 tablespoons paprika
8 garlic cloves, minced
2 tablespoons tomato paste
4 teaspoons ground cumin
½ teaspoon ground cardamom
¼ teaspoon cayenne pepper
1 (14.5-ounce) can diced tomatoes
1 cup chicken broth
3 tablespoons instant tapioca
2 tablespoons red wine vinegar
2 bay leaves
1 teaspoon sugar
4 pounds boneless lamb shoulder roast, pulled apart at seams, trimmed, and cut into 1½-inch pieces
   Salt and pepper
¼ cup minced fresh cilantro

1. Microwave onions, oil, paprika, garlic, tomato paste, cumin, cardamom, and cayenne in bowl, stirring occasionally, until onions are softened, about 5 minutes; transfer to slow cooker.

2. Stir tomatoes and their juice, broth, tapioca, vinegar, bay leaves, and sugar into slow cooker. Season lamb with salt and pepper and stir into slow cooker. Cover and cook until lamb is tender, 9 to 10 hours on low or 6 to 7 hours on high.

3. Discard bay leaves. Using large spoon, skim fat from surface of sauce. Adjust consistency with hot water as needed. Stir in cilantro and season with salt and pepper to taste. Serve.

SIMPLE SIDES

COUSCOUS

Toast couscous (see chart below for amounts and serving sizes) with extra-virgin olive oil in skillet over medium heat, stirring occasionally, until couscous is lightly browned, 3 to 5 minutes; transfer to medium bowl. Stir in boiling water, cover, and let sit until couscous is tender, about 12 minutes. Fluff with fork and season with salt and pepper to taste.

Serves	Couscous	Extra-Virgin Olive Oil	Boiling Water
4	1½ cups	2 tablespoons	2 cups
6	2¼ cups	2 tablespoons	3 cups
8	3 cups	3 tablespoons	4 cups
10	3¾ cups	4 tablespoons	5 cups

A ROAST IN EVERY POT

■ EASY PREP ■ LIGHT ■ COOK ALL DAY
Photo: Pork Loin with Fennel, Oranges, and Olives

A creamy dill sauce made with mayonnaise and yogurt plus a splash of red wine vinegar enhance this vegetable salad.

Herbed Chicken with Warm Spring Vegetable Salad

SERVES 4 **EASY PREP**

COOKING TIME 4 TO 5 HOURS ON LOW
SLOW COOKER SIZE 5 TO 7 QUARTS

WHY THIS RECIPE WORKS A fantastic method for making a whole "roast" chicken in the slow cooker comes in handy year-round. This flavorful recipe features a juicy whole chicken and crunchy, vibrant spring vegetables. A simple aromatic mixture of oil, shallot, garlic, and thyme was the perfect way to give the chicken layers of flavor. We rubbed the mixture under the skin to give it direct contact with the meat while it cooked. We placed the chicken breast side down into the slow cooker to keep the breast meat moist during cooking, and then we scattered seasoned radish halves around the chicken, which allowed for the chicken and the radishes to cook evenly in the same amount of time. While the chicken rested before carving, we stirred fresh sugar snap peas into the braised radishes in the slow cooker and cooked on high until the snap peas were crisp-tender yet still vibrant. A creamy dill dressing was the perfect flavorful accompaniment to our spring vegetable salad. Check the chicken's temperature after 4 hours of cooking and continue to monitor until the breast registers 160 degrees and the thighs register 175 degrees. You will need an oval slow cooker for this recipe.

¼ cup extra-virgin olive oil
1 shallot, minced
4 garlic cloves, minced
2 teaspoons minced fresh thyme or ½ teaspoon dried
  Salt and pepper
1 (4-pound) whole chicken, giblets discarded
1 pound radishes, trimmed and halved
1 pound sugar snap peas, strings removed
¼ cup plain whole-milk yogurt
¼ cup mayonnaise
2 tablespoons minced fresh dill
1 tablespoon red wine vinegar
1 teaspoon sugar
  Lemon wedges

1. Microwave 3 tablespoons oil, shallot, three-quarters of garlic, thyme, ½ teaspoon salt, and ¼ teaspoon pepper in bowl until fragrant, about 30 seconds; let cool slightly.

2. Using your fingers, gently loosen skin covering breast and thighs of chicken. Place half of oil mixture under skin, directly on meat in center of each side of breast and on thighs. Gently press skin to distribute oil mixture over meat. Rub entire exterior surface of chicken with remaining oil mixture. Place chicken, breast side down, into slow cooker.

3. Toss radishes with remaining 1 tablespoon oil, ¼ teaspoon salt, and ¼ teaspoon pepper in clean bowl, then arrange around chicken. Cover and cook until breast registers 160 degrees and thighs register 175 degrees, 4 to 5 hours on low.

4. Transfer chicken to carving board, tent loosely with aluminum foil, and let rest while finishing vegetables. Stir snap peas into slow cooker, cover, and cook on high until crisp-tender, about 20 minutes.

5. Whisk yogurt, mayonnaise, dill, vinegar, sugar, ⅛ teaspoon salt, and remaining garlic together in large bowl. Using slotted spoon, transfer vegetables to bowl with dressing and toss to coat; discard cooking liquid. Season salad with salt and pepper to taste. Carve chicken, discarding skin if desired. Serve with radish salad and lemon wedges.

Spice-Rubbed Chicken with Black Bean Salad

SERVES 4 **EASY PREP**

COOKING TIME 4 TO 5 HOURS ON LOW
SLOW COOKER SIZE 5 TO 7 QUARTS

WHY THIS RECIPE WORKS For this flavorful chicken recipe, we started with a Southwestern-inspired spice rub. We rubbed the mix under the skin to give it direct contact with the meat while it cooked. A simple black bean salad seemed like the perfect accompaniment to our chicken. Combining the beans with some chipotle chile and cooking them along with the chicken allowed the beans to absorb some of the chicken's juices and become even more flavorful and tender. While the chicken rested, we drained the beans and tossed them with bell pepper, corn, sliced scallions, lime juice, and olive oil to finish the salad. Check the chicken's temperature after 4 hours of cooking and continue to monitor until the breast registers 160 degrees and the thighs register 175 degrees. You will need an oval slow cooker for this recipe.

    5   teaspoons extra-virgin olive oil
    1   teaspoon ground cumin
    1   teaspoon paprika
    2   teaspoons grated lime zest plus ¼ cup juice (2 limes)
 1½   teaspoons packed brown sugar
        Salt and pepper
    1   (4-pound) whole chicken, giblets discarded
    1   (15-ounce) can black beans, rinsed
    1   teaspoon minced canned chipotle chile in adobo sauce
    1   red bell pepper, stemmed, seeded, and chopped fine
    1   cup frozen corn, thawed
    2   scallions, sliced thin

1. Microwave 2 teaspoons oil, cumin, and paprika in bowl until fragrant, about 30 seconds. Let spice mixture cool slightly, then stir in lime zest, sugar, ¼ teaspoon salt, and ¼ teaspoon pepper.

2. Using your fingers, gently loosen skin covering breast and thighs of chicken. Place half of spice mixture under skin, directly on meat in center of each side of breast and on thighs. Gently press skin to distribute spice mixture over meat. Rub entire exterior surface of chicken with remaining spice mixture.

3. Combine beans and chipotle in slow cooker. Place chicken, breast side down, on top of beans. Cover and cook until breast registers 160 degrees and thighs register 175 degrees, 4 to 5 hours on low.

4. Transfer chicken to carving board, tent loosely with aluminum foil, and let rest for 20 minutes.

5. Drain beans and transfer to large bowl. Stir in bell pepper, corn, scallions, lime juice, and remaining 1 tablespoon oil. Season with salt and pepper to taste. Carve chicken, discarding skin if desired. Serve with bean salad.

CARVING A WHOLE CHICKEN

1. Using chef's knife, remove leg quarters by cutting through joint that connects leg to carcass.

2. Cut through joint that connects drumstick to thigh.

3. Cut breast meat away from breastbone. Remove wing from breast by cutting through wing joint, then slice breasts crosswise.

NOTES FROM THE TEST KITCHEN

Buying Canned Black Beans

Most canned black beans have just three main ingredients: beans, water, and salt. So how different could they taste? Plenty different, we found out when 22 of our test cooks and editors sampled six nationally available products—three of them organic— in a blind taste test. Tasters sampled them plain (drained and rinsed) and in a test kitchen recipe for black bean soup. Our winning product was **Bush's Best Black Beans**. Tasters appreciated the "clean," "mild," and "slightly earthy" flavor of these beans, and several specifically called out their "good salt level." They liked the plain beans' "firm," "almost al dente" texture. In the soup, the beans were especially "creamy."

MAKE IT 5 WAYS CHICKEN IN A POT

Barbecue-Rubbed Chicken in a Pot

SERVES 4 **EASY PREP**
COOKING TIME 4 TO 5 HOURS ON LOW
SLOW COOKER SIZE 4 TO 7 QUARTS

Making a perfectly cooked whole chicken in a slow cooker is actually much easier than it sounds. We started by blooming a simple mixture of oil and aromatics in the microwave because we found it was the perfect way to give the chicken layers of flavor. Once the mixture was cool enough to handle, we then rubbed a portion of it under the skin to give it direct contact with the meat while it cooked, and massaged the remaining mixture directly onto the skin, coating the entire bird. Placing the chicken in the slow cooker upside down was key: As the meat rendered its juices and fat, they traveled over and through the breast (which can be notoriously dry), helping to maintain moistness. Additionally, as the juices pooled in the bottom of the cooker, they submerged the breast, enabling it to retain more moisture. Check the chicken's temperature after 4 hours of cooking and continue to monitor until the breast registers 160 degrees and the thighs register 175 degrees. You will need an oval slow cooker for these recipes.

1 LEMON-HERB CHICKEN IN A POT

3 tablespoons extra-virgin olive oil
1 shallot, minced
5 garlic cloves, minced
2 teaspoons minced fresh thyme
2 teaspoons grated lemon zest, plus lemon wedges for serving
Salt and pepper
2 tablespoons chopped fresh tarragon
1 (4-pound) whole chicken, giblets discarded

1. Microwave oil, shallot, garlic, thyme, lemon zest, 1½ teaspoons salt, and ½ teaspoon pepper in bowl until fragrant, about 30 seconds. Let oil mixture cool slightly, then stir in 1 tablespoon tarragon.

2. Using your fingers, gently loosen skin covering breast and thighs of chicken. Place half of oil mixture under skin, directly on meat in center of each side of breast and on thighs. Gently press on skin to distribute oil mixture over meat. Rub entire exterior surface of chicken with remaining oil mixture. Place chicken, breast side down, into slow cooker. Cover and cook until breast registers 160 degrees and thighs register 175 degrees, 4 to 5 hours on low.

3. Transfer chicken to carving board, tent loosely with aluminum foil, and let rest for 20 minutes. Carve chicken, discarding skin if desired. Sprinkle with remaining 1 tablespoon tarragon. Serve with lemon wedges.

2 BARBECUE-RUBBED CHICKEN IN A POT

3 tablespoons vegetable oil
4 teaspoons chili powder
2 teaspoons smoked paprika
1 teaspoon ground cumin
1 teaspoon garlic powder
½ teaspoon dry mustard
¼ teaspoon cayenne pepper
2 tablespoons packed brown sugar
Salt and pepper
1 (4-pound) whole chicken, giblets discarded

1. Microwave oil, chili powder, paprika, cumin, garlic powder, mustard, and cayenne in bowl until fragrant, about 30 seconds. Let oil mixture cool slightly, then stir in sugar, 1½ teaspoons salt, and ½ teaspoon pepper.

2. Using your fingers, gently loosen skin covering breast and thighs of chicken. Place half of oil mixture under skin, directly on meat in center of each side of breast and on thighs. Gently press on skin to distribute oil mixture over meat. Rub entire exterior surface of chicken with remaining oil mixture. Place chicken, breast side down, into slow cooker. Cover and cook until breast registers 160 degrees and thighs register 175 degrees, 4 to 5 hours on low.

3. Transfer chicken to carving board, tent loosely with aluminum foil, and let rest for 20 minutes. Carve chicken, discarding skin if desired. Serve.

3 THAI-SPICED CHICKEN IN A POT

2 tablespoons vegetable oil
1 shallot, minced
2 tablespoons red curry paste
1 tablespoon grated fresh ginger
4 garlic cloves, minced
1 teaspoon grated lime zest,
    plus lime wedges for serving
2 tablespoons packed brown sugar
2 tablespoons chopped
    fresh cilantro
4 teaspoons fish sauce
    Salt and pepper
1 (4-pound) whole chicken,
    giblets discarded

1. Microwave oil, shallot, curry paste, ginger, garlic, and lime zest in bowl until fragrant, about 30 seconds. Let oil mixture cool slightly, then stir in sugar, 1 tablespoon cilantro, fish sauce, 1½ teaspoons salt, and ½ teaspoon pepper.

2. Using your fingers, gently loosen skin covering breast and thighs of chicken. Place half of oil mixture under skin, directly on meat in center of each side of breast and on thighs. Gently press on skin to distribute oil mixture over meat. Rub entire exterior surface of chicken with remaining oil mixture. Place chicken, breast side down, into slow cooker. Cover and cook until breast registers 160 degrees and thighs register 175 degrees, 4 to 5 hours on low.

3. Transfer chicken to carving board, tent loosely with aluminum foil, and let rest for 20 minutes. Carve chicken, discarding skin if desired. Sprinkle with remaining 1 tablespoon cilantro. Serve with lime wedges.

4 HARISSA-SPICED CHICKEN IN A POT

3 tablespoons extra-virgin olive oil
4 garlic cloves, minced
4 teaspoons paprika
2 teaspoons ground coriander
    Salt and pepper
¾ teaspoon red pepper flakes
½ teaspoon ground cumin
½ teaspoon caraway seeds
1 (4-pound) whole chicken,
    giblets discarded
1 tablespoon chopped fresh mint

1. Microwave oil, garlic, paprika, coriander, 1½ teaspoons salt, ½ teaspoon pepper, pepper flakes, cumin, and caraway in bowl until fragrant, about 30 seconds; let cool slightly.

2. Using your fingers, gently loosen skin covering breast and thighs of chicken. Place half of oil mixture under skin, directly on meat in center of each side of breast and on thighs. Gently press on skin to distribute oil mixture over meat. Rub entire exterior surface of chicken with remaining oil mixture. Place chicken, breast side down, into slow cooker. Cover and cook until breast registers 160 degrees and thighs register 175 degrees, 4 to 5 hours on low.

3. Transfer chicken to carving board, tent loosely with aluminum foil, and let rest for 20 minutes. Carve chicken, discarding skin if desired. Sprinkle with mint and serve.

5 PESTO CHICKEN IN A POT

2 cups fresh basil leaves,
    lightly bruised
3 garlic cloves, minced
    Salt and pepper
⅓ cup extra-virgin olive oil
1 (4-pound) whole chicken,
    giblets discarded

1. Process basil, garlic, 1½ teaspoons salt, and ½ teaspoon pepper in food processor until finely ground, about 30 seconds, scraping down sides of bowl as needed. With processor running, slowly add oil and process until smooth, about 30 seconds.

2. Using your fingers, gently loosen skin covering breast and thighs of chicken. Place half of pesto under skin, directly on meat in center of each side of breast and on thighs. Gently press on skin to distribute pesto over meat. Rub entire exterior surface of chicken with remaining pesto. Place chicken, breast side down, into slow cooker. Cover and cook until breast registers 160 degrees and thighs register 175 degrees, 4 to 5 hours on low.

3. Transfer chicken to carving board, tent loosely with aluminum foil, and let rest 20 minutes. Carve chicken, discarding skin in desired. Serve.

APPLYING A RUB

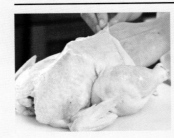

1. Separate skin from breast and thighs using your fingers.
2. Apply half of rub under skin; press on skin to distribute. Apply remaining rub on exterior of chicken.

Poultry Safety and Handling

It's important to follow some basic safety procedures when storing, handling, and cooking chicken, turkey, and other poultry.

REFRIGERATING Keep poultry refrigerated until just before cooking. Bacteria thrive at temperatures between 40 and 140 degrees. This means leftovers should also be promptly refrigerated.

FREEZING AND THAWING Poultry can be frozen in its original packaging or after repackaging. If you are freezing it for longer than two months, rewrap (or wrap over packaging) with foil or plastic wrap, or place inside a zipper-lock bag. You can keep poultry frozen for several months, but after two months the texture and flavor will suffer. Don't thaw frozen poultry on the counter; this puts it at risk of growing bacteria. Thaw it in its packaging in the refrigerator (in a container to catch its juices), or in the sink under cold running water. Count on one day of defrosting in the refrigerator for every 4 pounds of bird.

HANDLING RAW POULTRY When handling raw poultry, make sure to wash hands, knives, cutting boards, and counters (and anything else that has come into contact with the raw bird, its juices, or your hands) with hot, soapy water. Be careful not to let the poultry, its juices, or your unwashed hands touch foods that will be eaten raw. When seasoning raw poultry, touching the saltshaker or pepper mill can lead to cross-contamination. To avoid this, set aside the necessary salt and pepper before handling the poultry.

RINSING The U.S. Department of Agriculture advises against washing poultry. Rinsing poultry will not remove or kill much bacteria, and the splashing of water around the sink can spread the bacteria found in raw poultry.

COOKING AND LEFTOVERS Poultry should be cooked to an internal temperature of 160 degrees to ensure any bacteria have been killed (however, we prefer the flavor and texture of thigh meat cooked to at least 175 degrees). Leftover cooked poultry should be refrigerated and consumed within three days.

Turkey Breast with Cherry-Orange Sauce

SERVES 8 TO 10 `EASY PREP` `LIGHT`
COOKING TIME 5 TO 6 HOURS ON LOW
SLOW COOKER SIZE 5 TO 7 QUARTS

WHY THIS RECIPE WORKS We often think of turkey as being reserved for big holiday dinners, but some hands-off cooking in the slow cooker makes turkey breast a weeknight-friendly dinner. The bone-in turkey breast is prep free, and the gentle heat of the slow cooker produces juicy and tender meat every time. For a fresh accompaniment to our "roast" turkey, a cherry-orange sauce seemed like the perfect choice. To keep it simple, we started with frozen cherries, which we chopped, then added orange zest and a little thyme for aroma. By the time the turkey was fully cooked, the cherries were tender and the juices of the turkey had melded with the aromatics to create a flavorful sauce. To give it a thicker consistency, we added a small amount of instant tapioca. Many supermarkets are now selling "hotel-cut" turkey breasts, which still have the wings and rib cage attached. If this is the only type of breast you can find, you will need to remove the wings and cut away the rib cage with kitchen shears before proceeding with the recipe. Check the turkey's temperature after 5 hours of cooking and continue to monitor until the breast registers 160 degrees. You will need an oval slow cooker for this recipe.

12 ounces frozen sweet cherries, thawed and chopped
2 (2-inch) strips orange zest
1 teaspoon instant tapioca
½ teaspoon minced fresh thyme or ⅛ teaspoon dried
Salt and pepper
1 (6- to 7-pound) bone-in whole turkey breast, trimmed
½ cup apple butter
2 tablespoons unsalted butter
2 tablespoons lemon juice

1. Combine cherries, orange zest, tapioca, thyme, and ¼ teaspoon salt in slow cooker. Season turkey with salt and pepper and place skin side up into slow cooker. Cover and cook until breast registers 160 degrees, 5 to 6 hours on low.

2. Transfer turkey to carving board, tent loosely with aluminum foil, and let rest for 20 minutes.

3. Discard orange zest. Whisk apple butter, butter, and lemon juice into cherry mixture until combined. Season with salt and pepper to taste. Carve turkey and discard skin. Serve with sauce.

This slow-cooker recipe delivers moist and tender turkey and cooking liquid that is easily strained and turned into gravy.

Turkey Breast with Gravy

SERVES 8 TO 10   `LIGHT`
COOKING TIME 5 TO 6 HOURS ON LOW
SLOW COOKER SIZE 5 TO 7 QUARTS

WHY THIS RECIPE WORKS No one will ever guess that this dinner-table classic was turned out of a slow cooker as you serve up moist slices of turkey drizzled with a rich brown gravy. But it takes a little advance work (and a skillet) to get it right. We found that it was possible to skip the cumbersome step of browning the turkey breast, but to get a real gravy, we still needed the skillet to build a proper flavor base and make a roux. First we browned the onion, carrot, celery, and garlic. Then we added flour and cooked it until golden brown, deglazing the pan with water. Added to the slow cooker with the turkey and chicken broth and white wine, this base mingled with the juice released as the turkey cooked, resulting in a hearty gravy. Many supermarkets are now selling "hotel-cut" turkey breasts, which still have the wings and rib cage attached. If this is the only type of breast you can find, you will need to remove the wings and cut away the rib cage with kitchen shears before proceeding with

the recipe. Check the turkey's temperature after 5 hours of cooking and continue to monitor until the breast registers 160 degrees. You will need an oval slow cooker for this recipe.

- 3 tablespoons unsalted butter
- 1 onion, chopped
- 1 carrot, peeled and chopped
- 1 celery rib, chopped
- 6 garlic cloves, peeled and smashed
- ⅓ cup all-purpose flour
- 1 cup water
- 2 cups chicken broth
- ½ cup dry white wine
- 2 sprigs fresh thyme
- 2 bay leaves
- 1 (6- to 7-pound) bone-in whole turkey breast, trimmed
  Salt and pepper

1. Melt butter in 12-inch skillet over medium heat. Add onion, carrot, celery, and garlic and cook until softened and lightly browned, 8 to 10 minutes. Stir in flour and cook until golden brown, about 2 minutes. Stir in water, scraping up any browned bits and smoothing out any lumps; transfer to slow cooker.

2. Stir broth, wine, thyme sprigs, and bay leaves into slow cooker. Season turkey with salt and pepper and place skin side up into slow cooker. Cover and cook until breast registers 160 degrees, 5 to 6 hours on low.

3. Transfer turkey to carving board, tent loosely with aluminum foil, and let rest for 20 minutes.

4. Strain cooking liquid into saucepan; discard solids. Bring to simmer over medium heat and cook until thickened, about 15 minutes. Season with salt and pepper to taste. Carve turkey and discard skin. Serve with gravy.

CARVING A TURKEY BREAST

1. Cut down along 1 side following curvature of breastbone, pulling breast meat away from bone as you cut. Continue to cut and pry until breast has been removed.

2. Cut breast meat crosswise into thin slices for serving.

Roast Beef with Hearty Mushroom Gravy

SERVES 8 TO 10

COOKING TIME 1 TO 2 HOURS ON LOW

SLOW COOKER SIZE 4 TO 7 QUARTS

WHY THIS RECIPE WORKS The eye-round roast, an ultra-lean cut of beef, is perfectly suited to the low-and-slow heat of a slow cooker, which turns this otherwise tough cut tender. For an evenly cooked, medium-rare roast from the slow cooker, we first salted the roast overnight, browned it well in a skillet, and then built a gravy in the same pan. Cremini mushrooms formed the base of the gravy, along with onion, tomato paste, flour, and beef broth. To boost the mushroom flavor, we added potent porcini mushrooms. Look for an eye-round roast that is uniformly shaped to ensure even cooking. You will need an oval slow cooker for this recipe. Check the roast's temperature after 1 hour of cooking and continue to monitor until it registers 120 to 125 degrees (for medium-rare). We prefer this roast cooked to medium-rare, but if you prefer to cook it to medium, cook the roast until it registers 130 to 135 degrees. Note that the roast needs to rest for at least 18 hours after salting.

1 (4-pound) boneless eye-round roast, trimmed
  Kosher salt and pepper
3 tablespoons vegetable oil
8 ounces cremini mushrooms, trimmed, halved, and sliced thin
1 onion, chopped fine
2 tablespoons tomato paste
2 tablespoons all-purpose flour
1 teaspoon minced fresh thyme or ¼ teaspoon dried
⅛ ounce dried porcini mushrooms, rinsed and minced
1 cup beef broth, plus extra as needed
2 tablespoons unsalted butter
2 tablespoons minced fresh parsley

1. Sprinkle roast with 4 teaspoons salt. Wrap tightly in plastic wrap and refrigerate for at least 18 hours or up to 24 hours.

2. Pat roast dry with paper towels, rub with 1 tablespoon oil, and season with pepper. Heat 1 tablespoon oil in 12-inch skillet over medium-high heat until just smoking. Brown roast on all sides, 7 to 10 minutes; transfer to slow cooker.

3. Heat remaining 1 tablespoon oil in now-empty skillet over medium heat until shimmering. Add cremini mushrooms, onion, and ½ teaspoon salt and cook until vegetables are softened and lightly browned, 8 to 10 minutes. Stir in tomato paste, flour, thyme, and porcini mushrooms and cook until fragrant, about 1 minute. Slowly whisk in broth, scraping up any browned bits and smoothing out any lumps. Pour broth mixture over roast, cover, and cook until beef registers 120 to 125 degrees (for medium-rare), 1 to 2 hours on low.

4. Transfer roast to carving board, tent loosely with aluminum foil, and let rest for 20 minutes.

5. Whisk butter, parsley, and any accumulated meat juices into gravy. Adjust consistency with extra hot broth as needed. Season with salt and pepper to taste. Slice beef thin against grain. Serve with gravy.

SIMPLE SIDES

CLASSIC MASHED POTATOES

SERVES 4

For the smoothest mashed potatoes, use a food mill or a potato ricer. This recipe can be easily doubled.

2 pounds russet potatoes, peeled, quartered, and cut into 1-inch pieces
8 tablespoons unsalted butter, melted
¾ cup half-and-half, hot, plus extra as needed
  Salt and pepper

1. Place potatoes in large saucepan and add water to cover by 1 inch. Bring water to boil, then reduce to simmer and cook until potatoes are tender and paring knife can be inserted into potatoes with no resistance, 20 to 25 minutes.

2. Drain potatoes in colander, tossing to remove any excess water. Wipe now-empty saucepan dry with paper towels. Return potatoes to pot and mash to uniform consistency, or process through food mill or ricer and return to dry pot.

3. Using rubber spatula, fold in melted butter until just incorporated, then fold in half-and-half. Adjust consistency with extra hot half-and-half as needed. Season with salt and pepper to taste. Serve.

Roast Beef with Warm Garden Potato Salad

SERVES 8 TO 10

COOKING TIME 1 TO 2 HOURS ON LOW

SLOW COOKER SIZE 4 TO 7 QUARTS

WHY THIS RECIPE WORKS A juicy roast beef and potato dinner is always inviting and surprisingly well suited for the slow cooker. A quick sear in a skillet before transferring to the slow cooker gave the roast a flavorful dark crust before cooking all the way through. We cooked the roast at a low temperature, giving it a moist, even doneness and rosy color from edge to center. We gave the potatoes a head start in the microwave so they could finish cooking through

After searing this eye-round roast, we slow-cook it for 1 to 2 hours, along with the potatoes, for juicy, medium-rare beef.

perfectly in the slow cooker in the same time as the roast. However, to keep the green beans bright and crisp-tender, we kept them out of the slow cooker and briefly steamed them in the microwave. Look for an eye-round roast that is uniformly shaped to ensure even cooking. You will need an oval slow cooker for this recipe. Check the roast's temperature after 1 hour of cooking and continue to monitor until it registers 120 to 125 degrees (for medium-rare). We prefer this roast cooked to medium-rare, but if you prefer to cook it to medium, cook the roast until it registers 130 to 135 degrees. Note that the roast needs to rest for at least 18 hours after salting.

- 1 (4-pound) boneless eye-round roast, trimmed
  Kosher salt and pepper
- 2 pounds Yukon Gold potatoes, unpeeled, cut into 1-inch pieces
- 7 tablespoons extra-virgin olive oil
- 1½ teaspoons garlic powder
- 2 pounds green beans, trimmed and cut on bias into 1-inch lengths
- ¼ cup chopped fresh parsley

- 1 shallot, minced
- 2 tablespoons white wine vinegar
- 2 tablespoons Dijon mustard
- 2 tablespoons minced fresh chives

1. Sprinkle roast with 4 teaspoons salt. Wrap tightly in plastic wrap and refrigerate for at least 18 hours or up to 24 hours.

2. Microwave potatoes, 1 tablespoon oil, and ½ teaspoon salt in covered bowl, stirring occasionally, until almost tender, 8 to 10 minutes; transfer to slow cooker.

3. Pat roast dry with paper towels. Rub with 1 tablespoon oil, sprinkle with garlic powder, and season with pepper. Heat 1 tablespoon oil in 12-inch skillet over medium-high heat until just smoking. Brown roast on all sides, 7 to 10 minutes. Place roast on top of potatoes, cover, and cook until beef registers 120 to 125 degrees (for medium-rare), 1 to 2 hours on low.

4. Transfer roast to carving board, tent loosely with aluminum foil, and let rest for 20 minutes.

5. Microwave green beans and ¼ cup water in large covered bowl, stirring occasionally, until crisp-tender, 8 to 10 minutes. Drain green beans and return to now-empty bowl. Drain potatoes and transfer to bowl with green beans.

6. Whisk remaining ¼ cup oil, parsley, shallot, vinegar, mustard, chives, ¼ teaspoon salt, and ⅛ teaspoon pepper together in small bowl. Pour dressing over vegetables and gently toss to combine. Season with salt and pepper to taste. Slice beef thin against grain. Serve with potato salad.

Braised Brisket and Onions

SERVES 10 TO 12   `ALL DAY`

COOKING TIME 9 TO 10 HOURS ON LOW OR 6 TO 7 HOURS ON HIGH

SLOW COOKER SIZE 5 TO 7 QUARTS

WHY THIS RECIPE WORKS Brisket is a tough cut of meat and needs prolonged cooking to make it tender, which, of course, is just what the slow cooker does best. To avoid browning the brisket and still achieve loads of flavor we opted to use a dry rub—consisting of paprika, onion powder, salt, garlic powder, and cayenne—on the brisket and let the flavors mingle for at least 8 hours. To complement the spice rub, we sautéed onions with brown sugar, tomato paste, and garlic, achieving a deep, rich, caramelized flavor. Thickened with a little flour and finished with a bit of vinegar, the slightly sweet onion sauce paired perfectly with the meltingly tender brisket. Be sure to buy the brisket "first cut" or "flat cut," not "point cut," which is thicker and fattier. You will need an oval slow cooker for this recipe. Note that the roast needs to rest for at least 8 hours after seasoning.

This classic brisket recipe will feed a crowd, getting its big flavor from an overnight spice rub and lots of sliced onions.

1 tablespoon paprika
2 teaspoons onion powder
  Salt and pepper
1 teaspoon garlic powder
⅛ teaspoon cayenne pepper
1 (5-pound) beef brisket, flat cut,
  fat trimmed to ¼ inch
1 tablespoon vegetable oil
3 onions, halved and sliced ½ inch thick
3 tablespoons all-purpose flour
1 tablespoon tomato paste
3 garlic cloves, minced
1 cup chicken broth
2 tablespoons plus 1 teaspoon red wine vinegar
1 tablespoon packed brown sugar
3 sprigs fresh thyme
3 bay leaves

1. Combine paprika, onion powder, 1 teaspoon salt, garlic powder, and cayenne in bowl. Using fork, prick brisket all over. Rub spice mixture over brisket, wrap tightly in plastic wrap, and refrigerate for 8 to 24 hours.

2. Heat oil in 12-inch skillet over medium heat until shimmering. Add onions and cook until softened and lightly browned, 8 to 10 minutes. Stir in flour, tomato paste, and garlic and cook until fragrant, about 1 minute. Slowly stir in broth, scraping up any browned bits and smoothing out any lumps; transfer to slow cooker.

3. Stir 2 tablespoons vinegar, sugar, thyme sprigs, and bay leaves into slow cooker. Unwrap brisket and nestle fat side up into slow cooker. Spoon portion of onion mixture over brisket. Cover and cook until beef is tender, 9 to 10 hours on low or 6 to 7 hours on high.

4. Transfer brisket to carving board, tent loosely with aluminum foil, and let rest for 20 minutes.

5. Discard thyme sprigs and bay leaves. Using large spoon, skim fat from surface of sauce. Stir in remaining 1 teaspoon vinegar and season with salt and pepper to taste. Slice brisket against grain into ½-inch-thick slices and arrange on serving dish. Spoon 1 cup sauce over brisket and serve, passing remaining sauce separately.

Barbecued Beef Brisket

SERVES 10 TO 12   ALL DAY
COOKING TIME 9 TO 10 HOURS ON LOW OR 6 TO 7 HOURS ON HIGH
SLOW COOKER SIZE 5 TO 7 QUARTS

WHY THIS RECIPE WORKS To make a tender and moist barbecued brisket with robust spice and smoke flavor, we started out with a simple spice rub, often the hallmark of great barbecue. Salt, pepper, brown sugar, cumin, and paprika provided the backbone of flavor, while chipotle chiles lent a smoky dimension. To allow the rub to penetrate the meat we pierced the brisket all over with a fork and then refrigerated it overnight. Though brisket releases flavorful juices during cooking (used for serving), we wanted to bump up the flavors even more. We microwaved onions, more chipotles, tomato paste, garlic, and chili powder and added them to the slow cooker, along with a little water. The resulting braising liquid was sweet, smoky, and spicy; all we needed to do to finish the sauce was stir in ketchup, vinegar, and liquid smoke. Be sure to buy the brisket "first cut" or "flat cut," not "point cut," which is thicker and fattier. You will need an oval slow cooker for this recipe. Note that the roast needs to rest for at least 8 hours after seasoning.

½ cup packed dark brown sugar
3 tablespoons minced canned chipotle
  chile in adobo sauce
1 tablespoon ground cumin
1 tablespoon paprika
  Salt and pepper
1 (5-pound) beef brisket, flat cut,
  fat trimmed to ¼ inch

2 onions, chopped fine

2 tablespoons tomato paste

4 garlic cloves, minced

1 tablespoon vegetable oil

1 tablespoon chili powder

½ cup water

¼ cup ketchup

1 tablespoon cider vinegar

¼ teaspoon liquid smoke

1. Combine sugar, 2 tablespoons chipotle, cumin, paprika, 1 teaspoon salt, and 2 teaspoons pepper in bowl. Using fork, prick brisket all over. Rub sugar mixture over brisket, wrap tightly in plastic wrap, and refrigerate for 8 to 24 hours.

2. Microwave onions, tomato paste, garlic, oil, chili powder, and remaining 1 tablespoon chipotle in bowl, stirring occasionally, until onions are softened, about 5 minutes; transfer to slow cooker. Stir in water. Unwrap brisket and nestle fat side up into slow cooker. Spoon portion of onion mixture over brisket. Cover and cook until beef is tender, 9 to 10 hours on low or 6 to 7 hours on high.

3. Transfer brisket to carving board, tent loosely with aluminum foil, and let rest for 20 minutes.

4. Using large spoon, skim fat from surface of sauce. Whisk in ketchup, vinegar, and liquid smoke. Season with salt and pepper to taste. Slice brisket against grain into ½-inch-thick slices and arrange on serving dish. Spoon 1 cup sauce over brisket and serve, passing remaining sauce separately.

NOTES FROM THE TEST KITCHEN

Buying Beef Brisket

When buying brisket, be aware that butchers typically sell two types: flat cut and point cut. These two pieces together make up a full brisket, a large slab of muscle from the cow's chest. The knobby point cut (above) overlaps the rectangular flat cut (below). The point cut has more marbling, while the flat cut is lean but topped with a thick fat cap. Because the flat cut (sometimes labeled "first cut") is easy to find, cheap, and fairly uniform in shape, it's the cut we generally prefer. Make sure to trim the fat cap according to the instructions in whatever recipe you are using.

We break a large chuck-eye roast into smaller roasts and brown them for the ultimate slow-cooker pot roast.

Classic Pot Roast with Carrots and Potatoes

SERVES 8 TO 10   **ALL DAY**

COOKING TIME 9 TO 10 HOURS ON LOW OR 6 TO 7 HOURS ON HIGH

SLOW COOKER SIZE 5 TO 7 QUARTS

WHY THIS RECIPE WORKS The slow, even, moist heat of the slow cooker is perfect for creating a delicious fork-tender pot roast. We wanted a pot roast that had classic flavors and that was easy to assemble. We started with chuck-eye roast—our favorite cut for pot roast because it's well marbled with fat and connective tissue—and tied it around the center to help it cook more evenly. We found that pulling apart a large roast at the natural seam to make two smaller roasts (2 to 2½ pounds each) yielded fork-tender meat more consistently than cooking a single large roast. Searing the meat in a skillet first before transferring to the slow cooker proved crucial in developing the ultimate rich and savory pot roast flavor we wanted. Enhancing the cooking broth with classic aromatics like onion, celery, thyme, and garlic also gave the braising liquid some serious flavor. To make this roast into a hearty meal, we arranged small unpeeled potatoes and carrot pieces into the slow cooker before adding the roasts. This ensured the roasts would cook evenly as their juices were released, and the roasts submerged in their own flavorful liquid. We cooked the roasts until they were perfectly tender and our sauce had great body and flavor. Use small Yukon Gold potatoes measuring 1 to 2 inches in diameter; if your potatoes are larger, cut them into 1-inch pieces to ensure that they cook through properly.

1 (4- to 5-pound) boneless beef chuck-eye roast, pulled into 2 pieces at natural seam and trimmed
Salt and pepper
2 tablespoons vegetable oil
1 onion, chopped
2 celery ribs, chopped
2 tablespoons all-purpose flour
1 tablespoon tomato paste
3 garlic cloves, minced
1 teaspoon minced fresh thyme or ¼ teaspoon dried
½ cup dry red wine
½ cup beef broth
2 pounds small Yukon Gold potatoes, unpeeled
1 pound carrots, peeled and halved widthwise, thick ends halved lengthwise
2 bay leaves
2 tablespoons minced fresh parsley

1. Pat beef dry with paper towels and season with salt and pepper. Tie 3 pieces of kitchen twine around each piece of beef to create 2 evenly shaped roasts. Heat oil in 12-inch skillet over medium-high heat until just smoking. Brown roasts on all sides, 7 to 10 minutes; transfer to plate.

TYING A POT ROAST

1. Pull roast apart at major seams (delineated by lines of fat) into 2 halves, using knife as needed. Remove large knobs of fat from each piece, leaving thin layer of fat on meat.

2. Tie 3 pieces of kitchen twine around each piece of beef to create 2 evenly shaped roasts.

2. Add onion, celery, ½ teaspoon salt, and ¼ teaspoon pepper to fat left in skillet and cook over medium heat until vegetables are softened and lightly browned, 8 to 10 minutes. Stir in flour, tomato paste, garlic, and thyme and cook until fragrant, about 1 minute. Slowly stir in wine and broth, scraping up any browned bits and smoothing out any lumps; transfer to slow cooker.

3. Stir potatoes, carrots, and bay leaves into slow cooker. Nestle roasts into slow cooker, adding any accumulated juices. Cover and cook until beef is tender and fork slips easily in and out of meat, 9 to 10 hours on low or 6 to 7 hours on high.

4. Transfer roasts to carving board, tent loosely with aluminum foil, and let rest for 20 minutes.

5. Discard bay leaves. Transfer vegetables to serving dish and tent loosely with foil. Using large spoon, skim fat from surface of sauce. Stir in parsley and season with salt and pepper to taste.

6. Remove twine from roasts, slice meat against grain into ½-inch-thick slices, and arrange on serving dish with vegetables. Spoon 1 cup sauce over meat and serve, passing remaining sauce separately.

Italian Pot Roast

SERVES 8 TO 10   **ALL DAY**
COOKING TIME 9 TO 10 HOURS ON LOW OR 6 TO 7 HOURS ON HIGH
SLOW COOKER SIZE 5 TO 7 QUARTS

WHY THIS RECIPE WORKS A slow cooker, with its slow, even, and moist heat, is the perfect environment for braising a pot roast until fork-tender. We put an Italian spin on this pot roast with the addition of red wine, oregano, tomatoes, red pepper flakes, and dried porcini mushrooms. To get loads of flavor into our pot roast we first browned the meat, then sautéed some bacon and aromatics. Deglazing the skillet with wine helped capture all the flavorful browned bits. Boneless chuck-eye roast was our favorite cut for this dish, and we found that dividing a larger roast into two smaller ones (2 to 2½ pounds each) yielded fork-tender meat more consistently than cooking the roast whole.

1 (4- to 5-pound) boneless beef chuck-eye roast, pulled into 2 pieces at natural seam and trimmed
Salt and pepper
2 tablespoons extra-virgin olive oil
8 slices bacon, chopped
2 onions, chopped
4 carrots, peeled and cut into 1-inch pieces
6 garlic cloves, minced
½ ounce dried porcini mushrooms, rinsed and minced
2 tablespoons minced fresh oregano or 2 teaspoons dried
2 tablespoons tomato paste

½ teaspoon red pepper flakes
½ cup dry red wine
1 (28-ounce) can crushed tomatoes
1 cup chicken broth
2 bay leaves
¼ cup minced fresh parsley

1. Pat beef dry with paper towels and season with salt and pepper. Tie 3 pieces of kitchen twine around each piece of beef to create 2 evenly shaped roasts. Heat oil in 12-inch skillet over medium-high heat until just smoking. Brown roasts on all sides, 7 to 10 minutes; transfer to plate.

2. Add bacon to now-empty skillet and cook over medium heat until crisp, 5 to 7 minutes. Using slotted spoon, transfer bacon to slow cooker. Pour off all but 2 tablespoons fat from skillet.

3. Add onions and carrots to fat left in skillet and cook over medium heat until softened and lightly browned, 8 to 10 minutes. Stir in garlic, mushrooms, oregano, tomato paste, and pepper flakes and cook until fragrant, about 30 seconds. Stir in wine, scraping up any browned bits; transfer to slow cooker.

4. Stir tomatoes, broth, and bay leaves into slow cooker. Nestle roasts into slow cooker, adding any accumulated juices. Cover and cook until beef is tender and fork slips easily in and out of meat, 9 to 10 hours on low or 6 to 7 hours on high.

5. Transfer roasts to carving board, tent loosely with aluminum foil, and let rest for 20 minutes.

6. Discard bay leaves. Using large spoon, skim fat from surface of sauce. Stir in parsley and season with salt and pepper to taste.

7. Remove twine from roasts, slice meat against grain into ½-inch-thick slices, and arrange on serving dish. Spoon 1 cup sauce over meat and serve, passing remaining sauce separately.

Corned Beef and Cabbage Dinner

SERVES 6 TO 8 · EASY PREP · ALL DAY

COOKING TIME 9 TO 10 HOURS ON LOW OR 6 TO 7 HOURS ON HIGH

SLOW COOKER SIZE 5 TO 7 QUARTS

WHY THIS RECIPE WORKS In the States, corned beef and cabbage is rarely eaten outside of St. Patrick's Day—and maybe for good reason. When traditionally boiled, the meat often comes out salty and dry, and the vegetables are usually overcooked and bland. We wanted to use the steady, gentle heat of the slow cooker to get moist, tender corned beef and perfectly cooked vegetables. Placement of the ingredients in the slow cooker turned out to be the key to success. We put the meat in first, sprinkled the seasoning (pickling spice) over it, and placed the potatoes and carrots between the meat and the wall of the slow cooker. This arrangement gave

The arrangement of meat and vegetables in the slow cooker is the key to this one-pot corned beef dinner.

us enough room to be able to add the cabbage at the get-go, rather than at the end of cooking. Avoid buying a cabbage larger than 1½ pounds; it will be hard to fit into the slow cooker. Use red potatoes measuring about 2 inches in diameter. You will need an oval slow cooker for this recipe.

1 (3- to 4-pound) corned beef brisket, flat cut, fat trimmed to ¼ inch, rinsed
1 tablespoon pickling spice
1½ pounds small red potatoes, unpeeled
1 pound carrots, peeled and halved crosswise
1 head green cabbage (1½ pounds), cored and cut into 6 wedges
4 tablespoons unsalted butter, cut into ½-inch pieces

1. Place brisket into slow cooker and sprinkle with pickling spice. Arrange potatoes and carrots between meat and sides of slow cooker. Arrange cabbage over meat. Add 6 cups water to slow cooker. Cover and cook until beef is tender and fork slips easily in and out of meat, 9 to 10 hours on low or 6 to 7 hours on high.

2. Turn off slow cooker. Transfer brisket to carving board, tent loosely with aluminum foil, and let rest for 20 minutes. Cover slow cooker to keep vegetables warm while beef rests.

3. Slice brisket against grain into ½-inch-thick slices and arrange on serving dish. Using slotted spoon, transfer vegetables to dish with beef. Dot vegetables with butter. Serve.

NOTES FROM THE TEST KITCHEN

Pickling Spice

Jarred pickling spice typically includes a combination of whole and coarsely crushed spices such as bay leaves, cardamom, cinnamon, allspice, mustard seeds, cloves, coriander, and ginger, offering a whole lot of flavor in just one jar.

If you can't find pickling spice at the supermarket, you can make your own. Combine 1 cinnamon stick, broken into pieces, 2 tablespoons mustard seeds, 1 tablespoon peppercorns, 2 teaspoons allspice berries, 2 bay leaves, crushed, and 2 whole cloves. Makes about ¼ cup.

Pork Pot Roast

SERVES 8 TO 10 `ALL DAY`

COOKING TIME 9 TO 10 HOURS ON LOW OR 6 TO 7 HOURS ON HIGH

SLOW COOKER SIZE 5 TO 7 QUARTS

WHY THIS RECIPE WORKS Pork butt roast is a great candidate for braising in the slow cooker—its fat and connective tissue break down over the long cooking time, resulting in tender, silky meat. For our pot roast we found that halving a large roast to make two smaller roasts (2 to 2½ pounds each) yielded fork-tender meat more consistently and in less time than cooking a larger whole roast. To get enough flavor into our dish, we browned the roasts first, then browned onions deeply, along with tomato paste and more aromatics, which gave the sauce a meaty foundation. And since we had our skillet out, we decided to make a roux to thicken the sauce and deglazed the pan with a little white wine. We paired the rich pork with sweet and hearty root vegetables (carrots and parsnips) and diced tomatoes. Pork butt roast is often labeled Boston butt in the supermarket.

1 (4- to 5-pound) boneless pork butt roast, trimmed and halved
  Salt and pepper
1 tablespoon vegetable oil
2 onions, chopped fine
¼ cup all-purpose flour
6 garlic cloves, minced
1 tablespoon tomato paste
1 tablespoon minced fresh thyme or 1 teaspoon dried
½ cup dry white wine
1 (28-ounce) can diced tomatoes, drained
1 pound carrots, peeled and cut into 1-inch pieces
1 pound parsnips, peeled and cut into 1-inch pieces
2 bay leaves
2 teaspoons white wine vinegar

1. Pat pork dry with paper towels and season with salt and pepper. Tie 3 pieces of kitchen twine around each piece of pork to create 2 evenly shaped roasts. Heat oil in 12-inch skillet over medium-high heat until just smoking. Brown roasts on all sides, 7 to 10 minutes; transfer to plate.

2. Add onions, 1 teaspoon salt, and 1 teaspoon pepper to fat left in skillet and cook over medium heat until onions are softened and lightly browned, 8 to 10 minutes. Stir in flour, garlic, tomato paste, and thyme and cook until fragrant, about 1 minute. Stir in wine, scraping up any browned bits and smoothing out any lumps; transfer to slow cooker.

3. Stir tomatoes, carrots, parsnips, and bay leaves into slow cooker. Nestle roasts into slow cooker, adding any accumulated juices. Cover and cook until pork is tender and fork slips easily in and out of meat, 9 to 10 hours on low or 6 to 7 hours on high.

4. Transfer roasts to carving board, tent loosely with aluminum foil, and let rest for 20 minutes.

5. Discard bay leaves. Using slotted spoon, transfer vegetables to serving dish and tent loosely with foil. Strain sauce into fat separator, reserving solids, and let sit for 5 minutes. Combine reserved solids, defatted sauce, and vinegar in bowl, and season with salt and pepper to taste.

6. Remove twine from roasts, slice meat against grain into ½-inch-thick slices, and arrange on serving dish with vegetables. Spoon 1 cup sauce over meat and serve, passing remaining sauce separately.

Cider-Braised Pork Roast

SERVES 8 TO 10 `ALL DAY`

COOKING TIME 9 TO 10 HOURS ON LOW OR 6 TO 7 HOURS ON HIGH

SLOW COOKER SIZE 5 TO 7 QUARTS

WHY THIS RECIPE WORKS Whether it's apple wood–smoked bacon or pork chops served with applesauce, pork and apples are a classic combination. With this in mind, we set out to create a slow-cooker recipe for a pork roast that would slowly braise in a cider-based sauce and result in a tender roast infused with sweet-tart

Apple cider, apple butter, and cider vinegar ensure this braised pork roast is infused with apple flavor.

1. Pat pork dry with paper towels and season with salt and pepper. Tie 3 pieces of kitchen twine around each piece of pork to create 2 evenly shaped roasts. Heat oil in 12-inch skillet over medium-high heat until just smoking. Brown roasts on all sides, 7 to 10 minutes; transfer to plate.

2. Add onion and ½ teaspoon salt to fat left in skillet and cook over medium heat until onion is softened and lightly browned, 5 to 7 minutes. Stir in flour, garlic, and thyme sprigs and cook until fragrant, about 1 minute. Slowly whisk in apple cider, scraping up any browned bits and smoothing out any lumps; transfer to slow cooker.

3. Stir apple butter and bay leaves into slow cooker. Nestle roasts into slow cooker, adding any accumulated juices. Cover and cook until pork is tender and fork slips easily in and out of meat, 9 to 10 hours on low or 6 to 7 hours on high.

4. Transfer roasts to carving board, tent loosely with aluminum foil, and let rest for 20 minutes.

5. Strain sauce into fat separator and let sit for 5 minutes; discard solids. Combine defatted sauce and vinegar in bowl and season with salt and pepper to taste. Remove twine from roasts, slice meat against grain into ½-inch-thick slices, and arrange on serving dish. Spoon 1 cup sauce over meat and serve, passing remaining sauce separately.

Cuban Pork Roast with Mojo Sauce

SERVES 8 TO 10 ALL DAY
COOKING TIME 9 TO 10 HOURS ON LOW OR 6 TO 7 HOURS ON HIGH
SLOW COOKER SIZE 5 TO 7 QUARTS

WHY THIS RECIPE WORKS Boldly spiced slow-cooked meats are classic Caribbean fare, and Cuban slow-roasted pork is one of the best examples. Traditionally the pork is marinated in a flavorful mixture of citrus, garlic, and spices and cooked over a fire. We wanted to bring it indoors with a no-fuss slow-cooker version featuring tender, flavorful meat and a bracing garlic-citrus sauce. Well-marbled pork shoulder was our cut of choice; it turned meltingly tender in the slow cooker. To ensure that it cooked evenly, we cut the roast into two smaller roasts and tied them to ensure they retained a more uniform shape. To keep our prep time short, we skipped the lengthy marinating and simply cooked the roast in an aromatic mixture of orange juice, onion, chipotle, oregano, cumin, and garlic. To re-create the tart Cuban mojo sauce, we combined a portion of the pork cooking liquid with olive oil, orange juice, and a healthy dose of vinegar. With its citrusy spiced sauce and rich, tender pork, this dish will liven up any weeknight. Pork butt roast is often labeled Boston butt in the supermarket.

cider flavor. We started with pork butt—our favorite for low, slow cooking. Searing the meat built a flavorful and appealing deep golden crust and created valuable fond in the skillet that added flavor to our sauce. A small amount of flour added body and thickness to our sauce, while equal parts apple cider and apple butter finished out the sauce and provided the sweet apple flavor we wanted to complement our roast. A touch of cider vinegar added punch, creating the perfect cider sauce to accompany our pork. Pork butt roast is often labeled Boston butt in the supermarket.

1 (4- to 5-pound) boneless pork butt roast, trimmed and halved
  Salt and pepper
1 tablespoon vegetable oil
1 onion, chopped
¼ cup all-purpose flour
4 garlic cloves, minced
3 sprigs fresh thyme
½ cup apple cider
½ cup apple butter
2 bay leaves
1 tablespoon cider vinegar

A spiced, citrusy sauce livens up this rich Caribbean-inspired pork roast with little effort.

1 (4- to 5-pound) boneless pork butt roast, trimmed and halved
  Salt and pepper
5 tablespoons extra-virgin olive oil
1 onion, chopped
2 teaspoons dried oregano
1½ teaspoons ground cumin
6 garlic cloves, minced
½ cup water
1 tablespoon grated orange zest plus ½ cup juice
1 tablespoon minced canned chipotle chile in adobo sauce
¼ cup distilled white vinegar

1. Pat pork dry with paper towels and season with salt and pepper. Tie 3 pieces of kitchen twine around each piece of pork to create 2 evenly shaped roasts. Heat 1 tablespoon oil in 12-inch skillet over medium-high heat until just smoking. Brown roasts on all sides, 7 to 10 minutes; transfer to plate.

2. Add onion, 1 teaspoon salt, and 1 teaspoon pepper to fat left in skillet and cook over medium heat until onion is softened and lightly browned, 5 to 7 minutes. Stir in oregano, cumin, and two-thirds of garlic and cook until fragrant, about 30 seconds. Stir in water, scraping up any browned bits; transfer to slow cooker.

3. Stir orange zest and ¼ cup juice and chipotle into slow cooker. Nestle roasts into slow cooker, adding any accumulated juices. Cover and cook until pork is tender and fork slips easily in and out of meat, 9 to 10 hours on low or 6 to 7 hours on high.

4. Transfer roasts to carving board, tent loosely with aluminum foil, and let rest for 20 minutes.

5. Strain cooking liquid into fat separator and let sit for 5 minutes; discard solids. Pour ¼ cup defatted liquid into bowl; discard remaining liquid. Whisk in vinegar, remaining ¼ cup oil, remaining garlic, remaining ¼ cup orange juice, ¼ teaspoon salt, and ¼ teaspoon pepper. Remove twine from roasts and slice meat against grain into ½-inch-thick slices. Serve with sauce.

SIMPLE SIDES

CILANTRO RICE

SERVES 4

Basmati, jasmine, or Texmati rice can be substituted for the long-grain rice. A nonstick saucepan works best here, although a traditional saucepan will also work. This recipe can be easily doubled; increase broth to only 3¾ cups.

2¼ cups chicken broth
1½ cups fresh cilantro leaves, plus 2 tablespoons minced
2 tablespoons unsalted butter
1 small onion, chopped fine
  Salt and pepper
2 garlic cloves, minced
1½ cups long-grain white rice, rinsed

1. Process broth and cilantro leaves in blender until cilantro is finely chopped, about 15 seconds. Melt butter in large saucepan over medium heat. Add onion and ¼ teaspoon salt and cook until onion is softened, about 5 minutes. Stir in garlic and cook until fragrant, about 30 seconds. Add rice and cook, stirring often, until edges begin to turn translucent, about 3 minutes.

2. Stir in broth mixture and bring to simmer. Reduce heat to low, cover, and continue to simmer until rice is tender and water is absorbed, 16 to 18 minutes.

3. Off heat, lay clean folded dish towel underneath lid. Let sit for 10 minutes. Add minced cilantro and fluff rice with fork to incorporate. Season with salt and pepper to taste. Serve.

Southwestern Pork Roast

SERVES 8 TO 10 `ALL DAY`

COOKING TIME 9 TO 10 HOURS ON LOW OR 6 TO 7 HOURS
ON HIGH

SLOW COOKER SIZE 5 TO 7 QUARTS

WHY THIS RECIPE WORKS To put a Southwestern spin on a slow-cooker pork roast, we started with a well-marbled pork shoulder and seasoned it liberally with chili powder, oregano, salt, and pepper and quickly seared in the flavor for a well-browned crust before transferring to the slow cooker. We also added some of the spices to a mixture of canned tomato sauce and spicy chipotle chile to make a boldly flavored braising liquid. Cooking the onion and spices in rendered pork fat gave our sauce deeper, more complex flavors. Pork butt roast is often labeled Boston butt in the supermarket.

1 tablespoon chili powder
1 teaspoon dried oregano
   Salt and pepper
1 (4- to 5-pound) boneless pork butt roast, trimmed
   and halved
1 tablespoon vegetable oil
2 onions, chopped
2 tablespoons all-purpose flour
1 (15-ounce) can tomato sauce
2 teaspoons minced canned chipotle chile in adobo sauce
3 tablespoons minced fresh cilantro

1. Combine chili powder, oregano, 1 teaspoon salt, and 1 teaspoon pepper in bowl. Pat pork dry with paper towels and rub with half of spice mixture. Tie 3 pieces of kitchen twine around each piece of pork to create 2 evenly shaped roasts. Heat oil in 12-inch skillet over medium-high heat until just smoking. Brown roasts on all sides, 7 to 10 minutes; transfer to plate.

2. Add onions to fat left in skillet and cook over medium heat until softened and lightly browned, about 8 minutes. Stir in flour and remaining spice mixture and cook until fragrant, about 1 minute. Stir in tomato sauce and chipotle, scraping up any browned bits and smoothing out any lumps; transfer to slow cooker.

3. Nestle roasts into slow cooker, adding any accumulated juices. Cover and cook until pork is tender and fork slips easily in and out of meat, 9 to 10 hours on low or 6 to 7 hours on high.

4. Transfer roasts to carving board, tent loosely with aluminum foil, and let rest for 20 minutes.

5. Strain sauce into fat separator, reserving solids, and let sit for 5 minutes. Combine defatted sauce, reserved solids, and cilantro in bowl. Season with salt and pepper to taste. Remove twine from roasts, slice meat against grain into ½-inch-thick slices, and arrange on serving dish. Spoon 1 cup sauce over meat and serve, passing remaining sauce separately.

NOTES FROM THE TEST KITCHEN

All About Roasts in the Slow Cooker

Simply placing a roast in the slow cooker and walking away isn't likely going to give you the results you are after. Here are a few important tips to ensure your roasts are successful every time.

PICK THE RIGHT ROAST When selecting roasts for the slow cooker, our first choices are those that benefit the most from braising, namely the tougher, fattier roasts like beef chuck, beef brisket, and pork butt. These cuts are ideal for the slow cooker because low and slow cooking turns the meat meltingly tender after hours of cooking (when the collagen in the meat has broken down). Leaner roasts such as pork loin, whole chickens, and bone-in turkey breasts also work well, though they require a bit more attention to cooking time and temperature to turn out properly. To make sure these roasts remain moist, we cook them on low and monitor their temperature toward the end of cooking and take them out of the slow cooker as soon as they reach the desired temperature. Avoid premium cuts like beef tenderloin and rib-eye—they would be a waste of money. Save them for the grill or oven.

PAY ATTENTION TO POSITIONING In our testing, we learned that getting juicy roasts had a lot to do with how we positioned them in the slow cooker. Nestling two pork tenderloins side by side, alternating the narrow and thicker ends, helped to insulate the lean meat and prevent it from overcooking. Positioning larger roasts like brisket, pork loins, and turkey breasts fat and skin side up allowed more fat to render and baste the meat as it cooked. When it came to whole chickens, we found that the trick was to place them in the slow cooker breast side down. This allowed the fat from the legs and thighs to drip down onto the lean breast meat, and as the chicken released its juices the breast became partially submerged in the rendered fat and juices, which helped it to retain moisture.

SECURE POT ROASTS WITH TWINE Our favorite cuts for pot roast are beef chuck-eye roast and pork butt roast (also called Boston butt), because they are well marbled and become very tender over the long braising time. To ensure that they cook evenly, we tie them with kitchen twine to produce a more uniformly shaped roast that will cook through evenly.

Pork Loin with Dried Fig Compote

SERVES 6 TO 8 `LIGHT`
COOKING TIME 2 TO 3 HOURS ON LOW
SLOW COOKER SIZE 4 TO 7 QUARTS

WHY THIS RECIPE WORKS Cooking a lean roast like a pork loin in a slow cooker is tricky because it can quickly turn overcooked and dry. So the key to this recipe is to monitor the temperature of the roast after a couple of hours and take it out of the slow cooker as soon as it reaches 140 degrees. Here our goal was to pair a tender pork loin with a rich fruit compote. To keep it simple, we used unsweetened applesauce as the base for our compote, then stirred in chopped dried figs. Minced shallot and balsamic vinegar added complexity and balanced the sweetness. As the pork cooked, the figs hydrated and thickened the compote, resulting in a rich, flavorful accompaniment. You will need an oval slow cooker for this recipe. A wider, shorter pork loin (about 8 inches long) will fit best in the slow cooker. We found that leaving a ⅛-inch-thick layer of fat on top of the roast is ideal; if your roast has a thicker fat cap, trim it to be about ⅛ inch thick. Check the pork's temperature after 2 hours of cooking and continue to monitor until it registers 140 degrees.

1 (3- to 4-pound) boneless pork loin roast, trimmed and tied at 1-inch intervals
  Salt and pepper
2 tablespoons vegetable oil
1 shallot, minced
1 teaspoon minced fresh thyme
1 cup unsweetened applesauce
1 cup dried Black Mission figs, stemmed and chopped
2 tablespoons balsamic vinegar
2 bay leaves

1. Pat pork dry with paper towels and season with salt and pepper. Heat 1 tablespoon oil in 12-inch skillet over medium-high heat until just smoking. Brown pork on all sides, 7 to 10 minutes. Place pork, fat side up, into slow cooker.

2. Add remaining 1 tablespoon oil, shallot, and thyme to now-empty skillet and cook over medium heat until fragrant, about 1 minute. Off heat, stir in applesauce, figs, 1 tablespoon vinegar, ¼ teaspoon salt, and bay leaves, scraping up any browned bits; transfer to slow cooker. Cover and cook until pork registers 140 degrees, 2 to 3 hours on low.

3. Transfer roast to carving board, tent loosely with aluminum foil, and let rest for 20 minutes.

4. Discard bay leaves. Stir remaining 1 tablespoon vinegar into compote and season with salt and pepper to taste. Remove twine from roast and slice meat into ½-inch-thick slices. Serve with compote.

Pork loin and maple are an ideal combo, and here we use a full cup of maple syrup as the base of the flavorful glaze.

Maple-Glazed Pork Loin

SERVES 6 TO 8 `LIGHT`
COOKING TIME 2 TO 3 HOURS ON LOW
SLOW COOKER SIZE 4 TO 7 QUARTS

WHY THIS RECIPE WORKS Working off the success of our Pork Loin with Dried Fig Compote, we decided to develop another recipe, this time pairing a perfectly juicy pork loin with a sweet, spiced maple glaze. Once again it was necessary to brown the loin first, for flavor and color. Then we used the skillet to sauté onion and bloom our spices (a mix of cinnamon, ground cloves, and cayenne) before stirring in a cup of maple syrup and some chicken broth to deglaze the pan, after which we transferred everything to the slow cooker. After cooking the loin, we reduced the braising liquid until it became a sticky, sweet glaze that paired perfectly with our juicy pork loin. You will need an oval slow cooker for this recipe. A wider, shorter pork loin (about 8 inches long) will fit best in the slow cooker. We found that leaving a ⅛-inch-thick layer of fat on top of the roast is ideal; if your roast has a thicker fat cap, trim it to be about ⅛ inch thick. Check the pork's temperature after 2 hours of cooking and continue to monitor until it registers 140 degrees.

1 (3- to 4-pound) boneless pork loin roast,
  trimmed and tied at 1-inch intervals
  Salt and pepper
2 tablespoons vegetable oil
1 onion, chopped fine
½ teaspoon ground cinnamon
¼ teaspoon ground cloves
⅛ teaspoon cayenne pepper
1 cup maple syrup
½ cup chicken broth
1 tablespoon cider vinegar

1. Pat pork dry with paper towels and season with salt and pepper. Heat 1 tablespoon oil in 12-inch skillet over medium-high heat until just smoking. Brown roast on all sides, 7 to 10 minutes. Place pork, fat side up, into slow cooker.

2. Heat remaining 1 tablespoon oil in now-empty skillet over medium heat until shimmering. Add onion and cook until softened and lightly browned, 5 to 7 minutes. Stir in cinnamon, cloves, and cayenne and cook until fragrant, about 30 seconds. Stir in maple syrup and broth, scraping up any browned bits; transfer to slow cooker. Cover and cook until pork registers 140 degrees, 2 to 3 hours on low.

3. Transfer roast to carving board, tent loosely with aluminum foil, and let rest for 20 minutes.

4. Transfer cooking liquid to saucepan and bring to simmer over medium heat. Cook until thickened and measures 1¼ cups, 15 to 20 minutes. Stir in vinegar and season with salt and pepper to taste. Remove twine from roast and slice meat into ½-inch-thick slices. Serve with glaze.

Pork Loin with Warm Spiced Chickpea Salad

SERVES 6 TO 8 `LIGHT`
COOKING TIME 2 TO 3 HOURS ON LOW
SLOW COOKER SIZE 5 TO 7 QUARTS

WHY THIS RECIPE WORKS Inspired by the lively flavors of Moroccan cuisine, we set out to create a satisfying meal featuring moist pork and a warm-spiced salad. A combination of coriander, cumin, and cloves created an authentic and flavorful base for our side dish. Once the pork was done cooking, we let it rest while we finished our warm chickpea salad. We added dried apricots, roasted red peppers, and shallots at the end and allowed them to just warm through, keeping their flavors and textures distinct to balance the spice-infused chickpeas. A splash of vinegar and a generous sprinkling of mint rounded out the salad with bright freshness. You will need an oval slow cooker for this recipe. A wider, shorter pork loin (about 8 inches long) will fit best in the

The warm and colorful chickpea salad that accompanies this pork loin is infused with warm spices and is superflavorful.

slow cooker. We found that leaving a ⅛-inch-thick layer of fat on top of the roast is ideal; if your roast has a thicker fat cap, trim it to be about ⅛ inch thick. Check the pork's temperature after 2 hours of cooking and continue to monitor until it registers 140 degrees.

1 (3- to 4-pound) boneless pork loin roast,
  trimmed and tied at 1-inch intervals
  Salt and pepper
2 tablespoons extra-virgin olive oil
1 onion, chopped fine
2 garlic cloves, minced
1 teaspoon ground coriander
½ teaspoon ground cumin
¼ teaspoon ground cloves
½ cup chicken broth
3 (14-ounce) cans chickpeas, rinsed
½ cup dried apricots, chopped
½ cup jarred roasted red peppers, rinsed,
  patted dry, and chopped
1 shallot, sliced thin
¼ cup chopped fresh mint
1 tablespoon white wine vinegar

1. Pat pork dry with paper towels and season with salt and pepper. Heat 1 tablespoon oil in 12-inch skillet over medium-high heat until just smoking. Brown roast on all sides, 7 to 10 minutes; transfer to plate.

2. Heat remaining 1 tablespoon oil in now-empty skillet over medium heat until shimmering. Add onion and cook until softened and lightly browned, 5 to 7 minutes. Add garlic, coriander, cumin, and cloves and cook until fragrant, about 30 seconds. Stir in broth, scraping up any browned bits; transfer to slow cooker.

3. Stir chickpeas into slow cooker. Nestle roast, fat side up, into slow cooker, adding any accumulated juices. Cover and cook until pork registers 140 degrees, 2 to 3 hours on low.

4. Transfer roast to carving board, tent loosely with aluminum foil, and let rest for 20 minutes.

5. Stir apricots, red peppers, and shallot into chickpea mixture and let sit until heated through, about 5 minutes. Stir in mint and vinegar and season with salt and pepper to taste. Remove twine from roast and slice meat into ½-inch-thick slices. Serve with salad.

CUTTING CITRUS INTO PIECES

1. Slice off top and bottom of citrus, then cut away peel and pith using paring knife.

2. Cut citrus into wedges as directed in recipe. Working with 2 wedges at a time, slice into ½-inch-thick pieces.

Pork Loin with Fennel, Oranges, and Olives

SERVES 6 TO 8 LIGHT

COOKING TIME 2 TO 3 HOURS ON LOW

SLOW COOKER SIZE 5 TO 7 QUARTS

WHY THIS RECIPE WORKS Fennel, oranges, and olives are a classic Mediterranean combination that we wanted to pair with a tender pork loin roast. After quickly searing the roast to give it a deep color and more satisfying flavor, we sautéed fennel until softened and deglazed the pan with white wine before transferring the mixture and pork to the slow cooker. While the roast rested, we stirred orange segments and chopped kalamata olives into the fennel. You will need an oval slow cooker for this recipe. A wider, shorter pork loin (about 8 inches long) will fit best in the slow

Sprinkled with herbes de Provence and browned before slow cooking, this pork loin has a beautiful crust and great flavor.

cooker. We found that leaving a ⅛-inch-thick layer of fat on top of the roast is ideal; if your roast has a thicker fat cap, trim it to be about ⅛ inch thick. Check the pork's temperature after 2 hours of cooking and continue to monitor until it registers 140 degrees.

1 (3- to 4-pound) boneless pork loin roast, trimmed and tied at 1-inch intervals

1 teaspoon herbes de Provence
  Salt and pepper

2 tablespoons extra-virgin olive oil

3 fennel bulbs, stalks discarded, bulbs halved, cored, and sliced thin

2 garlic cloves, minced

½ cup dry white wine

4 oranges plus 1 tablespoon grated orange zest

½ cup pitted kalamata olives, chopped

2 tablespoons minced fresh tarragon

1. Pat pork dry with paper towels, sprinkle with herbes de Provence, and season with salt and pepper. Heat 1 tablespoon oil in 12-inch skillet over medium-high heat until just smoking. Brown roast on all sides, 7 to 10 minutes; transfer to plate.

2. Heat remaining 1 tablespoon oil in now-empty skillet over medium heat until shimmering. Add fennel and cook until softened and lightly browned, 8 to 10 minutes. Stir in garlic and cook until fragrant, about 30 seconds. Stir in wine, scraping up any browned bits; transfer to slow cooker. Nestle roast, fat side up, into slow cooker, adding any accumulated juices. Cover and cook until pork registers 140 degrees, 2 to 3 hours on low.

3. Transfer roast to carving board, tent loosely with aluminum foil, and let rest for 20 minutes.

4. Cut away peel and pith from oranges. Cut oranges into 8 wedges, then slice wedges crosswise into ½-inch-thick pieces. Stir oranges and zest and olives into fennel mixture and let sit until heated through, about 5 minutes. Stir in tarragon and season with salt and pepper to taste.

5. Remove twine from roast and slice meat into ½-inch-thick slices. Serve with fennel-orange mixture.

Glazed Ham

SERVES 10 TO 12　`EASY PREP`
COOKING TIME 5 TO 6 HOURS ON LOW
SLOW COOKER SIZE 5 TO 7 QUARTS

WHY THIS RECIPE WORKS We've all seen beautifully bronzed hams emerge from the oven, so why not from the slow cooker? We lacquered hams with every thick, sticky, sugary coating we could think of, but every glaze slid right off during slow cooking. The glaze definitely needed to be applied after the ham was brought to temperature in the slow cooker. Our goal was to make a stovetop glaze that would have a thick, coating consistency without having to make a trip to the oven. Ultimately we found that equal parts dark brown sugar and apple jelly thickened with a tablespoon of cornstarch gave us the ideal consistency, along with some Dijon mustard and pepper for balancing zest. Do not substitute spiral-cut ham, as it dries out during slow cooking. You will need an oval slow cooker for this recipe.

　1　(6- to 8-pound) bone-in half ham
½　cup packed dark brown sugar
½　cup apple jelly
　2　tablespoons Dijon mustard
　1　tablespoon cornstarch
　1　teaspoon pepper

1. Remove skin from exterior of ham and trim fat to ¼-inch thickness. Score remaining fat at 1-inch intervals in crosshatch pattern. Place ham cut side down into slow cooker. Add 1 cup water, cover, and cook until fat is rendered and ham registers 100 degrees, 5 to 6 hours on low.

Once our ham is cooked all the way through, we glaze it with a mixture of brown sugar, mustard, and apple jelly.

2. Bring sugar, jelly, mustard, cornstarch, and pepper to boil in small saucepan over medium-high heat. Cook, whisking often, until glaze begins to darken and is slightly thickened, 2 to 3 minutes. Let glaze cool for 5 minutes.

3. Transfer ham to carving board, brush evenly with glaze, and let rest for 20 minutes. Carve ham and serve.

PREPARING GLAZED HAM

1. Using chef's knife, remove tough skin or rind, then carefully trim fat to ¼-inch thickness.

2. Score remaining fat at 1-inch intervals in crosshatch pattern.

CHAPTER 6

FAVORITE WAYS WITH FISH AND SHELLFISH

■ EASY PREP ■ LIGHT ■ COOK ALL DAY
Photo: Shrimp with Spiced Quinoa and Corn Salad

Salmon with Mediterranean White Rice Salad

SERVES 4 **EASY PREP**

COOKING TIME 1 TO 2 HOURS ON LOW
SLOW COOKER SIZE 4 TO 7 QUARTS

WHY THIS RECIPE WORKS Cooking salmon in the slow cooker was a hurdle we didn't think we could overcome, but we had nailed the method (see Make it Five Ways Poached Salmon on page 178) and now wanted to raise the bar even higher. What if we could create a beautifully moist salmon and perfectly cooked rice combo in the slow cooker? We first tried cooking long-grain rice with parchment on top (a trick we used previously with success), and then laying the salmon on top of that and hoping for the best. Although this technique didn't work—we ended up with raw rice and cooked salmon—we knew the general ideas were solid. For our next attempt we cooked the rice for a few hours until mostly done, then added the salmon for the last little bit. While this worked, we were unhappy with the amount of time needed to tend to the dish. For our final trial, we switched to instant rice. Using this convenient ingredient, we found that we were able to cook both the rice and the salmon in the same amount of time, which was our original goal. Once we had our cooking method down pat, we turned to the flavors. Since we were keeping our salmon very simple, we knew that our rice needed some bold flavors to round out the meal. We decided on a Greek profile, using red wine vinegar, honey, garlic, and oregano as the base flavors for our vinaigrette. Once the rice was cooked, we then stirred cherry tomatoes, whole parsley leaves, feta, and vinaigrette into our rice. Look for salmon fillets of similar thickness to ensure that they cook at the same rate. Leave the skin on the salmon to keep the bottom of the fillets from overcooking and to make it easier to skin the fillets once done. Be sure to use instant rice (sometimes labeled minute rice); traditional rice takes much longer to cook and won't work here. You will need an oval slow cooker for this recipe. For an accurate measurement of boiling water, bring a full kettle of water to a boil and then measure out the desired amount. Check the salmon's temperature after 1 hour of cooking and continue to monitor until it registers 135 degrees.

1⅔ cups boiling water
1½ cups instant white rice
⅓ cup extra-virgin olive oil
Salt and pepper
4 (6- to 8-ounce) skin-on salmon fillets, 1 to 1½ inches thick
¼ cup red wine vinegar
1 tablespoon honey
2 teaspoons minced fresh oregano

2 garlic cloves, minced
8 ounces cherry tomatoes, quartered
½ cup fresh parsley leaves
2 ounces feta cheese, crumbled (½ cup)
Lemon wedges

1. Lightly coat slow cooker with vegetable oil spray. Combine boiling water, rice, 1 tablespoon oil, ½ teaspoon salt, and ½ teaspoon pepper in prepared slow cooker. Gently press 16 by 12-inch sheet of parchment paper onto surface of water, folding down edges as needed.

2. Season salmon with salt and pepper and arrange, skin side down, in even layer on top of parchment. Cover and cook until salmon is opaque throughout when checked with tip of paring knife and registers 135 degrees (for medium), 1 to 2 hours on low.

3. Using 2 metal spatulas, transfer salmon to serving dish; discard parchment and remove any white albumin from salmon. Whisk vinegar, honey, oregano, garlic, and remaining oil together in bowl. Fluff rice with fork, then gently fold in tomatoes, parsley, feta, and ½ cup vinaigrette. Season with salt and pepper to taste. Drizzle remaining vinaigrette over salmon and serve with salad and lemon wedges.

NOTES FROM THE TEST KITCHEN

Buying Salmon

WILD VERSUS FARMED SALMON In season, we've always preferred the more pronounced flavor of wild-caught salmon to that of farmed Atlantic salmon, traditionally the main farm-raised variety in this country. But with more wild and farmed species now available, we decided to reevaluate. We tasted three kinds of wild Pacific salmon and two farmed. While we love the stronger flavor of wild-caught fish, if you're going to spend the extra money, make sure it looks and smells fresh, and realize that high quality is available only from late spring through the end of summer.

CUTS OF SALMON There are many ways to buy salmon, but our preference is for thick, center-cut fillets. Cut from the head end or center, these fillets are the prime cut of the fish. They are thick enough to poach without overcooking and are easy to skin (if desired). You will also see thin fillets at the market. Stay away from these. These are cut from the tail end and cook unevenly because one end is very, very thin while the other is always much thicker.

Salmon cooks surprisingly well in the slow cooker, and with a few tricks you can cook rice at the same time.

Chili-Garlic Glazed Salmon with Brown Rice Salad

SERVES 4   EASY PREP

COOKING TIME 1 TO 2 HOURS ON LOW

SLOW COOKER SIZE 4 TO 7 QUARTS

WHY THIS RECIPE WORKS For a salmon and rice recipe with a distinctly Asian profile, we created a brown rice salad to go with a simple chili-glazed salmon. To keep things easy, we reserved half of the glaze to make a vinaigrette for our rice. We then stirred some orange segments and scallion greens into our rice salad to bolster our Asian theme. Look for salmon fillets of similar thickness to ensure that they cook at the same rate. Leave the skin on the salmon to keep the bottom of the fillets from overcooking and to make it easier to skin the fillets once done. Be sure to use instant rice (sometimes labeled minute rice); traditional rice takes much longer to cook and won't work here. You will need an oval slow cooker for this recipe. For an accurate measurement of boiling water, bring a full kettle of water to a boil and then measure out the desired amount. Check the salmon's temperature after 1 hour of cooking and continue to monitor until it registers 135 degrees.

1⅔ cups boiling water
1½ cups instant brown rice
3 tablespoons vegetable oil
  Salt and pepper
4 scallions, white parts minced, green parts sliced on bias ½ inch thick
3 tablespoons toasted sesame oil
2 tablespoons Asian chili-garlic sauce
2 tablespoons honey
4 (6- to 8-ounce) skin-on salmon fillets, 1 to 1½ inches thick
2 oranges
¼ cup rice vinegar
1 teaspoon grated fresh ginger

1. Lightly coat slow cooker with vegetable oil spray. Combine boiling water, rice, 1 tablespoon vegetable oil, ½ teaspoon salt, and ½ teaspoon pepper in prepared slow cooker. Gently press 16 by 12-inch sheet of parchment paper onto surface of water, folding down edges as needed.

2. Combine scallion whites, sesame oil, chili-garlic sauce, and honey in bowl; measure out and reserve half of scallion mixture in medium bowl until ready to use. Season salmon with salt and pepper, brush with remaining scallion mixture, and arrange, skin side down, in even layer on top of parchment. Cover and cook until salmon is opaque throughout when checked with tip of paring knife and registers 135 degrees (for medium), 1 to 2 hours on low.

3. Cut away peel and pith from oranges. Cut oranges into 8 wedges, then slice wedges crosswise into ½-inch-thick pieces. Using 2 metal spatulas, transfer salmon to serving dish; discard parchment and remove any white albumin from salmon. Whisk vinegar, ginger, and remaining 2 tablespoons vegetable oil into reserved scallion mixture. Fluff rice with fork, then gently fold in oranges (adding any accumulated juices), scallion greens, and half of vinaigrette. Season with salt and pepper to taste. Serve salmon with salad, passing remaining vinaigrette separately.

CREATING A PARCHMENT SHIELD

Press 16 by 12-inch sheet of parchment paper firmly onto rice or vegetables, folding down edges as needed.

MAKE IT 5 WAYS POACHED SALMON

Poached Salmon with Caper Relish

SERVES 4 **EASY PREP**
COOKING TIME 1 TO 2 HOURS ON LOW
SLOW COOKER SIZE 4 TO 7 QUARTS

A slow cooker is the perfect vehicle for poaching salmon, as it requires less monitoring than the classic stovetop method but yields comparable results with less chance of overcooking. To ensure success, we came up with a few tried-and-true techniques: a foil sling helped us with ease of removal once the fish was done, and elevating the fish on herb stems and citrus slices gave us more even cooking throughout. Each salmon dish uses its aromatics in two ways: as a base to elevate the fish, and as a component in the final sauce, salsa, or relish. Look for salmon fillets of similar thickness to ensure that they cook at the same rate. Leave the skin on the salmon to keep the bottom of the fillets from overcooking and to make it easier to skin the fillets once done. You will need an oval slow cooker for these recipes. For more information on making a foil sling, see page 180. Check the salmon's temperature after 1 hour of cooking and continue to monitor until it registers 135 degrees.

1 POACHED SALMON WITH AVOCADO AND GRAPEFRUIT SALSA

- 2 grapefruits
- 2 tablespoons minced fresh cilantro, stems reserved
- ¼ cup dry white wine
- 4 (6- to 8-ounce) skin-on salmon fillets, 1 to 1½ inches thick
  Salt and pepper
- 1 avocado, halved, pitted, and cut into ½-inch pieces
- 1 shallot, minced
- 2 tablespoons extra-virgin olive oil
- 1 tablespoon white wine vinegar
- 1 teaspoon honey

1. Fold sheet of aluminum foil into 12 by 9-inch sling; press widthwise into slow cooker. Slice 1 grapefruit ¼ inch thick; arrange slices in single layer in bottom of prepared slow cooker. Scatter cilantro stems over grapefruit slices. Add wine to slow cooker, then add water until liquid level is even with grapefruit slices (about ¼ cup). Season salmon with salt and pepper; arrange skin side down in even layer on top of cilantro stems. Cover and cook until salmon is opaque throughout when checked with tip of paring knife and registers 135 degrees (for medium), 1 to 2 hours on low.

2. Cut away peel and pith from remaining grapefruit. Cut grapefruit into 8 wedges, then slice wedges crosswise into ½-inch-thick pieces. Combine grapefruit and any accumulated juices, minced cilantro, avocado, shallot, oil, vinegar, and honey in bowl. Season with salt and pepper to taste.

3. Using sling, transfer salmon to baking sheet. Gently lift and tilt fillets with spatula to remove cilantro stems and grapefruit slices; transfer to serving dish. Discard poaching liquid and remove any white albumin from salmon. Serve with salsa.

2 POACHED SALMON WITH TANGERINE AND GINGER SALSA

- 4 tangerines
- 2 tablespoons minced fresh cilantro, stems reserved
- ¼ cup dry white wine
- 4 (6- to 8-ounce) skin-on salmon fillets, 1 to 1½ inches thick
  Salt and pepper
- 2 tablespoons extra-virgin olive oil
- 1 tablespoon white wine vinegar
- 2 teaspoons grated fresh ginger

1. Fold sheet of aluminum foil into 12 by 9-inch sling; press widthwise into slow cooker. Slice 1 tangerine ¼ inch thick; arrange slices in single layer in bottom of prepared slow cooker. Scatter cilantro stems over tangerine slices. Add wine to slow cooker, then add water until liquid level is even with tangerine slices (about ¼ cup). Season salmon with salt and pepper; arrange skin side down in even layer on top of cilantro stems. Cover and cook until salmon is opaque throughout when checked with tip of paring knife and registers 135 degrees (for medium), 1 to 2 hours on low.

2. Cut away peel and pith from remaining 3 tangerines. Cut tangerines into 8 wedges, then slice wedges crosswise into ½-inch-thick pieces. Combine tangerines and any accumulated juices, minced cilantro, oil, vinegar, and ginger in bowl. Season with salt and pepper to taste.

3. Using sling, transfer salmon to baking sheet. Gently lift and tilt fillets with spatula to remove cilantro stems and tangerine slices; transfer to serving dish. Discard poaching liquid and remove any white albumin from salmon. Serve with salsa.

3 POACHED SALMON WITH CAPER RELISH

1 lemon, sliced ¼ inch thick
2 tablespoons minced fresh parsley, stems reserved
2 tablespoons minced fresh tarragon, stems reserved
¼ cup dry white wine
4 (6- to 8-ounce) skin-on salmon fillets, 1 to 1½ inches thick
Salt and pepper
1 shallot, minced
2 tablespoons capers, rinsed and chopped
1 tablespoon honey
1 tablespoon cider vinegar
1 tablespoon extra-virgin olive oil

1. Fold sheet of aluminum foil into 12 by 9-inch sling; press widthwise into slow cooker. Arrange lemon slices in single layer in bottom of prepared slow cooker. Scatter parsley stems and tarragon stems over lemon slices. Add wine to slow cooker, then add water until liquid level is even with lemon slices (about ¼ cup). Season salmon with salt and pepper; arrange skin side down in even layer on top of herb stems. Cover and cook until salmon is opaque throughout when checked with tip of paring knife and registers 135 degrees (for medium), 1 to 2 hours on low.

2. Combine minced parsley, minced tarragon, shallot, capers, honey, vinegar, and oil in bowl. Season with salt and pepper to taste. Using sling, transfer salmon to baking sheet. Gently lift and tilt fillets with spatula to remove herb stems and lemon slices; transfer to serving dish. Discard poaching liquid and remove any white albumin from salmon. Serve with relish.

4 POACHED SALMON WITH CREAMY CHIPOTLE CHILE SAUCE

1 lime, sliced ¼ inch thick, plus 1 tablespoon lime juice
2 tablespoons minced fresh cilantro, stems reserved
¼ cup dry white wine
4 (6- to 8-ounce) skin-on salmon fillets, 1 to 1½ inches thick
Salt and pepper
¼ cup mayonnaise
¼ cup sour cream
2 teaspoons minced canned chipotle chile in adobo sauce
1 garlic clove, minced

1. Fold sheet of aluminum foil into 12 by 9-inch sling; press widthwise into slow cooker. Arrange lime slices in single layer in bottom of prepared slow cooker. Scatter cilantro stems over lime slices. Add wine to slow cooker, then add water until liquid level is even with lime slices (about ¼ cup). Season salmon with salt and pepper; arrange skin side down in even layer on top of cilantro stems. Cover and cook until salmon is opaque throughout when checked with tip of paring knife and registers 135 degrees (for medium), 1 to 2 hours on low.

2. Whisk mayonnaise, sour cream, chipotle, garlic, lime juice, and minced cilantro together in bowl. Season with salt and pepper to taste. Using sling, transfer salmon to baking sheet. Gently lift and tilt fillets with spatula to remove cilantro stems and lime slices; transfer to serving dish. Discard poaching liquid and remove any white albumin from salmon. Serve with sauce.

5 POACHED SALMON WITH YOGURT-DILL SAUCE

1 lemon, sliced ¼ inch thick, plus 2 tablespoons lemon juice
2 tablespoons minced fresh dill, stems reserved
¼ cup dry white wine
4 (6- to 8-ounce) skin-on salmon fillets, 1 to 1½ inches thick
Salt and pepper
1 cup plain whole-milk yogurt
2 garlic cloves, minced
1 cucumber, peeled, halved lengthwise, seeded, and sliced thin

1. Fold sheet of aluminum foil into 12 by 9-inch sling; press widthwise into slow cooker. Arrange lemon slices in single layer in bottom of prepared slow cooker. Scatter dill stems over lemon slices. Add wine to slow cooker, then add water until liquid level is even with lemon slices (about ¼ cup). Season salmon with salt and pepper; arrange skin side down in even layer on top of dill stems. Cover and cook until salmon is opaque throughout when checked with tip of paring knife and registers 135 degrees (for medium), 1 to 2 hours on low.

2. Whisk yogurt, garlic, lemon juice, minced dill, ¼ teaspoon salt, and ¼ teaspoon pepper together in bowl. Stir in cucumber. Season with salt and pepper to taste. Using sling, transfer salmon to baking sheet. Gently lift and tilt fillets with spatula to remove dill stems and lemon slices; transfer to serving dish. Discard poaching liquid and remove any white albumin from salmon. Serve with sauce.

We poach swordfish steaks on a bed of lemon slices and parsley stems so they cook evenly in a flavorful cooking liquid.

Poached Swordfish with Warm Tomato and Olive Relish

SERVES 4   `EASY PREP`

COOKING TIME 1 TO 2 HOURS ON LOW
SLOW COOKER SIZE 4 TO 7 QUARTS

WHY THIS RECIPE WORKS Hearty swordfish steaks are a great option for gentle poaching in the slow cooker because the low heat renders the fish exceptionally tender. To keep the bottoms of the steaks from overcooking, we propped the steaks up on lemon slices. A Mediterranean-style tomato and olive relish dressed up our swordfish and added big flavor. Look for swordfish steaks of similar thickness to ensure that they cook at the same rate. Halibut is a good substitute for swordfish. You will need an oval slow cooker for this recipe. Check the swordfish's temperature after 1 hour of cooking and continue to monitor until it registers 140 degrees.

  1 lemon, sliced ¼ inch thick
  2 tablespoons minced fresh parsley,
     stems reserved
  ¼ cup dry white wine

  4 (6- to 8-ounce) skinless swordfish steaks,
     1 to 1½ inches thick
     Salt and pepper
  1 pound cherry tomatoes, halved
  ½ cup pitted salt-cured black olives, rinsed
     and halved
  3 garlic cloves, minced
  ¼ cup extra-virgin olive oil

1. Fold sheet of aluminum foil into 12 by 9-inch sling and press widthwise into slow cooker. Arrange lemon slices in single layer in bottom of prepared slow cooker. Scatter parsley stems over lemon slices. Add wine to slow cooker, then add water until liquid level is even with lemon slices (about ¼ cup). Season swordfish with salt and pepper and arrange in even layer on top of parsley stems. Cover and cook until swordfish flakes apart when gently prodded with paring knife and registers 140 degrees, 1 to 2 hours on low.

2. Microwave tomatoes, olives, and garlic in bowl until tomatoes begin to break down, about 4 minutes. Stir in oil and minced parsley and season with salt and pepper to taste. Using sling, transfer swordfish to baking sheet. Gently lift and tilt steaks with spatula to remove parsley stems and lemon slices; transfer to serving dish. Discard poaching liquid and remove any white albumin from swordfish. Serve with relish.

MAKING A FOIL SLING

Fold sheet of aluminum foil into 12 by 9-inch rectangle and press it widthwise into slow cooker. Before serving, use edges of sling as handles to lift fish or other delicate items out of slow cooker fully intact.

Poached Swordfish with Papaya Salsa

SERVES 4   `EASY PREP`   `LIGHT`

COOKING TIME 1 TO 2 HOURS ON LOW
SLOW COOKER SIZE 4 TO 7 QUARTS

WHY THIS RECIPE WORKS Our method for poaching swordfish steaks delivers moist and tender fish every time, and while the cooking time is short, it still allows you some hands-off time to organize the rest of your dinner or just relax. And there are many ways to dress up these hearty steaks. Here, going with an island theme, we opted for a bright papaya salsa with sweet fruit, hot jalapeño, bright cilantro, and tangy lime juice. Look for swordfish steaks of similar thickness to ensure that they cook at the same rate. Halibut is a good substitute for swordfish. If your papaya is underripe, season the salsa with sugar to taste. You will need an oval slow cooker for this recipe. For more information on making a foil sling, see page 180. Check the swordfish's temperature after 1 hour of cooking and continue to monitor until it registers 140 degrees.

1 lime, sliced ¼ inch thick, plus ½ teaspoon grated lime zest plus 2 tablespoons juice

2 tablespoons minced fresh cilantro, stems reserved

¼ cup dry white wine

4 (6- to 8-ounce) skinless swordfish steaks, 1 to 1½ inches thick
    Salt and pepper

1 papaya, peeled, seeded, and cut into ½-inch pieces

1 jalapeño chile, stemmed, seeded, and minced

1 tablespoon extra-virgin olive oil

1. Fold sheet of aluminum foil into 12 by 9-inch sling and press widthwise into slow cooker. Arrange lime slices in single layer in bottom of prepared slow cooker. Scatter cilantro stems over lime slices. Add wine to slow cooker, then add water until liquid level is even with lime slices (about ¼ cup). Season swordfish with salt and pepper and arrange in even layer on top of cilantro stems. Cover and cook until swordfish flakes apart when gently prodded with paring knife and registers 140 degrees, 1 to 2 hours on low.

2. Combine papaya, jalapeño, oil, and lime zest and juice in bowl. Season with salt and pepper to taste. Using sling, transfer swordfish to baking sheet. Gently lift and tilt steaks with spatula to remove cilantro stems and lime slices; transfer to serving dish. Discard poaching liquid and remove any white albumin from swordfish. Serve with salsa.

PREPARING PAPAYA

1. Cut peeled papaya in half lengthwise and remove seeds with spoon.

2. Slice each half into evenly sized lengths, then cut lengths into pieces according to recipe.

Buying and Storing Fish

WHAT TO LOOK FOR Always buy fish from a trusted source (preferably one with high volume to help ensure freshness). The store, and the fish in it, should smell like the sea, not fishy or sour. And all the fish should be on ice or properly refrigerated. Fillets and steaks should look bright, shiny, and firm, not dull or mushy. Whole fish should have moist, taut skin, clear eyes, and bright-red gills.

WHAT TO ASK FOR It is always better to have your fish-monger slice steaks and fillets to order rather than buying precut pieces that may have been sitting around. Don't be afraid to be picky at the seafood counter; a ragged piece of hake or a tail end of sea bass will be difficult to cook properly. If you have a long ride home, ask for a bag of ice.

BUYING FROZEN FISH Thin fish fillets like flounder and sole are the best choice if you have to buy your fish frozen, because they freeze quickly, minimizing moisture loss. Firm fillets like halibut, snapper, and swordfish are acceptable to buy frozen if cooked beyond medium-rare, but at lower degrees of doneness they will have a dry, stringy texture. When buying frozen fish, make sure it is frozen solid, with no signs of freezer burn or excessive crystallization. The ingredients list should include only the name of the fish you are buying.

DEFROSTING FISH To defrost fish in the refrigerator overnight, remove the fish from its packaging, place it in a single layer on a rimmed plate or dish (to catch any water), and cover it with plastic wrap. You can also do a "quick thaw" by leaving the vacuum-sealed bags under cool running tap water for 30 minutes. Do not use a microwave to defrost fish; it will alter the texture of the fish or, worse, partially cook it.

HOW TO STORE IT Because fish is so perishable, it's best to buy it the day it will be cooked. If that's not possible, unwrap the fish, pat it dry, put it in a zipper-lock bag, press out the air, and seal the bag. Then set the fish on a bed of ice in a bowl or other container (one that can hold the water once the ice melts) and place it in the back of the fridge, where it is coldest. If the ice melts before you use the fish, replenish it. The fish should keep for one day.

A filling of ricotta and frozen spinach and an easy blender tomato sauce make a company-worthy stuffed sole.

Stuffed Sole with Creamy Tomato Sauce

SERVES 4

COOKING TIME 1 TO 2 HOURS ON LOW

SLOW COOKER SIZE 4 TO 7 QUARTS

WHY THIS RECIPE WORKS While it may seem implausible to create such a delicate dish in the slow cooker, we embraced the challenge. We poached the fish on top of lemon slices and basil stems, which imparted subtle flavor. And by rolling the fillets into bundles with a moist spinach filling, we reduced the likelihood of overcooking. Flounder is a good substitute for sole. You will need an oval slow cooker for this recipe. For more information on making a foil sling, see page 180. Be sure to squeeze the spinach dry thoroughly or the filling will be watery. Check the doneness of the sole after 1 hour of cooking and continue to monitor until it flakes apart when gently prodded with a paring knife.

1 lemon, sliced ¼ inch thick, plus ½ teaspoon grated lemon zest plus 1 tablespoon juice
¼ cup chopped fresh basil, stems reserved
¼ cup dry white wine
10 ounces frozen chopped spinach, thawed and squeezed dry
4 ounces (½ cup) whole-milk ricotta cheese
Pinch nutmeg
Salt and pepper
8 (2- to 3-ounce) skinless sole fillets, ¼ to ½ inch thick
8 ounces cherry tomatoes
1 shallot, peeled and quartered
2 tablespoons extra-virgin olive oil

1. Fold sheet of aluminum foil into 12 by 9-inch sling and press widthwise into slow cooker. Arrange lemon slices in single layer in bottom of prepared slow cooker. Scatter basil stems over lemon slices. Add wine to slow cooker, then add water until liquid level is even with lemon slices (about ¼ cup).

2. Combine spinach, ricotta, lemon zest, 2 tablespoons chopped basil, nutmeg, ¼ teaspoon salt, and ¼ teaspoon pepper in bowl. Season sole with salt and pepper and place skinned side up on cutting board. Mound filling evenly in center of fillets, fold tapered ends tightly over filling, then fold over thicker ends to make tidy bundles. Arrange bundles seam side down in even layer on top of basil sprigs. Cover and cook until sole flakes apart when gently prodded with paring knife, 1 to 2 hours on low.

3. Process tomatoes, shallot, oil, and lemon juice in blender until smooth, about 2 minutes, scraping down sides of blender jar as needed. Strain sauce through fine-mesh strainer into bowl, pressing on solids to extract as much liquid as possible; discard solids. Season with salt and pepper to taste.

4. Using sling, transfer sole bundles to baking sheet. Gently lift and tilt bundles with spatula to remove basil stems and lemon slices; transfer to serving dish. Discard poaching liquid and remove any white albumin from bundles. Spoon sauce over bundles and sprinkle with remaining 2 tablespoons basil. Serve.

MAKING SOLE BUNDLES

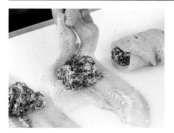

Divide spinach mixture equally among fillets, mounding in middle of each. Fold tapered end of sole tightly over filling, then fold thicker end over top to make tidy bundle.

Cod Poached in Grape Leaves

SERVES 4

COOKING TIME 1 TO 2 HOURS ON LOW

SLOW COOKER SIZE 4 TO 7 QUARTS

WHY THIS RECIPE WORKS Inspired by a popular Mediterranean dish of grape-leaf-wrapped fish, we came up with a version for the slow cooker that was streamlined and easy to make. We usually blanch grape leaves to tenderize them, but here we opted to skip this step, hoping that the moist, slow heat of the slow cooker would tenderize the leaves. To our delight, this method worked, allowing us to cut out a tedious preparation step. Once we had our method down solid, we turned to flavor profile. Playing off the brininess of the grape leaves, we found a strong salsa verde to be the perfect counterpoint. Its herbaciousness and brininess picked up on the flavor of the grape leaves without clashing. Adding a little into our packets helped to season the fish nicely, and we reserved the rest to serve alongside the finished dish. We've had good luck using Peloponnese and Krinos brand grape leaves. Take care when handling the grape leaves; they can be delicate and tear easily. Larger grape leaves can be trimmed to 6 inches. If using smaller leaves (about 4 inches in diameter), use 40 leaves; overlap nine leaves to create a 9-inch circle. Look for cod fillets of similar thickness to ensure that they cook at the same rate. You will need an oval slow cooker for this recipe. For more information on making a foil sling, see page 180. Check the cod's temperature after 1 hour of cooking and continue to monitor until it registers 140 degrees. Haddock and hake are good substitutes for the cod.

- 1 lemon, sliced ¼ inch thick, plus
  2 teaspoons lemon zest
- 3 cups fresh parsley leaves, stems reserved
- 1 cup fresh mint leaves, stems reserved
- ¼ cup dry white wine
- ½ cup extra-virgin olive oil
- 3 tablespoons white wine vinegar
- 2 tablespoons capers, rinsed
- 1 garlic clove, minced
  Salt and pepper
- 1 (16-ounce) jar grape leaves, rinsed
- 4 (6- to 8-ounce) skinless cod fillets,
  1 to 1½ inches thick

1. Fold sheet of aluminum foil into 12 by 9-inch sling and press widthwise into slow cooker. Arrange lemon slices in single layer in bottom of prepared slow cooker. Scatter parsley and mint stems over lemon slices. Add wine to slow cooker, then add water until liquid level is even with lemon slices (about ¼ cup).

2. Pulse lemon zest, parsley leaves, mint leaves, oil, vinegar, capers, garlic, and ⅛ teaspoon salt in food processor until finely chopped (mixture should not be smooth), about 10 pulses, scraping down sides of bowl as needed. Measure out and reserve ¼ cup salsa verde; transfer remaining salsa to bowl and refrigerate until ready to serve.

3. Reserve 24 intact grape leaves, roughly 6 inches in diameter; set aside remaining leaves for another use. Shingle 5 leaves smooth side down on counter into 9-inch circle, with stems pointing toward center of circle, then place 1 leaf smooth side down over opening in center. Place 1 fillet in center of leaf circle and spoon 1 tablespoon reserved salsa verde on top. Fold sides of leaf circle over cod, then fold up bottom of circle and continue to roll tightly into packet. Place packet seam side down on top of herb stems. Repeat with remaining grape leaves, fillets, and salsa, arranging packets in even layer.

4. Cover and cook until grape leaves are tender and cod registers 140 degrees, 1 to 2 hours on low. Using sling, transfer packets to baking sheet. Gently lift and tilt packets with spatula to remove herb stems and lemon slices; transfer to serving dish. Discard poaching liquid. Serve cod packets with reserved salsa verde.

MAKING GRAPE LEAF PACKETS

1. Reserve 24 intact grape leaves, roughly 6 inches in diameter.

2. Shingle 5 leaves smooth side down into 9-inch circle, then place 1 leaf smooth side down over opening in center.

3. After placing fillet in center of leaf circle, fold sides over cod, then fold up bottom of circle and continue to roll tightly into packet.

A mix of bell peppers, onions, and aromatics makes a savory base for the cod, which also gets a simple tomato sauce.

Cod Peperonata

SERVES 4
COOKING TIME 1 TO 2 HOURS ON LOW
SLOW COOKER SIZE 4 TO 7 QUARTS

WHY THIS RECIPE WORKS This sweet, simple fish dish is found all over the Mediterranean and highlights the fresh flavors of peppers, onions, and tomatoes. For our slow-cooker version of this dish we prepared the classic bell pepper base and added garlic, thyme, paprika, and wine for a deeper flavor. Thinly slicing the peppers and onions proved to be well worth the effort, as they cooked down to a soft, velvety consistency, while bigger slices still maintained some crunch and marred the smooth texture of the sauce. Once the sauce was prepared, we simply nestled the cod into the liquid and let the fish braise in the moist environment. We rounded out the peperonata with balsamic vinegar for a rich and slightly sweet finish. Look for cod fillets of similar thickness to ensure that they cook at the same rate. You will need an oval slow cooker for this recipe. Check the cod's temperature after 1 hour of cooking and continue to monitor until it registers 140 degrees. Haddock and hake are good substitutes for the cod.

2 red or yellow bell peppers, stemmed, seeded, and sliced thin
1 onion, halved and sliced thin
2 tablespoons extra-virgin olive oil, plus extra for drizzling
2 tablespoons tomato paste
4 garlic cloves, minced
1 tablespoon paprika
2 teaspoons minced fresh thyme or ½ teaspoon dried
¼ teaspoon red pepper flakes
Salt and pepper
1 (14.5-ounce) can diced tomatoes, drained
¼ cup dry white wine
4 (6- to 8-ounce) skinless cod fillets, 1 to 1½ inches thick
2 tablespoons coarsely chopped fresh basil
2 teaspoons balsamic vinegar

1. Microwave bell peppers, onion, oil, tomato paste, garlic, paprika, thyme, pepper flakes, ¼ teaspoon salt, and ¼ teaspoon pepper in bowl, stirring occasionally, until vegetables are softened, about 8 minutes; transfer to slow cooker.

2. Stir tomatoes and wine into slow cooker. Season cod with salt and pepper and nestle into slow cooker. Spoon portion of sauce over cod. Cover and cook until cod flakes apart when gently prodded with paring knife and registers 140 degrees, 1 to 2 hours on low.

3. Using 2 metal spatulas, transfer cod to serving dish. Stir basil and vinegar into sauce and season with salt and pepper to taste. Spoon sauce over cod and drizzle with extra oil. Serve.

Coconut Cod with Edamame

SERVES 4 `EASY PREP`
COOKING TIME 1 TO 2 HOURS ON LOW
SLOW COOKER SIZE 4 TO 7 QUARTS

WHY THIS RECIPE WORKS A nutty, Thai-inspired coconut sauce does wonders for lean, mild-flavored cod without requiring a lot of work. We combined coconut milk with fish sauce, ginger, garlic, and red pepper flakes for the slightest hint of heat. While cooking, the cod rested on top of a bed of edamame to prevent the bottom of the fish from overcooking. The nutty edamame base gave our meal the additional benefit of a side dish that soaked up the rich sauce. Look for cod fillets of similar thickness to ensure that they cook at the same rate. You will need an oval slow cooker for this recipe. Check the cod's temperature after 1 hour of cooking and continue to monitor until it registers 140 degrees. Haddock and hake are good substitutes for the cod.

2 shallots, minced
4 garlic cloves, minced
1 tablespoon grated fresh ginger
1 tablespoon vegetable oil
⅛ teaspoon red pepper flakes
2 cups frozen edamame, thawed
½ cup canned coconut milk
2 tablespoons fish sauce, plus extra for seasoning
4 (6- to 8-ounce) skinless cod fillets,
   1 to 1½ inches thick
   Salt and pepper
¼ cup chopped fresh cilantro
1 teaspoon rice vinegar

1. Microwave shallots, garlic, ginger, oil, and pepper flakes in bowl, stirring occasionally, until shallots are softened, about 2 minutes; transfer to slow cooker. Stir edamame, coconut milk, and fish sauce into slow cooker. Season cod with salt and pepper and nestle into slow cooker. Spoon portion of sauce over cod. Cover and cook until cod flakes apart when gently prodded with paring knife and registers 140 degrees, 1 to 2 hours on low.

2. Using 2 metal spatulas, transfer cod to serving dish. Stir cilantro and vinegar into edamame and season with extra fish sauce to taste. Spoon edamame and sauce over cod. Serve.

TUCKING THE TAIL

If you end up with a piece of fish with a thinner tail end, simply tuck the thinner end under before nestling it into the slow cooker so that it will cook at the same rate as the other pieces.

This tagine is so delicious because the sauce and all the aromatics simmer for hours before you even add the fish.

Moroccan Fish Tagine with Artichoke Hearts

SERVES 4 TO 6   LIGHT   ALL DAY
COOKING TIME 7 TO 8 HOURS ON LOW OR 4 TO 5 HOURS ON HIGH
SLOW COOKER SIZE 4 TO 7 QUARTS

WHY THIS RECIPE WORKS Making a slow-cooker fish tagine with moist and tender cod, an aromatic broth, and perfectly cooked vegetables seemed like a tall order. Our testing revealed that if we built the brothy base of the tagine first and let it and the vegetables simmer for a few hours, all we needed to do was add the fish at the end of the cooking time so it could absorb the tagine's flavors and poach gently until perfectly cooked through. The broth started with white wine, diced tomatoes, and chicken broth. Microwaving the onions and garlic with tomato paste and warm spices developed a complex Moroccan flavor for the tagine. We simmered this mixture with the artichoke hearts until the broth was deeply flavorful and the artichokes tender. Then we added the cod and allowed it to cook gently in the savory liquid for 30 minutes. Stirring in the olives with the cod allowed them to warm through and lightly flavor the broth. All the tagine needed was a sprinkle of fresh parsley to finish. Look for cod fillets of similar thickness to ensure that they cook at the same rate. While we prefer the flavor and texture of jarred whole baby artichokes, you can substitute 18 ounces frozen artichoke hearts, thawed and patted dry, for the jarred. You will need an oval slow cooker for this recipe. Haddock and hake are good substitutes for the cod.

2 onions, chopped fine
2 tablespoons tomato paste
4 garlic cloves, minced
1 tablespoon vegetable oil
2 teaspoons garam masala
1½ teaspoons paprika
¼ teaspoon cayenne pepper
3 cups jarred whole baby artichokes packed in water, halved, rinsed, and patted dry
2 cups chicken broth
1 (14.5-ounce) can diced tomatoes, drained
¼ cup dry white wine
Salt and pepper
1½ pounds skinless cod fillets, 1 to 1½ inches thick, cut into 2-inch pieces
½ cup pitted kalamata olives, chopped coarse
2 tablespoons minced fresh parsley

1. Microwave onions, tomato paste, garlic, oil, garam masala, paprika, and cayenne in bowl, stirring occasionally, until onions are softened, about 5 minutes; transfer to slow cooker. Stir in artichokes, broth, tomatoes, wine, and ½ teaspoon salt. Cover and cook until flavors meld, 7 to 8 hours on low or 4 to 5 hours on high.

2. Stir cod and olives into tagine, cover, and cook on high until cod flakes apart when gently prodded with paring knife, 30 to 40 minutes. Gently stir in parsley and season with salt and pepper to taste. Serve.

NOTES FROM THE TEST KITCHEN

Buying Kalamata Olives

Although kalamata olives are often packed in olive oil in their native Greece, on American soil we almost always find them swimming in a vinegary brine. We prefer the fresher kalamatas from the refrigerated section of the supermarket (also packed in brine) over the jarred, shelf-stable ones, which are bland and mushy in comparison. If you can't find kalamatas in the refrigerator section of your market, look for them at the salad bar.

Halibut with Warm Bean Salad

SERVES 4 `EASY PREP` `LIGHT`
COOKING TIME 1 TO 2 HOURS ON LOW
SLOW COOKER SIZE 4 TO 7 QUARTS

WHY THIS RECIPE WORKS For this healthy fish dinner we gently cooked meaty halibut fillets on a bed of creamy white beans flavored by shallot, lemon zest, and bay leaves. In the short time it took the fish to cook through perfectly, the beans absorbed the flavors of the cooking liquid. After removing the fish from the slow cooker, we finished our side dish by draining the beans and tossing them with a zesty dressing and green beans (which we steamed in the microwave, leaving them tender and not too crunchy). The final addition of briny kalamata olives paired well with fresh tarragon, intensifying the overall flavor of our dish. Look for halibut fillets of similar thickness to ensure that they cook at the same rate. You will need an oval slow cooker for this recipe. Check the halibut's temperature after 1 hour of cooking and continue to monitor until it registers 140 degrees. Sea bass is a good substitute for the halibut.

1 (15-ounce) can small white beans, rinsed
1 shallot, sliced thin
2 (2-inch) strips lemon zest, plus 1 tablespoon juice
2 bay leaves
4 (6- to 8-ounce) skinless halibut fillets, 1 to 1½ inches thick
2 tablespoons extra-virgin olive oil
Salt and pepper
8 ounces green beans, trimmed and cut into 1-inch lengths
2 tablespoons minced fresh tarragon
1 teaspoon Dijon mustard
1 teaspoon honey
2 tablespoons chopped pitted kalamata olives

1. Stir white beans, ½ cup water, shallot, lemon zest, and bay leaves into slow cooker. Rub halibut with 1 tablespoon oil and season with salt and pepper. Nestle halibut into slow cooker. Cover and cook until halibut flakes apart when gently prodded with paring knife and registers 140 degrees, 1 to 2 hours on low.

2. Microwave green beans with 1 tablespoon water in covered bowl, stirring occasionally, until tender, 4 to 6 minutes. Drain green beans and return to now-empty bowl. Whisk remaining 1 tablespoon oil, lemon juice, tarragon, mustard, and honey together in separate bowl.

3. Transfer halibut to serving dish; discard lemon zest and bay leaves. Drain white bean mixture and transfer to bowl with green beans. Add dressing and olives and toss to combine. Season with salt and pepper to taste. Serve.

Spice-rubbed halibut cooks perfectly in a slow cooker and pairs nicely with corn tortillas and a fresh cabbage slaw.

California-Style Fish Tacos

SERVES 4 **EASY PREP**

COOKING TIME 1 TO 2 HOURS ON LOW
SLOW COOKER SIZE 4 TO 7 QUARTS

WHY THIS RECIPE WORKS Simple and fresh fish tacos combine tender fish, crisp sliced cabbage, and a tangy sauce. We wanted a recipe for fish tacos that we could prepare in our slow cooker that offered the same great flavor. To start, we chose mild but sturdy halibut fillets and coated them with a spice rub that we bloomed in the microwave. The fillets sat on a bed of sliced limes, and we added just enough water to steam the fish, ensuring that it would be moist and flaky. After trying a variety of dairy products for our sauce, we settled on a combination of two—mayonnaise and sour cream— for tangy flavor and richness. Lime juice and chipotle chiles gave the sauce tang and a subtle, smoky heat. Cabbage salad mixed with fresh cilantro, scallions, and lime juice had a nice crunch and was the perfect finishing touch. Look for halibut fillets of similar thickness to ensure that they cook at the same rate. You will need an oval slow cooker for this recipe. For more information on making a foil sling, see page 180. Check the halibut's temperature after 1 hour of cooking and continue to monitor until it registers 140 degrees. Sea bass is a good substitute for the halibut.

1 lime, sliced ¼ inch thick, plus 3 tablespoons lime juice plus lime wedges for serving
6 tablespoons minced fresh cilantro, stems reserved
¼ cup dry white wine
2 tablespoons extra-virgin olive oil
1 tablespoon minced canned chipotle chile in adobo sauce
½ teaspoon ground coriander
¼ teaspoon ground cumin
Salt and pepper
4 (6- to 8-ounce) skinless halibut fillets, 1 to 1½ inches thick
4 cups shredded green cabbage
3 scallions, sliced thin
¼ cup mayonnaise
¼ cup sour cream
2 garlic cloves, minced
12 (6-inch) corn tortillas, warmed

1. Fold sheet of aluminum foil into 12 by 9-inch sling and press widthwise into slow cooker. Arrange lime slices in single layer in bottom of prepared slow cooker. Scatter cilantro stems over lime slices. Add wine to slow cooker, then add water until liquid level is even with lime slices (about ¼ cup).

2. Microwave 1 tablespoon oil, 2 teaspoons chipotle, coriander, cumin, ½ teaspoon salt, and ¼ teaspoon pepper in bowl until fragrant, about 30 seconds; let cool slightly. Rub halibut with spice mixture, then arrange in even layer on top of cilantro stems. Cover and cook until halibut flakes apart when gently prodded with paring knife and registers 140 degrees, 1 to 2 hours on low.

3. Combine cabbage, scallions, 2 tablespoons lime juice, ¼ cup cilantro, ¼ teaspoon salt, and remaining 1 tablespoon oil in bowl. In separate bowl, combine mayonnaise, sour cream, garlic, remaining 1 tablespoon lime juice, remaining 2 tablespoons cilantro, and remaining 1 teaspoon chipotle. Season with salt and pepper to taste.

4. Using sling, transfer halibut to cutting board. Gently lift and tilt fillets with spatula to remove cilantro stems and lime slices; discard poaching liquid and remove any white albumin from halibut. Cut each fillet into 3 equal pieces. Spread sauce evenly onto warm tortillas, top with fish and cabbage mixture, and serve with lime wedges.

Scallops with Creamy Braised Leeks

SERVES 4 `EASY PREP` `LIGHT`

COOKING TIME 3 TO 4 HOURS ON LOW OR 2 TO 3 HOURS
ON HIGH

SLOW COOKER SIZE 4 TO 7 QUARTS

WHY THIS RECIPE WORKS Taking inspiration from the French classic coquilles St. Jacques, we set out to create a lighter and more contemporary dish that paired briny, sweet scallops with a creamy sauce made primarily of leeks and white wine. Our main obstacle was finding the right dairy product to give our sauce richness and body. We tried a variety of options, from milk to yogurt, but were unsuccessful; every sauce was too thin or bland. In order to get the rich sauce we were looking for, we settled on a small amount of cream enriched with Pecorino Romano cheese. To further develop the flavor of our sauce, we cooked the leeks with the garlic, cream, and white wine until the leeks started to break down and sweeten the sauce. We then nestled the scallops into this hot leek mixture to poach for 30 minutes until tender. Topping it all with parsley at the end ensured a bright, fresh finish.

- 1 pound leeks, white and light green parts only, halved lengthwise, sliced thin, and washed thoroughly
- 4 garlic cloves, minced
- 1 teaspoon extra-virgin olive oil
- ⅓ cup heavy cream
- ¼ cup dry white wine
- 1½ pounds large sea scallops, tendons removed
  Salt and pepper
- ¼ cup grated Pecorino Romano cheese
- 2 tablespoons minced fresh parsley

1. Microwave leeks, garlic, and oil in bowl, stirring occasionally, until leeks are softened, about 5 minutes; transfer to slow cooker. Stir in cream and wine. Cover and cook until leeks are tender but not mushy, 3 to 4 hours on low or 2 to 3 hours on high.

2. Season scallops with salt and pepper and nestle into slow cooker. Spoon portion of sauce over scallops. Cover and cook on high until sides of scallops are firm and centers are opaque, 30 to 40 minutes.

3. Transfer scallops to serving dish. Stir Pecorino into sauce and season with salt and pepper to taste. Spoon sauce over scallops and sprinkle with parsley. Serve.

NOTES FROM THE TEST KITCHEN

All About Scallops

DRY VERSUS WET SCALLOPS Wet scallops are dipped in preservatives to extend their shelf life. Unfortunately, these watery preservatives dull the scallops' flavor and ruin their texture. Unprocessed, or dry, scallops have much more flavor and a creamy, smooth texture, plus they brown very nicely. Dry scallops will look ivory or pinkish; wet scallops are bright white.

DISTINGUISHING DRY FROM WET If your scallops are not labeled, you can determine if they are wet or dry with this quick microwave test: Place one scallop on a paper towel–lined plate and microwave for 15 seconds. A dry scallop will exude very little water, while a wet scallop will leave a sizable ring of moisture on the paper towel. (The microwaved scallop can be cooked as is.)

TREATING WET SCALLOPS When you can find only wet scallops, you can hide the off-putting taste of the preservative by soaking the scallops in a solution of 1 quart cold water, ¼ cup lemon juice, and 2 tablespoons salt for 30 minutes. Be sure to pat the scallops very dry after soaking them. Even with this treatment, these scallops will be harder to brown than untreated dry scallops.

Seafood Risotto

SERVES 6

COOKING TIME 2 TO 3 HOURS ON HIGH

SLOW COOKER SIZE 4 TO 7 QUARTS

WHY THIS RECIPE WORKS Risotto usually demands a cook's attention from start to finish, which is why slow-cooker risotto is so appealing. To start, we microwaved the onion and aromatics, which was easier than getting out a skillet and worked perfectly to soften the aromatics and toast the rice. We bolstered the rice with some white wine to increase depth of flavor, then stirred in a portion of a hot clam juice/chicken broth mixture, reserving the rest for later. We found that stirring it all in at once led to blown-out grains and mushy risotto. Once our rice was mostly cooked, we heated the remainder of the broth mixture and stirred it in to give the risotto a creamy texture. Now it was time for the seafood. Shrimp and scallops offered a brininess and sweetness that perfectly complemented the creamy rice, and they cooked through in just 30 to 40 minutes. Arborio rice, which is high in starch, gives risotto its characteristic creaminess; do not substitute other types of rice.

Making risotto in the slow cooker is easy, and using a parchment shield delivers foolproof results.

1. Lightly coat slow cooker with vegetable oil spray. Microwave onion, 2 tablespoons butter, garlic, thyme, and saffron in bowl, stirring occasionally, until onion is softened, about 5 minutes; transfer to prepared slow cooker.

2. Microwave 1 cup clam juice, 1 cup broth, and wine in 4-cup liquid measuring cup until steaming, about 5 minutes. Stir broth mixture and rice into slow cooker. Gently press 16 by 12-inch sheet of parchment paper onto surface of broth mixture, folding down edges as needed. Cover and cook until rice is almost fully tender and all liquid is absorbed, 2 to 3 hours on high.

3. Microwave remaining 2 cups clam juice and remaining 1 cup broth in now-empty measuring cup until steaming, about 5 minutes. Discard parchment. Slowly stream broth mixture into rice, stirring gently, until liquid is absorbed and risotto is creamy, about 1 minute. Gently stir in remaining 2 tablespoons butter until combined.

4. Season scallops and shrimp with salt and pepper and stir into risotto along with peas. Cover and cook on high until scallops and shrimp are opaque throughout, 30 to 40 minutes. Adjust risotto consistency with extra hot broth as needed. Season with salt and pepper to taste and sprinkle with chives. Serve.

PREPPING SCALLOPS

The small crescent-shaped muscle that is sometimes attached to the scallop will be incredibly tough when cooked. Use your fingers to peel this muscle away from the side of each scallop before cooking.

If you cannot find bay scallops, you can substitute 8 ounces sea scallops, quartered. You will need an oval slow cooker for this recipe. If using smaller or larger shrimp, be sure to adjust the cooking time as needed.

- 1 onion, chopped fine
- 4 tablespoons unsalted butter
- 3 garlic cloves, minced
- 1 teaspoon minced fresh thyme or ¼ teaspoon dried
- ⅛ teaspoon saffron threads, crumbled
- 3 (8-ounce) bottles clam juice
- 2 cups chicken broth, plus extra as needed
- ½ cup dry white wine
- 2 cups Arborio rice
- 8 ounces small bay scallops
- 8 ounces extra-large shrimp (21 to 25 per pound), peeled, deveined, and tails removed
  Salt and pepper
- ½ cup frozen peas, thawed
- 2 tablespoons minced fresh chives

We quickly toast the quinoa for this salad in the microwave, then slow-cook it until tender before nestling in the shrimp.

Shrimp with Spiced Quinoa and Corn Salad

SERVES 4 **EASY PREP** LIGHT

COOKING TIME 3 TO 4 HOURS ON LOW OR 2 TO 3 HOURS ON HIGH

SLOW COOKER SIZE 4 TO 7 QUARTS

WHY THIS RECIPE WORKS We wanted to make a main course quinoa seafood salad that was easy to prepare and that was tailored to the slow cooker. To keep the grains separate and fluffy during cooking, we quickly toasted them in the microwave before adding them to the slow cooker. The heat of the slow cooker further toasted our grains, giving a nicely caramelized flavor to our salad. We then added in some smaller shrimp and corn to round out our Southwestern-themed salad. A sprinkling of Cotija cheese was a delicious finishing touch. A fresh salsa made with tomatoes, cilantro, and some lime juice perfectly complemented our salad. You will need an oval slow cooker for this recipe. If you buy unwashed quinoa (or if you are unsure whether it's washed), be sure to rinse it before cooking to remove its bitter protective coating (called saponin).

1 cup white quinoa, rinsed
2 scallions, white parts minced, green parts cut into ½-inch pieces
2 jalapeño chiles, stemmed, seeded, and minced
5 teaspoons extra-virgin olive oil
1 teaspoon chili powder
1⅓ cups water
  Salt and pepper
1 pound medium-large shrimp (31 to 40 per pound), peeled, deveined, and tails removed
¾ cup frozen corn, thawed
3 tomatoes, cored and chopped
⅓ cup minced fresh cilantro
1 tablespoon lime juice
2 ounces Cotija cheese, crumbled (½ cup)

1. Lightly coat slow cooker with vegetable oil spray. Microwave quinoa, scallion whites, jalapeños, 2 teaspoons oil, and chili powder in bowl, stirring occasionally, until vegetables are softened, about 2 minutes; transfer to prepared slow cooker. Stir in water and ½ teaspoon salt. Cover and cook until water is absorbed and quinoa is tender, 3 to 4 hours on low or 2 to 3 hours on high.

2. Season shrimp with pepper. Fluff quinoa with fork, then nestle shrimp into quinoa and sprinkle with corn. Cover and cook on high until shrimp are opaque throughout, 30 to 40 minutes.

3. Combine tomatoes, cilantro, lime juice, scallion greens, remaining 1 tablespoon oil, ¼ teaspoon salt, and ¼ teaspoon pepper in bowl. Sprinkle quinoa and shrimp with Cotija and serve, passing salsa separately.

Spanish Braised Shrimp and Chorizo

SERVES 4 **EASY PREP** **ALL DAY**

COOKING TIME 7 TO 8 HOURS ON LOW OR 4 TO 5 HOURS ON HIGH

SLOW COOKER SIZE 4 TO 7 QUARTS

WHY THIS RECIPE WORKS To make this dish satisfying enough for a meal, we chose to pair the shrimp with some chorizo sausage and onion. We used a large can of fire-roasted diced tomatoes as the base for our dish, as well as another ingredient we found in many Spanish seafood recipes: beer. Beer added rounder, richer flavor than water or broth did; plus, it helped cut the acidity of the tomatoes. Two sliced serrano chiles added the perfect amount of heat to our base. As final touches, we stirred in some fresh cilantro and served the dish with lime wedges to add notes of freshness. Serve with crusty bread.

12 ounces Spanish-style chorizo sausage,
 halved lengthwise and sliced ¼ inch thick
1 onion, chopped fine
2 serrano chiles, stemmed and sliced thin
3 tablespoons tomato paste
3 garlic cloves, minced
1 tablespoon extra-virgin olive oil
1 (28-ounce) can fire-roasted diced tomatoes, drained
½ cup mild lager, such as Budweiser
1 pound extra-large shrimp (21 to 25 per pound),
 peeled, deveined, and tails removed
 Salt and pepper
2 tablespoons minced fresh cilantro
 Lime wedges

1. Microwave chorizo, onion, serranos, tomato paste, garlic, and oil in bowl, stirring occasionally, until onion is softened, about 5 minutes; transfer to slow cooker. Stir in tomatoes and beer, cover, and cook until flavors meld, 7 to 8 hours on low or 4 to 5 hours on high.

2. Season shrimp with salt and pepper and stir into slow cooker. Cover and cook on high until shrimp are opaque throughout, 30 to 40 minutes. Sprinkle with cilantro and serve with lime wedges.

Shrimp and Cheesy Polenta

SERVES 4   **EASY PREP**

COOKING TIME 3 TO 4 HOURS ON LOW OR 2 TO 3 HOURS ON HIGH

SLOW COOKER SIZE 4 TO 7 QUARTS

WHY THIS RECIPE WORKS This Southern favorite combo of shrimp and grits features rich-tasting polenta and tender shrimp with a hint of heat. The slow cooker is the perfect vehicle for cooking creamy polenta without the need to monitor the pot—the low, slow heat gently cooks the polenta, keeping it lump-free and creamy. We wanted a cheesy taste without using tons of cheese, so we added dry mustard powder, which enhanced the cheese flavor of the dish. To the mustard we added scallions, garlic, and chipotle to ensure that our polenta was anything but bland. We whisked in polenta with the water and milk and cooked it, without stirring, until tender, and we finished by stirring in cheddar for flavor. As for the shrimp, we simply nestled them into the polenta for just 30 to 40 minutes until cooked through. Be sure to use traditional polenta, not instant polenta. Coarse-ground degerminated cornmeal such as yellow grits (with uniform grains the size of couscous) works best in this recipe. Avoid instant or quick-cooking products, as well as whole-grain, stone-ground, and regular cornmeal. You will need an oval slow cooker for this recipe.

3 scallions, white parts minced, green parts
 sliced thin on bias
1 tablespoon unsalted butter
2 garlic cloves, minced
1 teaspoon minced canned chipotle chile in adobo sauce
½ teaspoon dry mustard
4 cups water
1 cup coarse-ground cornmeal
½ cup whole milk
 Salt and pepper
4 ounces cheddar cheese, shredded (1 cup)
1 pound extra-large shrimp (21 to 25 per pound),
 peeled, deveined, and tails removed

1. Lightly coat slow cooker with vegetable oil spray. Microwave scallion whites, butter, garlic, chipotle, and mustard in bowl, stirring occasionally, until scallions are softened, about 2 minutes; transfer to prepared slow cooker. Whisk in water, cornmeal, milk, and ¼ teaspoon salt. Cover and cook until polenta is tender, 3 to 4 hours on low or 2 to 3 hours on high.

2. Stir cheddar into polenta until melted, and season with salt and pepper to taste. Season shrimp with pepper and nestle into polenta. Cover and cook on high until shrimp are opaque throughout, 30 to 40 minutes. Sprinkle with scallion greens and serve.

NOTES FROM THE TEST KITCHEN

Buying Polenta

There are several different types of polenta available at the market—traditional, instant, and precooked—but they all are simply labeled "polenta." Here's how to tell them apart. The real deal (left) is labeled as either "polenta" or "traditional polenta," and it is nothing more than a package of coarse-ground cornmeal with a very even grind and no small floury bits. Don't be tempted to buy coarse-grain cornmeal without the term "polenta" clearly listed on the package, as it often includes a portion of fine, floury bits that will make the polenta taste gluey. Instant polenta (center) and precooked tubes of polenta (right) are parcooked convenience products that have short cooking times. Precooked polenta is easy to spot because of its tube-shaped packaging.

Shrimp and Green Chile Tacos

SERVES 4 TO 6   **EASY PREP**

COOKING TIME 6 TO 7 HOURS ON LOW OR 4 TO 5 HOURS ON HIGH

SLOW COOKER SIZE 4 TO 7 QUARTS

WHY THIS RECIPE WORKS We wanted to figure out a way to make appealingly simple shrimp and green chile tacos without a bunch of extraneous toppings—just the essential chiles and onions. For the vegetables, we took a cue from a traditional Mexican condiment, poblano *rajas*, where strips of poblano peppers are roasted along with onion, garlic, and herbs. We found we could easily make them in the slow cooker: tossed with garlic and oil, they cooked to an almost perfectly caramelized state. Once we achieved supertender vegetables, we added our shrimp and cooked it just until it was perfectly poached. We tried using whole shrimp, but tasters preferred chopped-up pieces to distribute the shrimp's brininess equally throughout the vegetable base. We then tossed the whole mixture with some lime zest, lime juice, and cilantro for brightness and freshness. Serve with your favorite taco toppings.

    4 poblano chiles, stemmed, seeded, and cut
       into ½-inch-wide strips
    3 onions, halved and sliced thin
    3 tablespoons extra-virgin olive oil
    4 garlic cloves, sliced thin
    ½ teaspoon dried oregano
       Salt and pepper
 1½ pounds extra-large shrimp (21 to 25 per pound),
       peeled, deveined, tails removed, and cut into
       1-inch pieces
    2 tablespoons minced fresh cilantro
    1 teaspoon grated lime zest plus 1 teaspoon juice
12–18 (6-inch) corn tortillas, warmed

   1. Toss poblanos and onions with 2 tablespoons oil, garlic, oregano, ½ teaspoon salt, and ½ teaspoon pepper in slow cooker. Cover and cook until vegetables are tender, 6 to 7 hours on low or 4 to 5 hours on high.

   2. Season shrimp with salt and pepper and stir into slow cooker. Cover and cook on high until shrimp pieces are opaque throughout, 30 to 40 minutes. Strain shrimp mixture, discarding cooking liquid, and return to now-empty slow cooker. Stir in cilantro, lime zest and juice, and remaining 1 tablespoon oil. Season with salt and pepper to taste. Serve with tortillas.

Everything for this classic shrimp boil goes into the slow cooker at once except the shrimp, which is added at the end.

Shrimp Boil with Corn and Potatoes

SERVES 6   **LIGHT**   **ALL DAY**

COOKING TIME 7 TO 8 HOURS ON LOW OR 4 TO 5 HOURS ON HIGH

SLOW COOKER SIZE 5 TO 7 QUARTS

WHY THIS RECIPE WORKS A classic South Carolina shrimp boil is made by simmering shrimp, smoked sausage, corn on the cob, and potatoes in a broth seasoned with Old Bay. In the moist environment of the slow cooker, we were able to cook everything gently to achieve perfectly cooked meat, seafood, and vegetables. We began by microwaving the sausage (to render fat) along with the spices (to bloom them). For the base, we replaced some of the cooking liquid (water, in this case) with clam juice to reinforce the taste of the sea. We cooked the sausage, potatoes, and corn until the potatoes were tender, then added the shrimp. This ensured intact potatoes, plump corn, and nicely cooked sausage and shrimp. Fresh corn on the cob is important to the success of this dish; do not substitute frozen corn on the cob. Use small red potatoes measuring 1 to 2 inches in diameter.

8 ounces andouille sausage, cut into 1-inch lengths

2 celery ribs, cut into 2-inch lengths

2 tablespoons tomato paste

4 teaspoons Old Bay seasoning

¼ teaspoon red pepper flakes

1½ pounds small red potatoes, unpeeled, halved

1 (8-ounce) bottle clam juice

3 ears corn, husks and silk removed, halved

3 bay leaves

1½ pounds extra-large shrimp (21 to 25 per pound), peeled, deveined, and tails removed
   Salt and pepper

1. Microwave andouille, celery, tomato paste, Old Bay, and pepper flakes in bowl, stirring occasionally, until celery is softened, about 5 minutes; transfer to slow cooker. Stir in 4 cups water, potatoes, clam juice, corn, and bay leaves. Cover and cook until potatoes are tender, 7 to 8 hours on low or 4 to 5 hours on high.

2. Season shrimp with salt and pepper and stir into slow cooker. Cover and cook on high until shrimp are opaque throughout, 30 to 40 minutes. Strain shrimp boil and discard bay leaves. Serve.

Thai Green Curry with Shrimp and Sweet Potatoes

SERVES 4 TO 6   **EASY PREP**   **LIGHT**

COOKING TIME 4 TO 5 HOURS ON LOW OR 3 TO 4 HOURS ON HIGH

SLOW COOKER SIZE 5 TO 7 QUARTS

WHY THIS RECIPE WORKS Thai curries usually get their complex flavor from a laundry list of aromatic ingredients—lemon grass, ginger, garlic, chiles, and other spices. To achieve the same great flavor without hunting down all those ingredients, we found a single ingredient that could substitute for them all: green curry paste, which contained all the ingredients of classic Thai curries and added big flavor to this dish in record time. All it needed was a little lime juice and fish sauce to round out the flavors. A combination of chicken broth and coconut milk gave us a rich, creamy base for our curry. To ensure that the delicate shrimp didn't overcook, we stirred them in toward the end of cooking. For snow peas that were perfectly crisp-tender, we microwaved them with a little oil, then added them to the finished curry. The sweet potatoes become very tender in this dish; be sure to stir the curry gently to prevent the potatoes from breaking up too much.

2 cups chicken broth, plus extra as needed

2 tablespoons Thai green curry paste

2 tablespoons instant tapioca

2 pounds sweet potatoes, peeled and cut into 1-inch pieces

Chicken broth and creamy coconut milk are the base for this curry, while Thai green curry paste gives it bold flavor.

1 (13.5-ounce) can coconut milk

1½ pounds large shrimp (26 to 30 per pound), peeled, deveined, and tails removed
   Salt and pepper

2 tablespoons lime juice

1 tablespoon fish sauce

8 ounces snow peas, strings removed and cut into 1-inch pieces

1 tablespoon vegetable oil

½ cup fresh cilantro leaves

1. Whisk broth, curry paste, and tapioca together in slow cooker, then stir in potatoes. Cover and cook until flavors meld and potatoes are tender, 4 to 5 hours on low or 3 to 4 hours on high.

2. Microwave coconut milk in bowl until hot, about 2 minutes. Season shrimp with salt and pepper. Stir shrimp, coconut milk, lime juice, and fish sauce into curry. Cover and cook on high until shrimp are opaque throughout, about 30 minutes.

3. Microwave snow peas and oil in bowl, stirring occasionally, until snow peas are tender, 3 to 5 minutes. Stir snow peas into curry. Adjust consistency with extra hot broth as needed. Stir in cilantro and season with salt and pepper to taste. Serve.

CHAPTER 7

CLASSIC COMFORT FOODS

■ EASY PREP ■ VEGETARIAN ■ LIGHT ■ COOK ALL DAY
Photo: Chicken Enchiladas

Chicken Pot Pie

SERVES 6
COOKING TIME 4 TO 5 HOURS ON LOW
SLOW COOKER SIZE 4 TO 7 QUARTS

WHY THIS RECIPE WORKS With its buttery, flaky topping and tender chicken and vegetables coated in a velvety sauce, chicken pot pie is a sure crowd-pleaser. A combination of mushrooms, carrots, and onion formed the base of our filling, which we bound with a flour-thickened sauce. Chicken thighs contributed more flavor compared with breasts and stayed moist even after the long cooking time. Boneless, skinless thighs were also a snap to pull into chunks after cooking. Adding just a little tomato paste and soy sauce to the filling helped ramp up its flavor even further, and finishing it with a small amount of heavy cream provided the right amount of richness. We found using frozen puff pastry and augmenting it with Parmesan and black pepper gave us an impressive, complex topping with a minimum of additional work. To thaw frozen puff pastry, let it sit either in the refrigerator for 24 hours or on the counter for 30 minutes to 1 hour.

2 pounds boneless, skinless chicken thighs, trimmed
  Salt and pepper
¼ cup extra-virgin olive oil
8 ounces cremini mushrooms, trimmed and
  sliced ¼ inch thick
4 carrots, peeled, halved lengthwise, and
  sliced ½ inch thick
1 onion, chopped fine
½ cup all-purpose flour
2 teaspoons minced fresh thyme or ½ teaspoon dried
1 teaspoon tomato paste
2½ cups chicken broth, plus extra as needed
1 tablespoon soy sauce
1 (9½ by 9-inch) sheet puff pastry, thawed
1 ounce Parmesan cheese, grated (½ cup)
1 cup frozen peas, thawed
¼ cup heavy cream
¼ cup chopped fresh parsley

CUTTING SLITS IN PUFF PASTRY

Using paring knife, cut four 1-inch slits in pastry.

1. Pat chicken dry with paper towels and season with salt and pepper. Heat 1 tablespoon oil in 12-inch skillet over medium-high heat until just smoking. Brown half of chicken, about 4 minutes per side; transfer to slow cooker. Repeat with 1 tablespoon oil and remaining chicken; transfer to slow cooker.

2. Heat 1 tablespoon oil in now-empty skillet over medium heat until shimmering. Add mushrooms, carrots, onion, and ½ teaspoon salt and cook until vegetables are softened and lightly browned, 8 to 10 minutes. Stir in flour, thyme, and tomato paste and cook until fragrant, about 1 minute. Slowly stir in 1½ cups broth, scraping up any browned bits and smoothing out any lumps; transfer to slow cooker.

3. Stir remaining 1 cup broth and soy sauce into slow cooker. Cover and cook until chicken is tender, 4 to 5 hours on low.

4. Adjust oven rack to middle position and heat oven to 400 degrees. Roll puff pastry into 12 by 9-inch rectangle on lightly floured counter. Using paring knife, cut pastry in half lengthwise, then into thirds widthwise to create 6 pieces. Cut four 1-inch slits in each piece and arrange upside down on parchment paper–lined baking sheet. Brush pieces with remaining 1 tablespoon oil, sprinkle with Parmesan and ¼ teaspoon pepper, and bake until puffed and lightly browned, 10 to 15 minutes, rotating sheet halfway through baking. Let pastry cool on sheet.

5. Transfer chicken to cutting board, let cool slightly, then pull apart into large chunks using 2 forks. Stir chicken, peas, and cream into filling and let sit until heated through, about 5 minutes. Adjust consistency with extra hot broth as needed. Stir in parsley and season with salt and pepper to taste. Top individual portions with pastry before serving.

Old-Fashioned Chicken and Dumplings

SERVES 8
COOKING TIME 4 TO 5 HOURS ON LOW
SLOW COOKER SIZE 5 TO 7 QUARTS

WHY THIS RECIPE WORKS Chicken and dumplings on the stovetop is a classic winter meal, but move it to a slow cooker and you get a slew of problems—chewy chicken, lackluster flavor, and gummy dumplings, to name a few. Since dark meat has more flavor and can stand up to long cooking without drying out, we started with boneless, skinless chicken thighs. We browned the meat, vegetables, and aromatics on the stovetop to build a base of flavor, and added tomato paste, dried herbs, and bay leaves—hardy ingredients that could stand up to the slow cooker. After the chicken and vegetables cooked for 4 to 5 hours, we arranged the dumplings around the perimeter of the slow-cooker insert (where heating elements are) to ensure that they cooked through. You will need an oval slow cooker for this recipe.

For our slow-cooker chicken and dumplings, we make the stew first and then cook the dumplings on top at the end.

FILLING

- 3 pounds boneless, skinless chicken thighs, trimmed
  Salt and pepper
- 3 tablespoons vegetable oil
- 2 onions, chopped fine
- 2 celery ribs, sliced ¼ inch thick
- 2 carrots, peeled and cut into ¼-inch pieces
- ¼ cup all-purpose flour
- 4 garlic cloves, minced
- 1 tablespoon tomato paste
- 1 tablespoon minced fresh thyme or 1 teaspoon dried
- 4 cups chicken broth, plus extra as needed
- ½ cup dry white wine
- 2 bay leaves
- 1 cup frozen peas, thawed

DUMPLINGS

- 1¾ cups (8¾ ounces) all-purpose flour
- 1 tablespoon baking powder
- 1 teaspoon salt
- 1 cup whole milk
- 4 tablespoons unsalted butter, melted

1. FOR THE FILLING Pat chicken dry with paper towels and season with salt and pepper. Heat 1 tablespoon oil in 12-inch skillet over medium-high heat until just smoking. Brown half of chicken, about 4 minutes per side; transfer to slow cooker. Repeat with 1 tablespoon oil and remaining chicken; transfer to slow cooker.

2. Heat remaining 1 tablespoon oil in now-empty skillet over medium heat until shimmering. Add onions, celery, and carrots and cook until softened and lightly browned, 8 to 10 minutes. Stir in flour, garlic, tomato paste, and thyme and cook until fragrant, about 1 minute. Slowly stir in 1 cup broth and wine, scraping up any browned bits and smoothing out any lumps; transfer to slow cooker.

3. Stir remaining 3 cups broth and bay leaves into slow cooker. Cover and cook until chicken is tender, 4 to 5 hours on low.

4. Discard bay leaves. Transfer chicken to cutting board, let cool slightly, then pull apart into large chunks using 2 forks. Stir chicken and peas into filling. Adjust consistency with extra hot broth as needed.

5. FOR THE DUMPLINGS Whisk flour, baking powder, and salt together in large bowl. Stir in milk and melted butter until just incorporated. Using greased ¼-cup measure, drop 8 dumplings around perimeter of filling. Cover and cook on high until dumplings have doubled in size, 30 to 40 minutes. Serve.

ARRANGING DUMPLINGS IN THE SLOW COOKER

Using ¼-cup measure, drop dumplings around perimeter of slow cooker.

Farmhouse Chicken Casserole

SERVES 6 **EASY PREP**
COOKING TIME 4 TO 5 HOURS ON LOW
SLOW COOKER SIZE 5 TO 7 QUARTS

WHY THIS RECIPE WORKS This satisfying rustic casserole combines moist chicken and tender potatoes and carrots in a velvety sauce, topped off with a layer of crunchy croutons. To keep our prep work to a minimum, we chose boneless, skinless chicken thighs, which remained moist and tender during the long cooking time. Once the chicken was tender, we pulled it into chunks then gently stirred them back into the slow cooker. To jump-start the cooking of our carrots and potatoes, we microwaved them briefly until they began to soften. For more color and a hint of sweetness, we added frozen peas, too. Boursin cheese, added when we set the chicken aside to cool, gave us the makings of an ultracreamy and flavor-packed sauce; a couple tablespoons of tapioca, added to the slow cooker with the chicken, ensured that the sauce was thick and clingy. Croutons, sprinkled over the top of the finished casserole, provided a big crunch.

- 1 pound red potatoes, unpeeled, cut into ½-inch pieces
- 3 carrots, peeled, halved lengthwise, and sliced ½ inch thick
- 3 tablespoons extra-virgin olive oil
- ¼ cup chicken broth, plus extra as needed
- 2 tablespoons instant tapioca
- 2 pounds boneless, skinless chicken thighs, trimmed
  Salt and pepper
- 1 (12-inch) baguette, cut into ½-inch pieces
- 1 (5.2-ounce) package Boursin Garlic and Fine Herbs cheese, crumbled
- ½ cup frozen peas, thawed

1. Microwave potatoes, carrots, and 1 tablespoon oil in covered bowl, stirring occasionally, until vegetables are softened, about 5 minutes; transfer to slow cooker. Stir in broth and tapioca. Season chicken with salt and pepper and nestle into slow cooker. Cover and cook until chicken is tender, 4 to 5 hours on low.

2. Adjust oven rack to middle position and heat oven to 450 degrees. Arrange bread in single layer on rimmed baking sheet and bake until browned and crisp, about 10 minutes, stirring halfway through baking. Toss croutons with remaining 2 tablespoons oil, and season with salt and pepper to taste; set aside for serving.

3. Transfer chicken to cutting board, let cool slightly, then pull apart into large chunks using 2 forks. Stir Boursin into filling until well combined. Stir in chicken and peas and let sit until heated through, about 5 minutes. Adjust consistency with extra hot broth as needed. Season with salt and pepper to taste. Top individual portions with croutons and serve.

Chicken Enchiladas

SERVES 4 TO 6   `EASY PREP`
COOKING TIME   4 TO 5 HOURS ON LOW
SLOW COOKER SIZE   4 TO 7 QUARTS

WHY THIS RECIPE WORKS Chicken enchiladas offer a rich and complex combination of flavors and textures, but traditional cooking methods can be tedious. We wanted a more streamlined recipe for chicken enchiladas—one that utilized our slow cooker to make the filling and that enabled the enchiladas to be quickly assembled

We make an ultraflavorful filling in the slow cooker and then assemble the enchiladas and bake them in a hot oven.

and finished in the oven. First we created a simple but flavorful red chile sauce with onion, garlic, spices, and tomato sauce, then braised chicken thighs directly in the sauce, which both enhanced the flavor of the sauce and ensured moist, flavorful meat for our enchilada filling. Monterey Jack cheese complemented the rich filling nicely, while canned jalapeños and fresh cilantro rounded out the flavors and provided tang and brightness. When it came time for assembly, we brushed the tortillas with oil and microwaved them to make them pliable. After experimenting with oven temperatures and times, we found that baking the assembled enchiladas covered for 15 minutes in a 450-degree oven resulted in perfectly melted cheese, and the edges of the tortillas did not dry out in the process. Serve with sour cream, diced avocado, sliced radishes, shredded romaine lettuce, and lime wedges.

- 1 onion, chopped fine
- ¼ cup vegetable oil
- 3 tablespoons chili powder
- 3 garlic cloves, minced
- 2 teaspoons ground coriander
- 2 teaspoons ground cumin

1 (15-ounce) can tomato sauce

2 teaspoons sugar

1 pound boneless, skinless chicken thighs, trimmed
   Salt and pepper

8 ounces Monterey Jack cheese, shredded (2 cups)

½ cup minced fresh cilantro

¼ cup jarred jalapeños, chopped

1 tablespoon lime juice

12 (6-inch) corn tortillas

1. Microwave onion, 2 tablespoons oil, chili powder, garlic, coriander, and cumin in bowl, stirring occasionally, until onions are softened, about 5 minutes; transfer to slow cooker. Stir in tomato sauce and sugar. Season chicken with pepper and nestle into slow cooker. Cover and cook until chicken is tender, 4 to 5 hours on low.

2. Transfer chicken to cutting board, let cool slightly, then shred into bite-size pieces using 2 forks. Combine chicken, ¾ cup sauce, 1½ cups Monterey Jack, cilantro, jalapeños, and lime juice in bowl. Season with salt and pepper to taste.

3. Adjust oven rack to middle position and heat oven to 450 degrees. Spread ¾ cup sauce over bottom of 13 by 9-inch baking dish. Brush both sides of tortillas with remaining 2 tablespoons oil. Stack tortillas, wrap in damp dish towel, and place on plate; microwave until warm and pliable, about 1 minute.

4. Working with 1 warm tortilla at a time, spread ⅓ cup chicken filling across center of tortilla. Roll tortilla tightly around filling and place seam side down in baking dish; arrange enchiladas in 2 columns across width of dish.

5. Pour remaining sauce over enchiladas to cover completely and sprinkle with remaining ½ cup Monterey Jack. Cover dish tightly with greased aluminum foil. Bake until enchiladas are heated through and cheese is melted, 15 to 20 minutes. Let cool for 5 minutes before serving.

ASSEMBLING ENCHILADAS

1. Spread chicken filling across center of tortilla, then roll tightly.

2. Place filled and rolled tortillas seam side down in 2 columns across width of prepared baking dish.

With a few tricks, it is surprisingly easy to turn out a first-rate, company-worthy paella in your slow cooker.

Paella

SERVES 6 TO 8
COOKING TIME 2 TO 3 HOURS ON HIGH
SLOW COOKER SIZE 5 TO 7 QUARTS

WHY THIS RECIPE WORKS We thought the opportunity to try making paella in a slow cooker was too good to be missed: Paella is a Spanish dish of rice, hearty meats, and seafood that are slowly simmered until they meld into one delicious whole. Heating clam juice, water, and sherry in the microwave gave us a complex yet simple base in which to cook our rice. Boneless, skinless chicken thighs were robust enough to withstand slightly higher heat than we usually apply to chicken. A hefty amount of garlic, tomato paste, chorizo, and spices bolstered the meatiness of the dish. We stirred everything together and waited; the meat cooked perfectly, but the rice was mushy in some places and undercooked in others. We found that the meat was interfering with the rice cooking evenly. By layering the chicken and chorizo on top of the rice, the rice could absorb just the right amount of liquid while the chicken would slowly steam from the liquid below and be basted by the flavorful fat rendering from the chorizo above. Placing a parchment shield on top of the meats before putting the lid on also helped to trap heat and allowed the rice and chicken to cook through properly. Shrimp are a traditional component of paella, and we added them at the end because they needed just 20 minutes to cook. You will need an oval slow cooker for this recipe. If using smaller or larger shrimp, be sure to adjust the cooking time as needed. For more information on making a parchment shield, see page 177. For more information on making a foil collar, see page 208.

    1 onion, chopped fine
    2 tablespoons extra-virgin olive oil
    6 garlic cloves, minced
    2 tablespoons tomato paste
    1 teaspoon smoked paprika
  ¼ teaspoon cayenne pepper
       Pinch saffron threads, crumbled
       Salt and pepper
    2 cups long-grain white rice, rinsed
    1 (8-ounce) bottle clam juice
  ⅔ cup water
  ⅓ cup dry sherry
 1½ pounds boneless, skinless chicken thighs,
       trimmed and halved
    8 ounces Spanish-style chorizo sausage,
       cut into ½-inch pieces
    1 pound extra-large shrimp (21 to 25 per pound),
       peeled, deveined, and tails removed
  ½ cup frozen peas, thawed
  ½ cup jarred roasted red peppers, rinsed,
       patted dry, and sliced thin
    2 tablespoons chopped fresh parsley
       Lemon wedges

1. Line slow cooker with aluminum foil collar and lightly coat with vegetable oil spray. Microwave onion, oil, garlic, tomato paste, paprika, cayenne, saffron, and 1 teaspoon salt in bowl, stirring occasionally, until onion is softened, about 5 minutes; transfer to prepared slow cooker. Stir in rice.

2. Microwave clam juice, water, and sherry in now-empty bowl until steaming, about 5 minutes; transfer to slow cooker. Season chicken with salt and pepper and arrange in even layer on top of rice. Scatter chorizo over chicken. Gently press 16 by 12-inch sheet of parchment paper onto surface of chorizo, folding down edges as needed. Cover and cook until liquid is absorbed and rice is just tender, 2 to 3 hours on high.

3. Discard parchment and foil collar. Season shrimp with salt and pepper and scatter on top of paella. Cover and cook on high until shrimp is opaque throughout, 20 to 30 minutes.

4. Sprinkle peas and red peppers over shrimp, cover, and let sit until heated through, about 5 minutes. Sprinkle with parsley and serve with lemon wedges.

We love using the slow cooker to make a delicious and rich beef pot pie filling that we top with browned puff pastry.

Hearty Beef and Vegetable Pot Pie

SERVES 6   ALL DAY

COOKING TIME 7 TO 8 HOURS ON LOW OR 4 TO 5 HOURS ON HIGH

SLOW COOKER SIZE 5 TO 7 QUARTS

WHY THIS RECIPE WORKS To make our version of beef pot pie in a slow cooker with all the nuances of a slow-simmered beef stew, we used beef chuck roast, which we've found to be the best cut for stews, and added a significant amount of vegetables. To deepen the meaty flavor of our vegetable-rich pie, we made sure to brown half of the beef to develop a nice fond before softening our vegetables. Tomato paste, garlic, and soy sauce enhanced the savory notes of the beef, and flour helped thicken the filling; we deglazed the pan with wine and a little of the broth to capture all of the flavorful browned bits on the bottom of the skillet. We liked the simplicity of the topping from our Chicken Pot Pie (page 196) so much that we used it here, brushing it with olive oil and sprinkling it with thyme before baking it. To thaw frozen puff pastry, let it sit either in the refrigerator for 24 hours or on the counter for 30 minutes to 1 hour.

3 pounds boneless beef chuck-eye roast, pulled apart at seams, trimmed, and cut into 1-inch pieces
  Salt and pepper
¼ cup extra-virgin olive oil
12 ounces portobello mushroom caps, gills removed, caps halved and sliced ¼ inch thick
4 carrots, peeled, halved lengthwise, and sliced ½ inch thick
½ cup all-purpose flour
2 tablespoons tomato paste
4 garlic cloves, minced
1 tablespoon minced fresh thyme or 1 teaspoon dried
3 cups beef broth, plus extra as needed
½ cup dry red wine
2 cups frozen pearl onions
2 tablespoons soy sauce
1 (9½ by 9-inch) sheet puff pastry, thawed
1½ cups frozen peas, thawed
¼ cup chopped fresh parsley

1. Pat beef dry with paper towels and season with salt and pepper. Heat 2 tablespoons oil in 12-inch skillet over medium-high heat until just smoking. Brown half of beef on all sides, about 8 minutes; transfer to slow cooker with remaining uncooked beef.

2. Heat 1 tablespoon oil in now-empty skillet over medium heat until shimmering. Add mushrooms, carrots, and ½ teaspoon salt, cover, and cook until vegetables are softened and mushrooms have released their liquid, about 5 minutes. Uncover and continue to cook until vegetables are dry and lightly browned, 5 to 7 minutes. Stir in flour, tomato paste, garlic, and 2 teaspoons thyme and cook until fragrant, about 1 minute. Slowly stir in 1 cup broth and wine, scraping up any browned bits and smoothing out any lumps; transfer to slow cooker.

3. Stir remaining 2 cups broth, onions, and soy sauce into slow cooker. Cover and cook until beef is tender, 7 to 8 hours on low or 4 to 5 hours on high.

4. Adjust oven rack to middle position and heat oven to 400 degrees. Roll puff pastry into 12 by 9-inch rectangle on lightly floured counter. Using paring knife, cut pastry in half lengthwise, then into thirds widthwise to create 6 pieces. Cut four 1-inch slits in each piece and arrange upside down on parchment paper–lined baking sheet. Brush pieces with remaining 1 tablespoon oil, sprinkle with remaining 1 teaspoon thyme and pinch salt, and bake until puffed and lightly browned, 10 to 15 minutes, rotating sheet halfway through baking. Let pastry cool on sheet.

5. Stir peas into filling and let sit until heated through, about 5 minutes. Adjust consistency with extra hot broth as needed. Stir in parsley and season with salt and pepper to taste. Top individual portions with pastry before serving.

NOTES FROM THE TEST KITCHEN

Thawing Puff Pastry

Homemade puff pastry is a laborious and time-intensive undertaking, but luckily convenient frozen puff pastry is readily available in grocery stores. Still, store-bought puff pastry can present the uninitiated with some minor obstacles, particularly when it comes to temperature.

For the perfect puff, the pastry should never come to room temperature. Most cooks thaw puff pastry on the counter, but it can quickly get too warm. We recommend letting the pastry defrost slowly in the refrigerator, where it can't overheat. When rolling or cutting the pastry on the counter, do so as quickly as possible. If the dough becomes too soft, return it to the refrigerator for 5 minutes or so to firm up. If it is warm in your kitchen and the dough has softened too much, chill the shaped dough thoroughly before baking—15 minutes in the freezer or 30 minutes in the refrigerator will do the trick.

Shepherd's Pie

SERVES 6
COOKING TIME 6 TO 7 HOURS ON LOW OR 4 TO 5 HOURS ON HIGH
SLOW COOKER SIZE 5 TO 7 QUARTS

WHY THIS RECIPE WORKS Shepherd's pie is certainly a classic among hearty casseroles, but achieving the characteristic tender meat and rich flavors in the filling can be a challenge in the slow cooker. Browning the beef to develop flavor is standard in most traditional recipes, but in the slow cooker this produced overcooked, gritty meat. To fix this, we found that mixing the raw beef with a panade—a mixture of bread and milk often used in meatballs but here we use chicken broth—before browning worked wonders. Tomato paste and Worcestershire sauce also helped to add meaty flavor and richness. As for the mashed potato topping, we simply whipped up a batch of our favorite spuds and spread then evenly over the top just before serving. You will need an oval slow cooker for this recipe. We prefer to make our own mashed potato topping; however, you can substitute 3 cups prepared mashed potatoes, if desired. Either way, be sure your mashed potatoes are warm and have a loose but not soupy texture; otherwise, they will be difficult to spread over the filling.

A panade made with bread and broth is the key to long-cooked ground beef that stays tender in our shepherd's pie.

FILLING

    2 slices hearty white sandwich bread, torn
       into 1-inch pieces
 2½ cups chicken broth
       Salt and pepper
    2 pounds 85 percent lean ground beef
    1 tablespoon vegetable oil
   10 ounces white mushrooms, trimmed and
       halved if small or quartered if large
    2 onions, chopped fine
    4 carrots, peeled and cut into ½-inch pieces
   ⅓ cup all-purpose flour
    2 tablespoons tomato paste
    3 garlic cloves, minced
    1 tablespoon minced fresh thyme or 1 teaspoon dried
    1 tablespoon Worcestershire sauce
    1 cup frozen peas, thawed

TOPPING

 1½ pounds russet potatoes, peeled and sliced ½ inch thick
   ½ cup warm half-and-half, plus extra as needed
    3 tablespoons unsalted butter, melted

   ¼ teaspoon salt
   ¼ teaspoon pepper
    2 tablespoons chopped fresh chives

1. FOR THE FILLING Mash bread, ¼ cup broth, ½ teaspoon salt, and ½ teaspoon pepper into paste in large bowl using fork. Add ground beef and knead with hands until well combined.

2. Heat oil in 12-inch nonstick skillet over medium heat until shimmering. Add half of beef mixture and cook, breaking up meat into rough 1-inch pieces with wooden spoon, until no longer pink, about 5 minutes. Using slotted spoon, transfer beef to slow cooker. Repeat with remaining beef mixture; transfer to slow cooker.

3. Add mushrooms, onions, carrots, and ½ teaspoon salt to fat left in skillet. Cover and cook until vegetables are softened and mushrooms have released their liquid, about 5 minutes. Uncover and continue to cook until vegetables are dry and lightly browned, 5 to 7 minutes.

4. Stir in flour, tomato paste, garlic, and thyme and cook until fragrant, about 1 minute. Slowly stir in remaining 2¼ cups broth and Worcestershire, scraping up any browned bits and smoothing out any lumps; transfer to slow cooker. Cover and cook until beef is tender, 6 to 7 hours on low or 4 to 5 hours on high.

5. Stir in peas and let sit until heated through, about 5 minutes. Adjust consistency with hot water as needed. Season with salt and pepper to taste.

6. FOR THE TOPPING Meanwhile, cover potatoes with 1 inch water in large saucepan. Bring to boil, then reduce to simmer and cook until tender, 18 to 20 minutes. Drain potatoes, wipe saucepan dry, then return potatoes to now-empty pot.

7. Mash potatoes thoroughly with potato masher. Fold in warm half-and-half, melted butter, salt, and pepper. Adjust consistency with extra warm half-and-half as needed until potatoes have a loose but not soupy texture. Transfer warm mashed potatoes to 1-gallon zipper-lock bag and snip off bottom corner to make 1-inch opening. Pipe potatoes evenly over filling, covering entire surface, and smooth with back of spoon. Sprinkle with chives and serve.

TOPPING SHEPHERD'S PIE

1. Transfer potato mixture to 1-gallon zipper-lock bag and snip off 1 corner.

2. Pipe mixture over filling, covering entire surface. Smooth with back of spoon.

Chopped bacon and boneless country-style pork ribs deliver meaty, smoky flavor to this cassoulet-inspired casserole.

Rustic Pork and White Bean Casserole

SERVES 6 TO 8   `LIGHT`   `ALL DAY`
COOKING TIME 6 TO 8 HOURS ON LOW OR 4 TO 6 HOURS ON HIGH
SLOW COOKER SIZE 4 TO 7 QUARTS

WHY THIS RECIPE WORKS Inspired by the French classic *cassoulet*, we set out to create a casserole in our slow cooker packed with vegetables and smoky pork flavor. For the meat we turned to easy-prep boneless country-style pork ribs, cutting them into 1½-inch pieces before adding them to the slow cooker. For smoky flavor, bacon was an easy choice, and we microwaved it along with the aromatics and vegetables. To bolster the flavor of the casserole, we microwaved chopped onions with plenty of garlic, as well as tomato paste for richness and body. To thicken the casserole, we processed a can of whole peeled tomatoes and half of the beans to a paste before adding them to the slow cooker. The remaining beans were left whole and simmered along with the vegetables and the aromatics. The finishing touch to our rustic casserole was crusty toasted croutons made from a small baguette; tossing the croutons with minced fresh oregano and a little olive oil added a welcome peppery taste.

1 (14.5-ounce) can whole peeled tomatoes
2 (15-ounce) cans cannellini beans, rinsed
2 onions, chopped fine
2 slices bacon, chopped fine
3 tablespoons tomato paste
3 tablespoons minced fresh oregano
6 garlic cloves, minced
  Salt and pepper
¼ cup dry white wine
8 ounces parsnips, peeled and cut into ½-inch pieces
4 carrots, peeled and cut into ½-inch pieces
1½ pounds boneless country-style pork ribs, trimmed and cut into 1½-inch pieces
1 (12-inch) baguette, cut into ½-inch pieces
2 tablespoons extra-virgin olive oil, plus extra for drizzling

1. Process tomatoes and their juice and half of beans in blender until smooth, about 30 seconds; transfer to slow cooker.

2. Microwave onions, bacon, tomato paste, 1 tablespoon oregano, garlic, and ½ teaspoon salt in bowl, stirring occasionally, until onions are softened, about 5 minutes; transfer to slow cooker. Stir in remaining beans, wine, parsnips, and carrots. Season pork with salt and pepper and stir into slow cooker. Cover and cook until pork is tender, 6 to 8 hours on low or 4 to 6 hours on high.

3. Adjust oven rack to middle position and heat oven to 450 degrees. Arrange bread in single layer on rimmed baking sheet and bake until browned and crisp, about 10 minutes, stirring halfway through baking. Toss croutons with oil and remaining 2 tablespoons oregano, and season with salt and pepper to taste; set aside for serving.

4. Adjust consistency of filling as needed with hot water. Season with salt and pepper to taste. Top individual portions with croutons and drizzle with extra oil. Serve.

NOTES FROM THE TEST KITCHEN

Buying Country-Style Pork Ribs

Country-style ribs aren't actually ribs at all. They're well-marbled pork chops cut from the upper  side of the rib cage, from the fatty blade end of the loin. Because they contain a good amount of intramuscular fat, they are a favorite for braising in the slow cooker, particularly when we want only a small amount of juicy, tender pork. At the meat counter, these "ribs" can have widely varying proportions of light and dark meat, so be sure to choose those with a greater amount of dark.

MAKE IT 5 WAYS MEATLOAF

Classic Meatloaf

SERVES 6 TO 8
COOKING TIME 2 TO 3 HOURS ON LOW
SLOW COOKER SIZE 5 TO 7 QUARTS

Our first tries at making meatloaf in the slow cooker turned out unattractive loaves, and although we liked the idea of pressing the loaf directly into the cooker, scooping out meatloaf at serving time was just not appealing. To alleviate some of the greasiness we tried using leaner beef, but this really dried out our meatloaf. By switching to rich, flavorful meatloaf mix we got something moist and delicious, albeit greasy. Then we hit upon using a foil sling to allow us to remove the loaf easily and leave the unwanted fat behind. What's more, we were now able to place our meatloaves under the broiler to ensure a bubbly, caramelized top. If you cannot find meatloaf mix, substitute 1 pound 85 percent lean ground beef and 1 pound ground pork. You will need an oval slow cooker for these recipes. Check the meatloaf's temperature after 2 hours of cooking and continue to monitor it until it registers 155 degrees. Be sure to pack the meat mixture well while shaping, so it doesn't break apart while cooking.

1 CLASSIC MEATLOAF

- 1 onion, chopped fine
- 1 tablespoon vegetable oil
- 2 teaspoons minced fresh thyme
- 2 slices hearty white sandwich bread, torn into 1-inch pieces
- ½ cup whole milk
- 2 large eggs
- ¼ cup chopped fresh parsley
- 2 tablespoons Worcestershire sauce
- 1 tablespoon Dijon mustard
  Salt and pepper
- 2 pounds meatloaf mix
- ½ cup ketchup
- 2 tablespoons cider vinegar
- 2 tablespoons packed brown sugar

1. Microwave onion, oil, and thyme in bowl, stirring occasionally, until onion is softened, about 5 minutes. Mash bread and milk into paste in large bowl using fork. Stir in onion mixture, eggs, parsley, Worcestershire, mustard, 1½ teaspoons salt, and ½ teaspoon pepper. Add meatloaf mix; knead with hands until well combined.

2. Fold sheet of aluminum foil into 12 by 9-inch sling; lightly coat with vegetable oil spray. Shape meat mixture into firm 9 by 5-inch loaf across center of foil sling using wet hands. Using sling, transfer meatloaf to slow cooker.

3. Combine ketchup, vinegar, and sugar. Brush meatloaf with half of ketchup mixture. Cover; cook until meatloaf registers 155 degrees, 2 to 3 hours on low.

4. Adjust oven rack 6 inches from broiler element and heat broiler. Using sling, transfer meatloaf to rimmed baking sheet, allowing juices to drain back into slow cooker; remove any albumin. Press edges of foil flat. Brush meatloaf with remaining ketchup mixture. Broil until spotty brown, 3 to 5 minutes. Let cool for 15 minutes before serving.

2 SMOKY BACON MEATLOAF

- 1 onion, chopped fine
- 1 tablespoon vegetable oil
- 2 slices hearty white sandwich bread, torn into 1-inch pieces
- ½ cup whole milk
- 2 large eggs
- ¼ cup chopped fresh parsley
- 2 tablespoons Worcestershire sauce
- 1 teaspoon salt
- 2 pounds meatloaf mix
- 8 slices bacon, chopped fine
- ½ cup ketchup
- 2 tablespoons cider vinegar
- 2 tablespoons packed brown sugar
- ½ teaspoon liquid smoke

1. Microwave onion and oil in bowl, stirring occasionally, until onion is softened, about 5 minutes. Mash bread and milk into paste in large bowl using fork. Stir in onion mixture, eggs, parsley, Worcestershire, and salt. Add meatloaf mix and bacon; knead with hands until well combined.

2. Fold sheet of aluminum foil into 12 by 9-inch sling; lightly coat with vegetable oil spray. Shape meat mixture into firm 9 by 5-inch loaf across center of foil sling using wet hands. Using sling, transfer meatloaf to slow cooker.

3. Combine ketchup, vinegar, sugar, and liquid smoke. Brush meatloaf with half of ketchup mixture. Cover; cook until meatloaf registers 155 degrees, 2 to 3 hours on low.

4. Adjust oven rack 6 inches from broiler element and heat broiler. Using sling, transfer meatloaf to rimmed baking sheet, allowing juices to drain back into slow cooker; remove any albumin. Press edges of foil flat. Brush meatloaf with remaining ketchup mixture. Broil until spotty brown, 3 to 5 minutes. Let cool for 15 minutes before serving.

3 SPICY KOREAN MEATLOAF

- 4 scallions, white and green parts separated and sliced thin on bias
- 1 tablespoon toasted sesame oil
- 2 teaspoons grated fresh ginger
- 2 slices hearty white sandwich bread, torn into 1-inch pieces
- ½ cup whole milk
- ½ cup cabbage kimchi, drained and chopped fine
- 2 large eggs
- 3 tablespoons soy sauce
- 2 pounds meatloaf mix
- ¼ cup Sriracha sauce
- 3 tablespoons packed brown sugar
- 2 tablespoons rice vinegar

1. Stir scallion whites, 2 teaspoons oil, and ginger together in small bowl and microwave until fragrant, about 1 minute. Mash bread and milk into paste in large bowl using fork. Stir in scallion mixture, kimchi, eggs, and soy sauce. Add meatloaf mix; knead with hands until well combined.

2. Fold sheet of aluminum foil into 12 by 9-inch sling; lightly coat with vegetable oil spray. Shape meat mixture into firm 9 by 5-inch loaf across center of foil sling using wet hands. Using sling, transfer meatloaf to slow cooker.

3. Combine Sriracha, sugar, vinegar, and remaining 1 teaspoon oil. Brush meatloaf with half of Sriracha mixture. Cover; cook until meatloaf registers 155 degrees, 2 to 3 hours on low.

4. Adjust oven rack 6 inches from broiler element and heat broiler. Using sling, transfer meatloaf to rimmed baking sheet, allowing juices to drain back into slow cooker; remove any albumin. Press edges of foil flat. Brush meatloaf with remaining Sriracha mixture. Broil until spotty brown, 3 to 5 minutes. Let cool for 15 minutes. Sprinkle with scallion greens and serve.

4 SOUTHWESTERN MEATLOAF

- 1 onion, chopped fine
- 1 tablespoon vegetable oil
- 2 slices hearty white sandwich bread, torn into 1-inch pieces
- ½ cup whole milk
- ½ cup frozen corn, thawed
- 2 large eggs
- ⅓ cup chopped fresh cilantro
- 1 tablespoon minced canned chipotle chile in adobo sauce
- 1½ teaspoons salt
- 2 pounds meatloaf mix
- ½ cup chili sauce
- 4 ounces pepper Jack cheese, shredded (1 cup)

1. Microwave onion and oil in bowl, stirring occasionally, until onion is softened, about 5 minutes. Mash bread and milk into paste in large bowl using fork. Stir in onions, corn, eggs, ¼ cup cilantro, chipotle, and salt. Add meatloaf mix; knead with hands until well combined.

2. Fold sheet of aluminum foil into 12 by 9-inch sling; lightly coat with vegetable oil spray. Shape meat mixture into firm 9 by 5-inch loaf across center of foil sling using wet hands. Using sling, transfer meatloaf to slow cooker.

3. Brush meatloaf with ¼ cup of chili sauce. Cover; cook until meatloaf registers 155 degrees, 2 to 3 hours on low.

4. Adjust oven rack 6 inches from broiler element and heat broiler. Using sling, transfer meatloaf to rimmed baking sheet, allowing juices to drain back into slow cooker; remove any albumin. Press edges of foil flat. Brush meatloaf with remaining ¼ cup chili sauce; sprinkle with pepper Jack. Broil until cheese is melted, 2 to 4 minutes. Let cool for 15 minutes. Sprinkle with remaining cilantro. Serve.

5 ITALIAN MEATLOAF

- 1 onion, chopped fine
- 8 garlic cloves, minced
- 1 tablespoon extra-virgin olive oil
- 2 slices hearty white sandwich bread, torn into 1-inch pieces
- ½ cup whole milk
- 2 ounces Parmesan cheese, grated (1 cup)
- ½ cup chopped fresh parsley
- 2 large eggs
- 1 teaspoon red pepper flakes
  Salt and pepper
- 2 pounds meatloaf mix
- 1 cup jarred pasta sauce

1. Microwave onion, garlic, and oil in bowl, stirring occasionally, until onion is softened, about 5 minutes. Mash bread and milk into paste in large bowl using fork. Stir in onion mixture, ¾ cup Parmesan, parsley, eggs, pepper flakes, 1½ teaspoons salt, and ½ teaspoon pepper. Add meatloaf mix; knead with hands until well combined.

2. Fold sheet of aluminum foil into 12 by 9-inch sling; lightly coat with vegetable oil spray. Shape meat mixture into firm 9 by 5-inch loaf across center of foil sling using wet hands. Using sling, transfer meatloaf to slow cooker.

3. Brush meatloaf with ½ cup pasta sauce. Cover; cook until meatloaf registers 155 degrees, 2 to 3 hours on low.

4. Adjust oven rack 6 inches from broiler element and heat broiler. Using sling, transfer meatloaf to rimmed baking sheet, allowing juices to drain back into slow cooker; remove any albumin. Press edges of foil flat. Brush meatloaf with remaining ½ cup pasta sauce. Broil until spotty brown, 3 to 5 minutes. Let cool for 15 minutes. Sprinkle with remaining ¼ cup Parmesan. Serve.

Turkey Meatloaf

SERVES 6 TO 8 `LIGHT`
COOKING TIME 2 TO 3 HOURS ON LOW
SLOW COOKER SIZE 5 TO 7 QUARTS

WHY THIS RECIPE WORKS For a lighter version of meatloaf, we started with ground turkey instead of the standard meatloaf mix. Adding coarsely chopped mushrooms gave us the same deep, meaty flavor as using a combination of meats, but without the additional fat. Be sure to use ground turkey, not ground turkey breast (also labeled 99 percent fat-free), in this recipe. You will need an oval slow cooker for this recipe. Check the meatloaf's temperature after 2 hours of cooking and continue to monitor it until it registers 160 degrees. Be sure to pack the meat mixture well while shaping so it doesn't break apart while cooking.

1 shallot, minced
2 garlic cloves, minced
1 tablespoon vegetable oil
1 teaspoon minced fresh thyme or ¼ teaspoon dried
¼ teaspoon cayenne pepper
2 slices hearty white sandwich bread,
    torn into 1-inch pieces
⅓ cup whole milk
1 large egg
2 tablespoons Worcestershire sauce
1 teaspoon salt
¾ teaspoon pepper
4 ounces white mushrooms, trimmed
2 pounds ground turkey
½ cup ketchup
2 tablespoons cider vinegar
2 tablespoons packed brown sugar
1 teaspoon hot sauce

1. Stir shallot, garlic, oil, thyme, and cayenne together in large bowl and microwave until fragrant, about 1 minute.

2. Process bread, milk, egg, Worcestershire, salt, and pepper in food processor to smooth paste, about 30 seconds, scraping down sides of bowl as needed. Add mushrooms and pulse until coarsely chopped, about 10 pulses; transfer to bowl with shallot mixture. Add ground turkey and knead with hands until well combined.

3. Fold sheet of aluminum foil into 12 by 9-inch sling; lightly coat with vegetable oil spray. Shape turkey mixture into firm 9 by 5-inch loaf across center of foil sling using wet hands. Using sling, transfer meatloaf to prepared slow cooker.

4. Combine ketchup, vinegar, sugar, and hot sauce in bowl. Brush meatloaf with half of ketchup mixture. Cover and cook until meatloaf registers 160 degrees, 2 to 3 hours on low.

5. Adjust oven rack 6 inches from broiler element and heat broiler. Using sling, transfer meatloaf to rimmed baking sheet, allowing juices to drain back into slow cooker; remove any albumin from meatloaf. Press edges of foil flat. Brush meatloaf with remaining ketchup mixture. Broil until bubbling and spotty brown, 3 to 5 minutes. Let meatloaf cool for 15 minutes before serving.

ASSEMBLING MEATLOAF FOR A SLOW COOKER

Fold sheet of aluminum foil into 12 by 9-inch rectangle, then shape meatloaf across center of sling into 9-inch-long loaf. Be sure to pack meat mixture well so it doesn't break apart while cooking.

Chili Mac

SERVES 6 TO 8
COOKING TIME 1 TO 2 HOURS ON HIGH
SLOW COOKER SIZE 5 TO 7 QUARTS

WHY THIS RECIPE WORKS Chili Mac is a classic American casserole in which a meaty, chili-flavored tomato sauce is blended with macaroni and cheese. Comfort food at its very best, this recipe was definitely one we wanted to translate to the slow cooker. To develop the meaty chili sauce, we knew that we'd need to brown the meat (to which we added a panade—a paste of milk and bread—for tenderness) for texture and flavor, so we used the Dutch oven instead of the microwave to also cook the onions along with a generous amount of chili powder, garlic, and cumin. A combination of crushed tomatoes and tomato sauce added to the pot after we browned the meat created the proper consistency for our casserole. We toasted the macaroni to set the proteins in our pasta and prevent it from becoming bloated. We reserved a cup of the cheese for an appealingly cheesy topping. You will need an oval slow cooker for this recipe. For more information on making a foil collar, see page 208.

1 slice hearty white sandwich bread,
    torn into 1-inch pieces
2 tablespoons whole milk
    Salt and pepper
1 pound 85 percent lean ground beef
3 tablespoons vegetable oil
2 onions, chopped fine
3 tablespoons chili powder

6 garlic cloves, minced
4 teaspoons ground cumin
1 pound elbow macaroni or small shells
1 (28-ounce) can crushed tomatoes
2½ cups water, plus extra as needed
1 (15-ounce) can tomato sauce
8 ounces pepper Jack cheese, shredded (2 cups)

1. Line slow cooker with aluminum foil collar and lightly coat with vegetable oil spray. Mash bread, milk, ¼ teaspoon salt, and ¼ teaspoon pepper into paste in large bowl using fork. Add ground beef and knead with hands until well combined.

2. Heat oil in Dutch oven over medium heat until shimmering. Add beef mixture and cook, breaking up meat into rough 1-inch pieces with wooden spoon, until no longer pink, about 5 minutes. Add onions, ½ teaspoon salt, and ¼ teaspoon pepper and cook until onions are softened, about 5 minutes. Stir in chili powder, garlic, and cumin and cook until fragrant, about 1 minute.

3. Reduce heat to medium-low. Add macaroni and cook, stirring occasionally, until edges are translucent, about 4 minutes. Off heat, stir in tomatoes, water, and tomato sauce, scraping up any browned bits. Stir in 1 cup pepper Jack. Transfer mixture to prepared slow cooker, cover, and cook until macaroni is tender, 1 to 2 hours on high.

4. Discard foil collar. Gently stir macaroni to recombine. Adjust consistency with extra hot water as needed. Season with salt and pepper to taste. Sprinkle with remaining 1 cup pepper Jack, cover, and let sit until melted, about 20 minutes. Serve.

Macaroni and Cheese

SERVES 6 TO 8   `EASY PREP`   `VEG`
COOKING TIME 1 TO 2 HOURS ON HIGH
SLOW COOKER SIZE 4 TO 7 QUARTS

WHY THIS RECIPE WORKS Slow-cooker macaroni and cheese is notoriously finicky—the pasta is usually overcooked and flabby, and the dairy-based sauce breaks and curdles during the long cooking time, resulting in a grainy, separated sauce. We found that toasting our macaroni with a little oil allowed its proteins to set, which prevented excessive swelling. By combining it with boiling water, we could jump-start its cooking and cut down on cooking time. As for the sauce, we found that evaporated milk and condensed cheddar cheese soup, because of their stabilizers, created a creamy base that didn't break. Shredded cheddar ramped up the flavor but brought back some of the graininess. Swapping in some Monterey Jack, which has a creamier texture when melted, produced a rich-tasting sauce with a smooth consistency; some dry mustard boosted the cheesy flavor. You will need an oval slow

For pasta with just the right texture, we toast it in the microwave and jump-start the cooking using boiling water.

cooker for this recipe. For an accurate measurement of boiling water, bring a full kettle of water to a boil and then measure out the desired amount. For more information on making a foil collar, see page 208.

1 pound elbow macaroni or small shells
1 tablespoon vegetable oil
3 cups boiling water, plus extra as needed
2 (12-ounce) cans evaporated milk
2 (11-ounce) cans condensed cheddar cheese soup
8 ounces mild cheddar cheese, shredded (2 cups)
8 ounces Monterey Jack cheese, shredded (2 cups)
1 teaspoon dry mustard
  Salt and pepper
1 recipe Bread-Crumb Topping (optional; page 209)

1. Line slow cooker with aluminum foil collar and lightly coat with vegetable oil spray. Microwave macaroni and oil in bowl at 50 percent power, stirring occasionally, until macaroni begin to look toasted and blistered, 5 to 8 minutes.

2. Transfer hot macaroni to prepared slow cooker and immediately stir in 2¾ cups boiling water. Stir in evaporated milk, condensed soup, cheddar, Monterey Jack, mustard, 1 teaspoon pepper, and ½ teaspoon salt. Cover and cook until macaroni are tender, 1 to 2 hours on high.

3. Discard foil collar. Gently stir remaining ¼ cup boiling water into macaroni until combined. Season with salt and pepper to taste. Adjust consistency with extra boiling water as needed. Sprinkle individual portions with bread-crumb topping, if using. Serve. (Macaroni can be held on warm or low setting for up to 30 minutes.)

MAKING A FOIL COLLAR

Fold sheets of aluminum foil to make six-layered foil rectangle that measures roughly 16 inches long by 4 inches wide. Press collar into back side of slow cooker; food will help hold collar in place.

NOTES FROM THE TEST KITCHEN

The Importance of Toasting Pasta

The main structural elements of pasta are starch and protein. When pasta is cooked in boiling water, the moisture causes the starch to swell up; simultaneously, the heat causes the protein to set, constraining the expansion of the starch and resulting in pasta with the proper texture. In the slow cooker, however, the liquid heats up slowly, so the starch has more time to swell before being checked by the protein, resulting in soggy, mushy pasta. Toasting our raw pasta—either on the stovetop or in the microwave—before adding it to the slow cooker helped to set the protein and prevented the pasta from becoming bloated.

When toasting pasta in the microwave, we found that using 50 percent power, and stirring the pasta occasionally, worked best; note that only a portion will look toasted and blistered. However, if you have a weaker microwave you may need to toast your pasta for a longer period than we've specified in the recipe. Also, if your microwave does not have a power-level button, you can toast the pasta on high power for half the amount of time given in the recipe, stirring the pasta more frequently.

Grown-Up Macaroni and Cheese with Comté and Porcini

SERVES 6 TO 8   `EASY PREP`   `VEG`

COOKING TIME 1 TO 2 HOURS ON HIGH
SLOW COOKER SIZE 4 TO 7 QUARTS

WHY THIS RECIPE WORKS Buoyed by the ease and comforting creaminess of our Macaroni and Cheese (page 207), we set out to boost its flavor and further broaden its appeal. Being almost entirely hands-off made it ideal for serving to company, and this dressed-up version fit the bill. For us, the meltiest, most grown-up cheese dish is a Swiss-style fondue–comprising a blend of Alpine cheeses, white wine, and, sometimes, wild mushrooms, with hunks of bread to sop up the dregs. We started with an aged Gruyère, a healthy dose of wine, and a handful of dried porcini; we ended up with a curdled mess, albeit a delicious one. We found that switching to a younger Comté, a cheese similar in flavor to Gruyère, and keeping the Monterey Jack (which was in our classic recipe) greatly improved our texture: Younger cheeses melt better due to their higher moisture levels and more flexible protein structures (both qualities diminish with age). Cutting back on the wine, and thus acidity, helped to prevent curdling, and substituting a little extra water aided meltability. Look for a Comté aged for about one year (avoid Comté aged for longer; it won't melt well). You can substitute an equal amount of fontina cheese for Comté. You will need an oval slow cooker for this recipe. For an accurate measurement of boiling water, bring a full kettle of water to a boil and then measure out the desired amount. For more information on making a foil collar, see left.

1 pound elbow macaroni or small shells
1 tablespoon extra-virgin olive oil
3 cups boiling water, plus extra as needed
2 (12-ounce) cans evaporated milk
2 (11-ounce) cans condensed onion soup
8 ounces Comté cheese, shredded (2 cups)
8 ounces Monterey Jack cheese, shredded (2 cups)
¼ cup dry white wine
¼ ounce dried porcini mushrooms, rinsed and minced
1 teaspoon dry mustard
  Salt and pepper
1 recipe Bread-Crumb Topping (optional)

1. Line slow cooker with aluminum foil collar and lightly coat with vegetable oil spray. Microwave macaroni and oil in bowl at 50 percent power, stirring occasionally, until macaroni begin to look toasted and blistered, 5 to 8 minutes.

2. Transfer hot macaroni to prepared slow cooker and immediately stir in 2¾ cups boiling water. Stir in evaporated milk, condensed soup, Comté, Monterey Jack, wine, mushrooms, mustard, 1 teaspoon pepper, and ½ teaspoon salt. Cover and cook until macaroni are tender, 1 to 2 hours on high.

3. Discard foil collar. Gently stir remaining ¼ cup boiling water into macaroni until combined. Season with salt and pepper to taste. Adjust consistency with extra boiling water as needed. Sprinkle individual portions with bread-crumb topping, if using. Serve. (Macaroni can be held on warm or low setting for up to 30 minutes.)

Our slow-cooker "baked" ziti features Italian sausage, creamy ricotta cheese, and a gooey topping of melted mozzarella.

SIMPLE ACCOMPANIMENTS

BREAD-CRUMB TOPPING
MAKES ABOUT 1 CUP

- 1 cup panko bread crumbs
- 2 tablespoons extra-virgin olive oil
  Salt and pepper
- 1 ounce Parmesan cheese, grated (½ cup)
- 2 tablespoons minced fresh chives

Toss panko with oil in bowl and season with salt and pepper. Microwave panko, stirring occasionally, until deep golden brown, 2 to 4 minutes; let cool completely. Stir in Parmesan and chives. (Topping can be refrigerated for up to 2 days; bring to room temperature before using.)

Baked Ziti

SERVES 6 TO 8
COOKING TIME 2 TO 3 HOURS ON HIGH
SLOW COOKER SIZE 5 TO 7 QUARTS

WHY THIS RECIPE WORKS Baked ziti usually requires multiple steps: cooking the pasta, making the sauce, layering in the cheese, and, finally, baking everything in the oven. Our goal was to simplify the process by making this classic dish in a slow cooker. But getting tender pasta and gooey melted cheese from the slow cooker required a few tricks. First there was the issue of the pasta: Precooked pasta turned mushy, and raw pasta didn't fare well either. Instead, we toasted raw ziti with a little oil before putting it into the slow cooker. For the sauce, we tried a variety of canned tomato products, but it was a combination of crushed tomatoes and tomato sauce that provided the right depth of flavor along with the aromatics. Topping the casserole with cheese after cooking and then letting it sit in the turned-off cooker allowed the cheese to melt and heat through without separating. You will need an oval slow cooker for this recipe. For more information on making a foil collar, see page 208.

- 2 tablespoons extra-virgin olive oil
- 1 pound hot or sweet Italian sausage, casings removed
- 1 onion, chopped fine
  Salt and pepper
- 3 garlic cloves, minced
- 2 teaspoons minced fresh oregano or ½ teaspoon dried
- 8 ounces (2½ cups) ziti
- 1 (28-ounce) can crushed tomatoes
- 1 (15-ounce) can tomato sauce
- 8 ounces (1 cup) whole-milk ricotta cheese
- 4 ounces mozzarella cheese, shredded (1 cup)
- 2 tablespoons shredded fresh basil

1. Line slow cooker with aluminum foil collar and lightly coat with vegetable oil spray. Heat oil in Dutch oven over medium-high heat until just smoking. Cook sausage, breaking up pieces with wooden spoon, until well browned, 6 to 8 minutes. Stir in onion, ½ teaspoon salt, and ½ teaspoon pepper and cook until onion is softened and lightly browned, 5 to 7 minutes. Stir in garlic and oregano and cook until fragrant, about 1 minute.

2. Reduce heat to medium-low. Add ziti and cook, stirring constantly, until edges of pasta become translucent, about 4 minutes. Off heat, stir in tomatoes and tomato sauce, scraping up any browned bits. Transfer mixture to prepared slow cooker. Cover and cook until pasta is tender, 2 to 3 hours on high.

3. Discard foil collar. Dollop ricotta over ziti and sprinkle with mozzarella. Cover and let sit until cheese is melted, about 20 minutes. Sprinkle with basil and serve.

SIMPLE SIDES

THE SIMPLEST GREEN SALAD
SERVES 4

It is important to use high-quality ingredients, as there are no bells or whistles to camouflage old lettuce, flavorless oil, or harsh vinegar. Be sure to use interesting leafy greens, such as mesclun, arugula, or Bibb lettuce, rather than those with a more neutral flavor, such as iceberg lettuce. This recipe can be easily doubled.

½ garlic clove, peeled
8 ounces (8 cups) lettuce, torn into
   bite-size pieces if necessary
   Extra-virgin olive oil
   Vinegar
   Salt and pepper

Rub inside of salad bowl with garlic. Add lettuce. Holding thumb over mouth of oil bottle to control flow, slowly drizzle lettuce with small amount of oil. Toss greens very gently. Continue to drizzle with oil and toss gently until greens are lightly coated and just glistening. Sprinkle with small amounts of vinegar, salt, and pepper to taste and toss gently to coat. Serve.

Sausage Lasagna
SERVES 6 TO 8
COOKING TIME 4 TO 5 HOURS ON LOW
SLOW COOKER SIZE 5 TO 7 QUARTS

WHY THIS RECIPE WORKS We think lasagna is the ultimate slow-cooker casserole, but our early attempts at slow-cooker lasagna yielded gummy noodles and washed-out flavors. With a few tricks, however, we were able to turn things around. First, we found that no-boil noodles simply didn't work in the slow cooker—they became much too soft. Turning to regular lasagna noodles, we found that

Traditional lasagna noodles, boiled in advance, are the key to a slow-cooker lasagna with just the right texture and heft.

precooking the noodles was the solution to gummy, underdone noodles. To simplify our assembly, we utilized the test kitchen's favorite jarred pasta sauce, Bertolli Tomato and Basil, and boosted the flavors of the ricotta filling with a hefty amount of Parmesan and some fragrant basil. Spooning dollops of ricotta over the noodles—instead of spreading it—and pinching off pieces of raw sausage helped to streamline assembly as well. You will need an oval slow cooker for this recipe. For more information on making a foil collar and a foil liner, see pages 208 and 211, respectively. This lasagna is great served right out of the slow cooker, or it can be transferred to a serving dish for a more impressive presentation.

8 curly-edged lasagna noodles, broken in half
   Salt and pepper
1 pound (2 cups) whole-milk ricotta cheese
2½ ounces Parmesan cheese, grated (1¼ cups)
½ cup chopped fresh basil
1 large egg
3 cups jarred pasta sauce
1 pound hot or sweet Italian sausage, casings removed
1 pound mozzarella cheese, shredded (4 cups)

1. Line slow cooker with aluminum foil collar, then press 2 large sheets of foil into slow cooker perpendicular to one another, with extra foil hanging over edges. Lightly coat prepared slow cooker with vegetable oil spray.

2. Bring 4 quarts water to boil in large pot. Add noodles and 1 tablespoon salt and cook, stirring often, until al dente. Drain noodles, rinse under cold water, then spread out in single layer over clean dish towels and let dry. (Do not use paper towels; they will stick to noodles.)

3. Combine ricotta, 1 cup Parmesan, basil, egg, ½ teaspoon salt, and ½ teaspoon pepper in bowl. Spread ½ cup pasta sauce into prepared slow cooker.

4. Arrange 4 noodle pieces in slow cooker (they may overlap), then dollop 10 rounded tablespoons of ricotta mixture over noodles. Pinch off one-third of sausage into tablespoon-size pieces and scatter over ricotta. Sprinkle with 1 cup mozzarella, then spoon ½ cup sauce over top. Repeat layering of noodles, ricotta mixture, sausage, mozzarella, and sauce twice more.

5. For final layer, arrange remaining 4 noodles in slow cooker, then top with remaining 1 cup sauce and sprinkle with remaining 1 cup mozzarella and remaining ¼ cup Parmesan. Cover and cook until lasagna is heated through, 4 to 5 hours on low.

6. Let lasagna cool for 20 minutes. (If desired, use sling to transfer lasagna to serving dish. Press edges of foil flat; discard any juices.) Serve.

Broccoli and Sun-Dried Tomato Lasagna

SERVES 6 TO 8 **VEG**

COOKING TIME 4 TO 5 HOURS ON LOW
SLOW COOKER SIZE 5 TO 7 QUARTS

WHY THIS RECIPE WORKS Following the success of our Sausage Lasagna (page 210), we decided to create a vegetarian version by swapping in broccoli and sun-dried tomatoes for the sausage. Blanching the broccoli in boiling water before cooking the lasagna noodles ensured it was perfectly tender and vibrant after 4 hours in the slow cooker. The test kitchen's favorite jarred pasta sauce is Bertolli Tomato and Basil. You will need an oval slow cooker for this recipe. For more information on making a foil collar and a foil liner, see page 208 and right, respectively. This lasagna is great served right out of the slow cooker, or it can be transferred to a serving dish for a more impressive presentation.

12 ounces broccoli florets, cut into 2-inch pieces
    Salt and pepper
8 curly-edged lasagna noodles, broken in half
1 pound (2 cups) whole-milk ricotta cheese

2½ ounces Parmesan cheese, grated (1¼ cups)
¾ cup oil-packed sun-dried tomatoes, patted dry and quartered
1 large egg
1 teaspoon minced fresh oregano
1 teaspoon garlic powder
½ teaspoon red pepper flakes
3 cups jarred pasta sauce
1 pound mozzarella cheese, shredded (4 cups)

1. Line slow cooker with aluminum foil collar, then press 2 large sheets of foil into slow cooker perpendicular to one another, with extra foil hanging over edges. Lightly coat prepared slow cooker with vegetable oil spray.

2. Bring 4 quarts water to boil in large pot. Add broccoli and 1 tablespoon salt and cook until broccoli is bright green and just tender, about 3 minutes; transfer to paper towel–lined plate. Let broccoli cool slightly, then chop coarse.

3. Return water to boil, add noodles, and cook, stirring often, until al dente. Drain noodles, rinse under cold water, then spread out in single layer over clean dish towels and let dry. (Do not use paper towels; they will stick to noodles.)

4. Combine ricotta, 1 cup Parmesan, tomatoes, egg, oregano, garlic powder, pepper flakes, ½ teaspoon salt, and ½ teaspoon pepper in bowl. Spread ½ cup pasta sauce into prepared slow cooker.

5. Arrange 4 noodle pieces in slow cooker (they may overlap), then dollop 10 rounded tablespoons of ricotta mixture over noodles. Scatter one-third of broccoli over ricotta. Sprinkle with 1 cup mozzarella, then spoon ½ cup sauce over top. Repeat layering of noodles, ricotta mixture, broccoli, mozzarella, and sauce twice more.

6. For final layer, arrange remaining 4 noodles in slow cooker, then top with remaining 1 cup sauce and sprinkle with remaining 1 cup mozzarella and remaining ¼ cup Parmesan. Cover and cook until lasagna is heated through, 4 to 5 hours on low.

7. Let lasagna cool for 20 minutes. (If desired, use sling to transfer lasagna to serving dish. Press edges of foil flat; discard any juices.) Serve.

MAKING A FOIL LINER

Press 2 large sheets of aluminum foil into slow cooker perpendicular to one another, with extra foil hanging over edges. Before serving, use edges of liner as handles to pull food out of slow cooker fully intact.

CHAPTER 8

DINNER FOR TWO

■ EASY PREP   ■ VEGETARIAN   ■ LIGHT   ■ COOK ALL DAY

Photo: Sweet and Sour Sticky Ribs

To keep our chicken and vegetable soup fresh-tasting, we add the peas and summer squash at the end.

Chicken and Garden Vegetable Soup

SERVES 2 `LIGHT`
COOKING TIME 2 TO 3 HOURS ON LOW
SLOW COOKER SIZE 1½ TO 7 QUARTS

WHY THIS RECIPE WORKS Creating anything garden-fresh in a slow cooker is a tall order, but we beat the odds by developing a recipe for a bright, lively-tasting chicken and vegetable soup. We found that the trick was adding the vegetables in stages. Onion, garlic, and carrot went in at the start so their flavors would deepen and meld into a richly flavored broth. We stirred in yellow squash and peas at the end of cooking so that they would turn tender but not mushy and dull-tasting. For a finishing touch of bright, herbal flavor, we stirred in fresh parsley just before serving. As with our other slow-cooker chicken soups, we chose a bone-in split breast. Although breast meat is lean, the bones helped protect the meat so it retained its moisture during cooking. We simply discarded the bones after shredding the cooked chicken, and then stirred the meat back into our soup, giving us juicy, flavorful bites of chicken to complement the soup's fresh vegetable flavor. You can substitute an equal amount of bone-in chicken thighs for the bone-in breast, if desired; increase the cooking time to 3 to 4 hours on low.

1 (12-ounce) bone-in split chicken breast, trimmed
  Salt and pepper
1 tablespoon extra-virgin olive oil
1 onion, chopped fine
1 carrot, peeled and sliced ¼ inch thick
1 tablespoon tomato paste
2 garlic cloves, minced
1 teaspoon minced fresh thyme or ¼ teaspoon dried
2 cups chicken broth, plus extra as needed
1 bay leaf
1 small yellow summer squash (6 ounces), quartered lengthwise and sliced ¼ inch thick
½ cup frozen peas, thawed
1 tablespoon chopped fresh parsley

1. Pat chicken dry with paper towels and season with salt and pepper. Heat oil in 12-inch skillet over medium-high heat until just smoking. Brown chicken, 3 to 4 minutes per side; transfer to plate and discard skin.

2. Add onion, carrot, and ¼ teaspoon salt to fat left in skillet and cook over medium heat until vegetables are softened, about 5 minutes. Stir in tomato paste, garlic, and thyme and cook until fragrant, about 30 seconds. Stir in 1 cup broth, scraping up any browned bits; transfer to slow cooker.

3. Stir remaining 1 cup broth and bay leaf into slow cooker. Nestle chicken into slow cooker, adding any accumulated juices. Cover and cook until chicken is tender, 2 to 3 hours on low.

4. Transfer chicken to cutting board, let cool slightly, then shred into bite-size pieces using 2 forks; discard bones.

5. Discard bay leaf. Stir squash into soup, cover, and cook on high until tender, 20 to 30 minutes. Stir chicken and peas into soup and let sit until heated through, about 5 minutes. Adjust consistency with extra hot broth as needed. Stir in parsley and season with salt and pepper to taste. Serve.

Beef and Noodle Soup

SERVES 2 `ALL DAY`
COOKING TIME 9 TO 10 HOURS ON LOW OR 6 TO 7 HOURS ON HIGH
SLOW COOKER SIZE 3½ TO 7 QUARTS

WHY THIS RECIPE WORKS For this old-fashioned soup we chose blade steak, which contributed beefy flavor. We found that cremini mushrooms gave our soup a rich dimension, and their earthy flavor held up even in the slow cooker. A traditional *mirepoix*, for which we jump-started the onion in the microwave with a little oil and tomato paste, formed the base of the soup while store-bought beef broth, enhanced with soy sauce, imparted deep flavor. You can substitute an equal amount of beef flat-iron steaks, if desired.

1 small onion, chopped fine
4 teaspoons vegetable oil
1 garlic clove, minced
1 teaspoon tomato paste
¾ teaspoon minced fresh thyme or ¼ teaspoon dried
3 cups beef broth
6 ounces cremini mushrooms, trimmed and sliced ½ inch thick
1 carrot, peeled and chopped
1 celery rib, chopped
2 teaspoons soy sauce
1 bay leaf
1 (8-ounce) beef blade steak, ¾ to 1 inch thick, trimmed
  Salt and pepper
1 ounce (⅔ cup) wide egg noodles
1 tablespoon chopped fresh parsley

1. Microwave onion, 1 tablespoon oil, garlic, tomato paste, and thyme in bowl, stirring occasionally, until onion is softened, about 5 minutes; transfer to slow cooker. Stir in broth, mushrooms, carrot, celery, soy sauce, and bay leaf. Season steak with salt and pepper and nestle into slow cooker. Cover and cook until beef is tender, 9 to 10 hours on low or 6 to 7 hours on high.

2. Bring 2 quarts water to boil in large saucepan. Add noodles and 1½ teaspoons salt and cook, stirring often, until al dente. Drain noodles, rinse with cold water, then toss with remaining 1 teaspoon oil in bowl.

3. Transfer steak to cutting board, let cool slightly, then shred into bite-size pieces using 2 forks; discard fat and gristle.

4. Discard bay leaf. Stir noodles and beef into soup and let sit until heated through, about 5 minutes. Stir in parsley and season with salt and pepper to taste. Serve.

NOTES FROM THE TEST KITCHEN

Egg Noodles

Egg noodles are the starchy soul of many of our favorite comfort foods like Beef and Noodle Soup. They should taste lightly wheaty, like traditional pasta, but with a richer flavor that comes from eggs in the pasta dough. Our favorite noodles, **Pennsylvania Dutch Wide Egg Noodles**, boast a "gentle egg flavor" that's "just rich enough." This product's high semolina content gave the noodles a firm yet tender bite with a "subtle chew." Their wide corkscrew shape worked in both soup and pasta.

Earthy butternut squash is paired with a sweet apple for this easy-to-make soup for two.

Creamy Butternut Squash and Apple Soup

SERVES 2 **EASY PREP** **VEG** **LIGHT**
COOKING TIME 6 TO 7 HOURS ON LOW OR 4 TO 5 HOURS ON HIGH
SLOW COOKER SIZE 3½ TO 7 QUARTS

WHY THIS RECIPE WORKS We wanted to make things easy and prepare this classic soup in the slow cooker. We started by microwaving onion in a bowl with butter and salt. After transferring that mixture to the slow cooker, we added freshly peeled butternut squash, which we cut into 1-inch pieces, chicken broth, and a Golden Delicious apple. After the soup had cooked for 6 to 7 hours on low (or 4 to 5 hours on high), we used a blender to puree it to a silky-smooth texture. A dollop of sour cream works really well on this soup, but you can also sprinkle it with crumbled blue cheese or goat cheese, or crispy bacon. Serve with Classic Croutons (page 56), if desired.

½ onion, chopped fine
2 tablespoons unsalted butter
  Salt and pepper

1 pound butternut squash, peeled, seeded, and cut into 1-inch pieces (3 cups)
1 Golden Delicious apple, peeled, cored, and chopped
2 cups chicken or vegetable broth
   Minced fresh chives

1. Microwave onion, butter, and ¼ teaspoon salt in bowl, stirring occasionally, until onion is softened, about 5 minutes; transfer to slow cooker. Stir in squash, apple, and broth. Cover and cook until squash is tender, 6 to 7 hours on low or 4 to 5 hours on high.

2. Process soup in blender until smooth, 1 to 2 minutes. Season with salt and pepper to taste. Sprinkle individual portions with chives before serving.

CUTTING UP BUTTERNUT SQUASH

1. After peeling squash, trim off top and bottom and cut squash in 2 between narrow neck and wide curved bottom.

2. Cut squash neck into evenly sized planks, then cut planks into evenly sized pieces, according to recipe.

3. Cut squash base in half lengthwise, then scoop out and discard seeds and fibers.

4. Slice each base half into evenly sized lengths. Cut lengths into evenly sized pieces, according to recipe.

Hearty Beef Stew

SERVES 2 `ALL DAY`

COOKING TIME 9 TO 10 HOURS ON LOW OR 6 TO 7 HOURS ON HIGH

SLOW COOKER SIZE 3½ TO 7 QUARTS

WHY THIS RECIPE WORKS In building a classic beef stew we started, naturally, with the beef. We found that tasters loved the silky, fall-part tender texture and deep meaty flavor of blade steak. To start building flavor, we browned the meat. Keeping the steaks whole while we seared them, and pulling them apart into chunks later, saved us labor but still produced the flavorful fond we wanted. We then enlisted the help of tomato paste—which we cooked with the other aromatics—along with wine and beef broth, to create a rich, complex base.

2 (6- to 8-ounce) beef blade steaks, ¾ to 1 inch thick, trimmed
   Salt and pepper
1 tablespoon vegetable oil
½ onion, chopped fine
2 tablespoons all-purpose flour
1 tablespoon tomato paste
¼ teaspoon minced fresh thyme
1 cup beef broth, plus extra as needed
½ cup water
¼ cup dry red wine
1 red potato, unpeeled, cut into 1-inch pieces
1 carrot, peeled, halved lengthwise, and sliced 1 inch thick
1 bay leaf
½ cup frozen peas, thawed
1 tablespoon chopped fresh parsley

1. Pat steaks dry with paper towels and season with salt and pepper. Heat oil in 12-inch skillet over medium-high heat until just smoking. Brown steaks, about 2 minutes per side; transfer to slow cooker.

2. Add onion to fat left in skillet and cook over medium heat until softened, about 5 minutes. Stir in flour, tomato paste, and thyme and cook until fragrant, about 1 minute. Slowly whisk in broth, water, and wine, scraping up any browned bits and smoothing out any lumps; transfer to slow cooker.

3. Stir potato, carrot, and bay leaf into slow cooker. Cover and cook until beef is tender, 9 to 10 hours on low or 6 to 7 hours on high. Transfer beef to cutting board, let cool slightly, then pull apart into large chunks using 2 forks; discard fat and gristle.

4. Discard bay leaf. Stir beef and peas into stew and let sit until heated through, about 5 minutes. Adjust consistency with extra hot broth as needed. Stir in parsley and season with salt and pepper to taste. Serve.

One large bone-in turkey thigh is all you need to make this delicious, for-two-size stew.

Hearty Turkey Stew with Squash and Spinach

SERVES 2 LIGHT
COOKING TIME 6 TO 7 HOURS ON LOW
SLOW COOKER SIZE 3½ TO 7 QUARTS

WHY THIS RECIPE WORKS For a twist on classic chicken stew, we turned to meaty turkey thighs, pairing them with earthy butternut squash and baby spinach. Garlic, thyme, and red pepper flakes added complex depth of flavor and worked nicely with the mellow taste and silky texture of the butternut squash. To bloom the seasonings and soften the onion, we gave them a jump start in the microwave before adding them to the slow cooker. Delicate baby spinach added freshness and needed to cook for just a few minutes at the end to warm through and wilt into the stew. A sprinkling of grated Parmesan cheese was a must here—its nutty and salty flavor enhanced the other flavors in the stew. The amount of spinach may seem like a lot at first, but the leaves wilt down substantially. You can substitute an equal amount of bone-in chicken thighs for the turkey.

1 onion, chopped fine
3 garlic cloves, minced
1 tablespoon tomato paste
1 tablespoon extra-virgin olive oil, plus extra for drizzling
1 teaspoon minced fresh thyme or ¼ teaspoon dried
⅛ teaspoon red pepper flakes
1 pound butternut squash, peeled, seeded, and cut into ½-inch pieces (3 cups)
2 cups chicken broth, plus extra as needed
2 teaspoons instant tapioca
1 bay leaf
1 pound bone-in turkey thighs, skin removed, trimmed
   Salt and pepper
2 ounces (2 cups) baby spinach
¼ cup grated Parmesan cheese

1. Microwave onion, garlic, tomato paste, oil, thyme, and pepper flakes in bowl, stirring occasionally, until onion is softened, about 5 minutes; transfer to slow cooker. Stir in squash, broth, tapioca, and bay leaf. Season turkey with salt and pepper and nestle into slow cooker. Cover and cook until turkey is tender, 6 to 7 hours on low.

2. Transfer turkey to cutting board, let cool slightly, then pull apart into large chunks using 2 forks; discard bones.

3. Discard bay leaf. Stir turkey into stew, then stir in spinach, 1 handful at a time, and let sit until wilted, about 5 minutes. Adjust consistency with extra hot broth as needed. Stir in Parmesan and season with salt and pepper to taste. Serve, drizzling individual portions with extra oil.

Red Lentil Stew

SERVES 2 EASY PREP VEG
COOKING TIME 3 TO 4 HOURS ON LOW OR 2 TO 3 HOURS ON HIGH
SLOW COOKER SIZE 1½ TO 7 QUARTS

WHY THIS RECIPE WORKS For a satisfying, flavorful lentil stew for two, we looked to Indian cuisine for inspiration. Deeply flavored, exotically spiced dals are comforting, hearty lentil dishes that have a thick consistency when cooked. For our scaled-down version, we started with red lentils, which are small and cooked down nicely in the slow cooker. Fork-friendly bites of carrot, chopped tomatoes, and sweet peas added color and substance. To capture the complex flavors of Indian cuisine without reaching for several spice jars, we opted for garam masala, a spice blend that contains dried chiles, cinnamon, cardamom, coriander, and other spices. Coconut milk ensured that our stew was rich and creamy. To prevent the flavor of the coconut milk from becoming muted over the long cooking time, and to keep the peas and tomatoes from disintegrating, we added them at the end and cooked our stew for 5 minutes to absorb the flavors and give the vegetables a chance to soften. Do not substitute other varieties of lentils for the red lentils here; red lentils produce a very different texture.

1 tablespoon vegetable oil
2 garlic cloves, minced
1½ teaspoons garam masala
    Pinch red pepper flakes
1¼ cups chicken or vegetable broth,
    plus extra as needed
2 carrots, peeled and cut into ¼-inch pieces
½ cup red lentils, picked over and rinsed
    Salt and pepper
2 tomatoes, cored and cut into ½-inch pieces
¾ cup canned coconut milk
⅓ cup frozen peas, thawed
1 tablespoon chopped fresh cilantro

1. Microwave oil, garlic, garam masala, and pepper flakes in bowl, stirring occasionally, until fragrant, about 1 minute; transfer to slow cooker. Stir in broth, carrots, lentils, ½ teaspoon salt, and ½ teaspoon pepper. Cover and cook until lentils are very tender and broken down, 3 to 4 hours on low or 2 to 3 hours on high.

2. Stir tomatoes, coconut milk, and peas into stew, cover, and cook on high until heated through, about 5 minutes. Adjust consistency with extra hot broth as needed. Stir in cilantro and season with salt and pepper to taste. Serve.

CORING AND SEEDING A TOMATO

1. To remove core, use tip of paring knife to cut around stem, angling tip of knife slightly inward. Remove cone-shaped piece of stem and core from top of tomato.

2. To seed tomato, first cut tomato in half crosswise, then use your finger to pull out seeds and surrounding gel.

Weeknight Beef Chili

SERVES 2

COOKING TIME 6 TO 7 HOURS ON LOW OR 4 TO 5 HOURS ON HIGH

SLOW COOKER SIZE 3½ TO 7 QUARTS

WHY THIS RECIPE WORKS To develop the all-American chili we were looking for, we started with the base, choosing a combination of tomato sauce and diced tomatoes to create the proper consistency. Next, we incorporated a generous combination of chili powder, cumin, oregano, and red pepper flakes, bumping up the flavors even further with smoky chipotles. Browning the beef to develop flavor is standard in most traditional chilis, but it produced overcooked, gritty meat in the slow cooker. To fix this, we found mixing the raw beef with a panade—usually a mixture of bread and milk often used in meatballs but here we sub in savory soy sauce—before browning worked wonders. The soy sauce may be a tad unconventional for chili, but it helped to boost the meaty flavor. Serve with your favorite chili garnishes.

½ slice hearty white sandwich bread,
    torn into 1-inch pieces
1 tablespoon water, plus extra as needed
1 tablespoon soy sauce
    Salt and pepper
8 ounces 85 percent lean ground beef
2 tablespoons vegetable oil
1 onion, chopped fine
1 tablespoon chili powder
1 tablespoon tomato paste
2 garlic cloves, minced
1 teaspoon ground cumin
¼ teaspoon dried oregano
¼ teaspoon red pepper flakes
1 (15-ounce) can tomato sauce
1 (15-ounce) can diced tomatoes, drained
1 (15-ounce) can red kidney beans, rinsed
1 teaspoon packed brown sugar
½ teaspoon minced canned chipotle chile in adobo sauce

1. Mash bread, water, soy sauce, and ¼ teaspoon pepper into paste in large bowl using fork. Add ground beef and knead with hands until well combined.

2. Heat oil in 12-inch skillet over medium heat until shimmering. Add onion and cook until softened and lightly browned, 5 to 7 minutes. Stir in chili powder, tomato paste, garlic, cumin, oregano, and pepper flakes and cook until fragrant, about 1 minute. Add beef mixture and cook, breaking up beef with wooden spoon, until no longer pink, about 5 minutes. Stir in tomato sauce, scraping up any browned bits; transfer to slow cooker.

3. Stir diced tomatoes, beans, sugar, and chipotle into slow cooker. Cover and cook until beef is tender, 6 to 7 hours on low or 4 to 5 hours on high.

4. Using large spoon, skim fat from surface of chili. Break up any remaining large pieces of beef with spoon. Adjust consistency with extra hot water as needed. Season with salt and pepper to taste. Serve.

Black Bean Chili

SERVES 2 `VEG` `LIGHT` `ALL DAY`
COOKING TIME 8 TO 9 HOURS ON HIGH
SLOW COOKER SIZE 3½ TO 7 QUARTS

WHY THIS RECIPE WORKS Black bean chili is a hearty, satisfying dish and a great option for the slow cooker. But vegetarian versions are a bit trickier since there are no ham products, like meaty, smoky ham hocks, to build flavor over the long cooking time. To achieve the full flavors we expected from a traditional black bean chili, we started by blooming a generous amount of aromatics and spices. This additional step was promising, but it got us only so far—the chili still seemed pretty lean. Though a bit odd for a chili, a surprise ingredient, mustard seeds, added an appealing pungency and the level of complexity we were looking for. To bulk up the chili, we added bell peppers, white mushrooms, and canned tomatoes. We added the tomatoes at the end because their acidity prevented the beans from cooking through fully when added at the beginning. And while canned diced tomatoes were convenient, they took more time to turn tender than hand-cut whole canned tomatoes, so we chose whole instead. Chopped cilantro finished the dish with welcome brightness. To make this dish spicier, add the chile seeds. Serve with your favorite chili garnishes.

1 tablespoon vegetable oil
½ onion, chopped fine
½ red bell pepper, minced
½ jalapeño chile, seeded and minced
2 garlic cloves, minced
1 tablespoon chili powder
1 teaspoon mustard seeds
1 teaspoon minced canned chipotle chile
  in adobo sauce
1 teaspoon ground cumin
1 teaspoon dried oregano
2 cups chicken or vegetable broth, plus extra
  as needed
¾ cup dried black beans, picked over and rinsed
3 ounces white mushrooms, trimmed and
  halved if small or quartered if large

Bell peppers and ordinary white mushrooms add heft to this black bean chili, while mustard seeds provide complexity.

1 bay leaf
1 (14.5-ounce) can whole peeled tomatoes,
  drained and chopped
1 tablespoon chopped fresh cilantro
  Salt and pepper

1. Heat oil in 12-inch skillet over medium heat until shimmering. Add onion and bell pepper and cook until vegetables are softened and lightly browned, 5 to 7 minutes. Stir in jalapeño, garlic, chili powder, mustard seeds, chipotle, cumin, and oregano and cook until fragrant, about 1 minute. Stir in 1 cup broth, scraping up any browned bits; transfer to slow cooker.

2. Stir remaining 1 cup broth, beans, mushrooms, and bay leaf into slow cooker. Cover and cook until beans are tender, 8 to 9 hours on high.

3. Discard bay leaf. Transfer ½ cup cooked beans to bowl and mash with potato masher until mostly smooth. Stir mashed beans and tomatoes into chili and let sit until heated through, about 5 minutes. Adjust consistency with extra hot broth as needed. Stir in cilantro and season with salt and pepper to taste. Serve.

Tomato paste and just a little heavy cream give the sauce for this Italian classic the right richness and texture.

Chicken Pomodoro

SERVES 2 `EASY PREP`
COOKING TIME 1 TO 2 HOURS ON LOW
SLOW COOKER SIZE 3½ TO 7 QUARTS

WHY THIS RECIPE WORKS Classic chicken pomodoro features tender chicken braised in a rich tomato sauce; gently simmering the chicken in the sauce helps it remain moist while enriching the flavors of both. It should be perfectly suited for the slow cooker, but most slow-cooker recipes result in a dull, waterlogged dish. For a pomodoro recipe with assertive tomato flavor, we'd need to perfect the sauce. Both fresh tomatoes and canned diced tomatoes released too much liquid during cooking. Compounded with the juices from the chicken, they created a thin, dull sauce. Switching to tomato paste proved to be the answer; the thick, concentrated paste, thinned with a little heavy cream and the chicken's juices, gave our sauce the perfect consistency and bold tomato flavor. Finishing the sauce with Parmesan contributed a nutty flavor, and a sprinkling

of fresh basil tied it all together. You will need an oval slow cooker for this recipe. Check the chicken's temperature after 1 hour of cooking and continue to monitor until it registers 160 degrees.

¼ cup finely chopped onion
¼ cup tomato paste
2 garlic cloves, minced
1 tablespoon extra-virgin olive oil
½ teaspoon minced fresh oregano or
⅛ teaspoon dried
Salt and pepper
Pinch red pepper flakes
¼ cup heavy cream
2 (6- to 8-ounce) boneless, skinless
chicken breasts, trimmed
¼ cup grated Parmesan cheese
2 tablespoons chopped fresh basil

1. Microwave onion, tomato paste, garlic, oil, oregano, ¼ teaspoon salt, and pepper flakes in bowl, stirring occasionally, until onion is softened, about 5 minutes; transfer to slow cooker. Stir in cream. Season chicken with salt and pepper and arrange in even layer in slow cooker. Cover and cook until chicken registers 160 degrees, 1 to 2 hours on low.

2. Sprinkle chicken with Parmesan, cover, and let sit until cheese is melted, about 5 minutes. Sprinkle with basil and serve.

Thai Chicken with Coconut Curry Sauce

SERVES 2 `EASY PREP` `LIGHT`
COOKING TIME 1 TO 2 HOURS ON LOW
SLOW COOKER SIZE 3½ TO 7 QUARTS

WHY THIS RECIPE WORKS For juicy and tender chicken breasts with a complexly aromatic Thai curry sauce, we developed a technique that resulted in big flavor—but with just a small amount of hands-on time. We added unsweetened shredded coconut to a small amount of Thai red curry paste, shallot, garlic, and chicken broth to flavor the chicken and create a wonderful sauce for our dish. As the coconut cooked, it became tender and added richness to the cooking liquid. Pureeing the coconut mixture after cooking gave us a vibrant and flavorful accompaniment with the perfect consistency. We stirred a small amount of fresh basil into the sauce at the end, which helped to bring the flavors to life. Using flaked coconut will yield a thicker sauce. You will need an oval slow cooker for this recipe. Check the chicken's temperature after 1 hour of cooking and continue to monitor until it registers 160 degrees.

1 shallot, chopped

2 teaspoons Thai red curry paste

1 teaspoon vegetable oil

1 garlic clove, minced

¼ cup chicken broth

3 tablespoons unsweetened shredded coconut

2 (6- to 8-ounce) boneless, skinless chicken breasts, trimmed

   Salt and pepper

1 tablespoon chopped fresh basil

1. Microwave shallot, curry paste, oil, and garlic in bowl, stirring occasionally, until fragrant, about 1 minute; transfer to slow cooker. Stir in broth and coconut. Season chicken with salt and pepper and arrange in even layer in slow cooker. Cover and cook until chicken registers 160 degrees, 1 to 2 hours on low.

2. Transfer chicken to individual plates, brushing any coconut that sticks to breasts back into slow cooker. Process cooking liquid in blender until almost smooth, about 30 seconds. Stir basil into sauce and season with salt and pepper to taste. Spoon sauce over chicken and serve.

NOTES FROM THE TEST KITCHEN

Unsweetened Shredded Coconut

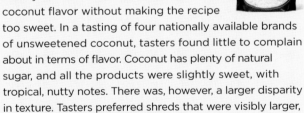

There are two types of shredded coconut—sweetened and unsweetened. We save the sweetened stuff to use as a form of added sugar in desserts like macaroons or coconut cake, and use the unsweetened variety when we want to maximize coconut flavor without making the recipe too sweet. In a tasting of four nationally available brands of unsweetened coconut, tasters found little to complain about in terms of flavor. Coconut has plenty of natural sugar, and all the products were slightly sweet, with tropical, nutty notes. There was, however, a larger disparity in texture. Tasters preferred shreds that were visibly larger, especially when used in recipes.

Top-ranked shreds weren't just larger; they were also more uniform in shape and size; we did a sifting test to prove it. We found that large, uniformly shaped shreds made for better, prettier pies and icing. Our winner was **NOW Real Food Organic Unsweetened Coconut, Shredded**; it had a strong coconut flavor and thick, fibrous pieces.

A tarragon vinaigrette, drizzled over the chicken and vegetables, elevates this humble slow-cooker dinner.

Orange-Tarragon Chicken with Potatoes and Carrots

SERVES 2   **EASY PREP**

COOKING TIME 2 TO 3 HOURS ON LOW

SLOW COOKER SIZE 3½ TO 7 QUARTS

WHY THIS RECIPE WORKS Chicken and potatoes are classic, easy weeknight fare, offering endless variations. We knew that, with enough ingenuity, this combination could make a successful transition out of the oven and into the slow cooker. We started by using the microwave to bloom an aromatic oil mixture, then letting it cool slightly before rubbing it directly onto bone-in chicken breasts (skin removed) for a big flavor boost. Microwaving the potatoes, along with some carrots, before placing them in the bottom of the slow cooker ensured that our vegetables would be fully tender when the chicken finished cooking. Once our chicken and vegetables were perfectly cooked, we whisked together tarragon and fresh orange juice for a sweet and herbal pantry-friendly dressing, creating a simple and satisfying slow-cooker meal with a vibrant appeal. You will need an oval slow cooker for this recipe. Check the chicken's temperature after 2 hours of cooking and continue to monitor until it registers 160 degrees.

5 tablespoons extra-virgin olive oil

2 garlic cloves, minced

1 teaspoon minced fresh thyme or ¼ teaspoon dried
Salt and pepper

12 ounces red potatoes, unpeeled, cut into 1-inch pieces

2 carrots, peeled and cut into 1-inch pieces

2 (12-ounce) bone-in split chicken breasts,
skin removed, trimmed

1 tablespoon minced fresh tarragon

2 teaspoons white wine vinegar

1 teaspoon Dijon mustard

¼ teaspoon grated orange zest plus 1 tablespoon juice

1. Microwave 1 tablespoon oil, garlic, thyme, ¼ teaspoon salt, and ¼ teaspoon pepper in small bowl until fragrant, about 30 seconds; let cool slightly.

2. Toss potatoes and carrots with 1 tablespoon oil, ¼ teaspoon salt, and ¼ teaspoon pepper in large bowl. Cover vegetables and microwave, stirring occasionally, until almost tender, 6 to 8 minutes; transfer to slow cooker. Rub chicken with oil mixture and arrange skinned side up in even layer in slow cooker. Cover and cook until chicken registers 160 degrees, 2 to 3 hours on low.

3. Whisk remaining 3 tablespoons oil, tarragon, vinegar, mustard, and orange zest and juice together in bowl. Season with salt and pepper to taste. Transfer chicken to individual plates. Using slotted spoon, transfer potatoes and carrots to plates; discard cooking liquid. Drizzle chicken and vegetables with dressing and serve.

Braised Chicken Thighs with Garlicky Spinach

SERVES 2   EASY PREP

COOKING TIME 4 TO 5 HOURS ON LOW

SLOW COOKER SIZE 3½ TO 7 QUARTS

WHY THIS RECIPE WORKS A specialty from the Catalonian region of Spain, this dish of sautéed spinach with garlic, raisins, and pine nuts is a simple yet satisfying combination of flavors and textures. To create a complete meal in the slow cooker inspired by this traditional tapas plate, we braised chicken thighs in an aromatic mixture of onion, garlic, and sweet paprika, along with a bit of tomato paste for depth. We then used the flavorful braising liquid to wilt the spinach and meld all of the flavors. Quick-cooking, delicate spinach may not seem like a good match for the slow cooker, but by adding it for just 20 minutes at the end of cooking, we had perfectly tender spinach without all of the oil typically needed for sautéing. We placed the cooked thighs on top of the spinach as the leaves cooked, which both kept the chicken warm and moist, and weighted down the spinach so it stayed submerged in the liquid.

We wilt the spinach, weighted down by the chicken, at the end of cooking—just long enough to pick up deep flavor.

1 onion, chopped fine

4 garlic cloves, sliced thin

2 teaspoons tomato paste

1 tablespoon vegetable oil

½ teaspoon paprika

⅛ teaspoon red pepper flakes

¼ cup chicken broth

4 (5- to 7-ounce) bone-in chicken thighs,
skin removed, trimmed
Salt and pepper

12 ounces (12 cups) baby spinach

¼ cup golden raisins

1 tablespoon lemon juice, plus lemon
wedges for serving

1 tablespoon pine nuts, toasted

1. Microwave onion, garlic, tomato paste, oil, paprika, and pepper flakes in bowl, stirring occasionally, until onion is softened, about 5 minutes; transfer to slow cooker. Stir in broth. Season chicken with salt and pepper, nestle into slow cooker, and turn to coat with onion mixture. Cover and cook until chicken is tender, 4 to 5 hours on low.

2. Transfer chicken to plate. Stir spinach, 1 handful at a time, into slow cooker until slightly wilted. Stir in raisins, then arrange chicken on top of spinach, adding any accumulated juices. Cover and cook on high until spinach is fully wilted, about 20 minutes.

3. Transfer chicken to individual plates. Stir lemon juice and pine nuts into spinach and season with salt and pepper to taste. Serve chicken and spinach with lemon wedges.

NOTES FROM THE TEST KITCHEN

Storing Baby Spinach

Baby spinach is sold in bags and plastic containers of various sizes. If you happen to have leftover spinach, store it either in its original bag with the open end folded over and taped shut, or in its original plastic container, as long as it has holes that allow air to pass through. These specially designed breathable bags and containers keep the spinach fresh as long as possible; if you transfer the spinach to a sealed airtight bag or container, it will spoil prematurely.

Southern Chicken and Dirty Rice

SERVES 2

COOKING TIME 4 TO 5 HOURS ON LOW

SLOW COOKER SIZE 3½ TO 7 QUARTS

WHY THIS RECIPE WORKS In the South, chicken is often paired with dirty rice—a side dish incorporating cured meats, vegetables, and seasonings that give the rice a "dirty" appearance. We wanted to transform this duo into a scaled-down slow-cooker casserole—we thought the moist environment would give all the robust flavors a chance to meld, for a richer-tasting dish overall. For the chicken, we selected bone-in thighs, which stayed moist even after a few hours of cooking. Onion, bell pepper, and garlic, plus some chili powder and thyme, provided a flavorful backbone, and microwaving the mix with bacon gave it a meaty, smoky depth and richness. Instant rice cooked up perfectly while absorbing the rich flavors of the broth, and, finally, sliced scallion added a touch of color and freshness. Be sure to use instant rice (sometimes labeled minute rice); traditional rice takes much longer to cook and won't work here.

½ onion, chopped fine

½ red bell pepper, cut into ½-inch pieces

1 celery rib, chopped

2 slices bacon, chopped

1 garlic clove, minced

For flavorful dirty rice we microwave the rice with the aromatics and bacon before adding it to the slow cooker.

1 tablespoon chili powder

1 teaspoon minced fresh thyme or
  ¼ teaspoon dried

¼ cup chicken broth

4 (5- to 7-ounce) bone-in chicken thighs,
  skin removed, trimmed
  Salt and pepper

1 cup instant white rice

1 scallion, sliced thin

1. Microwave onion, bell pepper, celery, bacon, garlic, chili powder, and thyme in bowl, stirring occasionally, until vegetables are softened, about 5 minutes; transfer to slow cooker. Stir in broth. Season chicken with salt and pepper and nestle into slow cooker. Cover and cook until chicken is tender, 4 to 5 hours on low.

2. Transfer chicken to plate. Stir rice into slow cooker. Arrange chicken on top of rice, adding any accumulated juices. Cover and cook on high until rice is tender, 20 to 30 minutes.

3. Transfer chicken to individual plates. Stir scallion into rice and season with salt and pepper to taste. Serve chicken with rice.

Cowboy Steaks and Beans

SERVES 2 `EASY PREP` `ALL DAY`

COOKING TIME 8 TO 9 HOURS ON LOW OR 5 TO 6 HOURS ON HIGH

SLOW COOKER SIZE 3½ TO 7 QUARTS

WHY THIS RECIPE WORKS To make a meal that would really satisfy, we braised juicy steaks in the slow cooker until they were meltingly tender and paired them with rich, smoky baked beans. We found that blade steaks were ideal for this dish because they have a relatively high and even distribution of fat; after hours of simmering in the slow cooker, the steaks were supremely moist and tender. We got a head start on our beans by using canned baked beans, which already had great sweet and smoky flavor. To give them more depth, we enhanced their flavor with barbecue sauce, molasses, and Dijon. The rich flavors of the meat and the saucy beans melded as they cooked to give us a hearty steak and baked beans supper. You can substitute an equal amount of beef flat-iron steaks, if desired.

    1   (16-ounce) can baked beans
    ¼   cup barbecue sauce
    1   tablespoon molasses
    2   teaspoons Dijon mustard
    2   (6- to 8-ounce) beef blade steaks,
        ¾ to 1 inch thick, trimmed
        Salt and pepper

1. Combine beans, barbecue sauce, molasses, and mustard in slow cooker. Season steaks with salt and pepper and nestle into slow cooker. Cover and cook until beef is tender and fork slips easily in and out of meat, 8 to 9 hours on low or 5 to 6 hours on high.

2. Transfer steaks to individual plates. Using large spoon, skim fat from surface of beans. Season with salt and pepper to taste. Serve steaks with beans.

Asian-Style Braised Short Ribs

SERVES 2 `EASY PREP` `ALL DAY`

COOKING TIME 8 TO 9 HOURS ON LOW OR 5 TO 6 HOURS ON HIGH

SLOW COOKER SIZE 3½ TO 7 QUARTS

WHY THIS RECIPE WORKS For a boldly flavored, ultrasatisfying dinner for two, we slow-cooked short ribs until meltingly tender in an Asian-style sauce that tasted sweet, spicy, and savory all at once. The well-marbled ribs cooked down significantly, so to compensate we started with over a pound of ribs for two diners. The duo of hoisin sauce and chili-garlic sauce provided an intensely flavored

It takes mere minutes to get these short ribs into the slow cooker, and they cook all day in the hoisin-based sauce.

sauce with a nice sweetness and subtle heat, and a small pour of chicken broth worked to thin the mixture slightly. To ensure an extra-clingy sauce by the end of the cooking time, we stirred in 2 teaspoons of tapioca. Minced scallion whites gave the sauce an aromatic presence. Once the ribs were tender, we took them out and let them rest while we defatted the sauce. A sprinkle of scallion greens over the finished dish added freshness and a burst of color. Look for boneless short ribs that are well marbled and measure about 2 inches wide and 1 inch thick.

    ½   cup chicken broth
    ⅓   cup hoisin sauce
    3   scallions, white parts minced, green
        parts sliced thin on bias
    1   tablespoon Asian chili-garlic sauce
    2   teaspoons instant tapioca
    1½ pounds boneless English-style short
        ribs, trimmed
        Salt and pepper

1. Combine broth, hoisin, scallion whites, chili-garlic sauce, and tapioca in slow cooker. Season short ribs with salt and pepper and nestle into slow cooker. Cover and cook until beef is tender and fork slips easily in and out of meat, 8 to 9 hours on low or 5 to 6 hours on high.

2. Transfer short ribs to individual plates, tent loosely with aluminum foil, and let rest for 5 minutes. Using large spoon, skim fat from surface of sauce. Spoon sauce over short ribs and sprinkle with scallion greens. Serve.

Smothered Pork Chops with Apples

SERVES 2

COOKING TIME 7 TO 8 HOURS ON LOW OR 4 TO 5 HOURS ON HIGH

SLOW COOKER SIZE 3½ TO 7 QUARTS

WHY THIS RECIPE WORKS For a lighter yet still hearty version of smothered pork chops, we traded in the usual bacon and buttery gravy for Golden Delicious apples, which held their shape but became tender and saucy in the slow cooker. To deliver the best flavor, we sautéed the apples and onion until they were softened and caramelized, then created a thickened sauce with flour and a little bit of chicken broth. Worcestershire sauce tempered the sweetness of the apples and deepened the flavor of the sauce. To get the tender chops we wanted, ¾-inch blade-cut pork chops were crucial. Because they contain more fat than other center-cut chops, they could handle hours of braising in the slow cooker without drying out. We nestled the chops in the apple mixture, and the juices released by the cooking apples and onion braised the chops, adding deep flavor. You will need an oval slow cooker for this recipe.

2 tablespoons unsalted butter
2 Golden Delicious apples, peeled, cored, and
   sliced ½ inch thick
1 onion, halved and sliced ¼ inch thick
2 tablespoons all-purpose flour
1 teaspoon minced fresh thyme or ¼ teaspoon dried
½ cup chicken broth
1 tablespoon Worcestershire sauce
1 bay leaf
2 (8- to 10-ounce) bone-in blade-cut pork chops,
   ¾ inch thick, trimmed
   Salt and pepper
1 tablespoon minced fresh parsley
1 teaspoon cider vinegar

1. Melt butter in 12-inch skillet over medium heat. Add apples and onion and cook until softened and lightly browned, 8 to 10 minutes. Stir in flour and thyme and cook until fragrant, about 1 minute. Slowly stir in broth, scraping up any browned bits and smoothing out any lumps; transfer to slow cooker.

2. Stir Worcestershire and bay leaf into slow cooker. Cut 2 slits about 2 inches apart through fat on edges of each pork chop. Season chops with salt and pepper and nestle into slow cooker. Cover and cook until pork is tender, 7 to 8 hours on low or 4 to 5 hours on high.

3. Transfer chops to individual plates, tent loosely with aluminum foil, and let rest for 5 minutes. Discard bay leaf. Using large spoon, skim fat from surface of sauce. Stir in parsley and vinegar and season with salt and pepper to taste. Spoon sauce over chops and serve.

SIMPLE SIDES

BUTTERMILK MASHED POTATOES

SERVES 2

For the smoothest mashed potatoes, use a food mill or potato ricer. This recipe can be easily doubled.

1 pound Yukon Gold potatoes, peeled,
   quartered, and cut into 1-inch pieces
2 tablespoons unsalted butter, melted
⅓ cup buttermilk, plus extra as needed
   Salt and pepper

1. Place potatoes in large saucepan and add water to cover by 1 inch. Bring water to boil, then reduce to simmer and cook until potatoes are tender and paring knife can be inserted into potatoes with no resistance, 12 to 15 minutes.

2. Drain potatoes in colander, tossing to remove any excess water. Wipe now-empty saucepan dry with paper towels. Return potatoes to pot and mash to uniform consistency, or process through food mill or ricer and back into dry pot.

3. Using rubber spatula, fold in melted butter until just incorporated, then fold in buttermilk. Adjust consistency with extra buttermilk as needed. Season with salt and pepper to taste. Serve.

Pomegranate seeds and mint are added to this bulgur salad just before serving, while a bright vinaigrette unites the dish.

Pork Tenderloin with Spiced Bulgur Salad

SERVES 2 EASY PREP LIGHT

COOKING TIME 1 TO 2 HOURS ON LOW
SLOW COOKER SIZE 4 TO 7 QUARTS

WHY THIS RECIPE WORKS Bulgur, a staple in Middle Eastern cooking, is a relatively fast-cooking grain, making it a particularly good choice to accompany a pork tenderloin in the slow cooker. We seasoned the pork with warm spices and cooked it in the slow cooker along with the bulgur until both were perfectly tender, the gentle cooking environment preserving the pork's moisture. To transform the bulgur into a satisfying side dish, we stirred in tart pomegranate seeds and fresh mint. When shopping, don't confuse bulgur with cracked wheat, which has a much longer cooking time and will not work in this recipe. You will need an oval slow cooker for this recipe. Because it is cooked gently and not browned, the tenderloin will be rosy throughout. Check the tenderloin's temperature after 1 hour of cooking and continue to monitor until it registers 145 degrees.

1 shallot, minced
4 teaspoons extra-virgin olive oil
1 garlic clove, minced
¼ teaspoon ground cinnamon
  Pinch cayenne pepper
1 cup chicken broth
½ cup medium-grind bulgur, rinsed
1 (12- to 16-ounce) pork tenderloin, trimmed
  Salt and pepper
¼ cup pomegranate seeds
2 tablespoons chopped fresh mint
1 tablespoon lemon juice
2 teaspoons molasses
1 teaspoon honey

1. Lightly coat slow cooker with vegetable oil spray. Microwave shallot, 1 teaspoon oil, garlic, cinnamon, and cayenne in bowl until fragrant, about 30 seconds; transfer to prepared slow cooker. Stir in broth and bulgur.

2. Season tenderloin with salt and pepper. Nestle tenderloin into slow cooker, cover, and cook until pork registers 145 degrees, 1 to 2 hours on low.

3. Transfer pork to carving board, brushing any bulgur that sticks to pork back into slow cooker; let rest while finishing salad.

4. Drain bulgur mixture, if necessary, and return to now-empty slow cooker. Add pomegranate seeds and mint and fluff with fork to combine. Season with salt and pepper to taste. Whisk lemon juice, molasses, honey, and remaining 1 tablespoon oil together in bowl. Slice tenderloin ¼ inch thick. Serve pork with bulgur salad and dressing.

NOTES FROM THE TEST KITCHEN

Bulgur

Bulgur is made from parboiled or steamed wheat kernels/berries that are then dried, partially stripped of their outer bran layer, and ground.

The result of this process is a relatively fast-cooking, highly nutritious grain that can be used in a variety of applications. Medium-grind bulgur is the most widely available size and our preferred choice for slow-cooker recipes because it cooks evenly and maintains its shape. Don't confuse bulgur with cracked wheat, which is often sold alongside bulgur but is not parcooked. Be sure to rinse bulgur to remove excess starches that can turn the grain gluey.

For a bright, glossy finish, these ribs are brushed with a glaze made with apricot preserves and then run under the broiler.

Sweet and Sour Sticky Ribs

SERVES 2 EASY PREP

COOKING TIME 5 TO 6 HOURS ON LOW OR 3 TO 4 HOURS ON HIGH

SLOW COOKER SIZE 3½ TO 7 QUARTS

WHY THIS RECIPE WORKS Chinese-style sweet-and-sour ribs are a party favorite, but we wanted to scale this irresistible dish down for two. Leaving the membrane attached to the underside of our baby back ribs helped the rack hold together as it cooked and, as a bonus, shortened our prep time. Rubbing the ribs with a mixture of garlic powder and ground ginger infused them with flavor. Once the ribs were tender, we brushed them with a tangy sauce and broiled them to develop a caramelized, lightly charred exterior. Avoid racks of baby back ribs that are larger than 2 pounds; they will be difficult to maneuver into the slow cooker.

1½ teaspoons garlic powder
 1 teaspoon ground ginger
   Salt and pepper
 1 (1½- to 2-pound) rack baby back ribs, trimmed

⅓ cup apricot preserves
 2 tablespoons ketchup
 2 tablespoons soy sauce
 2 tablespoons rice vinegar
 1 tablespoon chopped fresh cilantro

1. Lightly coat slow cooker with vegetable oil spray. Combine garlic powder, ginger, 1 teaspoon salt, and 1 teaspoon pepper in bowl. Pat ribs dry with paper towels and rub with spice mixture.

2. Arrange ribs meaty side down along bottom of prepared slow cooker. Cover and cook until ribs are just tender, 5 to 6 hours on low or 3 to 4 hours on high.

3. Adjust oven rack 4 inches from broiler element and heat broiler. Set wire rack in aluminum foil–lined rimmed baking sheet and coat with vegetable oil spray. Transfer ribs meaty side up to prepared rack; let sit until surface is dry, about 10 minutes.

4. Whisk preserves, ketchup, soy sauce, and vinegar together in bowl. Brush ribs with half of sauce and broil until sauce is bubbling and beginning to char, about 5 minutes. Brush ribs with remaining sauce, tent loosely with foil, and let rest for 10 minutes. Cut ribs in between bones to separate. Sprinkle with cilantro and serve.

ARRANGING A SINGLE RACK OF RIBS

Arrange rack with meaty side down across bottom of slow cooker (ends of rack will come up against sides).

Easy Pulled Pork

SERVES 2 EASY PREP

COOKING TIME 6 TO 7 HOURS ON LOW OR 4 TO 5 HOURS ON HIGH

SLOW COOKER SIZE 3½ TO 7 QUARTS

WHY THIS RECIPE WORKS Pulled pork is a cookout classic. To revamp the dish for two, we ditched the usual pork shoulder in favor of boneless country-style ribs, which are easy to purchase in smaller quantities; plus, the cut has plenty of marbling, which keeps the meat tender. Bottled barbecue sauce ensured that our recipe was effortless, since we didn't have to bother assembling umpteen ingredients for a simple sauce. To guarantee that our pork offered the big flavor of authentic recipes, we applied a dry spice rub made from brown sugar, paprika, and chili powder. Two slices of bacon, tossed into the slow cooker whole, infused the pork with smoky flavor. Adding the leftover braising liquid to the barbecue sauce enhanced its flavor and contributed meaty depth and richness. Look for country-style pork ribs with lots of fat and dark meat, and stay away from ribs that look overly lean with pale meat, as they will taste very dry after the extended cooking time. Don't shred the pork too fine in step 2; it will break up more as it is combined with the sauce. Serve on soft buns with pickle chips.

½ cup chicken broth
2 slices bacon
1 tablespoon packed brown sugar
1 tablespoon paprika
1½ teaspoons chili powder
   Salt and pepper
1 pound boneless country-style pork ribs, trimmed
¾ cup barbecue sauce

1. Combine broth and bacon in slow cooker. Combine sugar, paprika, chili powder, ½ teaspoon salt, and ½ teaspoon pepper in bowl. Pat ribs dry with paper towels and rub with spice mixture. Nestle ribs into slow cooker, cover, and cook until pork is tender, 6 to 7 hours on low or 4 to 5 hours on high.

2. Transfer ribs to cutting board, let cool slightly, then shred into bite-size pieces using 2 forks; discard fat.

3. Discard bacon. Transfer cooking liquid to fat separator and let sit for 5 minutes. Whisk ½ cup defatted liquid and barbecue sauce together in serving bowl. Toss pork with ½ cup sauce in now-empty slow cooker and season with salt and pepper to taste. Serve, passing remaining sauce separately.

Poached Salmon

SERVES 2 `EASY PREP`
COOKING TIME 1 TO 2 HOURS ON LOW
SLOW COOKER SIZE 3½ TO 7 QUARTS

WHY THIS RECIPE WORKS Poaching is a gentle cooking method that promises to deliver tender, delicately flavored salmon, thanks to a longer stint in a moist, gentle cooking environment. Rather than poach our salmon on the stovetop, where we'd have to carefully monitor the heat level, we decided to move this dish to the slow cooker to take advantage of its walk-away convenience. We started with two salmon fillets and kept the flavor profile simple, pairing our fish with lemon and dill for subtle flavor. To prevent the bottom of our salmon from overcooking, we rested our fillets on lemon slices and dill stems, then added a small amount of wine and water to the slow cooker to create a moist cooking environment. A foil sling made it easy to remove the delicate salmon from the slow cooker without the fillets breaking apart. For a simple serving sauce, we combined sour cream and Dijon mustard with more lemon and dill. Look for salmon fillets of similar thickness to ensure that they cook at the same rate. Leave the skin on the salmon to keep the bottom of the fillets from overcooking and to make it easier to skin the fillets once done. You will need an oval slow cooker for this recipe. For more information on making a foil sling, see page 180. Check the salmon's temperature after 1 hour of cooking and continue to monitor until it registers 135 degrees.

1 lemon, sliced ¼ inch thick, plus 1 tablespoon lemon juice
1½ teaspoons minced fresh dill, stems reserved
¼ cup dry white wine
2 (6- to 8-ounce) skin-on salmon fillets, 1 to 1½ inches thick
   Salt and pepper
¼ cup sour cream
1 teaspoon Dijon mustard

1. Fold sheet of aluminum foil into 12 by 9-inch sling and press widthwise into slow cooker. Arrange lemon slices in single layer in bottom of prepared slow cooker. Scatter dill stems over lemon slices. Add wine to slow cooker, then add water until liquid level is even with lemon slices (about ¼ cup). Season salmon with salt and pepper and arrange skin side down in even layer on top of herb stems. Cover and cook until salmon is opaque throughout when checked with tip of paring knife and registers 135 degrees (for medium), 1 to 2 hours on low.

2. Combine lemon juice, minced dill, sour cream, and mustard in bowl. Season with salt and pepper to taste. Using sling, transfer salmon to baking sheet. Gently lift and tilt fillets with spatula to remove dill stems and lemon slices; transfer to serving dish. Discard poaching liquid and remove any white albumin from salmon. Serve with sauce.

We use the slow cooker to create a French-inspired leek and cream sauce then poach the halibut to perfection in it.

Braised Halibut with Leeks and Mustard

SERVES 2 `EASY PREP` `LIGHT`
COOKING TIME 2 TO 3 HOURS ON LOW
SLOW COOKER SIZE 3½ TO 7 QUARTS

WHY THIS RECIPE WORKS The slow cooker is known for its prowess with conventional meat braises and hearty stews, but we knew its moist, gently heated environment also makes it the perfect cooking vessel for braising fish. We found it produced moist, succulent fish, and when we used just a small amount of flavorful cooking liquid and combined it with the juices released by the fish, we also had a potent sauce on the fly. We started with our sauce, choosing a classic, beautifully balanced combination of leeks, cream, and wine. After the leeks had softened, and sweetened and thickened our sauce, we added our fish, choosing halibut for its delicate flavor and firm texture. We finished off our rich sauce with a substantial hit of mustard and some bright fresh parsley for a slow-cooker braise that was anything but conventional. You will need an oval slow cooker for this recipe. Look for halibut fillets of similar thickness to ensure that they cook at the same rate. Sea bass is a good substitute for the halibut.

1 pound leeks, white and light green parts only, halved lengthwise, sliced thin, and washed thoroughly
1 tablespoon unsalted butter
  Salt and pepper
¼ cup dry white wine
2 tablespoons heavy cream
2 (6- to 8-ounce) skinless halibut fillets, 1 to 1½ inches thick
1 tablespoon minced fresh parsley
2 teaspoons Dijon mustard
  Lemon wedges

1. Microwave leeks, butter, and ¼ teaspoon salt in bowl, stirring occasionally, until leeks are softened, about 5 minutes; transfer to slow cooker. Stir in wine and cream, cover, and cook until leeks are tender but not mushy, 2 to 3 hours on low.

2. Season halibut with salt and pepper and nestle into slow cooker. Cover and cook on high until halibut flakes apart when gently prodded with paring knife and registers 140 degrees, about 30 minutes.

3. Transfer halibut to individual plates. Stir parsley and mustard into leek mixture and season with salt and pepper to taste. Spoon sauce over halibut. Serve with lemon wedges.

SIMPLE SIDES

SIMPLE WHITE RICE
SERVES 2
Basmati, jasmine, or Texmati rice can be substituted for the long-grain white rice. You will need a small saucepan with a tight-fitting lid for this recipe. A nonstick saucepan will help prevent the rice from sticking.

1 teaspoon vegetable oil
¾ cup long-grain white rice, rinsed
1¼ cups water
  Salt and pepper

1. Heat oil in small saucepan over medium heat until shimmering. Add rice and cook, stirring often, until grain edges begin to turn translucent, about 2 minutes. Stir in water and ¼ teaspoon salt and bring to simmer. Reduce heat to low, cover, and continue to simmer until rice is tender and all water is absorbed, 16 to 18 minutes.

2. Remove pot from heat and lay clean folded dish towel underneath lid. Let sit for 10 minutes. Fluff rice with fork, season with salt and pepper to taste, and serve.

Cod in Saffron Broth with Chorizo and Potatoes

SERVES 2

COOKING TIME 4 TO 5 HOURS ON LOW OR 3 TO 4 HOURS ON HIGH

SLOW COOKER SIZE 3½ TO 7 QUARTS

WHY THIS RECIPE WORKS We love saffron, with its bright yellow hue and distinctive aroma, and we especially love it paired with seafood. The Spanish have an especially rich tradition with this pairing, so we looked to that country for inspiration. Versatile cod is a favorite white fish in Spain, and its mild flavor was the perfect backdrop for the saffron. We created a flavorful saffron broth with aromatics, white wine, and clam juice. For additional flavor, we added spicy Spanish-style chorizo, lending a subtle heat and smoky flavor to the broth. Waxy red potatoes brought in just the right creaminess to soak up the flavorful broth. A sprinkle of parsley and a drizzle of olive oil brought it all together. You will need an oval slow cooker for this recipe. Look for cod fillets of similar thickness to ensure that they cook at the same rate. Haddock and hake are good substitutes for the cod. Serve with crusty bread.

- 1 tablespoon extra-virgin olive oil, plus extra for drizzling
- 4 ounces Spanish-style chorizo sausage, sliced ¼ inch thick
- 1 shallot, minced
- 4 garlic cloves, minced
- ⅛ teaspoon saffron threads, crumbled
- 8 ounces small red potatoes, unpeeled, halved
- 1 (8-ounce) bottle clam juice
- ¼ cup dry white wine
- 1 bay leaf
- 2 (6- to 8-ounce) skinless cod fillets, 1 to 1½ inches thick
  Salt and pepper
- 1 tablespoon minced fresh parsley
  Lemon wedges

1. Microwave oil, chorizo, shallot, garlic, and saffron in bowl, stirring occasionally, until fragrant, about 5 minutes; transfer to slow cooker. Stir in potatoes, clam juice, wine, and bay leaf. Cover and cook until potatoes are tender, 4 to 5 hours on low or 3 to 4 hours on high.

2. Season cod with pepper and nestle into slow cooker. Cover and cook on high until cod flakes apart when gently prodded with paring knife and registers 140 degrees, about 30 minutes.

3. Discard bay leaf. Using slotted spoon, carefully transfer cod, potatoes, and chorizo to individual bowls. Season broth with salt and pepper to taste. Spoon broth over cod, chorizo, and potatoes, sprinkle with parsley, and drizzle with extra oil. Serve with lemon wedges.

Meatballs and Marinara

MAKES 6 MEATBALLS AND 2½ CUPS SAUCE; ENOUGH FOR 8 OUNCES PASTA

COOKING TIME 3 TO 4 HOURS ON LOW

SLOW COOKER SIZE 3½ TO 7 QUARTS

WHY THIS RECIPE WORKS Our slow-cooker version of meatballs and marinara involves some prep work, but once everything is in the slow cooker, you've bought yourself hours of freedom with the promise of a great dinner waiting in the wings. To build a sauce with long-simmered flavor, we started by microwaving onion, tomato paste, garlic, and oregano. Clean-flavored crushed tomatoes were all we needed to add to this base. For the meatballs, a combination of ground beef, some of the sautéed aromatics, Parmesan, and parsley was a solid start, but they were still a bit dry. Adding a panade— a paste of bread and water—provided the moisture they needed. Microwaving the meatballs before adding them to the slow cooker helped render just enough fat to ensure that our sauce wasn't greasy.

- ½ onion, chopped fine
- 1 tablespoon tomato paste
- 1 tablespoon extra-virgin olive oil
- 2 garlic cloves, minced
- 2 teaspoons minced fresh oregano or ½ teaspoon dried
- ½ slice hearty white sandwich bread, torn into 1-inch pieces
- 2 tablespoons water
  Salt and pepper

We love the economy of this recipe, with the aromatics being microwaved and used in both the sauce and the meatballs.

¼ cup grated Parmesan cheese
1 tablespoon minced fresh parsley
1 large egg yolk
8 ounces 85 percent lean ground beef
1 (28-ounce) can crushed tomatoes
1 tablespoon chopped fresh basil
½ teaspoon sugar, plus extra for seasoning

1. Microwave onion, tomato paste, oil, garlic, and oregano in bowl, stirring occasionally, until onion is softened, about 5 minutes; transfer half of onion mixture to slow cooker.

2. Add bread, water, ¼ teaspoon salt, and ¼ teaspoon pepper to remaining onion mixture in bowl and mash into paste using fork. Stir in Parmesan, parsley, and egg yolk until combined. Add ground beef and knead with hands until well combined. Pinch off and roll mixture into 2-inch meatballs (about 6 meatballs) and arrange on large plate. Microwave meatballs until firm and no longer pink, about 5 minutes; discard rendered fat.

3. Add tomatoes and ¼ teaspoon salt to slow cooker. Gently nestle meatballs into slow cooker, cover, and cook until meatballs are tender, 3 to 4 hours on low. Stir in basil and sugar. Season with salt, pepper, and extra sugar to taste. Serve.

Easy Cherry Tomato Pasta Sauce

MAKES 2½ CUPS; ENOUGH FOR 8 OUNCES PASTA

EASY PREP **VEG** **LIGHT** **ALL DAY**

COOKING TIME 7 TO 8 HOURS ON LOW OR 4 TO 5 HOURS ON HIGH

SLOW COOKER SIZE 3½ TO 7 QUARTS

WHY THIS RECIPE WORKS For a fresh tomato sauce any time of the year, we turned to cherry tomatoes, which are reliably sweet even in the dead of winter. What we love about this recipe is how easy it is to assemble, as slow-cooked cherry tomatoes, when combined with lots of fresh herbs, needed little embellishment. First, we simply microwaved the aromatics—onion, garlic, and oregano—with tomato paste and a little oil until softened and added them to the slow cooker along with halved cherry tomatoes. In the slow cooker, the tomatoes collapsed and softened, becoming even sweeter and more flavorful as they absorbed some of the flavor of the aromatics. To ensure that our sauce had the right texture, we added a little tapioca. Still, the sauce wasn't quite thick enough, which wasn't surprising given that the slow cooker allows for almost no evaporation, so at the end of the cooking time we simply mashed the tomatoes a little with a potato masher. To finish, we added a dose of basil and parsley for freshness.

½ onion, chopped fine
3 tablespoons tomato paste
3 garlic cloves, minced
1 tablespoon extra-virgin olive oil
2 teaspoons minced fresh oregano or ½ teaspoon dried
   Salt and pepper
1¼ pounds cherry tomatoes, halved
1 tablespoon instant tapioca
2 tablespoons chopped fresh basil
2 tablespoons chopped fresh parsley

1. Microwave onion, tomato paste, garlic, oil, oregano, ¼ teaspoon salt, and ¼ teaspoon pepper in bowl, stirring occasionally, until onion is softened, about 5 minutes; transfer to slow cooker. Stir in tomatoes and tapioca. Cover and cook until tomatoes are very soft and beginning to disintegrate, 7 to 8 hours on low or 4 to 5 hours on high.

2. Using potato masher, mash tomatoes until mostly smooth. Stir in basil and parsley. Season with salt and pepper to taste. Serve.

Enriched with goat cheese, dried cranberries, and aromatics, the quinoa filling for this squash is anything but dull.

Stuffed Acorn Squash

SERVES 2 **VEG** **LIGHT**

COOKING TIME 3 TO 4 HOURS ON LOW OR 2 TO 3 HOURS ON HIGH

SLOW COOKER SIZE 4 TO 7 QUARTS

WHY THIS RECIPE WORKS For a simple stuffed squash recipe, we started with halved acorn squash and quinoa. To ensure that we achieved both tender squash and a perfectly cooked filling, we precooked the quinoa in the microwave. Shallot, garlic, and thyme added savory notes to the filling, and a small amount of goat cheese added a pleasant tang and richness. Dried cranberries complemented the nutty flavor of the quinoa and added a pop of color to the mixture. Once the squash halves were filled, we placed them in the slow cooker with a small amount of water to help them steam, and in just a few hours we had perfectly tender squash. A sprinkling of toasted pecans added a welcome crunch, and minced tarragon brought an herbal freshness. If you buy unwashed quinoa (or if you are unsure whether it's washed), be sure to rinse it before cooking to remove its bitter protective coating (called saponin).

⅓ cup white quinoa, rinsed
1 shallot, minced
2 garlic cloves, minced
1 teaspoon minced fresh thyme or ¼ teaspoon dried
  Salt and pepper
2 ounces goat cheese, crumbled (½ cup)
⅓ cup dried cranberries
1 small acorn squash (1 pound), halved pole to pole and seeded
2 tablespoons toasted chopped pecans
1 tablespoon minced fresh tarragon

1. Microwave 1 cup water, quinoa, shallot, garlic, thyme, and ¼ teaspoon salt in bowl, stirring occasionally, until almost all water is absorbed, 7 to 10 minutes. Cover quinoa and let sit until remaining water has been absorbed, about 10 minutes. Fluff quinoa with fork, then gently fold in goat cheese and cranberries.

2. Pour ½ cup water into slow cooker. Season squash with salt and pepper. Mound quinoa mixture into squash and pack lightly with spoon. Transfer squash to slow cooker, cover, and cook until squash is tender, 3 to 4 hours on low or 2 to 3 hours on high.

3. Using tongs, transfer squash to individual plates. Sprinkle with pecans and tarragon. Serve.

Creamy Farro with Swiss Chard

SERVES 2 **VEG** **LIGHT**

COOKING TIME 3 TO 4 HOURS ON LOW OR 2 TO 3 HOURS ON HIGH

SLOW COOKER SIZE 3½ TO 7 QUARTS

WHY THIS RECIPE WORKS A healthy whole-grain staple in Italian cooking, farro lends itself particularly well to the slow cooker. For extra-nutty flavor, we briefly toasted the grains in the microwave. Sweet, earthy carrots paired well with the nutty farro, and the dish required only the simplest of aromatics—onion, garlic, and fresh thyme—to round out the flavors. Thoroughly stirring the cooked farro with additional hot broth helped to release starches in the grains that gave the dish a pleasant creaminess. To balance the sweet, nutty flavors and boost the nutrition, we added slightly bitter Swiss chard. Since it required minimal cooking time, we stirred in the chard near the end of cooking so that it would turn just tender but retain its brightness. We prefer the flavor and texture of whole farro; pearled farro can be used, but the texture may be softer. Do not use quick-cooking or presteamed farro (the ingredient list on the package will specify the type) in this recipe.

1 onion, chopped fine
½ cup whole farro
1 tablespoon extra-virgin olive oil, plus extra for drizzling

1 garlic clove, minced
½ teaspoon minced fresh thyme or ⅛ teaspoon dried
2 cups chicken or vegetable broth, plus extra as needed
3 carrots, peeled and cut into ¼-inch pieces
¼ cup grated Parmesan cheese
8 ounces Swiss chard, stemmed and cut into 1-inch pieces
 Salt and pepper

1. Lightly coat slow cooker with vegetable oil spray. Microwave onion, farro, oil, garlic, and thyme in bowl, stirring occasionally, until onion is softened, about 5 minutes; transfer to prepared slow cooker.

2. Microwave 1½ cups broth in now-empty bowl until steaming, about 5 minutes. Stir broth and carrots into slow cooker. Cover and cook until farro is tender, 3 to 4 hours on low or 2 to 3 hours on high.

3. Microwave remaining ½ cup broth in bowl until steaming, about 2 minutes. Stir broth and Parmesan into farro until mixture is creamy but still somewhat thin. Stir in chard, 1 handful at a time, until slightly wilted. Cover and cook on high until chard is softened, about 20 minutes.

4. Adjust farro consistency with extra hot broth as needed. Season with salt and pepper to taste. Drizzle individual portions with extra oil before serving.

Southwestern Lentil and Bean Salad

SERVES 2 **EASY PREP** **VEG**

COOKING TIME 3 TO 4 HOURS ON LOW OR 2 TO 3 HOURS ON HIGH

SLOW COOKER SIZE 3½ TO 7 QUARTS

WHY THIS RECIPE WORKS The most important step in making a lentil salad is perfecting the cooking of the lentils so they maintain their shape and firm-tender bite. Adding a little salt and lime juice to the cooking liquid (we used water) gave us lentils that were firm yet creamy. Once we had perfectly cooked lentils, all we had left to do was to pair the healthy legumes with boldly flavored ingredients. We chose spicy chipotles in adobo sauce and earthy oregano and enhanced the Southwestern flavors at the end by adding corn, tomatoes, more lime juice, and queso fresco. To make this dish even heartier, we added canned pinto beans to the lentils. Fresh cilantro leaves and pepitas added brightness and crunch. We prefer French green lentils (*lentilles du Puy*), but this recipe will work with any type of lentil except red or yellow. For a heartier dish, serve over mixed greens.

⅔ cup French green lentils, picked over and rinsed
3 tablespoons lime juice
2 garlic cloves, minced

This foolproof, hands-off method for cooking lentils in the slow cooker makes assembling this bright salad supereasy.

 Salt and pepper
1 bay leaf
1 cup canned pinto beans, rinsed
6 ounces cherry tomatoes, halved
½ cup frozen corn, thawed
½ cup fresh cilantro leaves
1 shallot, sliced thin
3 tablespoons extra-virgin olive oil
1½ teaspoons minced canned chipotle chile in adobo sauce
1 teaspoon minced fresh oregano
1 ounce queso fresco, crumbled (¼ cup)
1 tablespoon roasted pepitas

1. Combine 4 cups water, lentils, 1 tablespoon lime juice, garlic, ¾ teaspoon salt, and bay leaf in slow cooker. Cover and cook until lentils are tender, 3 to 4 hours on low or 2 to 3 hours on high.

2. Discard bay leaf. Drain lentils and transfer to serving bowl. Stir in beans, tomatoes, corn, cilantro, shallot, oil, chipotle, oregano, ¼ teaspoon salt, and remaining 2 tablespoons lime juice. Season with salt and pepper to taste. Sprinkle with queso fresco and pepitas. Serve.

CHAPTER 9

HEARTY VEGETARIAN MAINS

■ EASY PREP ■ VEGETARIAN ■ LIGHT ■ COOK ALL DAY
Photo: Mushroom Biryani

Tofu and potatoes are the stars of this hearty Indian curry, to which we add heated coconut milk just before serving.

Indian-Style Vegetable Curry

SERVES 4 TO 6 **VEG**

COOKING TIME 4 TO 5 HOURS ON LOW OR 3 TO 4 HOURS ON HIGH

SLOW COOKER SIZE 4 TO 7 QUARTS

WHY THIS RECIPE WORKS Curries are especially well suited to the slow cooker. When the ingredients have the opportunity to cook for hours, the flavors meld and the result is a bold-tasting dish with complexity. And though many curries rely on chicken or shrimp for their centerpiece, swapping in tofu ensured an equally satisfying curry—plus, the tofu didn't require any extra prep. For a flavor-packed dish, we included a full tablespoon each of curry powder and grated fresh ginger, along with some fragrant garam masala. Blooming the aromatics in the microwave helped to intensify their flavors. For more savory depth, we included tomato paste; cubed red potatoes contributed heartiness. Precut frozen green beans added bulk and needed zero prep. For a rich, velvety sauce, we stirred in coconut milk; heating it in the microwave and adding it toward the end of cooking prevented it from cooling down our curry and preserved its flavor. Finally, minced cilantro offered a touch of

color and freshness. You can use firm tofu here if desired, but do not substitute softer varieties such as silken tofu; these varieties will break down during cooking.

- 1 onion, chopped fine
- 3 garlic cloves, minced
- 1 tablespoon vegetable oil
- 1 tablespoon grated fresh ginger
- 1 tablespoon tomato paste
- 1 tablespoon curry powder
- ½ teaspoon garam masala
  Salt and pepper
- 4 cups vegetable broth, plus extra as needed
- 1 pound red potatoes, unpeeled, cut into ½-inch pieces
- 14 ounces extra-firm tofu, cut into ½-inch pieces
- 1 tablespoon instant tapioca
- 1 (13.5-ounce) can coconut milk
- 2 cups frozen cut green beans, thawed
- ¼ cup minced fresh cilantro

1. Microwave onion, garlic, oil, ginger, tomato paste, curry powder, garam masala, and ½ teaspoon salt in bowl, stirring occasionally, until onion is softened, about 5 minutes; transfer to slow cooker. Stir in broth, potatoes, tofu, and tapioca. Cover and cook until potatoes are tender, 4 to 5 hours on low or 3 to 4 hours on high.

2. Microwave coconut milk in bowl, whisking occasionally, until hot, about 3 minutes. Stir coconut milk and green beans into curry and let sit until heated through, about 5 minutes. Adjust consistency with extra hot broth as needed. Stir in cilantro and season with salt and pepper to taste. Serve.

NOTES FROM THE TEST KITCHEN

Buying Tofu

Although freshly made tofu is common across the Pacific, in the United States tofu is typically sold in blocks packed in water and can be found in the refrigerated section of supermarkets. Tofu is available in a variety of textures, including silken, firm, and extra-firm. We prefer the latter two in our slow-cooker stews and braises because the tofu holds its shape well in the slow cooker. Like dairy products, tofu is perishable and should be kept well chilled. If you want to keep an open package of tofu fresh for several days, cover the tofu with fresh water and store it in the refrigerator in an airtight container, changing the water daily.

This fragrant Moroccan tagine makes great use of dried chickpeas, which require no presoaking.

Chickpea Tagine

SERVES 4 TO 6 `EASY PREP` `VEG` `LIGHT` `ALL DAY`

COOKING TIME 8 TO 9 HOURS ON HIGH

SLOW COOKER SIZE 4 TO 7 QUARTS

WHY THIS RECIPE WORKS This Moroccan-style stew gets its complex flavor from a combination of sweet paprika and garam masala (a blend of warm spices), along with onions, garlic, and orange zest, all of which perfume the sauce. Since many vegetables would be obliterated after hours in a slow cooker, we opted to stir in softened bell peppers and jarred artichokes at the end, cooking them just enough to heat through. To continue with the Mediterranean flavor profile, we added chopped kalamata olives and Greek yogurt to the stew. Golden raisins and honey added a touch of sweetness, while fresh cilantro brightened up the dish before serving. While we prefer the flavor and texture of jarred whole baby artichokes, you can substitute 12 ounces frozen artichoke hearts, thawed and patted dry, for the jarred.

2 onions, chopped fine
3 tablespoons extra-virgin olive oil, plus extra for drizzling
8 garlic cloves, minced
4 teaspoons paprika
2 teaspoons garam masala
4 cups vegetable broth, plus extra as needed
2 cups water
1 pound (2½ cups) dried chickpeas, picked over and rinsed
2 (2-inch) strips orange zest
2 red bell peppers, stemmed, seeded, and cut into ¼-inch-wide strips
2 cups jarred whole baby artichokes packed in water, halved, rinsed, and patted dry
½ cup pitted kalamata olives, chopped coarse
½ cup golden raisins
½ cup plain Greek yogurt
½ cup minced fresh cilantro
2 tablespoons honey
Salt and pepper

1. Microwave onions, 2 tablespoons oil, garlic, paprika, and garam masala in bowl, stirring occasionally, until onions are softened, about 5 minutes; transfer to slow cooker. Stir in broth, water, chickpeas, and orange zest. Cover and cook until chickpeas are tender, 8 to 9 hours on high.

2. Microwave bell peppers with remaining 1 tablespoon oil in bowl, stirring occasionally, until tender, about 5 minutes. Discard orange zest. Stir bell peppers, artichokes, olives, and raisins into tagine. Cover and cook on high until heated through, about 10 minutes.

3. Whisk ½ cup hot cooking liquid and yogurt together in bowl (to temper), then stir mixture back into slow cooker. Stir in cilantro and honey. Adjust consistency with extra hot broth as needed. Season with salt and pepper to taste. Serve, drizzling individual portions with extra oil.

MAKING CITRUS ZEST STRIPS

Using vegetable peeler, remove strips of zest from citrus, making sure to avoid bitter-tasting white pith.

FOOLPROOF BAKED BROWN RICE

SERVES 4 TO 6

To minimize any loss of water through evaporation, cover the saucepan and use the water as soon as it reaches a boil. An 8-inch square ceramic baking dish with a lid may be used instead of the glass baking dish and aluminum foil. To double the recipe, use a 13 by 9-inch baking dish; the baking time does not need to be increased. You can use long-, medium-, or short-grain brown rice for this recipe.

1½ cups brown rice
2⅓ cups water
2 teaspoons unsalted butter or vegetable oil
½ teaspoon salt

1. Adjust oven rack to middle position and heat oven to 375 degrees. Spread rice in 8-inch square baking dish.

2. Bring water and butter to boil, covered, in medium saucepan. Once boiling, immediately stir in salt and pour water mixture over rice in dish. Cover dish tightly with 2 layers of aluminum foil. Transfer dish to oven and bake until tender, about 1 hour.

3. Remove dish from oven and uncover. Fluff rice with fork, then cover dish with dish towel and let rice stand for 5 minutes. Uncover and let rice stand 5 minutes longer. Serve immediately.

Thai Braised Butternut Squash with Tofu

SERVES 4 TO 6 **EASY PREP** **VEG**

COOKING TIME 3 TO 4 HOURS ON LOW OR 2 TO 3 HOURS ON HIGH

SLOW COOKER SIZE 4 TO 7 QUARTS

WHY THIS RECIPE WORKS For this easy-to-make main dish, we braised tofu and chunks of butternut squash in a highly aromatic liquid base. Making sure this braising medium was loaded with flavor was key since tofu tends to absorb liquid as it cooks. We turned to a trio of aromatics (onion, ginger, and garlic), along with Thai red curry paste, and bloomed it all in the microwave to meld the flavors. At the end of the cooking time, we took this dish to the next level by adding coconut milk, lime juice, and cilantro. You can use firm tofu here if desired, but do not substitute softer varieties such as silken tofu; these varieties will break down during cooking.

Chunks of butternut squash and tofu soak up the aromatic broth infused with Thai red curry paste.

1 onion, chopped fine
3 tablespoons Thai red curry paste
2 tablespoons grated fresh ginger
4 garlic cloves, minced
4 teaspoons vegetable oil
2 pounds butternut squash, peeled, seeded, and cut into 1-inch pieces (6 cups)
14 ounces extra-firm tofu, cut into ¾-inch pieces
1 cup vegetable broth, plus extra as needed
2 teaspoons instant tapioca
1 red bell pepper, stemmed, seeded, and cut into ¼-inch-wide strips
1 cup canned coconut milk
1 tablespoon lime juice, plus extra for seasoning
  Salt and pepper
⅓ cup fresh cilantro leaves
¼ cup chopped dry-roasted peanuts

1. Microwave onion, curry paste, 1 tablespoon ginger, garlic, and 1 tablespoon oil in bowl, stirring occasionally, until onion is softened, about 5 minutes; transfer to slow cooker. Stir in squash, tofu, broth, and tapioca. Cover and cook until squash is tender, 3 to 4 hours on low or 2 to 3 hours on high.

2. Microwave bell pepper with remaining 1 teaspoon oil in bowl, stirring occasionally, until tender, about 5 minutes. Stir bell pepper, coconut milk, lime juice, and remaining 1 tablespoon ginger into slow cooker. Cover and cook on high until heated through, about 10 minutes.

3. Adjust sauce consistency with extra hot broth as needed. Season with salt, pepper, and extra lime juice to taste. Sprinkle individual portions with cilantro and peanuts before serving.

Summer Barley Salad

SERVES 4 TO 6   EASY PREP   VEG   LIGHT
COOKING TIME 3 TO 4 HOURS ON LOW OR 2 TO 3 HOURS ON HIGH
SLOW COOKER SIZE 4 TO 7 QUARTS

WHY THIS RECIPE WORKS To showcase the appealingly nutty taste of barley, we kept the flavors simple—just lemon and coriander—and constructed a salad that paired the barley with piles of fresh veggies and a yogurt-herb dressing. To get perfectly cooked barley, we needed to find the right liquid-to-barley ratio for the slow cooker. After a few tests, we found that 2¼ cups water to 1 cup barley produced barley that was cooked through once all the water had been absorbed, while leaving the texture still on the soft side. Reducing the amount of liquid wasn't an option because it resulted in unevenly cooked barley. To maintain a bit of the grains' toothsome structure and ensure even cooking, we briefly toasted the barley in the microwave before adding it to the slow cooker. Do not substitute hulled, hull-less, quick-cooking, or presteamed barley (read the ingredient list on the package to determine this) in this recipe.

 1 cup pearl barley, rinsed
 3 tablespoons extra-virgin olive oil
 1 teaspoon ground coriander
 1 tablespoon grated lemon zest plus 1 tablespoon juice
    Salt and pepper
 1 pound yellow summer squash or zucchini
10 ounces cherry tomatoes, halved
 ½ cup fresh parsley leaves
 ⅓ cup plain yogurt
 2 tablespoons minced fresh chives
 1 garlic clove, minced

1. Lightly coat slow cooker with vegetable oil spray. Microwave barley, 1 tablespoon oil, and coriander in bowl, stirring occasionally, until barley is lightly toasted and fragrant, about 3 minutes;

The base of this salad, tender barley infused with aromatics, cooks for hours in the slow cooker.

transfer to prepared slow cooker. Stir in 2¼ cups water, 2 teaspoons lemon zest, and ½ teaspoon salt. Cover and cook until barley is tender, 3 to 4 hours on low or 2 to 3 hours on high.

2. Drain barley, if needed, and transfer to large serving bowl; let cool slightly. Using vegetable peeler or mandoline, shave squash lengthwise into very thin ribbons. Add squash ribbons, tomatoes, and parsley to bowl with barley and gently toss to combine.

3. Whisk yogurt, chives, garlic, lemon juice, ¼ teaspoon salt, ¼ teaspoon pepper, remaining 2 tablespoons oil, and remaining 1 teaspoon lemon zest together in separate bowl. Add dressing to salad and toss to coat. Season with salt and pepper to taste. Serve.

MAKING SQUASH RIBBONS

Using vegetable peeler or mandoline, shave summer squash or zucchini lengthwise into very thin ribbons.

Quinoa, Black Bean, and Mango Salad

SERVES 4 TO 6 EASY PREP VEG LIGHT

COOKING TIME 3 TO 4 HOURS ON LOW OR 2 TO 3 HOURS ON HIGH

SLOW COOKER SIZE 4 TO 7 QUARTS

WHY THIS RECIPE WORKS We wanted to make a quinoa salad hearty enough for a main course while keeping it light and fresh-tasting. To ensure perfectly cooked, fluffy grains, we "toasted" the quinoa briefly in the microwave before adding it to the slow cooker. Canned black beans were an easy addition, and fresh mango and bell pepper stirred in before serving lent the salad heartiness, texture, and color. You will need an oval slow cooker for this recipe. Be sure to rinse the quinoa in a fine-mesh strainer before using; rinsing removes the quinoa's bitter protective coating (called saponins).

1½ cups prewashed white quinoa, rinsed
1 jalapeño chile, stemmed, seeded, and minced
3 tablespoons extra-virgin olive oil
1 garlic clove, minced
1 teaspoon ground cumin
1 teaspoon ground coriander
1¾ cups water
1 (15-ounce) can black beans, rinsed
Salt and pepper
2 red bell peppers, stemmed, seeded, and chopped
1 mango, peeled, pitted, and cut into ¼-inch pieces
⅓ cup fresh cilantro leaves
3 scallions, sliced thin
¼ cup lime juice (2 limes)

1. Lightly coat slow cooker with vegetable oil spray. Microwave quinoa, jalapeño, 1 tablespoon oil, garlic, cumin, and coriander in bowl, stirring occasionally, until quinoa is lightly toasted and fragrant, about 3 minutes; transfer to prepared slow cooker.

This quinoa salad couldn't be easier to make and is quite versatile: You can serve it over greens or top with avocado.

Stir in water, beans, and 1 teaspoon salt. Cover and cook until quinoa is tender and all water is absorbed, 3 to 4 hours on low or 2 to 3 hours on high.

2. Fluff quinoa with fork, transfer to large serving bowl, and let cool slightly. Add bell peppers, mango, cilantro, scallions, lime juice, and remaining 2 tablespoons oil and gently toss to combine. Season with salt and pepper to taste. Serve.

CUTTING UP A MANGO

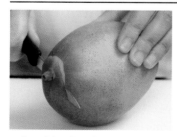

1. Cut thin slice from 1 end of mango so that it sits flat on counter.

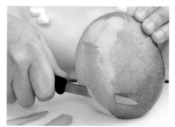

2. Rest mango on trimmed bottom, then cut off skin in thin strips, top to bottom.

3. Cut down along each side of flat pit to remove flesh

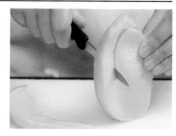

4. Trim around pit to remove any remaining flesh. Cut flesh as directed in recipe.

Beet and Wheat Berry Salad with Arugula and Apples

SERVES 4 TO 6   **EASY PREP**   **VEG**   **LIGHT**   **ALL DAY**

COOKING TIME 6 TO 8 HOURS ON LOW OR 4 TO 5 HOURS ON HIGH

SLOW COOKER SIZE 4 TO 7 QUARTS

WHY THIS RECIPE WORKS This hearty vegetarian entrée features nutty wheat berries, earthy beets, crisp apples, and fresh arugula, all tied together at the end with a lively vinaigrette and fresh goat cheese. The flavor of wheat berries works especially well in salads and pairs nicely with the sweet and rich beets. Even better, the wheat berries can be slowly simmered alongside the beets, which we wrapped in foil to keep the cooking even and the deep color from bleeding into the grain. Minced garlic and thyme, added right to the slow cooker, provided an aromatic backbone. Once the wheat berries were tender, we drained them and dressed them with a simple red wine vinaigrette. Baby arugula and Granny Smith apples rounded out our salad with their bitter and sweet-tart notes, respectively, and crumbled goat cheese provided a creamy, tangy counterpoint to the wheat berries and beets. To ensure even cooking, we recommend using beets that are similar in size—roughly 3 inches in diameter. If using quick-cooking or presteamed wheat berries (the ingredient list on the package specifies the type), you will need to decrease the cooking time. The wheat berries will retain a chewy texture once fully cooked.

- 1 cup wheat berries
- 2 garlic cloves, minced
- 2 teaspoons minced fresh thyme or ½ teaspoon dried
  Salt and pepper
- 1 pound beets, trimmed
- 1 Granny Smith apple, peeled, cored, halved, and sliced ¼ inch thick
- 4 ounces (4 cups) baby arugula
- 3 tablespoons extra-virgin olive oil
- 3 tablespoons red wine vinegar
  Pinch sugar
- 4 ounces goat cheese, crumbled (1 cup)

1. Combine 5 cups water, wheat berries, garlic, thyme, and ½ teaspoon salt in slow cooker. Wrap beets individually in aluminum foil and place in slow cooker. Cover and cook until wheat berries and beets are tender, 6 to 8 hours on low or 4 to 5 hours on high.

For this hearty salad, we cook the beets and wheat berries together but wrap the beets in foil for even cooking.

2. Transfer beets to cutting board, open foil, and let sit until cool enough to handle. Rub off beet skins with paper towels and cut beets into ½-inch-thick wedges.

3. Drain wheat berries, transfer to large serving bowl, and let cool slightly. Add beets, apple, arugula, oil, vinegar, ½ teaspoon salt, pinch pepper, and sugar and toss to combine. Season with salt and pepper to taste. Sprinkle with goat cheese and serve.

REMOVING BEET SKINS

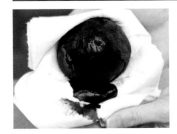

Once beets are cooled completely, cradle each beet in your hand with several layers of paper towels, then gently use towels to rub off skin.

MAKE IT 5 WAYS LENTIL SALADS

Lentil Salad with Radishes, Cilantro, and Pepitas

SERVES 4 `EASY PREP` `VEG`
COOKING TIME 3 TO 4 HOURS ON LOW OR 2 TO 3 HOURS ON HIGH
SLOW COOKER SIZE 4 TO 7 QUARTS

A lentil salad can be a hearty, impressive, and easy main course. But all too often the lentils overcook and break down, and you are left with something resembling more of a porridge than a salad. We found that the slow and even heat of the slow cooker was the perfect solution to great lentils every time. We discovered that cooking the lentils with plenty of liquid was necessary to ensure even cooking. Also adding a little salt and vinegar to the cooking liquid (we preferred water for a pure lentil flavor) gave us lentils that were firm yet creamy. We added aromatics to the cooking water for a flavorful backbone during cooking. Once the lentils were cooked to the ideal texture and drained, we added fresh and bright ingredients to create big flavor that turned this dish into a hearty main vegetarian course. We prefer French green lentils (lentilles du Puy) for this recipe, but it will work with any type of lentil except red or yellow.

1 MEDITERRANEAN LENTIL SALAD

1 cup French green lentils, picked over and rinsed
2½ tablespoons white wine vinegar
3 garlic cloves, minced
1 teaspoon herbes de Provence
1 bay leaf
Salt and pepper
1 (15-ounce) can chickpeas, rinsed
12 ounces cherry tomatoes, halved
½ cup fresh parsley leaves
¼ cup extra-virgin olive oil
2 ounces feta cheese, crumbled (½ cup)

1. Combine 4 cups water, lentils, 1 tablespoon vinegar, garlic, herbes de Provence, bay leaf, and ¾ teaspoon salt in slow cooker. Cover and cook until lentils are tender, 3 to 4 hours on low or 2 to 3 hours on high.

2. Drain lentils, discarding bay leaf, and transfer to large serving bowl; let cool slightly. Add chickpeas, tomatoes, parsley, oil, ¼ teaspoon salt, and remaining 1½ tablespoons vinegar; gently toss to combine. Season with salt and pepper to taste. Sprinkle with feta and serve.

2 SPICED LENTIL SALAD WITH CAULIFLOWER AND POMEGRANATE

1 cup French green lentils, picked over and rinsed
1 (3-inch) piece ginger, peeled and smashed
3 tablespoons lemon juice
3 garlic cloves, minced
2 teaspoons ground cumin
¾ teaspoon ground cinnamon
Salt and pepper
¼ teaspoon cayenne pepper
2 cups cauliflower florets, chopped coarse
½ cup pomegranate seeds
¼ cup extra-virgin olive oil
¼ cup fresh parsley leaves
4 scallions, sliced thin
2 teaspoons honey

1. Combine 4 cups water, lentils, ginger, 1 tablespoon lemon juice, garlic, cumin, cinnamon, ¾ teaspoon salt, and cayenne in slow cooker. Cover and cook until lentils are tender, 3 to 4 hours on low or 2 to 3 hours on high.

2. Microwave cauliflower and 2 tablespoons water in covered bowl, stirring occasionally, until cauliflower is tender, about 3 minutes. Drain cauliflower.

3. Drain lentils, discarding ginger, and transfer to large serving bowl; let cool slightly. Add cauliflower, pomegranate seeds, oil, parsley, scallions, honey, ½ teaspoon salt, and remaining 2 tablespoons lemon juice; gently toss to combine. Season with salt and pepper to taste. Serve.

3 LENTIL SALAD WITH RADISHES, CILANTRO, AND PEPITAS

1 cup French green lentils, picked over and rinsed
3 tablespoons lime juice
3 garlic cloves, minced
1 tablespoon ground cumin
1½ teaspoons dried oregano
Salt and pepper
6 radishes, trimmed, halved, and sliced thin
1 red bell pepper, stemmed, seeded, and cut into ½-inch pieces
¼ cup fresh cilantro leaves
¼ cup extra-virgin olive oil
1 jalapeño chile, stemmed, seeded, and minced
1 shallot, minced
2 tablespoons roasted pepitas
2 ounces queso fresco, crumbled (½ cup)

1. Combine 4 cups water, lentils, 1 tablespoon lime juice, garlic, cumin, oregano, and ¾ teaspoon salt in slow cooker. Cover and cook until lentils are tender, 3 to 4 hours on low or 2 to 3 hours on high.

2. Drain lentils and transfer to large serving bowl; let cool slightly. Add radishes, bell pepper, cilantro, oil, jalapeño, shallot, ¼ teaspoon salt, and remaining 2 tablespoons lime juice; gently toss to combine. Season with salt and pepper to taste. Sprinkle with pepitas and queso fresco. Serve.

4 LENTIL SALAD WITH DILL, ORANGE, AND SPINACH

1 cup French green lentils, picked over and rinsed
2½ tablespoons red wine vinegar
3 garlic cloves, minced
3 (2-inch) strips orange zest, plus 2 oranges
1 bay leaf
Salt and pepper
4 ounces (4 cups) baby spinach, chopped coarse
¼ cup extra-virgin olive oil
1 shallot, minced
2 tablespoons chopped fresh dill
2 tablespoons chopped toasted pecans

1. Combine 4 cups water, lentils, 1 tablespoon vinegar, garlic, orange zest, bay leaf, and ¾ teaspoon salt in slow cooker. Cover and cook until lentils are tender, 3 to 4 hours on low or 2 to 3 hours on high.

2. Cut away peel and pith from oranges. Cut oranges into 8 wedges, then slice wedges crosswise into ¼-inch-thick pieces.

3. Drain lentils, discarding orange zest and bay leaf, and transfer to large serving bowl; let cool slightly. Add oranges, along with any accumulated juices, spinach, oil, shallot, dill, ¼ teaspoon salt, and remaining 1½ tablespoons vinegar; gently toss to combine. Season with salt and pepper to taste. Sprinkle with pecans. Serve.

5 CURRIED LENTIL SALAD WITH KALE

1 cup French green lentils, picked over and rinsed
1 (3-inch) piece ginger, peeled and smashed
2½ tablespoons white wine vinegar
3 garlic cloves, minced
2 teaspoons curry powder
Salt and pepper
4 ounces kale, stemmed and chopped
1 Honeycrisp or Gala apple, cored and cut into ½-inch pieces
¼ cup extra-virgin olive oil
¼ cup fresh cilantro leaves
2 tablespoons toasted sliced almonds

1. Combine 4 cups water, lentils, ginger, 1 tablespoon vinegar, garlic, curry powder, and ¾ teaspoon salt in slow cooker. Cover and cook until lentils are tender, 3 to 4 hours on low or 2 to 3 hours on high.

2. Microwave kale and 2 tablespoons water in covered bowl, stirring occasionally, until kale is slightly wilted, about 5 minutes. Drain kale.

3. Drain lentils, discarding ginger, and transfer to large serving bowl; let cool slightly. Add kale, apple, oil, cilantro, ¼ teaspoon salt, and remaining 1½ tablespoons vinegar; gently toss to combine. Season with salt and pepper to taste. Sprinkle with almonds. Serve.

For these appealing vegetarian tacos, the sweet potatoes need to be wrapped in foil so they hold their shape.

Mustard Greens and Sweet Potato Tacos

SERVES 4   VEG

COOKING TIME 3 TO 4 HOURS ON LOW OR 2 TO 3 HOURS ON HIGH

SLOW COOKER SIZE 4 TO 7 QUARTS

WHY THIS RECIPE WORKS It's easy to get stuck in a rut when cooking vegetables, but we found that stuffing soft tacos with super-foods like mustard greens and sweet potatoes made even the most carnivorous among us excited to eat veggies. In order for the sweet potatoes to be a manageable size for folding into a taco, we cut them into ½-inch pieces. But these small pieces cooked quickly and lost their shape, so we wrapped the starchy tubers in foil to help tame the heat of the slow cooker and keep them from falling apart. The tender vegetables needed a crunchy counterpoint, so we put together some quickly pickled radishes. You can substitute an equal amount of Swiss chard for the mustard greens, if desired. For more information on making a foil packet, see page 76.

1 onion, chopped fine
2 tablespoons minced fresh oregano or 2 teaspoons dried
2 tablespoons extra-virgin olive oil
4 garlic cloves, minced
1 teaspoon ground cumin
1 teaspoon ground coriander
  Salt and pepper
1½ pounds mustard greens, stemmed and cut into 1-inch pieces
1 pound sweet potatoes, peeled and cut into ½-inch pieces
12 (6-inch) corn tortillas, warmed
1 recipe Spicy Pickled Radishes
4 ounces queso fresco, crumbled (1 cup)

1. Lightly coat slow cooker with vegetable oil spray. Microwave onion, oregano, 1 tablespoon oil, garlic, cumin, coriander, and ¾ teaspoon salt in bowl, stirring occasionally, until onion is softened, about 5 minutes; transfer to prepared slow cooker. Stir in mustard greens and ½ cup water. Season sweet potatoes with salt and pepper, wrap in aluminum foil packet, and place on top of greens. Cover and cook until greens and potatoes are tender, 3 to 4 hours on low or 2 to 3 hours on high.

2. Transfer foil packet to plate. Drain greens mixture and return to now-empty slow cooker. Carefully open foil packet and gently fold potatoes, along with any accumulated juices, into greens. Stir in remaining 1 tablespoon oil and season with salt and pepper to taste. Serve with tortillas, pickled radishes, and queso fresco.

SIMPLE ACCOMPANIMENTS

SPICY PICKLED RADISHES

MAKES ABOUT 1¾ CUPS

These easy-to-make spicy pickled radishes are the perfect garnish for numerous Mexican dishes including stews, tacos, enchiladas, and more.

10 radishes, trimmed and sliced thin
½ cup lime juice (4 limes)
½ jalapeño chile, stemmed and sliced thin
1 teaspoon sugar
¼ teaspoon salt

Combine all ingredients in bowl, cover, and let stand at room temperature for 30 minutes. (Mixture can be refrigerated for up to 24 hours.)

The magic behind this recipe is that we make the stuffing and cook the eggplant at the same time in the slow cooker.

Stuffed Spiced Eggplants with Tomatoes and Pine Nuts

SERVES 4 **VEG**

COOKING TIME 5 TO 6 HOURS ON LOW OR 3 TO 4 HOURS ON HIGH

SLOW COOKER SIZE 5 TO 7 QUARTS

WHY THIS RECIPE WORKS When cooked, eggplants turn rich and creamy, losing the bitterness they have when raw. Italian eggplants, which are slightly smaller than the ubiquitous globe eggplants, are the ideal size and shape for stuffing when halved, and two of them fit easily in a slow cooker. Inspired by the flavors of Turkey, where stuffed eggplant is a way of life, we created a simple stuffing with canned diced tomatoes, Pecorino Romano, pine nuts, and aromatics that included onion, garlic, oregano, and cinnamon. We simply nestled the halved eggplants cut side down in this fragrant mixture and let them cook until tender. After removing the eggplants from the slow cooker, we gently pushed the soft flesh to the sides to create a cavity, which we filled with the aromatic tomato mixture

left behind in the slow cooker. Topped with extra cheese and fresh minced parsley, these eggplants looked beautiful and were far easier to make than most traditional versions. Be sure to buy eggplants that are no more than 10 ounces; larger eggplants will not fit properly in your slow cooker. You may need to trim off the eggplant stems to help them fit. You will need an oval slow cooker for this recipe.

    1 onion, chopped fine
    2 tablespoons extra-virgin olive oil
    3 garlic cloves, minced
    2 teaspoons minced fresh oregano
       or ½ teaspoon dried
    ¼ teaspoon ground cinnamon
       Salt and pepper
    ⅛ teaspoon cayenne pepper
    1 (14.5-ounce) can diced tomatoes, drained
    2 ounces Pecorino Romano cheese, grated (1 cup)
    ¼ cup pine nuts, toasted
    1 tablespoon red wine vinegar
    2 (10-ounce) Italian eggplants, halved lengthwise
    2 tablespoons minced fresh parsley

1. Microwave onion, 1 tablespoon oil, garlic, oregano, cinnamon, ¼ teaspoon salt, and cayenne in bowl, stirring occasionally, until onion is softened, about 5 minutes; transfer to slow cooker. Stir in tomatoes, ¾ cup Pecorino, pine nuts, and vinegar. Season eggplant halves with salt and pepper and nestle cut side down into slow cooker (eggplants may overlap slightly). Cover and cook until eggplants are tender, 5 to 6 hours on low or 3 to 4 hours on high.

2. Transfer eggplant halves cut side up to serving dish. Using 2 forks, gently push eggplant flesh to sides of each half to make room for filling. Stir remaining 1 tablespoon oil into tomato mixture and season with salt and pepper to taste. Mound tomato mixture evenly into eggplants and sprinkle with parsley and remaining ¼ cup Pecorino. Serve.

PREPARING EGGPLANT FOR STUFFING

Using 2 forks, gently push flesh to sides of each eggplant half to make room in center for filling.

The layers of ingredients and flavors that define a great biryani can be easily replicated in the slow cooker.

Mushroom Biryani

SERVES 4 TO 6 | VEG

COOKING TIME 2 TO 3 HOURS ON HIGH

SLOW COOKER SIZE 5 TO 7 QUARTS

WHY THIS RECIPE WORKS The best biryani recipes place fragrant long-grain basmati center stage, enriching it with fresh herbs and pungent spices. However, most recipes take time to develop deep flavor by steeping whole spices and cooking each part of the dish separately before marrying them. We aimed to achieve a simple, streamlined, and hands-free slow cooker version of this dish that delivered on the big, bold flavors we expected from a biryani, without the fuss. We chose basmati rice for its nutty flavor and perfume-like aroma. A mixture of Indian-inspired aromatics were first bloomed with oil in the microwave to jump-start flavor development. We then combined the bloomed spice blend, rice, and hot vegetable broth in our slow cooker before topping the rice with hearty, earthy mushrooms. Layering the mushrooms on top of the rice mixture ensured even cooking of the rice. We found that basmati rice cooked best on high, and placing a piece of parchment paper over the mixture prevented the grains on top from drying out as the water was absorbed, and promoted even

steaming in the rice. Once the rice was cooked, fresh spinach, herbs, and raisins were added to the slow cooker before gently fluffing the rice to serve. Biryani is traditionally served with a cooling yogurt sauce; ideally, you should make it before starting the biryani to allow the flavors in the sauce to meld. We prefer the flavor of basmati rice in this recipe, but long-grain white rice can be substituted. You will need an oval slow cooker for this recipe. For more information on creating a parchment shield, see page 177.

SAUCE
¾ cup plain yogurt
2 tablespoons chopped fresh cilantro
2 tablespoons chopped fresh mint
1 garlic clove, minced
Salt and pepper

BIRYANI
1 onion, chopped fine
3 tablespoons extra-virgin olive oil
4 garlic cloves, minced
2 teaspoons garam masala
Salt and pepper
½ teaspoon turmeric
⅛ teaspoon cayenne pepper
1½ cups vegetable broth
1½ cups basmati rice, rinsed
1 pound cremini mushrooms, trimmed and sliced thin
6 ounces (6 cups) baby spinach, chopped coarse
¼ cup raisins
2 tablespoons chopped fresh cilantro
2 tablespoons chopped fresh mint
⅓ cup sliced almonds, toasted

1. FOR THE SAUCE: Combine all ingredients in bowl and season with salt and pepper to taste. Refrigerate until ready to serve.

2. FOR THE BIRYANI: Lightly coat slow cooker with vegetable oil spray. Microwave onion, oil, garlic, garam masala, 1 teaspoon salt, turmeric, and cayenne in bowl, stirring occasionally, until onion is softened, about 5 minutes; transfer to prepared slow cooker.

3. Microwave broth in bowl until steaming, about 5 minutes. Stir broth and rice into slow cooker. Spread mushrooms evenly on top of rice mixture. Gently press 16 by 12-inch sheet of parchment paper onto surface of mushrooms, folding down edges as needed. Cover and cook until rice is tender and all broth is absorbed, 2 to 3 hours on high.

4. Discard parchment. Sprinkle spinach and raisins on top of rice, cover, and let sit until spinach is wilted, about 5 minutes. Add cilantro and mint, and fluff rice with fork until combined. Season with salt and pepper to taste. Sprinkle with almonds and serve, passing sauce separately.

We use the slow cooker for an easy way to make scoopable quinoa for our lettuce cups, then add the toppings.

Greek Quinoa and Vegetable Lettuce Cups

SERVES 4 EASY PREP VEG

COOKING TIME 3 TO 4 HOURS ON LOW OR 2 TO 3 HOURS ON HIGH

SLOW COOKER SIZE 4 TO 7 QUARTS

WHY THIS RECIPE WORKS Lettuce cups—like tortillas—are great vessels for all sorts of fillings. For a vegetarian filling that could be made in the slow cooker, we turned to quinoa and paired it with fresh vegetables and an herbaceous yogurt dressing. Since we wanted a quinoa mixture that was easy to scoop into lettuce cups, we skipped the step of toasting the quinoa in the microwave. Putting the raw quinoa into the slow cooker gave it a softer, more cohesive texture. Our creamy dressing, flavored with tangy feta cheese and fresh mint, also helped to bind the quinoa mixture. Tomatoes and cucumber added healthy bulk to the mix, and shallot added a welcome bite. We tossed the quinoa and vegetables with part of the bold dressing and reserved the rest to drizzle on once we scooped our salad into the lettuce cups. You will need an oval slow cooker for this recipe. Be sure to rinse the quinoa in a fine-mesh strainer before using; rinsing removes the quinoa's bitter protective coating (called saponins).

2 tablespoons extra-virgin olive oil
1 tablespoon minced fresh oregano or 1 teaspoon dried
2 garlic cloves, minced
1½ cups vegetable broth
1 cup prewashed white quinoa, rinsed
⅔ cup plain yogurt
2 ounces feta cheese, crumbled (½ cup)
¼ cup minced fresh mint
2 tablespoons red wine vinegar
Salt and pepper
2 tomatoes, cored, seeded, and chopped
1 cucumber, peeled, halved lengthwise, seeded, and cut into ¼-inch pieces
1 small shallot, halved and sliced thin
2 heads Bibb lettuce (8 ounces each), leaves separated

1. Lightly coat slow cooker with vegetable oil spray. Microwave 1 tablespoon oil, oregano, and garlic in bowl until fragrant, about 1 minute; transfer to prepared slow cooker. Stir in broth and quinoa, cover, and cook until quinoa is tender and all broth is absorbed, 3 to 4 hours on low or 2 to 3 hours on high.

2. Fluff quinoa with fork, transfer to large serving bowl, and let cool slightly. Combine yogurt, feta, 2 tablespoons mint, vinegar, ½ teaspoon salt, ¼ teaspoon pepper, and remaining 1 tablespoon oil in separate bowl. Add half of dressing, tomatoes, cucumber, shallot, and remaining 2 tablespoons mint to quinoa and gently toss to combine. Season with salt and pepper to taste. Serve quinoa salad with lettuce leaves, passing remaining dressing separately.

Turkish Eggplant Casserole

SERVES 4 TO 6 VEG

COOKING TIME 3 TO 4 HOURS ON LOW OR 2 TO 3 HOURS ON HIGH

SLOW COOKER SIZE 5 TO 7 QUARTS

WHY THIS RECIPE WORKS Earthy and versatile, eggplant goes well with traditional Turkish spices, namely, paprika, cumin, cayenne pepper, and cinnamon. We paired eggplant, which we rubbed with a spice mixture and broiled before adding it to the slow cooker, thereby cooking off extra moisture and keeping the slices firm, with bulgur, a popular grain of the region that cooks perfectly in the steamy environment of the slow cooker. An herb-yogurt sauce added a welcome richness and tang to this spiced dish. When shopping, don't confuse bulgur with cracked wheat, which has a much longer cooking time and will not work in this recipe. You will need an oval slow cooker for this recipe.

SAUCE

- 1 cup plain yogurt
- ¼ cup chopped fresh parsley
- 2 tablespoons chopped fresh mint
- 1 garlic clove, minced
  Salt and pepper

BULGUR

- 2 teaspoons paprika
- 1½ teaspoons ground cumin
  Salt
- ⅛ teaspoon cayenne pepper
- ⅛ teaspoon ground cinnamon
- 1½ pounds eggplant, sliced into ½-inch-thick rounds
- ¼ cup extra-virgin olive oil
- 1 onion, chopped fine
- 4 garlic cloves, minced
- 1 tablespoon tomato paste
- 1 cup medium-grind bulgur, rinsed
- 1 cup vegetable broth
- 4 tomatoes, cored and sliced ½ inch thick

1. FOR THE SAUCE: Combine all ingredients in bowl and season with salt and pepper to taste. Refrigerate until ready to serve.

2. FOR THE BULGUR: Adjust oven rack 6 inches from broiler element and heat broiler. Combine paprika, cumin, ¾ teaspoon salt, cayenne, and cinnamon in bowl. Arrange eggplant in single layer on aluminum foil–lined rimmed baking sheet, brush both sides with 3 tablespoons oil, and sprinkle with spice mixture. Broil eggplant until softened and beginning to brown, 10 to 12 minutes, flipping eggplant halfway through broiling.

3. Lightly coat slow cooker with vegetable oil spray. Microwave onion, garlic, tomato paste, ¾ teaspoon salt, and remaining 1 tablespoon oil in bowl, stirring occasionally, until onion is softened, about 5 minutes; transfer to prepared slow cooker. Stir in bulgur and broth. Shingle alternating slices of eggplant and tomato into 3 tightly fitting rows on top of bulgur mixture. Cover and cook until eggplant and bulgur are tender and all broth is absorbed, 3 to 4 hours on low or 2 to 3 hours on high. Serve, passing sauce separately.

ASSEMBLING EGGPLANT CASSEROLE

After combining bulgur mixture in slow cooker, shingle alternating slices of eggplant and tomato into 3 tightly fitting rows on top. Vegetable rows may overlap slightly.

Farro Risotto with Carrots and Goat Cheese

SERVES 4 [VEG] [LIGHT]

COOKING TIME 3 TO 4 HOURS ON LOW OR 2 TO 3 HOURS ON HIGH

SLOW COOKER SIZE 4 TO 7 QUARTS

WHY THIS RECIPE WORKS Risotto usually demands a cook's attention from start to finish, which is why this hands-off slow-cooker version is so appealing. Instead of traditional Arborio rice, we chose nutrient-rich farro and added colorful carrots. Finely grating the carrots allowed them to overcook slightly and "melt" into the farro to help create a creamy base. When the farro was tender, we stirred in handfuls of bright, fresh baby spinach. We added an extra half-cup of broth to help wilt the spinach and keep the farro from becoming dry and sticky. A little bit of tangy goat cheese was the perfect finishing touch to give our risotto rich flavor and an ultracreamy texture. We prefer the flavor and texture of whole farro; pearled farro can be used, but the texture may be softer. Do not use quick-cooking or presteamed farro (the ingredient list on the package will specify the type) in this recipe. Use the small holes of a box grater to grate the carrots.

- 1 onion, chopped fine
- 1 tablespoon unsalted butter
- 2 garlic cloves, minced
  Salt and pepper
- 2½ cups vegetable broth, plus extra as needed
- ¼ cup dry white wine
- 1 cup whole farro
- 3 carrots, peeled and finely grated
- 4 ounces goat cheese, crumbled (1 cup)
- 4 ounces (4 cups) baby spinach

1. Lightly coat slow cooker with vegetable oil spray. Microwave onion, butter, garlic, and ¼ teaspoon salt in bowl, stirring occasionally, until onion is softened, about 5 minutes; transfer to prepared slow cooker.

2. Microwave 2 cups broth and wine in bowl until steaming, about 5 minutes. Stir broth mixture, farro, and carrots into slow cooker. Cover and cook until farro is tender, 3 to 4 hours on low or 2 to 3 hours on high.

3. Microwave remaining ½ cup broth in bowl until steaming, about 5 minutes. Stir broth and goat cheese into farro until mixture is creamy but still somewhat thin. Stir in spinach, 1 handful at a time, until slightly wilted. Cover and cook on high until spinach is completely wilted, about 15 minutes. Adjust risotto consistency with extra hot broth as needed. Season with salt and pepper to taste. Serve.

Nutty farro stands in for pasta in this rich-tasting dish, where the peas and asparagus are stirred in separately at the end.

Farro Primavera

SERVES 4 **VEG** LIGHT

COOKING TIME 3 TO 4 HOURS ON LOW OR 2 TO 3 HOURS ON HIGH

SLOW COOKER SIZE 4 TO 7 QUARTS

WHY THIS RECIPE WORKS For an interesting take on pasta primavera we swapped out pasta for whole-grain farro and nixed cream in favor of nutty Parmesan. Since most of the vegetables we had in mind, except the leek, would go into the slow cooker at the end to ensure bright colors and fresh flavors, the point of using a slow cooker was the hands-off approach to perfectly cooked farro. To mellow the potent allium flavor of the leek, we gave it a head start in the microwave. Once the farro was tender, we stirred in some additional broth to help steam the asparagus in the last few minutes of cooking. Peas rounded out the spring vegetables for our primavera, and a generous portion of Parmesan cheese turned our dish creamy and rich-tasting. We prefer the flavor and texture of whole farro; pearled farro can be used, but the texture may be softer. Do not use quick-cooking or presteamed farro (the ingredient list on the package will specify the type) in this recipe.

1 leek, white and light green parts only, halved lengthwise, sliced thin, and washed thoroughly
1 tablespoon extra-virgin olive oil
2 garlic cloves, minced
1 teaspoon minced fresh thyme or ¼ teaspoon dried
  Salt and pepper
2½ cups vegetable broth, plus extra as needed
1 cup whole farro
2 ounces Parmesan cheese, grated (1 cup), plus extra for serving
1 pound thin asparagus, trimmed and cut into 1-inch lengths
1 cup frozen peas, thawed

1. Lightly coat slow cooker with vegetable oil spray. Microwave leek, oil, garlic, thyme, and ¼ teaspoon salt in bowl, stirring occasionally, until leek is softened, about 5 minutes; transfer to prepared slow cooker.

2. Microwave 2 cups broth in bowl until steaming, about 5 minutes. Stir broth and farro into slow cooker, cover, and cook until farro is tender, 3 to 4 hours on low or 2 to 3 hours on high.

3. Microwave remaining ½ cup broth in bowl until steaming, about 5 minutes. Stir broth and Parmesan into farro until mixture is creamy but still somewhat thin. Stir in asparagus, cover, and cook on high until tender, about 20 minutes. Stir in peas and let sit until heated through, about 5 minutes. Adjust farro consistency with extra hot broth as needed. Season with salt and pepper to taste. Serve, passing extra Parmesan separately.

Rustic Braised Lentils with Eggplant

SERVES 4 TO 6 **VEG** LIGHT

COOKING TIME 3 TO 4 HOURS ON LOW OR 2 TO 3 HOURS ON HIGH

SLOW COOKER SIZE 4 TO 7 QUARTS

WHY THIS RECIPE WORKS For a hearty vegetarian main dish, we paired French green lentils, *lentilles du Puy*, with eggplant and created a braised dish overflowing with flavor. We broiled the eggplant with our aromatics to deepen its flavor and ensure that the eggplant cooked evenly and didn't turn mushy in the slow cooker. We added cherry tomatoes because they broke down and created a fresh tomato sauce to envelop the eggplant and lentils. We found it important to put the lentils and broth in the bottom of the slow cooker so that the lentils cooked thoroughly and evenly. We then layered the broiled eggplant and fresh tomatoes on top of the lentils, and stirred it all together at the end of cooking. Some extra-virgin olive oil stirred in, plus a sprinkling of crumbled feta cheese and parsley, completed this dish with rich, bright freshness. We prefer

French green lentils for this recipe, but it will work with any type of lentil except red or yellow. You will need an oval slow cooker for this dish.

2 pounds eggplant, cut into 1-inch pieces
1 onion, chopped fine
3 tablespoons extra-virgin olive oil
1 tablespoon tomato paste
2 garlic cloves, minced
2 teaspoons minced fresh thyme or ½ teaspoon dried
  Salt and pepper
2 cups vegetable broth
1 cup French green lentils, picked over and rinsed
2 tablespoons red wine vinegar
10 ounces cherry tomatoes, halved
2 ounces feta cheese, crumbled (½ cup)
¼ cup minced fresh parsley

1. Adjust oven rack 6 inches from broiler element and heat broiler. Line rimmed baking sheet with aluminum foil. Toss eggplant and onion with 1 tablespoon oil, tomato paste, garlic, thyme, and ½ teaspoon salt in bowl. Spread eggplant mixture evenly over prepared baking sheet. Broil until eggplant is softened and beginning to brown, 10 to 12 minutes, rotating sheet halfway through broiling.

2. Combine broth, lentils, and 1 tablespoon vinegar in slow cooker. Spread eggplant mixture and tomatoes evenly on top of lentils. Cover and cook until lentils are tender, 3 to 4 hours on low or 2 to 3 hours on high. Stir in remaining 2 tablespoons oil and remaining 1 tablespoon vinegar. Season with salt and pepper to taste. Sprinkle with feta and parsley and serve.

Southwestern Black Bean and Bulgur Bowls

SERVES 6   VEG   LIGHT   ALL DAY
COOKING TIME 8 TO 9 HOURS ON HIGH
SLOW COOKER SIZE 4 TO 7 QUARTS

WHY THIS RECIPE WORKS The low-and-slow heat of the slow cooker is ideal for cooking beans, and we wanted an easy dinner starring the protein-rich superfood black beans. To ensure perfectly cooked beans, we submerged them in 6 cups of liquid—half water and half vegetable broth—for added flavor. We infused our beans and cooking liquid with bold flavors, using

This healthy bean-bulgur bowl is easy to make in a slow cooker, which is the perfect way to infuse beans with flavor.

garlic, cumin, and chili powder. Once the beans were perfectly tender, we stirred in bulgur for another fiber-rich element. In the slow cooker, bulgur readily absorbed the extra cooking liquid and all of its rich flavors. To add freshness and textural variety to the dish, we made a quick tomato salsa. The brightness of the salsa, along with a sprinkling of smooth queso fresco, perfectly complemented the warm beans and bulgur for a hearty and healthy vegetarian dinner. When shopping, don't confuse bulgur with cracked wheat, which has a much longer cooking time and will not work in this recipe.

SALSA
6 ounces cherry tomatoes, quartered
2 tablespoons extra-virgin olive oil
2 tablespoons minced fresh cilantro
1 tablespoon lime juice
  Salt and pepper

BEANS

- 1 onion, chopped fine
- 4 garlic cloves, minced
- 1 tablespoon extra-virgin olive oil
- 1 tablespoon ground cumin
- 2 teaspoons chili powder
- 3 cups vegetable broth
- 3 cups water
- 1 pound (2½ cups) dried black beans, picked over and rinsed
  Salt and pepper
- 1 cup medium-grind bulgur, rinsed
- 4 ounces queso fresco, crumbled (1 cup)

1. FOR THE SALSA: Combine all ingredients in bowl and season with salt and pepper to taste. Refrigerate until ready to serve.

2. FOR THE BEANS: Microwave onion, garlic, oil, cumin, and chili powder in bowl, stirring occasionally, until onion is softened, about 5 minutes; transfer to slow cooker. Stir broth, water, beans, and 1 teaspoon salt into slow cooker. Cover and cook until beans are tender, 8 to 9 hours on high.

3. Stir bulgur into beans, cover, and cook on high until bulgur is tender and most of liquid is absorbed, 20 to 30 minutes. Season with salt and pepper to taste. Top individual portions with salsa and queso fresco before serving.

Red Beans and Rice with Okra and Tomatoes

SERVES 4 TO 6   `EASY PREP`   `VEG`   `LIGHT`   `ALL DAY`
COOKING TIME 8 TO 9 HOURS ON HIGH
SLOW COOKER SIZE 4 TO 7 QUARTS

WHY THIS RECIPE WORKS Rather than monitor the stovetop for an hour or two so we could enjoy this Cajun classic, we moved it to the slow cooker, where the moist environment and gentle heat could turn our red beans tender and creamy without a lot of effort. Though the beans cooked through perfectly with no advanced prep (we were able to skip the soaking step called for in many recipes), the rice presented a bit of a challenge. Raw rice didn't cook through evenly and was blown out and mushy by the time the beans were done. Instant rice, stirred in toward the end of cooking, held its shape and absorbed the rich flavors of the beans and broth. Using Cajun seasoning meant we didn't need to include a laundry list of spices, and frozen okra, added at the end with some fresh tomatoes, reinforced the Cajun identity of our dish. Be

sure to use instant rice (sometimes labeled minute rice); traditional rice takes much longer to cook and won't work here. Serve with hot sauce.

- 2 tablespoons Cajun seasoning
- 2 tablespoons extra-virgin olive oil
- 3 garlic cloves, minced
- 4 cups vegetable broth
- 8 ounces (1¼ cups) dried small red beans, picked over and rinsed
- 1 green bell pepper, stemmed, seeded, and cut into ½-inch pieces
- 1½ cups instant white rice
- 2 cups frozen cut okra, thawed
- 2 tomatoes, cored and cut into ½-inch pieces
- 4 scallions, sliced thin
  Salt and pepper

1. Microwave Cajun seasoning, oil, and garlic in bowl until fragrant, about 1 minute; transfer to slow cooker. Stir in broth, beans, and bell pepper. Cover and cook until beans are tender, 8 to 9 hours on high.

2. Stir in rice, cover, and cook on high until rice is tender, 20 to 30 minutes. Stir in okra and let sit until heated through, about 5 minutes. Stir in tomatoes and scallions, and season with salt and pepper to taste. Serve.

NOTES FROM THE TEST KITCHEN

Louisiana (Cajun or Creole) Seasoning

Whether called Cajun or Creole, most Louisiana spice blends contain a mix of paprika, garlic, thyme, salt, pepper, and cayenne—ingredients typically found in the region's signature dishes. We had 22 cooks and editors sample five seasonings labeled Creole or Cajun. Our tasters preferred saltier and spicier blends. We liked the "pungent" kick from products that list black pepper, cayenne, or chili powder high on their ingredient lists, and tasters also thought that products with more sodium had "more complex" flavors: Our favorite product, Tony Chachere's Original Creole Seasoning, contains 350 milligrams of sodium per ¼-teaspoon serving. Seasonings with less than 130 milligrams of sodium were "flat" and "bland," and one salt-free product was "completely boring."

CHAPTER 10

BIG BATCH PASTA SAUCES

■ EASY PREP ■ VEGETARIAN ■ LIGHT ■ COOK ALL DAY
Photo: Short Ribs and Red Wine Sauce

When you have access to lots of fresh plum tomatoes, the slow cooker makes it easy to turn them into a vibrant sauce.

All-Purpose Tomato Sauce

MAKES ABOUT 8 CUPS; ENOUGH FOR 2 POUNDS PASTA
`EASY PREP` `VEG` `LIGHT` `ALL DAY`
COOKING TIME 8 TO 10 HOURS ON LOW OR 5 TO 7 HOURS ON HIGH
SLOW COOKER SIZE 4 TO 7 QUARTS

WHY THIS RECIPE WORKS The beauty of this recipe is that you can put a bounty of fresh tomatoes into a slow cooker along with a little salt, walk away for up to 10 hours, and you end up with a brightly flavored tomato sauce—enough to serve a crowd (or plenty to freeze for later). This is the recipe to turn to when your local farmers' markets are overflowing with their late summer crops of field-grown tomatoes. Be sure to leave the lid slightly ajar—about ½ inch—to allow steam to escape and help concentrate the flavor.

  8 pounds plum tomatoes, cored and halved crosswise
      Salt and pepper
 ¼ cup extra-virgin olive oil
      Chopped fresh basil

1. Working over bowl, squeeze each tomato half to expel seeds and excess juice. Discard seeds and juice. Combine tomatoes and 1½ teaspoons salt in slow cooker. Cover, leaving lid about ½ inch ajar, and cook until tomatoes are very soft, 8 to 10 hours on low or 5 to 7 hours on high.

2. Transfer tomatoes to colander and let excess liquid drain (do not press on tomatoes). Working in batches, process tomatoes in blender until smooth, about 1 minute; return to now-empty slow cooker. Stir oil into sauce and season with salt and pepper to taste. Before serving, stir in 2 tablespoons basil for every 4 cups sauce.

Meaty Tomato Sauce

MAKES ABOUT 12 CUPS; ENOUGH FOR 2 POUNDS PASTA
`EASY PREP` `ALL DAY`
COOKING TIME 8 TO 10 HOURS ON LOW OR 5 TO 7 HOURS ON HIGH
SLOW COOKER SIZE 4 TO 7 QUARTS

WHY THIS RECIPE WORKS Nothing could be more welcoming on a cold night than coming home to a rustic, flavor-packed meat sauce ready to toss with some stick-to-your-ribs pasta. For our slow-cooker version, we relied on boneless pork butt, which turned meltingly tender during the long cooking time. Once the pork was fully cooked, it was easy to break it into shreds using a potato masher. To prevent the sauce from turning out watery, we relied on a trio of tomato products: tomato paste, diced tomatoes, and tomato puree. A dose of soy sauce further enhanced the sauce's meaty flavor. No one would ever guess that this rich-tasting and meaty sauce was so easy to make. Pork butt roast is often labeled Boston butt in the supermarket.

  2 onions, chopped fine
 12 garlic cloves, minced
 ¼ cup tomato paste
  2 tablespoons extra-virgin olive oil
  2 tablespoons minced fresh oregano
      or 2 teaspoons dried
 ¼ teaspoon red pepper flakes
  1 (28-ounce) can diced tomatoes, drained
  1 (28-ounce) can tomato puree
 ¾ cup dry red wine
 ⅓ cup soy sauce
  2 bay leaves
  3 pounds boneless pork butt roast, pulled apart
      at seams, trimmed, and cut into 1½-inch pieces
      Salt and pepper
      Sugar
      Chopped fresh parsley

1. Microwave onions, garlic, tomato paste, oil, oregano, and pepper flakes in bowl, stirring occasionally, until onions are softened, about 5 minutes; transfer to slow cooker. Stir in tomatoes, tomato puree, wine, soy sauce, and bay leaves. Season pork with salt and pepper and nestle into slow cooker. Cover and cook until pork is tender, 8 to 10 hours on low or 5 to 7 hours on high.

2. Discard bay leaves. Using large spoon, skim fat from surface of sauce. Using potato masher, smash pork until coarsely shredded. Season with salt, pepper, and sugar to taste. Before serving, stir in 2 tablespoons parsley for every 6 cups sauce.

Sausage Ragu with Red Peppers

MAKES ABOUT 12 CUPS; ENOUGH FOR 2 POUNDS PASTA

`ALL DAY`

COOKING TIME 8 TO 10 HOURS ON LOW OR 5 TO 7 HOURS ON HIGH

SLOW COOKER SIZE 4 TO 7 QUARTS

WHY THIS RECIPE WORKS Sausages and sweet bell peppers are a classic pairing that we thought would translate perfectly into a bright, slightly sweet, and deeply flavored slow-cooker pasta sauce. We liked the flavor that Italian sausages imparted, and a few minutes spent browning them and breaking them up in a skillet gave the sauce an even deeper and richer flavor. Since we had our skillet out, we sautéed our aromatics (onions, garlic, oregano, and red pepper flakes) and deglazed the pan with red wine. Tomato paste, crushed tomatoes, diced tomatoes, and tomato puree were the perfect combination of tomato products with which to build our sauce—neither too watery nor too thick. As for the bell peppers, which rounded out the flavors and cut a little of the heat, we simply softened them in the microwave and stirred them into the sauce just before serving.

2 tablespoons extra-virgin olive oil

2 pounds hot or sweet Italian sausage, casings removed

2 onions, chopped fine

6 garlic cloves, minced

2 tablespoons tomato paste

2 tablespoons minced fresh oregano or 2 teaspoons dried

1 teaspoon red pepper flakes

1 cup dry red wine

1 (28-ounce) can crushed tomatoes

1 (28-ounce) can diced tomatoes, drained

1 (28-ounce) can tomato puree

2 red bell peppers, stemmed, seeded, and cut into ½-inch pieces

This luxuriously rich ragu features the classic combo of Italian sausage and red peppers plus lots of onion and garlic.

Salt and pepper

Sugar

Chopped fresh parsley

1. Heat 1 tablespoon oil in 12-inch skillet over medium-high heat until just smoking. Brown sausage, breaking up large pieces with wooden spoon, about 5 minutes. Using slotted spoon, transfer sausage to slow cooker.

2. Add onions, garlic, tomato paste, oregano, and pepper flakes to fat left in skillet and cook over medium heat until onions are softened and lightly browned, 5 to 7 minutes. Stir in wine, scraping up any browned bits, and simmer until thickened, about 5 minutes; transfer to slow cooker. Stir in crushed tomatoes, diced tomatoes, and tomato puree. Cover and cook until sauce is deeply flavored, 8 to 10 hours on low or 5 to 7 hours on high.

3. Using large spoon, skim fat from surface of sauce. Microwave bell peppers with remaining 1 tablespoon oil in bowl, stirring occasionally, until tender, about 5 minutes. Stir bell peppers into sauce and season with salt, pepper, and sugar to taste. Before serving, stir in 2 tablespoons parsley for every 6 cups sauce.

MAKE IT 5 WAYS MARINARA SAUCE

Classic Marinara Sauce

MAKES ABOUT 10 CUPS; ENOUGH FOR 2 POUNDS PASTA

`EASY PREP` `ALL DAY`

COOKING TIME 8 TO 10 HOURS ON LOW OR 5 TO 7 HOURS ON HIGH

SLOW COOKER SIZE 4 TO 7 QUARTS

There are many classic pasta sauces that are basically variations on marinara, and we wanted to come up with a formula for making them in the slow cooker, where the long simmering time would render them rich and flavorful. The biggest hurdle was choosing the right tomato products to create sauces that were neither watery nor too thick. Our solution was a combination of three different tomato products (paste, crushed, and puree). The concentrated products (paste and puree) provided strong, complex flavor without unwanted water—no need for evaporation. For all these sauces we microwaved onions and aromatics along with tomato paste to create a flavor-packed sauce base, adding other ingredients like anchovies, red pepper flakes, or pancetta to the mix to suit the particular sauce. Seasoning at the end, and adding additional herbs or other ingredients like capers and olives, provided the finishing touches.

1 CLASSIC MARINARA SAUCE

2 onions, chopped fine
6 garlic cloves, minced
2 tablespoons tomato paste
2 tablespoons extra-virgin olive oil
2 tablespoons minced fresh oregano or 2 teaspoons dried
Salt and pepper
2 (28-ounce) cans crushed tomatoes
1 (28-ounce) can tomato puree
½ cup dry red wine
2 teaspoons sugar, plus extra for seasoning
Chopped fresh basil

1. Microwave onions, garlic, tomato paste, oil, oregano, and 1 teaspoon salt in bowl, stirring occasionally, until onions are softened, about 5 minutes; transfer to slow cooker. Stir in tomatoes, tomato puree, and wine. Cover and cook until sauce is deeply flavored, 8 to 10 hours on low or 5 to 7 hours on high.

2. Stir sugar into sauce. Season with salt, pepper, and extra sugar to taste. Before serving, stir in 2 tablespoons basil for every 5 cups sauce.

2 AMATRICIANA SAUCE

2 onions, chopped fine
8 ounces pancetta, chopped fine
6 garlic cloves, minced
2 tablespoons tomato paste
2 tablespoons extra-virgin olive oil
2 tablespoons minced fresh oregano or 2 teaspoons dried
1 teaspoon red pepper flakes
Salt and pepper
2 (28-ounce) cans fire-roasted crushed tomatoes
1 (28-ounce) can tomato puree
½ cup dry red wine
2 ounces Pecorino Romano cheese, grated (1 cup)
2 teaspoons sugar, plus extra for seasoning
Chopped fresh basil

1. Microwave onions, pancetta, garlic, tomato paste, oil, oregano, pepper flakes, and 1 teaspoon salt in bowl, stirring occasionally, until onions are softened, about 5 minutes; transfer to slow cooker. Stir in tomatoes, tomato puree, and wine. Cover and cook until sauce is deeply flavored, 8 to 10 hours on low or 5 to 7 hours on high.

2. Stir Pecorino and sugar into sauce. Season with salt, pepper, and extra sugar to taste. Before serving, stir in 2 tablespoons basil for every 5 cups sauce.

3 PUTTANESCA SAUCE

2 onions, chopped fine

8 anchovy fillets, rinsed and minced

6 garlic cloves, minced

2 tablespoons tomato paste

2 tablespoons extra-virgin olive oil

1 tablespoon minced fresh oregano or 1 teaspoon dried

½ teaspoon red pepper flakes
   Salt and pepper

2 (28-ounce) cans crushed tomatoes

1 (28-ounce) can tomato puree

½ cup pitted kalamata olives, chopped

¼ cup capers, rinsed and minced

2 teaspoons sugar, plus extra for seasoning
   Chopped fresh basil

1. Microwave onions, anchovies, garlic, tomato paste, oil, oregano, pepper flakes, and ½ teaspoon salt in bowl, stirring occasionally, until onions are softened, about 5 minutes; transfer to slow cooker. Stir in tomatoes and tomato puree, cover, and cook until sauce is deeply flavored, 8 to 10 hours on low or 5 to 7 hours on high.

2. Stir olives, capers, and sugar into sauce. Season with salt, pepper, and extra sugar to taste. Before serving, stir in 2 tablespoons basil for every 5 cups sauce.

4 ARRABBIATA SAUCE

2 onions, chopped fine

6 anchovy fillets, rinsed and minced

6 garlic cloves, minced

2 tablespoons tomato paste

2 tablespoons extra-virgin olive oil

1 teaspoon red pepper flakes
   Salt and pepper

2 (28-ounce) cans crushed tomatoes

1 (28-ounce) can tomato puree

¼ cup pepperoncini, stemmed and minced

2 teaspoons sugar, plus extra for seasoning
   Chopped fresh basil

1. Microwave onions, anchovies, garlic, tomato paste, oil, pepper flakes, and 1 teaspoon salt in bowl, stirring occasionally, until onions are softened, about 5 minutes; transfer to slow cooker. Stir in tomatoes, tomato puree, and pepperoncini. Cover and cook until sauce is deeply flavored, 8 to 10 hours on low or 5 to 7 hours on high.

2. Stir sugar into sauce and season with salt, pepper, and extra sugar to taste. Before serving, stir in 2 tablespoons basil for every 5 cups sauce.

5 VODKA CREAM SAUCE

2 onions, chopped fine

8 garlic cloves, minced

2 tablespoons tomato paste

2 tablespoons extra-virgin olive oil

1 tablespoon minced fresh oregano or 1 teaspoon dried

½ teaspoon red pepper flakes
   Salt and pepper

2 (28-ounce) cans crushed tomatoes

1 (28-ounce) can tomato puree

½ cup vodka

1 cup heavy cream

1 ounce Parmesan cheese, grated (½ cup)

2 teaspoons sugar, plus extra for seasoning
   Chopped fresh basil

1. Microwave onions, garlic, tomato paste, oil, oregano, pepper flakes, and 1 teaspoon salt in bowl, stirring occasionally, until onions are softened, about 5 minutes; transfer to slow cooker. Stir in tomatoes, tomato puree, and vodka. Cover and cook until sauce is deeply flavored, 8 to 10 hours on low or 5 to 7 hours on high.

2. Stir cream, Parmesan, and sugar into sauce. Season with salt, pepper, and extra sugar to taste. Before serving, stir in 2 tablespoons basil for every 5 cups sauce.

Rustic Sausage, Lentil, and Swiss Chard Sauce

MAKES ABOUT 8 CUPS; ENOUGH FOR 1 POUND PASTA `ALL DAY`

COOKING TIME 9 TO 11 HOURS ON LOW OR 6 TO 8 HOURS ON HIGH

SLOW COOKER SIZE 4 TO 7 QUARTS

WHY THIS RECIPE WORKS Pasta and lentils are a classic pairing—add sausage and Swiss chard and you have the ultimate cold-weather pasta dish: earthy, deeply flavored, and totally satisfying. To build flavor into this humble dish, we started by browning Italian sausage and then sautéing the aromatics in the fat left in the skillet. This gave us a chance to build a flour-thickened sauce, which formed the base of this dish. Added at the end, Swiss chard retained its earthy flavor and color. We prefer French green lentils, or *lentilles du Puy*, for this recipe, but it will work with any type of lentil except red or yellow.

- 1 tablespoon extra-virgin olive oil
- 1 pound hot or sweet Italian sausage, casings removed
- 2 onions, chopped fine
- 2 carrots, peeled and chopped
- 1 celery rib, minced
- ⅓ cup all-purpose flour
- 6 garlic cloves, minced
- 1 tablespoon minced fresh oregano or 1 teaspoon dried
- 5 cups chicken broth
- ½ cup dry white wine
- ¾ cup French green lentils, picked over and rinsed
- 2 bay leaves
- 1 pound Swiss chard, stemmed and cut into ½-inch pieces
  Salt and pepper

1. Heat oil in 12-inch skillet over medium-high heat until just smoking. Brown sausage, breaking up large pieces with wooden spoon, about 5 minutes. Using slotted spoon, transfer sausage to slow cooker.

2. Add onions, carrots, and celery to fat left in skillet and cook over medium heat until softened and lightly browned, 8 to 10 minutes. Stir in flour, garlic, and oregano and cook until fragrant, about 1 minute. Slowly stir in 1 cup broth and wine, scraping up any browned bits and smoothing out any lumps; transfer to slow cooker.

3. Stir remaining 4 cups broth, lentils, and bay leaves into slow cooker. Cover and cook until lentils are tender, 9 to 11 hours on low or 6 to 8 hours on high.

4. Discard bay leaves. Using large spoon, skim fat from surface of sauce. Gently stir in chard, cover, and cook on high until tender, 20 to 30 minutes. Season with salt and pepper to taste. Serve.

NOTES FROM THE TEST KITCHEN

Pairing Pasta Shapes and Sauces

Pairing a pasta shape with the right sauce might be an art form in Italy, but we think there's only one basic rule to follow: Thick, chunky sauces go with short pastas, and thin, smooth, or light sauces with strand pasta. Short tubular or molded pasta shapes do an excellent job of trapping chunky sauces. Sauces with very large chunks are best with large tubes such as rigatoni. Sauces with small chunks pair better with fusilli or penne. Long strands are best with smooth sauces or thinner sauces. In general, wider noodles, such as pappardelle and fettuccine, can support slightly chunkier sauces like Bolognese or ragu.

Braised Fennel and Turkey Sausage Sauce

MAKES ABOUT 8 CUPS; ENOUGH FOR 1 POUND PASTA `LIGHT`

COOKING TIME 4 TO 5 HOURS ON LOW OR 3 TO 4 HOURS ON HIGH

SLOW COOKER SIZE 4 TO 7 QUARTS

WHY THIS RECIPE WORKS We set out to create a hearty yet healthy creamy meat sauce in the slow cooker that married the rich flavor of sausage with aromatic fennel. We decided on turkey sausage, as it is leaner than other options but still has great flavor. In order to maximize this flavor, we got out the skillet to brown the meat, which provided welcome savory and rich undertones. Keeping things streamlined, we moved on to cook the carrots and fennel in the leftover fat of the sausage, which enhanced their already-bold flavors. To make sure we got every last drop of that flavor, we sprinkled flour into the pan and stirred it around with the vegetables. This also helped thicken our sauce. Deglazing with a little broth and white wine allowed us to scrape up any flavorful browned bits in the pan before we transferred everything to the slow cooker. Finishing the sauce with just a quarter-cup of cream added extra richness while keeping it relatively lean. Minced fresh tarragon and orange zest complemented the flavors of the sausage and fennel, and added fresh notes.

- 1 tablespoon extra-virgin olive oil
- 1 pound hot or sweet Italian turkey sausage, casings removed
- 2 fennel bulbs, ¼ cup fronds minced, stalks discarded, bulbs halved, cored, and sliced ¼ inch thick
- 2 carrots, peeled and chopped
- ⅓ cup all-purpose flour
- 4 garlic cloves, minced

Pinch red pepper flakes
3 cups chicken broth
¼ cup dry white wine
1 bay leaf
¼ cup heavy cream
1 tablespoon grated orange zest
1 tablespoon minced fresh tarragon
Salt and pepper

1. Heat oil in Dutch oven over medium-high heat until just smoking. Brown sausage, breaking up large pieces with wooden spoon, about 5 minutes. Using slotted spoon, transfer sausage to slow cooker.

2. Add fennel and carrots to fat left in pot and cook over medium heat until softened and lightly browned, 8 to 10 minutes. Stir in flour, garlic, and pepper flakes and cook until fragrant, about 1 minute. Slowly stir in 1 cup broth and wine, scraping up any browned bits and smoothing out any lumps; transfer to slow cooker.

3. Stir remaining 2 cups broth and bay leaf into slow cooker. Cover and cook until sausage is tender, 4 to 5 hours on low or 3 to 4 hours on high.

4. Discard bay leaf. Stir cream, orange zest, tarragon, and reserved fennel fronds into sauce. Season with salt and pepper to taste. Serve.

Bolognese Sauce

MAKES ABOUT 14 CUPS; ENOUGH FOR 3 POUNDS PASTA

`ALL DAY`

COOKING TIME 9 TO 10 HOURS ON LOW OR 6 TO 7 HOURS ON HIGH

SLOW COOKER SIZE 5 TO 7 QUARTS

WHY THIS RECIPE WORKS Unlike meat sauces in which tomatoes dominate, a Bolognese sauce is all about the meat, with the tomatoes in a supporting role. We wanted an easy big-batch recipe with all the flavor and rich meatiness of traditional versions, but without all the work required to incorporate first the milk and then the wine into the meat, not to mention the long simmering time. To build a flavorful base, we sautéed the aromatics in butter and then deglazed the pan with white wine. As for the meat, meatloaf mix, with its mixture of ground beef, pork, and veal, was a simple solution. The problem was how to incorporate the dairy that gives Bolognese its hallmark richness and appeal. To tenderize the meat, we tried something unconventional: a panade, a mixture of bread and milk—but here we used cream instead for extra richness. This worked perfectly—we simply mixed the meat and the panade and added it raw to the slow cooker. At the end of hours of hands-off cooking, we had a rich Bolognese with concentrated

This hands-off Bolognese sauce is a godsend for busy home cooks—go ahead and stock your freezer with it!

flavor and a tender texture that rivaled our stovetop version. And better yet, this version could cook all day and gave us enough for a crowd or batches to freeze for busy nights. If you cannot find meatloaf mix, substitute 1½ pounds 85 percent lean ground beef and 1½ pounds ground pork.

3 tablespoons unsalted butter
1 onion, chopped fine
1 carrot, peeled and chopped fine
¼ cup minced celery
¼ cup tomato paste
3 garlic cloves, minced
1 teaspoon minced fresh thyme or ¼ teaspoon dried
½ cup dry white wine
3 slices hearty white sandwich bread, torn into 1-inch pieces
1 cup heavy cream
Salt and pepper
3 pounds meatloaf mix
2 (28-ounce) cans crushed tomatoes

1. Melt butter in 12-inch skillet over medium heat. Add onion, carrot, and celery and cook until softened and lightly browned, 8 to 10 minutes. Stir in tomato paste, garlic, and thyme and cook until fragrant, about 1 minute. Stir in wine, scraping up any browned bits; transfer to slow cooker.

2. Mash bread, cream, ½ teaspoon salt, and ½ teaspoon pepper into paste in large bowl using fork. Add meatloaf mix and knead with hands until well combined. Stir meatloaf mixture and tomatoes into slow cooker until combined. Cover and cook until meat is tender, 9 to 10 hours on low or 6 to 7 hours on high.

3. Using large spoon, skim fat from surface of sauce. Break up any remaining large pieces of meat with spoon. Season with salt and pepper to taste. Serve.

Short Ribs and Red Wine Sauce

MAKES ABOUT 12 CUPS; ENOUGH FOR 2 POUNDS PASTA

`ALL DAY`

COOKING TIME 8 TO 10 HOURS ON LOW OR 5 TO 7 HOURS ON HIGH

SLOW COOKER SIZE 4 TO 7 QUARTS

WHY THIS RECIPE WORKS The classic pairing of short ribs and red wine sauce struck us as the perfect basis for a slow-cooker pasta sauce. Here boneless short ribs were cooked until tender and shreddable in a rich red wine–based sauce. To build our sauce we first sautéed aromatics (onions, carrots, celery, garlic, and tomato paste), then deglazed the pan with a healthy dose of red wine. To further complement the rich flavor of the meat and wine, we stirred diced tomatoes and tomato puree into the slow cooker, which gave our sauce just the right body and flavor. At the end of cooking we simply shredded the meat and stirred in some parsley before serving the sauce over our favorite pasta.

  2 tablespoons extra-virgin olive oil
  2 onions, chopped fine
  2 carrots, peeled and chopped fine
  1 celery rib, minced
  ¼ cup tomato paste
  6 garlic cloves, minced
  ½ cup dry red wine
  1 (28-ounce) can diced tomatoes, drained
  1 (28-ounce) can tomato puree
  2 bay leaves

We brown the aromatics for this rich sauce but add the short ribs directly to the slow cooker to braise until tender.

2½ pounds boneless English-style short ribs, trimmed and cut into 1½-inch pieces
    Salt and pepper
    Chopped fresh parsley

1. Heat oil in 12-inch skillet over medium heat until shimmering. Add onions, carrots, and celery and cook until softened and lightly browned, 8 to 10 minutes. Stir in tomato paste and garlic and cook until fragrant, about 1 minute. Stir in wine, scraping up any browned bits; transfer to slow cooker.

2. Stir tomatoes, tomato puree, and bay leaves into slow cooker. Season short ribs with salt and pepper and nestle into slow cooker. Cover and cook until beef is tender, 8 to 10 hours on low or 5 to 7 hours on high.

3. Discard bay leaves. Using large spoon, skim fat from surface of sauce. Using potato masher, smash beef until coarsely shredded. Season with salt and pepper to taste. Before serving, stir in 2 tablespoons parsley for every 6 cups sauce.

Beef Ragu with Warm Spices

MAKES ABOUT 6 CUPS; ENOUGH FOR 1 POUND PASTA

EASY PREP **ALL DAY**

COOKING TIME 8 TO 9 HOURS ON LOW OR 5 TO 6 HOURS
ON HIGH

SLOW COOKER SIZE 4 TO 7 QUARTS

WHY THIS RECIPE WORKS Making a true long-simmered Italian meat sauce requires tending the stovetop for hours—so we decided to move ours to the slow cooker. Boneless beef short ribs turned meltingly tender after several hours of low, slow cooking and were easy enough to break apart into fork-friendly pieces right in the slow cooker once they were done. Onion and garlic provided essential aromatic notes, and a generous amount of tomato paste—2 tablespoons—added depth of flavor. To infuse our sauce with warmth, we included cinnamon and cloves, blooming them in the microwave with the aromatics. Tomato puree ensured that our sauce had the right consistency. Though untraditional in pasta sauce, a big dose of soy sauce enhanced the meaty flavor of our ragu. At the end of cooking we stirred in some chopped parsley for a fresh finish. No one would ever guess that this rich-tasting sauce was so easy to make.

- 1 onion, chopped fine
- 2 tablespoons tomato paste
- 1 tablespoon extra-virgin olive oil
- 2 garlic cloves, minced
- ⅛ teaspoon ground cinnamon
  Pinch ground cloves
- 1 (28-ounce) can tomato puree
- 2 tablespoons soy sauce
  Salt and pepper
- 1½ pounds boneless English-style short ribs, trimmed
  and cut into 1½-inch pieces
- ¼ cup chopped fresh parsley

1. Microwave onion, tomato paste, oil, garlic, cinnamon, and cloves in bowl, stirring occasionally, until onion is softened, about 5 minutes; transfer to slow cooker. Stir in tomato puree, soy sauce, 1 teaspoon salt, and ½ teaspoon pepper. Season short ribs with salt and pepper and nestle into slow cooker. Cover and cook until beef is tender, 8 to 9 hours on low or 5 to 6 hours on high.

2. Using large spoon, skim fat from surface of sauce. Using potato masher, smash beef until coarsely shredded. Stir in parsley and season with salt and pepper to taste. Serve.

NOTES FROM THE TEST KITCHEN

Cooking Pasta 101

Cooking pasta seems simple, but perfect pasta takes some finesse. Here's how we do it in the test kitchen.

USE PLENTY OF WATER To prevent sticking, you'll need 4 quarts of water to cook up to 1 pound of dried pasta. Pasta leaches starch as it cooks; without plenty of water to dilute it, the starch will coat the noodles and they will stick. Use a pot with at least a 6-quart capacity so that the water won't boil over.

SALT THE WATER Adding salt to the pasta cooking water is essential; it seasons the pasta and adds flavor. Add 1 tablespoon of salt per 4 quarts of water. Be sure to add the salt with the pasta, not before, so it will dissolve and not stain the pot.

SKIP THE OIL It's a myth that adding oil to pasta cooking water prevents the pasta from sticking together as it cooks. Adding oil to cooking water just creates a slick on the surface of the water, doing nothing for the pasta. And after you drain the pasta, the oil prevents the pasta sauce from adhering. To prevent pasta from sticking, simply stir the pasta for a minute or two when you add it to the boiling water, then stir occasionally while it's cooking.

CHECK OFTEN FOR DONENESS The timing instructions given on the package are almost always too long and will result in mushy, overcooked pasta. Tasting is the best way to check for doneness. We typically prefer pasta cooked al dente, when it still has a little bite left in the center.

RESERVE SOME WATER Reserve about ½ cup cooking water before draining the pasta—the water is flavorful and can help loosen a thick sauce.

DON'T RINSE Drain the pasta in a colander, but don't rinse the pasta; it washes away starch and makes the pasta taste watery. Do let a little cooking water cling to the cooked pasta to help the sauce adhere.

SAUCE IN THE POT Return the drained pasta to the now-empty pot, add the sauce, and toss using tongs or a pasta fork. Add pasta cooking water as needed until the sauce reaches the proper consistency. Saucing pasta in the pot ensures evenly coated, hot pasta.

Beef and Onion Ragu

MAKES ABOUT 12 CUPS; ENOUGH FOR 2 POUNDS PASTA

`ALL DAY`

COOKING TIME 8 TO 10 HOURS ON LOW OR 5 TO 7 HOURS ON HIGH

SLOW COOKER SIZE 4 TO 7 QUARTS

WHY THIS RECIPE WORKS We capitalized on the slow cooker's low, slow, moist cooking environment to make this meaty peasant-style pasta sauce. The long simmer that is required to break down the collagen and melt the fatty pockets of chuck-eye roast is easy work in the slow cooker. To ensure that the mixture didn't become too soupy, we drew excess water out of the onions before adding them to the pot.

- 2 pounds onions, chopped
  Salt and pepper
- 2 ounces pancetta, chopped
- 2 ounces salami, chopped
- 1 small carrot, peeled and chopped
- 1 small celery rib, chopped
- ⅓ cup dry white wine
- ⅓ cup water
- ¼ cup extra-virgin olive oil
- 2 tablespoons tomato paste
- 1 tablespoon dried oregano
- 1 pound boneless beef chuck-eye roast, trimmed and cut into 1½-inch pieces
- 2 ounces Pecorino Romano cheese, grated (1 cup)

1. Working in batches, pulse onions in food processor until finely chopped, about 15 pulses, scraping down sides of bowl as needed; transfer to large bowl. Stir in ¼ teaspoon salt, cover, and microwave for 5 minutes. Drain onions in fine-mesh strainer, pressing with rubber spatula to extract excess liquid; transfer to slow cooker.

2. Process pancetta, salami, carrot, and celery in now-empty processor until ground to paste, about 45 seconds, scraping down sides of bowl as needed; transfer to slow cooker. Stir in wine, water, 2 tablespoons oil, tomato paste, oregano, ¾ teaspoon salt, and ½ teaspoon pepper until thoroughly combined.

3. Season beef with salt and pepper and stir into slow cooker. Cover and cook until beef is tender, 8 to 10 hours on low or 5 to 7 hours on high.

4. Using potato masher, smash beef until coarsely shredded. Stir in Pecorino and remaining 2 tablespoons oil. Season with salt and pepper to taste. Serve.

To make Sunday Gravy in the slow cooker we turned to country-style spareribs, flank steak, and Italian sausage.

Italian Sunday Gravy

MAKES ABOUT 16 CUPS; ENOUGH FOR 3 POUNDS PASTA

`ALL DAY`

COOKING TIME 9 TO 10 HOURS ON LOW OR 6 TO 7 HOURS ON HIGH

SLOW COOKER SIZE 5 TO 7 QUARTS

WHY THIS RECIPE WORKS We love the flavor and heartiness of Sunday gravy, but not the laundry list of ingredients or the hours of stovetop monitoring. For a streamlined recipe, we turned to our slow cooker and narrowed the meat selection down to three: flank steak, for meaty flavor; country-style spareribs, for porky, fall-off-the-bone meat; and sausage, for its spicy, sweet kick. Using the flavorful drippings left behind from browning the sausage to sauté our aromatics infused the whole dish with flavor. And a combination of drained diced tomatoes, tomato puree, and tomato paste ensured a rich, thick sauce.

- 1 tablespoon extra-virgin olive oil
- 2 pounds hot or sweet Italian sausage
- 2 onions, chopped fine

1 (6 ounce) can tomato paste
12 garlic cloves, minced
2 tablespoons minced fresh oregano or 2 teaspoons dried
½ cup dry red wine
1 (28-ounce) can diced tomatoes, drained
1 (28-ounce) can tomato puree
2 pounds bone-in country-style pork ribs, trimmed
1½ pounds flank steak, trimmed
Salt and pepper
Chopped fresh basil

1. Heat oil in Dutch oven over medium-high heat until just smoking. Brown half of sausage on all sides, about 5 minutes; transfer to slow cooker. Repeat with remaining sausage; transfer to slow cooker.

2. Add onions to fat left in pot and cook over medium heat until softened and lightly browned, 5 to 7 minutes. Stir in tomato paste, garlic, and oregano and cook until fragrant, about 1 minute. Stir in wine, scraping up any browned bits; transfer to slow cooker. Stir in tomatoes and tomato puree.

3. Season spareribs and steak with salt and pepper and nestle into slow cooker. Cover and cook until pork and beef are tender and fork slips easily in and out of meat, 9 to 10 hours on low or 6 to 7 hours on high.

4. Transfer sausages, spareribs, and steak to cutting board and let cool slightly. Using 2 forks, shred ribs and steak into rough 1-inch pieces; discard fat and bones. Slice sausages in half crosswise.

5. Using large spoon, skim fat from surface of sauce. Stir in shredded meat and sausages and season with salt and pepper to taste. Before serving, stir in 2 tablespoons basil for every 8 cups sauce.

NOTES FROM THE TEST KITCHEN

Freezing Pasta Sauce

One of the greatest things about making a large batch of pasta sauce is that you can freeze it in smaller batches for easy last-minute dinners in the future. We've found that the best way to freeze pasta sauce is to spoon it into zipper-lock freezer bags, then lay the bags flat in the freezer to save space. To reheat the sauce, simply cut away the bag, place the frozen block of sauce in a large pot with several tablespoons of water, and reheat gently over medium-low heat, stirring occasionally, until hot. Alternatively, you can microwave the frozen sauce in a covered bowl, stirring occasionally, until hot. Before serving, stir in any additional fresh herbs, if needed, and season with salt and pepper to taste.

SIMPLE SIDES

GARLIC BREAD
SERVES 8
A 12 by 5-inch loaf of Italian bread from the bakery section of the supermarket has a soft, thin crust and fine crumb, and works best in this recipe. We do not recommend using a rustic or crusty artisan-style loaf. A rasp-style grater makes quick work of turning the garlic into a paste. If you bake the bread on a dark baking sheet, start checking for doneness 4 minutes after flipping the bread in step 3.

1 teaspoon garlic powder
1 teaspoon water
8 tablespoons unsalted butter
½ teaspoon salt
⅛ teaspoon cayenne pepper
1 tablespoon garlic, minced to paste
1 (1-pound) loaf soft Italian bread, halved horizontally

1. Adjust oven rack to lower-middle position and heat oven to 450 degrees. Combine garlic powder and water in medium bowl. Add 4 tablespoons butter, salt, and cayenne to bowl; set aside.

2. Place remaining 4 tablespoons butter in small bowl and microwave, covered, until melted, about 30 seconds. Stir in garlic and continue to microwave, covered, until mixture is bubbling around edges, about 1 minute, stirring halfway through. Transfer garlic-butter mixture to bowl with garlic powder mixture and whisk together until it forms homogenous loose paste. (If mixture melts, set aside until it solidifies before using.)

3. Spread cut sides of loaf evenly with butter mixture. Transfer bread cut side up to rimmed baking sheet. Bake until butter has melted into surface of bread and bread is hot, 3 to 4 minutes. Remove baking sheet from oven. Flip bread, cut side down, place second rimmed baking sheet on top and gently press. Return bread to oven, with second baking sheet on top of bread, and continue to bake until cut side of bread is golden brown and crisp, 8 to 12 minutes longer, rotating bread halfway through baking. Transfer bread to cutting board. Using serrated knife, cut each half into 8 slices and serve immediately.

Meatballs must be partially cooked before they go into the slow cooker—otherwise they will fall apart.

Meatballs and Marinara

MAKES 24 MEATBALLS AND ABOUT 10 CUPS SAUCE;
ENOUGH FOR 2 POUNDS PASTA
COOKING TIME 4 TO 5 HOURS ON LOW
SLOW COOKER SIZE 5 TO 7 QUARTS

WHY THIS RECIPE WORKS For our slow-cooker spaghetti and meatballs, we wanted nothing short of great meatballs: crusty and dark brown on the outside, soft and moist on the inside. We first microwaved the aromatics (including tomato paste, olive oil, and oregano) to bloom their flavors, which gave the sauce a meaty base. Then we combined half of the onion mixture with crushed tomatoes, tomato puree, and wine to create a rich, flavorful sauce in which to gently braise the meatballs. To punch up the flavor of the meatballs, we added the remaining half of the onion mixture. Adding a simple panade (milk and bread mixed to a paste) kept the meat moist and prevented it from getting tough. The addition of egg yolks was also important for both texture and

flavor; their fats and emulsifiers contributed moisture and richness. Before placing the meatballs in the slow cooker, we found that roasting them on a wire rack for about 10 minutes allowed for even browning and a firm exterior texture; this enabled them to hold their shape during the long cooking time as they absorbed the flavor of sauce while lending even more meaty flavor to it. At the end of cooking, we stirred in a little sugar to provide subtle sweetness, and some chopped basil to add just the right amount of freshness.

    2 onions, chopped fine
    6 garlic cloves, minced
    2 tablespoons tomato paste
    2 tablespoons extra-virgin olive oil
    2 tablespoons minced fresh oregano or
       2 teaspoons dried
       Salt and pepper
    2 (28-ounce) cans crushed tomatoes
    1 (28-ounce) can tomato puree
  ½ cup dry red wine
    2 slices hearty white sandwich bread,
       torn into 1-inch pieces
  ⅓ cup whole milk
    1 ounce Parmesan cheese, grated (½ cup)
  ¼ cup minced fresh parsley
    2 large egg yolks
    2 pounds 85 percent lean ground beef
    2 teaspoons sugar, plus extra for seasoning
       Chopped fresh basil

1. Adjust oven rack to middle position and heat oven to 475 degrees. Set wire rack in aluminum foil–lined rimmed baking sheet and coat with vegetable oil spray.

2. Microwave onions, garlic, tomato paste, oil, oregano, and ½ teaspoon salt in bowl, stirring occasionally, until onions are softened, about 5 minutes. Transfer half of onion mixture to slow cooker. Stir in tomatoes, tomato puree, and wine.

3. Mash bread, milk, and ½ teaspoon salt to paste in large bowl using fork. Stir in remaining onion mixture, Parmesan, parsley, egg yolks, and ½ teaspoon pepper. Add ground beef and knead with hands until well combined. Pinch off and roll mixture into 1½-inch meatballs (about 24 meatballs) and arrange on prepared rack. Bake until firm and no longer pink, about 10 minutes.

4. Gently nestle meatballs into slow cooker, cover, and cook until meatballs are tender, 4 to 5 hours on low. Stir in sugar and season with salt, pepper, and extra sugar to taste. Before serving, stir in 2 tablespoons basil for every 5 cups sauce.

This fresh take on meatballs and sauce has chopped spinach in the meatballs and handfuls of spinach in the sauce.

Meatballs Florentine

MAKES 12 MEATBALLS AND ABOUT 6 CUPS SAUCE;
ENOUGH FOR 1 POUND PASTA
COOKING TIME 4 TO 5 HOURS ON LOW
SLOW COOKER SIZE 4 TO 7 QUARTS

WHY THIS RECIPE WORKS This twist on classic spaghetti and meatballs features tender meatballs made ultraflavorful with a mixture of spinach, Parmesan, and garlic, and a robust marinara to which we also added fresh spinach. A panade, which is bread and milk combined to form a paste, was added to the meat to help keep it moist and prevent it from getting tough. Raw meatballs added directly to the sauce have a tendency to disintegrate while in the slow cooker, so we first gave them a quick spin in the microwave to help them firm up. For our marinara, we needed three tomato products to achieve the right balance of flavor and texture: chunky crushed tomatoes, smooth tomato puree, and rich tomato paste. Stirring in more spinach at the end kept the sauce fresh and bright, resulting in a colorful and delicious sauce to accompany our alternative take on classic meatballs.

1 (28-ounce) can crushed tomatoes
1 (14.5-ounce) can tomato puree
2 tablespoons tomato paste
6 garlic cloves, minced
2 teaspoons sugar
  Salt and pepper
½ teaspoon red pepper flakes
1 slice hearty white sandwich bread, torn into 1-inch pieces
¼ cup whole milk
5 ounces (5 cups) baby spinach, 1 cup chopped
¼ cup grated Parmesan cheese
1 pound 85 percent lean ground beef
¼ cup chopped fresh basil

1. Combine tomatoes, tomato puree, tomato paste, two-thirds of garlic, sugar, 1 teaspoon salt, and ¼ teaspoon pepper flakes in slow cooker.

2. Mash bread, milk, and ¼ teaspoon salt to paste in large bowl using fork. Stir in chopped spinach, Parmesan, remaining garlic, and remaining ¼ teaspoon pepper flakes. Add ground beef and knead with hands until well combined. Pinch off and roll mixture into 1½-inch meatballs (about 12 meatballs) and arrange on large plate.

3. Microwave meatballs until firm and no longer pink, about 5 minutes. Gently nestle meatballs into slow cooker, adding any accumulated juices. Cover and cook until meatballs are tender, 4 to 5 hours on low.

4. Gently stir in remaining 4 cups spinach, 1 handful at a time, and let sit until wilted, about 5 minutes. Stir in basil and season with salt and pepper to taste. Serve.

NOTES FROM THE TEST KITCHEN

Buying Spaghetti

Besides convenience, the other draw of dried spaghetti is that it's inexpensive—or at least it used to be. When we recently browsed the options at the supermarket, we discovered that while you can still pick up a 1-pound package for as little as a dollar and change, you can also spend more than three times that amount. How much better could a pound of pasta costing more than $4 really be? To answer that question, we tasted several products ranging in price from $1.39 to $4.17 per pound. So when it comes to spaghetti, do you get what you pay for? Not necessarily: Our winner, **De Cecco Spaghetti No. 12**, stood out for its particularly good texture and flavor—and at $1.39 a pound, it was one of the two least expensive spaghettis we tasted.

These turkey meatballs get big flavor from chopped sun-dried tomatoes plus their packing oil.

Sun-Dried Tomato and Basil Turkey Meatballs

MAKES 24 MEATBALLS AND ABOUT 10 CUPS SAUCE;
ENOUGH FOR 2 POUNDS PASTA
COOKING TIME 4 TO 5 HOURS ON LOW
SLOW COOKER SIZE 5 TO 7 QUARTS

WHY THIS RECIPE WORKS Turkey meatballs often turn out bland and dry, so we set out to develop a recipe that rivaled those made from beef or pork in terms of tenderness and flavor. To start we wanted to pack them with a bright savoriness, and decided to try adding a hefty dose of chopped basil, sun-dried tomatoes, and Parmesan along with the usual aromatics. We microwaved a large amount of aromatics first, thinking we'd split it between the sauce and the meatballs. This worked perfectly, infusing their flavors throughout the whole dish. The addition of a panade (milk and bread mixed to a paste) and egg yolks helped bind the turkey mixture while keeping it moist and tender. But if we tried to place our meatballs directly into the slow cooker, they were apt to fall apart during the long cooking time. An extra step solved the problem: just 10 minutes in the oven browned them perfectly and

firmed them up just enough to withstand the simmering time in the slow cooker, where they imparted flavor to the sauce. The sauce was supersimple to make—we simply combined crushed tomatoes, tomato puree, and wine, along with half the onion mix. Sugar stirred in at the end balanced out any sharpness in the sauce, and chopped basil gave the meatballs a fresh finishing touch. Be sure to use ground turkey, not ground turkey breast (also labeled 99 percent fat-free), in this recipe.

2 onions, chopped fine
6 garlic cloves, minced
2 tablespoons tomato paste
½ cup oil-packed sun-dried tomatoes, chopped fine, plus 2 tablespoons packing oil
2 tablespoons minced fresh oregano or 2 teaspoons dried
½ teaspoon red pepper flakes
Salt and pepper
2 (28-ounce) cans crushed tomatoes
1 (28-ounce) can tomato puree
½ cup dry red wine
2 slices hearty white sandwich bread, torn into 1-inch pieces
⅓ cup whole milk
1 ounce Parmesan cheese, grated (½ cup)
¼ cup chopped fresh basil, plus extra for serving
2 large egg yolks
2 pounds ground turkey
2 teaspoons sugar, plus extra for seasoning

1. Adjust oven rack to middle position and heat oven to 475 degrees. Set wire rack in aluminum foil–lined rimmed baking sheet and coat with vegetable oil spray.

2. Microwave onions, garlic, tomato paste, tomato packing oil, oregano, pepper flakes, and ½ teaspoon salt in bowl, stirring occasionally, until onions are softened, about 5 minutes. Transfer half of onion mixture to slow cooker. Stir in tomatoes, tomato puree, and wine.

3. Mash bread, milk, and ½ teaspoon salt to paste in large bowl using fork. Stir in sun-dried tomatoes, remaining onion mixture, Parmesan, basil, egg yolks, and ½ teaspoon pepper. Add ground turkey and knead with hands until well combined. Pinch off and roll mixture into 1½-inch meatballs (about 24 meatballs) and arrange on prepared rack. Bake until firm and no longer pink, about 10 minutes.

4. Gently nestle meatballs into slow cooker, cover, and cook until meatballs are tender, 4 to 5 hours on low. Stir in sugar and season with salt, pepper, and extra sugar to taste. Before serving, stir in 2 tablespoons basil for every 5 cups sauce.

The combo of cremini and dried porcini mushrooms delivers undeniable flavor in this satisfying shredded chicken sauce.

Chicken and Mushroom Sauce

MAKES ABOUT 8 CUPS; ENOUGH FOR 1 POUND PASTA **LIGHT**
COOKING TIME 4 TO 5 HOURS ON LOW
SLOW COOKER SIZE 4 TO 7 QUARTS

WHY THIS RECIPE WORKS This dish was inspired by the classic flavors of chicken cacciatore, a savory Italian braise that includes mushrooms, tomatoes, onions, and herbs. We didn't skimp on the mushrooms, settling on two bold types to ensure a hearty sauce: cremini and porcini. Microwaving the cremini with our aromatics—onion, garlic, and tomato paste—was an easy way to bloom the aromatics and soften the mushrooms before adding them to the slow cooker. For the base of our sauce we chose crushed tomatoes, which allowed the earthiness of the mushrooms to shine through. Boneless, skinless chicken thighs gave the sauce richness, and they were moist enough to shred easily by the end of the cooking time. Finally, a sprinkling of chopped parsley, stirred in just before serving, contributed a hit of freshness.

1 pound cremini mushrooms, trimmed and sliced ¼ inch thick
1 onion, halved and sliced thin
2 tablespoons tomato paste
6 garlic cloves, minced
1 tablespoon extra-virgin olive oil
¼ ounce dried porcini mushrooms, rinsed and minced
1 (28-ounce) can crushed tomatoes
Salt and pepper
1½ pounds boneless, skinless chicken thighs, trimmed
2 tablespoons chopped fresh parsley

1. Microwave cremini mushrooms, onion, tomato paste, garlic, oil, and porcini mushrooms in covered bowl, stirring occasionally, until vegetables are softened, about 10 minutes; transfer to slow cooker. Stir in tomatoes, ½ teaspoon salt, and ½ teaspoon pepper. Season chicken with salt and pepper and nestle into slow cooker. Cover and cook until chicken is tender, 4 to 5 hours on low.

2. Transfer chicken to cutting board, let cool slightly, then pull apart into large chunks using 2 forks. Stir chicken into sauce and let sit until heated through, about 5 minutes. Stir in parsley and season with salt and pepper to taste. Serve.

NOTES FROM THE TEST KITCHEN

Mushrooms: Wash or Brush?

Culinary wisdom holds that raw mushrooms must never touch water, lest they soak up the liquid and become soggy. Many sources call for cleaning dirty mushrooms with a soft bristled brush or a damp cloth. These fussy techniques may be worth the effort if you plan to eat the mushrooms raw, but we wondered whether mushrooms destined for the sauté pan could be simply rinsed and patted dry. To test this, we submerged 6 ounces of white mushrooms in a bowl of water for 5 minutes. We drained and weighed the mushrooms and found that they had soaked up only ¼ ounce (about 1½ teaspoons) of water, not nearly enough to affect their texture. So when we plan to cook mushrooms, we don't bother with the brush. Instead, we place the mushrooms in a salad spinner, rinse the dirt and grit away with cold water, and spin to remove excess moisture.

This slow-cooker take on chicken, broccolini, and penne takes a fresher route to a satisfying pasta dinner.

Chicken and Broccolini Sauce

MAKES ABOUT 8 CUPS; ENOUGH FOR 1 POUND PASTA LIGHT
COOKING TIME 3 TO 4 HOURS ON LOW
SLOW COOKER SIZE 4 TO 7 QUARTS

WHY THIS RECIPE WORKS With its enticing combination of moist chicken, fresh broccolini, and sweet red bell pepper, this rich sauce perfectly complements pasta. We chose bone-in chicken breasts, which stayed moist throughout the cooking time and also added a deep chicken flavor to the sauce. To build the base, we microwaved the aromatics—onion and garlic—along with oregano, red pepper flakes, and a little olive oil. Then we added the chicken broth and the chicken. For a little more depth and brightness, we added a splash of white wine. And to thicken the sauce so that it would coat the pasta properly, we simply added a little tapioca at the outset. As this flavorful base simmered with the chicken, it took on a deep, complex flavor. Once the chicken was tender, we

removed it from the slow cooker, let it rest briefly, then shredded it into small pieces. Meanwhile, we microwaved the broccolini and then added it and some grated Parmesan to the sauce along with the chicken for a bright, fresh, and healthy pasta dinner.

 1 onion, chopped fine
 6 garlic cloves, minced
 2 tablespoons extra-virgin olive oil
 1 tablespoon minced fresh oregano or 1 teaspoon dried
   Salt and pepper
 ¼ teaspoon red pepper flakes
 2 cups chicken broth
 1 red bell pepper, stemmed, seeded, and cut into
   ½-inch pieces
 ¼ cup dry white wine
 2 tablespoons instant tapioca
 2 (12-ounce) bone-in split chicken breasts,
   skin removed, trimmed
 12 ounces broccolini, trimmed and cut into 1-inch pieces
 2 ounces Parmesan cheese, grated (1 cup)

1. Microwave onion, garlic, 1 tablespoon oil, oregano, ½ teaspoon salt, and pepper flakes in bowl, stirring occasionally, until onion is softened, about 5 minutes; transfer to slow cooker. Stir in broth, bell pepper, wine, and tapioca. Season chicken with salt and pepper and nestle into slow cooker. Cover and cook until chicken is tender, 3 to 4 hours on low.

2. Microwave broccolini and 1 tablespoon water in covered bowl, stirring occasionally, until tender, about 5 minutes. Drain broccolini.

3. Transfer chicken to cutting board, let cool slightly, then pull apart into large chunks using 2 forks; discard bones. Stir chicken and broccolini into sauce and let sit until heated through, about 5 minutes. Stir in Parmesan and remaining 1 tablespoon oil and season with salt and pepper to taste. Serve.

GRATING HARD CHEESE

When grating Parmesan and other hard cheeses, we use a rasp-style grater because it produces lighter, fluffier shreds of cheese that melt seamlessly into pasta dishes and sauces.

Shrimp Fra Diavolo Sauce

MAKES ABOUT 8 CUPS; ENOUGH FOR 1 POUND PASTA

`EASY PREP` `LIGHT` `ALL DAY`

COOKING TIME 8 TO 9 HOURS ON LOW OR 5 TO 6 HOURS ON HIGH

SLOW COOKER SIZE 4 TO 7 QUARTS

WHY THIS RECIPE WORKS Shrimp Fra Diavolo, a restaurant favorite, at first glance seems like an unlikely candidate for a slow-cooker recipe, but in truth it works exceedingly well. *Fra Diavolo* (which translates from Italian to "brother devil") is simply a super-spicy tomato sauce that is often paired with seafood. To create a tomato sauce with a definite kick, we gave traditional aromatics a boost with a heaping amount of garlic and red pepper flakes. We achieved fresh tomato flavor with a combination of crushed and diced tomatoes. White wine instead of red kept the sauce bright and light and over the long cooking time the flavors melded into a robust sauce. Because shrimp need only a brief moment to cook through, tossing them in right at the end allowed them to poach in the flavorful base in the time it took the pasta to cook on the stovetop. Parsley's earthiness finished off this garlicky and spicy sauce studded with sweet, plump shrimp. If using smaller or larger shrimp, be sure to adjust the cooking time as needed.

1 onion, chopped fine
6 garlic cloves, minced
2 tablespoons tomato paste
2 tablespoons extra-virgin olive oil
1 tablespoon minced fresh oregano or 1 teaspoon dried
½ teaspoon red pepper flakes
1 (28-ounce) can crushed tomatoes
1 (14.5-ounce) can diced tomatoes, drained
¼ cup dry white wine
2 teaspoons sugar
   Salt and pepper
1½ pounds large shrimp (26 to 30 per pound), peeled, deveined, and tails removed
¼ cup chopped fresh parsley

1. Microwave onion, garlic, tomato paste, 1 tablespoon oil, oregano, and pepper flakes in bowl, stirring occasionally, until onion is softened, about 5 minutes; transfer to slow cooker. Stir in crushed tomatoes, diced tomatoes, wine, sugar, and ½ teaspoon pepper. Cover and cook until sauce is deeply flavored, 8 to 9 hours on low or 5 to 6 hours on high.

2. Stir shrimp into sauce, cover, and cook on high until opaque throughout, 30 to 40 minutes. Stir in parsley and remaining 1 tablespoon oil, and season with salt and pepper to taste. Serve.

NOTES FROM THE TEST KITCHEN

All About Canned Tomatoes

Since canned tomatoes are processed at the height of freshness, they deliver more flavor than off-season fresh tomatoes. But with all the options lining supermarket shelves, it's not always clear what you should buy. We tested a variety of canned tomato products to determine the best uses for each.

WHOLE TOMATOES Whole tomatoes are peeled tomatoes packed in either their own juice or puree. They are best when fresh tomato flavor is a must. Whole tomatoes are quite soft and break down quickly when cooked. In taste tests, we preferred **Muir Glen** for their lively, fresh flavor.

DICED TOMATOES Diced tomatoes are peeled, machine-diced, and packed in either their own juice or puree. Many brands contain calcium chloride, a firming agent that helps the chunks maintain their shape. Diced tomatoes are best for rustic tomato sauces with a chunky texture, and in long-cooked stews and soups in which you want the tomatoes to hold their shape. We favor diced tomatoes packed in juice because they have a fresher flavor than those packed in puree; our favorite is **Hunt's**.

CRUSHED TOMATOES Crushed tomatoes are whole tomatoes ground very finely, then enriched with tomato puree. They work well in smoother sauces, and their thicker consistency makes them ideal when you want to make a sauce quickly. We like **Tuttorosso**, but you can also make your own by pulsing canned diced tomatoes in a food processor.

TOMATO PUREE Tomato puree is made from cooked tomatoes that have been strained to remove their seeds and skins. Tomato puree works well in long-simmered, smooth, thick sauces with a deep, hearty flavor. Our favorite brand is **Muir Glen Organic**.

TOMATO PASTE Tomato paste is tomato puree that has been cooked to remove almost all moisture. Because it's naturally full of glutamates, tomato paste brings out subtle depths and savory notes. We use it in a variety of recipes, including both long-simmered sauces and quicker-cooking dishes, to lend a deeper, well-rounded tomato flavor and color. Our preferred brand is **Goya**.

Even diehard meat eaters will tuck away this savory mushroom-based take on classic Bolognese.

Mushroom Bolognese

MAKES ABOUT 6 CUPS; ENOUGH FOR 2 POUNDS PASTA

VEG **LIGHT** **ALL DAY**

COOKING TIME 7 TO 8 HOURS ON LOW OR 4 TO 5 HOURS ON HIGH

SLOW COOKER SIZE 4 TO 7 QUARTS

WHY THIS RECIPE WORKS For a vegetarian take on classic Bolognese with long-cooked flavor, we turned to mushrooms, deciding on cremini for their firm texture and porcini for savory flavor. To keep things simple, we used the food processor to chop the cremini and the vegetables. Since mushrooms take on more flavor when browned, and because there is no opportunity for evaporation in a slow cooker, we sautéed them and the other vegetables in a skillet to drive off excess moisture and build flavor. We first tried tomato puree as the tomato base for our sauce, but we found it was a little too thick; the mushrooms required more liquid in which to cook. We discovered that processing whole peeled tomatoes gave us the extra liquid we needed while keeping the fresh tomato flavor. Finishing this hearty sauce with a little heavy cream helped smooth out any sharpness and gave it a nice creaminess, and parsley and lemon juice brightened it up.

2 pounds cremini mushrooms, trimmed and quartered
1 onion, chopped
1 carrot, peeled and chopped
1 (28-ounce) can whole peeled tomatoes
2 teaspoons extra-virgin olive oil
½ ounce dried porcini mushrooms, rinsed and minced
2 tablespoons tomato paste
3 garlic cloves, minced
1 tablespoon minced fresh oregano or 1 teaspoon dried
½ cup dry red wine
  Salt and pepper
1 teaspoon sugar
1 bay leaf
¼ cup heavy cream
1 tablespoon lemon juice
  Chopped fresh parsley

1. Working in batches, pulse cremini mushrooms in food processor until pieces are no larger than ½ inch, 5 to 7 pulses; transfer to large bowl. Pulse onion and carrot in now-empty processor until finely chopped, 5 to 7 pulses; transfer to bowl with mushrooms. Pulse tomatoes and their juice in again-empty processor until almost smooth, 6 to 8 pulses; set aside in separate bowl.

2. Heat oil in 12-inch skillet over medium heat until shimmering. Add processed vegetables and porcini mushrooms, cover, and cook until softened, about 5 minutes. Uncover and continue to cook until vegetables are dry and browned, 12 to 14 minutes. Stir in tomato paste, garlic, and oregano and cook until fragrant, about 1 minute. Stir in wine, scraping up any browned bits, and simmer until nearly evaporated, about 3 minutes; transfer to slow cooker.

3. Stir tomatoes, 1 teaspoon salt, sugar, ½ teaspoon pepper, and bay leaf into slow cooker. Cover and cook until sauce is deeply flavored, 7 to 8 hours on low or 4 to 5 hours on high.

4. Discard bay leaf. Stir in cream and lemon juice. Season with salt and pepper to taste. Before serving, stir in 2 tablespoons parsley for every 3 cups sauce.

Alla Norma Sauce

MAKES ABOUT 10 CUPS; ENOUGH FOR 2 POUNDS PASTA

COOKING TIME 5 TO 6 HOURS ON LOW OR 3 TO 4 HOURS ON HIGH

SLOW COOKER SIZE 4 TO 7 QUARTS

WHY THIS RECIPE WORKS *Rigatoni alla norma* is a pasta dish with a gutsy tomato sauce studded with chunks of eggplant. We tried adding the eggplant to the slow cooker without parcooking it, but we ended up with mushy, flavorless chunks of eggplant floating in our sauce. We found that a quick stint under the broiler after a toss with oil and our aromatics was all it took to rid the

Broiling the eggplant before adding it to the slow cooker gives this alla norma sauce just the right firm texture.

eggplant of moisture and add flavor. To build the base for our sauce, we started with crushed tomatoes and added tomato puree, which gave the sauce the right clingy consistency. For a spicy backbone, we included a generous amount of red pepper flakes. Anchovy fillets provided deep, savory flavor without unwanted fishiness. Fresh basil and olive oil added at the end rounded out the flavors of this easy sauce. This sauce is traditionally served on rigatoni and topped with shredded ricotta salata, a slightly aged ricotta cheese.

    3 pounds eggplant, cut into 1-inch pieces
    2 tablespoons extra-virgin olive oil, plus extra for serving
    6 garlic cloves, minced
 1½ tablespoons tomato paste
    1 tablespoon sugar
    1 (28-ounce) can crushed tomatoes
    1 (14.5-ounce) can tomato puree
    6 anchovy fillets, rinsed and minced
       Salt and pepper
  ¼ teaspoon red pepper flakes
       Chopped fresh basil

1. Adjust oven rack 6 inches from broiler element and heat broiler. Toss eggplant with oil, garlic, tomato paste, and sugar in bowl. Spread eggplant mixture evenly over aluminum foil–lined rimmed baking sheet. Broil eggplant until softened and beginning to brown, 10 to 12 minutes, rotating sheet halfway through broiling; transfer to slow cooker.

2. Stir tomatoes, tomato puree, anchovies, ¼ teaspoon salt, ¼ teaspoon pepper, and pepper flakes into slow cooker. Cover and cook until flavors meld and eggplant is tender, 5 to 6 hours on low or 3 to 4 hours on high. Season with salt and pepper to taste. Before serving, stir in 2 tablespoons basil and 1 tablespoon oil for every 5 cups sauce.

CUTTING UP EGGPLANT

1. To cut eggplant into tidy pieces, first cut eggplant crosswise into 1-inch-thick rounds.

2. Then cut each round into pieces as directed in recipe.

SOFT AND CHEESY BREADSTICKS
MAKES 12

Feel free to use your favorite pizza dough recipe here or purchase ready-made pizza dough from the local pizzeria or supermarket. This recipe can be easily doubled.

    1 pound pizza dough, room temperature
    2 tablespoons extra-virgin olive oil
  ¼ cup grated Parmesan cheese
       Salt and pepper

Adjust oven rack to middle position and heat oven to 400 degrees. Roll dough into 12 by 6-inch rectangle on lightly floured counter. Using pizza cutter or chef's knife, cut dough crosswise into 1-inch-wide strips. Arrange dough strips evenly on greased rimmed baking sheet, brush with oil, sprinkle with Parmesan, and season with salt and pepper. Bake until golden, about 20 minutes. Serve warm.

It takes only a little butter to make a satisfying sage sauce to pair with pasta, squash, and spinach.

Butternut Squash and Sage Sauce

MAKES ABOUT 6 CUPS; ENOUGH FOR 1 POUND PASTA   VEG
COOKING TIME 5 TO 6 HOURS ON LOW OR 3 TO 4 HOURS ON HIGH
SLOW COOKER SIZE 4 TO 7 QUARTS

WHY THIS RECIPE WORKS Pasta paired with butternut squash and a sage-infused butter sauce is always a winner, but often this dish loses its focus with too much butter overwhelming the delicate nuttiness of the squash. We were hoping to create a lighter and more brothy version of this sauce in the slow cooker. To start, we got out a skillet to create our base, sautéing the onion in butter, then adding the aromatics and flour. Once the aromatics were softened and the raw flavor cooked out of the flour, we deglazed the pan with broth and wine, making sure to scrape up any flavorful browned bits on the bottom of the pan. To this base we added more broth and the squash; as it simmered in the slow cooker, the mixture became superflavorful, making the perfect delicate sauce for the pasta. At the end of the cooking time we added spinach, which gave the dish a bright green color and healthy kick.

4 tablespoons unsalted butter
1 onion, chopped fine
3 tablespoons all-purpose flour
3 tablespoons minced fresh sage
2 garlic cloves, minced
¼ teaspoon red pepper flakes
2½ cups vegetable broth
¼ cup dry white wine
1½ pounds butternut squash, peeled, seeded, and cut into ½-inch pieces (4 cups)
Salt and pepper
3 ounces (3 cups) baby spinach
2 ounces Parmesan cheese, grated (1 cup)

1. Melt butter in 12-inch skillet over medium heat. Add onion and cook until softened and lightly browned, 5 to 7 minutes. Stir in flour, 1½ tablespoons sage, garlic, and pepper flakes and cook until fragrant, about 1 minute. Slowly whisk in 1 cup broth and wine, scraping up any browned bits and smoothing out any lumps; transfer to slow cooker.

2. Stir remaining 1½ cups broth, squash, ¾ teaspoon salt, and ¼ teaspoon pepper into slow cooker. Cover and cook until squash is tender, 5 to 6 hours on low or 3 to 4 hours on high.

3. Stir in spinach, Parmesan, and remaining 1½ tablespoons sage and toss until spinach is slightly wilted. Season with salt and pepper to taste. Serve.

This easy-to-prepare vegetarian pasta sauce packs a pound of kale into the mix along with two sliced fennel bulbs.

Braised Kale, Fennel, and Sun-Dried Tomato Sauce

MAKES ABOUT 4 CUPS; ENOUGH FOR 1 POUND PASTA

EASY PREP **VEG**

COOKING TIME 5 TO 6 HOURS ON LOW OR 3 TO 4 HOURS ON HIGH

SLOW COOKER SIZE 5 TO 7 QUARTS

WHY THIS RECIPE WORKS Pasta and braised kale are a popular pairing for a reason—the earthy, meaty notes of the tender greens add depth and flavor to the mild-tasting pasta, creating a simple yet incredibly satisfying dish. To prepare our kale for the slow cooker, we cut it into pieces and tossed it in along with chopped onion, minced garlic, and red pepper flakes. This combination tasted good, but swapping out the onion for fennel promised a more filling and flavorful dish. Rather than water, we used vegetable broth for our cooking liquid, which imparted salty, savory notes to our sauce. For some much-needed brightness, we added chopped sun-dried tomatoes. A big drizzle of extra-virgin olive oil along with some grated Parmesan enriched this fairly lean sauce, and toasted pine nuts offered a welcome crunch. We stirred these last ingredients in just before serving so that their flavors wouldn't dull in the slow cooker. Be sure to use high-quality extra-virgin olive oil here.

1 pound kale, stemmed and cut into 1-inch pieces
2 fennel bulbs, stalks discarded, bulbs halved, cored, and sliced ¼ inch thick
2 cups vegetable or chicken broth
1 cup oil-packed sun-dried tomatoes, rinsed, patted dry, and chopped coarse
6 garlic cloves, minced
Salt and pepper
¼ teaspoon red pepper flakes
1 ounce Parmesan cheese, grated (½ cup)
½ cup extra-virgin olive oil
¼ cup pine nuts, toasted

1. Lightly coat slow cooker with vegetable oil spray. Combine kale, fennel, broth, tomatoes, garlic, 1 teaspoon salt, ½ teaspoon pepper, and pepper flakes in prepared slow cooker. Cover and cook until kale is tender, 5 to 6 hours on low or 3 to 4 hours on high.

2. Stir in Parmesan, oil, and pine nuts. Season with salt and pepper to taste. Serve.

NOTES FROM THE TEST KITCHEN

Sun-Dried Tomatoes

Sun-dried tomatoes are made by—not surprisingly—drying tomatoes in the sun or through artificial means. The drying process turns the tomatoes dark red, makes their flesh chewy, and gives them an intense, concentrated flavor. Sun-dried tomatoes are sold either dry-packed in small plastic containers or bags or oil-packed in jars. We prefer oil-packed sun-dried tomatoes because the dry-packed variety are often leathery. Plus, the former provides a flavorful oil that can be used for cooking.

A little bacon gives this sauce smoky undertones, while pureed chickpeas give it the right body.

Braised Kale and Chickpea Sauce

MAKES ABOUT 6 CUPS; ENOUGH FOR 1 POUND PASTA
COOKING TIME 5 TO 6 HOURS ON LOW OR 3 TO 4 HOURS ON HIGH
SLOW COOKER SIZE 5 TO 7 QUARTS

WHY THIS RECIPE WORKS Classic pasta sauces that marry hearty greens and beans usually rely on lots of oil and often cream to make the dish cohesive and rich-tasting, but we were after a healthier version, one we could make in a slow cooker. Tackling it head-on, we started by adding just a little bacon to the mix, which infused the sauce with smoky undertones; to keep things easy, we microwaved it along with the aromatics, which included a hefty dose of garlic and pungent minced rosemary. As for the chickpeas, whose nutty flavor paired well with the earthy kale, we found that pureeing half of them in the blender with some of the broth

gave the sauce body that would otherwise have come from cream. The kale was added raw to the slow cooker along with the bacon mixture, the pureed and whole beans, and the remaining chicken broth. At the end of the cooking time, we had a flavorful, brothy pasta sauce that needed just lemon zest and juice for brightening and Parmesan cheese for added richness.

    1 onion, chopped fine
    2 slices bacon, chopped fine
    6 garlic cloves, minced
    2 teaspoons minced fresh rosemary or ½ teaspoon dried
  ¼ teaspoon red pepper flakes
    2 (15-ounce) cans chickpeas, rinsed
2¼ cups chicken broth
    1 pound kale, stemmed and cut into 1-inch pieces
       Salt and pepper
    2 ounces Parmesan cheese, grated (1 cup)
    1 tablespoon grated lemon zest plus 1 teaspoon juice

1. Lightly coat slow cooker with vegetable oil spray. Microwave onion, bacon, garlic, rosemary, and pepper flakes in bowl, stirring occasionally, until onion is softened, about 5 minutes; transfer to prepared slow cooker.

2. Process half of chickpeas and 1 cup broth in blender until smooth, about 30 seconds; transfer to slow cooker. Stir remaining chickpeas, remaining 1¼ cups broth, kale, and ½ teaspoon pepper into slow cooker. Cover and cook until kale is tender, 5 to 6 hours on low or 3 to 4 hours on high.

3. Stir in Parmesan and lemon zest and juice. Season with salt and pepper to taste. Serve.

A Parmesan rind adds nutty richness to this rustic sauce, to which we add bright, assertive chopped escarole at the end.

Escarole and White Bean Sauce

MAKES ABOUT 6 CUPS; ENOUGH FOR 1 POUND PASTA　**ALL DAY**
COOKING TIME 8 TO 9 HOURS ON HIGH
SLOW COOKER SIZE 5 TO 7 QUARTS

WHY THIS RECIPE WORKS The moist cooking environment of the slow cooker turns beans perfectly creamy and tender, so we set about using the slow cooker to create a sauce that paid homage to the classic dish of beans, greens, and pasta. Cannellini beans offered an earthy flavor and ultracreamy texture after simmering in chicken broth for several hours. Borrowing a trick used in many stew recipes, we mashed some of the beans to help thicken the sauce. For the greens, we opted for escarole, which we chopped and added to the slow cooker for the last 20 minutes of cooking so it would wilt but retain its color. Diced tomatoes and dried thyme, cooked with the beans, contributed brightness and woodsy notes, and a Parmesan cheese rind (another trick used in stews and sauces) offered complexity and bolstered the flavor of our

sauce—and made use of an often-overlooked byproduct of pasta night. For an easy garnish, we stirred crisp bacon pieces into the finished sauce for some crunch and salty, savory bites.

　4　slices bacon, chopped
　1　onion, chopped fine
　1　tablespoon minced fresh thyme or 1 teaspoon dried
　5　cups chicken broth
　8　ounces (1¼ cups) dried cannellini beans, picked over and rinsed
　1　(14.5-ounce) can diced tomatoes, drained
　1　Parmesan cheese rind (optional)
　　　Salt and pepper
　½　head escarole, chopped coarse (8 cups)
　¼　cup extra-virgin olive oil

1. Cook bacon in 12-inch skillet over medium heat until crisp, 5 to 7 minutes. Using slotted spoon, transfer bacon to paper towel-lined bowl; set aside.

2. Add onion to fat left in skillet and cook over medium heat until softened and lightly browned, 5 to 7 minutes. Stir in thyme and cook until fragrant, about 30 seconds. Stir in 1 cup broth, scraping up any browned bits; transfer to slow cooker.

3. Stir remaining 4 cups broth, beans, tomatoes, Parmesan rind (if using), ½ teaspoon salt, and ½ teaspoon pepper into slow cooker. Cover and cook until beans are tender, 8 to 9 hours on high.

4. Discard Parmesan rind, if using. Transfer 1 cup of bean-tomato mixture to separate bowl and mash with potato masher until mostly smooth. Stir escarole and mashed bean mixture into slow cooker, cover, and cook on high until escarole is tender, 20 to 30 minutes. Stir in bacon and oil, and season with salt and pepper to taste. Serve.

NOTES FROM THE TEST KITCHEN

Escarole

Escarole, a kind of chicory, is a leafy green that looks like green leaf lettuce. Its bitter flavor makes it a great choice for peppery salads, a good accent for romaine, or delicious with just a simple vinaigrette. Unlike lettuce, however, escarole stands up well to cooking, which makes it a great addition to this hearty soup. Make sure to slice or chop the escarole before washing it well. Use a salad spinner to wash it, as the fine, feathery leaves tend to hold a lot of soil.

■ EASY PREP   ■ VEGETARIAN   ■ LIGHT   ■ COOK ALL DAY
Photo: Wild Rice Pilaf with Cranberries and Pecans

Boiling water and a parchment shield are the secrets to making brown rice in a slow cooker.

Brown Rice with Parmesan and Herbs

SERVES 6 **EASY PREP** **VEG** **LIGHT**
COOKING TIME 2 TO 3 HOURS ON HIGH
SLOW COOKER SIZE 5 TO 7 QUARTS

WHY THIS RECIPE WORKS It's true that brown rice takes longer than white rice to cook, and that it can be trickier to cook evenly. We wondered if the steady, gentle heat of the slow cooker would take the challenge out of cooking brown rice. After some experiments that resulted in burnt rice and undercooked grains, we learned that while brown rice needs a head start with boiling water in the slow cooker, it can indeed emerge with light and fluffy grains every time. Cooking on high was best, and we laid a piece of parchment paper over the rice to protect the grains on top from drying out as the water was absorbed. You will need an oval slow cooker for this recipe. For more information on creating a parchment shield, see page 177. For an accurate measurement of boiling water, bring a full kettle of water to a boil and then measure out the desired amount.

3 cups boiling water
2 cups long-grain brown rice, rinsed
1 tablespoon unsalted butter
  Salt and pepper
2 ounces Parmesan cheese, grated (1 cup)
½ cup chopped fresh basil, dill, or parsley
2 teaspoons lemon juice

1. Lightly coat slow cooker with vegetable oil spray. Combine boiling water, rice, butter, ½ teaspoon salt, and ½ teaspoon pepper in prepared slow cooker. Gently press 16 by 12-inch sheet of parchment paper onto surface of water, folding down edges as needed. Cover and cook until rice is tender and all water is absorbed, 2 to 3 hours on high.

2. Discard parchment. Fluff rice with fork, then gently fold in Parmesan, basil, and lemon juice. Season with salt and pepper to taste. Serve.

Mexican Rice

SERVES 6 **VEG** **LIGHT**
COOKING TIME 2 TO 3 HOURS ON HIGH
SLOW COOKER SIZE 5 TO 7 QUARTS

WHY THIS RECIPE WORKS This easy variation on plain white rice is the perfect accompaniment to enchiladas and tacos, as well as to many simply prepared meat and fish dishes. Cumin, tomato paste, and minced garlic infused the rice with flavor as it cooked, while a few ingredients stirred in before serving—cilantro, scallions, and lime juice—provided bright, zesty flavor. As with our other rice dishes, we found that long-grain white rice cooked best on high, and we laid a piece of parchment paper over the mixture to prevent the grains on top from drying out as the water was absorbed. Basmati rice can be substituted for the long-grain white rice. You will need an oval slow cooker for this recipe. For more information on creating a parchment shield, see page 177.

1 onion, chopped fine
2 jalapeño chiles, stemmed, seeded, and minced
3 tablespoons tomato paste
2 tablespoons extra-virgin olive oil
4 garlic cloves, minced
½ teaspoon ground cumin
  Salt and pepper
3 cups vegetable or chicken broth
2 cups long-grain white rice, rinsed
¼ cup chopped fresh cilantro
2 scallions, sliced thin
1 tablespoon lime juice

1. Lightly coat slow cooker with vegetable oil spray. Microwave onion, jalapeños, tomato paste, oil, garlic, cumin, and ½ teaspoon salt in bowl, stirring occasionally, until vegetables are softened, about 5 minutes; transfer to prepared slow cooker.

2. Microwave broth in bowl until steaming, about 5 minutes. Stir broth and rice into slow cooker. Gently press 16 by 12-inch sheet of parchment paper onto surface of broth, folding down edges as needed. Cover and cook until rice is tender and all broth is absorbed, 2 to 3 hours on high.

3. Discard parchment. Fluff rice with fork, then gently fold in cilantro, scallions, and lime juice. Season with salt and pepper to taste. Serve.

RINSING RICE AND GRAINS

Place rice or grains in fine-mesh strainer and rinse under cool water until water runs clear, occasionally stirring lightly with your hand. Let drain briefly.

Middle Eastern Basmati Rice Pilaf

SERVES 6   EASY PREP   VEG   LIGHT
COOKING TIME 2 TO 3 HOURS ON HIGH
SLOW COOKER SIZE 5 TO 7 QUARTS

WHY THIS RECIPE WORKS For an easy aromatic side dish that's big on flavor, we paired basmati rice with warm spices, dried currants, and crunchy toasted almonds. As with other rice dishes, we found that basmati cooked best on high, and we laid a piece of parchment paper over the mixture to prevent the grains on top from drying out as the water was absorbed. We prefer the flavor of basmati rice in this recipe, but long-grain white rice can be substituted. You will need an oval slow cooker for this recipe. For more information on creating a parchment shield, see page 177. For an accurate measurement of boiling water, bring a full kettle of water to a boil and then measure out the desired amount.

1 tablespoon extra-virgin olive oil
2 garlic cloves, minced
½ teaspoon ground turmeric
¼ teaspoon ground cinnamon
3 cups boiling water

2 cups basmati rice, rinsed
⅓ cup dried currants
Salt and pepper
¼ cup sliced almonds, toasted

1. Lightly coat slow cooker with vegetable oil spray. Microwave oil, garlic, turmeric, and cinnamon in bowl until fragrant, about 1 minute, stirring halfway through microwaving; transfer to prepared slow cooker.

2. Stir boiling water, rice, currants, and ½ teaspoon salt into slow cooker. Gently press 16 by 12-inch sheet of parchment paper onto surface of water, folding down edges as needed. Cover and cook until rice is tender and all water is absorbed, 2 to 3 hours on high.

3. Fluff rice with fork, then gently fold in almonds. Season with salt and pepper to taste. Serve.

Wild Rice Pilaf with Cranberries and Pecans

SERVES 6 TO 8   VEG   LIGHT
COOKING TIME 2 TO 3 HOURS ON HIGH
SLOW COOKER SIZE 5 TO 7 QUARTS

WHY THIS RECIPE WORKS We love wild rice, with its chewy outer husk and nutty, savory flavor, but it can be a chore to cook on the stovetop. We wanted to take advantage of the slow cooker to make wild rice an easy, hands-off affair. Since wild rice can easily go from tough to pasty, it was crucial to find the ratio of liquid to rice that would give our slow-cooker wild rice pilaf the right texture. After several tests, we found that 2½ cups broth to 1½ cups wild rice produced rice that was evenly cooked and not wet or mushy. In pinning down the cooking time, we discovered that heating the broth improved the texture of the rice and also contributed to evenly cooked grains. We also laid a piece of parchment paper over the mixture to prevent the grains on top from drying out as the water was absorbed. To keep this dish simple yet flavorful, we stirred in dried cranberries, which plumped nicely as the rice cooked, and their sweetness provided a good counterpoint to the nutty rice. A handful of toasted pecans and a sprinkling of fresh parsley added at the end of cooking contributed texture and color without much fuss, enabling this dish to go from slow cooker to table in no time. Do not use quick-cooking or presteamed wild rice in this recipe; you may need to read the ingredient list on the package carefully to determine if the wild rice is presteamed. You will need an oval slow cooker for this recipe. For more information on creating a parchment shield, see page 177.

For great-tasting wild rice, we cook it along with heated broth, aromatics, and dried cranberries.

1 onion, chopped fine
1 tablespoon extra-virgin olive oil
1½ teaspoons minced fresh thyme or ¼ teaspoon dried
Salt and pepper
2½ cups vegetable or chicken broth
1½ cups wild rice, picked over and rinsed
⅔ cup dried cranberries
½ cup pecans, toasted and chopped
2 tablespoons chopped fresh parsley

1. Lightly coat slow cooker with vegetable oil spray. Microwave onion, oil, thyme, and ½ teaspoon salt in bowl, stirring occasionally, until onion is softened, about 5 minutes; transfer to prepared slow cooker.

2. Microwave broth in bowl until steaming, about 5 minutes. Stir broth, rice, and cranberries into slow cooker. Gently press 16 by 12-inch sheet of parchment paper onto surface of broth, folding down edges as needed. Cover and cook until rice is tender and all broth is absorbed, 2 to 3 hours on high.

3. Discard parchment. Fluff rice with fork, then gently fold in pecans and parsley. Season with salt and pepper to taste. Serve.

Parmesan Risotto

SERVES 6 `VEG`
COOKING TIME 2 TO 3 HOURS ON HIGH
SLOW COOKER SIZE 4 TO 7 QUARTS

WHY THIS RECIPE WORKS Risotto demands attention from start to finish, which is why this hands-off version is so appealing. Instead of sautéing, we gave our risotto rich flavor by microwaving onion with garlic, thyme, and butter before adding the mixture to the slow-cooker. Adding all the broth at once led to blown-out grains and a mushy risotto, so we stirred in 2 cups of hot broth at the outset and gently stirred in more at the end to guarantee an ultracreamy texture. Arborio rice, which is high in starch, gives risotto its characteristic creaminess; do not substitute other types of rice here. You will need an oval slow cooker for this recipe. For more information on creating a parchment shield, see page 177.

1 onion, chopped fine
4 tablespoons unsalted butter
3 garlic cloves, minced
1 teaspoon minced fresh thyme or ¼ teaspoon dried
Salt and pepper
5 cups vegetable or chicken broth, plus extra as needed
½ cup dry white wine
2 cups Arborio rice
2 ounces Parmesan cheese, grated (1 cup)
2 tablespoons minced fresh chives
1 teaspoon lemon juice

1. Lightly coat slow cooker with vegetable oil spray. Microwave onion, 2 tablespoons butter, garlic, thyme, and ½ teaspoon salt in bowl, stirring occasionally, until onion is softened, about 5 minutes; transfer to prepared slow cooker.

2. Microwave 2 cups broth and wine in 4-cup liquid measuring cup until steaming, about 5 minutes. Stir broth mixture and rice into slow cooker. Gently press 16 by 12-inch sheet of parchment paper onto surface of broth mixture, folding down edges as needed. Cover and cook until rice is almost fully tender and all liquid is absorbed, 2 to 3 hours on high.

3. Microwave remaining 3 cups broth in now-empty measuring cup until steaming, about 5 minutes. Discard parchment. Slowly stream broth into rice, stirring gently, until liquid is absorbed and risotto is creamy, about 1 minute. Gently stir in remaining 2 tablespoons butter, Parmesan, chives, and lemon juice until combined. Adjust consistency with extra hot broth as needed. Season with salt and pepper to taste. Serve.

Butternut Squash Risotto

SERVES 6 TO 8 **VEG**
COOKING TIME 2 TO 3 HOURS ON HIGH
SLOW COOKER SIZE 4 TO 7 QUARTS

WHY THIS RECIPE WORKS Risotto usually demands a cook's attention from start to finish, which is why our slow-cooker version is so appealing. We microwaved garlic and chopped onion and then stirred in white wine, allowing the grains to absorb the liquid. Since adding all the broth at once led to blown-out grains and a mushy risotto, we stirred in 2 cups of hot broth at the outset and gently stirred in more at the end for an ultracreamy texture. Butternut squash offered sweetness and color, and butter, Parmesan, and fresh sage ramped up the richness and flavor of our effortless risotto. Arborio rice, which is high in starch, gives risotto its characteristic creaminess; do not substitute other types of rice here. You will need an oval slow cooker for this recipe. For more information on creating a parchment shield, see page 177.

1 onion, chopped fine
4 tablespoons unsalted butter
3 garlic cloves, minced
  Salt and pepper
5 cups vegetable or chicken broth, plus
  extra as needed
½ cup dry white wine
1 pound butternut squash, peeled, seeded,
  and cut into ½-inch pieces (3 cups)
2 cups Arborio rice

It is far easier to make risotto in the slow cooker than on the stove, as you need to add more broth only at the end.

2 ounces Parmesan cheese, grated (1 cup)
1 tablespoon minced fresh sage
1 teaspoon lemon juice

1. Lightly coat slow cooker with vegetable oil spray. Microwave onion, 2 tablespoons butter, garlic, and ½ teaspoon salt in bowl, stirring occasionally, until onion is softened, about 5 minutes; transfer to prepared slow cooker.

2. Microwave 2 cups broth and wine in 4-cup liquid measuring cup until steaming, about 5 minutes. Stir broth mixture, squash, and rice into slow cooker. Gently press 16 by 12-inch sheet of parchment paper onto surface of broth mixture, folding down edges as needed. Cover and cook until rice is almost fully tender and all liquid is absorbed, 2 to 3 hours on high.

3. Microwave remaining 3 cups broth in now-empty measuring cup until steaming, about 5 minutes. Discard parchment. Slowly stream broth into rice, stirring gently, until liquid is absorbed and risotto is creamy, about 1 minute. Gently stir in remaining 2 tablespoons butter, Parmesan, sage, and lemon juice until combined. Adjust consistency with extra hot broth as needed. Season with salt and pepper to taste. Serve.

For this pilaf, we first toast the barley in the microwave, which sets its structure and keeps it from turning mushy.

Herbed Barley Pilaf

SERVES 6   EASY PREP   VEG   LIGHT

COOKING TIME 3 TO 4 HOURS ON LOW OR 2 TO 3 HOURS ON HIGH

SLOW COOKER SIZE 4 TO 7 QUARTS

WHY THIS RECIPE WORKS For an everyday barley pilaf, we needed to find the right liquid-to-barley ratio for the slow cooker. After a few tests, we found that 3½ cups broth to 1½ cups barley produced barley that was cooked through once all the broth had been absorbed, though the texture was on the soft side. Reducing the amount of liquid wasn't an option because it resulted in unevenly cooked barley. To maintain a bit of the grains' toothsome structure and ensure even cooking, we briefly toasted the barley in the microwave before adding it to the slow cooker. All this pilaf needed was a bit of fresh herbs before serving. Do not substitute hulled, hull-less, quick-cooking, or presteamed barley (read the ingredient list on the package to determine this) in this recipe.

    1 onion, chopped fine
1½ cups pearl barley, rinsed
    2 tablespoons extra-virgin olive oil
    2 garlic cloves, minced
    1 teaspoon minced fresh thyme or ¼ teaspoon dried
      Salt and pepper
3½ cups vegetable or chicken broth
    ¼ cup chopped fresh basil, dill, or parsley

1. Lightly coat slow cooker with vegetable oil spray. Microwave onion, barley, 1 tablespoon oil, garlic, thyme, and ½ teaspoon salt in bowl, stirring occasionally, until onion is softened and barley is lightly toasted, about 5 minutes; transfer to prepared slow cooker. Stir in broth, cover, and cook until barley is tender and all broth is absorbed, 3 to 4 hours on low or 2 to 3 hours on high.

2. Fluff barley with fork, then gently fold in basil and remaining 1 tablespoon oil. Season with salt and pepper to taste. Serve.

Spiced Barley Pilaf with Dates and Parsley

SERVES 6   EASY PREP   VEG   LIGHT

COOKING TIME 3 TO 4 HOURS ON LOW OR 2 TO 3 HOURS ON HIGH

SLOW COOKER SIZE 4 TO 7 QUARTS

WHY THIS RECIPE WORKS For a distinctive variation on our easy Herbed Barley Pilaf, we added a potent blend of Indian-inspired spices—ginger, cinnamon, and cardamom—plus dates for sweetness. Do not substitute hulled, hull-less, quick-cooking, or presteamed barley (read the ingredient list on the package to determine this) in this recipe.

    1 onion, chopped fine
1½ cups pearl barley, rinsed
    2 tablespoons extra-virgin olive oil
    2 teaspoons grated fresh ginger
      Salt and pepper
    ⅛ teaspoon ground cinnamon
    ⅛ teaspoon ground cardamom
3½ cups vegetable or chicken broth
    3 ounces pitted dates, chopped (½ cup)
    ⅓ cup chopped fresh parsley
    2 teaspoons lemon juice

1. Lightly coat slow cooker with vegetable oil spray. Microwave onion, barley, 1 tablespoon oil, ginger, ½ teaspoon salt, cinnamon, and cardamom in bowl, stirring occasionally, until onion is softened and barley is lightly toasted, about 5 minutes; transfer to prepared slow cooker. Stir in broth, cover, and cook until barley is tender and all broth is absorbed, 3 to 4 hours on low or 2 to 3 hours on high.

2. Fluff barley with fork, then gently fold in dates, parsley, lemon juice, and remaining 1 tablespoon oil. Season with salt and pepper to taste. Serve.

CHOPPING DRIED FRUIT

To prevent dried fruit from sticking to knife, coat blade with thin film of vegetable oil spray before chopping.

Barley

While barley might be most familiar as a key ingredient in beer, in fact it is a nutritious high-fiber, high-protein, and low-fat cereal grain with a nutty flavor similar to that of  brown rice. It is great in soups and salads, as risotto, and as a simple side dish. Barley is available in multiple forms. Hulled barley, which is sold with the hull removed and the fiber-rich bran intact, is considered a whole grain and is higher in nutrients in comparison with pearl (or pearled) barley, which is hulled barley that has been polished to remove the bran. There is also quick-cooking barley, which is available as kernels or flakes. Hulled barley takes a long time to cook and should be soaked prior to cooking. Pearl barley cooks much more quickly, making it a more versatile choice when you are adding it to soups or making risotto or pilaf.

Farro turns luxuriously creamy in the slow cooker, and here we boost its flavor with mushrooms, thyme, and Parmesan.

Creamy Farro with Mushrooms and Thyme

SERVES 4 TO 6   VEG   LIGHT
COOKING TIME 3 TO 4 HOURS ON LOW OR 2 TO 3 HOURS ON HIGH
SLOW COOKER SIZE 4 TO 7 QUARTS

WHY THIS RECIPE WORKS Farro's nutty, mild flavor will happily lend itself to almost any culinary direction, but as it's a popular ingredient in Tuscan cuisine, we decided to give this dish a simple and fresh Italian profile. We started by softening our aromatics— shallots, porcini mushrooms, garlic, and thyme—in the microwave. Cremini mushrooms lent the dish meatiness, and sherry was a natural complement and added complexity. Once our farro was tender, we stirred in just enough Parmesan to create a luxurious, creamy texture without overwhelming our well-balanced dish. Finishing with a couple tablespoons of fresh parsley added brightness and freshness that balanced the hearty, savory flavors. Do not use quick-cooking or presteamed farro (the ingredient list on the package will specify the type) in this recipe.

2 shallots, minced
   ½ ounce dried porcini mushrooms, rinsed and minced
   2 tablespoons extra-virgin olive oil
   3 garlic cloves, minced
   2 teaspoons minced fresh thyme or ½ teaspoon dried
      Salt and pepper
2½ cups vegetable or chicken broth, plus extra as needed
   ¼ cup dry sherry
   8 ounces cremini mushrooms, trimmed and sliced thin
   1 cup whole farro
   1 ounce Parmesan cheese, grated (½ cup)
   2 tablespoons chopped fresh parsley

   1. Lightly coat slow cooker with vegetable oil spray. Microwave shallots, porcini mushrooms, 1 tablespoon oil, garlic, thyme, ½ teaspoon salt, and ½ teaspoon pepper in bowl, stirring occasionally, until shallots are softened, about 5 minutes; transfer to prepared slow cooker.

   2. Microwave 2 cups broth and sherry in bowl until steaming, about 5 minutes. Stir broth mixture, cremini mushrooms, and farro into slow cooker. Cover and cook until farro is tender, 3 to 4 hours on low or 2 to 3 hours on high.

   3. Microwave remaining ½ cup broth in bowl until steaming, about 2 minutes. Stir broth and Parmesan into farro until mixture is creamy. Adjust consistency with extra hot broth as needed. Stir in parsley and remaining 1 tablespoon oil. Season with salt and pepper to taste. Serve.

This creamy orzo dish is great served alongside roasted chicken or fish.

Creamy Orzo with Parmesan and Peas

SERVES 4 TO 6 VEG
COOKING TIME 1 TO 2 HOURS ON HIGH
SLOW COOKER SIZE 4 TO 7 QUARTS

WHY THIS RECIPE WORKS For a side dish of tender—not mushy—orzo, we toasted our pasta in butter in the microwave before moving it to the slow cooker, then added hot broth to jump-start its cooking. Grated Parmesan and a couple more pats of butter, added at the end, gave us a rich-tasting dish with a creamy texture. Stirring frozen peas in at the end of cooking ensured they stayed bright and fresh-tasting. You will need an oval slow cooker for this recipe.

   1 cup orzo
   1 onion, chopped fine
   6 garlic cloves, minced
   3 tablespoons unsalted butter
      Salt and pepper
2½ cups vegetable or chicken broth,
      plus extra as needed
   ¼ cup dry white wine
   1 cup frozen peas, thawed
   2 ounces Parmesan cheese, grated (1 cup)
1½ teaspoons grated lemon zest

   1. Microwave orzo, onion, garlic, 1 tablespoon butter, and ½ teaspoon salt in bowl, stirring occasionally, until orzo is lightly toasted and onion is softened, 5 to 7 minutes; transfer to slow cooker.

   2. Microwave 2 cups broth and wine in bowl until steaming, about 5 minutes. Stir broth mixture into slow cooker, cover, and cook until orzo is al dente, 1 to 2 hours on high.

   3. Sprinkle peas over orzo, cover, and let sit until heated through, about 5 minutes. Microwave remaining ½ cup broth in bowl until steaming, about 2 minutes. Stir broth, Parmesan, lemon zest, and remaining 2 tablespoons butter into orzo until mixture is creamy. Adjust consistency with extra hot broth as needed. Season with salt and pepper to taste. Serve.

Creamy Parmesan Polenta

SERVES 6 `EASY PREP` `VEG` `LIGHT`

COOKING TIME 3 TO 4 HOURS ON LOW OR 2 TO 3 HOURS
ON HIGH

SLOW COOKER SIZE 4 TO 7 QUARTS

WHY THIS RECIPE WORKS Many polenta recipes deliver rich
creaminess by piling on hefty amounts of cheese and butter. Not
wanting to sacrifice creaminess or texture, we focused on getting
the polenta perfectly tender. Remarkably, thanks to the gentle heat
of the slow cooker, our typical ratio of liquid to polenta worked
just fine. Instead of using all water and stirring in lots of butter
at the end, we added 1 cup of whole milk up front. This helped to
deliver the same rich, creamy texture but with substantially less
fat and calories. We finished the dish by steeping a sprig of rosemary in the polenta to infuse herbal flavor without adding bits
of herbs to disturb the smooth texture of the dish. Just a cup of
nutty Parmesan and a couple pats of butter stirred in at the end
gave the polenta richness and flavor while keeping the dish light.
Coarse-ground degerminated cornmeal such as yellow grits (with
uniform grains the size of couscous) works best in this recipe.
Avoid instant or quick-cooking products, as well as whole-grain,
stone-ground, and regular cornmeal.

3 cups water, plus extra as needed
1 cup whole milk
1 cup coarse-ground cornmeal
2 garlic cloves, minced
  Salt and pepper
1 sprig fresh rosemary (optional)
2 ounces Parmesan cheese, grated (1 cup)
2 tablespoons unsalted butter

1. Lightly coat slow cooker with vegetable oil spray. Whisk water,
milk, cornmeal, garlic, and 1 teaspoon salt together in prepared
slow cooker. Cover and cook until polenta is tender, 3 to 4 hours
on low or 2 to 3 hours on high.

2. Nestle rosemary sprig into polenta, if using, cover, and let
steep for 10 minutes; discard rosemary sprig. Whisk Parmesan
and butter into polenta until combined. Season with salt and
pepper to taste. Serve. (Polenta can be held on warm or low setting for up to 2 hours; adjust consistency with extra hot water as
needed before serving.)

NOTES FROM THE TEST KITCHEN

All About Parmesan Cheese

Parmesan is a hard, grainy cheese made from cow's milk.
It has a rich, sharp flavor and a melt-in-your-mouth texture.
We frequently reach for it to sprinkle on top of pasta dishes
or to add a rich, salty flavor to sauces, soups, and stews.

BUYING PARMESAN We recommend authentic Italian
Parmigiano-Reggiano. Most of the other Parmesan-
type cheeses are too salty and one-dimensional. When
shopping, make sure some portion of the words
"Parmigiano-Reggiano" is stenciled on the golden rind.
To ensure that you're buying a properly aged cheese,
examine the condition of the rind. It should be a few
shades darker than the straw-colored interior and
penetrate about ½ inch deep. And closely scrutinize the
center of the cheese. Those small white spots found on
many samples are actually good things—they signify
the presence of calcium phosphate crystals, which are
formed only after the cheese has been aged for the
proper amount of time.

STORING PARMESAN The best way to preserve the flavor
and texture of Parmesan is to wrap it first in parchment
paper, then aluminum foil. However, if you have just
a small piece of cheese, tossing it in a zipper-lock bag
works almost as well; just be sure to squeeze out as
much air as possible before sealing the bag. Note that
these methods also work for Pecorino Romano.

PARMESAN VERSUS PECORINO ROMANO While Parmesan
is a cow's-milk cheese, Pecorino Romano is made
from sheep's milk, but the two do have a similar texture
and flavor. We have found that Parmesan and Pecorino
Romano generally can be used interchangeably, especially when the amount called for is moderate. However,
when Parmesan is called for in larger quantities, it is
best to stick with the Parmesan, as Pecorino Romano
can be fairly pungent.

CAN YOU PREGRATE YOUR OWN PARMESAN? Tasters were
hard-pressed to detect any difference between freshly
grated Parmesan and cheese that had been grated and
stored for up to three weeks. To grind Parmesan, cut
a block into 1-inch chunks. Place the chunks in a food
processor and process until ground into coarse particles,
about 20 seconds. Refrigerate in an airtight container
until ready to use.

No-Fuss Quinoa with Lemon

SERVES 6 `EASY PREP` `VEG` `LIGHT`

COOKING TIME 3 TO 4 HOURS ON LOW OR 2 TO 3 HOURS
ON HIGH

SLOW COOKER SIZE 4 TO 7 QUARTS

WHY THIS RECIPE WORKS We love quinoa for its nutty taste and ease of preparation. To keep the grains separate and fluffy during cooking, we toasted them in the microwave before adding them to the slow cooker. We dressed the quinoa simply, with lemon and parsley, to make a universally appealing side dish. You will need an oval slow cooker for this recipe. Be sure to rinse the quinoa in a fine-mesh strainer before using; rinsing removes the quinoa's bitter protective coating (called saponins).

1½ cups prewashed white quinoa, rinsed
1 onion, chopped fine
2 tablespoons extra-virgin olive oil
   Salt and pepper
1¾ cups water
2 (2-inch) strips lemon zest plus 1 tablespoon juice
2 tablespoons minced fresh parsley

1. Lightly coat slow cooker with vegetable oil spray. Microwave quinoa, onion, 1 tablespoon oil, and 1 teaspoon salt in bowl, stirring occasionally, until quinoa is lightly toasted and onion is softened, about 5 minutes; transfer to prepared slow cooker. Stir in water and lemon zest. Cover and cook until quinoa is tender and all water is absorbed, 3 to 4 hours on low or 2 to 3 hours on high.

2. Discard lemon zest. Fluff quinoa with fork, then gently fold in lemon juice, parsley, and remaining 1 tablespoon oil. Season with salt and pepper to taste. Serve.

No-Fuss Quinoa with Corn and Jalapeño

SERVES 6 `EASY PREP` `VEG` `LIGHT`

COOKING TIME 3 TO 4 HOURS ON LOW OR 2 TO 3 HOURS
ON HIGH

SLOW COOKER SIZE 4 TO 7 QUARTS

WHY THIS RECIPE WORKS For this quinoa side dish we turned to Southwestern flavors, adding jalapeños, lime, and corn. You will need an oval slow cooker for this recipe. Be sure to rinse the quinoa in a fine-mesh strainer before using; rinsing removes the quinoa's bitter protective coating (called saponins).

It is supereasy to make fluffy quinoa in the slow cooker, and here we jazz it up with minced chiles, corn, and cilantro.

1½ cups prewashed white quinoa, rinsed
1 onion, chopped fine
2 jalapeño chiles, stemmed, seeded, and minced
2 tablespoons extra-virgin olive oil
   Salt and pepper
1¾ cups water
1 cup frozen corn, thawed
⅓ cup minced fresh cilantro
2 tablespoons lime juice

1. Lightly coat slow cooker with vegetable oil spray. Microwave quinoa, onion, jalapeños, 1 tablespoon oil, and 1 teaspoon salt in bowl, stirring occasionally, until quinoa is lightly toasted and vegetables are softened, about 5 minutes; transfer to prepared slow cooker. Stir in water, cover, and cook until quinoa is tender and all water is absorbed, 3 to 4 hours on low or 2 to 3 hours on high.

2. Sprinkle corn over quinoa, cover, and let sit until heated through, about 5 minutes. Fluff quinoa with fork, then gently fold in cilantro, lime juice, and remaining 1 tablespoon oil. Season with salt and pepper to taste. Serve.

Wheat Berries with Carrots and Oranges

SERVES 6 TO 8 **EASY PREP** **VEG** **LIGHT**

COOKING TIME 4 TO 5 HOURS ON LOW OR 3 TO 4 HOURS
ON HIGH

SLOW COOKER SIZE 4 TO 7 QUARTS

WHY THIS RECIPE WORKS Orange and tarragon are a classic pairing, and it's easy to understand why: sweet-tart orange boosts and brightens tarragon's grassy licorice notes, creating a remarkably vibrant flavor. This combination shone against a backdrop of mildly nutty wheat berries, especially after we added shredded carrots for crunch and orange zest for a deeper citrus flavor. A simple red wine vinaigrette finished off this fresh, crowd-pleasing salad with a sophisticated mix of flavors. We found cooking our wheat berries in a large amount of water, much as we would cook pasta, worked best and produced the most evenly cooked results. If using quick-cooking or presteamed wheat berries (the ingredient list on the package specifies the type), you will need to decrease the cooking time in step 1. The wheat berries will retain a chewy texture once fully cooked.

1½ cups wheat berries
1 bay leaf
 Salt and pepper
⅛ teaspoon grated orange zest, plus 1 orange
1 shallot, minced
3 tablespoons red wine vinegar
2 tablespoons extra-virgin olive oil
1½ tablespoons Dijon mustard
1½ teaspoons honey
1 garlic clove, minced
3 carrots, peeled and shredded
1 tablespoon chopped fresh tarragon

1. Combine 5 cups water, wheat berries, bay leaf, and ½ teaspoon salt in slow cooker. Cover and cook until wheat berries are tender, 4 to 5 hours on low or 3 to 4 hours on high.

2. Drain wheat berries, transfer to large serving bowl, and let cool slightly. Cut away peel and pith from orange. Quarter orange, then slice crosswise into ¼-inch-thick pieces.

3. Whisk shallot, vinegar, oil, mustard, honey, garlic, ½ teaspoon salt, and orange zest together in separate bowl. Add orange and any accumulated juices, vinaigrette, carrots, and tarragon to wheat berries, and toss to combine. Season with salt and pepper to taste. Serve.

Braised Lentils with Escarole

SERVES 6 TO 8 **EASY PREP** **VEG**

COOKING TIME 3 TO 4 HOURS ON LOW OR 2 TO 3 HOURS
ON HIGH

SLOW COOKER SIZE 5 TO 7 QUARTS

WHY THIS RECIPE WORKS Lentils are amazingly versatile: Their mild earthiness makes it easy to pair them with a wide range of flavors, and, depending on the variety of lentil and the cooking method, their consistency can range from a silky, smooth dal to the just barely toothsome bite of a French lentil salad. For this side we envisioned something in between—distinct, tender lentils in a brothy sauce thickened by the lentils themselves. We started by deliberately veering away from our slow-cooker technique for perfect salad lentils. Usually, to ensure they cook evenly without blowing out, we use abundant liquid, often with a touch of acid (which helps keep them firm while cooking), and then drain them. In this case, since we actually wanted to release some starches, we wouldn't mind a few burst lentils. So we skipped the acid and used just enough broth, fortified with some simple aromatics, to submerge our lentils. The result was just what we had hoped for—tender lentils in a ready-made sauce. We wanted to keep the dish simple, just wilting in escarole for some heft, and found its bitterness the perfect foil to the lentils' earthy base. A final stir-in of olive oil and lemon juice, and a sprinkling of Parmesan, brought our dish into perfect balance. We prefer French green lentils, *lentilles du Puy*, for this recipe, but it will work with any type of lentil except red or yellow.

1 onion, chopped fine
3 tablespoons extra-virgin olive oil
3 garlic cloves, minced
½ teaspoon red pepper flakes
2½ cups vegetable or chicken broth
1 cup French green lentils, picked over and rinsed
1 head escarole (1 pound), trimmed and sliced 1 inch thick
1 ounce Parmesan cheese, grated (½ cup)
1 tablespoon lemon juice, plus extra for seasoning
 Salt and pepper

1. Microwave onion, 1 tablespoon oil, garlic, and pepper flakes in bowl, stirring occasionally, until onion is softened, about 5 minutes; transfer to slow cooker. Stir in broth and lentils, cover, and cook until lentils are tender, 3 to 4 hours on low or 2 to 3 hours on high.

2. Stir in escarole, 1 handful at a time, until slightly wilted. Cover and cook on high until escarole is completely wilted, about 10 minutes. Stir in Parmesan, lemon juice, and remaining 2 tablespoons oil. Season with salt, pepper, and extra lemon juice to taste. Serve.

MAKE IT 5 WAYS BAKED BEANS

Boston Baked Beans

SERVES 6 `EASY PREP` `ALL DAY`
COOKING TIME 8 TO 9 HOURS ON HIGH
SLOW COOKER SIZE 4 TO 7 QUARTS

Traditional baked beans rely on a long, slow cooking time in a low oven and require careful adjustment of the cooking liquid in order to get perfectly cooked beans with just the right amount of syrupy, but not cloyingly sweet, sauce. While the gentle, steady heat of the slow cooker seemed like the perfect fit for beans, we were in for a surprise. While we were able to get silky, tender beans after 8 to 9 hours of cooking on the high setting, we weren't able to replicate those results on low; even after 16 hours of cooking, we still had crunchy, inconsistent beans. So we settled on cooking the beans exclusively on high. Our method perfected, we next created five baked bean recipes, ranging from tried-and-true Boston Baked Beans to unconventional Peach-Bourbon Baked Beans, showcasing the best of this sweet and savory comfort food. The finished beans can be held on the warm or low setting for up to 2 hours; adjust their consistency with hot water as needed before serving.

1 BOSTON BAKED BEANS

1 onion, chopped fine
6 ounces salt pork, rind removed, cut into ½-inch pieces
  Salt and pepper
6 cups water, plus extra as needed
1 pound dried navy beans (2½ cups), picked over and rinsed
¼ cup plus 1 tablespoon molasses
¼ cup packed dark brown sugar
2 bay leaves
1 tablespoon soy sauce
4 teaspoons cider vinegar
2 teaspoons dry mustard

1. Microwave onion, salt pork, and ½ teaspoon salt in bowl, stirring occasionally, until onion is softened, about 5 minutes; transfer to slow cooker. Stir in water, beans, 2 tablespoons molasses, 2 tablespoons sugar, and bay leaves. Cover and cook until beans are tender, 8 to 9 hours on high.

2. Discard bay leaves. Drain beans, reserving ¾ cup cooking liquid. Return beans to now-empty slow cooker. Stir in reserved cooking liquid, soy sauce, vinegar, mustard, remaining 3 tablespoon molasses, and remaining 2 tablespoons sugar. Cover and cook on high until beans are thickened slightly, about 10 minutes. Season with salt and pepper to taste. Serve.

2 BARBECUED BAKED BEANS

1 onion, chopped fine
6 slices bacon, chopped
4 garlic cloves, minced
1 tablespoon vegetable oil
  Salt and pepper
5½ cups water, plus extra as needed
1 pound dried navy beans (2½ cups), picked over and rinsed
½ cup barbecue sauce
½ cup brewed coffee
2 bay leaves
1 tablespoon cider vinegar
2 teaspoons dry mustard
  Hot sauce

1. Microwave onion, bacon, garlic, oil, and ½ teaspoon salt in bowl, stirring occasionally, until onion is softened, about 5 minutes; transfer to slow cooker. Stir in water, beans, ¼ cup barbecue sauce, coffee, and bay leaves. Cover and cook until beans are tender, 8 to 9 hours on high.

2. Discard bay leaves. Drain beans, reserving ¾ cup cooking liquid. Return beans to now-empty slow cooker. Stir in reserved cooking liquid, vinegar, mustard, and remaining ¼ cup barbecue sauce. Cover and cook on high until beans are thickened slightly, about 10 minutes. Season with salt, pepper, and hot sauce to taste. Serve.

3 COUNTRY-STYLE BAKED BEANS

1 pound bratwurst, casings removed
1 onion, chopped fine
6 slices bacon, chopped
2 garlic cloves, minced
   Salt and pepper
¼ teaspoon cayenne pepper
6 cups water, plus extra as needed
1 pound dried navy beans
   (2½ cups), picked over and rinsed
1 (10-ounce) can Ro-tel Original
   Diced Tomatoes & Green Chilies,
   drained
¼ cup plus 2 tablespoons
   barbecue sauce
¼ cup plus 2 tablespoons ketchup
2 tablespoons spicy brown mustard
1 tablespoon cider vinegar

1. Microwave bratwurst, onion, bacon, garlic, ½ teaspoon salt, and cayenne in bowl, stirring and occasionally breaking up meat with wooden spoon, until sausage is no longer pink, 6 to 8 minutes; transfer to slow cooker. Stir in water, beans, tomatoes, ¼ cup barbecue sauce, and ¼ cup ketchup. Cover and cook until beans are tender, 8 to 9 hours on high.

2. Drain beans, reserving ¾ cup cooking liquid. Return beans to now empty slow cooker. Stir in reserved cooking liquid, mustard, vinegar, remaining 2 tablespoons barbecue sauce, and remaining 2 tablespoons ketchup. Cover and cook on high until beans are thickened slightly, about 10 minutes. Season with salt and pepper to taste. Serve.

4 PEACH-BOURBON BAKED BEANS

1 onion, chopped fine
6 slices bacon, chopped
2 teaspoons minced fresh thyme
   or ½ teaspoon dried
   Salt and pepper
6 cups water, plus extra as needed
1 pound dried navy beans
   (2½ cups), picked over and rinsed
2 cups frozen peaches, thawed and
   cut into 2-inch pieces
¼ cup packed dark brown sugar
2 bay leaves
2 tablespoons peach preserves
2 tablespoons bourbon
4 teaspoons cider vinegar
2 teaspoons dry mustard

1. Microwave onion, bacon, thyme, and ½ teaspoon salt in bowl, stirring occasionally, until onion is softened, about 5 minutes; transfer to slow cooker. Stir in water, beans, peaches, 2 tablespoons sugar, and bay leaves. Cover and cook until beans are tender, 8 to 9 hours on high.

2. Discard bay leaves. Drain beans, reserving ¾ cup cooking liquid. Return beans to now-empty slow cooker. Stir in reserved cooking liquid, peach preserves, bourbon, vinegar, mustard, ½ teaspoon salt, and remaining 2 tablespoons sugar. Cover and cook on high until beans are thickened slightly, about 10 minutes. Season with salt and pepper to taste. Serve.

5 HONEY-MUSTARD BAKED BEANS

1 onion, chopped fine
1 tablespoon vegetable oil
1 teaspoon minced fresh thyme
   or ¼ teaspoon dried
1 teaspoon ground ginger
1 teaspoon ground coriander
   Salt and pepper
6 cups water, plus extra as needed
1 pound dried navy beans
   (2½ cups), picked over and rinsed
¼ cup honey
2 bay leaves
2 tablespoons yellow mustard
1 tablespoon cider vinegar

1. Microwave onion, oil, thyme, ginger, coriander, and ½ teaspoon salt in bowl, stirring occasionally, until onion is softened, about 5 minutes; transfer to slow cooker. Stir in water, beans, 2 tablespoons honey, and bay leaves. Cover and cook until beans are tender, 8 to 9 hours on high.

2. Discard bay leaves. Drain beans, reserving ¾ cup cooking liquid. Return beans to now-empty slow cooker. Stir in reserved cooking liquid, mustard, vinegar, ½ teaspoon salt, and remaining 2 tablespoons honey. Cover and cook on high until beans are thickened slightly, about 10 minutes. Season with salt and pepper to taste. Serve.

We mash a portion of the cooked chickpeas with the braising liquid for a side dish with just the right creamy texture.

Braised Chickpeas

SERVES 6　**EASY PREP**　**VEG**　**LIGHT**　**ALL DAY**
COOKING TIME 8 TO 9 HOURS ON HIGH
SLOW COOKER SIZE 4 TO 7 QUARTS

WHY THIS RECIPE WORKS Chickpeas have a great buttery texture, and they easily soak up the flavors of other ingredients they're cooked with, making them ideal for cooking in a flavor-packed broth over a long, slow stint in the slow cooker. We infused broth with distinctive sweet smoked paprika and a sliced red onion for flavor and texture. Once our chickpeas were perfectly tender and creamy, we drained away all but a cup of the cooking liquid, using what we reserved to create a simple, smoky sauce. Mashing a portion of the beans enhanced the creamy consistency of the dish, and citrusy cilantro added brightness and a simple colorful finish.

1 red onion, halved and sliced thin
1 tablespoon extra-virgin olive oil
1 tablespoon smoked paprika
　Salt and pepper

3 cups vegetable or chicken broth, plus
　extra as needed
3 cups water
1 pound (2½ cups) dried chickpeas,
　picked over and rinsed
¼ cup minced fresh cilantro

1. Microwave onion, oil, paprika, and 1 teaspoon salt in bowl, stirring occasionally, until onion is softened, about 5 minutes; transfer to slow cooker. Stir in broth, water, and chickpeas. Cover and cook until chickpeas are tender, 8 to 9 hours on high.

2. Drain chickpeas, reserving 1 cup cooking liquid. Return one-third of chickpeas and reserved cooking liquid to now-empty slow cooker and mash with potato masher until smooth. Stir in remaining chickpeas and cilantro. Season with salt and pepper to taste. Serve. (Chickpeas can be held on warm or low setting for up to 2 hours; adjust consistency with extra hot broth as needed before serving.)

Braised White Beans with Olive Oil and Sage

SERVES 6　**EASY PREP**　**VEG**　**ALL DAY**
COOKING TIME 8 TO 9 HOURS ON HIGH
SLOW COOKER SIZE 4 TO 7 QUARTS

WHY THIS RECIPE WORKS Perfect alongside pork, chicken, or fish, these slow-cooked beans deliver rich flavor and a creamy, tender texture. The beans themselves—we found that small white beans worked well here—required no prep, other than being picked over and rinsed. To ensure that the beans took on robust flavor during their long stint in the slow cooker, we cooked them with onion, a hefty amount of garlic, and a little sage. Once the beans were perfectly cooked, we drained the mixture and reserved a cup of the flavorful cooking liquid to stir back into the beans. We then mashed a portion of the beans to thicken the sauce and enhance the creamy consistency of the dish. Extra olive oil and fresh sage stirred in at the end enhanced the earthy, herbaceous flavors.

1 onion, chopped fine
5 garlic cloves, minced
3 tablespoons extra-virgin olive oil
2 teaspoons minced fresh sage
　Salt and pepper
3 cups vegetable or chicken broth, plus
　extra as needed
3 cups water
1 pound (2½ cups) dried small white beans,
　picked over and rinsed

1. Microwave onion, garlic, 1 tablespoon oil, 1 teaspoon sage, and 1 teaspoon salt in bowl, stirring occasionally, until onion is softened, about 5 minutes; transfer to slow cooker. Stir in broth, water, and beans. Cover and cook until beans are tender, 8 to 9 hours on high.

2. Drain beans, reserving 1 cup cooking liquid. Return one-third of beans and reserved cooking liquid to now-empty slow cooker and mash with potato masher until smooth. Stir in remaining beans, remaining 2 tablespoons oil, and remaining 1 teaspoon sage. Season with salt and pepper to taste. Serve. (Beans can be held on warm or low setting for up to 2 hours; adjust consistency with extra hot broth as needed before serving.)

All About Dried Beans

Canned beans are undeniably convenient, and in many cases they work as well as or even better than dried. However, there are instances when dried beans are central to the success of a recipe. Here's what to know about them.

BUYING When shopping for beans, it's essential to select "fresh" dried beans. Buy those that are uniform in size and have a smooth exterior. When dried beans are fully hydrated and cooked, they should be plump, with taut skins, and have creamy insides; spent beans will have wrinkled skin and a dry, almost gritty texture.

STORING Uncooked beans should be stored in a cool, dry place in a sealed plastic or glass container. Beans are less susceptible than rice and grains to pests and spoilage, but it is still best to use them within a month or two.

SORTING AND RINSING Prior to cooking, you should pick over dried beans for any small stones or debris and then rinse the beans to wash away any dust or impurities. The easiest way to check for small stones is to spread the beans on a large plate or rimmed baking sheet.

SOAKING While we typically recommend salt-soaking beans for traditional stovetop recipes to soften their skins and encourage even cooking, we find the low, slow cooking of the slow cooker allows us to skip this step without any negative results.

Simmered all day in the slow cooker, black beans become perfectly tender and here are flavored with a ham hock.

Cuban-Style Black Beans

SERVES 6 `EASY PREP` `ALL DAY`
COOKING TIME 8 TO 9 HOURS ON HIGH
SLOW COOKER SIZE 4 TO 7 QUARTS

WHY THIS RECIPE WORKS Served at almost every meal, black beans are at the heart of Cuban cuisine. Prior testing left us confident in our method for cooking the beans, so we turned our attention to building layers of flavor. Pork is commonly added to the beans for much-needed depth, so we began there. After trying bacon, ham, and a ham hock, we liked the smoky depth the ham hock lent. Instead of adding aromatics to the beans at the start of cooking, we favored the custom of stirring a *sofrito* (typically sautéed onion, garlic, and green bell pepper) into the cooked beans instead. Microwaving the sofrito until the vegetables were tender saved us time and did not compromise flavor. This addition, along with minced cilantro and lime juice, provided a fresh layer of flavor without overwhelming the beans. Some recipes suggested pureeing the sofrito with some of the beans to thicken the sauce, but we preferred simply mashing the sofrito along with a portion of the beans and a little of the cooking liquid. The texture of these beans is typically looser than that achieved in other bean recipes.

6 cups water, plus extra as needed
1 pound dried black beans (2½ cups), picked over
   and rinsed
1 (12-ounce) smoked ham hock, rinsed
2 bay leaves
1 onion, chopped fine
1 green bell pepper, stemmed, seeded, and minced
6 garlic cloves, minced
2 tablespoons extra-virgin olive oil
2 tablespoons minced fresh oregano or 2 teaspoons dried
1½ teaspoons ground cumin
½ cup minced fresh cilantro
1 tablespoon lime juice, plus extra for seasoning
   Salt and pepper

1. Combine water, beans, ham hock, and bay leaves in slow cooker. Cover and cook until beans are tender, 8 to 9 hours on high.

2. Transfer ham hock to cutting board, let cool slightly, then shred into bite-size pieces using 2 forks; discard fat, skin, and bones. Discard bay leaves.

3. Microwave onion, bell pepper, garlic, oil, oregano, and cumin in bowl, stirring occasionally, until vegetables are tender, 8 to 10 minutes.

4. Drain beans, reserving 1½ cups cooking liquid. Add vegetable mixture, one-third of beans, and reserved cooking liquid to now-empty slow cooker and mash with potato masher until mostly smooth. Stir in remaining beans, ham, cilantro, and lime juice. Season with salt, pepper, and extra lime juice to taste. Serve. (Beans can be held on warm or low setting for up to 2 hours; adjust consistency with extra hot water as needed before serving.)

CUTTING UP A BELL PEPPER

1. Slice off top and bottom of pepper and remove seeds and stem. Slice down through side of pepper.

2. Lay pepper flat and trim away remaining ribs and seeds. Cut pepper as directed in recipe.

Smoky chipotle chiles and beer form the flavor backbone of these assertive Mexican beans.

Mexican-Style Beans

SERVES 6 `EASY PREP` `VEG` `ALL DAY`
COOKING TIME 8 TO 9 HOURS ON HIGH
SLOW COOKER SIZE 4 TO 7 QUARTS

WHY THIS RECIPE WORKS To deliver flavorful, robust Mexican-style beans from the slow cooker we needed to amp up the aromatics and spices. Since the beans required a full 6 cups of liquid to cook evenly in the slow cooker, we knew that we would need to drain away some of that cooking liquid. To ensure that our beans remained full of flavor, we boosted the amount of garlic, oregano, and chili powder. For an extra dimension of flavor, we also added smoky chipotle chiles in adobo sauce and exchanged 1 cup of water for beer. When we stirred 1 cup of reserved cooking liquid back into the tender beans, we created a sauce that was rich and bold. A little bit of brown sugar rounded things out, and a hit of fresh lime juice and cilantro added brightness at the end.

1 onion, chopped fine
2 tablespoons extra-virgin olive oil
4 garlic cloves, minced
1 tablespoon minced fresh oregano or 1 teaspoon dried

1 tablespoon chili powder
2 teaspoons minced canned chipotle chile in adobo sauce
Salt and pepper
5 cups water, plus extra as needed
1 pound (2½ cups) dried pinto beans, picked over and rinsed
1 cup mild lager, such as Budweiser
2 tablespoons minced fresh cilantro
1 tablespoon packed brown sugar
1 tablespoon lime juice, plus extra for seasoning

1. Microwave onion, 1 tablespoon oil, garlic, oregano, chili powder, chipotle, and 1 teaspoon salt in bowl, stirring occasionally, until onion is softened, about 5 minutes; transfer to slow cooker. Stir in water, beans, and beer. Cover and cook until beans are tender, 8 to 9 hours on high.

2. Drain beans, reserving 1 cup cooking liquid. Return beans and reserved cooking liquid to now-empty slow cooker. Stir in cilantro, sugar, lime juice, and remaining 1 tablespoon oil. Season with salt, pepper, and extra lime juice to taste. Serve. (Beans can be held on warm or low setting for up to 2 hours; adjust consistency with extra hot water as needed before serving.)

Refried Beans

SERVES 6   EASY PREP   ALL DAY

COOKING TIME 8 TO 9 HOURS ON HIGH
SLOW COOKER SIZE 4 TO 7 QUARTS

WHY THIS RECIPE WORKS Homemade refried beans, infused with rich pork flavor, a subtle heat, and warm spice notes, are worlds apart from the canned stuff, but making them takes time. For great refried beans for our tacos, tostadas, and nachos, we put our slow cooker to work and developed a recipe that was flavor-packed but hands-off. We started with dried pintos (the usual pick for refried beans) and added them right to the slow cooker—no advance soaking or simmering needed. Chicken broth provided a flavorful cooking liquid, and garlic, onion, and cumin offered the requisite aromatic and warm spice notes. A poblano chile upped the heat level, and two slices of bacon infused the beans with smoky, savory depth. To jump-start the cooking of the aromatics and spices and deepen their flavor, we microwaved them briefly with the bacon, which rendered some fat and took the place of any vegetable oil. Once the beans were tender, we discarded the spent bacon strips and mashed the beans. Cilantro and lime juice added brightness and gave our dish authentic south-of-the-border flavor.

1 onion, chopped fine
1 poblano chile, stemmed, seeded, and minced
2 slices bacon

Canned refried beans pale in comparison to this ultraflavorful version infused with aromatics and bacon.

3 garlic cloves, minced
1 tablespoon ground cumin
1 pound (2½ cups) dried pinto beans, picked over and rinsed
6 cups chicken broth, plus extra as needed
3 tablespoons minced fresh cilantro
1 tablespoon lime juice, plus extra as needed
Salt and pepper

1. Microwave onion, poblano, bacon, garlic, and cumin in bowl, stirring occasionally, until vegetables are softened, about 5 minutes; transfer to slow cooker. Stir in beans and broth, cover, and cook until beans are tender, 8 to 9 hours on high.

2. Discard bacon. Drain beans, reserving 1 cup cooking liquid. Return beans and reserved cooking liquid to now-empty slow cooker and mash with potato masher until smooth. Stir in cilantro, lime juice, and ½ teaspoon salt. Season with salt, pepper, and extra lime juice to taste. Serve. (Beans can be held on warm or low setting for up to 2 hours; adjust consistency with extra hot broth as needed before serving.)

VEGETABLE SIDES

■ EASY PREP ■ VEGETARIAN ■ LIGHT ■ COOK ALL DAY
Photo: Braised Artichokes

Once trimmed, whole artichokes sit nicely in the slow cooker and cook perfectly in the moist heat environment.

Braised Artichokes

SERVES 4 **EASY PREP** **VEG** **ALL DAY**

COOKING TIME 8 TO 9 HOURS ON LOW OR 5 TO 6 HOURS ON HIGH

SLOW COOKER SIZE 5 TO 7 QUARTS

WHY THIS RECIPE WORKS Whole artichokes with drawn butter make for an impressive side dish or starter. To ensure that we didn't have to prep or cook them while also getting dinner going, we moved the artichokes to the slow cooker so the leaves could simmer unattended until tender. Prep was easy: We simply trimmed the artichokes and placed them upright in the slow cooker with a little water. Tossing them with a bit of lemon juice and olive oil beforehand helped to preserve their color. For a simple yet boldly flavored dipping sauce, we melted butter with more lemon juice and some minced garlic. If your artichokes are larger than 8 to 10 ounces, strip away another layer or two of the toughest outer leaves. The tender inner leaves, heart, and stem are entirely edible. To eat the tough outer leaves, use your teeth to scrape the flesh out from the underside of each leaf. These artichokes taste great warm or at room temperature. You will need an oval slow cooker for this recipe.

4 artichokes (8 to 10 ounces each)
¼ cup lemon juice (2 lemons)
1 tablespoon extra-virgin olive oil
6 tablespoons unsalted butter
3 garlic cloves, minced
¼ teaspoon salt

1. Using chef's knife, cut off stems so artichokes sit upright, then trim off top quarter of each artichoke. Using kitchen shears, trim off top portion of outer leaves. Toss artichokes with 2 tablespoons lemon juice and oil in bowl, then place right side up in slow cooker. Add ½ cup water, cover, and cook until outer leaves of artichokes pull away easily and tip of paring knife inserted into stem end meets no resistance, 8 to 9 hours on low or 5 to 6 hours on high.

2. Microwave remaining 2 tablespoons lemon juice, butter, garlic, and salt in bowl until butter is melted, about 30 seconds. Whisk butter mixture to combine, then divide evenly among 4 serving bowls. Remove artichokes from slow cooker, letting any excess cooking liquid drain back into insert, and place artichokes in bowls with butter. Serve.

TRIMMING ARTICHOKES

1. Cut stem off each artichoke with chef's knife so that base is even, then trim off top quarter of artichoke.

2. Using kitchen shears, cut off dry, sharp tips from remaining outer leaves.

NOTES FROM THE TEST KITCHEN

Assessing Artichokes

When selecting fresh artichokes at the market, look for leaves that are tight, compact, and bright green; they should not appear dried out or feathery at the edges. If you give an artichoke a squeeze, its leaves should squeak as they rub together (evidence that the artichoke still possesses much of its moisture). The leaves should also snap off cleanly; if they bend, the artichoke is old.

Mediterranean Braised Green Beans

SERVES 4 TO 6 **VEG** **LIGHT** **ALL DAY**

COOKING TIME 7 TO 8 HOURS ON LOW OR 4 TO 5 HOURS
ON HIGH

SLOW COOKER SIZE 5 TO 7 QUARTS

WHY THIS RECIPE WORKS Using the slow cooker to gently braise green beans with the bold flavors of the Mediterranean turned them meltingly tender and infused them with big taste. Canned tomatoes made this dish too watery, so we used tomato paste to provide deep flavor and minimize the amount of liquid. Onion and garlic, along with oregano, provided an aromatic backbone. For subtle heat, we included a small amount of red pepper flakes. Briny capers, added at the end of cooking, made them stand out among the beans and provided a salty kick. For extra richness, we simply stirred in a second tablespoon of olive oil just before serving. You will need an oval slow cooker for this recipe.

- 1 onion, halved and sliced thin
- 2 tablespoons extra-virgin olive oil
- 3 garlic cloves, sliced thin
- 2 teaspoons minced fresh oregano or ½ teaspoon dried
  Salt and pepper
- ⅛ teaspoon red pepper flakes
- ½ cup water
- ⅓ cup tomato paste
- 2 pounds green beans, trimmed
- 2 tablespoons capers, rinsed and minced
- 1 tablespoon chopped fresh parsley

1. Microwave onion, 1 tablespoon oil, garlic, oregano, ¾ teaspoon salt, and pepper flakes in bowl, stirring occasionally, until onion is softened, about 5 minutes; transfer to slow cooker. Stir in water and tomato paste, then stir in green beans. Cover and cook until green beans are tender, 7 to 8 hours on low or 4 to 5 hours on high.

2. Stir in remaining 1 tablespoon oil, capers, and parsley. Season with salt and pepper to taste. Serve. (Green beans can be held on warm or low setting for up to 2 hours.)

TRIMMING GREEN BEANS QUICKLY

Instead of trimming the ends from one green bean at a time, line up the beans on a cutting board and trim all the ends with just one slice.

For perfectly cooked beets, we wrap them in foil before placing them in the slow cooker, then add water.

Beets with Oranges and Walnuts

SERVES 4 TO 6 **EASY PREP** **VEG**

COOKING TIME 6 TO 7 HOURS ON LOW OR 4 TO 5 HOURS
ON HIGH

SLOW COOKER SIZE 4 TO 7 QUARTS

WHY THIS RECIPE WORKS Roasting beets can take up to an hour, which is a long time for the oven to be occupied by a simple side, and steaming them can lead to a loss in flavor. Moving ours to the slow cooker both freed up the oven and guaranteed beets with an undiluted, earthy flavor. Wrapping the beets in aluminum foil and including ½ cup of water in the slow cooker ensured that they cooked through evenly. Rather than skin the beets when they were raw—which can be a messy endeavor—we waited until they were cooked and simply rubbed the skins off with paper towels. Cutting our beets into fork-friendly wedges made them easy to eat, and a simple white wine vinaigrette added brightness. Orange pieces, toasted walnuts, and minced chives turned our slow-cooked vegetable into an impressive bistro-style side dish. To ensure even cooking, we recommend using beets that are similar in size—roughly 3 inches in diameter. You will need an oval slow cooker for this recipe.

    1½ pounds beets, trimmed
    2 oranges
    ¼ cup white wine vinegar
    2 tablespoons extra-virgin olive oil
    1 tablespoon honey
      Salt and pepper
    ¼ cup walnuts, toasted and chopped
    2 tablespoons minced fresh chives

1. Wrap beets individually in aluminum foil and place in slow cooker. Add ½ cup water, cover, and cook until beets are tender, 6 to 7 hours on low or 4 to 5 hours on high.

2. Transfer beets to cutting board and carefully remove foil (watch for steam). When beets are cool enough to handle, rub off skins with paper towels and cut into ½-inch-thick wedges.

3. Cut away peel and pith from oranges. Quarter oranges, then slice crosswise into ½-inch-thick pieces. Whisk vinegar, oil, and honey together in large bowl. Add beets and orange pieces, along with any accumulated juices, and toss to coat. Season with salt and pepper to taste. Sprinkle with walnuts and chives. Serve.

Brussels Sprouts with Lemon, Thyme, and Bacon

SERVES 4 TO 6 `EASY PREP`
COOKING TIME 2 TO 3 HOURS ON HIGH
SLOW COOKER SIZE 5 TO 7 QUARTS

WHY THIS RECIPE WORKS These dressed-up Brussels sprouts are perfect for any table—and because we use the slow cooker, they leave the oven open for the main course. Chicken broth and thyme added savory depth, and a bit of lemon zest and juice contributed brightness. For added richness, we quickly crisped some bacon in the microwave and sprinkled it on top. When trimming the Brussels sprouts, be careful not to cut off too much of the stem end or the leaves will fall away from the core.

    2 pounds Brussels sprouts, trimmed and halved
      through root end
    2 cups chicken broth
      Salt and pepper
    4 slices bacon, chopped
    2 tablespoons unsalted butter, melted
    2 teaspoons grated lemon zest plus 1 tablespoon juice
    1 teaspoon minced fresh thyme

We dress up perfectly tender Brussels sprouts with crisp bacon, butter, lemon, and fresh thyme.

1. Combine Brussels sprouts, broth, and ½ teaspoon salt in slow cooker. Cover and cook until Brussels sprouts are tender, 2 to 3 hours on high.

2. Line plate with double layer of coffee filters. Spread bacon in even layer on filters and microwave until crisp, about 5 minutes. Drain Brussels sprouts and return to now-empty slow cooker. Stir in melted butter, lemon zest and juice, and thyme. Season with salt and pepper to taste. Sprinkle with bacon and serve.

Sweet and Sour Braised Red Cabbage

SERVES 4 TO 6
COOKING TIME 5 TO 6 HOURS ON LOW OR 3 TO 4 HOURS ON HIGH
SLOW COOKER SIZE 5 TO 7 QUARTS

WHY THIS RECIPE WORKS The slow cooker, with its moist heat environment, is perfect for braising cabbage. However, adding the cabbage directly to the slow cooker left it too crunchy for our liking. To get the texture just right, we had to precook it in the microwave to soften it slightly. This step had the added benefit of getting rid of excess moisture that was otherwise detracting from the flavors of the dish. For the braising medium we selected sweet and fruity apple cider, enhancing it with traditional spices such as cinnamon, caraway seeds, and allspice. A bit of sugar rounded out the sweetness, while vinegar perked up the flavors and added balance. Since tasters found the cabbage a little lean, we added bacon, which imparted a smoky depth and richness.

    1 head red cabbage (2 pounds), cored and sliced thin
    1 tablespoon vegetable oil
      Salt and pepper
    4 slices bacon, chopped fine
    1 onion, chopped fine
    1 teaspoon minced fresh thyme or ¼ teaspoon dried
    ½ teaspoon caraway seeds, toasted
    ¼ teaspoon ground cinnamon
    ¼ teaspoon ground allspice
  1½ cups apple cider
    2 tablespoons packed brown sugar, plus extra
      for seasoning
    3 bay leaves
    2 tablespoons cider vinegar, plus extra for seasoning

SLICING CABBAGE

1. Cut cabbage into quarters, then trim and discard core.

2. Separate cabbage into small stacks of leaves that flatten when pressed.

3. Use chef's knife to cut each stack of cabbage leaves into thin shreds.

1. Microwave cabbage, oil, and ½ teaspoon salt in covered bowl, stirring occasionally, until cabbage is softened, 15 to 20 minutes. Drain cabbage and transfer to slow cooker.

2. Cook bacon in 12-inch skillet over medium-high heat until crisp, about 5 minutes. Add onion and cook until softened and lightly browned, 5 to 7 minutes. Stir in thyme, caraway seeds, cinnamon, and allspice and cook until fragrant, about 30 seconds. Stir in ½ cup cider, scraping up any browned bits; transfer to slow cooker.

3. Stir remaining 1 cup cider, sugar, and bay leaves into slow cooker. Cover and cook until cabbage is tender, 5 to 6 hours on low or 3 to 4 hours on high.

4. Discard bay leaves. Stir in vinegar and season with salt, pepper, extra sugar, and extra vinegar to taste. Serve. (Cabbage can be held on warm or low setting for up to 2 hours.)

Glazed Carrots

SERVES 6 TO 8 `EASY PREP` `VEG` `LIGHT`
COOKING TIME 5 TO 6 HOURS ON LOW OR 3 TO 4 HOURS ON HIGH
SLOW COOKER SIZE 4 TO 7 QUARTS

WHY THIS RECIPE WORKS Glazed carrots are one of those reliable side dishes we often turn to when hosting a holiday meal, and using the slow cooker eliminated all the last-minute fuss involved (and freed up the stovetop). Initially we tried cooking the carrots in broth, but it detracted from their delicate, sweet flavor. In the end, water that had been seasoned with a little sugar and salt was best for gently simmering the carrots. Once they were tender, we simply drained them and tossed them with tart orange marmalade and a pat of butter. The marmalade and butter melted to form a mock "glaze" that conveniently did not need to be reduced on the stovetop first. Simple, sweet, and delicious—nothing could be easier.

    3 pounds carrots, peeled and sliced ¼ inch thick on bias
    1 tablespoon sugar
      Salt and pepper
    ½ cup orange marmalade
    2 tablespoons unsalted butter, softened

1. Combine carrots, ¾ cup water, sugar, and ¼ teaspoon salt in slow cooker. Cover and cook until carrots are tender, 5 to 6 hours on low or 3 to 4 hours on high.

2. Drain carrots and return to now-empty slow cooker. Stir in marmalade and butter. Season with salt and pepper to taste. Serve. (Carrots can be held on warm or low setting for up to 2 hours.)

Mashed Cauliflower

SERVES 8 TO 10 `EASY PREP` `VEG` `LIGHT` `ALL DAY`

COOKING TIME 7 TO 8 HOURS ON LOW OR 4 TO 5 HOURS ON HIGH

SLOW COOKER SIZE 5 TO 7 QUARTS

WHY THIS RECIPE WORKS For a simple alternative to mashed potatoes, we decided to use cauliflower. Since cauliflower is low in fiber, it easily breaks down when cooked for an extended period of time, making it perfect for the slow cooker. This meant a creamy textured side dish could easily be achieved using only a potato masher. With just three key ingredients—cauliflower, water instead of broth, and salt—we aimed to keep the flavor of the cauliflower at the fore. Because the cooking liquid isn't drained, a mere half-cup of water proved to be just enough to allow the cauliflower to cook perfectly without causing the sweet, nutty flavor developed during the long cooking time to become washed out. But tasters felt our cauliflower mash was too lean to be considered a mashed potato alternative. We solved this with a splash of heavy cream (a tablespoon of cream per pound of vegetables), which provided richness, while a sprinkle of chives added a bright, fresh finish. If you prefer to buy bagged cauliflower florets, rather than a head, you will need 3 pounds of florets. For more information on creating a parchment shield, see page 177. For an accurate measurement of boiling water, bring a full kettle of water to a boil and then measure out the desired amount.

- 2 heads cauliflower (4 pounds), cored and cut into 2-inch florets
- ½ cup boiling water, plus extra as needed
  Salt and pepper
- ¼ cup heavy cream
- 3 tablespoons minced fresh chives

1. Combine cauliflower, boiling water, and 1½ teaspoons salt in slow cooker. Press 16 by 12-inch sheet of parchment paper firmly onto cauliflower, folding down edges as needed. Cover and cook until cauliflower is very tender, 7 to 8 hours on low or 4 to 5 hours on high.

2. Discard parchment. Mash cauliflower with potato masher until almost completely broken down. Stir in cream and chives and season with salt and pepper to taste. Serve. (Cauliflower can be held on warm or low setting for up to 2 hours; adjust consistency with extra hot water as needed before serving.)

Made on the side, a zesty vinaigrette with capers and lemon is the perfect finishing touch to easy braised cauliflower.

Braised Cauliflower with Lemon-Caper Dressing

SERVES 4 TO 6 `EASY PREP` `VEG` `LIGHT`

COOKING TIME 2 TO 3 HOURS ON HIGH

SLOW COOKER SIZE 5 TO 7 QUARTS

WHY THIS RECIPE WORKS We wanted to add flavor to cauliflower without drowning it in a heavy blanket of cheese sauce, so we developed a recipe for braised cauliflower in our slow cooker. Since cauliflower can quickly go from perfectly tender to completely broken down we avoided small florets and instead sliced a head of cauliflower into thick wedges. A small amount of water seasoned with a little salt was best for gently braising the cauliflower. We also included a few smashed garlic cloves, thyme sprigs, and pepper flakes for added flavor. A bright dressing put a fresh Mediterranean spin on this simple side. You will need an oval slow cooker for this recipe.

- 4 garlic cloves, peeled and smashed
- 2 sprigs fresh thyme
  Salt and pepper

⅛ teaspoon red pepper flakes
1 head cauliflower (2 pounds)
2 tablespoons extra-virgin olive oil
2 teaspoons grated lemon zest plus 1 tablespoon juice
2 teaspoons capers, rinsed and minced
1 tablespoon minced fresh parsley

1. Combine 1 cup water, garlic, thyme sprigs, ½ teaspoon salt, and pepper flakes in slow cooker. Trim outer leaves of cauliflower and cut stem flush with bottom of head. Cut head into 8 equal wedges, keeping core and florets intact. Place wedges cut side down in slow cooker (wedges may overlap). Cover and cook until cauliflower is tender, 2 to 3 hours on high.

2. Whisk oil, lemon zest and juice, capers, and parsley together in bowl. Season with salt and pepper to taste. Using slotted spoon, transfer cauliflower to serving dish, brushing away any garlic cloves or thyme sprigs that stick to cauliflower. Drizzle cauliflower with dressing. Serve.

CUTTING CAULIFLOWER INTO WEDGES

1. Remove outer leaves from cauliflower and cut stalk flush with bottom. Place head upside down and cut cauliflower crown in half through stalk.

2. Cut each half of crown in half to make 4 wedges, and cut each of those in half again to make 8 equal wedges.

Creamed Corn

SERVES 6 TO 8 **EASY PREP** **VEG**

COOKING TIME 3 TO 4 HOURS ON LOW OR 2 TO 3 HOURS ON HIGH

SLOW COOKER SIZE 4 TO 7 QUARTS

WHY THIS RECIPE WORKS Taste this homemade slow-cooker version of creamed corn, with its rich flavor and lush texture, and you'll never dream of reaching for the canned alternative again. With loads of sweet corn flavor, this comforting side comes together with a minimum of prep and just a handful of pantry staples—shallot, garlic, thyme, and cayenne pepper. We knew fresh corn would be essential for flavor here. To get the best in both texture and flavor we used a combination of whole kernels cut away from the cobs and grated corn (the large holes of a box grater work best for this task). The kernels became tender yet maintained a slight bite owing to the gentle cooking environment of the slow cooker, while the grated corn contributed to a thicker body in the dish. Before discarding them, don't forget to scrape the cobs with the back of a knife to collect the flavorful corn pulp and "milk." This important step dramatically improves the corn flavor. Because heavy cream, unlike milk or half-and-half, can be simmered without curdling, it is essential here. For information on making an aluminum foil collar, see page 208.

1 shallot, minced
2 tablespoons unsalted butter, melted
1 garlic clove, minced
½ teaspoon minced fresh thyme or ⅛ teaspoon dried
    Pinch cayenne pepper
5 ears corn, husks and silk removed
1½ cups heavy cream
    Salt and pepper

1. Line slow cooker with aluminum foil collar and lightly coat with vegetable oil spray. Microwave shallot, melted butter, garlic, thyme, and cayenne in bowl, stirring occasionally, until shallot is softened, about 2 minutes.

2. Cut kernels from 3 ears of corn into large bowl, reserving cobs. Grate remaining 2 ears of corn over large holes of box grater into bowl with kernels, reserving cobs. Firmly scrape all cobs with back of butter knife into bowl with corn to collect pulp and milk.

3. Stir cream, shallot mixture, ¼ teaspoon salt, and ⅛ teaspoon pepper into bowl with corn; transfer to prepared slow cooker. Cover and cook until corn is tender, 3 to 4 hours on low or 2 to 3 hours on high.

4. Discard foil collar. Stir corn mixture to recombine and season with salt and pepper to taste. Serve. (Corn can be held on warm or low setting for up to 2 hours; adjust consistency with hot water as needed before serving.)

PREPARING FRESH CORN

To remove the kernels from an ear of corn, stand the cob upright inside a large bowl; this will help catch any flying kernels. Then, using a paring knife, slice down along the sides of the cob to remove the kernels.

To keep the vegetables for our ratatouille from becoming soggy, we broil them before adding them to the slow cooker.

Ratatouille

SERVES 8 TO 10 VEG

COOKING TIME 3 TO 4 HOURS ON LOW OR 2 TO 3 HOURS ON HIGH

SLOW COOKER SIZE 5 TO 7 QUARTS

WHY THIS RECIPE WORKS The slow cooker is tailor-made for long-cooked stews, but this Provençal dish is chock-full of watery vegetables, and the cooker doesn't allow for any evaporation—a recipe for bland, runny ratatouille. Draining the canned tomatoes was a good start, and adding some instant tapioca at the outset helped, too. In the end, tossing the chopped vegetables with olive oil and a little sugar and broiling them before they went into the slow cooker not only added flavorful browning but also drove off moisture, creating a stewy—not soupy—dish. Garlic and herbes de Provence seasoned the ratatouille as it cooked, and Parmesan cheese and fresh basil finished it off. Herbes de Provence is a French blend that usually includes rosemary, marjoram, thyme, lavender, and fennel. If you can't find it, you can use 1 teaspoon each of dried rosemary and dried thyme.

2 pounds eggplant, cut into ½-inch pieces

1½ pounds zucchini, cut into 1-inch pieces

2 red bell peppers, stemmed, seeded, and cut into ½-inch pieces

2 onions, chopped

½ cup extra-virgin olive oil

1 tablespoon sugar

2 garlic cloves, minced

2 teaspoons herbes de Provence

1 (28-ounce) can diced tomatoes, drained

1 teaspoon instant tapioca

Salt and pepper

¼ cup grated Parmesan cheese

¼ cup chopped fresh basil

1. Adjust oven rack 4 inches from broiler element and heat broiler. Line 2 rimmed baking sheets with aluminum foil and spray with vegetable oil spray. Toss eggplant, zucchini, bell peppers, and onions with 6 tablespoons oil, sugar, garlic, and herbes de Provence in large bowl. Divide vegetables evenly between prepared sheets and spread in single layer. Broil, 1 sheet at a time, until vegetables begin to brown, 10 to 12 minutes, rotating sheet halfway through broiling. Transfer vegetables and tomatoes to slow cooker.

2. Stir tapioca, 2½ teaspoons salt, and 1 teaspoon pepper into vegetables. Cover and cook until vegetables are tender, 3 to 4 hours on low or 2 to 3 hours on high. Stir in Parmesan, basil, and remaining 2 tablespoons oil. Season with salt and pepper to taste. Serve. (Ratatouille can be held on warm or low setting for up to 2 hours; adjust consistency with hot water as needed before serving.)

Braised Fennel with Orange-Tarragon Dressing

SERVES 4 TO 6 EASY PREP VEG LIGHT ALL DAY

COOKING TIME 8 TO 9 HOURS ON LOW OR 5 TO 6 HOURS ON HIGH

SLOW COOKER SIZE 5 TO 7 QUARTS

WHY THIS RECIPE WORKS We wanted a recipe for braised fennel that would infuse the fennel with rich, savory flavor. Cutting the fennel into wedges turned out to be the key to evenly cooked fennel, and we made sure to braise it long enough to deliver uniformly tender but not mushy results. A combination of water, garlic, juniper berries, and thyme provided a base of seasoning for this appealing side dish, and we finished it off with a simple orange-tarragon dressing. Don't core the fennel bulb before cutting it into wedges; the core will help hold the layers of fennel together during cooking. You will need an oval slow cooker for this recipe.

A braising liquid with smashed garlic cloves, fresh thyme, and juniper berries adds flavor to these fennel wedges.

2 garlic cloves, peeled and smashed
2 sprigs fresh thyme
1 teaspoon juniper berries
  Salt and pepper
2 fennel bulbs, stalks discarded, bulbs halved and
  each half cut into 4 wedges
2 tablespoons extra-virgin olive oil
2 teaspoons grated orange zest plus 1 tablespoon juice
1 teaspoon minced fresh tarragon

1. Combine 1 cup water, garlic, thyme sprigs, juniper berries, and ½ teaspoon salt in slow cooker. Place fennel wedges cut side down in slow cooker (wedges may overlap). Cover and cook until fennel is tender, 8 to 9 hours on low or 5 to 6 hours on high.

2. Whisk oil, orange zest and juice, and tarragon together in bowl. Season with salt and pepper to taste. Using slotted spoon, transfer fennel to serving dish, brushing away any garlic cloves, thyme sprigs, or juniper berries that stick to fennel. Drizzle fennel with dressing. Serve.

Southern Braised Collard Greens

SERVES 4 TO 6 **EASY PREP** **ALL DAY**
COOKING TIME 9 TO 10 HOURS ON LOW OR 6 TO 7 HOURS ON HIGH
SLOW COOKER SIZE 5 TO 7 QUARTS

WHY THIS RECIPE WORKS Any Southerner will tell you that "lip-smacking" collard greens require long cooking and the smokiness of cured pork, and we tend to agree. Slow-cooking this hearty green in liquid tempers its assertive bitterness, making it perfectly suited to the slow cooker. Upon testing varying amounts of liquid, we found 4 cups to be ideal for 2 pounds of greens. This may not sound like a lot of liquid, but given the lack of significant evaporation and the slow cooker's moist environment, this amount went a long way to ensure properly cooked collards without the need for them to be fully submerged. A combination of chicken broth (rather than water) and aromatics (onion and garlic) helped the greens develop great flavor, while a ham hock imparted characteristic smokiness. To round things out, pepper flakes were added for some subtle heat. We brightened up the liquid at the end of cooking with cider vinegar, and the leftover cooking liquid, traditionally called pot "liquor" (or "likker"), can be sopped up with cornbread or biscuits, or used to cook a second batch of collard greens, as is traditionally done in the South.

1 onion, chopped fine
6 garlic cloves, minced
1 tablespoon vegetable oil
  Salt and pepper
½ teaspoon red pepper flakes
2 pounds collard greens, stemmed and cut
  into 1-inch pieces
4 cups chicken broth
1 (12-ounce) smoked ham hock, rinsed
2 tablespoons cider vinegar, plus extra for seasoning
  Hot sauce

1. Lightly coat slow cooker with vegetable oil spray. Microwave onion, garlic, oil, 1 teaspoon salt, and pepper flakes in bowl, stirring occasionally, until onion is softened, about 5 minutes; transfer to prepared slow cooker. Stir in collard greens and broth. Nestle ham hock into slow cooker. Cover and cook until collard greens are tender, 9 to 10 hours on low or 6 to 7 hours on high.

2. Transfer ham hock to cutting board, let cool slightly, then shred into bite-size pieces using 2 forks; discard fat, skin, and bones. Stir ham and vinegar into collard greens. Season with salt, pepper, and extra vinegar to taste. Serve with hot sauce. (Collard greens can be held on warm or low setting for up to 2 hours.)

Here hearty kale gets a big flavor boost from chorizo, which we microwave with garlic and oil before slow cooking.

Braised Kale with Garlic and Chorizo

SERVES 4 TO 6 `ALL DAY`

COOKING TIME 7 TO 8 HOURS ON LOW OR 4 TO 5 HOURS ON HIGH

SLOW COOKER SIZE 5 TO 7 QUARTS

WHY THIS RECIPE WORKS Using the slow cooker to prepare our hearty kale was a no-brainer—after all, a long cooking time helps to turn kale meltingly tender and tempers its assertive flavor. With the texture right where we wanted it, all we had to do was come up with a few flavorful ingredients to add to the pot. We liked a simple combination of chorizo and garlic, which gave these simple greens a meaty, spicy kick.

    8 ounces Spanish-style chorizo sausage, halved
       lengthwise and sliced ½ inch thick
    2 garlic cloves, minced
    1 tablespoon extra-virgin olive oil
  1½ cups chicken broth
       Salt and pepper
    2 pounds kale, stemmed and cut into 1-inch pieces

1. Lightly coat slow cooker with vegetable oil spray. Microwave chorizo, garlic, and oil in bowl, stirring occasionally, until fragrant, about 1 minute; transfer to prepared slow cooker. Stir in broth and ¼ teaspoon salt.

2. Microwave half of kale in covered bowl until slightly wilted, about 5 minutes; transfer to slow cooker. Stir in remaining kale, cover, and cook until kale is tender, 7 to 8 hours on low or 4 to 5 hours on high. Season with salt and pepper to taste. Serve. (Kale can be held on warm or low setting for up to 2 hours.)

Braised Swiss Chard with Shiitakes and Peanuts

SERVES 4 TO 6 `EASY PREP` `VEG` `LIGHT`

COOKING TIME 1 TO 2 HOURS ON HIGH

SLOW COOKER SIZE 5 TO 7 QUARTS

WHY THIS RECIPE WORKS For an Asian take on braised Swiss chard, we turned to toasted sesame oil, a hefty dose of grated fresh ginger, and minced garlic as our aromatic base. And for heartiness we added shiitake mushrooms, braising them along with the chard. Once the chard was perfectly tender, we stirred in rice vinegar and some additional ginger, keeping the flavors fresh and vibrant. A little butter added richness.

    2 pounds Swiss chard, stems chopped fine,
       leaves cut into 1-inch pieces
    4 ounces shiitake mushrooms, stemmed and
       sliced ¼ inch thick
    3 garlic cloves, minced
    2 teaspoons grated fresh ginger
    2 teaspoons toasted sesame oil
       Salt and pepper
   ⅛ teaspoon red pepper flakes
    1 tablespoon rice vinegar
    1 tablespoon unsalted butter
    1 teaspoon sugar
    2 tablespoons chopped dry-roasted peanuts
    2 scallions, sliced thin

1. Lightly coat slow cooker with vegetable oil spray. Microwave chard stems, mushrooms, garlic, 1 teaspoon ginger, 1 teaspoon oil, ¼ teaspoon salt, and pepper flakes in bowl, stirring occasionally, until vegetables are softened, about 5 minutes; transfer to prepared slow cooker. Stir in chard leaves, cover, and cook until chard is tender, 1 to 2 hours on high.

2. Stir in vinegar, butter, sugar, remaining 1 teaspoon ginger, and remaining 1 teaspoon oil. Season with salt and pepper to taste. (Swiss chard can be held on warm or low setting for up to 2 hours.) Sprinkle with peanuts and scallions before serving.

All About Hearty Greens

No longer just a farmers' market specialty item, hearty greens are now widely available in grocery stores across the country. There are many types of hearty greens, but the ones we use most often are Swiss chard, collard greens, kale, and mustard greens. Here is some basic information on each.

SWISS CHARD Swiss chard has dark, ruffled leaves and a tough stem that can be crimson red, orange, yellow, or white. The leaves and stems need to be cooked separately, as the stems take much longer to soften. Look for bunches with bright-stemmed leaves that are firm and undamaged.

COLLARD GREENS Collard greens have dark green, very wide leaves and a thick stem. Look for bunches with trimmed stems and no sign of yellowing or wilting. Unless you plan to slice the leaves thinly, it is best to braise collard greens until tender. Be sure to strip the leaves from the stems, which are tough and woody.

KALE Kale comes in many varieties: curly green kale, red kale, more delicate Tuscan kale, and baby kale. Its hearty leaves have a surprisingly sweet undertone. Kale is easy to find both in bunches and in prewashed bags. Tender baby kale can be eaten raw in salads without any special treatment, but mature kale is tougher. To eat it raw, cut it into pieces, then vigorously knead it for about 5 minutes.

MUSTARD GREENS There are many varieties of mustard greens, but the most common one has crisp, bright green leaves and thin stems. These greens have a medium-hot flavor with a fairly strong bite, which makes them especially well suited to spicy Asian noodle dishes.

Creamy Braised Leeks

SERVES 4 TO 6 **VEG**
COOKING TIME 3 TO 4 HOURS ON LOW OR 2 TO 3 HOURS ON HIGH
SLOW COOKER SIZE 5 TO 7 QUARTS

WHY THIS RECIPE WORKS The unique onion-like sweetness of leeks makes them a delicious accompaniment to a fish or poultry entrée, especially when braised. The key to this dish was cooking the leeks to the ideal doneness so they'd be nicely tender with a creamy texture and great flavor. Utilizing the slow cooker's relatively low heat and slow cooking time helped to coax out their delicate flavor. First, we jump-started the leeks in the microwave for a few minutes, along with garlic and thyme, to build even more complex flavor. Prior to cooking in the slow cooker, we added a generous amount of cream to ensure a rich, velvety texture while a splash of wine added acidity. Pecorino stirred in at the end of cooking enriched the dish further and provided an even creamier texture. Because heavy cream, unlike milk or half-and-half, can be simmered without curdling, it is essential here.

3 pounds leeks, white and light green parts only, halved lengthwise, sliced thin, and washed and dried thoroughly
1 tablespoon vegetable oil
2 garlic cloves, minced
2 teaspoons minced fresh thyme or ½ teaspoon dried
  Salt and pepper
1 cup heavy cream
½ cup dry white wine
¼ cup grated Pecorino Romano cheese

1. Microwave leeks, oil, garlic, thyme, 1 teaspoon salt, and ¼ teaspoon pepper in bowl, stirring occasionally, until leeks are softened, 8 to 10 minutes; transfer to slow cooker. Stir in cream and wine, cover, and cook until leeks are tender but not mushy, 3 to 4 hours on low or 2 to 3 hours on high.

2. Stir Pecorino into leek mixture and season with salt and pepper to taste. Let sit for 5 minutes until slightly thickened. Serve. (Leeks can be held on warm or low setting for up to 2 hours; adjust consistency with hot water as needed before serving.)

PREPARING LEEKS

1. Trim and discard root and dark green leaves, then cut trimmed leek in half lengthwise.

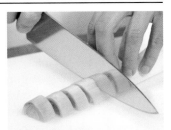

2. Slice leek crosswise as directed. Wash cut leeks thoroughly to remove dirt and sand.

Classic Mashed Potatoes

SERVES 10 TO 12   `EASY PREP`
COOKING TIME 5 TO 6 HOURS ON LOW
OR 3 TO 4 HOURS ON HIGH
SLOW COOKER SIZE 5 TO 7 QUARTS

For evenly cooked potatoes in the slow
cooker, we used a small amount of water
and a parchment shield to create a moist,
steamy environment. Thinly sliced potatoes cooked more evenly than chunks,
and boiling the water first jump-started
the cooking process. We brushed the top
layer of potatoes with melted butter to
help prevent discoloration, and mashed
in the rest of the butter for additional
flavor about 4 hours later, when the potatoes were tender. (The top layer of
potatoes may discolor slightly, but this
won't be noticeable upon mashing.) To
simplify things further, we did away with
the extra step of draining the potatoes in
favor of just mashing them in the cooking
liquid. Along with the added butter (or
olive oil), the cooking liquid easily created
a nice smooth texture when incorporated. For more information on creating
a parchment shield, see page 177. The
potatoes can be held on the warm or
low setting for up to 2 hours; adjust the
consistency with extra hot water as
needed before serving.

1 CLASSIC MASHED POTATOES

- 5 pounds russet potatoes, peeled and sliced ¼ inch thick
- 2¾ cups boiling water, plus extra as needed
  Salt and pepper
- 12 tablespoons unsalted butter, melted
- ½ cup sour cream
- 3 tablespoons minced fresh chives

1. Combine potatoes, boiling water, and 2 teaspoons salt in slow cooker. Brush top layer of potatoes with 3 tablespoons melted butter. Press 16 by 12-inch sheet of parchment paper firmly onto potatoes, folding down edges as needed. Cover and cook until potatoes are tender, 5 to 6 hours on low or 3 to 4 hours on high.

2. Discard parchment. Mash potatoes with potato masher until smooth. Stir in sour cream, chives, and remaining 9 tablespoons melted butter until combined. Season with salt and pepper to taste. Serve.

2 LOADED MASHED POTATOES

- 5 pounds russet potatoes, peeled and sliced ¼ inch thick
- 2¾ cups boiling water, plus extra as needed
- 3 garlic cloves, peeled and smashed
  Salt and pepper
- 12 tablespoons unsalted butter, melted
- 6 slices bacon, chopped
- 8 ounces cheddar cheese, shredded (2 cups)
- ½ cup sour cream
- 3 scallions, sliced thin

1. Combine potatoes, boiling water, garlic, and 2 teaspoons salt in slow cooker. Brush top layer of potatoes with 3 tablespoons melted butter. Press 16 by 12-inch sheet of parchment paper firmly onto potatoes, folding down edges as needed. Cover and cook until potatoes are tender, 5 to 6 hours on low or 3 to 4 hours on high.

2. Line plate with double layer of coffee filters. Spread bacon in even layer on filters and microwave until crisp, about 5 minutes.

3. Discard parchment. Mash potatoes with potato masher until smooth. Stir in bacon, cheddar, sour cream, scallions, and remaining 9 tablespoons melted butter until combined. Season with salt and pepper to taste. Serve.

3 GARLIC AND PARMESAN MASHED POTATOES

5 pounds russet potatoes, peeled and sliced ¼ inch thick
2¾ cups boiling water, plus extra as needed
8 garlic cloves, peeled and smashed
Salt and pepper
12 tablespoons unsalted butter, melted
3 ounces Parmesan cheese, grated (1½ cups)

1. Combine potatoes, boiling water, garlic, and 2 teaspoons salt in slow cooker. Brush top layer of potatoes with 3 tablespoons melted butter. Press 16 by 12-inch sheet of parchment paper firmly onto potatoes, folding down edges as needed. Cover and cook until potatoes are tender, 5 to 6 hours on low or 3 to 4 hours on high.

2. Discard parchment. Mash potatoes with potato masher until smooth. Stir in Parmesan and remaining 9 tablespoons melted butter until combined. Season with salt and pepper to taste. Serve.

4 MASHED POTATOES AND ROOT VEGETABLES

3 pounds russet potatoes, peeled and sliced ¼ inch thick
1 pound parsnips, peeled and sliced ¼ inch thick
1 celery root (14 ounces), peeled, quartered, and sliced ¼ inch thick
2¾ cups boiling water, plus extra as needed
Salt and pepper
12 tablespoons unsalted butter, melted
½ cup sour cream
3 tablespoons minced fresh chives

1. Combine potatoes, parsnips, celery root, boiling water, and 2 teaspoons salt in slow cooker. Brush top layer of vegetables with 3 tablespoons melted butter. Press 16 by 12-inch sheet of parchment paper firmly onto vegetables, folding down edges as needed. Cover and cook until vegetables are tender, 5 to 6 hours on low or 3 to 4 hours on high.

2. Discard parchment. Mash vegetables with potato masher until smooth. Stir in sour cream, chives, and remaining 9 tablespoons melted butter until combined. Season with salt and pepper to taste. Serve.

5 OLIVE OIL–ROSEMARY MASHED POTATOES

5 pounds russet potatoes, peeled and sliced ¼ inch thick
2¾ cups boiling water, plus extra as needed
Salt and pepper
10 tablespoons extra-virgin olive oil
1 teaspoon minced fresh rosemary
½ teaspoon grated lemon zest plus 1 tablespoon juice

1. Combine potatoes, boiling water, and 2 teaspoons salt in slow cooker. Brush top layer of potatoes with 2 tablespoons oil. Press 16 by 12-inch sheet of parchment paper firmly onto potatoes, folding down edges as needed. Cover and cook until potatoes are tender, 5 to 6 hours on low or 3 to 4 hours on high.

2. Discard parchment. Mash potatoes with potato masher until smooth. Stir in rosemary, lemon zest and juice, and remaining ½ cup oil until combined. Season with salt and pepper to taste. Serve.

We love using the slow cooker to make no-fuss mashed sweet potatoes with a perfect texture.

Mashed Sweet Potatoes

SERVES 6 TO 8 **EASY PREP** **VEG** **LIGHT**

COOKING TIME 5 TO 6 HOURS ON LOW OR 3 TO 4 HOURS ON HIGH

SLOW COOKER SIZE 5 TO 7 QUARTS

WHY THIS RECIPE WORKS Smooth and velvety, and with a buttery finish, these slow-cooker mashed sweet potatoes will keep you coming back for more. Pressing a piece of parchment on top of the potatoes resulted in even cooking, without any dry edges. For more information on creating a parchment shield, see page 177. For an accurate measurement of boiling water, bring a full kettle of water to a boil and then measure out the desired amount. This recipe can be easily doubled in a 7-quart slow cooker; you will need to increase the cooking time range by 1 hour.

    3 pounds sweet potatoes, peeled and sliced ¼ inch thick
    ½ cup boiling water, plus extra as needed
    1 teaspoon sugar
       Salt and pepper
    6 tablespoons half-and-half, warmed
    3 tablespoons unsalted butter, melted

1. Combine potatoes, boiling water, sugar, and ¾ teaspoon salt in slow cooker. Press 16 by 12-inch sheet of parchment paper firmly onto potatoes, folding down edges as needed. Cover and cook until potatoes are tender, 5 to 6 hours on low or 3 to 4 hours on high.

2. Discard parchment. Mash potatoes with potato masher until smooth. Stir in warm half-and-half and melted butter, and season with salt and pepper to taste. Serve. (Sweet potatoes can be held on warm or low setting for up to 2 hours; adjust consistency with extra hot water as needed before serving.)

Buttermilk Smashed Red Potatoes

SERVES 4 TO 6 **EASY PREP** **VEG**

COOKING TIME 5 TO 6 HOURS ON LOW OR 3 TO 4 HOURS ON HIGH

SLOW COOKER SIZE 4 TO 7 QUARTS

WHY THIS RECIPE WORKS Bold flavors and a rustic, chunky texture make smashed potatoes a satisfying side dish that pairs well with a range of entrées. Low-starch, high-moisture red potatoes were the best choice, as their compact structure held up well under pressure from mashing, and their red skins provided nice contrasting color. For the best chunky texture, we cooked the potatoes whole with olive oil, garlic, and thyme, then smashed them with a potato masher. A combination of buttermilk and sour

For just the right ratio of skins to flesh in these smashed potatoes we use small red potatoes and cut them in half.

cream gave our potatoes a unified creamy consistency. Look for small red potatoes measuring 1 to 2 inches in diameter. This recipe can easily be doubled in a 7-quart slow cooker; you will need to increase the cooking time range by 1 hour.

    2 pounds small red potatoes, unpeeled, halved
    3 tablespoons extra-virgin olive oil
    3 garlic cloves, peeled and smashed
    2 teaspoons minced fresh thyme or ½ teaspoon dried
       Salt and pepper
    ⅔ cup buttermilk
    ¼ cup sour cream
    2 tablespoons minced fresh chives

1. Combine potatoes, oil, garlic, thyme, 1 teaspoon salt, and ¼ teaspoon pepper in slow cooker. Cover and cook until potatoes are tender, 5 to 6 hours on low or 3 to 4 hours on high.

2. Add buttermilk and sour cream to potatoes and, using potato masher, mash until combined and chunks of potatoes remain. Fold in chives and season with salt and pepper to taste. Serve. (Potatoes can be held on warm or low setting for up to 2 hours; adjust consistency with hot water as needed before serving.)

All About Potatoes

Since potatoes have varying textures (determined by starch level), you can't just reach for any potato and expect great results. Potatoes fall into three main categories—baking, boiling, or all-purpose—depending on texture.

BAKING POTATOES These dry, floury potatoes contain more total starch (20 to 22 percent) than that in other categories, giving these varieties a dry, mealy texture. These potatoes are the best choice when baking and frying. In our opinion, they are also the best potatoes for mashing because they can drink up butter and cream. They work well when you want to thicken a stew or soup, but not when you want distinct chunks of potatoes. Common varieties: russet, Russet Burbank, and Idaho.

ALL-PURPOSE POTATOES These potatoes contain less total starch (18 to 20 percent) than that in dry, floury potatoes but more than the total starch in firm boiling potatoes. Although they are considered "in-between" potatoes, in comparison to boiling potatoes their texture is more mealy, putting them closer to dry, floury potatoes. All-purpose potatoes can be mashed or baked but won't be as fluffy as dry, floury potatoes. They can be used in salads and soups but won't be quite as firm as boiling potatoes. Common varieties: Yukon Gold, Yellow Finn, Purple Peruvian, Kennebec, and Katahdin.

BOILING POTATOES These potatoes contain a relatively low amount of total starch (16 to 18 percent), which means they have a firm, smooth, waxy texture. Often they are called "new" potatoes because they are less-mature potatoes harvested in late spring and summer. They are less starchy than "old" potatoes because they haven't had time to convert their sugar to starch. They also have thinner skins. Firm, waxy potatoes are perfect when you want the potatoes to hold their shape, as with potato salad. They are also a good choice when roasting or boiling. Common varieties: Red Bliss, French Fingerling, Red Creamer, and White Rose.

Red Potatoes with Rosemary and Garlic

SERVES 4 TO 6 `EASY PREP` `VEG`

COOKING TIME 5 TO 6 HOURS ON LOW OR 3 TO 4 HOURS
ON HIGH

SLOW COOKER SIZE 4 TO 7 QUARTS

WHY THIS RECIPE WORKS Moving small red potatoes to the
slow cooker gave us another simple side that goes well with any
number of entrées. Since our spuds were small, they cooked
through evenly on their own—no need to wrap them in foil. We
simply tossed them with extra-virgin olive oil and minced garlic
for richness and flavor. Minced fresh rosemary added at the end
of cooking infused our supertender, ultracreamy spuds with
woodsy notes. Look for small red potatoes measuring 1 to 2 inches
in diameter. This recipe can easily be doubled in a 7-quart slow
cooker; you will need to increase the cooking time range by 1 hour.

  2 pounds small red potatoes, unpeeled
  2 tablespoons extra-virgin olive oil
  3 garlic cloves, minced
     Salt and pepper
  1 teaspoon minced fresh rosemary

1. Combine potatoes, 1 tablespoon oil, garlic, ½ teaspoon salt,
and ¼ teaspoon pepper in slow cooker. Cover and cook until
potatoes are tender, 5 to 6 hours on low or 3 to 4 hours on high.

2. Stir in rosemary and remaining 1 tablespoon oil. Season with
salt and pepper to taste. Serve. (Potatoes can be held on warm or
low setting for up to 2 hours.)

Lemon-Herb Fingerling Potatoes

SERVES 6 `EASY PREP` `VEG` `LIGHT`

COOKING TIME 5 TO 6 HOURS ON LOW OR 3 TO 4 HOURS
ON HIGH

SLOW COOKER SIZE 4 TO 7 QUARTS

WHY THIS RECIPE WORKS Widely available at farm stands and
now at many grocery stores too, fingerling potatoes are a nice
alternative to standard white or red potatoes. They are creamy and
dense and feel somehow special because of their small, narrow
shape. So for a supereasy and attractive side dish, we turned to
fingerlings, which required no prep work and turned perfectly
tender in the slow cooker. Although they are traditionally roasted
because boiling them dilutes their flavor and turns them mushy,
we found that we could add them to the slow cooker without
any liquid whatsoever, just some olive oil, garlic, and scallions
for flavor, and they retained their delicate sweetness without a
hint of mushiness. Unlike some other slow-cooker potato dishes,
they cooked through properly without covering them first with a

There is almost no prep work required to turn out these
elegant fingerling potatoes using the slow cooker.

sheet of parchment paper. Look for fingerling potatoes measuring
approximately 3 inches long and 1 inch in diameter. This recipe
can easily be doubled in a 7-quart slow cooker; you will need to
increase the cooking time range by 1 hour.

  2 pounds fingerling potatoes, unpeeled
  2 tablespoons extra-virgin olive oil
  2 scallions, white parts minced, green parts sliced thin
  3 garlic cloves, minced
     Salt and pepper
  1 tablespoon chopped fresh parsley
  1 teaspoon grated lemon zest plus 1 tablespoon juice

1. Combine potatoes, 1 tablespoon oil, scallion whites, garlic,
1 teaspoon salt, and ¼ teaspoon pepper in slow cooker. Cover
and cook until potatoes are tender, 5 to 6 hours on low or 3 to
4 hours on high.

2. Stir in parsley, lemon zest and juice, scallion greens, and
remaining 1 tablespoon oil. Season with salt and pepper to taste.
Serve. (Potatoes can be held on warm or low setting for up to
2 hours.)

Easy Baked Potatoes

SERVES 4 TO 6 `EASY PREP` `VEG`

COOKING TIME 6 TO 7 HOURS ON LOW OR 4 TO 5 HOURS ON HIGH

SLOW COOKER SIZE 5 TO 7 QUARTS

WHY THIS RECIPE WORKS Forget about preheating the oven to achieve perfectly cooked baked potatoes with a creamy interior— we moved this dish to the slow cooker, leaving the oven available for other things (like the main course). Wrapping the potatoes in foil and including a little water in the slow cooker helped them cook through more evenly. Spritzing the potatoes with vegetable oil spray ensured that our seasonings adhered (salt and pepper did the trick). Serve with your favorite baked potato toppings. You will need an oval slow cooker for this recipe.

4–6 russet potatoes, unpeeled
     Vegetable oil spray
     Salt and pepper

Spray potatoes with oil spray and season with salt and pepper. Wrap potatoes individually in aluminum foil and place in slow cooker. Add ½ cup water, cover, and cook until potatoes are tender, 6 to 7 hours on low or 4 to 5 hours on high. Transfer potatoes to serving dish and carefully remove foil (watch for steam). Serve.

For scalloped potatoes, we use the microwave to parcook both the potatoes and the cheesy, creamy sauce.

Scalloped Potatoes

SERVES 6 TO 8 `VEG`

COOKING TIME 4 TO 5 HOURS ON LOW OR 3 TO 4 HOURS ON HIGH

SLOW COOKER SIZE 5 TO 7 QUARTS

WHY THIS RECIPE WORKS Tender potatoes and a smooth, creamy sauce with lots of cheese flavor are the hallmarks of well-made scalloped potatoes. They are hard enough to make perfectly in an oven, so could we find a way to make a slow-cooker version that rivaled the best an oven could offer? To start, cream and broth—plus garlic and fresh thyme—guaranteed that the sauce was rich and flavorful. To thicken it, we tried adding flour, but this led to a pasty sauce that separated. Thickening the sauce with cornstarch worked much better, ensuring our sauce stayed stable over the long cooking time; melting shredded sharp cheddar and creamy Monterey Jack into the sauce ensured a smooth texture and robust flavor. To avoid the stovetop altogether, we heated the sauce base in the microwave for a few minutes before adding the cheese. We selected russet potatoes for their fluffy texture, but they cooked unevenly: The bottom layer was tender after the cooking time, while the top remained crunchy. Giving the potatoes a head start in the microwave solved this problem, and a little cream prevented them from sticking together. Lining the side of the slow cooker with foil helped protect our casserole from burning. Extra-sharp cheddar, which becomes grainy during slow cooking, should not be substituted for the sharp cheddar. You will need an oval slow cooker for this recipe. Don't soak the potatoes in water before using or the dish will be watery. For information on making a foil collar and creating a parchment shield, see pages 208 and 177, respectively.

    3 pounds russet potatoes, peeled and sliced ¼ inch thick
 1¼ cups heavy cream
 1¼ cups vegetable or chicken broth
 4½ tablespoons cornstarch
    4 garlic cloves, minced
    2 teaspoons minced fresh thyme or ½ teaspoon dried
  ½ teaspoon salt
  ½ teaspoon pepper
    3 ounces sharp cheddar cheese, shredded (¾ cup)
    3 ounces Monterey Jack cheese, shredded (¾ cup)
    2 tablespoons minced fresh chives

1. Line slow cooker with aluminum foil collar and lightly coat with vegetable oil spray. Microwave potatoes with 2 tablespoons cream in large covered bowl, stirring occasionally, until nearly tender, 8 to 10 minutes; let cool slightly.

2. Whisk remaining cream, broth, cornstarch, garlic, thyme, salt, and pepper together in medium bowl. Microwave, whisking occasionally, until mixture is thickened, about 5 minutes. Slowly whisk in ½ cup cheddar and ½ cup Monterey Jack until melted.

3. Gently fold cheese mixture into potatoes. Transfer potato-cheese mixture to prepared slow cooker and press gently to compress layers. Grease 16 by 12-inch sheet of parchment paper and press firmly onto potatoes, folding down edges as needed. Cover and cook until potatoes are tender, 4 to 5 hours on low or 3 to 4 hours on high.

4. Discard parchment and foil collar. Sprinkle potatoes with remaining ¼ cup cheddar and remaining ¼ cup Monterey Jack. Cover and let sit until cheese is melted, about 20 minutes. Sprinkle with chives and serve. (Potatoes can be held on warm or low setting for up to 2 hours.)

Mixing in melted butter, warm cream, and brown sugar just before serving takes this squash puree to the next level.

Butternut Squash Puree

SERVES 6 TO 8 EASY PREP VEG
COOKING TIME 5 TO 6 HOURS ON LOW OR 3 TO 4 HOURS ON HIGH
SLOW COOKER SIZE 5 TO 7 QUARTS

WHY THIS RECIPE WORKS With its silky-smooth texture and earthy, slightly sweet flavor, pureed butternut squash is one of our favorite side dishes. Since the flavor of butternut squash is quite delicate, our goal was to bump up its flavor so it would taste great even after hours in the slow cooker. At first we tried cooking the squash in water to cover but this washed away some of the squash's subtle flavor, leaving us with a bland, watery puree. Since the squash exuded a lot of moisture during cooking we thought we could take down the amount of water dramatically. In the end it took only a bare minimum—½ cup—to properly braise the squash. Even this small amount of water, however, seemed to be diluting the squash flavor significantly. We considered alternative braising liquids and settled on apple cider, which accented the squash's innate sweetness and added a brightness tasters liked. A small amount of heavy cream and some butter rounded out the flavors and added richness without overpowering the squash flavor. For more information on creating a parchment shield, see page 177. This recipe can easily be doubled in a 7-quart slow cooker; you will need to increase the cooking time range by 1 hour.

3 pounds butternut squash, peeled, seeded, and cut into 1-inch pieces (8 cups)

½ cup apple cider, plus extra as needed

 Salt and pepper

4 tablespoons unsalted butter, melted

2 tablespoons heavy cream, warmed

2 tablespoons packed brown sugar, plus extra for seasoning

1. Combine squash, cider, and ½ teaspoon salt in slow cooker. Press 16 by 12-inch sheet of parchment paper firmly onto squash, folding down edges as needed. Cover and cook until squash is tender, 5 to 6 hours on low or 3 to 4 hours on high.

2. Discard parchment. Mash squash with potato masher until smooth. Stir in melted butter, cream, and sugar. Season with salt, pepper, and extra sugar to taste. Serve. (Squash can be held on warm or low setting for up to 2 hours; adjust consistency with extra hot cider as needed before serving.)

Braised Butternut Squash with Pecans and Cranberries

SERVES 4 TO 6 `EASY PREP` `VEG`

COOKING TIME 4 TO 5 HOURS ON LOW OR 3 TO 4 HOURS ON HIGH

SLOW COOKER SIZE 5 TO 7 QUARTS

WHY THIS RECIPE WORKS Cooking this popular winter squash in a slow cooker makes for a wonderful everyday vegetable, but slow-cooked butternut squash is truly a great contribution to the holiday dinner table, freeing up valuable oven space. We found that a small amount of liquid in the bottom of the slow cooker, plus a couple of aromatics, was all it took to deeply flavor and perfectly steam butternut squash. Pecans and dried cranberries dressed up the squash, and a quick vinaigrette tied the elements of this vegetable side together. You will need an oval slow cooker for this recipe.

1 cup vegetable or chicken broth

2 garlic cloves, peeled and smashed

2 sprigs fresh thyme

Dressed up with an easy vinaigrette plus pecans and cranberries, braised squash takes center stage on the table.

 Salt and pepper

2 pounds butternut squash, peeled, halved lengthwise, seeded, and sliced 1 inch thick

2 tablespoons extra-virgin olive oil

1 teaspoon grated lemon zest plus 2 teaspoons juice

¼ cup pecans, toasted and chopped

¼ cup dried cranberries

1 tablespoon minced fresh parsley

1. Combine broth, garlic, thyme sprigs, and ¼ teaspoon salt in slow cooker. Nestle squash into slow cooker. Cover and cook until squash is tender, 4 to 5 hours on low or 3 to 4 hours on high.

2. Using slotted spoon, transfer squash to serving dish, brushing away any garlic cloves or thyme sprigs that stick to squash. Whisk oil and lemon zest and juice together in bowl. Season with salt and pepper to taste. Drizzle squash with dressing and sprinkle with pecans, cranberries, and parsley. Serve.

Quartered acorn squashes cook perfectly in the slow cooker in a base of water, orange juice, and spices.

Maple-Orange Glazed Acorn Squash

SERVES 4 TO 6   **EASY PREP**   **VEG**   **LIGHT**

COOKING TIME 3 TO 4 HOURS ON LOW OR 2 TO 3 HOURS ON HIGH

SLOW COOKER SIZE 5 TO 7 QUARTS

WHY THIS RECIPE WORKS A quintessential fall vegetable, acorn squash takes forever to roast and often emerges dry and a bit grainy. In the slow cooker, however, it turns tender easily without over-cooking or drying out. And as an added bonus, you can perfume it with warm spices as it cooks. Here we created a cooking base made up of water, orange juice, cloves, and cinnamon and placed the squash cut side down in this flavorful mixture. And since we think a glaze greatly enhances acorn squash, we made a quick one in the microwave by combining maple syrup with coriander, cayenne pepper, and orange zest; toasted hazelnuts provided great crunch and flavor. You will need an oval slow cooker for this recipe.

2 teaspoons grated orange zest plus ½ cup juice
5 whole cloves
1 cinnamon stick

2 small acorn squashes (1 pound each), quartered pole to pole and seeded
   Salt and pepper
¼ cup maple syrup
⅛ teaspoon ground coriander
   Pinch cayenne pepper
¼ cup hazelnuts, toasted, skinned, and chopped
1 tablespoon chopped fresh parsley

1. Combine 1 cup water, orange juice, cloves, and cinnamon stick in slow cooker. Season squashes with salt and pepper and shingle cut side down in slow cooker. Cover and cook until squashes are tender, 3 to 4 hours on low or 2 to 3 hours on high.

2. Using tongs, transfer squashes to serving dish, brushing away any cloves that stick to squashes. Microwave maple syrup, coriander, cayenne, and orange zest in bowl until heated through, about 1 minute. Season with salt and pepper to taste. Drizzle glaze over squashes and sprinkle with hazelnuts and parsley. Serve.

SKINNING HAZELNUTS

Transfer hot toasted hazelnuts to center of dish towel. Fold towel around hazelnuts to seal them inside; rub them together in towel to scrape off as much brown skin as possible. Some small patches of skin may remain.

NOTES FROM THE TEST KITCHEN

Toasting Nuts and Seeds

Toasting nuts and seeds maximizes their flavor, so whether you are adding them to a salad or tossing them into a pasta dish or baked good, it pays to spend a few minutes toasting them.

To toast a small amount (less than 1 cup) of nuts or seeds, put them in a dry skillet over medium heat. Shake the skillet occasionally to prevent scorching, and toast until they are lightly browned and fragrant, 3 to 8 minutes. Watch the nuts closely because they can go from golden to burnt very quickly. To toast a large quantity of nuts, spread the nuts in a single layer on a rimmed baking sheet and toast in a 350-degree oven. To promote even toasting, shake the baking sheet every few minutes, and toast until the nuts are lightly browned and fragrant, 5 to 10 minutes.

Fragrant, garlic-infused olive oil is a great added bonus when making these sweet and easy slow-cooked tomatoes.

Slow-Cooked Tomatoes with Olive Oil

SERVES 4 TO 6   EASY PREP   VEG

COOKING TIME 5 TO 6 HOURS ON LOW OR 3 TO 4 HOURS ON HIGH

SLOW COOKER SIZE 5 TO 7 QUARTS

WHY THIS RECIPE WORKS A perfectly ripe, freshly picked August tomato needs no more preparation than slicing and sprinkling with salt. But if you are lucky enough to have an overabundance of them, or if you're just looking for a way to improve average supermarket tomatoes, slow roasting is the way to go. In the best versions, the tomato's juices are concentrated by the slow, steady heat of the oven and become one with the olive oil in which it is roasted. We were after a foolproof method for "slow roasting" tomatoes in the slow cooker, one that would deliver a sweet, intense tomato flavor and a melt-in-your-mouth texture. To start, we cored the tomatoes, then halved them crosswise (tasters felt this cut made for a more visually pleasing presentation). We gently tossed them with just enough extra-virgin olive oil to infuse them with bright, fruity flavor as they released their juices into the slow cooker, creating a flavorful cooking liquid. The addition of smashed garlic cloves, which mellowed and softened during the long cooking time, lent a rich, nutty flavor to the oil and paired well with the fresh thyme that we also added. Aside from a little salt and pepper, no other seasoning was needed for this uncomplicated dish. We recommend serving these tomatoes alongside roasted meat or fish with plenty of crusty bread for dipping into the extra cooking liquid. You can also use the seriously flavorful tomato oil to make a salad dressing.

6 ripe tomatoes, cored and halved crosswise
½ cup extra-virgin olive oil
6 garlic cloves, peeled and smashed
2 teaspoons minced fresh thyme or ¾ teaspoon dried
  Salt and pepper

1. Combine tomatoes, oil, garlic, thyme, ¾ teaspoon salt, and ¼ teaspoon pepper in slow cooker. Cover and cook until tomatoes are tender and slightly shriveled around edges, 5 to 6 hours on low or 3 to 4 hours on high.

2. Let tomatoes cool in oil for at least 15 minutes or up to 4 hours. Season with salt and pepper to taste. Serve.

NOTES FROM THE TEST KITCHEN

Buying Fresh Tomatoes

Buying tomatoes at the height of summer won't guarantee juicy, flavorful fruit, but keeping these guidelines in mind will help ensure a flavorful tomato: The shorter the distance a tomato has to travel, the riper it can be when it's picked. And commercial tomatoes are engineered to be sturdier, with thicker walls and less of the flavorful jelly and seeds. When selecting tomatoes, oddly shaped tomatoes are fine, and even cracked skin is OK. Avoid tomatoes that are overly soft or leaking juice. Choose tomatoes that smell fruity and feel heavy. And consider trying heirloom tomatoes; grown from naturally pollinated plants and seeds, they are some of the best local tomatoes you can find. If supermarket tomatoes are your only option, look for tomatoes sold on the vine. Although this does not mean that these tomatoes were fully ripened on the vine, they are better than regular supermarket tomatoes.

CHAPTER 13

HOW ABOUT BRUNCH?

■ EASY PREP ■ VEGETARIAN ■ LIGHT ■ COOK ALL DAY
Photo: Irish Oatmeal

A hefty dose of whole-milk ricotta cheese plus shredded fontina gives these egg casseroles tons of richness.

Individual Ricotta, Spinach, and Egg Casseroles

SERVES 4 EASY PREP VEG

COOKING TIME 2 TO 3 HOURS ON LOW

SLOW COOKER SIZE 5 TO 7 QUARTS

WHY THIS RECIPE WORKS Perfect for a late breakfast or light supper, these individual egg casseroles are ready for the slow cooker in mere minutes with little effort. Whole-milk ricotta and shredded fontina ensured a dish that was plenty rich, and frozen spinach balanced the richness and needed no chopping—we simply thawed it and squeezed out the excess moisture so it wouldn't water down our eggs. Assembly was easy: We started by microwaving our aromatics (garlic and onion), then stirred in the spinach, ricotta, fontina, and eggs and portioned the mixture into four ramekins. Thin slices of tomato, placed on top, provided bright flavor and color, and a water bath guaranteed that our eggs cooked through gently and evenly. You will need an oval slow cooker and four 6-ounce round ramekins for this recipe.

1 onion, chopped fine
1 tablespoon extra-virgin olive oil
3 garlic cloves, minced
10 ounces (1¼ cups) whole-milk ricotta cheese
8 ounces frozen chopped spinach, thawed and squeezed dry
4 ounces fontina cheese, shredded (1 cup)
4 large eggs, lightly beaten
¼ teaspoon salt
¼ teaspoon pepper
2 plum tomatoes, cored and sliced crosswise ¼ inch thick

1. Grease four 6-ounce ramekins. Microwave onion, oil, and garlic in large bowl, stirring occasionally, until onion is softened, about 5 minutes. Stir in ricotta, spinach, fontina, eggs, salt, and pepper until well combined. Divide mixture evenly among prepared ramekins and shingle tomatoes over top.

2. Fill slow cooker with ½ inch boiling water (about 2 cups water) and set ramekins in slow cooker. Cover and cook until casseroles are set, 2 to 3 hours on low. Using tongs and sturdy spatula, remove ramekins from slow cooker and let cool for 15 minutes before serving.

SQUEEZING SPINACH DRY

To rid thawed spinach of excess water before adding it to recipes, simply wrap it in cheesecloth and squeeze it firmly.

Individual Ricotta, Broccoli, and Egg Casseroles

SERVES 4 EASY PREP VEG

COOKING TIME 2 TO 3 HOURS ON LOW

SLOW COOKER SIZE 5 TO 7 QUARTS

WHY THIS RECIPE WORKS For another take on easy individual egg casseroles, we decided to pair cheddar cheese and broccoli with the eggs. Frozen broccoli kept prep to a minimum, and chopped onion, minced garlic, and fresh thyme ensured our custard was anything but bland. Assembly was easy: We microwaved our aromatics (garlic and onion), then stirred in the broccoli, ricotta, cheddar, and eggs before portioning the mixture into four rame-kins. Adding water to the slow cooker turned the slow cooker into an even-cooking water bath. This guaranteed that our casseroles cooked through gently and evenly every time. You will need an oval slow cooker and four 6-ounce round ramekins for this recipe.

1 onion, chopped fine
1 tablespoon extra-virgin olive oil
3 garlic cloves, minced
1 teaspoon minced fresh thyme
8 ounces frozen broccoli spears, thawed, patted dry, and chopped
8 ounces (1 cup) whole-milk ricotta cheese
4 ounces cheddar cheese, shredded (1 cup)
4 large eggs, lightly beaten
¼ teaspoon salt
¼ teaspoon pepper
1 tablespoon minced fresh chives

1. Grease four 6-ounce ramekins. Microwave onion, oil, garlic, and thyme in large bowl, stirring occasionally, until onion is soft-ened, about 5 minutes. Stir in broccoli, ricotta, cheddar, eggs, salt, and pepper until well combined. Divide mixture evenly among prepared ramekins.

2. Fill slow cooker with ½ inch boiling water (about 2 cups water) and set ramekins in slow cooker. Cover and cook until casseroles are set, 2 to 3 hours on low. Using tongs and sturdy spatula, remove ramekins from slow cooker and let cool for 15 minutes. Sprinkle with chives and serve.

SHREDDING SEMISOFT CHEESE

To prevent the grater from becoming clogged when shredding mozzarella and other semisoft cheeses, use vegetable oil spray to lightly coat the holes, then shred away.

Buying Eggs

Here's what we've learned in the test kitchen about buying eggs.

COLOR The shell's hue depends on the breed of the chicken. The run-of-the-mill leghorn chicken produces the typical white egg. Brown-feathered birds, such as Rhode Island Reds, produce ecru- to coffee-colored eggs. Despite marketing hype extolling the virtues of nonwhite eggs, our tests proved that shell color has no effect on flavor.

FARM-FRESH AND ORGANIC In our taste tests, farm-fresh eggs were standouts. The large yolks were bright orange and sat very high above the comparatively small whites, and the flavor of these eggs was exceptionally rich and complex. The organic eggs followed in second place, with eggs from hens raised on a vegetarian diet in third, and the standard supermarket eggs last. Differ-ences were easily detected in egg-based dishes such as omelets or frittatas, but not in cakes or cookies.

EGGS AND OMEGA-3S Several companies are marketing eggs with a high level of omega-3 fatty acids, the healthful unsaturated fats also found in some fish. In our taste test, we found that more omega-3s translated into a richer egg flavor and a deeper yolk color. Why? Commercially raised chickens usually peck on corn and soy, while chickens on a diet enriched in omega-3 have supplements of greens, flaxseeds, and algae, which also add flavor, complexity, and color to their eggs. Read labels carefully and look for brands that guarantee at least 200 milligrams omega-3s per egg.

HOW OLD ARE MY EGGS? Egg cartons are marked with both a sell-by date and a pack date. The pack date is the day the eggs were graded and packed, which is generally within a week of when they were laid but may be as much as 30 days later. The sell-by date is within 30 days of the pack date, which is the legal limit set by the U.S. Department of Agriculture (USDA). In short, a carton of eggs may be up to two months old by the end of the sell-by date. Even so, according to the USDA, eggs are still fit for consumption for an additional three to five weeks past the sell-by date.

MAKE IT 5 WAYS STRATA

Smoky Southwestern Strata

SERVES 8 TO 10
COOKING TIME 3 TO 4 HOURS ON LOW
SLOW COOKER SIZE 5 TO 7 QUARTS

We wanted a savory and rich-tasting strata with a balanced, well-seasoned filling, a foolproof technique, and lots of ways to vary the basic recipe to keep things interesting. The key to producing the perfect strata with great texture was using stale bread pieces. We also found that the trick to a surefire strata was using the slow cooker's gentle low heat setting, which ensured a silky-smooth custard. To prevent uneven cooking and to make the strata easy to remove and serve, we placed a foil collar and sling in the slow cooker before building the strata (see pages 208 and 180). If you don't have stale bread in hand, you can dry out fresh bread pieces by baking them on a rimmed baking sheet in a 225-degree oven for about 40 minutes, stirring occasionally. You will need an oval slow cooker for these recipes. These stratas are great served right out of the slow cooker, or they can be transferred to a serving dish for a more impressive presentation.

1 CLASSIC STRATA WITH SAUSAGE

- 8 ounces bulk breakfast sausage
- 1 onion, chopped fine
- 1 tablespoon vegetable oil
- 2 garlic cloves, minced
- 2 teaspoons minced fresh thyme or ½ teaspoon dried
- 14 ounces French or Italian bread, cut into ½-inch pieces (12 cups), staled overnight
- 6 ounces sharp cheddar cheese, shredded (1½ cups)
- 2½ cups half-and-half
- 9 large eggs
  Salt and pepper
- 2 tablespoons minced fresh chives

1. Line slow cooker with aluminum foil collar, then press 2 large sheets of foil into slow cooker perpendicular to one another, with extra foil hanging over edges. Lightly coat prepared slow cooker with vegetable oil spray.

2. Microwave sausage, onion, oil, garlic, and thyme in bowl, stirring and breaking up meat with wooden spoon occasionally, until sausage is no longer pink, 6 to 8 minutes.

3. Spread half of stale bread into prepared slow cooker, then sprinkle with half of sausage mixture and ½ cup cheddar. Repeat layering with remaining stale bread, remaining sausage mixture, and remaining 1 cup cheddar. Whisk half-and-half, eggs, 1 teaspoon salt, and ½ teaspoon pepper together in bowl, then pour mixture evenly over bread. Press gently on bread to submerge. Cover and cook until center of strata is set, 3 to 4 hours on low.

4. Turn off slow cooker and let strata cool, covered, for 20 minutes. Sprinkle with chives and serve.

2 MUSHROOM AND SPINACH STRATA

- 12 ounces white mushrooms, trimmed and sliced thin
- 1 onion, chopped fine
- 2 tablespoons vegetable oil
- 2 garlic cloves, minced
- 2 teaspoons minced fresh thyme or ½ teaspoon dried
- 10 ounces frozen chopped spinach, thawed and squeezed dry
- 14 ounces French or Italian bread, cut into ½-inch pieces (12 cups), staled overnight
- 6 ounces Gruyère cheese, shredded (1½ cups)
- 2½ cups half-and-half
- 9 large eggs
  Salt and pepper

1. Line slow cooker with aluminum foil collar, then press 2 large sheets of foil into slow cooker perpendicular to one another, with extra foil hanging over edges. Lightly coat prepared slow cooker with vegetable oil spray.

2. Microwave mushrooms, onion, oil, garlic, and thyme in bowl, stirring occasionally, until vegetables are softened, 6 to 8 minutes. Stir in spinach.

3. Spread half of stale bread into prepared slow cooker, then sprinkle with half of mushroom mixture and ½ cup Gruyère. Repeat layering with remaining stale bread, remaining mushroom mixture, and remaining 1 cup Gruyère. Whisk half-and-half, eggs, 1½ teaspoons salt, and ½ teaspoon pepper together in bowl, then pour mixture evenly over bread. Press gently on bread to submerge. Cover and cook until center of strata is set, 3 to 4 hours on low.

4. Turn off slow cooker and let strata cool, covered, for 20 minutes. Serve.

3 DENVER-STYLE STRATA

2 red or green bell peppers, stemmed, seeded, and cut into ½-inch pieces
1 onion, chopped fine
2 tablespoons vegetable oil
2 garlic cloves, minced
2 teaspoons minced fresh thyme or 1 teaspoon dried
8 ounces ham steak, cut into ½-inch pieces
14 ounces French or Italian bread, cut into ½-inch pieces (12 cups), staled overnight
6 ounces Monterey Jack cheese, shredded (1½ cups)
2½ cups half-and-half
9 large eggs
Salt and pepper

1. Line slow cooker with aluminum foil collar, then press 2 large sheets of foil into slow cooker perpendicular to one another, with extra foil hanging over edges. Lightly coat prepared slow cooker with vegetable oil spray.

2. Microwave bell peppers, onion, oil, garlic, and thyme in bowl, stirring occasionally, until vegetables are softened, 5 to 8 minutes. Stir in ham.

3. Spread half of stale bread into prepared slow cooker, then sprinkle with half of ham mixture and ½ cup Monterey Jack. Repeat layering with remaining stale bread, remaining ham mixture, and remaining 1 cup Monterey Jack. Whisk half-and-half, eggs, 1 teaspoon salt, and ½ teaspoon pepper together in bowl, then pour mixture evenly over bread. Press gently on bread to submerge. Cover and cook until center of strata is set, 3 to 4 hours on low.

4. Turn off slow cooker and let strata cool, covered, for 20 minutes. Serve.

4 SMOKY SOUTHWESTERN STRATA

14 ounces French or Italian bread, cut into ½-inch pieces (12 cups), staled overnight
1 (28-ounce) can diced tomatoes, drained
6 ounces pepper Jack cheese, shredded (1½ cups)
6 scallions, sliced thin
2½ cups half-and-half
9 large eggs
4 teaspoons chili powder
1 teaspoon ground cumin
Salt and pepper
2 tablespoons chopped fresh cilantro

1. Line slow cooker with aluminum foil collar, then press 2 large sheets of foil into slow cooker perpendicular to one another, with extra foil hanging over edges. Lightly coat prepared slow cooker with vegetable oil spray.

2. Spread half of stale bread into prepared slow cooker, then sprinkle with half of tomatoes, ½ cup pepper Jack, and half of scallions. Repeat layering with remaining stale bread, remaining tomatoes, remaining 1 cup Pepper Jack, and remaining scallions. Whisk half-and-half, eggs, chili powder, cumin, 1½ teaspoons salt, and ½ teaspoon pepper together in bowl, then pour mixture evenly over bread. Press gently on bread to submerge. Cover and cook until center of strata is set, 3 to 4 hours on low.

3. Turn off slow cooker and let strata cool, covered, for 20 minutes. Sprinkle with cilantro and serve.

5 LEEK, BACON, AND GOAT CHEESE STRATA

1 pound leeks, white and light green parts only, halved lengthwise, sliced thin, and washed thoroughly
10 slices bacon, chopped fine
2 garlic cloves, minced
2 teaspoons minced fresh thyme or ½ teaspoon dried
14 ounces French or Italian bread, cut into ½-inch pieces (12 cups), staled overnight
6 ounces goat cheese, crumbled (1½ cups)
2½ cups half-and-half
9 large eggs
Salt and pepper
2 tablespoons minced fresh chives

1. Line slow cooker with aluminum foil collar, then press 2 large sheets of foil into slow cooker perpendicular to one another, with extra foil hanging over edges. Lightly coat prepared slow cooker with vegetable oil spray.

2. Microwave leeks, bacon, garlic, and thyme in bowl, stirring occasionally, until leeks are softened, 8 to 10 minutes.

3. Spread half of stale bread into prepared slow cooker, then sprinkle with half of leek mixture and ¾ cup goat cheese. Repeat layering with remaining stale bread, remaining leek mixture, and remaining ¾ cup goat cheese. Whisk half-and-half, eggs, 1 teaspoon salt, and ½ teaspoon pepper together in bowl, then pour mixture evenly over bread. Press gently on bread to submerge. Cover and cook until center of strata is set, 3 to 4 hours on low.

4. Turn off slow cooker and let strata cool, covered, for 20 minutes. Sprinkle with chives and serve.

It's easy to make huevos rancheros in a slow cooker; you're simply building a fragrant sauce, then poaching eggs.

Huevos Rancheros

SERVES 6 VEG

COOKING TIME 5 TO 6 HOURS ON LOW OR 3 TO 4 HOURS ON HIGH

SLOW COOKER SIZE 5 TO 7 QUARTS

WHY THIS RECIPE WORKS Huevos rancheros are a welcome addition to any brunch, but preparing the dish's many components often requires a lot of effort. Our goal was to create a flavorful version of this hearty tomato sauce and egg dish by letting the slow cooker do the work for us. To evoke the charred deep flavors in traditional huevos rancheros, first we bloomed a healthy dose of chili powder that we microwaved along with onions, oil, and garlic. We then stirred in canned fire-roasted tomatoes, brown sugar, lime juice, and green chiles for a tangy punch of flavor. Cracking eggs into wells we had created in the cooked sauce allowed us to cook all six servings at once. The final touch to this zesty breakfast was some spicy pepper Jack cheese. You will need an oval slow cooker for this recipe. For more information on making a foil collar, see page 208. Serve with warm tortillas and diced avocado.

1 onion, chopped
¼ cup extra-virgin olive oil
3 tablespoons chili powder
4 garlic cloves, minced
Salt and pepper
2 (28-ounce) cans fire-roasted diced tomatoes, drained
½ cup canned chopped green chiles
1 tablespoon packed brown sugar
1 tablespoon lime juice
4 ounces pepper Jack cheese, shredded (1 cup)
6 large eggs
½ cup fresh cilantro leaves
3 scallions, sliced thin

1. Line slow cooker with aluminum foil collar and lightly coat with vegetable oil spray.

2. Microwave onion, oil, chili powder, garlic, and ½ teaspoon salt in bowl, stirring occasionally, until onion is softened, about 5 minutes; transfer to prepared slow cooker. Stir in tomatoes, green chiles, sugar, and lime juice. Cover and cook until tomato mixture is deeply flavored, 5 to 6 hours on low or 3 to 4 hours on high.

3. Discard foil collar. Smooth tomato mixture into even layer and sprinkle evenly with pepper Jack. Using back of spoon, make 6 indentations (about 2½ inches wide) into tomato mixture. Crack 1 egg into each indentation and season with salt and pepper. Cover and cook on high until egg whites are just beginning to set but still have some movement when slow cooker is gently shaken, 20 to 30 minutes.

4. Turn off slow cooker and let eggs sit, covered, for 5 minutes. Sprinkle with cilantro and scallions. Serve immediately.

This vegetarian take on red flannel hash uses a combination of beets and russet potatoes, with a little cream for richness.

Red Flannel Hash with Poached Eggs

SERVES 6 `VEG`

COOKING TIME 5 TO 6 HOURS ON LOW OR 3 TO 4 HOURS ON HIGH

SLOW COOKER SIZE 5 TO 7 QUARTS

WHY THIS RECIPE WORKS For a healthier but still hearty hash, we took out the meat altogether and increased the amount of vegetables. Red beets cooked perfectly along with potatoes and provided a ruby hue, which is where this dish gets its name. To give our vegetables that real hash texture, we stirred just a quarter-cup of cream into a portion of the cooked vegetables, mashed them, and then stirred the mashed vegetables back into the rest of the hash. Dimpling the finished hash with the back of a spoon provided the perfect nests to hold eggs as they slowly cooked to perfection. You will need an oval slow cooker for this recipe. To avoid staining your hands, hold beets in layers of paper towels while peeling them with a vegetable peeler. For more information on making a foil collar, see page 208.

½ onion, chopped fine
2 garlic cloves, minced
1 tablespoon vegetable oil
2 teaspoons minced fresh thyme or ½ teaspoon dried
1 teaspoon paprika
  Salt and pepper
2 pounds russet potatoes, peeled and cut into ½-inch pieces
12 ounces beets, peeled and cut into ½-inch pieces
½ cup vegetable or chicken broth
¼ cup heavy cream
6 large eggs
2 scallions, sliced thin
  Hot sauce

1. Line slow cooker with aluminum foil collar and lightly coat with vegetable oil spray. Microwave onion, garlic, oil, thyme, paprika, and 1 teaspoon salt in large bowl, stirring occasionally, until onion is softened, about 3 minutes. Add potatoes and beets and toss to combine; transfer to prepared slow cooker. Pour broth over vegetables, cover, and cook until vegetables are tender, 5 to 6 hours on low or 3 to 4 hours on high.

2. Discard foil collar. Transfer 2 cups vegetables to medium bowl. Add cream and mash with potato masher until smooth. Fold mashed vegetable mixture into remaining vegetables in slow cooker, then smooth into even layer.

3. Using back of spoon, make 6 indentations (about 2½ inches wide) into hash. Crack 1 egg into each indentation and season with salt and pepper. Cover and cook on high until egg whites are just beginning to set but still have some movement when slow cooker is gently shaken, 20 to 30 minutes.

4. Turn off slow cooker and let eggs sit, covered, for 5 minutes. Sprinkle with scallions and serve with hot sauce.

PREPPING FRESH THYME

For thin-stemmed thyme, chop stems along with leaves. If stems are thick, hold sprig upright and run your thumb and forefinger along stem to release leaves.

With just a few humble pantry ingredients, plus deli corned beef, you can make a great hash in your slow cooker.

Corned Beef Hash with Poached Eggs

SERVES 6

COOKING TIME 5 TO 6 HOURS ON LOW OR 3 TO 4 HOURS ON HIGH

SLOW COOKER SIZE 5 TO 7 QUARTS

WHY THIS RECIPE WORKS This slow-cooker version of corned beef hash captures what everyone loves about this diner classic, but with much less fuss. First we microwaved the aromatics before tossing them with the chunks of potatoes. Once everything was in the slow cooker, including deli counter corned beef, we let it cook until the potatoes were tender. We mashed a portion of the cooked potato mixture with a little cream to give our hash a cohesive texture. You will need an oval slow cooker for this recipe. For more information on making a foil collar, see page 208.

2 onions, chopped fine
6 garlic cloves, minced
1 tablespoon vegetable oil
1 tablespoon minced fresh thyme or
   1 teaspoon dried
2 teaspoons paprika
   Salt and pepper
2 pounds russet potatoes, peeled and
   cut into ½-inch pieces
1 pound thinly sliced deli corned beef,
   cut into ½-inch pieces
½ cup chicken broth
¼ cup heavy cream
6 large eggs
2 scallions, sliced thin
   Hot sauce

1. Line slow cooker with aluminum foil collar and lightly coat with vegetable oil spray. Microwave onions, garlic, oil, thyme, paprika, 1 teaspoon salt, and ¼ teaspoon pepper in large bowl, stirring occasionally, until onions are softened, about 5 minutes. Add potatoes and corned beef and toss to combine; transfer to prepared slow cooker. Pour broth over potato mixture, cover, and cook until potatoes are tender, 5 to 6 hours on low or 3 to 4 hours on high.

2. Discard foil collar. Transfer 2 cups potato mixture to medium bowl. Add cream and mash with potato masher until smooth. Fold mashed mixture into remaining potato mixture in slow cooker, then smooth into even layer.

3. Using back of spoon, make 6 indentations (about 2½ inches wide) into hash. Crack 1 egg into each indentation and season with salt and pepper. Cover and cook on high until egg whites are just beginning to set but still have some movement when slow cooker is gently shaken, 20 to 30 minutes.

4. Turn off slow cooker and let eggs sit, covered, for 5 minutes. Sprinkle with scallions and serve with hot sauce.

ADDING EGGS TO HASH

1. Using back of large spoon, make 6 indentations in surface of vegetable mixture, about 2½ inches wide and 1½ inches deep.

2. Carefully crack egg into each hole and season with salt and pepper. Cover and cook on high for about 20 minutes.

A combo of rye flour, whole-wheat flour, and cornmeal gives our slow-cooker Boston brown bread a hearty flavor.

Boston Brown Bread

MAKES 4 SMALL LOAVES; SERVES 6 TO 8

`EASY PREP` `VEG`

COOKING TIME 3 TO 4 HOURS ON HIGH

SLOW COOKER SIZE 4 TO 7 QUARTS

WHY THIS RECIPE WORKS A New England breakfast staple, brown bread is a cross between a cake and a quick bread in both texture and taste. It has a unique flavor that is rich in molasses, raisins, and complex whole grains. While most brown bread recipes are traditionally steamed in tin cans in a water bath on the stovetop, we moved the process to the slow cooker for a fuss-free version. For the batter, we used easy-to-find whole-wheat flour, rye flour, and finely ground cornmeal in equal amounts to give our bread balanced whole-grain flavor. Molasses, the traditional sweetener in brown bread, added a hint of bitterness. Baking soda and baking powder reacted with the acid in the batter to lighten the bread, and melted butter gave some richness to the lean loaves. To prevent the metal cans from staining the bottom of the slow cooker insert, we first lined the insert with parchment. We prefer Quaker white cornmeal in this recipe, though other types will work; do not use coarse grits. Any style of molasses will work except blackstrap. You will need an oval slow cooker and four empty 15-ounce cans for this recipe. Use cans that are labeled BPA-free. Brown bread is great as is or toasted and buttered.

¾ cup (4⅛ ounces) rye flour
¾ cup (4⅛ ounces) whole-wheat flour
¾ cup (3¾ ounces) fine white cornmeal
1¾ teaspoons baking soda
½ teaspoon baking powder
1 teaspoon salt
1⅔ cups buttermilk
½ cup molasses
3 tablespoons butter, melted and cooled slightly
¾ cup raisins
2 cups boiling water

1. Fold four 12 by 8-inch pieces of aluminum foil in half twice to yield rectangles that measure 6 by 4 inches, and grease 1 side with vegetable oil spray. Coat inside of 4 clean 15-ounce cans with oil spray.

2. Whisk rye flour, whole-wheat flour, cornmeal, baking soda, baking powder, and salt together in large bowl. Whisk buttermilk, molasses, and melted butter together in second bowl. Stir raisins into buttermilk mixture. Add buttermilk mixture to flour mixture and stir until combined and no dry flour remains. Divide batter evenly among prepared cans and smooth top with back of greased spoon. Wrap tops of cans tightly with prepared foil, greased side facing batter.

3. Line bottom of slow cooker with parchment paper. Fill slow cooker with ½ inch boiling water (about 2 cups water) and set cans in slow cooker. Cover and cook until skewer inserted in center of loaves comes out clean, 3 to 4 hours on high.

4. Using tongs and sturdy spatula, transfer cans to wire rack and let cool, uncovered, for 20 minutes. Invert cans and slide loaves onto rack and let cool completely, about 1 hour. Slice and serve. (Bread can be wrapped tightly in plastic wrap and stored at room temperature for up to 3 days.)

Monkey Bread

SERVES 6 TO 8 **VEG**

COOKING TIME 2 TO 4 HOURS ON HIGH

SLOW COOKER SIZE 5 TO 7 QUARTS

WHY THIS RECIPE WORKS We wanted a slow-cooker recipe for monkey bread that didn't compromise on its sticky, sweet appeal. To expedite the rising and proofing in this recipe we used a generous amount of instant yeast and added sugar to the dough, which jump-started the yeast. Before assembling the bread, we rolled the balls of dough in melted butter and sugar to give them a thick, caramel-like coating. After shaping, dipping, and assembling the monkey bread directly into the foil-lined slow cooker, we cooked the bread on high for 3 to 4 hours. We didn't need to wait for a second proofing of the dough after it was shaped; the gentle heat of the slow cooker properly proofed the dough as it came up to temperature, allowing us to walk away and enjoy the sweet smell of cinnamon. To prevent uneven cooking and possible overbrowning, and to make the monkey bread easy to remove and serve, we placed both a foil collar and double-layered sling in the slow cooker. When the bread was finished cooking, we used the foil sling to remove it to cool slightly before inverting, showing off the gooey, caramelized coating of brown sugar, butter, and cinnamon. A final drizzle of glaze was all this decadent breakfast treat needed before serving. You will need an oval slow cooker for this recipe. For more information on making a foil collar and a foil sling, see pages 208 and 180, respectively.

After rolling the proofed balls of dough in melted butter and sugar, you simply arrange them in the slow cooker to cook.

DOUGH

3¼ cups (16¼ ounces) all-purpose flour

2¼ teaspoons instant or rapid-rise yeast

2 teaspoons salt

1 cup whole milk, room temperature

⅓ cup water, room temperature

¼ cup (1¾ ounces) granulated sugar

2 tablespoons unsalted butter, melted

BROWN SUGAR COATING

1 cup packed (7 ounces) light brown sugar

2 teaspoons ground cinnamon

8 tablespoons unsalted butter, melted and cooled

GLAZE

1 cup (4 ounces) confectioners' sugar

2 tablespoons whole milk

1. FOR THE DOUGH Whisk flour, yeast, and salt together in bowl of stand mixer. Whisk milk, water, sugar, and melted butter in 4-cup liquid measuring cup until sugar has dissolved. Using dough hook on low speed, slowly add milk mixture to flour mixture and mix until cohesive dough starts to form and no dry flour remains, about 2 minutes, scraping down bowl as needed. Increase speed to medium-low and knead until dough is smooth and elastic and clears sides of bowl but sticks to bottom, 8 to 10 minutes.

2. Transfer dough to lightly floured counter and knead by hand to form smooth, round ball, about 30 seconds. Place dough, seam side down, in lightly greased large bowl or container, cover tightly with plastic wrap, and let rise until doubled in size, 1½ to 2 hours. (Unrisen dough can be refrigerated for at least 8 hours or up to 16 hours; let sit at room temperature for 1 hour before shaping in step 4.)

3. FOR THE BROWN SUGAR COATING Line slow cooker with aluminum foil collar, then press 2 double-layered large sheets of foil into slow cooker perpendicular to one another, with extra foil hanging over edges. Lightly coat prepared slow cooker with vegetable oil spray. Combine sugar and cinnamon in bowl. Place melted butter in second bowl.

4. Transfer dough to lightly floured counter and press into rough 8-inch square. Using pizza cutter or chef's knife, cut dough into 6 even strips. Cut each strip into 6 pieces (36 pieces total). Cover dough pieces loosely with greased plastic.

5. Working with a few pieces of dough at a time (keep remaining pieces covered), dip pieces in melted butter, then roll in sugar mixture to coat. Place coated pieces in prepared slow cooker, staggering seams where dough balls meet as you build layers. Once dough is layered, sprinkle remaining sugar mixture on top.

6. Cover and cook until dough is set and registers 190 degrees, 2 to 4 hours on high. (Top of monkey bread will be pale and slightly tacky to touch.) Using foil sling, transfer monkey bread to wire rack and let cool for 20 minutes.

7. FOR THE GLAZE Whisk sugar and milk in bowl until smooth. Invert monkey bread onto serving dish; discard foil. Drizzle glaze over bread, letting it run down sides. Serve warm.

ASSEMBLING MONKEY BREAD

Place coated pieces in prepared slow cooker, staggering seams where dough balls meet as you build layers.

Irish Oatmeal

SERVES 8 **VEG** LIGHT

COOKING TIME 4 TO 5 HOURS ON LOW OR 3 TO 4 HOURS ON HIGH

SLOW COOKER SIZE 4 TO 7 QUARTS

WHY THIS RECIPE WORKS We love the chewy texture and fuller flavor of steel-cut oats (and also their health benefits). Although we set out to create an overnight version of these oats so they'd be ready the next morning, we found that the oats were mushy and blown-out after such a long cooking time. For perfectly cooked oats in the slow cooker, 3 to 5 hours of cooking time were key. Also, toasting the oats before putting them in the slow cooker brought out their nutty flavor. This oatmeal reheats well, so you can quickly serve it up again later in the week. Serve with your favorite toppings such as brown sugar, butter, maple syrup, cinnamon, dried fruit, and nuts.

2 tablespoons unsalted butter
2 cups steel-cut oats
8 cups water
1 teaspoon salt

1. Melt butter in 12-inch skillet over medium heat. Add oats and toast, stirring constantly, until golden and fragrant, about 2 minutes; transfer to slow cooker.

Since making steel-cut oats takes time, it's handy to make a big batch in the slow cooker and reheat portions as needed.

2. Stir water and salt into slow cooker. Cover and cook until oats are softened and thickened, 4 to 5 hours on low or 3 to 4 hours on high. Stir oatmeal to recombine. Turn off slow cooker and let oatmeal sit for 10 minutes. Serve. (Oatmeal can be refrigerated for up to 4 days. Reheat oatmeal in microwave or in saucepan over medium-low heat; stir often and adjust consistency with hot water as needed.)

NOTES FROM THE TEST KITCHEN

Steel-Cut Oats

Steel-cut oats are made by slicing whole oat groats with steel blades into nubby grains. These grainy-textured oats take a little longer than rolled oats to cook, but their chewy texture and fuller oat flavor are worth the wait. Our favorite brand is **Bob's Red Mill Organic Steel Cut Oats,** which tasters praised for its outstanding nutty oat flavor and "creamy, toothsome" texture.

These creamy slow-cooker grits are a lifesaver when you're trying to orchestrate a brunch, since they free up your oven.

Cheesy Grits

SERVES 6 **EASY PREP** **VEG**

COOKING TIME 3 TO 4 HOURS ON LOW OR 2 TO 3 HOURS ON HIGH

SLOW COOKER SIZE 4 TO 7 QUARTS

WHY THIS RECIPE WORKS A staple of the Southern table, grits can be a substantial start to the day, or a good addition to the dinner plate. But often grits cook up bland and watery or too thick and gluey. The slow cooker proved to be the perfect vehicle for cooking up consistently creamy and flavorful grits without a need to monitor the pot. The low, gradual heat of the slow cooker gently cooked the grits, keeping them lump-free and creamy. In the search for the best recipe, we began by looking at the variety of grits available and found two forms: instant grits and old-fashioned. Instant grits were too gummy in texture and tasted overprocessed. We found that old-fashioned grits worked best in the slow cooker. The old-fashioned grits were velvety, but at the same time they

retained a slightly coarse texture. We kept the recipe simple by whisking together water, milk, grits, and salt in the slow cooker and cooking until the grits were tender, without any need to stir. To create big flavor after cooking, we finished the dish by stirring in sharp cheddar for deep cheesy flavor, butter for richness, and scallions and a splash of hot sauce for a savory boost. The grits will retain a little bite once fully cooked.

3 cups water, plus extra as needed
1 cup whole milk
1 cup old-fashioned grits
Salt and pepper
8 ounces sharp cheddar cheese, shredded (2 cups)
4 tablespoons butter, softened
4 scallions, sliced thin
½ teaspoon hot sauce

1. Lightly coat slow cooker with vegetable oil spray. Whisk water, milk, grits, and 1 teaspoon salt together in prepared slow cooker. Cover and cook until grits are tender, 3 to 4 hours on low or 2 to 3 hours on high.

2. Whisk cheddar, butter, scallions, and hot sauce into grits until combined. Season with salt and pepper to taste. Serve. (Grits can be held on warm or low setting for up to 2 hours; adjust consistency with hot water as needed before serving.)

NOTES FROM THE TEST KITCHEN

Sharp Cheddar Cheese

Traditionally, cheddar is made by a process called "cheddaring": The curd (made by adding acid-producing cultures and clotting agents to unpasteurized whole milk) is cut into slabs, then stacked, cut, pressed, and stacked again. Along the way a large amount of liquid, called whey, is extracted. The remaining compacted curd is what gives farmhouse cheddars their hard and fine-grained characteristics. When it comes to flavor and sharpness, the longer a cheddar is aged, which can be anywhere from a couple of months to a couple of years, the firmer in texture and the more concentrated in flavor (and sharper) it gets. In a recent taste test, **Cabot Vermont Sharp Cheddar** came out on top. This cheese, which is aged for five to eight months, was praised for its "sharp," "clean," and "tangy" flavor.

Although you have to stir this granola every hour, it is otherwise a dump-and-go recipe with foolproof results.

Almond-Raisin Granola

MAKES ABOUT 9 CUPS **EASY PREP** **VEG**
COOKING TIME 4 TO 5 HOURS ON HIGH
SLOW COOKER SIZE 5 TO 7 QUARTS

WHY THIS RECIPE WORKS Store-bought granola is often chock-full of pale oats and dried-out nuts, and is underwhelming when it comes to dried fruit. We knew we could do better, and so we set out to create an easy-to-make, foolproof recipe for granola with big flavor and a crisp texture. The sweetened oat mixture burns easily when cooked in the oven, but the slow cooker was the perfect alternative. For a chewy, crisp, and pleasantly sweet granola, we started by whisking a mixture of maple syrup, honey, and brown sugar together. A small amount of salt, vanilla, and cinnamon boosted the flavor of the mixture. We then drizzled the flavorful mixture over the oats and almonds in the slow cooker to ensure even coating. During cooking, we made sure to stir the granola every hour so it browned evenly. As soon as it was done we turned it out of the slow cooker to cool. Raisins and coarsely chopped almonds added a welcome sweetness and crunch to the granola—and we didn't skimp on the amounts. Do not use quick or instant oats here. You will need an oval slow cooker for this recipe. We prefer to chop the almonds by hand for even texture and superior crunch.

> 5 cups old-fashioned rolled oats
> 2 cups whole almonds, chopped
> ½ cup vegetable oil
> ⅓ cup maple syrup
> ⅓ cup honey
> ⅓ cup packed light brown sugar
> 4 teaspoons vanilla extract
> 1 teaspoon ground cinnamon
> ½ teaspoon salt
> 2 cups raisins

1. Lightly coat slow cooker with vegetable oil spray. Combine oats and almonds in prepared slow cooker. Whisk oil, maple syrup, honey, sugar, vanilla, cinnamon, and salt together in bowl. Drizzle oil mixture over oat mixture and gently toss until evenly coated. Cover and cook, stirring every hour, until oat mixture is deep golden brown and fragrant, 4 to 5 hours on high.

2. Transfer oat mixture to rimmed baking sheet and spread into even layer. Let cool to room temperature, about 30 minutes. Transfer cooled granola to large bowl, add raisins, and gently toss to combine. Serve. (Granola can be stored in airtight container for up to 2 weeks.)

NOTES FROM THE TEST KITCHEN

Buying Maple Syrup

There's no cheap substitute for maple syrup. We confirmed this when we compared maple syrups with pancake syrups; the latter, corn syrup–based products that are one-fifth the price of maple syrup, tasted cloying and candy-like. This time, we decided to home in on pure maple syrup and gathered eight products, all grade A dark amber. Some were dark, while others were only faintly golden. Surprisingly, these color differences did not correlate to the syrups' flavors. Most of the lighter-colored products tasted as robust as the darker ones, and we were hard-pressed to find distinct differences besides color. Due to blending, supermarket grade A dark amber syrups have a similar taste, so our advice is to buy the least expensive all-maple product you can find.

■ EASY PREP ■ LIGHT ■ COOK ALL DAY
Photo: Applesauce Spice Cake

A 6-inch round cake pan fits perfectly into the slow cooker and is the perfect size for our slow-cooker brownies.

Fudgy Brownies

SERVES 6
COOKING TIME 3 TO 4 HOURS ON HIGH
SLOW COOKER SIZE 5 TO 7 QUARTS

WHY THIS RECIPE WORKS The low heat and moist environment of the slow cooker are good not just for preparing richly flavored stews and braises; we found we could also take advantage of this appliance to make easy, from-scratch brownies. And because the flavor compounds in chocolate are extremely volatile and cook off easily in a hot oven, the gentle heat of the slow cooker preserves more chocolate flavor and practically guarantees a fudgy texture. In fact, when we made our classic brownie recipe in a slow cooker they were too fudgy, so we cut back on the sugar and eggs. Simply pouring the batter into the slow cooker led to unevenly cooked brownies that were hard to remove. Instead, we "baked" our brownies in a small springform pan, which fit nicely in the slow cooker. A water bath ensured that they would cook through gently and evenly, and a foil rack elevated the pan so no water would seep in. You will need an oval slow cooker for this recipe. A 6-inch round cake pan can be substituted for the springform pan. For more information on making a foil rack, see page 333.

½ cup (2½ ounces) all-purpose flour
½ teaspoon baking powder
⅛ teaspoon salt
2 ounces unsweetened chocolate, chopped
5 tablespoons unsalted butter
⅔ cup packed (4⅔ ounces) brown sugar
1 large egg plus 1 large yolk, room temperature
½ teaspoon vanilla extract
⅓ cup walnuts, toasted and chopped (optional)

1. Fill slow cooker with ½ inch water (about 2 cups) and place aluminum foil rack in bottom. Grease 6-inch springform pan and line with parchment paper.

2. Whisk flour, baking powder, and salt together in bowl. In large bowl, microwave chocolate and butter at 50 percent power, stirring occasionally, until melted, 1 to 2 minutes; let cool slightly. Whisk sugar, egg and yolk, and vanilla into cooled chocolate mixture until well combined. Stir in flour mixture until just incorporated.

3. Scrape batter into prepared pan, smooth top, and sprinkle with walnuts, if using. Set pan on prepared rack, cover, and cook until toothpick inserted into center comes out with few moist crumbs attached, 3 to 4 hours on high.

4. Let brownies cool completely in pan on wire rack, 1 to 2 hours. Run small knife around edge of brownies, then remove sides of pan. Remove brownies from pan bottom, discarding parchment, and transfer to cutting board. Cut into wedges and serve.

NOTES FROM THE TEST KITCHEN

Pure Vanilla versus Imitation Vanilla

Pure vanilla extract is made by soaking vanilla beans in a solution of water and alcohol and then aging the mixture in holding tanks prior to bottling. This process contributes to the high cost of pure vanilla extract. The less-expensive imitation extract, on the other hand, relies primarily on the synthetic compound vanillin to mimic the smell and taste of real vanilla.

We compared batches of chocolate chip cookies and pastry cream made with each extract. When the extract was baked into the cookies, most tasters preferred the artificial vanilla, claiming that its "mild, natural" flavor melded nicely with the chocolaty cookies. In the pastry cream (where the extracts were added after cooking), the opinions were more varied. Some tasters lauded the "clean, floral" aroma of the pure vanilla, but others found it to be "too strong" and "boozy."

The choice of which one to use comes down to cost and personal philosophy about using imitation products.

Made in a small springform pan, this chocolate cake gets bold flavor from unsweetened chocolate and cocoa powder.

Chocolate Snack Cake

SERVES 6

COOKING TIME 1 TO 2 HOURS ON HIGH

SLOW COOKER SIZE 5 TO 7 QUARTS

WHY THIS RECIPE WORKS By creating a supersteamy environment in the slow cooker, we were able to easily turn out a moist and tender chocolate cake. As we did with many of our slow-cooker cakes, we added water to the slow cooker and then elevated the pan on an aluminum foil rack. A combination of unsweetened chocolate and cocoa powder ensured there would be plenty of chocolate flavor. A little instant espresso reinforced the chocolate flavor, and sour cream added moisture and just the right amount of tang. You will need an oval slow cooker for this recipe. A 6-inch round cake pan can be substituted for the springform pan. For an accurate measurement of boiling water, bring a kettle of water to a boil and then measure out the desired amount.

½ cup (2½ ounces) all-purpose flour
½ teaspoon salt
½ teaspoon baking soda
⅛ teaspoon baking powder
1½ ounces unsweetened chocolate, chopped
3 tablespoons unsweetened cocoa powder
3 tablespoons unsalted butter, cut into 3 pieces
¼ teaspoon instant espresso powder
¼ cup boiling water
½ cup packed (3½ ounces) light brown sugar
¼ cup sour cream
1 large egg, room temperature
½ teaspoon vanilla extract
  Confectioners' sugar

1. Fill slow cooker with ½ inch water (about 2 cups) and place aluminum foil rack in bottom. Grease 6-inch springform pan and line with parchment paper.

2. Whisk flour, salt, baking soda, and baking powder together in bowl. In large bowl, combine chocolate, cocoa, butter, and espresso powder. Pour boiling water over chocolate mixture, cover, and let sit until chocolate and butter are melted, 3 to 5 minutes. Whisk mixture until smooth; let cool slightly. Whisk brown sugar, sour cream, egg, and vanilla into cooled chocolate mixture until well combined. Stir in flour mixture until just incorporated.

3. Scrape batter into prepared pan and smooth top. Gently tap pan on counter to release air bubbles. Set pan on prepared rack, cover, and cook until toothpick inserted in center comes out with few moist crumbs attached, 1 to 2 hours on high.

4. Let cake cool in pan on wire rack for 10 minutes. Run small knife around edge of cake, then remove sides of pan. Remove cake from pan bottom, discarding parchment, and let cool completely on rack, 1 to 2 hours. Transfer to serving dish and dust with confectioners' sugar. Serve.

MAKING A FOIL RACK

Loosely roll 24 by 12-inch piece of foil into 1-inch cylinder, then bend sides in to form oval ring that measures 8 inches long by 5 inches wide. After adding water to slow cooker, place foil rack in center.

This apple-y snack cake cooks to moist perfection in a springform pan set over a water bath in the slow cooker.

Applesauce Spice Cake

SERVES 6   **EASY PREP**

COOKING TIME 3 TO 4 HOURS ON HIGH
SLOW COOKER SIZE 5 TO 7 QUARTS

WHY THIS RECIPE WORKS For a simple dessert that would also satisfy that afternoon craving, we set our sights on a moist snack cake permeated with the sweet flavor of apples and infused with warm spice notes. A water bath ensured that it cooked through gently and evenly. Half a cup of applesauce guaranteed robust apple flavor throughout, and small amounts of cinnamon, nutmeg, and cloves offered subtle spice flavor. To finish our easy cake, we dusted it with a bit of confectioners' sugar. You will need an oval slow cooker for this recipe. A 6-inch round cake pan can be substituted for the springform pan. For more information on making a foil rack, see page 333.

  1 cup (5 ounces) all-purpose flour
  ½ teaspoon baking soda
  ¼ teaspoon ground cinnamon

  ¼ teaspoon salt
    Pinch ground nutmeg
    Pinch ground cloves
  ½ cup (3½ ounces) granulated sugar
  ½ cup unsweetened applesauce
  1 large egg, room temperature
  ½ teaspoon vanilla extract
  6 tablespoons unsalted butter, melted and cooled
    Confectioners' sugar

1. Fill slow cooker with ½ inch water (about 2 cups) and place aluminum foil rack in bottom. Grease 6-inch springform pan and line with parchment paper.

2. Whisk flour, baking soda, cinnamon, salt, nutmeg, and cloves together in bowl. In large bowl, whisk granulated sugar, applesauce, egg, and vanilla until smooth, then slowly whisk in melted butter until well combined. Stir in flour mixture until just incorporated.

3. Scrape batter into prepared pan and smooth top. Gently tap pan on counter to release air bubbles. Set pan on prepared rack, cover, and cook until toothpick inserted in center comes out clean, 3 to 4 hours on high.

4. Let cake cool in pan on wire rack for 10 minutes. Run small knife around edge of cake, then remove sides of pan. Remove cake from pan bottom, discarding parchment, and let cool completely on rack, 1 to 2 hours. Transfer to serving dish and dust with confectioners' sugar. Serve.

NOTES FROM THE TEST KITCHEN

Baking in the Slow Cooker

Scooping cakes or flan out of the bottom of a slow cooker just isn't that appealing, which is why we turn to a variety of baking vessels, including 6-inch cake pans, 6-inch springform pans, loaf pans, and ramekins for desserts like cheesecake, crème brûlée, snack cakes, and flan. For cake and cheesecake recipes, we found elevating the baking vessels on an easy-to-make aluminum foil rack and adding water to the slow cooker created a moist environment, providing an oven-like atmosphere for our cakes. This ensured even, slow baking, giving us consistent texture throughout. For our custards, we used the slow cooker as a water bath and simply placed the vessels on the bottom of the insert.

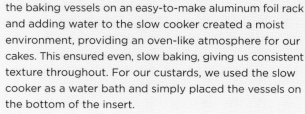

We use a loaf pan in the slow cooker to shape desserts like this delicate blueberry quick bread.

Blueberry Cornmeal Tea Cake

SERVES 6

COOKING TIME 2 TO 3 HOURS ON HIGH

SLOW COOKER SIZE 5 TO 7 QUARTS

WHY THIS RECIPE WORKS Fresh fruit is too often lost in heavy, overwhelmingly sweet desserts, so we set our sights on a versatile cake that would highlight the classically light combination of summery blueberries and moist cornbread. This cake is easy to assemble and works as both an afternoon coffee accompaniment and a welcome dessert for a summer meal. We used a quick-bread method of mixing, combining just 4 tablespoons of melted (instead of creamed) butter with sugar, egg, leaveners, and flour, which gave the cake good height and a substantial crumb. For soft and creamy results, we mixed in yogurt, which contributed a subtle sweetness and moisture for a delicate texture. The addition of lemon zest gave our cake the final brightness that we wanted,

pairing well with the juicy blueberries. Do not use stone-ground cornmeal here; it will yield a drier and less tender cake. You will need an oval slow cooker for this recipe. The test kitchen's preferred loaf pan measures 8½ by 4½ inches, but you can substitute a 9 by 5-inch loaf pan. For more information on making a foil rack, see page 333.

    1 cup (5 ounces) all-purpose flour
    ¼ cup (1¼ ounces) cornmeal
    ½ teaspoon baking powder
    ½ teaspoon baking soda
      Salt
    ½ cup plain yogurt
    ⅓ cup (2⅓ ounces) granulated sugar
    1 large egg, room temperature
    2 teaspoons grated lemon zest plus 4 teaspoons juice
    ½ teaspoon vanilla extract
    4 tablespoons unsalted butter, melted and cooled
    5 ounces (1 cup) blueberries
    ¾ cup (3 ounces) confectioners' sugar

1. Fill slow cooker with ½ inch water (about 2 cups) and place aluminum foil rack in bottom. Make foil sling for 8½ by 4½-inch loaf pan by folding 2 long sheets of foil; first sheet should be 8½ inches wide and second sheet should be 4½ inches wide. Lay sheets of foil in pan perpendicular to each other, with extra foil hanging over edges of pan. Push foil into corners and up sides of pan, smoothing foil flush to pan. Lightly grease foil.

2. Whisk flour, cornmeal, baking powder, baking soda, and ½ teaspoon salt together in bowl. In large bowl, whisk yogurt, granulated sugar, egg, lemon zest, and vanilla until smooth, then slowly whisk in melted butter until well combined. Stir in flour mixture until just incorporated. Gently fold in blueberries.

3. Scrape batter into prepared pan and smooth top. Gently tap pan on counter to release air bubbles. Set pan on prepared rack, cover, and cook until toothpick inserted in center comes out clean, 2 to 3 hours on high.

4. Let cake cool in pan on wire rack for 10 minutes. Using foil overhang, lift cake out of pan and transfer to rack; discard foil. Let cake cool completely, 1 to 2 hours.

5. Whisk confectioners' sugar, pinch salt, and lemon juice in bowl until smooth. Flip cake over onto serving dish. Drizzle top and sides with glaze and let glaze set before serving, about 25 minutes.

The trick to scaling down this carrot cake for the slow cooker was the ratio of ¾ cup carrots to 7 tablespoons oil.

Carrot Cake

SERVES 6   **EASY PREP**

COOKING TIME 3 TO 4 HOURS ON HIGH
SLOW COOKER SIZE 5 TO 7 QUARTS

WHY THIS RECIPE WORKS This humble cake really shines when the balance of sweet, shredded carrots and vegetable oil is just right, ensuring a moist, tender crumb. All too often, however, this cake dries out in the oven, unless you use a lot of oil. It turns out the slow cooker makes it far easier to produce a moist carrot cake without using all that oil. For a flavorful carrot cake with a moist, but not wet, texture, we tested different amounts of grated carrots and oil, both of which can weigh down the batter. In the end, ¾ cup of shredded carrots and 7 tablespoons of oil provided enough flavor and richness, respectively, without making the cake soggy or greasy. As for the spices, we found that a small amount of cinnamon and a pinch of cloves offered ample spice notes. Finally, the combination of baking powder and baking soda gave our cake the right amount

of lift. You will need an oval slow cooker for this recipe. A 6-inch round cake pan can be substituted for the springform pan. For more information on making a foil rack, see page 333.

CAKE
- ¾ cup (3¾ ounces) plus 2 tablespoons all-purpose flour
- ½ teaspoon baking powder
- ½ teaspoon baking soda
- ½ teaspoon ground cinnamon
  - Pinch ground cloves
  - Pinch salt
- ½ cup packed (3½ ounces) brown sugar
- 1 large egg, room temperature
- 7 tablespoons vegetable oil
- ¾ cup shredded carrots

FROSTING
- 4 ounces cream cheese, softened
- 2 tablespoons unsalted butter, softened
- 1 teaspoon vanilla extract
  - Pinch salt
- ½ cup (2 ounces) confectioner's sugar

1. FOR THE CAKE Fill slow cooker with ½ inch water (about 2 cups) and place aluminum foil rack in bottom. Grease 6-inch springform pan and line with parchment paper.

2. Whisk flour, baking powder, baking soda, cinnamon, cloves, and salt together in bowl. In large bowl, whisk sugar and egg until smooth, then slowly whisk in oil until well combined. Stir in flour mixture until just incorporated. Gently fold in carrots.

3. Scrape batter into prepared pan and smooth top. Gently tap pan on counter to release air bubbles. Set pan on prepared rack, cover, and cook until toothpick inserted in center comes out clean, 3 to 4 hours on high.

4. Let cake cool in pan on wire rack for 10 minutes. Run small knife around edge of cake, then remove sides of pan. Remove cake from pan bottom, discarding parchment, and let cool completely on rack, 1 to 2 hours. Transfer cake to serving dish.

5. FOR THE FROSTING Using handheld mixer set at medium-high speed, beat cream cheese, butter, vanilla, and salt in medium bowl until smooth, 1 to 2 minutes, scraping down sides of bowl as needed. Reduce speed to medium-low, gradually add sugar, and beat until smooth, 2 to 3 minutes. Increase speed to medium-high and beat until frosting is pale and fluffy, 2 to 3 minutes. Spread frosting evenly over top of cake. Serve.

This fudgy, indulgent cake firms up as it cools, so temping it will ensure that you don't overcook it.

Flourless Chocolate Cake

SERVES 8

COOKING TIME 1 TO 2 HOURS ON HIGH

SLOW COOKER SIZE 5 TO 7 QUARTS

WHY THIS RECIPE WORKS This decadent cake requires just a handful of ingredients (chocolate, butter, eggs, and coffee) and can be made ahead of time, for an elegant and fuss-free finale. Removing the cake from the slow cooker when it was just slightly underdone (when it registered 140 degrees on an instant-read thermometer) was key because the cake continued to cook and firm up as it cooled. You will need an oval slow cooker and a 6-inch springform pan for this recipe. For more information on making a foil rack, see page 333. Check the temperature of the cake after 1 hour of cooking and continue to monitor until it registers 140 degrees. To make neat slices, dip the knife blade into hot water and wipe it clean with a dish towel after each cut.

8 ounces bittersweet or semisweet chocolate, chopped
8 tablespoons unsalted butter
2 tablespoons brewed coffee
4 large eggs
   Confectioners' sugar

1. Fill slow cooker with ½ inch water (about 2 cups) and place aluminum foil rack in bottom. Grease 6-inch springform pan and line with parchment paper.

2. Microwave chocolate and butter in large bowl at 50 percent power, stirring occasionally, until melted, 1 to 2 minutes. Stir in coffee and let chocolate mixture cool slightly.

3. Using handheld mixer set at medium-low speed, whip eggs in separate bowl until foamy, about 1 minute. Increase speed to medium-high and whip eggs until very thick and pale yellow, 5 to 10 minutes. Gently fold one-third of whipped eggs into chocolate mixture until few streaks remain. Repeat folding twice more with remaining whipped eggs and continue to fold batter until no streaks remain. Scrape batter into prepared pan and smooth top. Set pan on prepared rack, cover, and cook until cake registers 140 degrees, 1 to 2 hours on high.

4. Transfer cake to wire rack. Run small knife around edge of cake and gently blot away condensation using paper towels. Let cake cool in pan to room temperature, about 1 hour. Cover with plastic wrap and refrigerate until well chilled, at least 3 hours or up to 3 days.

5. About 30 minutes before serving, run small knife around edge of cake, then remove sides of pan. Invert cake onto sheet of parchment paper. Peel off and discard parchment baked onto cake. Turn cake right side up onto serving dish. Dust with confectioners' sugar and serve.

SIMPLE ACCOMPANIMENTS

WHIPPED CREAM

MAKES ABOUT 2 CUPS

1 cup heavy cream
1 tablespoon sugar
1 teaspoon vanilla extract

Using handheld mixer set at medium-low speed, whip cream, sugar, and vanilla until foamy, about 1 minute. Increase speed to high and whip until soft peaks form, 1 to 3 minutes.

Rich and Creamy Cheesecake

SERVES 8
COOKING TIME 1½ TO 2½ HOURS ON HIGH
SLOW COOKER SIZE 5 TO 7 QUARTS

WHY THIS RECIPE WORKS Moving this luxurious dessert to the slow cooker ensures that it "bakes" through perfectly every time—no need to worry about cracks on the top. For a supremely creamy texture, we turned off the slow cooker once the cake registered 150 degrees on an instant-read thermometer and let the cheesecake sit in the slow cooker for an hour so it could gently finish cooking. A simple crust of graham crackers, butter, and sugar was a snap to make in a food processor and, with the processor already out, we could easily reuse it to attain a super-smooth filling. By mixing the cream cheese with sugar, sour cream, and a couple of eggs, we achieved the perfect balance of richness and sweetness. You will need an oval slow cooker and a 6-inch springform pan for this recipe. For more information on making a foil rack, see page 333. Check the temperature of the cheesecake after 1½ hours of cooking and continue to monitor until it registers 150 degrees. To make neat slices, dip the knife blade into hot water and wipe it clean with a dish towel after each cut.

  6 whole graham crackers, broken into 1-inch pieces
  2 tablespoons unsalted butter, melted and cooled
  ⅔ cup (4⅔ ounces) plus 1 tablespoon sugar
  ½ teaspoon ground cinnamon
     Salt
 18 ounces cream cheese, softened
  1 teaspoon vanilla extract
  ¼ cup sour cream
  2 large eggs, room temperature

1. Pulse graham crackers in food processor to fine crumbs, about 20 pulses. Add melted butter, 1 tablespoon sugar, cinnamon, and pinch salt and pulse to combine, about 4 pulses. Sprinkle crumbs into 6-inch springform pan and press into even layer using bottom of dry measuring cup. Wipe out processor bowl.

2. Process cream cheese, vanilla, ¼ teaspoon salt, and remaining ⅔ cup sugar in now-empty processor until combined, about 15 seconds, scraping down sides of bowl as needed. Add sour cream and eggs and process until just incorporated, about 15 seconds; do not overmix. Pour filling into prepared pan and smooth top.

3. Fill slow cooker with ½ inch water (about 2 cups) and place aluminum foil rack in bottom. Set pan on prepared rack, cover, and cook until cheesecake registers 150 degrees, 1½ to 2½ hours on high. Turn off slow cooker and let cheesecake sit, covered, for 1 hour.

This rich slow-cooker cheesecake is easy to whip up: Both crust and filling can be made in the food processor.

4. Transfer cheesecake to wire rack. Run small knife around edge of cake and gently blot away condensation using paper towels. Let cheesecake cool in pan to room temperature, about 1 hour. Cover with plastic wrap and refrigerate until well chilled, at least 3 hours or up to 3 days.

5. About 30 minutes before serving, run small knife around edge of cheesecake, then remove sides of pan. Invert cheesecake onto sheet of parchment paper, then turn cheesecake right side up onto serving dish. Serve.

Chocolate Cheesecake

SERVES 8
COOKING TIME 1½ TO 2½ HOURS ON HIGH
SLOW COOKER SIZE 5 TO 7 QUARTS

WHY THIS RECIPE WORKS For the ultimate in decadence, we added melted semisweet chocolate and cocoa powder to our Rich and Creamy Cheesecake. Swapping out the graham crackers for chocolate sandwich cookies ensured a flavorful crust. Any brand of chocolate sandwich cookies will work well here, but avoid any "double-filled" cookies because the crust won't set properly. You will need an oval slow cooker and a 6-inch springform pan for this recipe. For more information on making a foil rack, see page 333. Check the temperature of the cheesecake after 1½ hours of cooking and continue to monitor until it registers 150 degrees. To make neat slices, dip the knife blade into hot water and wipe it clean with a dish towel after each cut.

- 8 chocolate sandwich cookies
- 2 tablespoons unsalted butter, melted and cooled
- 4 ounces semisweet chocolate, chopped
- 18 ounces cream cheese, softened
- ⅔ cup (4⅔ ounces) sugar
- ¼ teaspoon salt
- ¼ cup sour cream
- 2 large eggs, room temperature
- 2 tablespoons unsweetened cocoa powder
- 1 teaspoon vanilla extract

1. Pulse cookies in food processor to fine crumbs, about 20 pulses. Add melted butter and pulse to combine, about 4 pulses. Sprinkle crumbs into 6-inch springform pan and press into even layer using bottom of dry measuring cup. Wipe out processor bowl.

2. Microwave chocolate in bowl at 50 percent power, stirring occasionally, until melted, 1 to 2 minutes; let cool slightly. Process cream cheese, sugar, and salt in now-empty processor until combined, about 15 seconds, scraping down sides of bowl as needed. Add cooled chocolate, sour cream, eggs, cocoa, and vanilla and process until just incorporated, about 15 seconds; do not overmix. Pour filling into prepared pan and smooth top.

3. Fill slow cooker with ½ inch water (about 2 cups) and place aluminum foil rack in bottom. Set pan on prepared rack, cover, and cook until cheesecake registers 150 degrees, 1½ to 2½ hours on high. Turn off slow cooker and let cheesecake sit, covered, for 1 hour.

4. Transfer cheesecake to wire rack. Run small knife around edge of cake and gently blot away condensation using paper towels. Let cheesecake cool in pan to room temperature, about 1 hour. Cover with plastic wrap and refrigerate until well chilled, at least 3 hours or up to 3 days.

5. About 30 minutes before serving, run small knife around edge of cheesecake, then remove sides of pan. Invert cheesecake onto sheet of parchment paper, then turn cheesecake right side up onto serving dish. Serve.

Cream Cheese

Supermarket shelves aren't exactly overflowing with cream cheese options. Whenever we need cream cheese in the test  kitchen, we instinctively reach for Philadelphia brand. But is Philadelphia the best or just the most familiar and widely available?

To find out, we gathered all the types of cream cheese we could find—a paltry five, three of which were Philadelphia brand. We tasted the samples plain on bagels and in a cheesecake recipe and judged the cream cheeses on richness, tanginess, creaminess, and overall quality. One product swept both the plain and the cheesecake taste tests in all categories: **Philadelphia Original**. Though some liked the easy spreadability of Philadelphia Whipped, and most were enthusiastic about buttery Organic Valley (our second-place finisher), the familiar Philadelphia Original was appointed the cream cheese of choice in the test kitchen. All but one of the products we tasted can be recommended. Despite our best hopes, Philadelphia ⅓ Less Fat tanked, coming in last. While we would have been thrilled to offer a low-fat cream cheese as a suitable option, its artificial flavor and stiff texture forced it out of consideration.

Spiced Pumpkin Cheesecake

SERVES 8
COOKING TIME 1½ TO 2½ HOURS ON HIGH
SLOW COOKER SIZE 5 TO 7 QUARTS

WHY THIS RECIPE WORKS For a seasonal take on our Rich and Creamy Cheesecake (page 333), we found we could substitute a little pumpkin puree for some of the cream cheese. Thoroughly drying the puree before mixing enabled the filling to remain indulgently creamy and dense. We eschewed store-bought pumpkin spice for a judicious custom blend so that the flavor of the pumpkin would shine through even as the blend invoked the warmth of fall. The gentle heat of the slow cooker eliminated the risk of overcooking the center and cracking on top while also freeing up the oven. You will need an oval slow cooker and a 6-inch springform pan for this recipe. For more information on making a foil rack, see page 333.

Check the temperature of the cheesecake after 1½ hours of cooking and continue to monitor until it registers 150 degrees. To make neat slices, dip the knife blade into hot water and wipe it clean with a dish towel after each cut.

  6 whole graham crackers, broken into 1-inch pieces
  2 tablespoons unsalted butter, melted and cooled
  ⅔ cup (4⅔ ounces) plus 1 tablespoon sugar
 1½ teaspoons ground cinnamon
     Salt
  1 cup canned unsweetened pumpkin puree
 12 ounces cream cheese, softened
  ½ teaspoon ground ginger
  ⅛ teaspoon ground cloves
  ¼ cup sour cream
  2 large eggs, room temperature

1. Pulse graham crackers in food processor to fine crumbs, about 20 pulses. Add melted butter, 1 tablespoon sugar, ½ teaspoon cinnamon, and pinch salt and pulse to combine, about 4 pulses. Sprinkle crumbs into 6-inch springform pan and press into even layer using bottom of dry measuring cup. Wipe out processor bowl.

2. Spread pumpkin puree over baking sheet lined with several layers of paper towels and press dry with additional towels. Transfer puree to now-empty processor bowl (puree will separate easily from towels). Add cream cheese, ginger, cloves, ½ teaspoon salt, remaining ⅔ cup sugar, and remaining 1 teaspoon cinnamon and process until combined, about 15 seconds, scraping down sides of bowl as needed. Add sour cream and eggs and process until just incorporated, about 15 seconds; do not overmix. Pour filling into prepared pan and smooth top.

3. Fill slow cooker with ½ inch water (about 2 cups) and place aluminum foil rack in bottom. Set pan on prepared rack, cover, and cook until cheesecake registers 150 degrees, 1½ to 2½ hours on high. Turn off slow cooker and let cheesecake sit, covered, for 1 hour.

4. Transfer cheesecake to wire rack. Run small knife around edge of cake and gently blot away condensation using paper towels. Let cheesecake cool in pan to room temperature, about 1 hour. Cover with plastic wrap and refrigerate until well chilled, at least 3 hours or up to 3 days.

5. About 30 minutes before serving, run small knife around edge of cheesecake, then remove sides of pan. Invert cheesecake onto sheet of parchment paper, then turn cheesecake right side up onto serving dish. Serve.

We replace an egg yolk with cream cheese for a filling that emerges from the slow cooker silken and sliceable.

Key Lime Pie

SERVES 8
COOKING TIME 1 TO 2 HOURS ON HIGH
SLOW COOKER SIZE 5 TO 7 QUARTS

WHY THIS RECIPE WORKS We think a great Key lime pie is defined not just by the fragile balance of sweet and sour but also by its creamy, just-set filling. We knew we had to be gentle in our slow-cooker "bake," so we used a water bath to cook the classic Key lime pie constituents of condensed milk, limes, and egg yolks. Results were mixed at first, as the delicate filling rapidly went from soupy to overcooked, and we didn't fancy hovering over our slow cooker to catch that fleeting moment of perfection. To solve our dilemma, we employed a trick we've used in baking bars—replacing some of the egg yolks with just 2 ounces of cream cheese—which gave us a more resilient filling that remained silken and sliced perfectly. For our crust, a simple graham cracker press-in gave us enough structure and buttery indulgence to counter our zesty filling. Pressing toasty shredded coconut onto the edge of the pie made for a beautiful presentation and added further complexity to this sweet-sour custard creation. You will need an oval slow cooker and a 6-inch springform pan for this recipe.

For more information on making a foil rack, see page 333. Check the temperature of the pie after 1 hour of cooking and continue to monitor until it registers 150 degrees. To make neat slices, dip the knife blade into hot water and wipe it clean with a dish towel after each cut.

6 whole graham crackers, broken into 1-inch pieces
2 tablespoons unsalted butter, melted and cooled
1 tablespoon sugar
  Salt
1 (14-ounce) can sweetened condensed milk
1 tablespoon grated lime zest plus ½ cup juice (4 limes)
2 ounces cream cheese, softened
1 large egg yolk, room temperature
¼ cup (¾ ounce) sweetened shredded coconut, toasted

1. Pulse graham crackers in food processor to fine crumbs, about 20 pulses. Add melted butter, sugar, and pinch salt and pulse to combine, about 4 pulses. Sprinkle crumbs into 6-inch springform pan and press into even layer using bottom of dry measuring cup. Wipe out processor bowl.

2. Process condensed milk, lime zest and juice, and cream cheese in now-empty processor until combined, about 15 seconds, scraping down sides of bowl as needed. Add egg yolk and process until just incorporated, about 5 seconds. Pour filling into prepared pan and smooth top.

3. Fill slow cooker with ½ inch water (about 2 cups) and place aluminum foil rack in bottom. Set pan on prepared rack, cover, and cook until pie registers 150 degrees, 1 to 2 hours on high. Turn slow cooker off and let pie sit, covered, for 1 hour.

4. Transfer pie to wire rack. Run small knife around edge of pie and gently blot away condensation using paper towels. Let pie cool in pan to room temperature, about 1 hour. Cover with plastic wrap and refrigerate until well chilled, at least 3 hours or up to 3 days.

5. About 30 minutes before serving, run small knife around edge of pie, then remove sides of pan. Invert pie onto sheet of parchment paper, then turn pie right side up onto serving dish. Press coconut gently against sides of pie to adhere; wipe away excess coconut. Serve.

ASSEMBLING A CRUMB CRUST

Sprinkle crumbs into 6-inch springform pan and press into even layer using bottom of dry measuring cup.

The alchemy of this cake is magical and delivers both pudding and cake for the ultimate comfort food.

Chocolate Pudding Cake

SERVES 6 TO 8
COOKING TIME 1 TO 2 HOURS ON HIGH
SLOW COOKER SIZE 4 TO 7 QUARTS

WHY THIS RECIPE WORKS This recipe for slow-cooker Chocolate Pudding Cake may sound, well, like a recipe for disaster—combine dry ingredients with wet, scrape into the slow cooker, sprinkle with sugar and cocoa powder, and then pour boiling water over the whole thing—but trust us, all will be well and delicious. The cocoa and sugar on top of the batter bubble as they cook to form a pudding-style chocolate sauce on the bottom, while a chewy, brownie-like cake rises to the top. The batter is a simple mixture of pantry staples— flour, sugar, cocoa, baking powder, and salt combined with milk, melted butter, egg yolk, and vanilla. We folded in a handful of semi-sweet chocolate chips to add another layer of flavor and ensure plenty of gooey pockets in the baked cake. You will need an oval slow cooker for this recipe. For more information on making a foil collar, see page 208. For an accurate measurement of boiling water, bring a full kettle of water to a boil and then measure out the desired amount.

1 cup (5 ounces) all-purpose flour

1 cup (7 ounces) sugar

½ cup (1½ ounces) unsweetened cocoa powder

2 teaspoons baking powder

¼ teaspoon salt

½ cup whole milk

4 tablespoons unsalted butter, melted and cooled

1 large egg yolk, room temperature

2 teaspoons vanilla extract

½ cup (3 ounces) semisweet chocolate chips

1 cup boiling water

1. Line slow cooker with aluminum foil collar and lightly coat with vegetable oil spray. Whisk flour, ½ cup sugar, ¼ cup cocoa, baking powder, and salt together in large bowl. In separate bowl, whisk together milk, melted butter, egg yolk, and vanilla. Stir milk mixture into flour mixture until just combined. Fold in chocolate chips (batter will be stiff).

2. Scrape batter into prepared slow cooker and spread to edges. Combine remaining ½ cup sugar and remaining ¼ cup cocoa in clean bowl and sprinkle evenly over top. Slowly pour boiling water evenly over top. Do not stir. Cover and cook until cake is puffed, top is lightly set, and center is gooey when pierced with toothpick, 1 to 2 hours on high.

3. Discard foil collar. Turn off slow cooker and let cake sit, covered, for 10 minutes before serving.

NOTES FROM THE TEST KITCHEN

Cocoa Powder

This potent source of chocolate flavor is nothing more than unsweetened chocolate with much of the fat removed. Cocoa powder comes in natural and Dutched versions. Dutch-processed cocoa has been treated with an alkaline substance to make it less acidic (Dutching also darkens the cocoa's color). In some cases, the type of cocoa can make a noticeable difference, but for the recipes in this book we had good results with both regular (natural) products and Dutched cocoas. Our favorite natural cocoa is **Hershey's Natural Unsweetened Cocoa**; our favorite Dutch-processed cocoa is **Droste Cocoa**.

These tart lemon pudding cakes are easier to make in the slow cooker than in the oven: no fussy water bath needed.

Individual Lemon Pudding Cakes

SERVES 4
COOKING TIME 1 TO 2 HOURS ON LOW
SLOW COOKER SIZE 5 TO 7 QUARTS

WHY THIS RECIPE WORKS During cooking, these magical little cakes separate into two layers: a rich pudding underneath, and a delicate, tender cake on top. We began by combining sugar, melted butter, and egg yolks, then added milk and a good amount of lemon zest and juice for brightness. Next, we folded in whipped egg whites and portioned our batter into ramekins. A water bath ensured that they cooked through gently and evenly. After about an hour, these individual cakes offered the perfect mix of tender cake, creamy custard, and intense lemon flavor. You will need an oval slow cooker and four 6-ounce round ramekins for this recipe.

6 tablespoons (2⅔ ounces) sugar

2 tablespoons unsalted butter, melted and cooled

2 large eggs, separated, plus 1 large white, room temperature

Pinch salt

2 tablespoons all-purpose flour

⅔ cup whole milk
2 teaspoons grated lemon zest plus 3 tablespoons juice
¼ teaspoon cream of tartar

1. In large bowl, whisk sugar, melted butter, egg yolks, and salt until smooth. Whisk in flour, then whisk in milk and lemon zest and juice until just incorporated.

2. Using handheld mixer set at medium-low speed, whip egg whites and cream of tartar in separate bowl until foamy, about 1 minute. Increase speed to medium-high and whip until stiff peaks form, 2 to 4 minutes. Gently fold one-third of whipped egg whites into batter until few streaks remain. Fold remaining egg whites into batter until no streaks remain.

3. Divide batter evenly among four 6-ounce ramekins and smooth tops. Fill slow cooker with ½ inch water (about 2 cups) and set ramekins in slow cooker. Cover and cook until cakes are domed and tops are just firm to touch, 1 to 2 hours on low. Using tongs and sturdy spatula, remove ramekins from slow cooker. Serve warm.

NOTES FROM THE TEST KITCHEN

Whipping Egg Whites

Lemon pudding cakes rely on perfectly whipped whites for their lightness, so it's important to whip them right. Egg whites whipped to soft peaks, which droop slightly  from the tip of the whisk or beater, will not have the structure to support the cake properly. Egg whites whipped to stiff peaks (shown), standing up tall on their own on the tip of the whisk or beater, have the ideal structure to support a light-as-air pudding cake. Over-whipped egg whites, which will look curdled and separated, will not incorporate well into the cake base and will often result in flat cakes. (If your whites are over-whipped, start over with new whites and a clean bowl.)

Individual Chocolate Fudge Cakes

SERVES 4
COOKING TIME 1 TO 2 HOURS ON LOW
SLOW COOKER SIZE 5 TO 7 QUARTS

WHY THIS RECIPE WORKS With a flavor that's intense and rich, and a texture that's cakey yet soufflé-like, these little desserts are utterly satisfying. Plus they're easy enough to get into the slow cooker for a sweet finish on a busy weeknight. For ours, we whipped

two eggs and an egg yolk, then added sugar, melted chocolate and butter, vanilla, and a single tablespoon of flour before portioning our batter into four ramekins. To ensure that each cake had a dense, superfudgy center, we simply pressed a small piece of chocolate into the middle of each ramekin before cooking. You will need an oval slow cooker and four 6-ounce round ramekins for this recipe.

6 ounces semisweet chocolate, 4 ounces chopped and 2 ounces broken into 4 (½-ounce) pieces
4 tablespoons unsalted butter
½ teaspoon vanilla extract
2 large eggs plus 1 large yolk, room temperature
¼ cup (1¾ ounces) granulated sugar
⅛ teaspoon salt
1 tablespoon all-purpose flour
Confectioners' sugar

1. Microwave chopped chocolate and butter in large bowl at 50 percent power, stirring occasionally, until melted, 1 to 2 minutes. Stir in vanilla and let chocolate mixture cool slightly.

2. Using handheld mixer set at medium-low speed, whip eggs and yolk in separate bowl until foamy, about 1 minute. Gradually whip in granulated sugar and salt, about 30 seconds. Increase speed to medium-high and continue to whip mixture until very thick and pale yellow, 5 to 10 minutes. Scrape whipped egg mixture on top of cooled chocolate mixture, then sift flour over top. Gently fold together until no streaks remain.

3. Divide batter evenly among four 6-ounce ramekins. Gently press 1 piece broken chocolate into center of each ramekin to submerge, and smooth tops. Fill slow cooker with ½ inch water (about 2 cups) and set ramekins in slow cooker. Cover and cook until cakes are domed and tops are just firm to touch, 1 to 2 hours on low. Using tongs and sturdy spatula, remove ramekins from slow cooker. Dust with confectioners' sugar and serve warm.

Crème Brûlée

SERVES 4 **EASY PREP**
COOKING TIME 2 TO 3 HOURS ON LOW
SLOW COOKER SIZE 5 TO 7 QUARTS

WHY THIS RECIPE WORKS For this easy, foolproof slow-cooker version of crème brûlée, we simply whisked a good amount of cream and egg yolks together with some sugar and vanilla extract. These custards cooked to creamy perfection thanks to the gentle heat of the slow cooker. Cooking the custards on low until the centers were just barely set and then chilling them also ensured a smooth, rich texture. Turbinado sugar, sprinkled over the top and heated with a kitchen torch, gave our crème brûlée a picture-perfect crust. You will need an oval slow cooker and four 6-ounce round ramekins for this recipe. Check the temperature of the custards after 2 hours of cooking and continue to monitor until they register 185 degrees. While we prefer turbinado or Demerara sugar for the sugar crust, regular granulated sugar will work.

2 cups heavy cream
5 large egg yolks
⅓ cup (2⅓ ounces) granulated sugar
1 teaspoon vanilla extract
Pinch salt
4 teaspoons turbinado or Demerara sugar

1. Whisk cream, egg yolks, granulated sugar, vanilla, and salt in bowl until sugar has dissolved. Strain custard through fine-mesh strainer into 4-cup liquid measuring cup. Divide custard evenly among four 6-ounce ramekins. Fill slow cooker with ½ inch water (about 2 cups) and set ramekins in slow cooker. Cover and cook until centers are just barely set and register 185 degrees, 2 to 3 hours on low.

2. Using tongs and sturdy spatula, transfer ramekins to wire rack and let cool to room temperature, about 2 hours. Cover with plastic wrap and refrigerate until well chilled, at least 4 hours or up to 2 days.

3. To serve, gently blot away condensation using paper towels. Sprinkle each ramekin with 1 teaspoon turbinado sugar. Tilt and tap each ramekin to distribute sugar evenly, then dump out excess sugar and wipe rims of ramekins clean. Ignite torch and caramelize sugar. Refrigerate ramekins, uncovered, to rechill custard before serving, 30 to 45 minutes.

CARAMELIZING CRÈME BRÛLÉE

1. After sprinkling sugar over surface of each custard, tilt and tap ramekin to distribute sugar into thin, even layer. Pour out any excess sugar and wipe inside rim clean.

2. To caramelize sugar, sweep flame of torch from perimeter of custard toward middle, keeping flame about 2 inches above ramekin, until sugar is bubbling and deep golden brown.

Cooking our rich and creamy flan in a narrow loaf pan makes it easier to unmold without cracking.

Flan

SERVES 6 TO 8
COOKING TIME 2 TO 3 HOURS ON LOW
SLOW COOKER SIZE 5 TO 7 QUARTS

WHY THIS RECIPE WORKS Flan is a classic Spanish dessert, slightly sweeter than a traditional baked custard, and with a crowning touch of thin, sweet caramel that pools over the dish once unmolded. To create our slow-cooker version we opted for a base of sweetened condensed milk and whole milk. Mixing the dairy with a combination of whole eggs, egg yolks, and sugar resulted in a tender, rich custard. We tried to make our caramel topping in the microwave but could not achieve the right texture or color, so we moved it to the stovetop. A water bath ensured that the custard cooked evenly. You will need an oval slow cooker for this recipe. Check the temperature of the custard after 2 hours and continue to monitor until it registers 180 degrees. The test kitchen's preferred loaf pan measures 8½ by 4½ inches, but you can substitute a 9 by 5-inch loaf pan. Serve the flan on a dish with a raised rim to contain the liquid caramel.

¼ cup water plus 2 tablespoons
⅔ cup (4⅔ ounces) sugar
2 large eggs plus 3 large yolks
1½ cups whole milk
1 (14-ounce) can sweetened condensed milk
¼ teaspoon grated lemon zest

1. Place ¼ cup water in large saucepan. Pour sugar into center of pan, taking care not to let sugar crystals touch pan sides. Gently stir with spatula to moisten sugar thoroughly. Bring mixture to boil over medium heat, without stirring, until it begins to turn golden, 4 to 7 minutes. Gently swirling pan, continue to cook until sugar is color of peanut butter, 1 to 2 minutes.

2. Remove pan from heat and continue to swirl pan until sugar is reddish-amber and fragrant, 15 to 20 seconds. Immediately add remaining 2 tablespoons water (mixture will bubble) and swirl pan until water is incorporated. Pour caramel into 8½ by 4½-inch loaf pan; do not scrape out saucepan.

3. Whisk eggs and yolks together in medium bowl. Whisk in milk, condensed milk, and lemon zest until incorporated, then pour into prepared pan. Fill slow cooker with ½ inch water (about 2 cups) and set pan in slow cooker. Cover and cook until center of flan jiggles slightly when shaken and registers 180 degrees, 2 to 3 hours on low.

4. Transfer pan to wire rack and let cool to room temperature, about 2 hours. Cover with plastic wrap and refrigerate until well chilled, at least 8 hours or up to 4 days.

5. To serve, slide paring knife around edges of pan. Invert serving dish on top of pan, and turn pan and dish over. When flan is released, remove loaf pan. Use rubber spatula to scrape residual caramel onto flan. Slice and serve.

Rice Pudding

SERVES 6 TO 8 **EASY PREP**
COOKING TIME 2 TO 3 HOURS ON HIGH
SLOW COOKER SIZE 4 TO 7 QUARTS

WHY THIS RECIPE WORKS At its best, rice pudding boasts intact, tender grains bound loosely in a subtly sweet, milky sauce. For our slow-cooker version, we set out to determine how much and what types of liquid to use. Milk (often used in traditional recipes) did not fare well, leaving us with unappealing curdled flecks throughout the pudding. Cream, on the other hand, was too rich and obscured the flavor of the rice. In the end, equal parts water and half-and-half worked best, providing a satisfying but not too rich consistency. Placing a parchment shield over the surface of the rice while it cooked—a technique we honed through our rice pilafs—ensured that the rice was more evenly cooked. We prefer pudding made from medium-grain rice, though long-grain rice works too. For more

A mixture of water and half-and-half gives this rice pudding perfect texture, and a parchment shield aids in even cooking.

information on creating a parchment shield, see page 177. For an accurate measurement of boiling water, bring a full kettle of water to a boil and then measure out the desired amount.

3 cups boiling water, plus extra as needed
3 cups half-and-half
1 cup medium-grain rice
⅔ cup (4⅔ ounces) sugar
¼ teaspoon salt
½ cup raisins
1½ teaspoons vanilla extract
1 teaspoon ground cinnamon

1. Lightly coat slow cooker with vegetable oil spray. Combine boiling water, half-and-half, rice, sugar, and salt in prepared slow cooker. Gently press 16 by 12-inch sheet of parchment paper onto surface of water mixture, folding down edges as needed. Cover and cook until rice is tender and mixture is creamy, 2 to 3 hours on high.

2. Discard parchment. Stir raisins, vanilla, and cinnamon into rice and let sit until heated through, about 5 minutes. Adjust consistency with extra hot water as needed. Serve.

MAKE IT 5 WAYS BREAD PUDDING

Classic Bread Pudding

SERVES 8 TO 10
COOKING TIME 3 TO 4 HOURS ON LOW
SLOW COOKER SIZE 5 TO 7 QUARTS

Our slow-cooker bread pudding boasts tender bread cubes enveloped by a rich custard and accented with a few stir-ins and a simple topping. Getting the texture of this company-worthy dessert just right was a challenge; early tests yielded mushy or dry puddings. After testing types of bread, we settled on challah for its rich flavor. Using staled bread was key as it was much better at soaking up our custard. By soaking and pressing the bread into the custard for just 10 minutes prior to cooking we ensured that the bread absorbed the custard evenly. After 3 hours in the slow cooker, we had moist, evenly cooked bread pudding that was definitely luxurious. Hearty white sandwich bread can be substituted for the challah. If you don't have stale bread, you can dry fresh bread pieces by baking them on a rimmed baking sheet in a 225-degree oven for about 40 minutes, stirring occasionally. You will need an oval slow cooker for this recipe. For more information on making a foil collar, see page 208.

1 CLASSIC BREAD PUDDING

2½ cups heavy cream
2½ cups whole milk
9 large egg yolks
¾ cup (5¼ ounces) granulated sugar
4 teaspoons vanilla extract
2 teaspoons grated lemon zest
¾ teaspoon salt
1 pound challah, cut into 1-inch pieces (12 cups), staled overnight
2 tablespoons packed brown sugar
½ teaspoon ground cinnamon
   Pinch ground nutmeg

1. Line slow cooker with aluminum foil collar and lightly coat with vegetable oil spray. Whisk cream, milk, egg yolks, granulated sugar, vanilla, lemon zest, and salt in large bowl until sugar has dissolved. Stir in challah and let sit, pressing on bread occasionally, until custard is mostly absorbed, about 10 minutes.

2. Transfer challah mixture to prepared slow cooker and spread into even layer. Combine brown sugar, cinnamon, and nutmeg in bowl and sprinkle over top. Cover and cook until center of bread pudding is set, 3 to 4 hours on low.

3. Turn off slow cooker and let bread pudding cool, covered, for 30 minutes. Discard foil collar. Serve.

2 BOURBON BREAD PUDDING

2½ cups heavy cream
2½ cups whole milk
9 large egg yolks
¾ cup packed (5¼ ounces) plus 2 tablespoons brown sugar
⅓ cup bourbon
1 tablespoon vanilla extract
¾ teaspoon salt
¼ teaspoon cardamom
1 pound challah, cut into 1-inch pieces (12 cups), staled overnight
½ cup pecans, toasted and chopped

1. Line slow cooker with aluminum foil collar and lightly coat with vegetable oil spray. Whisk cream, milk, egg yolks, ¾ cup sugar, bourbon, vanilla, salt, and cardamom in large bowl until sugar has dissolved. Stir in challah and let sit, pressing on bread occasionally, until custard is mostly absorbed, about 10 minutes.

2. Transfer challah mixture to prepared slow cooker and spread into even layer. Sprinkle with remaining 2 tablespoons sugar. Cover and cook until center of bread pudding is set, 3 to 4 hours on low.

3. Turn off slow cooker and let bread pudding cool, covered, for 30 minutes. Discard foil collar and sprinkle with pecans. Serve.

3   NUTELLA BREAD PUDDING

2 cups heavy cream

2 cups whole milk

9 large egg yolks

1 cup Nutella

¾ cup (5¼ ounces) sugar

1 tablespoon vanilla extract

¾ teaspoon salt

1 pound challah, cut into 1-inch pieces (12 cups), staled overnight

¾ cup (4½ ounces) chocolate chips

1. Line slow cooker with aluminum foil collar and lightly coat with vegetable oil spray. Whisk cream, milk, egg yolks, Nutella, sugar, vanilla, and salt in large bowl until sugar has dissolved and mixture is well combined. Stir in challah and ½ cup chocolate chips and let sit, pressing on bread occasionally, until custard is mostly absorbed, about 10 minutes.

2. Transfer challah mixture to prepared slow cooker and spread into even layer. Sprinkle with remaining ¼ cup chocolate chips. Cover and cook until center of bread pudding is set, 3 to 4 hours on low.

3. Turn off slow cooker and let bread pudding cool, covered, for 30 minutes. Discard foil collar. Serve.

4   WHITE CHOCOLATE AND CHERRY BREAD PUDDING

2½ cups heavy cream

2½ cups whole milk

9 large egg yolks

¾ cup (5¼ ounces) sugar

1 tablespoon vanilla extract

¾ teaspoon salt

1 pound challah, cut into 1-inch pieces (12 cups), staled overnight

1 cup dried cherries

¾ cup (4½ ounces) white chocolate chips

½ cup shelled pistachios, toasted and chopped

1. Line slow cooker with aluminum foil collar and lightly coat with vegetable oil spray. Whisk cream, milk, egg yolks, sugar, vanilla, and salt in large bowl until sugar has dissolved. Stir in challah, cherries, and ½ cup chocolate chips and let sit, pressing on bread occasionally, until custard is mostly absorbed, about 10 minutes.

2. Transfer challah mixture to prepared slow cooker and spread into even layer. Sprinkle with remaining ¼ cup chocolate chips. Cover and cook until center of bread pudding is set, 3 to 4 hours on low.

3. Turn off slow cooker and let bread pudding cool, covered, for 30 minutes. Discard foil collar and sprinkle with pistachios. Serve.

5   RUM-RAISIN BREAD PUDDING

⅔ cup raisins

¼ cup dark rum

2½ cups heavy cream

2½ cups whole milk

9 large egg yolks

¾ cup packed (5¼ ounces) plus 2 tablespoons brown sugar

1 tablespoon vanilla extract

¾ teaspoon salt

1 pound challah, cut into 1-inch pieces (12 cups), staled overnight

1. Line slow cooker with aluminum foil collar and lightly coat with vegetable oil spray. Microwave raisins and rum in small bowl until hot, about 45 seconds; let cool slightly.

2. Whisk cream, milk, egg yolks, ¾ cup sugar, vanilla, and salt in large bowl until sugar has dissolved. Stir in challah and raisin mixture and let sit, pressing on bread occasionally, until custard is mostly absorbed, about 10 minutes.

3. Transfer challah mixture to prepared slow cooker and spread into even layer. Sprinkle with remaining 2 tablespoons sugar. Cover and cook until center of bread pudding is set, 3 to 4 hours on low.

4. Turn off slow cooker and let bread pudding cool, covered, for 30 minutes. Discard foil collar. Serve.

We cook the topping for this crisp in the oven, which keeps things simple because it can be made ahead.

Apple-Oat Crisp

SERVES 6 TO 8 **EASY PREP**

COOKING TIME 3 TO 4 HOURS ON LOW OR 2 TO 3 HOURS ON HIGH

SLOW COOKER SIZE 4 TO 7 QUARTS

WHY THIS RECIPE WORKS A great fruit crisp marries sweet, almost fall-apart-tender fruit with a buttery-rich and crisp topping, so there is no wonder that it is an appealing dessert option. What's tricky about making a fruit crisp is ensuring that the filling and topping are perfectly cooked and ready to serve when dinner is over. Turns out that using the slow cooker makes this feat easier and more streamlined. We knew from the outset that we'd have to cook the topping separately—it would simply steam on top of the filling. But all that moist heat made the slow cooker the perfect vessel for making the apple filling: As the apples cooked, they were infused with flavor from the mixture of brown sugar, cinnamon, and cider. Cutting the apples into thick wedges ensured that they did not turn to mush during the long cooking time. And as they cooked and released their juice, they formed a delicious sauce, which was thickened by a little instant tapioca that we had added at the outset. For the crisp topping, we made a simple dough using rolled oats, almonds, a little butter, honey, and spices. After cooking it separately in the oven, we crumbled it over the top before serving.

FILLING

- 1½ pounds Granny Smith apples, peeled, cored, and cut into ½-inch-thick wedges
- 1½ pounds Golden Delicious apples, peeled, cored, and cut into ½-inch-thick wedges
- ½ cup apple cider
- 2 tablespoons packed light brown sugar
- 4 teaspoons instant tapioca
- 2 teaspoons lemon juice
- ¼ teaspoon ground cinnamon

TOPPING

- ½ cup sliced almonds
- ½ cup (2½ ounces) all-purpose flour
- ¼ cup packed (1¾ ounces) light brown sugar
- ¼ teaspoon ground cinnamon
- ¼ teaspoon salt
- ⅛ teaspoon ground nutmeg
- 5 tablespoons unsalted butter, melted and cooled
- ¾ cup (2¼ ounces) old-fashioned rolled oats
- 2 tablespoons honey

1. FOR THE FILLING Combine all ingredients in slow cooker. Cover and cook until apples are tender and sauce is thickened, 3 to 4 hours on low or 2 to 3 hours on high.

2. FOR THE TOPPING Adjust oven rack to upper-middle position and heat oven to 400 degrees. Pulse almonds, flour, sugar, cinnamon, salt, and nutmeg in food processor until nuts are finely chopped, about 10 pulses. Drizzle melted butter over top and pulse until mixture resembles crumbly wet sand, about 5 pulses. Add oats and honey and pulse until evenly incorporated, about 3 pulses.

3. Spread topping evenly over parchment paper–lined rimmed baking sheet and pinch it between your fingers into small pea-size pieces (with some smaller loose bits). Bake until golden brown, 8 to 12 minutes, rotating sheet halfway through baking; let cool slightly. (Topping can be stored in airtight container for up to 1 day.)

4. Turn off slow cooker and let apple filling cool for 20 minutes. Gently stir apples to coat with sauce. Sprinkle individual portions of filling with crumbles before serving.

Peach-Ginger Crisp

SERVES 8 TO 10 | **EASY PREP**

COOKING TIME 3 TO 4 HOURS ON LOW OR 2 TO 3 HOURS ON HIGH

SLOW COOKER SIZE 5 TO 7 QUARTS

WHY THIS RECIPE WORKS One of our all-time favorite fruit desserts is peach crisp, which should taste like summer, full of juicy peach flavor, with a buttery, nutty topping. We tried using fresh peaches, but we had trouble getting a consistent texture; some peaches turned out mushy while others refused to soften even after hours in our cooker. To get a consistent peach texture and flavor we opted to use frozen peaches, which are quickly frozen at the height of ripeness, ensuring their quality and flavor and making this dish possible any time of year. We decided to complement the sweet peach flavor with the spicy heat of ginger by using crystallized ginger in the filling and ground ginger in the topping. For the cookie-like crisp topping, we made a simple dough, cooked it separately in the oven, and crumbled it over the top before serving.

FILLING

- 4 pounds frozen sliced peaches, thawed and drained (7 cups)
- ¾ cup (5¼ ounces) granulated sugar
- 3 tablespoons crystallized ginger, chopped
- 4 teaspoons instant tapioca
- 1 teaspoon lemon juice
- 1 teaspoon vanilla extract

TOPPING

- 1 cup (5 ounces) all-purpose flour
- ¼ cup (1¾ ounces) granulated sugar
- ¼ cup packed (1¾ ounces) light brown sugar
- 2 teaspoons vanilla extract
- ¾ teaspoon ground ginger
- ⅛ teaspoon salt
- 8 tablespoons unsalted butter, cut into 6 pieces and softened
- ½ cup sliced almonds

1. FOR THE FILLING Combine all ingredients in slow cooker. Cover and cook until peaches are tender and sauce is thickened, 3 to 4 hours on low or 2 to 3 hours on high.

2. FOR THE TOPPING Adjust oven rack to lower-middle position and heat oven to 350 degrees. Pulse flour, granulated sugar, brown sugar, vanilla, ginger, and salt in food processor until combined, about 5 pulses. Sprinkle butter and ¼ cup almonds over top and process until mixture clumps together into large crumbly balls, about 30 seconds. Sprinkle remaining ¼ cup almonds over top and pulse to incorporate, about 2 pulses.

3. Spread topping evenly over parchment paper–lined rimmed baking sheet and pinch it between your fingers into small pea-size pieces (with some smaller loose bits). Bake until golden brown, about 18 minutes, rotating sheet halfway through baking; let cool slightly. (Topping can be stored in airtight container for up to 1 day.)

4. Turn off slow cooker and let peach filling cool for 20 minutes. Gently stir peaches to coat with sauce. Sprinkle individual portions of filling with crumbles before serving.

NOTES FROM THE TEST KITCHEN

Tapioca: Slow Cooking Secret Ingredient

When we're making stews or braises, or when we want thickened sauces, we usually reach for flour. But we've found that flour requires cooking on the stovetop to remove its raw flavor. In search of a thickener that we could simply stir into the slow cooker, we hit upon tapioca, which is made from starch extracted from the root of the cassava plant (also called manioc or yuca).

Tapioca is available in several forms, but flour, pearl, and instant are the most common. After the cassava starch grains are removed from the root's cells, they are heated and ruptured, which converts the starches into small, irregular masses. These masses are then baked into flakes that are finely ground to make tapioca flour, or they're forced through sieves and baked again to form pearl tapioca. Tapioca pearls are gelatinous spheres; they come in various sizes ranging from 1 to 8 millimeters in diameter and must be rehydrated before using. Minute, or instant, tapioca is made from tapioca flour and is precooked, then coarsely ground. It dissolves quickly and doesn't require presoaking, making it our favorite choice for thickening. It is also the most widely available. Tapioca flour and pearl tapioca can be substituted for instant tapioca, but pearl tapioca will not fully dissolve and will lend a slightly grainy texture to the dish. Stored in a cool, dark place, all types of tapioca will keep indefinitely.

Blueberry Cobbler

SERVES 6 **EASY PREP**

COOKING TIME 3 TO 4 HOURS ON LOW OR 2 TO 3 HOURS
ON HIGH

SLOW COOKER SIZE 5 TO 7 QUARTS

WHY THIS RECIPE WORKS It doesn't get much easier or tastier than our slow-cooker blueberry cobbler, full of sweet, juicy blueberries offset with some fragrant lemon zest and juice, and topped with tender biscuits. But getting the filling just to our liking took a little investigative work. We started by testing different types of blueberries (frozen and fresh) and ultimately found both worked well. Our final issue was the texture—we couldn't get the filling thick enough without adding excessive tapioca, which made it too gloppy. We borrowed a trick from our blueberry pie recipe and added an apple into the mix; the gentle heat of the slow cooker activated the apple's pectin—which is a natural thickener. Our biscuit topping (cooked separately in the oven) started out as a fairly standard drop biscuit: a mix of flour, butter, baking powder and soda, sugar, salt, and buttermilk. However, we added a dash of vanilla to the dough and sprinkled the shaped dough with cinnamon sugar before baking to create crisp but tender biscuits with hints of vanilla and cinnamon—perfect for serving with our blueberry filling. You will need an oval slow cooker for this recipe.

FILLING

- 30 ounces (6 cups) fresh or frozen blueberries
- 1 Granny Smith apple, peeled, cored, and finely shredded
- ½ cup (3½ ounces) sugar
- 2 tablespoons instant tapioca
- ½ teaspoon grated lemon zest plus 1 tablespoon juice
  Pinch salt

BISCUITS

- 1 cup (5 ounces) all-purpose flour
- ¼ cup (1¾ ounces) plus 2 teaspoons sugar
- 2 teaspoons baking powder
- ¼ teaspoon baking soda
- ¼ teaspoon salt
- ⅓ cup buttermilk
- 4 tablespoons unsalted butter, melted and cooled
- ½ teaspoon vanilla extract
- ⅛ teaspoon ground cinnamon

1. FOR THE FILLING Combine all ingredients in slow cooker. Cover and cook until blueberries are softened and sauce is thickened, 3 to 4 hours on low or 2 to 3 hours on high.

2. FOR THE BISCUITS Adjust oven rack to middle position and heat oven to 400 degrees. Whisk flour, ¼ cup sugar, baking powder, baking soda, and salt together in large bowl. In separate bowl, whisk buttermilk, melted butter, and vanilla together. Gently stir buttermilk mixture into flour mixture until dough is just combined.

3. Divide dough into 6 equal pieces, round gently into biscuits, and place on parchment paper–lined rimmed baking sheet, spaced about 1½ inches apart. Combine remaining 2 teaspoons sugar and cinnamon in bowl and sprinkle over top of biscuits. Bake until biscuits are golden and cooked through, 12 to 15 minutes, rotating sheet halfway through baking. Transfer biscuits to wire rack and set aside. (Biscuits can be stored at room temperature for up to 8 hours.)

4. Turn off slow cooker. Arrange biscuits on top of blueberry filling, cover, and let cool for 20 minutes. Serve.

NOTES FROM THE TEST KITCHEN

Using Frozen Blueberries

You can use either fresh or frozen blueberries in our muffins and scones. During the summer, when blueberries are ripe, it's a no-brainer what you'd choose. But these days you can find fresh berries in your supermarket almost year-round.

Last winter, the test kitchen tried fresh berries from Chile as well as five frozen brands in a cobbler. The frozen wild berries easily beat the fresh imported berries as well as the other frozen contenders. (Compared with cultivated berries, wild berries are smaller, more intense in color, firmer in texture, and sweeter and tangier.) While frozen cultivated berries trailed in the tasting, all but one brand received decent scores.

Why did frozen wild berries beat fresh berries? To help them survive the long trip north, the imported berries are picked before they have a chance to fully ripen. As a result, they are often tart and not so flavorful. Frozen berries have been picked at their peak—when perfectly ripe—and are then individually quick frozen (IQF) at −20 degrees. The quick freezing preserves their sweetness, letting us enjoy them year-round.

Cherry Grunt

SERVES 8

COOKING TIME 3 TO 4 HOURS ON LOW OR 2 TO 3 HOURS
ON HIGH

SLOW COOKER SIZE 5 TO 7 QUARTS

WHY THIS RECIPE WORKS A grunt is an old-fashioned summer fruit dessert topped with sweet, tender dumplings. The fruit is traditionally simmered in a pot, and the dumplings are dropped on top and steamed until fluffy and light. Using frozen cherries

Easy-to-make and sturdy dumplings cook best atop this fruit dessert when arranged around the perimeter of the insert.

makes this rustic dessert an option even in the dead of winter, and it cuts down on prep time. For a filling that was thick and jammy, we microwaved the cherries with some of the flour (along with sugar and other flavorings) so the released juice would be absorbed by the flour, then moved the mixture to the slow cooker. Positioning the dumplings around the perimeter of the slow cooker—where it's hottest—guaranteed that they were completely cooked through by the time the filling was done. A sprinkle of cinnamon sugar added flavor and a slight crunch to our dumplings. You will need an oval slow cooker for this recipe.

2¼ pounds frozen sweet cherries, thawed
  2 cups (10 ounces) all-purpose flour
  1 cup (7 ounces) plus 3 tablespoons sugar
  1 tablespoon lemon juice
1¼ teaspoons ground cinnamon
  1 teaspoon almond extract
  1 tablespoon baking powder
  ½ teaspoon salt
  ½ cup plus 2 tablespoons milk
  4 tablespoons unsalted butter, melted and cooled

1. Combine cherries, ¼ cup flour, 1 cup sugar, lemon juice, 1 teaspoon cinnamon, and almond extract in bowl. Microwave until cherries begin to release their liquid, about 5 minutes, stirring halfway through microwaving. Stir cherry mixture well, transfer to slow cooker, and spread into even layer.

2. In large bowl, combine remaining 1¾ cups flour, 2 tablespoons sugar, baking powder, and salt. Stir in milk and melted butter until just combined; do not overmix. In small bowl, combine remaining 1 tablespoon sugar and remaining ¼ teaspoon cinnamon.

3. Using greased ¼ cup measure, drop 8 dumplings around perimeter of slow cooker on top of cherries, leaving center empty. Sprinkle dumplings with cinnamon-sugar mixture. Cover and cook until toothpick inserted in center of dumplings comes out clean, 3 to 4 hours on low or 2 to 3 hours on high. Turn off slow cooker and let grunt cool for 20 minutes before serving.

ASSEMBLING CHERRY GRUNT

Using greased ¼-cup dry measuring cup, arrange dumplings around perimeter of slow cooker to ensure that they cook through completely.

Stuffed Apples with Dried Cherries and Hazelnuts

SERVES 6
COOKING TIME 4 TO 5 HOURS ON LOW
SLOW COOKER SIZE 5 TO 7 QUARTS

WHY THIS RECIPE WORKS This homey dessert is often plagued with a mushy texture and cloyingly sweet flavor. We wanted cooked apples that were tender and firm, and a filling that perfectly complemented their sweet-tart flavor. We knew picking the right variety of apple was paramount to our success and, after extensive testing, we arrived at a surprising winner: Granny Smith was the best apple for the job, with its firm flesh and tart, fruity flavor. To ensure our fruit avoided even the occasional collapse, we peeled the apples after cutting off their tops. The skin on top trapped steam released by the breakdown of the apples' interior cells, and removing the rest of it allowed the steam to escape and the apple to retain its firm texture. By keeping the heat low, the apples cooked evenly and didn't turn mushy. Our filling base of tangy dried cherries, brown sugar, and hazelnuts benefited from some finessing by way of black pepper, orange zest, and a few pats of butter. To punch up

A complex filling with hazelnuts, dried cherries, and oats turns humble Granny Smiths into a pleasing dessert.

the flavor even more, we added chewy rolled oats and diced apple. We then capped the filled apples with the tops we had lopped off. A drizzle of maple syrup commingled with the cooking juices, which, when emulsified with more butter at the end, turned into a complex sauce and topped off a surprisingly elegant dish. A melon baller helps to create a cavity that fits plenty of filling. You will need an oval slow cooker for this recipe.

    7 large Granny Smith apples
    8 tablespoons unsalted butter, softened
    ¼ cup packed (1¾ ounces) brown sugar
    ⅓ cup dried cherries, chopped
    ⅓ cup hazelnuts, toasted, skinned, and chopped
    3 tablespoons old-fashioned rolled oats
    1 teaspoon grated orange zest
    ½ teaspoon pepper
       Pinch salt
    ⅓ cup maple syrup

1. Peel and core 1 apple and cut into ¼-inch pieces. Combine apple, 5 tablespoons butter, sugar, cherries, hazelnuts, oats, orange zest, pepper, and salt in bowl; set aside.

2. Shave thin slice off bottom (blossom end) of remaining 6 apples to allow them to sit flat. Cut top ½ inch off stem end of apples and reserve. Peel apples and use melon baller or small measuring spoon to cut 1½-inch diameter opening from core, being careful not to cut through bottom of apple. Spoon filling inside apples, mounding excess filling over cavities; top with reserved apple caps.

3. Lightly coat slow cooker with vegetable oil spray. Arrange stuffed apples in prepared slow cooker. Drizzle with maple syrup, cover, and cook until skewer inserted into apples meets little resistance, 4 to 5 hours on low.

4. Using tongs and sturdy spatula, transfer apples to serving dish. Whisk remaining 3 tablespoons butter into cooking liquid, 1 tablespoon at a time, until incorporated. Spoon sauce over apples and serve.

PREPARING APPLES FOR STUFFING

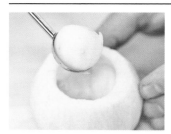

After peeling apples, use melon baller or small measuring spoon to remove 1½-inch diameter opening from core, being careful not to cut through bottom of apples.

White Wine–Poached Pears

SERVES 6 **EASY PREP**

COOKING TIME 3 TO 4 HOURS ON LOW OR 2 TO 3 HOURS ON HIGH

SLOW COOKER SIZE 4 TO 7 QUARTS

WHY THIS RECIPE WORKS Here we poached pears in sugar-sweetened white wine with fresh herbs, lemon zest, vanilla, and cinnamon. But for a sauce thick enough to coat the pears, we needed to reduce it on the stovetop. Chilling the pears in the sauce allowed the fruit to absorb even more flavor while taking on a lovely translucent appearance. For the best texture, look for pears that are neither fully ripe nor rock hard; choose those that yield just slightly when pressed. We recommend a medium-bodied dry white wine such as Sauvignon Blanc or Chardonnay. You will need an oval slow cooker for this recipe.

    1 (750-ml) bottle dry white wine
    ¾ cup (5¼ ounces) sugar
    ½ vanilla bean
    6 (2-inch) strips lemon zest
    5 sprigs fresh mint

3 sprigs fresh thyme

½ cinnamon stick

⅛ teaspoon salt

6 ripe but firm Bosc or Bartlett pears (8 ounces each), peeled, halved, and cored

1. Whisk wine and sugar together in slow cooker until sugar has dissolved. Cut vanilla bean in half lengthwise. Using tip of paring knife, scrape out seeds. Stir vanilla bean and seeds, lemon zest, mint sprigs, thyme sprigs, cinnamon stick, and salt into wine mixture. Nestle pears into slow cooker, cover, and cook until skewer inserted into pears meets little resistance, 3 to 4 hours on low or 2 to 3 hours on high.

2. Using slotted spoon, transfer pears to shallow casserole dish. Strain cooking liquid into large saucepan. Bring to simmer over medium heat and cook until thickened and measures about 1⅓ cups, about 15 minutes. Pour sauce over pears, cover, and refrigerate until well chilled, at least 2 hours or up to 3 days. Serve.

CORING PEARS

1. Peel pear and cut in half through core.

2. Guide melon baller in circular motion to cut around central core. Draw melon baller to top of pear, then remove blossom end.

Tea-Poached Pears

SERVES 6 LIGHT

COOKING TIME 3 TO 4 HOURS ON LOW OR 2 TO 3 HOURS ON HIGH

SLOW COOKER SIZE 4 TO 7 QUARTS

WHY THIS RECIPE WORKS Poaching pears in tea creates a fragrant and delicate dessert. We created a poaching liquid strong enough to add flavor but not bitterness; a ratio of four tea bags to 3 cups water worked best. A cinnamon stick and star anise added subtle complexity. We reduced the flavorful liquid on the stovetop to create a warm spiced sauce to pour over the pears. For a rich and creamy topping we combined confectioners' sugar with Greek yogurt and Grand Marnier. For the best texture, look for pears that

The tea-infused poaching liquid was so delicious that we decided to reduce it on the stovetop for a sauce.

are neither fully ripe nor rock hard; choose those that yield just slightly when pressed. You will need an oval slow cooker for this recipe. For an accurate measurement of boiling water, bring a full kettle of water to a boil and then measure out the desired amount.

3 cups boiling water

4 black tea bags

1 cinnamon stick

2 star anise pods

Salt

¼ cup packed (1¾ ounces) brown sugar

6 ripe but firm Bosc or Bartlett pears (8 ounces each), peeled, halved, and cored

¾ cup plain Greek yogurt

3 tablespoons confectioners' sugar

1 teaspoon Grand Marnier

1. Combine boiling water, tea bags, cinnamon stick, star anise, and ½ teaspoon salt in slow cooker and let steep for 8 minutes; discard tea bags. Whisk in brown sugar until dissolved. Nestle pears into slow cooker, cover, and cook until skewer inserted into pears meets little resistance, 3 to 4 hours on low or 2 to 3 hours on high.

2. Using slotted spoon, transfer pears to shallow casserole dish. Strain cooking liquid into large saucepan. Bring to simmer over medium heat and cook until thickened and measures about 1 cup, 15 to 20 minutes. Pour sauce over pears, cover, and refrigerate until well chilled, at least 2 hours or up to 3 days.

3. Whisk yogurt, confectioners' sugar, Grand Marnier, and ⅛ teaspoon salt in bowl until combined. Dollop individual portions with yogurt topping before serving.

Bananas Foster

SERVES 6 **EASY PREP**

COOKING TIME 1 TO 2 HOURS ON HIGH
SLOW COOKER SIZE 4 TO 7 QUARTS

WHY THIS RECIPE WORKS This iconic New Orleans dessert is usually served flambéed at tableside. To save effort, stove space, and our eyebrows, we adapted it for the slow cooker, and it could hardly have been easier. Simply whisking together sugar, rum, and cinnamon in the slow cooker and then nestling in the bananas kept prep time to a minimum. After cooking the fruit for an hour or so on high, we found we had partially caramelized bananas and the makings of a flavorful sauce. Whisking some butter into the cooking liquid gave us a rich emulsion, and a little lemon juice balanced the sweetness with some acidity. Look for yellow bananas with just a few spots; overripe bananas will fall apart during cooking. We prefer the flavor of gold rum, but you can substitute white or dark rum if desired. You will need an oval slow cooker for this recipe.

½ cup packed (3½ ounces) dark brown sugar
¼ cup gold rum
½ teaspoon ground cinnamon
¼ teaspoon salt
3 ripe bananas, peeled, halved crosswise, then halved lengthwise
2 tablespoons unsalted butter, cut into 2 pieces
1 teaspoon lemon juice
2 pints vanilla ice cream
½ cup pecans or walnuts, toasted and chopped (optional)

1. Lightly coat slow cooker with vegetable oil spray. Whisk sugar, rum, cinnamon, and salt in prepared slow cooker until sugar has dissolved. Nestle bananas cut side down into slow cooker. Cover and cook until skewer inserted into bananas meets little resistance, 1 to 2 hours on high. (Bananas can be held on warm or low setting for up to 1 hour.)

2. Using tongs and sturdy spatula, transfer bananas to individual bowls. Whisk butter and lemon juice into sauce until incorporated. Portion ice cream on top of bananas, spoon sauce over top, and sprinkle with pecans, if using. Serve.

Warm Peach-Raspberry Compote

SERVES 6 **EASY PREP**

COOKING TIME 3 TO 4 HOURS ON LOW OR 2 TO 3 HOURS ON HIGH
SLOW COOKER SIZE 4 TO 7 QUARTS

WHY THIS RECIPE WORKS Ideal for entertaining, this effortless yet brightly flavored compote takes a simple bowl of vanilla ice cream from ordinary to extraordinary. Frozen sliced peaches offer consistent quality, and so they guaranteed a compote that thickened to just the right texture with the help of a little tapioca. Raspberries, stirred in at the end, provided a lively, tart punch, and chopped mint added freshness. You do not need to thaw the peaches for this recipe.

2 pounds frozen sliced peaches, cut into 1-inch pieces
⅓ cup (2⅓ ounces) sugar
2 tablespoons instant tapioca
1 teaspoon lemon juice
1 teaspoon vanilla extract
⅛ teaspoon salt
10 ounces (2 cups) raspberries
¼ cup chopped fresh mint
2 pints vanilla ice cream or frozen yogurt

1. Combine peaches, sugar, tapioca, lemon juice, vanilla, and salt in slow cooker. Cover and cook until peaches are tender and sauce is thickened, 3 to 4 hours on low or 2 to 3 hours on high. (Compote can be held on warm or low setting for up to 2 hours.)

2. Stir raspberries into compote and let sit until heated through, about 5 minutes. Stir in mint. Portion ice cream into individual bowls and spoon compote over top. Serve.

Warm Strawberry-Rhubarb Compote

SERVES 6 **EASY PREP**

COOKING TIME 1 TO 2 HOURS ON HIGH
SLOW COOKER SIZE 4 TO 7 QUARTS

WHY THIS RECIPE WORKS When developing this classic strawberry-rhubarb duo, we found that just a small amount of honey added to the slow cooker with the rhubarb provided a hint of sweetness and tamed the acidity in the rhubarb. It also thickened the fruit juice into a light syrup that was perfect for spooning over ice cream. For big, distinct strawberry flavor we stirred the berries in at the end, which also prevented them from turning to mush. To finish the compote we stirred in butter for richness.

1 pound rhubarb, peeled and sliced 1 inch thick
¼ cup honey
2 tablespoons water
1 teaspoon vanilla extract
   Pinch salt
20 ounces strawberries, hulled and quartered (4 cups)
1 tablespoon unsalted butter
2 pints vanilla ice cream or frozen yogurt

1. Combine rhubarb, honey, water, vanilla, and salt in slow cooker. Cover and cook until rhubarb is softened and sauce is thickened, 1 to 2 hours on high. (Compote can be held on warm or low setting for up to 2 hours.)

2. Stir strawberries and butter into compote and let sit until heated through, about 5 minutes. Portion ice cream into individual bowls and spoon compote over top. Serve.

PEELING RHUBARB

1. Trim ends of stalk. Slice thin disk from bottom, being careful not to cut through stalk. Gently pull partially attached disk away to peel off fibrous outer layers.

2. Working from bottom of stalk again, repeat in reverse direction to remove outer layers on opposite side.

Chocolate Fondue

SERVES 8 TO 10   `EASY PREP`
COOKING TIME 1 TO 2 HOURS ON LOW
SLOW COOKER SIZE 1½ TO 7 QUARTS

WHY THIS RECIPE WORKS Dipping a fresh strawberry into warm melted chocolate is guaranteed to make just about anybody happy. For our version, we first chopped chocolate into small pieces before combining it with heavy cream and a pinch of salt. (Our recipe uses more chocolate than cream because it results in a thick, velvety fondue.) The chocolate melted gently as the cream heated, and after about an hour all we needed to do was whisk the steaming mixture until smooth. At this point the fondue was rich and thick. Adding a tablespoon of corn syrup made all the difference; the fondue became satiny—the perfect consistency for

Making this chocolate dipping sauce in a slow cooker is a party trick that should be in everyone's repertoire.

dipping—and retained a beautiful gloss. We found that semisweet chocolate produced both the most reliable consistency and the best flavor to pair with an array of accompaniments. We tested more than eight brands of semisweet chocolate (including chips), and they all worked fine, though there were minor flavor differences between brands. (Be sure to taste the chocolate before making the fondue to make sure you like its flavor.) By comparison, white, milk, and bittersweet chocolates were neither consistent nor liked by all tasters; we don't recommend using them. For dipping, we like to use bite-size pieces of fruit, pound cake, or bread; make sure you have long skewers on hand to make things easy.

12 ounces semisweet chocolate, chopped
1⅓ cups heavy cream, plus extra as needed
1 tablespoon light corn syrup
   Pinch salt

Combine all ingredients in slow cooker. Cover and cook until chocolate has melted and mixture is hot, 1 to 2 hours on low. Whisk chocolate mixture together until smooth and serve. (Fondue can be held on warm or low setting for up to 2 hours; adjust consistency with extra hot cream as needed.)

NUTRITIONAL INFORMATION FOR OUR LIGHT RECIPES

Analyzing recipes for their nutritional values is a tricky business, and we did our best to be as realistic and accurate as possible throughout this book. We were absolutely strict about measuring when cooking and never resorted to guessing or estimating. We also didn't play games when analyzing the light recipes in the nutritional program to make the numbers look better. To calculate the nutritional values of our recipes per serving, we used The Food Processor SQL by ESHA Research. When using this program, we entered all the ingredients, using weights for important ingredients such as meat, cheese, and most vegetables. We also used all of our preferred brands in these analyses. When the recipe called for seasoning with an unspecified amount of salt and pepper (often raw meat), we added ½ teaspoon of salt and ¼ teaspoon of pepper to the analysis. We did not, however, include additional salt or pepper when the food was seasoned "to taste" at the end of cooking.

NOTE: Unless otherwise indicated, information applies to a single serving. If there is a range in the serving size in the recipe, we used the highest number of servings to calculate the nutritional values.

	Cal	Fat (g)	Sat Fat (g)	Chol (mg)	Carb (g)	Protein (g)	Fiber (g)	Sodium (mg)
Chapter 1. Easy Appetizers								
Easy Spiced Nuts	190	15	1	0	11	7	4	170
Rosemary and Garlic White Bean Dip	150	7	1	0	17	7	5	350
Turkey-Pesto Cocktail Meatballs	190	8	2.5	55	10	20	1	290
Chapter 2. Bottomless Bowls								
Italian Meatball and Escarole Soup	240	6	3	65	18	30	5	930
Old-Fashioned Chicken Noodle Soup	160	4	0.5	40	11	19	2	1090
Spring Vegetable Chicken Soup	220	5	1	45	19	23	3	1250
Spicy Chipotle Chicken Noodle Soup	200	4.5	0.5	50	19	20	2	1260
Curried Chicken and Couscous Soup	160	4	0.5	40	12	20	2	1180
Chinese Chicken and Ramen Soup	290	5	0.5	40	38	24	5	1350
Turkey and Rice Soup	220	4	0.5	45	27	19	3	980
Hearty Turkey and Vegetable Soup	160	4	1	45	13	19	2	1070
Spanish Seafood Soup	240	7	1	120	19	23	4	890
Spicy Thai Shrimp Soup	160	2.5	0	120	14	19	1	1300
Manhattan Clam Chowder	230	6	1.5	30	30	13	3	950
Garden Minestrone	200	3	0.5	0	32	12	7	970
Miso Soup with Shiitakes and Sweet Potatoes	180	6	0	0	23	10	3	930
Tuscan White Bean Soup	300	9	2.5	15	38	19	20	670
Black Bean Soup	300	6	1	20	42	19	7	640
15-Bean Soup with Sausage and Spinach	230	3	1	30	30	20	4	840
Moroccan Lentil Soup with Mustard Greens	260	6	2	5	39	16	8	800
Fisherman's Stew	280	12	4.5	90	14	27	2	890
Sicilian Fish Stew	230	12	2	60	11	19	2	650
Quinoa and Vegetable Stew	370	13	3.5	10	50	17	9	930
French Lentil Stew	290	6	1.5	5	47	17	10	990
Farro and Butternut Squash Stew	250	4	0	0	45	12	6	770

	Cal	Fat (g)	Sat Fat (g)	Chol (mg)	Carb (g)	Protein (g)	Fiber (g)	Sodium (mg)
Wheat Berry and Wild Mushroom Stew	320	8	1	0	45	14	7	740
Hearty Vegetarian Chili	300	5	0.5	0	51	16	13	580
Black Bean Chili	290	4.5	0.5	0	48	15	9	430
Cuban White Bean and Plantain Chili	500	7	1	0	92	23	23	750
Chapter 3. Chicken Every Way								
Cranberry-Orange Chicken	410	8	1.5	125	39	40	1	670
Chicken with "Roasted" Garlic Sauce	400	13	2.5	160	11	52	1	750
Latin Chicken with Tomatoes and Olives	350	11	2	160	10	51	2	770
Chicken Provençal	370	12	2.5	160	22	38	4	890
Chicken Adobo	280	11	6	160	8	35	0	1040
Chicken Mole	330	12	3	160	19	37	4	770
Chicken Cacciatore	390	11	2.5	160	26	41	5	1040
Kimchi-Braised Chicken Thighs	300	11	2.5	160	13	36	2	960
Chicken Thighs with Swiss Chard and Mustard	310	12	2.5	160	14	39	5	1090
Curried Chicken Thighs with Acorn Squash	380	11	2.5	160	37	36	4	460
Chicken Thighs with Black-Eyed Pea Ragout	410	12	2.5	160	31	45	8	1050
Sweet and Tangy Pulled Chicken	240	7	1	80	19	26	2	740
Tomatillo Chicken Soft Tacos	500	14	4.5	215	38	51	3	1150
Italian Braised Turkey Sausages	280	11	2.5	75	27	23	5	1030
Chapter 4. Steaks, Chops, Ribs, and More								
Teriyaki Pork Tenderloin	310	6	2	110	22	37	0	1640
Herbed Pork Tenderloin with Ratatouille	400	14	3	110	28	42	5	880
Chapter 5. A Roast in Every Pot								
Turkey Breast with Cherry-Orange Sauce	310	5	2	130	12	51	1	420
Turkey Breast with Gravy	300	6	2.5	130	4	52	0	460
Pork Loin with Dried Fig Compote	320	13	4	85	17	33	2	320
Maple-Glazed Pork Loin	360	13	4	85	27	33	0	280
Pork Loin with Warm Spiced Chickpea Salad	360	14	4	85	21	37	4	530
Pork Loin with Fennel, Oranges, and Olives	330	13	4	85	15	34	4	320
Chapter 6. Favorite Ways with Fish and Shellfish								
Poached Swordfish with Papaya Salsa	290	12	3	110	11	34	1	460
Moroccan Fish Tagine with Artichoke Hearts	210	4	0.5	50	18	26	3	1100
Halibut with Warm Bean Salad	340	12	1.5	55	19	41	5	690
Scallops with Creamy Braised Leeks	260	10	6	65	15	23	1	1020
Shrimp with Spiced Quinoa and Corn Salad	380	15	4	120	40	22	5	1150
Shrimp Boil with Corn and Potatoes	260	7	2	130	29	23	3	800
Thai Green Curry with Shrimp and Sweet Potatoes	350	13	9	105	38	18	5	1180

	Cal	Fat (g)	Sat Fat (g)	Chol (mg)	Carb (g)	Protein (g)	Fiber (g)	Sodium (mg)
Chapter 7. Classic Comfort Foods								
Rustic Pork and White Bean Casserole	410	11	3	70	46	29	6	820
Turkey Meatloaf	210	4.5	3	70	13	30	0	660
Chapter 8. Dinner for Two								
Chicken and Garden Vegetable Soup	310	10	1.5	80	21	33	5	940
Creamy Butternut Squash and Apple Soup	260	11	7	30	38	6	6	1100
Hearty Turkey Stew with Squash and Spinach	380	12	3	100	37	36	6	1170
Black Bean Chili	410	8	1	0	62	22	4	960
Thai Chicken with Coconut Curry Sauce	300	12	6	125	7	40	2	630
Pork Tenderloin with Spiced Bulgur Salad	480	15	2.5	110	43	43	6	650
Braised Halibut with Leeks and Mustard	350	13	7	115	16	34	2	840
Easy Cherry Tomato Pasta Sauce	180	8	1	0	26	4	6	390
Stuffed Acorn Squash	420	13	5	15	69	12	8	440
Creamy Farro with Swiss Chard	380	12	2	5	58	17	6	940
Chapter 9. Hearty Vegetarian Mains								
Chickpea Tagine	430	13	3	5	84	19	3	910
Summer Barley Salad	220	9	1.5	0	32	5	7	310
Quinoa, Black Bean, and Mango Salad	300	11	1.5	0	44	9	6	540
Beet and Wheat Berry Salad with Arugula and Apples	260	12	4	10	32	9	6	420
Farro Risotto with Carrots and Goat Cheese	340	11	6	20	48	13	3	810
Farro Primavera	330	10	2.5	10	49	16	3	870
Rustic Braised Lentils with Eggplant	250	10	2.5	10	33	10	10	560
Southwestern Black Bean and Bulgur Bowls	420	8	1	0	70	18	4	900
Red Beans and Rice with Okra and Tomatoes	290	5	0.5	0	48	11	7	640
Chapter 10. Big Batch Pasta Sauces								
All-Purpose Tomato Sauce (per 1 cup)	140	8	1	0	18	4	5	460
Braised Fennel and Turkey Sausage Sauce (per 1 cup)	160	8	3	35	12	10	2	520
Chicken and Mushroom Sauce	140	4	1	50	12	13	1	390
Chicken and Broccolini Sauce (per 1 cup)	180	7	2	45	8	18	1	510
Shrimp Fra Diavolo Sauce (per 1 cup)	140	4	0.5	80	13	11	1	640
Mushroom Bolognese (per 1 cup)	160	6	2.5	10	18	5	1	690

	Cal	Fat (g)	Sat Fat (g)	Chol (mg)	Carb (g)	Protein (g)	Fiber (g)	Sodium (mg)
Chapter 11. Rice, Grains, and Beans								
Brown Rice with Parmesan and Herbs	290	7	3	10	47	9	2	370
Mexican Rice	280	5	0.5	0	53	5	1	600
Middle Eastern Basmati Rice Pilaf	270	4.5	0.5	0	54	5	1	200
Wild Rice Pilaf with Cranberries and Pecans	230	7	0.5	0	38	5	2	380
Herbed Barley Pilaf	240	6	0.5	0	43	5	9	630
Spiced Barley Pilaf with Dates and Parsley	280	6	0.5	0	53	6	10	630
Creamy Farro with Mushrooms and Thyme	220	8	1.5	5	30	8	1	600
Creamy Parmesan Polenta	190	8	4.5	20	20	7	1	580
No-Fuss Quinoa with Lemon	210	8	1	0	30	6	4	390
No-Fuss Quinoa with Corn and Jalapeño	240	8	1	0	35	7	4	390
Wheat Berries with Carrots and Oranges	180	4	0.5	0	32	5	6	300
Braised Chickpeas	310	7	0	0	49	15	14	780
Chapter 12. Vegetable Sides								
Mediterranean Braised Green Beans	110	5	0.5	0	15	3	4	480
Glazed Carrots	150	3	2	10	31	2	5	200
Mashed Cauliflower	40	2.5	1.5	5	4	2	1	370
Braised Cauliflower with Lemon-Caper Dressing	80	5	1	0	8	3	3	170
Braised Fennel with Orange-Tarragon Dressing	70	5	0.5	0	6	1	2	140
Braised Swiss Chard with Shiitakes and Peanuts	90	5	1.5	5	9	4	3	420
Mashed Sweet Potatoes	180	5	3.5	15	31	3	5	320
Lemon-Herb Fingerling Potatoes	170	4.5	0.5	0	28	4	0	400
Maple-Orange Glazed Acorn Squash	130	3	0	0	26	2	3	105
Chapter 13. How About Brunch?								
Irish Oatmeal	200	6	2.5	10	29	7	0	300
Chapter 14. There's Dessert!								
Tea-Poached Pears	200	3.5	2.5	5	40	3	5	110

CONVERSIONS AND EQUIVALENTS

Some say cooking is a science and an art. We would say that geography has a hand in it, too. Flours and sugars manufactured in the United Kingdom and elsewhere will feel and taste different from those manufactured in the United States. So we cannot promise that the loaf of bread you bake in Canada or England will taste the same as a loaf baked in the States, but we can offer guidelines for converting weights and measures. We also recommend that you rely on your instincts when making our recipes. Refer to the visual cues provided. If the dough hasn't "come together, in a ball" as described, you may need to add more flour—even if the recipe doesn't tell you to. You be the judge.

The recipes in this book were developed using standard U.S. measures following U.S. government guidelines. The charts below offer equivalents for U.S. and metric measures. All conversions are approximate and have been rounded up or down to the nearest whole number.

EXAMPLE

1 teaspoon = 4.9292 milliliters, rounded up to 5 milliliters
1 ounce = 28.3495 grams, rounded down to 28 grams

VOLUME CONVERSIONS	
U.S.	METRIC
1 teaspoon	5 milliliters
2 teaspoons	10 milliliters
1 tablespoon	15 milliliters
2 tablespoons	30 milliliters
¼ cup	59 milliliters
⅓ cup	79 milliliters
½ cup	118 milliliters
¾ cup	177 milliliters
1 cup	237 milliliters
1¼ cups	296 milliliters
1½ cups	355 milliliters
2 cups (1 pint)	473 milliliters
2½ cups	591 milliliters
3 cups	710 milliliters
4 cups (1 quart)	0.946 liter
1.06 quarts	1 liter
4 quarts (1 gallon)	3.8 liters

WEIGHT CONVERSIONS	
OUNCES	GRAMS
½	14
¾	21
1	28
1½	43
2	57
2½	71
3	85
3½	99
4	113
4½	128
5	142
6	170
7	198
8	227
9	255
10	283
12	340
16 (1 pound)	454

CONVERSION FOR COMMON BAKING INGREDIENTS

Baking is an exacting science. Because measuring by weight is far more accurate than measuring by volume, and thus more likely to produce reliable results, in our recipes we provide ounce measures in addition to cup measures for many ingredients. Refer to the chart below to convert these measures into grams.

INGREDIENT	OUNCES	GRAMS
Flour		
1 cup all-purpose flour*	5	142
1 cup cake flour	4	113
1 cup whole-wheat flour	5½	156
Sugar		
1 cup granulated (white) sugar	7	198
1 cup packed brown sugar (light or dark)	7	198
1 cup confectioners' sugar	4	113
Cocoa Powder		
1 cup cocoa powder	3	85
Butter†		
4 tablespoons (½ stick, or ¼ cup)	2	57
8 tablespoons (1 stick, or ½ cup)	4	113
16 tablespoons (2 sticks, or 1 cup)	8	227

*U.S. all-purpose flour, the most frequently used flour in this book, does not contain leaveners, as some European flours do. These leavened flours are called self-rising or self-raising. If you are using self-rising flour, take this into consideration before adding leavening to a recipe.

†In the United States, butter is sold both salted and unsalted. We generally recommend unsalted butter. If you are using salted butter, take this into consideration before adding salt to a recipe.

OVEN TEMPERATURES

FAHRENHEIT	CELSIUS	GAS MARK
225	105	¼
250	120	½
275	135	1
300	150	2
325	165	3
350	180	4
375	190	5
400	200	6
425	220	7
450	230	8
475	245	9

CONVERTING TEMPERATURES FROM AN INSTANT-READ THERMOMETER

We include doneness temperatures in many of the recipes in this book. We recommend an instant-read thermometer for the job. Refer to the above table to convert Fahrenheit degrees to Celsius. Or, for temperatures not represented in the chart, use this simple formula:

Subtract 32 degrees from the Fahrenheit reading, then divide the result by 1.8 to find the Celsius reading.

EXAMPLE
"Roast chicken until thighs register 175 degrees."
To convert:
$175°F - 32 = 143°$
$143° \div 1.8 = 79.44°C$, rounded down to 79°C

INDEX

Note: Page references in *italics* indicate photographs.

■ indicates easy prep   ■ indicates vegetarian   ■ indicates light   ■ indicates all day